Lecture Notes in Artificial Intelligence 10621

Subseries of Lecture Notes in Computer Science

More information about this series at http://www.springer.com/series/1244

Bo An · Ana Bazzan
João Leite · Serena Villata
Leendert van der Torre (Eds.)

PRIMA 2017:
Principles and Practice
of Multi-Agent Systems

20th International Conference
Nice, France, October 30 – November 3, 2017
Proceedings

 Springer

Editors
Bo An (iD)
Nanyang Technological University
Singapore
Singapore

Ana Bazzan (iD)
Universidade Federal Rio Grande do Sul
Porto Alegre, Rio Grande do Sul
Brazil

João Leite (iD)
Universidade Nova de Lisboa
Caparica
Portugal

Serena Villata (iD)
Université Côte d'Azur
Sophia Antipolis
France

Leendert van der Torre (iD)
University of Luxembourg
Esch-sur-Alzette
Luxembourg

ISSN 0302-9743   ISSN 1611-3349   (electronic)
Lecture Notes in Artificial Intelligence
ISBN 978-3-319-69130-5   ISBN 978-3-319-69131-2   (eBook)
https://doi.org/10.1007/978-3-319-69131-2

Library of Congress Control Number: 2017956066

LNCS Sublibrary: SL7 – Artificial Intelligence

Printed on acid-free paper

This Springer imprint is published by Springer Nature
The registered company is Springer International Publishing AG
The registered company address is: Gewerbestrasse 11, 6330 Cham, Switzerland

Preface

Welcome to the proceedings of the 20th International Conference on Principles and Practice of Multi-Agent Systems (PRIMA 2017) held in Nice, France, from October 30 to November 3.

Originally started as a regional (Asia-Pacific) workshop in 1998, PRIMA has become one of the leading and influential scientific conferences for research on multi-agent systems. Each year since 2009, PRIMA has brought together active researchers, developers, and practitioners from both academia and industry to show-case, share, and promote research in several domains, ranging from foundations of agent theory and engineering aspects of agent systems, to emerging interdisciplinary areas of agent-based research. PRIMA's previous editions were held in Nagoya, Japan (2009), Kolkata, India (2010), Wollongong, Australia (2011), Kuching, Malaysia (2012), Dunedin, New Zealand (2013), Gold Coast, Australia (2014), Bertinoro, Italy (2015), and Phuket, Thailand (2016).

We received 88 submissions from 34 countries, including five papers submitted to the social science track, chaired by Michael Mäs, whose accepted papers will be fast-tracked into the *Journal of Artificial Societies and Social Simulation* (these are not included in the present proceedings). Each submission was carefully reviewed by at least three members of the Program Committee (PC) composed of 121 prominent world-level researchers and 37 additional reviewers. The PC and senior PC (SPC) in-cluded researchers from all continents. This year, we were proud to be able to provide four or more reviews to 79 papers, in the hope of offering more feedback to the authors. In total, 350 reviews were sent to authors.

The review period was followed by PC discussions moderated by SPC members. The PRIMA SPC has been part of the PRIMA reviewing scheme since 2010, and this year it included 19 members. At the end of the reviewing process, in addition to the technical reviews, authors received a summary meta-review by an SPC member.

Of the 88 submissions, PRIMA 2017 accepted 24 full papers (an acceptance rate of 27%). An additional 11 submissions whose core ideas were judged innovative, perhaps even disruptive, but which were not fully polished to make it as a full papers, were selected to appear as short papers. Two papers were accepted to be presented in the social science track.

In addition to the paper presentations and poster sessions, the conference also included a demo session and three keynote talks: the first by Jorge M. Pacheco titled "Evolutionary Game Theory of Cooperation: From Cells to Societies," the second by Wolfram Burgard on "Deep Learning for Robot Navigation and Perception," and the third by Massimiliano Giacomin titled "Handling Heterogeneous Disagreements Through Abstract Argumentation."

We would like to thank all individuals, institutions, and sponsors that supported PRIMA 2017. Mainly we thank the conference delegates and the authors, who answered our call for papers by submitting state-of-the-art research papers from all over the world, confirming the role that PRIMA has gained as a leading international conference in multi-agent system research. Without them, none of this would have been possible. We also thank EasyChair for the use of their conference management system, which allowed us to handle the reviewing process of a conference of this size, from the early stages until the production of the present volume. We are indebted to our PC and SPC members and additional reviewers for spending their valuable time by providing careful reviews and recommendations on the submissions, and for taking part in follow-up discussions.

We also thank the demo session chair, Viviana Mascardi, and the web chair, Jeremie Dauphin, for their hard work. Finally, we are very grateful to the sponsors who supported PRIMA financially, making the conference accessible to a larger number of delegates, and supporting the participation of keynote speakers: Université Côte d'Azur, Laboratoire I3S Sophia Antipolis, and Inria.

September 2017

Bo An
Ana L.C. Bazzan
João Leite
Serena Villata
Leendert van der Torre

Organization

PRIMA 2017 was organized by the Université Côte d'Azur in Nice, France.

General Chairs

Leendert van der Torre   University of Luxembourg, Luxembourg
Serena Villata   Université Côte d'Azur, France

Program Chairs

Bo An   Nanyang Technological University, Singapore
Ana Bazzan   Universidade Federal do Rio Grande do Sul, Brazil
João Leite   Universidade Nova de Lisboa, Portugal

Social Science Track Chair

Michael Mäs   University of Groningen, The Netherlands

Demo Chair

Viviana Mascardi   University of Genoa, Italy

Web Chair

Jérémie Dauphin   University of Luxembourg, Luxembourg

Local Organizing Co-chairs

Andrea G.B. Tettamanzi   Université Côte d'Azur, France
Celia da Costa Pereira   Université Côte d'Azur, France
Catherine Faron-Zucker   Université Côte d'Azur, France

PRIMA Steering Committee

Aditya Ghose   University of Wollongong, Australia (Chair)
Takayuki Ito   Nagoya Institute of Technology, Japan (Deputy Chair)
Makoto Yokoo   Kyushu University, Japan (Past Chair and Ex Officio
                                Member)
Abdul Sattar   Griffith University, Australia (Treasurer)
Guido Governatori   NICTA, Australia
Sandip Sen   University of Tulsa, USA
Toshiharu Sugawara   Waseda University, Japan

Iyad Rahwan	Masdar Institute of Science and Technology, United Arab Emirates
Wayne Wobcke	University of New South Wales, Australia
Frank Dignum	Utrecht University, The Netherlands
Martin Purvis	University of Otago, New Zealand
Guido Boella	Università degli Studi di Torino, Italy
Edith Elkind	University of Oxford, UK
Bastin Tony Roy Savarimuthu	University of Otago, New Zealand
Hoa Dam	University of Wollongong, Australia
Jeremy Pitt	Imperial College, UK
Yang Xu	University of Electronic Science and Technology, China
Jane Hsu	National Taiwan University, Taiwan
Andrea Omicini	Università di Bologna, Italy
Qingliang Chen	Jinan University, Guangzhou, China
Paolo Torroni	Università di Bologna, Italy
Serena Villata	Université Côte d'Azur, France
Katsutoshi Hirayama	Kobe University, Japan
Matteo Baldoni	University of Turin, Italy
Amit K. Chopra	Lancaster University, UK
Tran Cao Son	New Mexico State University, USA
Michael Mäs	University of Groningen, The Netherlands

Senior Program Committee

Matteo Baldoni	University of Turin, Italy
Tina Balke	University of Surrey, UK
Jamal Bentahar	Concordia University, Canada
Rafael H. Bordini	PUCRS
Mehdi Dastani	Utrecht University, The Netherlands
Paul Davidsson	Malmö University, Sweden
Yves Demazeau	CNRS - LIG
Frank Dignum	Utrecht University, The Netherlands
Amal El Fallah Seghrouchni	LIP6 - University of Pierre and Marie Curie, France
Ulle Endriss	University of Amsterdam, The Netherlands
Rino Falcone	Institute of Cognitive Sciences and Technologies-CNR
Katsutoshi Hirayama	Kobe University, Japan
Nicolas Maudet	Université Pierre et Marie Curie, France
Felipe Meneguzzi	Pontifical Catholic University of Rio Grande do Sul, Brazil
Zinovi Rabinovich	Nanyang Technological University, Singapore
Bastin Tony Roy Savarimuthu	University of Otago, New Zealand
Paolo Torroni	Università di Bologna, Italy

Bo Yang   Jilin University, China
Makoto Yokoo   Kyushu University, Japan

Program Committee

Diana Francisca Adamatti	Universidade Federal do Rio Grande, Brazil
Natasha Alechina	University of Nottingham, UK
Giulia Andrighetto	ISTC-CNR, Italy
Grigoris Antoniou	University of Huddersfield, UK
Luis Antunes	GUESS/LabMAg/University of Lisbon, Portugal
Quan Bai	Auckland University of Technology, New Zealand
Cristina Baroglio	Università di Torino, Italy
Chiara Bassetti	ISTC-CNR, Italy
Salem Benferhat	Cril, CNRS UMR8188, Université d'Artois, France
Floris Bex	Utrecht University, The Netherlands
Elizabeth Black	King's College London, UK
Olivier Boissier	Mines Saint-Etienne, Institut Henri Fayol, France
Elise Bonzon	LIPADE, Université Paris Descartes, France
Elena Cabrio	Université Côte d'Azur, France
Sara Casare	University of São Paulo, Brazil
Federico Cerutti	Cardiff University, UK
Qingliang Chen	Sun Yat-sen University, China
Massimo Cossentino	National Research Council, Italy
Stefania Costantini	University of l'Aquila, Italy
Célia Da Costa Pereira	Université Côte d'Azur, France
Dave De Jonge	Western Sydney University, Australia
Nirmit Desai	IBM T.J. Watson Research Center, USA
Virginia Dignum	Delft University of Technology, The Netherlands
Isabella Distinto	Municipia Spa
Sylvie Doutre	University of Toulouse 1, IRIT, France
Catherine Faron Zucker	Université Côte d'Azur, France
Michael Fisher	University of Liverpool, UK
Nicoletta Fornara	Università della Svizzera Italiana
Katsuhide Fujita	Tokyo University of Agriculture and Technology
Naoki Fukuta	Shizuoka University, Japan
Amineh Ghorbani	Delft University of Technology, The Netherlands
Ricardo Gonçalves	NOVA LINCS, Universidade Nova de Lisboa, Portugal
Davide Grossi	University of Liverpool, UK
Akin Gunay	Lancaster University, UK
The Anh Han	Teesside University, UK
James Harland	RMIT University, Australia
Mohammad Hasan	University of North Carolina at Charlotte, USA
Hiromitsu Hattori	College of Computer Science and Engineering
Koen Hindriks	Delft University of Technology, The Netherlands
Xiaowei Huang	University of Oxford, UK
Jomi Fred Hubner	Federal University of Santa Catarina, Brazil

Fuyuki Ishikawa	National Institute of Informatics, Japan
Wojtek Jamroga	Polish Academy of Sciences, Poland
Yichuan Jiang	Southeast University, China
Ozgur Kafali	North Carolina State University, USA
Shohei Kato	Nagoya Institute of Technology, Japan
Thomas Christopher King	Lancaster University, UK
Yasuhiko Kitamura	Kwansei Gakuin University, Japan
Matthias Knorr	NOVA LINCS, Universidade Nova de Lisboa, Portugal
Sébastien Konieczny	CRIL - CNRS, France
Andrew Koster	IIIA-CSIC, Spain
Jérôme Lang	CNRS, LAMSADE, Université Paris-Dauphine, France
Kate Larson	University of Waterloo, Canada
Ho-Fung Leung	The Chinese University of Hong Kong, SAR China
Beishui Liao	Zhejiang University, China
Churn-Jung Liau	Academia Sinica, Taipei, Taiwan
Fenrong Liu	Tsinghua University, Bejing, China
Rey-Long Liu	Tzu Chi University, Taiwan
Brian Logan	University of Nottingham, UK
Maite Lopez-Sanchez	University of Barcelona, Spain
Emiliano Lorini	IRIT, France
Xudong Luo	Guangxi Normal University, China
Marco Lützenberger	Technische Universität Berlin/DAI Labor, Germany
Samhar Mahmoud	King's College London, UK
Elisa Marengo	Free University of Bozen-Bolzano, Italy
Viviana Mascardi	University of Genoa, Italy
Shigeo Matsubara	Kyoto University, Japan
Roberto Micalizio	Università di Torino, Italy
Tim Miller	University of Melbourne, Australia
Tsunenori Mine	Kyushu University, Japan
Pavlos Moraitis	LIPADE, Paris Descartes University, France
Yohei Murakami	Kyoto University, Japan
Michael Mäs	University of Groningen, The Netherlands
Yuu Nakajima	Toho University, Japan
Mariusz Nowostawski	Norwegian University of Science and Technology, Norway
Ingrid Nunes	Universidade Federal do Rio Grande do Sul, Brazil
Andrea Omicini	Università di Bologna, Italy
Nir Oren	University of Aberdeen, UK
Sascha Ossowski	Rey Juan Carlos University, Spain
Julian Padget	University of Bath, UK
Simon Parsons	King's College London, UK
Gauthier Picard	Institut Henri Fayol, Mines Saint-Etienne, France
Enrico Pontelli	New Mexico State University, USA
David Pynadath	Institute for Creative Technologies, University of Southern California, USA
Hongyang Qu	University of Sheffield, UK

Franco Raimondi	Middlesex University, UK
David Rajaratnam	The University of New South Wales, Australia
Sarvapali Ramchurn	University of Southampton, UK
Fenghui Ren	University of Wollongong, Australia
Ji Ruan	Auckland University of Technology, New Zealand
Yuko Sakurai	Kyushu University, Japan
Francesco Santini	University of Perugia, Italy
Ken Satoh	National Institute of Informatics and Sokendai, Japan
Francois Schwarzentruber	École normale supérieure de Rennes, France
Sandip Sen	University of Tulsa, USA
Guillermo Ricardo Simari	Universidad del Sur in Bahia Blanca, Brazil
Marija Slavkovik	University of Bergen, Norway
Tran Cao Son	New Mexico State University, USA
Leandro Soriano Marcolino	Lancaster University, UK
Jan-Philipp Steghofer	University of Gothenburg, Sweden
Leon Sterling	Swinburne University of Technology, Australia
Kaile Su	Griffith University, Australia
Yuqing Tang	Microsoft
Matthias Thimm	Universität Koblenz-Landau, Germany
Nicolas Troquard	KRDB Research Centre, Free University of Bozen-Bolzano, Italy
Rainer Unland	University of Duisburg-Essen, ICB, Germany
Maria Esther Vidal	Universidad Simon Bolivar, Venezuela
Meritxell Vinyals	Commissariat à l'énergie atomique et aux énergies alternatives (CEA)
Wanyuan Wang	Southeast University, China
Brendon J. Woodford	University of Otago, New Zealand
Feng Wu	University of Science and Technology, China
Nitin Yadav	University of Melbourne, Australia
William Yeoh	Washington University in St. Louis, USA
Logan Yliniemi	University of Nevada, Reno, USA
Neil Yorke-Smith	Delft University of Technology, The Netherlands
Yifeng Zeng	Teesside University, UK
Zhiqiang Zhuang	Griffith University, Australia
Thomas Ågotnes	University of Bergen, Norway

Additional Reviewers

Alechina, Natasha	Niu, Lei
De Sanctis, Martina	Pedersen, Truls
Garcia, Laurent	Sapienza, Alessandro
Koeman, Vincent Jaco	Stocker, Richard
Liu, Chanjuan	Takahashi, Kazuko
Murphy, Josh	Wang, Wanyuan

Zhang, Jihang
Charrier, Tristan
Flavien, Balbo
Hao, Jianye
Li, Weihua
Lopes, Salvatore
Nguyen, Hoang Nga
Paglieri, Fabio
Rönnholm, Raine
Seidita, Valeria
Su, Che-Ping
Testerink, Bas
Wang, Yuchen

Chen, Siqi
Gainer, Paul
Kido, Hiroyuki
Linker, Sven
Masuch, Nils
Nguyen, Tung
Payette, Nicolas
Sakama, Chiaki
Smyrnakis, Michalis
Tachmazidis, Ilias
Vilone, Daniele
Zhan, Jieyu

Contents

Applications of Agents and Multiagent Systems

Cooperation and Negotiation in Multiagent Systems

Organizations, Institutions and Norms in Multiagent Systems

Argumentation in Multiagent Systems

Early Innovation Short Papers

XVI   Contents

Invited Talk

Handling Heterogeneous Disagreements Through Abstract Argumentation (Extended Abstract)

Massimiliano Giacomin[✉]

University of Brescia, Brescia, Italy
massimiliano.giacomin@unibs.it

Abstract. Agents disagree in many situations and in many ways on their beliefs, preferences and goals. Abstract argumentation frameworks are a formal model to handle disagreement, which is represented as a conflict relation between a set of arguments. To solve the conflict and identify justified arguments, a single argumentation semantics is applied at a global level, under the assumption that the involved conflicts are essentially homogeneous. In the talk I will argue that disagreements are in general heterogeneous and thus should be treated in different ways according both to their nature and to the specific agents features. Accordingly, a general model of abstract argumentation will be discussed, able to handle heterogeneous disagreements by means of multiple argumentation semantics at a local level.

Keywords: Abstract argumentation · Heterogeneous disagreement · Multiple semantics

1 Background in Abstract Argumentation

Formal argumentation can be considered as a model concerned with how assertions are proposed, discussed and resolved in the context of disagreement [5]. The idea is that reasoning is defeasible and corresponds to a process of production and evaluation of *arguments*, each representing a reason to support (or oppose) a given statement. In general, arguments may be in conflict since the validity of an argument can be disputed by other arguments, which may support an opposite conclusion or attack one of its premises or the validity of an inferential step. As a result, the acceptability of a claim does not only depend on the arguments supporting it, but also on the presence of counterarguments, which in turn can be attacked by counterarguments and so on.

The argumentation model has been proved general and flexible enough to accommodate various kinds of disagreement. In multi-agent systems, such disagreement arises in many situations and in many ways on agents beliefs, preferences and goals, both during their individual reasoning activity (e.g. to revise beliefs in front of perceptual information [7] or to deliberate among a set of possible actions [10]) and in their mutual interaction (as e.g. in negotiation [1]).

© Springer International Publishing AG 2017
B. An et al. (Eds.): PRIMA 2017, LNAI 10621, pp. 3–11, 2017.
https://doi.org/10.1007/978-3-319-69131-2_1

While arguments can have different internal structures giving rise to a variety of argumentation approaches (e.g. [11,13,18]), in order to evaluate the status of arguments their structure may be abstracted away and the attacks between them can be represented simply as a binary relation. This corresponds to the model of *abstract argumentation frameworks* [8], specifically devoted to conflict management, where arguments are the nodes of a directed graph $AF = (Ar, att)$ whose edges correspond to their conflict relation: we say that argument a attacks argument b if $(a, b) \in att$. To solve the conflict and identify justified arguments, various *argumentation semantics* have been devised that can be introduced by means of the notion of *extension*, intuitively representing a set of arguments that can survive the conflict together. Given an $AF = (Ar, att)$, an argumentation semantics $\mathcal{S}$ associates to AF a set of extensions, i.e. subsets of Ar, denoted as $\mathcal{E}_\mathcal{S}(AF)$. An argument is then skeptically justified if it belongs to all extensions, while it is credulously justified if it belongs to at least one of them.

Specific argumentation semantics differ in the definition of extension adopted. Most of them are based on the notion of admissibility: a set of arguments $\mathcal{A}rgs$ is *admissible* if it is conflict-free, i.e. $\neg\exists a, b \in \mathcal{A}rgs : a$ attacks b, and able to *defend* all of its elements, i.e. for any argument b which attacks an argument $a \in \mathcal{A}rgs$, there is an argument $c \in \mathcal{A}rgs$ such that c attacks b. Intuitively, admissible sets feature a sort of internal coherence and are able to provide a counterargument to any opposite argument that may be advanced. A further requirement for extensions is *completeness*, i.e. one should not abstain about an argument which is defended: a *complete extension* is an admissible set including all arguments it defends. Most argumentation semantics then identify their extensions among complete extensions, by introducing additional conditions on them. In particular[1]:

- *Grounded semantics* (**GR**) identifies as its unique extension the least (w.r.t. $\subseteq$) complete extension;
- *Stable semantics* (**ST**) identifies as its extensions the complete extensions each of them able to attack all arguments outside it;
- *Preferred semantics* (**PR**) identifies as its extensions the maximal (w.r.t. $\subseteq$) complete extensions;
- *Ideal semantics* (**ID**) identifies as its unique extension the maximal set (w.r.t. $\subseteq$) which is admissible and contained in all preferred extensions [9].

In the following, **GR** and **ID** will be called unique-status semantics, while stable and preferred semantics will be called multiple-status semantics. Intuitively, **GR** corresponds to the most skeptical semantics among those based on complete extensions, as it justifies the smallest possible set of arguments. Conversely, **ST** and **PR** are able to justify more arguments by exploiting multiple extensions. In particular, **ST** is more committed than **PR**, by adopting a definition of extension where any argument is either in the extension or is attacked by it, while **PR** adopts a weaker definition which, differently from **ST**, always guarantee

---

[1] The reader is referred to [3] for an introduction to argumentation semantics also including additional proposals.

the existence of extensions [8]. **ID** can be considered a unique-status semantics which is more committed than **GR**, as it always justifies a (sometimes strict) superset of the grounded extension, but also more skeptical than **PR**, as it adds the requirement of admissibility to the set of skeptically justified arguments according to **PR**.

Whereas in the brief introduction above I have used the term *skepticism* informally to characterize argumentation semantics, in [4] several partial orders have been defined to provide a formal counterpart to the tendency of making more or less committed choices about argument justification. Here I need to recall the following relations, with reference to two argumentation semantics S_1 and S_2:

- $S_1 \preceq_{\cap+}^{S} S_2$ iff for any AF where both S_1 and S_2 identify a non empty set of extensions, $\forall E_2 \in \mathcal{E}_{S_2}(AF) \, \exists E_1 \in \mathcal{E}_{S_1}(AF) : E_1 \subseteq E_2$.
- $S_1 \preceq_{\cup+}^{S} S_2$ iff for any AF where both S_1 and S_2 identify a non empty set of extensions, $\forall E_1 \in \mathcal{E}_{S_1}(AF) \, \exists E_2 \in \mathcal{E}_{S_2}(AF) : E_1 \subseteq E_2$.

Intuitively, $S_1 \preceq_{\cap+}^{S} S_2$ indicates that S_1 is more skeptical w.r.t. S_2 according to a skeptical viewpoint on argument justification, since every extension in $\mathcal{E}_{S_2}(AF)$ has a more skeptical counterpart in $\mathcal{E}_{S_1}(AF)$, while $\mathcal{E}_{S_1}(AF)$ can include additional unrelated extensions (that can only lead to less committed choices on argument justification). Dually, $S_1 \preceq_{\cup+}^{S} S_2$ indicates that S_1 is more skeptical w.r.t. S_2 according to a credulous viewpoint on argument justification.

Referring to the argumentation semantics introduced above, it turns out that **GR** $\prec_{\cap+}^{S}$ **ID** $\prec_{\cap+}^{S}$ **PR** $\prec_{\cap+}^{S}$ **ST** and **GR** $\prec_{\cup+}^{S}$ **ID** $\prec_{\cup+}^{S}$ **ST** $\prec_{\cup+}^{S}$ **PR** (where $S_1 \prec_{\cap+}^{S} S_2$ denotes that $S_1 \preceq_{\cap+}^{S} S_2$ and $S_2 \npreceq_{\cap+}^{S} S_1$, and similarly for $\prec_{\cup+}^{S}$).

2   Handling Heterogeneous Disagreements: Introduction and Motivation

While various argumentation semantics have appeared in the literature, with the exception of [17] no proposal has been made to mix different semantics in the same argumentation framework. However, there are several motivations for this.

From a general point of view, it has to be noted that no semantics has prevailed over the others, rather different proposals are meant to satisfy specific properties and/or fulfill some desired behavior in problematic examples [3,6]. It is then likely that which semantics to adopt should depend on the application context. For the same reason, it is reasonable to make it possible to apply specific semantics in different parts of the same argumentation framework, reflecting the heterogeneous nature of the corresponding conflicts.

In this respect, different semantic treatments have been advocated in the literature, either directly or indirectly. In the context of single agents, one reason for this concerns the nature of arguments involved in conflicts. In particular, a distinction has been advocated in [16] between epistemic and practical reasoning, i.e. reasoning over beliefs vs reasoning about what to do (where the latter concerns goals, desires and intentions). While in the first case conflicts between arguments arise mainly from uncertainty and incompleteness of information, in the second case distinct goals may conflict since they cannot all be fulfilled due to resource limitations. As a consequence, in [16] grounded semantics is proposed to deal with epistemic arguments, on the grounds that truth is at stake and a skeptical approach ensures that only well established arguments can be justified. The idea is that in case of indecision it is better to do further investigations (e.g. acquiring additional information) to solve the conflicts, rather than making an arbitrary choice between conflicting arguments. On the other hand, a very credulous approach is advocated for practical arguments, i.e. selecting a preferred extension at random, in order to always enforce a choice over equally preferable alternatives.

Focusing on epistemic reasoning, it can be noted that to achieve a skeptical behavior there are several alternatives to grounded semantics. In this respect, a paradigmatic example is a modification of the so-called "Nixon Diamond", where two conflicting arguments support the same conclusion that Nixon is politically extreme. In particular, one of the arguments is based the premise that Nixon is a Quaker, implying that he is presumably a dove thus politically extreme, while the other argument yields the same conclusion based on the premise that he is Republican, thus presumably a hawk. To get the shared conclusion as justified, we have to adopt a multiple-status semantics (such as preferred semantics) and justify all those propositions that appear as conclusions of at least an argument in any preferred extension. These include the so-called "floating conclusions" which turn out to be justified even if not supported by any skeptically justified argument.

On the other hand, John Horty in [12] provides some examples where this solution appears as counterintuitive, i.e. there are cases where the conflict arising between extensions seems to undermine the assumption, underlying multiple-status semantics, that one of them is correct. In these cases, rather than considering multiple extensions it seems more appropriate to doubt about them and adopt a single-status approach such as the grounded semantics. A rebuttal to this conclusion is provided in [15], where the problematic examples in [12] are modelled by adding extra-information in such a way that the intuitive results can still be obtained with the approach based on multiple extensions. I note however that the corresponding modelling is relatively complex, thus depending on the audience an equivalent formalization based on multiple semantics may be more intuitive.

In general, the choice of the appropriate semantics seems to depend on practical considerations. Besides those outline above, the cost of evaluation errors may play a role in this choice [12], i.e. more skeptical semantics should be adopted for the more critical arguments in this respect. Moreover, since different semantics feature different computational complexities, most complex ones may be devoted to most relevant arguments w.r.t. the focus of attention towards a specific issue [17].

Finally, considering multi-agent systems it may well be the case that different agents feature different reasoning attitudes, being e.g. more confident or thoughtful [14]. In the context of argumentation-based reasoning, different attitudes correspond to the adoption of semantics featuring different degrees of skepticism. In this respect, multiple semantics play a role both to model the interaction among individual agents, and when an agent represents the reasoning of another agent and selects a corresponding semantics based e.g. on its estimated sincerity and competence [17].

3   Multiple Argumentation Semantics: A Basic Requirement and Preliminary Results

Based on the above considerations, given an argumentation framework $AF = (Ar, att)$ it makes sense to consider a partition $\mathcal{P} = \{P_1, \ldots, P_n\}$ of Ar where each element P_i is associated to a specific semantics[2] $S(P_i)$. The question is then how to properly introduce a definition of extension arising from the application of different semantics at a local level.

To this purpose, we may first consider the limit case where all the elements of the partition are associated to the same semantics $\mathcal{S}$: in this case, a sensible requirement[3], that we call *uniform semantics equivalence*, is that the novel definition should return the same extensions as $\mathcal{S}$ applied to the whole argumentation framework. This limit case is strongly related to the notion of *semantics decomposability* which has been extensively investigated in [2]. Intuitively, a semantics $\mathcal{S}$ is fully decomposable if, given a partition of an argumentation framework into a set of sub-frameworks, the outcomes produced by $\mathcal{S}$ can be obtained as a combination of the outcomes produced by a local counterpart of $\mathcal{S}$ applied separately on each sub-framework, and vice versa.

To simplify the formal treatment, it is convenient to adopt a labelling-based counterpart of semantics definitions [3] where an extension E is replaced by a corresponding *labelling*, i.e. a total function that associates to each argument a label in $\{\text{in}, \text{out}, \text{undec}\}$, such that an argument a is labelled in iff $a \in E$; it is labelled out iff $\exists\, b \in E$ such that b attacks a; it is labelled undec if neither of the above conditions holds. Thus, a semantics $\mathcal{S}$ returns for any AF a set of labellings $\mathcal{L}_\mathcal{S}(AF)$ instead of a set of extensions. Given a set of arguments Ar, we denote as $\mathfrak{L}_{Ar}$ the set including all possible labellings of Ar.

In order to formally describe the interactions between the sub-frameworks induced by the arbitrary partition, we exploit the notion of *argumentation framework with input*, namely a tuple $(AF_L, \mathcal{I}, \mathcal{L}ab_\mathcal{I}, att_\mathcal{I})$, including an argumentation framework $AF_L = \langle Ar, att \rangle$, a set of arguments $\mathcal{I}$ such that $\mathcal{I} \cap Ar = \emptyset$ (playing the role of *input* arguments, i.e. affecting AF_L from the outside), a labelling $\mathcal{L}ab_\mathcal{I} \in \mathfrak{L}_\mathcal{I}$ (i.e. a labelling assigned to $\mathcal{I}$, to be taken into account in the local semantics evaluation inside AF_L) and a relation $att_\mathcal{I} \subseteq \mathcal{I} \times Ar$ (i.e. the attack relation from input arguments to Ar). The local semantics evaluation for the arguments of AF_L is then expressed by a *local function* F, which assigns to any

---

[2] This has been first proposed in [17] and called sorting.
[3] Focusing on extension-based semantics, this has been called *Uniform Case Extension Equivalence* in [17].

argumentation framework with input a (possibly empty) set of labellings, i.e. $F(AF_L, \mathcal{I}, \mathcal{L}ab_{\mathcal{I}}, att_{\mathcal{I}}) \in 2^{\mathfrak{L}_{Ar}}$, where $\mathfrak{L}_{Ar}$ is the set of all labellings of AF_L.

A semantics $\mathcal{S}$ is *fully decomposable* iff there is a local function F such that for every argumentation framework $AF = \langle Ar, att \rangle$ and every partition $\mathcal{P} = \{P_1, \ldots, P_n\}$ of Ar it holds that $\mathcal{L}_{\mathcal{S}}(AF) = \mathcal{U}(\mathcal{P}, AF, F)$ with $\mathcal{U}(\mathcal{P}, AF, F) \triangleq \{\mathcal{L}ab_{P_1} \cup \ldots \cup \mathcal{L}ab_{P_n} \mid \mathcal{L}ab_{P_i} \in F(AF\!\downarrow_{P_i}, P_i^{\text{inp}}, (\bigcup_{j=1\ldots n, j \neq i} \mathcal{L}ab_{P_j})\!\downarrow_{P_i^{\text{inp}}}, P_i^R)\}$,

where $AF\!\downarrow_{P_i} = (P_i, att \cap (P_i \times P_i))$ is the restriction of AF to P_i, $P_i^{\text{inp}} = \{a \notin P_i \mid \exists b \in P_i : (a, b) \in att)\}$ includes the external arguments attacking P_i, $(\bigcup_{j=1\ldots n, j \neq i} \mathcal{L}ab_{P_j})\!\downarrow_{P_i^{\text{inp}}}$ is the labelling externally assigned[4] to P_i^{inp}, and $P_i^R = att \cap (P_i^{\text{inp}} \times P_i)$ is the attack relation from P_i^{inp} to P_i.

It is proven in [2] that, under some mild conditions, if a semantics $\mathcal{S}$ is fully decomposable then the local function used to compute the local labellings is unique, and corresponds to the so called *canonical local function* $F_{\mathcal{S}}$. The latter can be identified by applying $\mathcal{S}$, for any argumentation framework with input, to a corresponding *standard argumentation framework* where the input labelling is enforced through the addition of arguments attacking out-labelled arguments and self-attacks for all undec-labelled arguments.

We can then generalize the above definition to the case of multiple semantics. Considering an $AF = (Ar, att)$ and a partition $\mathcal{P} = \{P_1, \ldots, P_n\}$ of Ar with associated semantics $S(P_i)$, one is led to define the resulting labellings as $\{\mathcal{L}ab_{P_1} \cup \ldots \cup \mathcal{L}ab_{P_n} \mid \mathcal{L}ab_{P_i} \in F_{S(P_i)}(AF\!\downarrow_{P_i}, P_i^{\text{inp}}, (\bigcup_{j=1\ldots n, j \neq i} \mathcal{L}ab_{P_j})\!\downarrow_{P_i^{\text{inp}}}, P_i^R)\}$. It is then easy to see that the basic requirement of uniform semantics equivalence w.r.t. a semantics $\mathcal{S}$ coincides with the property of full decomposability of $\mathcal{S}$.

Table 1 reports some results from [2] concerning the decomposability properties of argumentation semantics, also including **CO** that denotes the semantics identifying as its labellings all complete labellings. In the table, top-down decomposability holds iff for any AF and any partition $\mathcal{P}$, $\mathcal{L}_{\mathcal{S}}(AF) \subseteq \mathcal{U}(\mathcal{P}, AF, F_{\mathcal{S}})$, while bottom-up decomposability holds iff $\mathcal{L}_{\mathcal{S}}(AF) \supseteq \mathcal{U}(\mathcal{P}, AF, F_{\mathcal{S}})$. Top-down and bottom-up decomposability can be viewed as two partial decomposability properties, indicating that the combination of the labellings locally computed by $F_{\mathcal{S}}$ on the partition is complete and correct w.r.t. the globally computed labellings, respectively. Table 1 also reports the decomposability properties restricting the allowed partitions so that every element is the union of some strongly connected components (SCCs). From the perspective of mixing semantics, we can summarize these results as follows:

- admissibility and completeness are preserved by the definition introduced above: due to full decomposability of **CO**, mixing semantics based on complete labellings (such as those considered in this paper) always yields a set of complete labellings;

---

[4] More precisely, given a labelling $\mathcal{L}$ and a set of arguments $\mathcal{A}rgs$, $\mathcal{L}\!\downarrow_{\mathcal{A}rgs} \equiv \mathcal{L} \cap (\mathcal{A}rgs \times \{\text{in}, \text{out}, \text{undec}\})$.

- only stable semantics is fully decomposable with arbitrary partitions, thus the uniform semantics equivalence is not satisfied in the general case;
- on the other hand, full decomposability is recovered for all semantics besides **ID** if partitions based on SCCs are considered.

It should be noted that the partitions based on SCCs include the case where an argumentation framework is partitioned in two sets, i.e. a set without attacks from external arguments and the remainder of the framework. This is the case e.g. of the approach recalled in the previous section integrating epistemic and practical reasoning. Actually, in [16] epistemic arguments identify an unattacked set, since they can attack the practical ones but not vice versa.

Table 1. Decomposability properties of argumentation semantics.

	CO	ST	GR	PR	ID
Full decomposability	Yes	Yes	No	No	No
Top-down decomposability	Yes	Yes	Yes	Yes	No
Bottom-up decomposability	Yes	Yes	No	No	No
Full decomposability w.r.t. SCC	Yes	Yes	Yes	Yes	No
Top-down decomposability w.r.t. SCC	Yes	Yes	Yes	Yes	No
Bottom-up decomposability w.r.t. SCC	Yes	Yes	Yes	Yes	No

Finally, on the basis of top-down decomposability of **GR** and **PR**, it can be proved that uniform semantics equivalence is recovered for **GR** and **PR** by adding to $\mathcal{U}(\mathcal{P}, AF, F_{\mathcal{S}})$ a minimality and maximality condition, respectively. More specifically, let us denote with $\sqsubseteq$ the commitment relation between labellings such that $\mathcal{L}_1 \sqsubseteq \mathcal{L}_2$ iff $\mathbf{in}(\mathcal{L}_1) \subseteq \mathbf{in}(\mathcal{L}_2)$ and $\mathbf{out}(\mathcal{L}_1) \subseteq \mathbf{out}(\mathcal{L}_2)$, where $\mathbf{in}(\mathcal{L})$ and $\mathbf{out}(\mathcal{L})$ denote the arguments labelled **in** and **out** by $\mathcal{L}$, respectively. Then, for grounded semantics it holds that $\mathcal{L}_{\mathbf{GR}}(AF) = \min_{\sqsubseteq} \mathcal{U}(\mathcal{P}, AF, F_{\mathcal{S}})$, and for preferred semantics it holds that $\mathcal{L}_{\mathbf{PR}}(AF) = \max_{\sqsubseteq} \mathcal{U}(\mathcal{P}, AF, F_{\mathcal{S}})$.

4   Discussion and Open Issues

The results of the previous section show that, under some restrictions on the allowed partitions, the local semantics computation proposed in [2] can be extended to multiple semantics. This raises several research issues, both from the perspective of adopting such schema and along the direction of revising it.

As to the first perspective, an interesting issue is to identify further restrictions on the partitions that guarantee uniform semantics equivalence, possibly considering also ideal semantics. Moreover, it would be interesting to formally characterize the labellings obtained by mixing semantics w.r.t. the skepticism relations. In particular, one may expect the resulting semantics to feature a somewhat intermediate level of skepticism w.r.t. individual semantics, and the level of skepticism to monotonically depend on that of individual semantics. As to the last point, replacing a semantics associated to a sub-framework e.g. with a more skeptical one should correspondingly result in a more skeptical semantics.

As to the revision of the proposed computation schema, a starting point may be the minimization/maximization of labellings, which as shown above yields uniform semantics equivalence for **GR** and **PR** in the general case. However, it is not really clear how this can be applied in case of multiple semantics. Another option would be to modify the "interface" between sub-frameworks by increasing the amount of information exchanged between them (currently including only the labels assigned to external attackers). This would require a significant revision of the proposed computation schema, paving the way for significant further research.

References

1. Amgoud, L., Dimopolous, Y., Moraitis, P.: A unified and general framework for argumentation-based negotiation. In: Proceedings of AAMAS 2007, pp. 113–124 (2007)
2. Baroni, P., Boella, G., Cerutti, F., Giacomin, M., van der Torre, L.W.N., Villata, S.: On the input/output behavior of argumentation frameworks. Artif. Intell. **217**, 144–197 (2014)
3. Baroni, P., Caminada, M., Giacomin, M.: An introduction to argumentation semantics. Knowl. Eng. Rev. **26**(4), 365–410 (2011)
4. Baroni, P., Giacomin, M.: Skepticism relations for comparing argumentation semantics. Int. J. Approximate Reasoning **50**(6), 854–866 (2009)
5. Bench-Capon, T., Prakken, H., Sartor, G.: Argumentation in legal reasoning. In: Simari, G., Rahwan, I. (eds.) Argumentation in Artificial Intelligence, pp. 363–382. Springer, Boston (2009). doi:10.1007/978-0-387-98197-0_18
6. Caminada, M., Amgoud, L.: On the evaluation of argumentation formalisms. Artif. Intell. **171**, 286–310 (2007)
7. Capobianco, M., Chesñevar, C.I., Simari, G.R.: Argumentation and the dynamics of warranted beliefs in changing environments. Auton. Agent. Multi-Agent Syst. **11**(2), 127–151 (2005)
8. Dung, P.M.: On the Acceptability of Arguments and Its Fundamental Role in Nonmonotonic Reasoning, Logic Programming, and n-Person Games. Artif. Intell. **77**(2), 321–357 (1995)
9. Dung, P.M., Mancarella, P., Toni, F.: A dialectic procedure for sceptical, assumption-based argumentation. In: Proceedings of COMMA 2006, pp. 145–156. IOS Press, Liverpool (2006)
10. Fox, J., Parsons, S.: Arguing about beliefs and actions. In: Hunter, A., Parsons, S. (eds.) Applications of Uncertainty Formalisms. LNCS, vol. 1455, pp. 266–302. Springer, Heidelberg (1998). doi:10.1007/3-540-49426-X_13
11. García, A.J., Simari, G.R.: Defeasible logic programming: an argumentative approach. Theor. Pract. Log. Program. **4**(1–2), 95–138 (2004)
12. Horty, J.F.: Skepticism and floating conclusions. Artif. Intell. **135**, 55–72 (2002)
13. Modgil, S., Prakken, H.: A general account of argumentation with preferences. Artif. Intell. **195**, 361–397 (2013)

14. Parsons, S., Wooldridge, M., Amgoud, L.: An analysis of formal inter-agent dialogues. In: Proceedings of AAMAS 2002, pp. 394–401 (2002)
15. Prakken, H.: Intuitions and the modelling of defeasible reasoning: some case studies. In: Proceedings of NMR-2002, pp. 91–99. Toulouse, France (2002)
16. Prakken, H.: Combining sceptical epistemic reasoning with credulous practical reasoning. In: Proceedings of COMMA 2006, pp. 311–322. IOS Press (2006)
17. Rienstra, T., Perotti, A., Villata, S., Gabbay, D.M., van der Torre, L.: Multi-sorted argumentation. In: Modgil, S., Oren, N., Toni, F. (eds.) TAFA 2011. LNCS, vol. 7132, pp. 215–231. Springer, Heidelberg (2012). doi:10.1007/978-3-642-29184-5_14
18. Toni, F.: A tutorial on assumption-based argumentation. Argum. Comput. 5(1), 89–117 (2014)

Agent and Multiagent Theories, Architectures, and Languages

Other-Condemning Anger = Blaming Accountable Agents for Unattainable Desires

Mehdi Dastani[1]([✉]), Emiliano Lorini[2], John-Jules Meyer[1], and Alexander Pankov[1]

[1] Utrecht University, Utrecht, The Netherlands
{m.m.dastani,j.j.c.meyer}@uu.nl, a.pankov@students.uu.nl
[2] IRIT-CNRS, Toulouse, France
emiliano.lorini@irit.fr

Abstract. This paper provides a formalization of the other-condemning anger emotion which is a social type of anger triggered by the behaviour of other agents. Other-condemning anger responds to frustration of committed goals by others, and motivates goal-congruent behavior towards the blameworthy agents. Understanding this type of anger is crucial for modelling human behavior in social settings as well as designing socially aware artificial systems. We utilize existing psychological theories on other-condemning anger and propose a logical framework to formally specify this emotion. The logical framework is based on dynamic multi-agent logic with graded cognitive attitudes.

1 Introduction

Other-condemning anger is a reaction to the frustration of goals to which agents are committed, and motivates goal congruent behavior towards the agents believed to be accountable for the goal frustration [7,10,15,21]. Imagine someone who has to upload his paper in a submission system just before the deadline, but notices that the Internet connection is broken for some maintenance operations without a notice. The frustration of not having submitted the paper makes the author angry and motivates him to write a letter of complaint to the Internet company. Situations like this may also occur for autonomous software agents where similar responses are desirable, not only because of the believability of the agents' behaviours, but also because of the efficiency and effectiveness of goal-congruent responses. Imagine a situation where autonomous robots commit themselves to transport containers from one place to another in an environment such as harbours. A robot R_1 that aims at picking up its container at a designated position may notice the container is removed by another robot R_2. A desirable response of the robot R_1 would be to send a request to the robot R_2, who is believed by R_1 to be accountable for the removal of the container, to make the container accessible to R_1 and/or to send a warning message to the manager of the environment to report this irregularity. We stress that it is the general function of anger, i.e., specific type of response to specific type of situation, that we aim at integrating in the model of autonomous agents, rather than

© Springer International Publishing AG 2017
B. An et al. (Eds.): PRIMA 2017, LNAI 10621, pp. 15–33, 2017.
https://doi.org/10.1007/978-3-319-69131-2_2

the physiological aspects of anger that is characteristic to human body. In this sense, it is the coordination role of emotions in agents' behaviour that motivates our work. For autonomous software agents that interact in social settings, the other-condemning anger emotion can be considered as a behavioural pattern or a heuristic that steers their behaviours.

There are reasons to believe that emotions in general, and other-condemning anger in particular, play an important role in rational behavior and in maintaining social order within societies [4,6,8,23]. Although there have been some efforts in artificial intelligence to provide a precise specification of emotions in general [5,17,18,28], there has not been, to our knowledge, a precise and adequate specification dedicated to the other-condemning anger emotion. We follow psychological literature [7,10,15,20,25] that explain other-condemning emotions in terms of complex social constructs such as controllability, accountability and blameworthiness. These social concepts require an adequate formalization of notions such as actions, control, causality, and their relations with the agents' cognitive states. As the above robot example illustrates, the angry robot R_1 believes its transportation goal being frustrated and that this is due to the removal action of robot R_2 who had control over its removal action (in the sense that R_2 could have chosen not to remove the container) and thus accountable for the caused consequences (i.e., R_1 cannot accomplish its transportation goal). The overtly social nature (being concerned with other agents) of this type of anger and its potential to influence others' behavior, make them essential for modelling human-like social interaction and designing socially aware artificial systems, which can be used for example in entertainment and serious games, crowd simulations, and human-computer interaction.

This paper proposes a logical model of multi-agent systems (Sect. 3) in which agents are specified by means of their knowledge, beliefs, desires, intentions, and actions. The logical model allows us to formally specify agents' anger. We present a logical specification of the appraisal and coping processes involved in other-condemning anger (Sect. 4). The specification is provided gradually by first specifying the underlying social and cognitive concepts such as control, accountability, blameworthiness, beliefs, goals, intentions and actions. We distinguish two types of anger. The first type of anger, called *plain anger*, involves two agents and captures the setting where an agent's committed goals is frustrated by another agent. The second type of anger, called *social anger*, involves three agents and captures the situation where the first agent gets angry at the second agent because the second agent harms a third agent who is in some social relation with the first agent. For social anger, we assume some social rules the existence of which are due to (or depend on) some norms or organisation governing the multi-agent environment. These assumed social rules may relate the goals of the first and the third agents such that the frustration of the third agent's goals by the second agent indirectly frustrates the goals of the first agent. For example, consider an extension of the robot example with a new manager agent that is responsible for the distribution and accomplishment of the transportation goals of all transport robots, including robot R_1. In this setting, the manager agent and robot R_1 are in an organisational setting where the achievement of the transportation goals of R_1 may contribute to the achievement of the manager goals. If R_2 frustrates the goal of R_1, then R_2 will indirectly and through the existence of the social rule frustrate the manager's goals and therefore make this agent angry. The theoretical and empirical supports for our formalization are derived from cognitive psychology [7,10,15,21,25,26]. We first provide an informal description of the other-condemning anger emotion, followed by a presentation of the syntax, semantics, axiomatization and decidability of a *dynamic multi-agent logic of graded attitudes*, which will be used to ground the informal description of the anger emotion.

2   Other-Condemning Anger

Other-condemning anger is commonly viewed as a negatively valenced reaction to the actions of other agents [21]. It is an instance of the *other-condemning* emotions [10], and triggered by frustration of a goal commitment [15,21]. In our robot example, the goal that the transport robot is committed to, i.e., the goal to have the container at its designated position, is frustrated. This broad view of other-condemning anger has been refined by emotion theories to distinguish it from other negative emotions such as sadness, guilt and remorse that also can arise from *goal incongruence*.

Most emotion theories distinguish other-condemning anger from other negative emotions by attributing *blame* for goal incongruence to other agents [7,15]. As a result, blame towards someone else becomes a necessary condition for other-condemning anger, for without the attribution of blame we can expect an emotion such as sadness. What does it mean, however, to blame someone for goal incongruence? According to [15], blame is an appraisal based on *accountability* and imputed *control*. To attribute accountability is to know who caused the relevant goal-frustrating event, and to attribute control is to believe that the accountable agent could have acted differently without causing the goal-incongruence. In our example, robot R_1 believes that robot R_2 is accountable for removing the container and that R_2 has the choice not to remove the container. According to Lazarus, anger is triggered if, in addition to above conditions, the *coping potential* (the evaluation of the possible responses) is viable. In our running example, the robot R_1 can send a request to R_2 to make the container accessible to R_1 and/or to report this irregularity to the environment manager. The prototypical *coping strategy* of other-condemning anger generally involves attack, or other means of getting back at the blameworthy agent, with the intention of restoring a goal congruent state of affairs [7,13,15].

The second type of other-condemning anger, i.e., social anger, is similar to what is often called *moral anger*, where a first agent is morally angry at a second agent because the second agent harms a third agent by violating some moral norm [23]. In such cases, an agent can rightfully be angry without any of his own goals being directly frustrated. In our extended example, the manager agent, which may be a software agent as well, may get angry at robot R_2, because R_2

has frustrated the goal of R_1. The actual reason for an agent to get angry at the third agent is the existence of a social rule that prescribes and promotes cooperation. For example, in case of human agents the reason for being angry can be the violation of a moral rule that prescribes agents not to harm the autonomy of each other. The typical coping strategy for social anger is similar to the coping strategy for the plain anger and promotes socially congruent behavior. Combining this aspect of social anger with the elicitation conditions of plain anger allows us to informally describe other-condemning anger in psychological terms as follows:

Displeasure from thwarting of a personal goal, or a social rule aimed at preserving the goal commitment of other agents, combined with attribution of blame for the goal-thwarting state of affairs to another agent, and an estimate of one's own coping potential as favouring attack towards *the blameworthy agent.*

3   The Logical Framework

In this section we define the logic DMAL-GA (*Dynamic Multi-Agent Logic of Graded Beliefs*). This logic serves as the basis for the formalization of the other-condemning anger emotion. The logic is a multi-agent extension of the DL-GA logic developed by Dastani and Lorini in [5]. However, there are substantial differences in the syntax and semantics of the system. Most importantly, here atomic actions are considered as special type of assignments, whereas Dastani and Lorini take an approach similar to that of Situation Calculus [24]. The consideration allows us to model the converse of actions in DMAL-GA and to define it as the reverse of the effects of atomic actions. The converse of actions is a prerequisite for formalizing concepts such as accountability and blame, which in turn play a central role in defining the other-condemning anger emotion. In particular, for the characterization of the accountability we need to refer to the action that has just occurred and look at the state from which the action is performed. The converse of the actions allows us to do this. We also need to refer to the actions that can possibly occur next.

Syntax. We assume a non-empty finite set of agents $Agt = \{1, \ldots, n\}$ and a non-empty finite set of atomic propositions $Atm = \{p, q, \ldots\}$ describing the environment in which the agents act. Because we aim at modelling the intensity of the anger emotion, we also assume a non-empty finite set of natural numbers $Num^+ = \{x \in \mathbb{N} : 0 \leq x \leq max\}$ with $max \in \mathbb{N} \backslash \{0\}$. Let also $Num^- = \{-x : x \in Num^+ \backslash \{0\}\}$ and $Num = Num^+ \cup Num^-$. The set of literals is defined in the usual way as follows: $Lit = Atm \cup \{\neg p : p \in Atm\}$. Let $Act = \{toggle(p) : p \in Atm\}$ be the set of atomic actions. Specifically, $toggle(p)$ should be read as "toggle the truth value of p", and understood as changing the truth value of p. This construct represents a simple notion of atomic action consisting in changing the truth value of a specific atomic proposition. We assume that changing the truth value of an atomic proposition in not always feasible such that a specific toggle action may not be available/executable at every state. For notational convenience, elements of Act are denoted by $a, b, \ldots$ For every agent

$i \in Agt$, agent i's set of events is defined to be $Evt_i = \{(i, a) : a \in Act\}$ and the set of all agents' events is defined to be $Evt = \bigcup_{i \in Agt} Evt_i$. An event (i, a) indicates that action a is performed by agent i. For notational convenience, elements of Evt are denoted by $e, e', \ldots$ Following [22], we use $-e$ to denote the converse of event $e \in Evt$, which allows us to describe properties of states before an atomic action of type $toggle(p)$ has been performed by an agent. We use $\alpha, \beta, \ldots$ to denote an event or its converse, i.e., $\alpha, \beta, \ldots$ denote the elements of $Evt \cup \{-e : e \in Evt\}$. We define $SeqEvt$ to be the set of all possible finite sequences of events or their converse. Elements of $SeqEvt$ are denoted by $\epsilon, \epsilon', \ldots$ The empty sequence of events is denoted by nil.

The language $\mathcal{L}$ of the logic DMAL-GA is defined by the following grammar:

$$\varphi, \psi ::= p \mid \neg\varphi \mid \varphi \wedge \psi \mid exc_i^h \mid Des_i^k l \mid Int_i(\epsilon, a) \mid$$
$$Fut(\epsilon, e) \mid Past(\epsilon, e) \mid K_i\varphi \mid [\alpha]\varphi$$

where p ranges over Atm, i ranges over Agt, h ranges over Num^+, k ranges over Num, a ranges over Act, e ranges over Evt, ϵ ranges over $SeqEvt$ and α ranges over $Evt \cup \{-e : e \in Evt\}$. The other Boolean constructions on formulae ($\vee$, $\rightarrow$, $\leftrightarrow$, $\top$ and $\bot$) are defined in the standard way using $\neg$ and $\wedge$.

The set of formulae contains special constructions exc_i^h, $Des_i^k l$ and $Int_i(\epsilon, a)$ which are used to represent agents' mental states. Formulae exc_i^h is used to identify the degree of exceptionality of a given world for a given agent i. Following [27], the worlds that are assigned the smallest numbers are the least exceptional and therefore the most plausible ones. Therefore, formula exc_i^h can be read as "the current world has a degree of exceptionality h for agent i" or "the current world has a degree of plausibility $max - h$ for agent i". In the following we will use exc_i^h to define graded beliefs of agent i. The formula $Des_i^k l$ represents the desires, or preferences, of agent i, and has to be read as "the state of affairs l has a degree of desirability k for agent i". For notational convenience, the following abbreviations are used in the rest of the paper: $AchG_i^k l \overset{def}{=} Des_i^k l$ and $AvdG_i^k l \overset{def}{=} Des_i^{-k} l$ for $k > 0$, where $AchG$ and $AvdG$ respectively stand for achievement goal and avoidance goal. Formulae $Int_i(\epsilon, a)$ represent the agents' intentions or commitments about atomic actions. Specifically, $Int_i(\epsilon, a)$ has to be read "after the sequence of events ϵ, agent i intends to perform action a".

The formulae $Fut(\epsilon, e)$ and $Past(\epsilon, e)$ represent the dynamics of the system by means of its action structure. They are introduced to refer to respectively the event (i.e., an action of an agent) that can possibly occur next in a state and the event that has just occurred in a state. In particular, $Fut(\epsilon, e)$ denotes the fact that event e is an option in the state reached after the execution of event sequence ϵ, and $Past(\epsilon, e)$ denotes the fact that event e has just occurred in the state reached after the execution of event sequence ϵ. These two formulae allow us to reason about options and performed actions after the execution of arbitrary sequence of events. The formula $Fut(\epsilon, e)$ has to be read as "the event e can possibly occur in the state reached by the sequence of events ϵ", while the formula $Past(\epsilon, e)$ has to be read as "the event e has just occurred in the state reached after the sequence of events ϵ". Note the use of nil in formulae $Fut(nil, e)$

and $Past(nil, e)$ which have the interpretation that the event e possibly occurs next to the "current state" and the event e has just occurred prior to the "current state", respectively.

Furthermore, the logic has an epistemic operator K_i for each agent. The formula $K_i\varphi$ should be read as "agent i knows that φ is true". This concept of knowledge is the standard S5-notion of knowledge. Finally, the formula $[\alpha]\varphi$ covers the dynamic nature of the formalism by referring to the state of the world after the occurrence of an event or its converse. It should be read as "the occurrence of event α leads to φ" or "the occurrence of event α results in φ". For notational convenience, we use special dynamic operators of the form $\langle\langle e \rangle\rangle$ and $\langle\langle -e \rangle\rangle$ where $\langle\langle e \rangle\rangle\, \varphi$ and $\langle\langle -e \rangle\rangle\, \varphi$ have to be read as, respectively, "the event e is going to possibly occur next and φ will be true afterwards" and "the event e has just occurred and φ was true before":

$$\langle\langle e \rangle\rangle\, \varphi \stackrel{def}{=} Fut(nil, e) \wedge [e]\varphi \qquad \& \qquad \langle\langle -e \rangle\rangle\, \varphi \stackrel{def}{=} Past(nil, e) \wedge [-e]\varphi$$

We also define the concept of present-directed intention, denoted by $Int_i a$, that is, the intention to do the action a now:

$$Int_i a \stackrel{def}{=} Int_i(nil, a)$$

An important aspect of the language is the possibility of defining *graded beliefs* using the formulae exc_i^h and the epistemic operators K_i. First, we introduce the following abbreviation: $exc_i^{\leq k} \stackrel{def}{=} \bigvee_{0 \leq l \leq k} exc_i^l$ for all $i \in Agt$ and for all $k \in Num^+$. Now, following [14,27], we define the following concept of belief:

$$B_i\varphi \stackrel{def}{=} K_i(exc_i^0 \to \varphi)$$

The formula $B_i\varphi$ says that agent i believes a formula φ *if and only if* φ is true in all worlds that are maximally plausible (or minimally exceptional) for the agent. We moreover define the following concept of graded belief, for $h > 0$:

$$B_i^{\geq h}\varphi \stackrel{def}{=} K_i(exc_i^{\leq h-1} \to \varphi)$$

The formula $B_i^{\geq h}\varphi$ says that agent i believes a formula φ with strength at least h *if and only if* φ is true in all worlds with exceptionality degree for the agent of less than h. Finally, we define the following concept of *exact* degree of belief, for $h > 0$:

$$B_i^h\varphi \stackrel{def}{=} \begin{cases} B_i^{\geq h}\varphi \wedge \neg B_i^{\geq h+1}\varphi & \text{if } 0 < h < max \\ B_i^{\geq max}\varphi & \text{if } h = max \end{cases}$$

The formula $B_i^h\varphi$ says that an agent believes that φ exactly with strength h *if and only if* the agent believes φ with strength at least h and the agent does not believe φ with strength at least $h + 1$.

Models. The language $\mathcal{L}$ is interpreted relative to a possible world semantics with special functions that represent the dynamic structure of the model. These functions are defined to ensure models with linear past and branching future, which are tree-like structures. Given a state of the model, these structures allow us to refer to the event that has just occurred and the events that can possible occur next. Specifically, the language $\mathcal{L}$ is interpreted on structures called DMAL-GA models.

Definition 1. *The tuple* $\mathfrak{M} = \Big(W, (\sim_i)_{i \in Agt}, (\mathcal{E}_i)_{i \in Agt}, (\mathcal{D}_i)_{i \in Agt}, (\mathcal{I}_i)_{i \in Agt},$ $\mathcal{F}, \mathcal{P}, \mathcal{V} \Big)$ *is a* DMAL-GA *model where:*

- W *is a nonempty set of worlds or states;*
- $\sim_i \subseteq W \times W$ *is an equivalence relation representing knowledge*
- $\mathcal{E}_i : W \longrightarrow Num^+$ *is a total function representing exceptionality degrees of states*
- $\mathcal{D}_i : W \times Lit \longrightarrow Num$ *is a total function representing desirability of facts*
- $\mathcal{I}_i : W \times SeqEvt \longrightarrow 2^{Act}$ *is a total function representing agents' intentions*
- $\mathcal{F} : W \times SeqEvt \longrightarrow 2^{Evt}$ *is a total function indicating future events;*
- $\mathcal{P} : W \times SeqEvt \longrightarrow Evt$ *is a partial function indicating past events;*
- $\mathcal{V} : W \longrightarrow 2^{Atm}$ *is a valuation function*

$\sim_i$ is an equivalence relation used to interpret the epistemic operator K_i. The set $\sim_i (w) = \{v \in W \mid w \sim_i v\}$ is the agent's information state at world w: the set of worlds the agent considers possible at world w. As $\sim_i$ is an equivalence relation, if $w \sim_i v$, then $\sim_i (w) = \sim_i (v)$: being at w or v is indistinguishable for agent i. The function $\mathcal{E}_i$ is the plausibility grading of the possible worlds for agent i, and is used to interpret the atomic formulae exc_i^h. $\mathcal{E}_i(w) = h$ means that, according to agent i, the world w has a degree of exceptionality h, or alternatively, degree of plausibility $max - h$. The function $\mathcal{E}_i$, together with the epistemic equivalence relation, allow to model the notion of graded belief: among the worlds agent i can not distinguish from, there are worlds the agent considers more plausible. We assume that DMAL-GA models satisfy the following *normality* condition with respect to the $\mathcal{E}_i$ functions:

(Norm) for all $i \in Agt$ and for all $w \in W$, there is $v \in W$ s.t. $w \sim_i v$ and $\mathcal{E}_i(v) = 0$.

This condition ensures that the real world, the world with exceptionality zero, is among possible worlds. The function $\mathcal{D}_i$ is the desirability grading of literals for agent i, and is used to interpret the atomic formulae $Des_i^k l$. $\mathcal{D}_i(w, l) = k$, means that, at world w, for agent i, l has a degree of desirability k. Positive values of k denote positive desirability, whereas negative values of k denote negative desirability (undesirability). A value of 0 means that agent i is indifferent about l at world w.

$\mathcal{I}_i(w, \epsilon)$ represents the set of actions that agent i intends to perform in the state that is reached after the sequence of events ϵ performed at world w. In other words, for every possible sequence of events ϵ and for every agent i, we describe the set of intentions that agent i will have in the state that is reached after this sequence. $\mathcal{I}_i(w, \epsilon) = \emptyset$ means that agent i will have no intention in the state that is reached after the sequence of events ϵ performed at world w.

$\mathcal{F}(w, \epsilon)$ and $\mathcal{P}(w, \epsilon)$ represent, respectively, the events which *can possibly* occur in the state reached after the sequence of events ϵ is performed at world w and the event which has just occurred in the state that is reached after the sequence of events ϵ is performed at world w. We call $\mathcal{F}$ and $\mathcal{P}$ *agenda* functions, given their similarity with the agenda function in [19]. $\mathcal{F}(w, \epsilon) = \emptyset$ means that no event can possibly occur in the state reached after the execution of the sequence ϵ at world w. If $\mathcal{P}(w, \epsilon)$ is undefined (since $\mathcal{P}$ is assumed to be a partial function), then it means that no event has just occurred in the state reached after the sequence of events ϵ is performed at world w. When ϵ is the empty sequence *nil*, then $\mathcal{F}(w, nil)$ and $\mathcal{P}(w, nil)$ denote, respectively, the events which *can possibly* occur at w (i.e., the options available at w) and the event which has just occurred at w (i.e., the event leads to w). Figure 1 illustrates how the dynamic structure of a *DMAL-GA* model can be specified by means of these two functions.

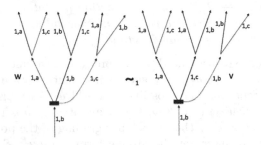

Fig. 1. Representation of the epistemic-temporal aspects of a *DMAL-GA* model

Figure 1 represents two worlds w and v that are indistinguishable from agent 1's perspective. Each world is associated with a particular evolution of the system that is specified by the functions $\mathcal{F}$ and $\mathcal{P}$. The small black rectangle in each world represents the reference point, which corresponds to the empty event sequence *nil*. Full arrows represent *possible* transitions (i.e., transitions corresponding to the execution of available actions) while dotted arrows represent counterfactual *impossible* transitions (i.e., transitions corresponding to the execution of non-available/non-executable actions). The following is a partial presentation of $\mathcal{F}$ and $\mathcal{P}$ applied to world w.

$$\mathcal{F}(w, nil) = \{(1, a), (1, b)\} \qquad \mathcal{P}(w, nil) = \{(1, b)\}$$
$$\mathcal{F}(w, (1, b)) = \{(1, b), (1, c)\} \qquad \mathcal{F}(w, (1, c)) = \{(1, a), (1, b)\}$$

It should be emphasized that Fig. 1 is not complete as it does not show all possible and impossible transitions. This is done to keep the figure simple and clear. Assuming the set of actions $Act = \{a, b, c\}$, other possible and impossible transitions should be drawn at each choice point. In particular, a complete figure should have all events at each choice point, either as a possible or as an impossible transition.

We assume that DMAL-GA models satisfy the following *equivalence* condition for intention and agenda functions:

(Equiv) for all $i \in Agt$, $\epsilon, \epsilon' \in SeqEvt$, $e \in Evt$, and $w \in W$, $\mathcal{I}_i(w, \epsilon;e; -e;\epsilon') = \mathcal{I}_i(w, \epsilon;\epsilon') = \mathcal{I}_i(w, \epsilon; -e;e;\epsilon')$, $\mathcal{F}(w, \epsilon;e; -e;\epsilon') = \mathcal{F}(w, \epsilon;\epsilon') = \mathcal{F}(w, \epsilon; -e;e;\epsilon')$ and $\mathcal{P}(w, \epsilon;e; -e;\epsilon') = \mathcal{P}(w, \epsilon;\epsilon') = \mathcal{P}(w, \epsilon; -e;e;\epsilon')$.

The previous constraint just means that the consecutive occurrences of a event e and its corresponding converse event $-e$ is ineffective. We also assume that DMAL-GA models satisfy the following *temporal coherence* condition between events and their converse counterparts:

(Coh) for all $\epsilon \in SeqEvt$, for all $e \in Evt$, and for all $w \in W$, $e \in \mathcal{F}(w, \epsilon; -e)$, and $\mathcal{P}(w, \epsilon;e) = e$.

For instance, suppose that $\epsilon = nil$. Then, the previous condition says that (i) before e has occurred, it was possible that e occurs, and (ii) after e occurs, it is the case that e has just occurred.

Given the structures for interpreting the DMAL-GA language, we specify truth conditions of formulae.

Definition 2. *Given a model* $\mathfrak{M} = \Big(W, (\sim_i)_{i \in Agt}, (\mathcal{E}_i)_{i \in Agt} (\mathcal{D}_i)_{i \in Agt}, (\mathcal{I}_i)_{i \in Agt},$ $\mathcal{F}, \mathcal{P}, \mathcal{V} \Big)$ *The truth conditions of formulae are defined as follows:*

- $\mathfrak{M}, w \models p$ iff $p \in \mathcal{V}(w)$;
- $\mathfrak{M}, w \models Des_i^k l$ iff $\mathcal{D}_i(w, l) = k$;
- $\mathfrak{M}, w \models exc_i^h$ iff $\mathcal{E}_i(w) = h$;
- $\mathfrak{M}, w \models Int_i(\epsilon, a)$ iff $a \in \mathcal{I}_i(w, \epsilon)$;
- $\mathfrak{M}, w \models Fut(\epsilon, e)$ iff $e \in \mathcal{F}(w, \epsilon)$;
- $\mathfrak{M}, w \models Past(\epsilon, e)$ iff $\mathcal{P}(w, \epsilon) = e$;
- $\mathfrak{M}, w \models \neg\varphi$ iff *not* $\mathfrak{M}, w \models \varphi$;
- $\mathfrak{M}, w \models \varphi \wedge \psi$ iff $\mathfrak{M}, w \models \varphi$ *and* $\mathfrak{M}, w \models \psi$;
- $\mathfrak{M}, w \models K_i\varphi$ iff $\mathfrak{M}, v \models \varphi$ *for all* $v \in W$ *s.t.* $v \sim_i w$;
- $\mathfrak{M}, w \models [\alpha]\varphi$ iff $\mathfrak{M}^\alpha, w \models \varphi$;

where $\mathfrak{M}^\alpha$ *is defined according to Definition 3.*

We write $\models \varphi$ to say that φ is valid and say that φ is satisfiable if $\neg\varphi$ is not valid. Before defining the updated model $\mathfrak{M}^\alpha$ let us briefly illustrate the interpretation epistemic formulas by means of the model given in Fig. 1. We have the following:

$$\mathfrak{M}, w \models K_1 Fut(nil, (1, a))$$
$$\mathfrak{M}, w \models K_1 Past(nil, (1, b))$$
$$\mathfrak{M}, w \models \neg K_1 Fut(nil, (1, b)) \wedge \neg K_1 \neg Fut(nil, (1, b))$$
$$\mathfrak{M}, w \models K_1 Fut((1, b), (1, b))$$

For instance, $\mathfrak{M}, w \models \neg K_1 Fut(nil, (1, b)) \wedge \neg K_1 \neg Fut(nil, (1, b))$ means that at w in the model of Fig. 1, agent 1 is uncertain whether she can possibly perform action b. Moreover, at w in the model of Fig. 1, agent 1 knows that, after having performed action b, she can possibly perform it again.

Definition 3. *Given a model* $\mathfrak{M} = \Big(W, (\sim_i)_{i \in Agt}, (\mathcal{E}_i)_{i \in Agt} (\mathcal{D}_i)_{i \in Agt}, (\mathcal{I}_i)_{i \in Agt},$
$\mathcal{F}, \mathcal{P}, \mathcal{V} \Big)$ *and an event* $\alpha \in \{(i, toggle(p)), -(i, toggle(p)) : i \in Agt \text{ and } p \in$
$Atm\}$, *the update of* $\mathfrak{M}$ *by* α, *is* $\mathfrak{M}^\alpha = \Big(W, (\sim_i)_{i \in Agt}, (\mathcal{E}_i)_{i \in Agt}, (\mathcal{D}_i)_{i \in Agt},$
$(\mathcal{I}_i^\alpha)_{i \in Agt}, \mathcal{F}^\alpha, \mathcal{P}^\alpha, \mathcal{V}^\alpha \Big)$ *where for all* $w \in W$, $i \in Agt$ *and* $\epsilon \in SeqEvt$:

$$\mathcal{I}_i^\alpha(w, \epsilon) = \mathcal{I}_i(w, \alpha; \epsilon) \qquad \mathcal{F}^\alpha(w, \epsilon) = \mathcal{F}(w, \alpha; \epsilon) \qquad \mathcal{P}^\alpha(w, \epsilon) = \mathcal{P}(w, \alpha; \epsilon)$$

$$\mathcal{V}^\alpha(w) = \begin{cases} \mathcal{V}(w) \cup \{p\} & \text{if } p \notin \mathcal{V}(w) \\ \mathcal{V}(w) \setminus \{p\} & \text{if } p \in \mathcal{V}(w) \end{cases}$$

The update of model $\mathfrak{M}$ by the event α just consists in: (i) updating the intention functions $\mathcal{I}_i$ as well as the agenda functions $\mathcal{F}$ and $\mathcal{P}$, and (ii) modifying the valuation function $\mathcal{V}$. In particular, if $a = toggle(p)$, then the truth value of p should be toggled. To illustrate the update of $\mathcal{F}$ let us consider an example. Suppose $F(w, \alpha; \beta) = \{e, e'\}$. This means that after performing the sequence of events $\alpha; \beta$ in state w we arrive in a state in which two events can possibly occur, namely, e and e'. The event α makes us to move one step right along the sequence $\alpha; \beta$ and to eliminate the first element (α) from it. Therefore, $F^\alpha(w, \beta) = F(w, \alpha; \beta) = \{e, e'\}$. The updates of $\mathcal{I}_i$ and $\mathcal{P}$ can be illustrated in a similar way. The following proposition guarantees that $\mathfrak{M}^\alpha$ is indeed a DMAL-GA model.

Proposition 1. *Let* $\mathfrak{M}$ *be a DMAL-GA model and* $\alpha \in Evt$. *Then,* $\mathfrak{M}^\alpha$ *is a DMAL-GA model too.*

We now present some interesting validities of the logic DMAL-GA.

Proposition 2. *For all* $i \in Agt$ *and for all* $e \in Evt$, *we have:*

$$\models \varphi \leftrightarrow [e][-e]\varphi \tag{1}$$
$$\models \varphi \leftrightarrow [-e][e]\varphi \tag{2}$$

Validities (1) and (2) in the preceding proposition capture the dependence between events and their converse counterparts. Similarly to [5], we have the following set of validities related to beliefs.

Proposition 3. *For all* $i \in Agt$, *and for all* $h, k \in Num^+$ *such that* $h \geq 1$ *and* $k \geq 1$:

$$\models K_i\varphi \rightarrow B_i^{\geq h}\varphi \tag{3}$$
$$\models B_i\varphi \leftrightarrow B_i^{\geq 1}\varphi \tag{4}$$
$$\models \neg(B_i\varphi \wedge B_i\neg\varphi) \tag{5}$$
$$\models (B_i^{\geq h}\varphi \wedge B_i^{\geq k}\psi) \rightarrow B_i^{\geq min[h,k]}(\varphi \wedge \psi) \tag{6}$$
$$\models (B_i^{\geq h}\varphi \wedge B_i^{\geq k}\psi) \rightarrow B_i^{\geq max[h,k]}(\varphi \vee \psi) \tag{7}$$

3.1 Axiomatization and Decidability

In this section we present an axiomatics and a decidability result for the logic DMAL-GA. The following theorem establish the axiomatization of the logic.

Theorem 1. *The logic DMAL-GA is axiomatized as an extension of the proposition multimodal logic $S5^n$ for the epistemic operators K_i with: (i) a theory describing the constraints imposed on agents' mental states and actions given in Fig. 2, (ii) reduction axioms of the dynamic operators $[\alpha]$ given in Fig. 3, and (iii) the following rule of replacement of equivalents:*

$$\frac{\psi_1 \leftrightarrow \psi_2}{\varphi \leftrightarrow \varphi[\psi_1/\psi_2]}$$

Proof (Sketch). To prove soundness of the principles in Figs. 2 and 3 is just a routine exercise. The completeness proof proceeds as follows. By standard canonical model argument, it is routine to show that the axioms and rules of inference of the multimodal logic $S5^n$ for every epistemic operator K_i together with the principles in Fig. 2 and all principles of classical propositional logic provide a complete axiomatization for the fragment of DMAL-GA with no dynamic operators. Let us call DMAL-GA$^-$ this fragment and $\mathcal{L}^-$ its corresponding language. Call *red* the mapping which iteratively applies the equivalences in Figure 3 from the left to the right, starting from one of the innermost modal operators. *red* pushes the dynamic operators inside the formula, and finally eliminates them when facing an atomic formula. By the rule of replacement of equivalents, it is routine to prove that $red(\varphi) \leftrightarrow \varphi$ is DMAL-GA valid. Now, suppose φ is DMAL-GA valid. Hence, $red(\varphi)$ is valid in DMAL-GA. By the completeness of DMAL-GA$^-$, $red(\varphi)$ is also provable there. DMAL-GA being a conservative extension of DMAL-GA$^-$, $red(\varphi)$ is provable in DMAL-GA, too. As the reduction axioms and the rule of replacement of equivalents are part of our axiomatics, the formula φ must also be provable in DMAL-GA. $\square$

$\bigvee_{h \in Num^+} exc_i^h$	$\bigvee_{k \in Num} Des_i^k l$
$\neg K_i \neg exc_i^0$	$Past(\epsilon, e, e)$
$exc_i^h \rightarrow \neg exc_i^{h'}$ if $h \neq h'$	$Des_i^k l \rightarrow \neg Des_i^{k'} l$ if $k \neq k'$
$Past(\epsilon, e) \rightarrow \neg Past(\epsilon, e')$ if $e \neq e'$	$Int_i(\epsilon; e'; - e'; \epsilon', a) \leftrightarrow Int_i(\epsilon; \epsilon', a)$
$Fut(\epsilon; e'; - e'; \epsilon', e) \leftrightarrow Fut(\epsilon; \epsilon', e)$	$Past(\epsilon; e'; - e'; \epsilon', e) \leftrightarrow Past(\epsilon; \epsilon', e)$
$Int_i(\epsilon; - e'; \epsilon'; \epsilon', a) \leftrightarrow Int_i(\epsilon; \epsilon', a)$	$Fut(\epsilon; - e'; e'; \epsilon', e) \leftrightarrow Fut(\epsilon; \epsilon', e)$
$Past(\epsilon; - e'; e'; \epsilon', e) \leftrightarrow Past(\epsilon; \epsilon', e)$	$Fut(\epsilon; - e, e)$

Fig. 2. Theory of the agents' mental states and actions

$$[\alpha]p \leftrightarrow \begin{cases} \neg p & \text{if } \alpha \in \{(i, toggle(p)), -(i, toggle(p))\} \\ & \text{for some } i \in Agt \\ p & \text{otherwise} \end{cases}$$

$$[\alpha]Int_i(\epsilon, a) \leftrightarrow Int_i(\alpha; \epsilon, a) \qquad\qquad [\alpha]Fut(\epsilon, e) \leftrightarrow Fut(\alpha; \epsilon, e)$$

$$[\alpha]Past(\epsilon, e) \leftrightarrow Past(\alpha; \epsilon, e) \qquad\qquad [\alpha]exc_i^h \leftrightarrow exc_i^h$$

$$[\alpha]Des_i^k l \leftrightarrow Des_i^k l \qquad\qquad\qquad [\alpha]\neg\varphi \leftrightarrow \neg[\alpha]\varphi$$

$$[\alpha](\varphi_1 \wedge \varphi_2) \leftrightarrow ([\alpha]\varphi_1 \wedge [\alpha]\varphi_2) \qquad\quad [\alpha]K_i\varphi \leftrightarrow K_i[\alpha]\varphi$$

Fig. 3. Reduction axiom schemas for the operators $[\alpha]$

Theorem 2. *The satisfiability problem of the logic DMAL-GA is decidable.*

Proof. (*Sketch*) Hardness just follows from the fact that the satisfiability problem of the multimodal logic $S5^n$ is PSPACE-hard [11] and that DMAL-GA extends the multimodal logic $S5^n$. As in the proof of Theorem 1 above let us call DMAL-GA$^-$ the fragment of DMAL-GA with no dynamic operators and let *red* be the mapping which allows us to eliminate the dynamic operators. The problem of checking the validity of a DMAL-GA$^-$ formula φ is reducible to the problem of *global* logical consequence in $S5^n$ with a finite set of global axioms Γ, Γ includes all principles in Fig. 2 which are relevant for $Sub(\varphi)$, the set of subformulas of φ. That is, we have $\models_{DMAL-GA^-} \varphi$ if and only if $\Gamma \models_{S5^n} \varphi$. The problem of global logical consequence in $S5^n$ with a finite set of global axioms is reducible to the problem of validity checking in $S5^n$ and these two problems are decidable. Thus, it follows that the problem of validity checking in the logic DMAL-GA$^-$ is decidable too. From the fact that $red(\varphi) \leftrightarrow \varphi$ is DMAL-GA valid and the fact that DMAL-GA is a conservative extension of DMAL-GA$^-$, it follows that *red* provides an effective procedure for reducing a DMAL-GA formula φ into an equivalent DMAL-GA$^-$ formula $red(\varphi)$. Thus, since the problem of validity checking in DMAL-GA$^-$ is decidable, it follows that the problem of validity checking in DMAL-GA is decidable too. □

4 Formalizing Anger

We are now well-equipped to formalize the other-condemning anger emotion. This requires translating our informal definitions into the language of DMAL-GA. The appraisal behind the elicitation of other-condemning anger is *blame*. According to the appraisal theories of emotion, there are two more basic concepts behind blame: *accountability* and *control*. For an agent to attribute blame to someone for something, he has to determine, first, if the other agent is accountable for (or having caused) the state of affairs, and second, if the other agent had control over it (or was able to prevent it). Formally, in the language of DMAL-GA, for agent i to attribute blame to agent j for a state of affairs, i must believe that j is (1) accountable for the state of affairs, and (2) had control over it (or was able to prevent it).

We first define what it means to have control over a state of affairs φ, denoted as $Control_i(\varphi)$ and read as "agent i has control over state of affairs φ". We say that agent i has control over state of affairs φ *if and only if* there exists an event $e \in Evt_i$ such that e can possibly occur next (i.e., if e is an option) and the occurrence of e maintains the truth value of φ. In other words, "agent i has control over the state of affairs φ if i is able to maintain its truth value". Formally,

$$Control_i(\varphi) \stackrel{def}{=} (\varphi \wedge \bigvee_{e \in Evt_i} \langle\langle e \rangle\rangle \varphi) \vee (\neg\varphi \wedge \bigvee_{e \in Evt_i} \langle\langle e \rangle\rangle \neg\varphi)$$

An instance of the $Control_i(\varphi)$ formula is $Control_{R_2}(XatY)$, where R_2 is one of the robots from our example, and $XatY$ denotes the state of affairs where container X is at some spacial location Y. This formula states that R_2 has control over the position of container X because it can ensure to maintain the position of X, i.e., if X is currently at Y then I can ensure that X is at Y in the next state and if X is currently not at Y then X will not be at Y at the next state.

For the notion of accountability, we assume an agent being accountable for a state of affair if and only if the state of affair is realized because of the action of the agent. In order to express accountability, we use the formula $Account_i(a, \varphi)$ which should be read as "agent i is accountable for (has caused) φ by doing a". By definition, this is the case *if and only if* φ is true now and was not true before event (i, a) occurred,[1] i.e.,

$$Account_i(a, \varphi) \stackrel{def}{=} \varphi \wedge \langle\langle -(i, a) \rangle\rangle \neg\varphi$$

An instance of this formula is $Account_{R_2}(pickXatY, \neg XatY)$, where $pickXatY$ denotes an action (or a complete plan) for picking up container X from location Y. This formula states that R_2 can be held accountable for container X not being at position Y because R_2 has picked up X from Y. The appraisal of blame can now be defined.

$$Blame^k_{i,j}(a, \varphi) \stackrel{def}{=} B^k_i(Account_j(a, \varphi) \wedge [-(j, a)]Control_j(\varphi))$$

The formula $Blame^k_{i,j}(a, \varphi)$ should be read as "agent i blames with strength k agent j for doing a and causing φ". By definition, this is the case *if and only if* agent i believes agent j is accountable for φ by doing a, and that before the event (j, a), j had control over φ. Going back to our robot example, we can speak of R_1 blaming R_2 for picking up the container from its location. Formally expressed as $Blame^k_{R_1, R_2}(pickXatY, XatY)$, for some $k > 0$. It is important to stress that we define blame without any negative connotations. Instead, it is viewed as a belief about the accountability of an agent for, and his control over,

---

[1] We assume that only one agent acts at each moment.

a given state of affairs. This is much in the spirit of how Lazarus talks about blame in his discussion on anger [15, p. 219].

Before defining other-condemning anger, we need a way of talking about the practical possibility of an agent to make a formula true. For this we use:

$$Pos_i(\varphi) \stackrel{def}{=} \bigvee_{e \in Evt_i} \langle\langle e \rangle\rangle \varphi$$

The formula $Pos_i(\varphi)$ should be read as "there is a practical possibility for agent i to make φ true". By definition, this is the case *if and only if* there exists an event $e \in Evt_i$ such that e can possibly occur next and φ will be true after its occurrence. In our example, this can be understood as robot R_1 being able to obtain the removed container, by say, sending a message to R_2 requesting the container to be returned, and thus making the formula $Pos_{R_1}(R_1 holds X)$ true.

4.1 Plain Anger

We can now define plain anger in the logic DMAL-GA as follows. $Anger^l_{i,j}(a, \varphi, b) \stackrel{def}{=}$
    $\bigvee_{l=merge(h,k)} (AchG^k_i(\varphi) \wedge Int_i b \wedge Blame^h_{i,j}(a, \neg \langle\langle (i,b) \rangle\rangle \varphi) \wedge B_i Pos_i(\varphi))$
where $merge$ is a monotonically increasing function of its two arguments, h and k.[2] Its range being the set $EmoInt = \{y : \exists x_1, x_2 \in Num^+ \text{ s.t. } merge(x_1, x_2) = y\}$. The formula $Anger^l_{i,j}(a, \varphi, b)$ should be read as "agent i is angry with intensity l at agent j for doing a and preventing i from achieving φ by doing b". By definition, this is the case *if and only if* agent i has an achievement goal φ, intends to do b, and blames agent j for performing the action a, thus preventing him from achieving φ by doing b".

Let us dissect the definition of plain anger and see how it matches our informal definition. The first conjunct, $AchG^k_i(\varphi)$, captures the prototypical feature of any emotion, i.e., to be about goal state φ. The next two conjuncts, $Int_i b$ and $Blame^h_{i,j}(a, \neg \langle\langle (i,b) \rangle\rangle \varphi)$, represent the anger-specific appraisal of blaming someone else for a goal-thwarting state of affairs. Here the goal-thwarting state is represented as the belief of agent i not to be able to achieve his goal by executing the intended plan b, which is expressed by $\neg \langle\langle (i,b) \rangle\rangle \varphi$, although i believes this was possible before action a was performed by agent j, which is expressed by $[-(j,a)] \langle\langle (i,b) \rangle\rangle \varphi$. This observation about the agent's attitudes is expressed as the following simple proposition:

Proposition 4. *Let* $\mathfrak{M}$ *be a DMAL-GA model,* $w \in W$; $a, b \in Act$; $i, j \in Agt$; $l \in EmoInt$ *and* $\varphi \in Lit$. *If* $\mathfrak{M}, w \models Anger^l_{i,j}(a, \varphi, b)$, *then*
    $\mathfrak{M}, w \models B^h_i(\neg \langle\langle (i,b) \rangle\rangle \varphi \wedge [-(j,a)] \langle\langle (i,b) \rangle\rangle \varphi)$ *for some* $h \in Num^+$

---

[2] As suggested by some appraisal theorists [15,21], the function $merge$ models the intensity of emotions by merging the strength of the negative belief behind blame and the desirability of φ. Possible instances of such a merging function are $\frac{h+k}{2}$ and $h \times k$.

Finally, $B_i Pos_i(\varphi)$, the last conjunct in the definition, highlights the positive evaluation by the agent of his coping potential – the type of secondary appraisal claimed to be an indispensable part of anger. Note that this practical possibility of achieving φ does not involve performing b, for agent i believes, according to Proposition 4, of not being able to achieve φ by means of b, i.e., $B_i^h \neg \langle\langle (i, b) \rangle\rangle \varphi$. For our robot example we can assume the following facts to hold:

- $AchG_{R_1}^k (R_1 holds X)$: robot R_1 wants with strength k to obtain container X;
- $Int_{R_1}(pickXatY)$: robot R_1 intends to pick up container X from its location Y;
- $B_{R_1} Pos_{R_1}(R_1 holds X)$: robot R_1 believes it has the practical possibility to achieve its goal of obtaining container X;
- $B_{R_1}^h Account_{R_2}(pickXatY, \neg \langle\langle (R_1, pickXatY) \rangle\rangle R_1 holds X)$: robot R_1 believes with strength h that robot R_2 is accountable for R_1 not being able to obtain container X by picking it up from location Y;
- $B_{R_1}^h [\neg (R_2, pickXatY)] Control_{R_2}(\langle\langle (R_1, pickXatY) \rangle\rangle R_1 holds X)$: robot R_1 believes, with strength h, that before R_2 obtained container X from location Y, R_2 had control over R_1 obtaining container X by picking it up from location Y; in other words, R_2 could have done something else.

Combining these assumptions with our definitions above one can conclude that $Anger_{R_1, R_2}^l(pickXatY, R_1 holds X, pickXatY)$, where $l = merge(h, k)$. That is, robot R_1 is angry with intensity l at robot R_2 for picking up container X from location Y, and thus preventing R_1 to pick it up instead in order to hold it (presumably with the intention of transporting it somewhere else).

4.2 Social Anger

Social settings are often governed by specific social rules or norms, which causes agents to become related to each other. For example, in a social setting governed by the norm to respect the autonomy of each other, one agent can get angry at a second one, not because of the negative consequence of the action of the second agent for the first agent, but because the second agent has violated the norm by restricting the autonomy of a third agent. Similarly, in an organisational setting, a manager agent can get angry at one agent because the agent ignores an organisational rule with respect to a third agent. In our robot example, the manager agent gets angry at R_2 because R_2 has frustrated the goals of R_1.

Proceeding to the social anger, we reassert that it is a flavor of other-condemning anger with its content related to the harm done to other agents. Although there are different types of harm distinguished in the literature [12,20], what they all have in common is the violation of personal preferences by others. We represent now the emotion of social anger, together with the concept of harm, in the language of DMAL-GA.

$$Harm_{i,j}^k(a, \varphi) \stackrel{def}{=} AchG_j^k \varphi \wedge Account_i(a, \neg Pos_j(\varphi))$$

The formula $Harm_{i,j}^k(a, \varphi)$ should be read as "agent i harmed with strength k agent j by doing a and preventing him from achieving φ". By definition, this is the case *if and only if* j has an achievement goal φ and i is accountable for j not having the practical possibility to achieve its goal φ. In our robot example, R_2 harmed R_1 preventing R_1 from achieving its goal of obtaining the container: $Harm_{R_2, R_2}^k(pickXatY, R_1 holdsX)$. Social anger can now be defined as follows:

$$SAnger_{i,j,k}^l(a, \varphi, \psi) \stackrel{def}{=} \bigvee_{l=merge(m,n)} (\bigvee_{b \in Act} Anger_{i,j}^m(a, \varphi, b) \wedge B_i(Harm_{j,k}^n(a, \psi) \wedge (\varphi \to \psi)))$$

The formula $SAnger_{i,j,k}^l(a, \varphi, \psi)$ should be read as "agent i is socially angry with intensity l at agent j for harming agent k preventing k from achieving ψ by doing a and preventing i from following his social concern φ". By definition, $SAnger_{i,j,k}^l(a, \varphi, \psi)$ is true *if and only if* (1) $Anger_{i,j}^m(a, \varphi, b)$ for some $b \in Act$, i.e., agent i is angry at agent j for doing a and thereby preventing him from achieving φ by some action b, (2) agent i believes $Harm_{j,k}^n(a, \psi)$, i.e., agent i believes agent j has harmed agent k by preventing the achievement of k's goal ψ, and (3) agent i believes ψ holds if φ holds.

To illustrate, let us consider again our robot example. For social anger, agent k from the definition above translates to robot R_1, j translates to robot R_2, and i to the manager agent M, who is socially angry. Furthermore, ψ is R_1's wish to obtain the container, φ is the wish of the manager that the autonomy of other agents should be respected, and a the act of picking up the container.

4.3 Anger Related Validities

Our formalization of anger and other concepts respects the following intuitive validities.

- After the occurrence of an event an agent is accountable for a state of affairs iff the state of affair does currently not hold, the state of affair is the case after the event, and the event creates the history.
  $\models [(i, a)]Account_i(a, \phi) \leftrightarrow \neg\phi \wedge [(i, a)]\phi \wedge [(i, a)]Past(nil, (i, a))$
- Blame requires choices in the direct past.
  $\models Blame_{i,j}^k(a, \phi) \to B_i^k([-(j, a)] \bigvee_{e \in Evt_j} [e]\neg\phi)$
- No blame for unavoidable.
  $\models B_i^k(\phi \wedge \bigwedge_{e \in Evt_j} [e]\neg\phi) \to [(j, b)]\neg Blame_{i,j}^k(b, \phi)$ for $(j, b) \in Evt_j$
- No blame for trivialities and impossibilities.
  $\models \neg Blame_{i,j}^k(a, \top)$
  $\models \neg Blame_{i,j}^k(a, \bot)$
- Decomposition of accountability.
  $\models Account_i(a, \neg\phi) \leftrightarrow \neg Account_i(a, \phi)$
  $\models Account_i(a, \phi \vee \psi) \leftrightarrow Account_i(a, \phi) \vee Account_i(a, \psi)$
  $\models Account_i(a, \phi \wedge \psi) \to Account_i(a, \phi) \vee Account_i(a, \psi)$
  $\models Account_i(a, \phi) \wedge Account_i(a, \psi) \to Account_i(a, \phi \wedge \psi)$

- No anger at those who are not accountable for your disability or desired outcome of your choice.
  $$\models \quad (\neg B_i^k Account_j(a, \neg Fut(nil, (i, b)) \quad \wedge \quad \neg B_i^k Account_j(a, \neg[(i, b)]\phi)) \quad \rightarrow$$
  $$\neg Anger_{i,j}^l(a, \phi, b)$$
  for $l = merge(h, k)$ and $h \in Num^+$
- Social Anger with respect to oneself implies Anger, but not vice versa.
  $$\models SAnger_{i,j,i}^l(a, \varphi, \varphi) \rightarrow Anger_{i,j}^l(a, \varphi, b) \text{ for some } (i, b) \in Evt_i$$
  $$\not\models Anger_{i,j}^l(a, \varphi, b) \rightarrow SAnger_{i,j,i}^l(a, \varphi, \varphi) \text{ for any } (i, b) \in Evt_i$$

4.4 Coping with (Social) Anger

Most psychologists agree that the innate coping strategy in anger is *aggression* towards the blameworthy agent [2,3], including *attack* and *threat* with the goal being the removal of the obstruction that caused anger. When planning an attack the agent chooses between types of attack (e.g., verbal versus physical, or punishment versus warning) based on coping potential. For instance, in our example, the participant's decision to report the irregularity to an environment administrator is based on the evaluation of his inability to ensure robot R_2 makes the container accessible to robot R_1: an estimate of his coping potential.

Following [5], coping is specified in terms of a function $Trg : Agt \times CStr \rightarrow \mathcal{L}$ that maps agents Agt and strategies $CStr$ to formulae from $\mathcal{L}$: for every agent i and coping strategy β, $Trg(i, \beta)$ denotes the conditions for i that triggers the strategy. We consider coping strategies $CStr$ for social anger as *intention-affecting* strategies a^+ (adopting intention a) and a^- (removing intention a). As social anger is elicited when an agent is harmed, we specify coping with social anger as adopting the intention a for which it is known to lead to $Harm_{j,k}(a, \psi)$ being false, i.e.,

$$Tr(i, b^+) = SAnger_{i,j,k}^l(a, \varphi, \psi) \wedge K_i[(i, b)]\neg Harm_{j,k}^n(a, \psi)$$

where $b \in Act$ and all the other variables as used for social anger. An immediate observation is the following:

Proposition 5. *Let $\mathfrak{M}$ be a model, $w \in W$, $a, b \in Act$, $i, j, k \in Agt$ and $\varphi \in \mathcal{L}$. If $\mathfrak{M}, w \models K_i[(i, b)]\neg Harm_{j,k}(a, \psi)$, then $\mathfrak{M}, w \models [(i, b)]\neg SAnger_{i,j,k}^l(a, \varphi, \psi)$ for $l \in EmoInt$.*

That is, successfully triggering the coping strategy b^+ for agent i, and executing the action b, removes the presence of social anger – a property necessary for successful coping [16]. In our example, this amounts to saying that in case of social anger one should expect attacking behavior (banning, warning) towards the violating robot R_2. This way the problem of harming robot R_1 will be mitigated by repairing the transportation task of R_1 or banning robot R_2 from operating in the transportation environment. It is important to note that the triggering condition is not the same as the selecting/executing the strategy. The selection/execution of a strategy is a separate issue which should take the intensity of the involved social anger emotion and its corresponding harm into account. This issue is not discussed as it is outside the scope of this paper.

5 Concluding Remarks

Although the focus of this paper is other-condemning anger, the presented logical framework is powerful enough to model various other-condemning social emotions such as disgust and contempt. We left out a formalization of other social emotions due to space limitation. The characteristic features of the presented framework are its multi-agent flavor and the inclusion of emotion intensity. Although the importance of emotion intensity has been stressed by appraisal theorist, most of the formal models in the literature have ignored at least one of them. For example, [1,18] ignores emotion intensity and [5] does not have multi-agent flavor. Our proposed model is inspired by [5], but we consider other-condemning and socially oriented anger, which requires extending the single agent framework proposed in [5] to a multi-agent framework with the converse of actions to reason about the state of the world before action execution. This feature is of crucial importance to some components of anger, e.g., responsibility and blame. Another influencing work on the topic has been [28]. Unlike our approach, [28] take emotion intensity as primitive, without explaining how it depends on belief and goal strengths. Furthermore, [28] does not provide any decidability results or axiomatization, whereas the current work does provide axiomatization and a decidability result. Finally, [9] proposes a formal model of emotions which incorporates both emotion intensities and coping. However, the authors do not provide any details on the underlying logic, which makes comparing the two approaches difficult.

We intend to extend the set of other-condemning emotions in future work and provide an analysis on the relation between various moral emotions. We also aim at extending the dynamic nature of our proposed logic by allowing more complex actions and extend the accountability not to actions that have been performed in previous state, but to some state in the past.

References

1. Adam, C., Herzig, A., Longin, D.: A logical formalization of the occ theory of emotions. Synthese **168**, 201–248 (2009)
2. Averill, J.R.: Studies on anger and aggression: Implications for theories of emotion. Am. Psychol. **38**(1), 1145–1160 (1983)
3. Averill, J.R.: Anger and Aggression: An Essay on Emotion. Springer, New York (1982)
4. Blackburn, S.: Ruling Passions. Clarendon Press, Oxford (1998)
5. Dastani, M., Lorini, E.: A logic of emotions: from appraisal to coping. In: Proceedings of the 11th International Conference on Autonomous Agents and Multiagent Systems, vol. 2, pp. 1133–1140 (2012)
6. Elster, J.: Rationality, emotions, and social norms. Synthese **98**(1), 21–49 (1994)
7. Frijda, N.H.: The Emotions. Cambridge Univ. Pr., Cambridge (1986)
8. Gewirth, A.: Reason and Morality. University of Chicago Press, Chicago (1981)
9. Gratch, J., Marsella, S.: A domain-independent framework for modeling emotion. Cogn. Syst. Res. **5**(4), 269–306 (2004)
10. Haidt, J.: The moral emotions. Handbook Affect. Sci. **11**, 852–870 (2003)

11. Halpern, J., Moses, Y.: A guide to completeness and complexity for modal logics of knowledge and belief. Artif. Intell. **54**, 319–379 (1992)
12. Helwig, C.C., Zelazo, P.D., Wilson, M.: Children's judgments of psychological harm in normal and noncanonical situations. Child Dev. **72**(1), 66–81 (2001)
13. Izard, C.E.: Human Emotions. Plenum, New York (1977)
14. Laverny, N., Lang, J.: From knowledge-based programs to graded belief-based programs, part i: On-line reasoning*. Synthese **147**, 277–321 (2005)
15. Lazarus, R.S.: Emotion and Adaptation. Oxford University Press, USA (1991)
16. Lazarus, R.S., Folkman, S.: Stress, Appraisal, and Coping. Springer, New York (1984)
17. Lorini, E.: A dynamic logic of knowledge, graded beliefs and graded goals and its application to emotion modelling. In: van Ditmarsch, H., Lang, J., Ju, S. (eds.) LORI 2011. LNCS, vol. 6953, pp. 165–178. Springer, Heidelberg (2011). doi:10.1007/978-3-642-24130-7_12
18. Lorini, E., Schwarzentruber, F.: A logic for reasoning about counterfactual emotions. Artif. Intell. **175**, 814–847 (2010)
19. Meyer, J.-J.C., van der Hoek, W., van Linder, B.: A logical approach to the dynamics of commitments. Artif. Intell. **113**, 1–40 (1999)
20. Ohbuchi, K., Kameda, M., Agarie, N.: Apology as aggression control: its role in mediating appraisal of and response to harm. J. Pers. Soc. Psychol. **56**(2), 219 (1989)
21. Ortony, A., Clore, G., Collins, A.: The Cognitive Structure of Emotions. Camb. Uni. Pr., Cambridge (1990)
22. Parikh, R.: The completeness of propositional dynamic logic. In: Winkowski, J. (ed.) MFCS 1978. LNCS, vol. 64, pp. 403–415. Springer, Heidelberg (1978). doi:10.1007/3-540-08921-7_88
23. Prinz, J.: The Emotional Construction of Morals. Oxford University Press, Oxford (2007)
24. Reiter, R.: Knowledge in Action: Logical Foundations for Specifying and Implementing Dynamical Systems. MIT Press, Cambridge (2001)
25. Rozin, P., Lowery, L., Imada, S., Haidt, J., et al.: The cad triad hypothesis: a mapping between three moral emotions (contempt, anger, disgust) and three moral codes (community, autonomy, divinity). J. Personal. Soc. Psychol. **76**, 574–586 (1999)
26. Scherer, K.R.: Appraisal considered as a process of multilevel sequential checking: a component process approach. Apprais. Process. Emot. Theory Methods Res. **92**, 120 (2001)
27. Spohn, W.: Ordinal conditional functions: a dynamic theory of epistemic states. Causation Dec. Belief Change Stat. **2**, 105–134 (1988)
28. Steunebrink, B.R., Dastani, M., Meyer, J.-J.C.: A formal model of emotion-based action tendency for intelligent agents. In: Lopes, L.S., Lau, N., Mariano, P., Rocha, L.M. (eds.) EPIA 2009. LNCS, vol. 5816, pp. 174–186. Springer, Heidelberg (2009). doi:10.1007/978-3-642-04686-5_15

Group Decision Making in a Bipolar Leveled Framework

Florence Dupin de Saint-Cyr$^{(\boxtimes)}$ and Romain Guillaume

IRIT, Toulouse University, Toulouse, France
bannay@irit.fr

Abstract. We study the use of a bipolar decision structure called BLF (bipolar leveled framework) in the context of collective decision making where the vote consists in giving factual information about a candidate which the group should accept or reject. A BLF defines the set of possible decision principles that may be used in order to evaluate the admissibility of a given candidate. A decision principle is a rule that relates some observations about the candidate to a given goal that the selection of this candidate may achieve or miss. The decision principles are ordered accordingly to the importance of the goal they support. Oppositions to decision principles are also described in the BLF under the form of observations that contradict the realization of the decision principles. We show how the use of a common BLF may reduce the impact of manipulation strategies in the context of group decision making.

Keywords: Group decision making · Qualitative decision theory · Arguments

1 Introduction

A standard way [16] to handle a decision problem is to define a utility function which enables the decision maker to evaluate the quality of each decision and select the one that have the best utility. This utility function should be designed in order to take into account the multi-criteria aspects of the problem. The classical approaches for handling collective decision problems under uncertainty are based on (i) the identification of a decision making theory under uncertainty that captures the decision makers' behaviour with respect to uncertainty and (ii) the specification of a collective utility function (CUF) as it may be used when the problem is not pervaded with uncertainty [5].

In classical decision problems, all candidates are available to the decision maker simultaneously and he must choose one preferred candidate among them. Our approach deals with a different case of decision like the "secretary problem" (see e.g. [15]) where an administrator wants to hire the best secretary. In this case, only one candidate is evaluated at a time and a decision about each particular applicant is to be made immediately after the interview. Once rejected, an applicant cannot be recalled. Hence the decision maker should decide whether

© Springer International Publishing AG 2017
B. An et al. (Eds.): PRIMA 2017, LNAI 10621, pp. 34–52, 2017.
https://doi.org/10.1007/978-3-319-69131-2_3

to make a final choice or continue searching for better candidates. In this kind of problem, the aim is not to compute the best candidate among all the possible candidates, but rather to select a candidate that is convenient wrt some criterias. We capture the notion of convenience by introducing "admissibility statuses" where the admissibility of a candidate is given in terms of the goals that would be achieved by accepting her, the goals are positive or negative and some are more important to achieve than others.

Recently, a framework based on default rules have been proposed by [12] for decision under uncertainty. Its aim was to propose a new rational model for decision making in the presence of incomplete knowledge, through the definition of clear admissibility criteria by taking advantage of the notions of efficiency and simplicity that are central in industrial domain. In particular the authors were inspired from the protocols promoted in business practices guidelines like the "Collaborative Planning, Forecasting and Replenishment" model [14]. This protocol aims at coordinating the supply chain from strategic to operational decision: at the end, the agents should select a production plan (the candidate) that will be convenient for all the members of the supply chain. In this context the knowledge is incomplete and distributed since all the consequences of a production policy (i.e. the selection of a given production plan) are not known by all the particular participants of the supply chain and agents usually do not want to make all their knowledge public. This paper has defined a new representation framework for decision making, called Bipolar Leveled Framework (BLF), which was first introduced in [3]. The BLF is a bipolar structure that enables the decision maker to *visualize the attributes and goals that are involved in the decision problem, together with their inhibitors and their importance levels.* Informally, a BLF may be viewed as a kind of qualitative utility function with some extra features: (1) the defeasible links between attributes and goals are made explicit into what is called "decision principles", (2) an opposition to a decision principle, called "inhibitor", is represented by an arc directed towards it, (3) the importance levels of decision principles are represented by the height of their position in the structure. The BLF can be established either by one person or by a group of people in order to define a decision making framework which will be instantiated when candidates will be evaluated.

In this paper we propose to use a BLF in the collective decision problem to accept or reject a candidate. We propose to organize the decision by letting agents vote about the features that hold for the candidate but agents are never allowed to vote about the goals that would be achieved by selecting the candidate. Hence we separate the decision into three phases, the phase where the criteria associated to a good decision are defined (the BLF construction which is out of the scope of this paper), the phase where the candidates are evaluated by the voters, and the final decision to accept or reject the candidate (which is an automatic phase using the BLF with the precise features concerning the current candidate). In the literature the specification of a CUF is an aggregation of the agent preferences hence this is somewhat mixing the three phases. Moreover, in order to show that this rich and visual framework is well founded we show how the use of a common BLF may reduce the impact of manipulation strategies in the context of group decision making. The term manipulation is used in a weak sense, since the results presented are not of a game-theoretic nature, in particular, they do not admit deviating behavior. However since agents have the right to omit some information we consider that this behavior is a kind of manipulation.

2   Decision Making with a BLF

2.1   BLF: A Structure Encoding Decision Criteria

We consider a set $\mathscr{C}$ of candidates[1] about which some information is available and two languages $\mathscr{L}_F$ (a propositional language based on a vocabulary $\mathcal{V}_F$) representing information about some features that are believed to hold for a candidate and $\mathscr{L}_G$ (another propositional language based on a distinct vocabulary $\mathcal{V}_G$) representing information about the achievement of some goals when a candidate is selected. In the propositional languages used here, the logical connectors "or", "and", "not" are denoted respectively by $\vee$, $\wedge$, and $\neg$. A *literal* is a propositional symbol x or its negation $\neg x$, the set of literals of $\mathscr{L}_G$ are denoted by LIT_G. Classical inference, logical equivalence and contradiction are denoted respectively by $\models$, $\equiv$, $\perp$. The reason why we propose two distinct languages is to clearly differentiate beliefs (coming from observations) from desires (goals to be achieved when selecting a candidate). In the following we denote by K a set of formulas representing features that are believed to hold: hence $K \subseteq \mathscr{L}_F$ is the available information. Using the inference operator $\models$, the fact that a formula $\varphi \in \mathscr{L}_F$ holds[2] in K is written $K \models \varphi$.

The BLF is a structure that contains two kinds of information: decision principles and inhibitors. A decision principle can be viewed as a defeasible reason enabling to reach a conclusion about the achievement of a goal. More precisely, a decision principle is a pair (φ, g), it represents the default rule meaning that "if the formula φ is believed to hold for a candidate then the goal g is a priori believed to be achieved by selecting this candidate":

Definition 1 (decision principle (DP)). A *decision principle* p is a pair $(\varphi, g) \in \mathscr{L}_F \times LIT_G$, where φ is the reason denoted $reas(p)$ and g the conclusion of p denoted $concl(p)$. $\mathcal{P}$ denotes the set of decision principles.

We illustrate the BLF notions on a toy example concerning a recruitment problem.

Example 1. *If the candidates are people applying for a job then the decision principle (CV good readability, ability to well present herself) could be understood as "if the candidate has a CV easy to read then a priori the goal to have a person able to well present herself is achieved".*

---

[1] Candidates are also called alternatives in the literature.

[2] The agent's knowledge K being considered to be certain, we write "φ holds" instead of "φ is believed to hold".

Depending on whether the achievement of its goal is wished or dreaded, a decision principle may have either a positive or a negative polarity. Moreover some decision principles are more important than others because their goal is more important. The decision principles are totally ordered accordingly.

Definition 2 (polarity and importance). A function $pol : \mathcal{V}_G \rightarrow \{\oplus, \ominus\}$ gives the polarity of a goal $g \in \mathcal{V}_G$, this function is extended to goal literals by $pol(\neg g) = -pol(g)$ with $-\oplus = \ominus$ and $-\ominus = \oplus$. Decision principles are polarized accordingly: $pol(\varphi, g) = pol(g)$. The set of positive and negative goals are abbreviated $\overline{\oplus}$ and $\overline{\ominus}$ respectively: $\overline{\oplus} = \{g \in LIT_G : pol(g) = \oplus\}$ and $\overline{\ominus} = \{g \in LIT_G : pol(g) = \ominus\}$.

LIT_G is totally ordered by the relation $\preceq$ ("less or equally important than"). Decision principles are ordered accordingly: $(\varphi, g) \preceq (\psi, g')$ iff $g \preceq g'$.

The polarities and the relative importances of the goals in $\mathcal{V}_G$ are supposed to be given by the decision maker. In the following example, the decision maker (our agent) may want to avoid to select an anti-social person (hence ap is a negative goal), while selecting a candidate who is efficient for the job is a positive goal, moreover he may give more importance to the efficiency for the job than to the ability to present oneself. In this example we propose to affect the same importance to the negative goal to have a person not efficient for the job $\neg ej$ and to the positive goal to have an easy to train person et, since when a candidate has those features it is difficult to say whether the positive outweights the negative or the reverse.

Example 2. *Let us consider a recruitment problem. The recruitment is done according to the following goals, listed with their abbreviation and polarity:*

goal	meaning	polarity
ap	we do not want someone with an anti-social personality	$\ominus$
ej	we want to hire an efficient person for the job	$\oplus$
ph	we want to find a person able to present herself	$\oplus$
et	we want to find a person easy to train	$\oplus$
st	we want to hire a stable person	$\oplus$

Hence in this example $LIT_G = \{ap, \neg ap, ej, \neg ej, ph, \neg ph, et, \neg et, st, \neg st\}$. The levels of the goals of LIT_G are s.t.[3] $et \simeq \neg ej \succ \neg et \succ ap \succ ph \simeq \neg ph \succ \neg st \succ \neg ap \simeq ej \simeq st$. These levels of importance translate e.g. that finding an efficient and easy to train person is strictly more important than achieving any of the three other goals.

The set of features $\mathcal{V}_F$ describing a candidate is summarized in the following tables:

---

[3] The equivalence relation associated to $\preceq$ is denoted $\simeq$ ($x \simeq y \Leftrightarrow x \preceq y$ and $y \preceq x$) and the strict order is denoted $\prec$ ($x \prec y \Leftrightarrow x \preceq y$ and not $y \preceq x$) hence $x \simeq y$ represents the fact that the goals x and y are equally important, $x \succ y$ that x is strictly more important than y.

Feature	Meaning
cbs	CV bad spelling
eb	educational background
i	introverted candidate
lpe	long professional experience
u	unmotivated candidate

Feature	Meaning
cgr	CV good readability
gp	good personality
jhop	job hopper
spe	professional experience in the specialty of the job

A decision principle (φ, g) is a defeasible piece of information because sometimes there may exist some reason φ' to believe that it does not apply in the situation, this reason is called an *inhibitor*.

The fact that φ' inhibits a decision principle (φ, g) is interpreted as follows: "when the decision maker only knows $\varphi \wedge \varphi'$ then he is no longer certain that g is achieved". In that case, the inhibition is represented with an arc towards the decision principle. The decision principles and their inhibitors are supposed to be given by the decision maker. An interpretation in terms of possibility theory is described in [12].

We are now in position to define the structure BLF.

Definition 3 (BLF). Given a set of goals $\mathcal{V}_G$, a BLF is a quadruplet $(\mathcal{P}, \mathcal{R}, pol, \preceq)$ where $\mathcal{P}$ is a set of decision principles ordered accordingly to their goals by $\preceq$ and with a polarity built on *pol* as defined in Definition 2, $\mathcal{R} \subseteq (\mathscr{L}_F \times \mathcal{P})$ is an inhibition relation.

The four elements of the BLF are supposed to be available prior to the decision and to be settled for future decisions as if it was a kind of utility function. A graphical representation of a BLF is given below, it is a tripartite graph represented in three columns, the DPs with a positive level are situated on the right column, the inhibitors are in the middle, and the DPs with a negative polarity are situated on the left. The more important (positive and negative) DPs are in the higher part of the graph, equally important DPs are drawn at the same horizontal level. By convention the highest positive level is at the top right of the figure and the lowest negative level is at the top left. The height of the inhibitors is not significant only their existence is used.

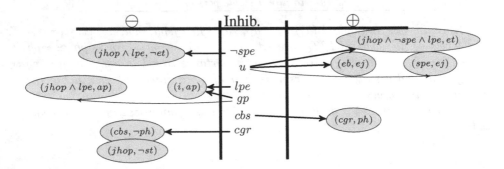

Fig. 1. Recruitment BLF

Example 2 (continued): *Figure 1 illustrates the BLF corresponding to Example 2. In this example, we can see that it is different to have a decision principle with the negation of a goal like ¬et (not easy to train) in (jhop ∧ lpe, ¬et) (a job hopper with a long experience is not easy to train) from having an inhibition u towards a DP with the goal et, here (jhop ∧ ¬spe ∧ lpe, et) (a job hopper non specialist with a long experience is generally easy to train except when he is unmotivated). Note that the utility of ¬et is considered, it has a disutility (at a lower level than the utility of et), but sometimes the utility of the opposite goal is not considered as it is done for ¬ap here (which is translated by an attribution of the lowest utility).*

In the following, the BLF $(\mathcal{P}, \mathcal{R}, pol, \preceq)$ is set and we show how it can be used for analyzing the acceptability of a candidate. First, we present the available information and the notion of instantiated BLF, called valid-BLF.

Given a candidate $c \in \mathscr{C}$, we consider that the knowledge of the decision maker about c has been gathered in a knowledge base K_c with $K_c \subseteq \mathscr{L}_F$. Given a formula φ describing a configuration of features ($\varphi \in \mathscr{L}_F$), the decision maker can have three kinds of knowledge about c: φ holds for candidate c (i.e., $K_c \models \varphi$), or not ($K_c \models \neg\varphi$) or the feature φ is unknown for c ($K_c \not\models \varphi$ and $K_c \not\models \neg\varphi$). When there is no ambiguity about the candidate c, K_c is denoted K.

Definition 4 (K-valid-BLF). Given a *consistent* knowledge base K, a K-valid-BLF is a quadruplet $(\mathcal{P}_K, \mathcal{R}_K, pol, \preceq)$ where

- $\mathcal{P}_K = \{(\varphi, g) \in \mathcal{P},$ s.t. $K \models \varphi\}$ is the set of DPs in $\mathcal{P}$ whose reason φ holds in K, called *valid-DPs*.
- $\mathcal{R}_K = \{(\varphi, p) \in \mathcal{R},$ s.t. $K \models \varphi$ and $p \in \mathcal{P}_K\}$ is the set of *valid inhibitions* according to K.

When there is no ambiguity, we simply use "valid-BLF" instead of "K-valid-BLF". The validity of a DP only depends on the fact whether the features that constitute its reason φ hold or not, it does not depend on its goal g since the link between the reasons and the goal is given in the BLF (hence it is no longer questionable).

Example 2 (continued): *The agent has information about a candidate c_0: she is a job hopper jhop, with a long personal experience, lpe, this experience is not in the specialty of the job ¬spe and the candidate is unmotivated u but she has a CV with a good readability cgr. Figure 2 is the valid-BLF representing the knowledge about c_0.*

Now in the valid-BLF the principles that are not inhibited are the ones that are going to be trusted. A goal in $\mathcal{V}_G$ is said to be *realized* if there is a valid-DP that is not inhibited by any valid-inhibitor.

Definition 5 (realized goal). Let g be a goal in LIT_G, g is *realized* w.r.t. a K-valid-BLF $B = (\mathcal{P}_K, \mathcal{R}_K, pol, \preceq)$ iff $\exists(\varphi, g) \in \mathcal{P}_K$ and $\nexists(\varphi', (\varphi, g)) \in \mathcal{R}_K$.

The set of realized goals w.r.t. B is denoted $\mathbf{R}(B)$, the positive and negative realized goals are denoted by $\mathbf{R}(B)^\oplus = \mathbf{R}(B) \cap \overline{\oplus}$ and $\mathbf{R}(B)^\ominus = \mathbf{R}(B) \cap \overline{\ominus}$ respectively.

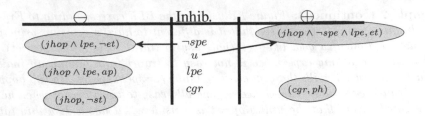

Fig. 2. Valid BLF with $K = \{jhop, lpe, \neg spe, u, cgr\}$

When there is no ambiguity about the BLF B, $\text{R}(B)$ is simply denoted by R.

Example 2 (continued): *The goals $\neg et$ and et are not realized for candidate c_0 since the inhibitions $\neg spe$ and u are valid. Two negative goals, ap and $\neg st$, and one positive goal, ph, are realized.*

In Sect. 2.2 we explain how to use a BLF in order to make a decision. The decision consists in saying whether or not a candidate is admissible based on the goals that are realized in its corresponding valid-BLF.

2.2 Admissibility Statuses of Candidates

The admissibility status of a candidate c is computed from a BLF and a knowledge base K_c describing what is known about c, its corresponding K_c-valid-BLF should be denoted $\langle \mathcal{P}_{K_c}, \mathcal{R}_{K_c}, pol, \preceq \rangle$. However, when there is no ambiguity about the knowledge available, $\mathcal{P}_{K_c}$ is denoted $\mathcal{P}$ and $\mathcal{R}_{K_c}$ is abbreviated $\mathcal{R}$.

We first define the notion of order of magnitude which requires to define the levels of a set of goals. We attribute levels to sets of goals starting from the least important ones that are assigned a level 1 and stepping by one each time the importance grows.

Definition 6 (levels and order of magnitude). Given a set of goals $G \subseteq LIT_G$ and the relation $\preceq$ on LIT_G, the levels of G are defined by induction:

- $G_1 = \{g \in G : \nexists g' \in G \text{ s.t. } g' \prec g\}$
- $G_{i+1} = \{g \in G : \nexists g' \in G \setminus (\bigcup_{k=1}^{i} G_k) \text{ s.t. } g' \prec g\}$

The order of magnitude of G is: $\text{OM}(G) = \max_{g \in G}\{\lambda : g \in G_\lambda\}$ with $\text{OM}(\varnothing) = 0$.

Definition 7 (admissibility status). Given a candidate $c \in \mathscr{C}$, given the knowledge K_c about c and given a K_c-valid-BLF $\langle \mathcal{P}, \mathcal{R}, pol, \preceq \rangle$. The status of c is:

- *necessarily admissible* if $\text{R}_M^\oplus \neq \varnothing$ and $\text{R}_M^\ominus = \varnothing$
- *possibly admissible* if $\text{R}_M^\oplus \neq \varnothing$
- *indifferent* if $\text{R} = \varnothing$
- *possibly inadmissible* if $\text{R}_M^\ominus \neq \varnothing$

– *necessarily inadmissible* if $R_M^\ominus \neq \varnothing$ and $R_M^\oplus = \varnothing$
– *controversial* if $R_M^\oplus \neq \varnothing$ and $R_M^\ominus \neq \varnothing$

where $M = \mathrm{OM}(R)$ (hence R_M is the set of most important realized goals).

We respectively denote by N_{ad}, Π_{ad}, Id, $\Pi_{\neg ad}$, $N_{\neg ad}$ and Ct the set of necessarily admissible, possibly admissible, indifferent, possibly inadmissible, necessarily inadmissible and controversial candidates.

In other words, a *necessarily admissible* candidate is supported by positive principles with goals of maximum importance that are realized (*i.e.,* uninhibited) and all the negative goals of the same importance do not hold. A *possibly admissible* candidate has at least one uninhibited positive principle of maximum importance in its favor. An *indifferent candidate*[4] is not concerned by any uninhibited principle (nor positive nor negative), while a *controversial candidate* is both supported and criticized by uninhibited DPs of maximum importance We define three sets of admissibility:

– $S1 = N_{ad}$, in this set, the candidates are admissible with no doubt, there are uninhibited principles about the candidates which are all positive.
– Since there are two ways to have doubts about a candidate, namely when she is indifferent (Id) or controversial (Ct), we define two weaker sets:
  • $S2a = N_{ad} \cup Id$ (*i.e.,* $S2a = \mathscr{C} \setminus \Pi_{\neg ad}$). In this set, we place candidates of S1 together with those for which no uninhibited principle is available (neither positive nor negative),
  • $S2b = N_{ad} \cup Ct$ (*i.e.,* $S2b = \Pi_{ad}$). It gathers S1 together with the candidates that are concerned by negative uninhibited principles provided that they are also concerned at least by one positive uninhibited principle.
– $S3 = Id \cup Ct \cup N_{ad}$ (*i.e.,* $\Pi_{ad} \cup Id = \mathscr{C} \setminus N_{\neg ad}$). It contains also S1.

Note that in this paper we focus on the question whether to accept or not a given candidate. Regarding the question about the selection of one candidate among a set of candidates, different rules [7] have been proposed for comparing candidates in a qualitative bipolar decision framework and have been adapted to the BLF setting [12].

Example 2 (continued): *The status of the candidate c_0 is* necessarily inadmissible *since only ap, ph and ¬st are realized in her valid BLF, but $ap \succ ph$ and $pol(ap) = \ominus$. Hence c_0 will not be accepted since the most important realized goal for her is negative.*

3   Vote Between Several Agents Under a Common BLF

The BLF demonstrates the full extent of its usefulness in the case where knowledge is distributed over several agents who have personal preferences but who want to collaborate in order to make a good decision for the group. In this paper,

---

[4] Note that the indifference definition uses R and not R_M.

we focus on the case where the agents vote in order to accept or reject one candidate. The vote action consists in revealing that some feature holds or not (wrt to the agent knowledge).

In order to evaluate the BLF with regard to manipulation, we are going to consider that each agent has some private preferences about the candidates i.e. she may want to support one candidate or not. However, we assume that the common knowledge is consistent and that agent can not lie, hence, two agents cannot utter contradictory facts.

More formally, we consider a set $\mathcal{V}$ of agents (voters), each agent $v \in \mathcal{V}$ divides the set of candidates $\mathscr{C}$ into two subsets $\mathscr{C}_v^+$ and $\mathscr{C}_v^-$. $c \in \mathscr{C}_v^+$ means that the agent v is in favor of the candidate c and $c \in \mathscr{C}_v^-$ means that the agent v is against accepting c. In this section we propose several vote strategies and study the relation between the strategies and the admissible thresholds. Each agent has her own private knowledge, K_v, and we suppose that the set of all the available knowledge K ($K = \bigcup_{v \in \mathcal{V}} K_v$) is consistent, however each agent does not know the private knowledge of the other agents.

Let $Voted_v^s \subseteq \mathscr{L}_F$ be the set of voted formulas under strategy s by the agent v i.e. $f \in Voted_v^s$ if under strategy s the agent v gives the information that f holds to the group (the subscript v will be forgotten when there is no ambiguity about the agent). In this paper we define two strategies, the optimistic strategy (Definition 8) and the pessimistic strategy (Definition 9). In the vote procedure, we impose that the agents are only allowed to use literals extracted from the BLF: more formally, let $LIT_{\mathcal{F}} = \bigcup_{a \in \mathcal{P}, x \in reas(a)} \{x, \neg x\}$, $\forall s, \forall v \in V, Voted_v^s \subseteq LIT_{\mathcal{F}}$. In other words, the BLF defines the vocabulary that can be used for voting.

3.1   Optimistic and Pessimistic Strategies

In the following definition we slightly abuse notations by using $f \in \varphi$ with f being a literal, it means that the variable on which f is built appears in φ, i.e., $\forall f \in LIT_F$, $f \in \varphi$ is a shortcut for $((f$ is a variable and $f \in \varphi)$ or $(f = \neg x$ and x is a variable s.t. $x \in \varphi))$. We call optimistic strategy Definition 8 (or Confident strategy) a strategy in which as soon as something is in a positive decision principle or in an inhibitor of a negative decision principle the agent will utter it without looking at the possible negative effect of this utterance. More formally:

Definition 8 (Optimistic strategy).   Let $v \in \mathcal{V}$ be a agent and $c \in \mathscr{C}$ a candidate such that $c \in \mathscr{C}_v^+$, let $K_{v,c}$ the facts that are known by v about c. Let us consider $(\mathcal{P}, \mathcal{R}, pod, \preceq)$ a BLF with $(\mathcal{P}_c, \mathcal{R}_c, pod, \preceq)$ the associated $K_{v,c}$-valid BLF. The *optimistic strategy* is: $\forall f \in LIT_{\mathcal{F}}$,

$$f \in Voted_v^o \text{ iff } \begin{cases} K_{v,c} \vdash f \\ \text{and} & (\exists p \in \mathcal{P}_c^{\oplus} \text{ s.t. } f \in reas(p) \text{ and } f \wedge reas(p) \nvdash \bot \\ \text{or} & \exists(\varphi, p) \in \mathcal{R}_c^{\ominus} \text{ s.t. } f \in \varphi \text{ and } f \wedge \varphi \nvdash \bot) \end{cases}$$

where $\mathcal{P}_c^{\oplus} = \{(\varphi, g) \in \mathcal{P}_c \text{ s.t. } g \in \oplus\}$ is the set of DPs in the $K_{v,c}$-valid BLF that have a positive goal and $\mathcal{R}_c^{\ominus} = \{(\varphi', (\varphi, g)) \in \mathcal{R}_c \text{ s.t. } g \in \ominus\}$ denotes the set of inhibition that inhibit a DP with a negative goal in the $K_{v,c}$-valid BLF.

In other words the optimistic strategy consists in giving *all*[5] the literals that are known to hold and that appear either in a positive DP or in a inhibitor of a negative DP as long as they are not inconsistent with the reason of this positive DP, nor inconsistent with this inhibitor. Hence by using an optimistic strategy the agent will give a lot of information, hoping that it will help to validate at least one positive DP or to invalidate at least one negative DP.

Example 2 (continued): *Let us suppose that the agent wants to accept the candidate c_0. If she uses the optimistic strategy then she will omit to say u because it does not appear in a positive DP nor in a Inhibitor against a negative DP. The valid BLF obtained by the vote of this agent is described in Fig. 3 with a cross on the omitted literal. In this case the candidate becomes necessarily admissible.*

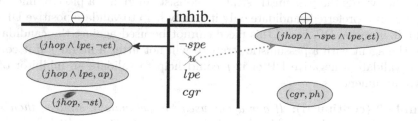

Fig. 3. Optimistic BLF with $K = \{jhop, lpe, \neg spe, u, cgr\}$

Note that with the optimistic strategy, the agent would tell everything she knows as soon as there is a possibility that other agents complete her vote in a favorable way.

Example 2 (continued): *The agent utters $jhop$ even if there is a negative uninhibited DP $(jhop \wedge lpe, ap)$. Unfortunately, in our case, we know that lpe holds, hence by saying $jhop$ it opens the way to validate the negative DP, moreover the agent herself has uttered lpe (since she is a naive optimistic, a more skilled strategy would reason more globally on the whole set of voted formulas, which would require a more complex computation). Besides since the most important DP is inhibited by u, the agent takes the risk that another agent utters u, in that case the candidate c_0 would be necessarily rejected.*

As we have seen, by using the optimistic strategy the agent may validate some negative DP. She can also inhibit other positive DPs when the literal is present both in a reason for a positive DP and in an inhibitor. The pessimistic approach is more cautious and check (naively) if a voted literal cannot create collateral damages.

---

[5] Due to the use of "iff" in Definition 8.

Definition 9 (Pessimistic strategy). Let $v \in \mathcal{V}$ be a agent and $c \in \mathscr{C}$ a candidate such that $c \in \mathscr{C}_v^+$ and let $K_{v,c}$ the facts that are known by v about c. Let us consider $(\mathcal{P}, \mathcal{R}, pol, \preceq)$ a BLF with $(\mathcal{P}_c, \mathcal{R}_c, pol, \preceq)$ the associated $K_{v,c}$-valid BLF. The *pessimistic strategy* is: $\forall f \in LIT_{\mathcal{F}}$,

$$\forall f \in LIT_{\mathcal{F}}, f \in Voted_v^p \text{ iff } \begin{cases} K_{v,c} \vdash f \\ and \quad (\exists p \in \mathcal{P}_c^{\oplus} \text{ s.t. } f \in reas(p) \text{ and } f \wedge reas(p) \nvdash \bot \\ or \, \exists(\varphi, p) \in \mathcal{R}_c^{\ominus} \text{ s.t. } f \in \varphi \text{ and } f \wedge \varphi \nvdash \bot) \\ and \quad \nexists p \in \mathcal{P}_c^{\ominus} \text{ such that } f \in reas(p) \text{ and } f \wedge reas(p) \nvdash \bot \\ and \quad \nexists(\varphi, p) \in \mathcal{R}_c^{\oplus} \text{ s.t. } f \in \varphi \text{ and } f \wedge \varphi \nvdash \bot) \end{cases}$$

where $\mathcal{P}_c^{\oplus}$ is defined as before and $P_c^{\ominus} = \{(\varphi, g) \in \mathcal{P}_c \text{ s.t. } g \in \ominus\}$ is the set of DPs in the $K_{v,c}$-valid BLF that have a negative goal and $\mathcal{R}_c^{\ominus}$ is defined as before and $\mathcal{R}_c^{\oplus} = \{(\varphi', (\varphi, g)) \in \mathcal{R}_c \text{ s.t. } g \in \oplus\}$ denotes the set of inhibition that inhibit a DP with a positive goal in the $K_{v,c}$-valid BLF.

In other words the pessimistic strategy consists in giving a piece of information f about a preferred candidate only if it may help to validate positive DP or to inhibit negative DP, but if this piece cannot be used against the candidate. Hence the agent with a pessimistic strategy will not utter a literal f if it could help to validate a negative DP or if f could help to validate an inhibitor of a positive argument.

Example 2 (continued): *If our agent uses the pessimistic strategy then she would omit to say u but would also omit jhop and lpe. The valid BLF obtained by the vote of this agent is described in Fig. 4 with the only valid DP encircled by solid lines. In this case the candidate becomes necessarily admissible.*

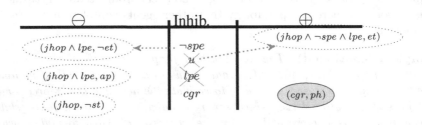

Fig. 4. Pessimistic BLF with $K = \{jhop, lpe, \neg spe, u, cgr\}$

We can notice that the pessimistic strategy is hiding a lot of information. Note that we have shown the BLF obtained after the vote of only one agent, let us see in the next section what happens in presence of several agents. The previous strategies are naive in the sense that they focus on each literal independently while they could focus on achieving the goals. More complex strategy could be defined, namely we could propose to select a set of literals which can be uttered together in order to influence admissibility statuses. However, we are going to show that no strategy can guarantee to obtain the desired admissibility status.

3.2 Analysis of the Strategies

In this section, we study the properties of the optimistic and pessimistic strategies. First, let us recall that global knowledge is assumed to be consistent. We also assume that the agents cannot lie (except by omission). This comes from two reasons: first, ideally agents are gathered in order to take the best decision for the group, hence they have a moral duty to do it honestly, second a lie may lead to an inconsistency hence could be discovered by the group and cause the agent to be ashame. Hence the only way to manipulate the vote is to omit to declare some pieces of information that they know.

Proposition 1. [6]$\forall v \in \mathcal{V}, \forall s \in \{o, p\}$ $K_v \vdash Voted_v^s$ and $Voted_v^s \nvdash \perp$.

Proposition 1 states that under optimistic and pessimistic strategy what is voted should be deduced from the knowledge of the voters and it is consistent. The following proposition shows that the pessimistic strategy cannot reveal more information than the optimistic one.

Proposition 2. $\forall v \in \mathcal{V}$, $Voted_v^p \subseteq Voted_v^o$.

In the following, $Voted$ is the set of voted knowledge and R_K and R_{Voted} denotes the set of realized goals under total knowledge and voted knowledge respectively. We are now going to study the link between strategies and the admissibility thresholds. Note that if all the agents use the optimistic strategy then $Voted = \bigcup_{v \in \mathcal{V}} Voted_v^o$. The following propositions concern basic admissibility.

Proposition 3. $\forall c \in \mathscr{C}$ s.t. $\forall v \in \mathcal{V}$, $c \in \mathscr{C}_v^+$, if all the agents use the optimistic strategy, then $\mathrm{R}_K^\oplus \subseteq \mathrm{R}_{Voted}^\oplus$.

Note that the inclusion maybe strict since there maybe some positive goals which are realized by an optimistic strategy made by all the agents but which are not realized under total knowledge, since they can have inhibitors that would be omitted by the strategical agents. Hence there can be more positive realized goals by using a global optimistic strategy than by sharing all the knowledge.

Proposition 4. $\forall c \in \mathscr{C}$ s.t. $\forall v \in \mathcal{V}$, $c \in \mathscr{C}_v^+$, if all the agents use the optimistic strategy then $\mathrm{R}_{Voted}^\ominus \subseteq \mathrm{R}_K^\ominus$.

Similarly as before, the inclusion maybe strict since there maybe some negative DP that are not validated by the vote. Hence there can be less negative realized goals by using a global optimistic strategy than by sharing all the knowledge. From Propositions 3 and 4, it follows that under the optimistic strategy used by all the agents, a candidate that is preferred by all the agents is not guaranteed to be accepted, this depends on how the complete knowledge is shared and on the BLA structure. More precisely, we have:

---

[6] The proofs are in Annex.

Theorem 1. $\forall c \in \mathscr{C}$ s.t. $\forall v \in \mathcal{V}$, $c \in \mathscr{C}_v^+$, if all the agents use the optimistic strategy

- $c \in N_{ad}$ under total knowledge then $c \in N_{ad}$ under voted knowledge
- $c \in Ct$ under total knowledge then $c \in N_{ad} \cup Ct$ under voted knowledge
- $c \in Id$ under total knowledge then $c \in N_{ad} \cup Id$ under voted knowledge
- $c \in N_{\neg ad}$ under total knowledge then c may have any status under voted knowledge ($c \in N_{ad} \cup Id \cup Ct \cup N_{\neg ad}$).

The last point of Theorem 1 shows that a unanimity of personal preferences may lead to accept a candidate which is not admissible for the group according to the BLF.

Example 3. To illustrate Theorem 1, we propose an example with 4 agents with $c \in \mathscr{C}_v^+$ with $K_1 = \{eb, \neg spe\}$, $K_2 = \{lpe, i\}$, $K_3 = \{eb, cgr\}$ and $K_4 = \{i, u, cbs\}$. Using optimistic strategy $Voted = \{eb, \neg spe, lpe, cgr\}$. Hence, $R_K^\oplus = \{ej, ph\}$ and $R_K^\ominus = \varnothing$ so the candidate is N_{ad} while the candidate is Id under total knowledge (see Fig. 5). Note that Agent 4's preferences are totally in contradiction with its valid-BLF. This contradiction allows Agent 4 to omit information in order to increase the accepted status of the candidate. One can see that if Agent 4 changes its personal preferences the candidate becomes Id.

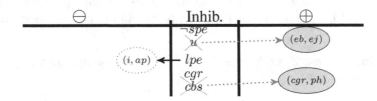

Fig. 5. $K = \{eb, \neg spe\} \cup \{lpe, i\} \cup \{eb, cgr\} \cup \{i, u, cbs\}$, Voted=$\{eb, \neg spe, lpe, cgr\}$

Let us study the pessimistic strategy. Note that under this strategy, the realized goals may e pessimistic differ from what could have been obtained by having the whole information.

Proposition 5. If all the agents use the pessimistic strategy then $R_{Voted}^\ominus = \varnothing$.

$R_{Voted}^\oplus$ can be different from $R_K^\oplus$ (i.e., we can have $R_{Voted}^\oplus \not\subseteq R_K^\oplus$ and $R_K^\oplus \not\subseteq R_{Voted}^\oplus$). Since we may have some positive DPs that can be uninhibited by voted DPs while they are inhibited under complete knowledge, and we may also have some positive DPs that contains facts that belong to inhibitors of positive DPs or that belong to negative DPs that will not be valid under voted knowledge while they would be validated by sharing the complete knowledge.

From Proposition 5 it follows that a candidate that is preferred by all agents is either necessary admissible or indifferent when the pessimistic strategy is used by everyone:

Corollary 1. $\forall c \in \mathscr{C}$, if all the agents use pessimistic strategy and if c is s.t. $\forall v \in \mathcal{V}$, $c \in \mathscr{C}_v^+$ then $c \in N_{ad} \cup Id$ under voted knowledge.

Theorem 1 and Corollary 1 show the impact of the unanimity of the agents' preferences on the satisfaction of the group. Optimistic strategy can increase the evaluation of a candidate but this may be impossible to do if there is no feature that holds (under total knowledge) that can help to produce a DP in favor of the candidate. Concerning pessimistic strategy, even if it is naive, the possibilities of manipulation of the results are limited, i.e., it cannot transform a candidate which is preferred by all the agents into a necessary admissible candidate, sometimes the best they can obtain will be Id (for instance when the agents possess only bad features for this candidate, then they will say nothing, hence the candidate will be considered as indifferent).

We are now in position to relate the choice of a strategy and the choice of an admissibility threshold. Indeed, from Theorem 1, it follows that given an admissibility threshold in the set $\{1, 2a, 2b, 3\}$, if a candidate would have been selected according to that threshold under total knowledge and if this candidate is preferred by all the agents then it would also have been selected by these agents playing all the optimistic strategy and using the same threshold:

Corollary 2. $\forall c \in Ad$ under total knowledge with $Ad \in \{1, 2a, 2b, 3\}$, if $\forall v \in \mathcal{V}$, v uses the optimistic strategy and $c \in \mathscr{C}_v^+$ then $c \in Ad$ under voted knowledge.

It follows from Corollary 1 that with the pessimistic strategy used by all the agents, the common utility modeled by a BLF is ignored in favor of a unanimity of personal preferences if the admissibility threshold is 2a (hence a good way to lower manipulation would be to rather choose the 2b threshold, forbidding the pessimistic strategies to act against the common utility).

Corollary 3. If the group uses the threshold 2a $(N_{ad} \cup Id)$ and if all agents are using the pessimistic strategy and if c is s.t. $\forall v \in \mathcal{V}$, $c \in \mathscr{C}_v^+$ then the candidate is accepted.

In a symmetric way, if no one wants to accept the candidate and if the threshold is 2a, the candidate can be accepted in the Voted BLF.

The use of a BLF reflects that knowledge is power: since knowledge gives the power to advance facts for triggering or inhibits DPs, this is why we are going to use a framework in which all the agents have the same knowledge. More formally, $K = K_v, \forall v \in \mathcal{V}$. With equal knowledge the optimistic strategy is more efficient since if there are pros and cons it will be the consensual BLF that will make the decision.

Proposition 6. $\forall c \in \mathscr{C}$ s.t. $\exists v \in \mathcal{V}$, $c \in \mathscr{C}_v^+$ and $\exists v' \in \mathcal{V}$, $c \in \mathscr{C}_{v'}^-$, if all the agents use the optimistic strategy and $K = K_v, \forall v \in \mathcal{V}$ then $Voted = K$.

In the case where an agent is pro and another agent is con and the knowledge is the same for all agents, the vote amounts to share all the knowledge in a neutral way, hence the candidate will have the same admissibility as if there were no strategy.

Corollary 4 (Statuses under optimistic strategy 2). $\forall c \in \mathscr{C}$ *s.t.* $\exists v \in \mathcal{V}$, $c \in \mathscr{C}_v^+$ *and* $\exists v' \in \mathcal{V}$, $c \in \mathscr{C}_{v'}^-$, $\forall Ad \in \{1, 2a, 2b, 3\}$, *if* $c \in Ad$ *under total knowledge then* $c \in Ad$ *under voted knowledge.*

Let us consider now the pessimistic strategy under a shared equal knowledge.

Proposition 7. $\forall c \in \mathscr{C}$ *s.t.* $\exists v \in \mathcal{V}$, $c \in \mathscr{C}_v^+$ *and* $\exists v' \in \mathcal{V}$, $c \in \mathscr{C}_v^-$, *if all the agents use the pessimistic strategy and* $K = K_v, \forall v \in \mathcal{V}$ *then* $\forall Ad \in \{1, 2a, 2b, 3\}$, *if* $c \in Ad$ *under total knowledge then* $c \in N_{ad} \cup Id \cup Ct \cup N_{\neg ad}$ *under voted knowledge.*

From Corollary 4 and Proposition 7 it appears that the optimistic strategy is more rational and does not depend on the structure of the BLF, since with pessimistic strategy c can have any status under voted knowledge.

We are now going to compare the use of the optimistic or pessimistic strategy in the case where the knowledge is the same for all and some agents are pro others are con. For this, we consider a problem with two agents, the first one is pro the candidate and uses the optimistic strategy and the second one is con and uses the pessimistic strategy.

Proposition 8. *Let* $\mathcal{V} = \{v_1, v_2\}$ *with* $K = K_{v1} = K_{v2}$, $\forall c \in \mathscr{C}$ *s.t.* $c \in \mathscr{C}_{v_1}^+$ *and* $c \in \mathscr{C}_{v_2}^-$ *with* v_1 *(resp.* v_2*) using optimistic (resp. pessimistic) strategy, it holds that* $\mathrm{R}_K^\oplus \subseteq \mathrm{R}_{Voted}^\oplus$ *and* $\mathrm{R}_{Voted}^\ominus \subseteq \mathrm{R}_K^\ominus$ *and:*

- $c \in N_{ad}$ *under total knowledge then* $c \in N_{ad}$ *under voted knowledge*
- $c \in Ct$ *under total knowledge then* $c \in N_{ad} \cup Ct$ *under voted knowledge*
- $c \in Id$ *under total knowledge then* $c \in N_{ad} \cup Id$ *under voted knowledge*
- $c \in N_{\neg ad}$ *under total knowledge then* c *may have any status under voted knowledge* $(c \in N_{ad} \cup Id \cup Ct \cup N_{\neg ad})$.

Before closing this section about naive strategies, let us underline the fact that strategies are not well suited with the collaborative spirit of the BLF, since, by strategy, a agent can choose to hide some information that have been judged to be relevant for the realization of a common goal by all the group. Hence using a strategy in order to favor a candidate may be viewed as a betrayal with respect to the group welfare.

4   Discussion and Related Work

In AI literature the bipolar view has often been used, inspired by the fact that human usually evaluate the possible alternatives considering positive and negative aspects separately [9]. In the domain of multi-criteria decision, Dubois and Fargier [10] propose a qualitative bipolar approach in which a candidate is associated with two distinct sets of positive "arguments" (pros) and negative "arguments" (cons). This polarity is given wrt the decision goal. The arguments are abstract and there is no relation between them, but their level of importance is given. The papers [8,11] study the use of decision rules in practice by human decision makers, and show that the bipolar lexicographic rule is largely favored by humans. Another way to deal with this kind of situation can be based on the matching between a post profile and each candidate. When uncertainty is taken into account, this matching can be expressed by criteria based on the possibility or necessity measure that the candidate matches the profile [13]. A drawback of these approaches is that it requires to dispose of a precise possibility distribution about candidates and it implies a commensurability between the preferences about the research profile and the uncertainty about the candidate. Moreover it is difficult to define the threshold over which the candidate could be accepted.

The notion of "argument" in favor or against a decision has also been developed in practical argumentation domain which has been widely studied (see e.g. [1,17]). Practical argumentation aims at answering the question "what is the right thing to do in a given situation" which is clearly related to a decision problem. Several works are using argumentative approaches to tackle it: for instance [6] have a very similar view of what we call Principles, since they use defeasible rules in favor or against a given action, Amgoud and Prade [2] propose a bipolar argumentation-based approach distinguishing epistemic and practical arguments. Our decision principle can be viewed as a pair of (epistemic information, practical information) which defines the practical conclusion that should be fired under the epistemic information.

Another theoretical framework has been proposed for multi-criteria/multi-agent (non sequential) decision making under possibilistic uncertainty [4,5]. Our approach differs from classical approaches of group decision under uncertainty on the following points: (i) our BLF is a kind of CUF, but it is a richer qualitative bipolar structure that takes into account available knowledge and not only agents' utilities; (ii) our BLF is based on justifications of why we should take one decision (since a DP contains the reasons for saying that a given goal is achieved) while in standard CUF, utilities are given with no structured explanation; (iii) we assume that agents have no uncertainty about what they know but they are uncertain about what the other agents know.

In this paper, we consider that agents can provide only factual information and no information about their preferences, since the BLF contains already importance levels and polarities that are assumed to reflect the group utility. Hence the agents has only access to the information describing the candidates which differs from classical utilitarian approaches. In this context, our paper studies what happens when agents are not purely acting for the wellfare of the group, hence we take into account a second type of private utility: the fact that an agent wants secretly to accept a candidate without considering the common BLF. In this case, this kind of utility is personal and the agent does not want to aggregate this information. This differs from the aim to aggregate the utilities of the different agents used in the literature about collective decision making. Our study shows that the BLF may help to reduce the possibilities of agents to influence the decision that would have been taken for the wellfare of the group. Indeed for an agent it is very difficult in our context to know what the other agents know and what they will utter hence to compute what goal will be achieved after the vote of the group, and moreover to know the status that will get the candidate.

Concerning vote and manipulability, we plan to introduce reputation and blame, i.e., if an agent has always access to some information and does not deliver it for a given candidate, then he can be accused of attempting to manipulate the group decision. This could enforce agents to utter all the information they know in order to behave better for the group. Another direction would be to extend the expressivity of a BLF in order to incorporate the strength of a decision principle (which will both have an importance relative to its goal, and a strength relative to the certainty of its conclusion when the reasons hold). A possible extension would be to handle the agent's uncertain knowledge about the situation, hence to allow for features associated with uncertainty degrees. The question of how to build a BLF from different points of view has been evoked in [12] but has not been developed yet. We plan to work on the subject of BLF building with health decision makers in order to see how complicated it is for them to define decision principles, inhibitors and importance relations.

Annex: Proofs

Proof of Proposition 1: In both definitions (Definitions 8 and 9) $\forall f \in Voted_v^s$ it holds that $K_v \vdash f$. Moreover K is supposed to be consistent and $K_v \subseteq K$. □

Proof of Proposition 2: It is straightforward from the definition of the pessimistic strategy that is based on the optimistic one on which some more constraints are added. □

Proof of Proposition 3: Let us show that $\mathrm{R}_K^\oplus \subseteq \mathrm{R}_{Voted}^\oplus$, if $g \in \mathrm{R}_K^\oplus$ then there exists an unhibited positive DP with conclusion g, i.e., $\exists (\varphi, g) \in \mathcal{P}_K^\oplus$ s.t. $K \vdash \varphi$ and $g \in \oplus$ and $\nexists (\varphi', (\varphi, g)) \in \mathcal{R}_K$ s.t. $K \vdash \varphi'$, hence, $\forall l \in LIT_K$, s.t. $K \vdash l$, if $l \in \varphi$ then $l \wedge \varphi \nvdash \bot$ (since K is consistent), so l is voted with the optimistic strategy. Moreover if $\nexists (\varphi', (\varphi, g)) \in \mathcal{R}_K$ s.t. $K \vdash \varphi'$ then it is not possible that $Voted \vdash \varphi'$ s.t. φ' inhibits (φ, g) since $K \vdash Voted$ and K is consistent. □

Proof of Proposition 4: If g is in $\mathrm{R}_{Voted}^\ominus$ then it means that g is the conclusion of a negative DP (φ, g) such that $Voted \vdash \varphi$ and forall inhibitor φ' s.t. $(\varphi', (\varphi, g)) \in \mathcal{R}_K$, $Voted \nvdash \varphi'$, which means that $K \nvdash \varphi'$ unless by strategy agents would have inhibit the negative DP. It means that $K \vdash \varphi$ since $K \vdash Voted$, and $K \nvdash \varphi'$ for any inhibitor φ' of the negative DP. Hence $g \in \mathrm{R}_K$. □

Proof of Theorem 1

- $c \in N_{ad}$ under total knowledge implies $\mathrm{R}_{eK}^\oplus \neq \varnothing$ and $\mathrm{R}_{eK}^\ominus = \varnothing$. Using Proposition 3 we have $\mathrm{R}_{eVoted}^\oplus \neq \varnothing$ and due to Proposition 4, $\mathrm{R}_{eVoted}^\ominus = \varnothing$, hence the result.
- $c \in Ct$ under total knowledge implies $\mathrm{R}_{eK}^\oplus \neq \varnothing$ and $\mathrm{R}_{eK}^\ominus \neq \varnothing$. Using Proposition 3, we have $\mathrm{R}_{eVoted}^\oplus \neq \varnothing$ and due to Proposition 4, $\mathrm{R}_{eVoted}^\ominus = \varnothing$ or $\mathrm{R}_{eVoted}^\ominus \neq \varnothing$, hence the result.

- $c \in Id$ under total knowledge implies $R_K^{\oplus} = \varnothing$ and $R_K^{\ominus} = \varnothing$. Using Proposition 3, we have $R_{Voted}^{\oplus} \neq \varnothing$ or $R_{Voted}^{\oplus} = \varnothing$ and due to Proposition 4, $R_{Voted}^{\ominus} = \varnothing$, hence the result.
- $c \in N_{\neg ad}$ under total knowledge implies $R_{eK}^{\oplus} = \varnothing$ and $R_{eK}^{\ominus} \neq \varnothing$. Using Proposition 3 we have $R_{eVoted}^{\oplus} \neq \varnothing$ or $R_{eVoted}^{\oplus} = \varnothing$ and due to Proposition 4 $R_{eVoted}^{\ominus} = \varnothing$ or $R_{eVoted}^{\ominus} \neq \varnothing$. □

Proof of Proposition 5: If $g \in R_{Voted}^{\ominus}$ then $\exists (\varphi, g) \in \mathcal{P}_K^{\ominus}$ s.t. $K \vdash \varphi$ hence for all $f \in LIT_K$ s.t. $K \vdash f$, if $f \in \varphi$ then $f \wedge \varphi \nvdash \bot$ hence f is not voted, hence $Voted \nvdash \varphi$ i.e., $g \notin R_{Voted}^{\ominus}$. □

Proof of Corollary 1: From Proposition 5 we know that $R_{Voted}^{\ominus} = \varnothing$, hence the result. □

Proof of Corollary 3: Follows from Corollary 1. □

Proof of Proposition 6: Since v and v' have the same knowledge K, and v is pro c it means that all facts that appear in a positive DP or that inhibits a negative DP will be uttered. Symmetrically, v' being con c' means that all facts appearing in a negative DP or inhibiting a positive one will be uttered as well. Hence $Voted = K$. □

Proof of Proposition 7: The proof consists in giving examples of all the possibilities. □

Proof of Proposition 8: Let us prove that $R_K^{\oplus} \subseteq R_{Votcd}^{\oplus}$, if $g \in R_K^{\oplus}$ then it means that $\exists (\varphi, g) \in \mathcal{P}_K^{\oplus}$ s.t. (φ, g) is not inhibited in the K-valid BLF. Hence $v1$ has voted every literal in φ and (φ, g) is not inhibited in $Voted$ (since $v2$ has no way to inhibit it). Thus, $g \in R_{Voted}^{\oplus}$.

Let us proove that $R_{Voted}^{\ominus} \subseteq R_K^{\ominus}$, if $g \in R_{Voted}^{\ominus}$ then $\exists (\varphi, g) \in \mathcal{P}_{Voted}o^{\ominus}$ s.t. (φ, g) is not inhibited in the $Voted$-valid BLF. This DP can come from v_2's or v_1's votes since v_2 may have utter facts against c when none of those facts can be used positively, but it can also come from v_1 if these facts belong also to positive DPs. There are two possibilities when (φ, g) is not inhibited in the Voted-valid BLF, either there is no inhibitor in K then $g \in R_K^{\ominus}$ or the inhibitor exists in K but it has not been voted. However, since v_1 has an optimistic strategy and is pro c, v_1 would have voted any fact that appear in an inhibitor of a negative DP, hence this case is impossible. □

References

1. Amgoud, L., Devred, C., Lagasquie-Schiex, M.-C.: A constrained argumentation system for practical reasoning. In: Rahwan, I., Moraitis, P. (eds.) ArgMAS 2008. LNCS, vol. 5384, pp. 37–56. Springer, Heidelberg (2009). doi:10.1007/978-3-642-00207-6_3
2. Amgoud, L., Prade, H.: Comparing decisions on the basis of a bipolar typology of arguments. In: Della, R.G., Dubois, D., Kruse, R., Lenz, H.J. (eds.) Preferences and Similarities, pp. 249–264. Springer, Vienna (2008). doi:10.1007/978-3-211-85432-7_10

3. Bannay, F., Guillaume, R.: Towards a transparent deliberation protocol inspired from supply chain collaborative planning. In: Laurent, A., Strauss, O., Bouchon-Meunier, B., Yager, R.R. (eds.) IPMU 2014. CCIS, vol. 443, pp. 335–344. Springer, Cham (2014). doi:10.1007/978-3-319-08855-6_34

4. Ben Amor, N., Essghaier, F., Fargier, H.: Solving multi-criteria decision problems under possibilistic uncertainty using optimistic and pessimistic utilities. In: Laurent, A., Strauss, O., Bouchon-Meunier, B., Yager, R.R. (eds.) IPMU 2014. CCIS, vol. 444, pp. 269–279. Springer, Cham (2014). doi:10.1007/978-3-319-08852-5_28

5. Ben Amor, N., Essghaier, F., Fargier, H.: Egalitarian collective decision making under qualitative possibilistic uncertainty: principles and characterization. In: AAAI Conference on Artificial Intelligence, pp. 3482–3488 (2015)

6. Bonet, B., Geffner, H.: Arguing for decisions: a qualitative model of decision making. In: Proceedings of the Twelfth UAI, pp. 98–105. Morgan Kaufmann Publishers Inc. (1996)

7. Bonnefon, J., Dubois, D., Fargier, H.: An overview of bipolar qualitative decision rules. In: Della Riccia, G., Dubois, D., Kruse, R., Lenz, H.J. (eds.) Preferences and Similarities. CISM, vol. 504, pp. 47–73. Springer, Vienna (2008). doi:10.1007/978-3-211-85432-7_3

8. Bonnefon, J.-F., Dubois, D., Fargier, H., Leblois, S.: Qualitative heuristics for balancing the pros and cons. Theor. Decis. 65, 71–95 (2008)

9. Cacioppo, J., Berntson, G.: Relationship between attitudes and evaluative space: a critical review, with emphasis on the separability of positive and negative substrates. Psychol. Bull. 115(3), 401 (1994)

10. Dubois, D., Fargier, H.: Qualitative bipolar decision rules: toward more expressive settings. In: Greco, S., Marques Pereira, R.A., Squillante, M., Yager, R.R., Kacprzyk, J. (eds.) Preferences and Decisions, pp. 139–158. Springer, Heidelberg (2010). doi:10.1007/978-3-642-15976-3_9

11. Dubois, D., Fargier, H., Bonnefon, J.-F.: On the qualitative comparison of decisions having positive and negative features. J. Artif. Intell. Res. 32, 385–417 (2008)

12. De Saint-Cyr, F.D., Guillaume, R.: Analyzing a bipolar decision structure through qualitative decision theory. KI - Künstliche Intelligenz 31, 53–62 (2017)

13. Guillaume, R., Houé, R., Grabot, B.: Robust competence assessment for job assignment. Eur. J. Oper. Res. 238(2), 630–644 (2014)

14. Ireland, R., Crum, C., Collaboration, S.C.: How To Implement CPFR and Other Best Collaborative Practices. Integrated Business Management Series. J. Ross Publishing Inc., Boca Raton (2005)

15. Mak, V., Rapoport, A., Seale, D.: Sequential search by groups with rank-dependent payoffs: an experimental study. Org. Behav. Hum. Decis. Proc. 124(2), 256–267 (2014)

16. Raiffa, H.: Decision Analysis: Introductory Lectures on Choices Under Uncertainty. Addison-Wesley, Reading (1970)

17. Wooldridge, M.J.: Reasoning About Rational Agents. MIT Press, Cambridge (2000)

Revision and Updates in Possibly Action-Occurrence-Incomplete Narratives

Chitta Baral[1] and Tran Cao Son[2]([⊠])

[1] Arizona State University, Tempe, AZ 85281, USA
chitta@asu.edu
[2] New Mexico State University, Las Cruces, NM 88003, USA
tson@cs.nmsu.edu

Abstract. We propose a framework for integrating belief revision with action narratives whose observations about properties of the world might be inaccurate. We define the notion of an acceptable revision of a narrative as a sequence of revision-candidate formulas which is used in revising the observations and creates a consistent narrative. We propose a more preferred relation among revisions and prove that this relation is transitive and irreflexive. We also define a notion of most preferred models of a narrative when likelihood of action occurrences are available and discuss an alternative characterization that takes into consideration preferences over revisions. We show that the more preferred relation among models is also transitive and irreflexive. We conclude the paper with a discussion on the related work.

1 Introduction

Physical states of the world change due to (world altering) actions and an agent's knowledge and beliefs about the world changes by the agent "knowing about occurrence of world altering actions" as well as by the agent "knowing about the value of some of the properties of the world at certain times." The agent gets to "know either through sensing or by other means" such as being told. Revision and Updates are two different (but related) formulations to address such changes and the difference between them is well-studied [18]. A simple way to describe their difference is that updates formulate the change in the world due to a world-altering action while revisions formulate the change in the beliefs of an agent when it acquires new beliefs (that may contradict with the agent's original beliefs due to wrong beliefs and inaccurate perceptions). In this paper our focus is on action narratives and the role of revision and update in reasoning about action narratives.

An action narrative is defined (in [5]) as a collection of observations about action occurrences and properties of the world along a timeline. An action narrative is considered to be action-occurrence-complete if there is complete knowledge about all the actions that occurred. Otherwise it is referred as action-occurrence-incomplete. In [5] action-occurrence-incomplete narratives were considered and were characterized by a set of models which filled in the incomplete

© Springer International Publishing AG 2017
B. An et al. (Eds.): PRIMA 2017, LNAI 10621, pp. 53–70, 2017.
https://doi.org/10.1007/978-3-319-69131-2_4

aspects by filling in missing action occurrences that were not observed. If no such models were found, then the original narrative was considered to be inconsistent. In essence, the formulation in [5] only incorporated the concept of updates. In recent years there have been many works [9,16,17] where narratives are characterized using both updates and revisions; updates formalizing and addressing the world changing action occurrences, and revision formalizing and addressing belief change due to wrong beliefs and inaccurate perceptions being revised. *However, these later works only consider action-occurrence-complete narratives.* This assumption is too restrictive as often agents may miss observing some actions.

In this paper our goal is to allow action-occurrence-incomplete narratives but at the same time overcome labeling narratives as inconsistent (as was done in [5]) as well as wrong beliefs and inaccurate perceptions. This requires the use of both the notions of update and revision and in certain cases the incompleteness may be addressed by alternative means, one using updates by adding missing action occurrences, and the other by doing revision. In such cases the alternative could be presented as different models or one can use additional knowledge about the probability of action occurrences to assign a likelihood measure for the alternative models.

In a broad sense, the paper is related to attempts to integrate belief revision into action formalisms to deal with inaccurate sensing actions or approaches to combining belief revision and belief update since observations considered as results of sensing actions mentioned above [9,16,17]. Detailed comparison will be discussed in Sect. 4. We now present several motivating examples.

Example 1. Consider an agent in an environment with a single property f. The agent observes the environment and comes to the conclusion that f is true. Suppose that after a while, the agent observes that $\neg f$ is true.

Scenario 1: The agent also knows that there exists no action that can cause $\neg f$ to be true. According to the definition in [5], the story can be described by two situations s_0 and s_1 with s_0 preceding s_1 and two observations f at s_0 and $\neg f$ at s_1. Under the assumption that observations are accurate, this narrative is *inconsistent* since it is not possible for f to change its value. This is reasonable.

The above conclusion is not so reasonable when the agent has to rely on imprecise means to observe the world. In this case, a different but reasonable view of the scenario is as follows. Initially, the agent observed f and believed that f is true. Later, s/he observed $\neg f$. Since the agent knows that nothing can make f false, s/he concludes that the initial observation is inaccurate. He/she *revises* the initial belief to $\neg f$, i.e., the agent *revises* the narrative. This reasoning exemplifies the process of *belief revision* in which the agent revises his/her beliefs given new information. It also demonstrates that belief revision can be used to restore the consistency of narratives when observations might be inaccurate. □

Scenario 2: The agent has the knowledge of an action, say a, that makes f false. In this case, the narrative is consistent since it has a model in which a occurs at s_0 (and the agent did not observe it!). According to the definition in [5], the revision model discussed above (f is initially false and a does not occur) is not a model of the modified narrative. Yet, there is no reason for not believing that it is a possible model of the narrative if observations might be inaccurate. Obviously, the likelihood of being the true model of the modified narrative depends on the likelihood of the action a occurs, e.g., how difficult/easy for a to occur? For example, if f denotes that a turkey is alive and a is the action of a meteoroid falling from the sky and killing it, then the likelihood of the model that a occurs being the true model of the narrative is rather small; however, if a is the action of someone shooting the turkey, then the likelihood is much higher.   □

The purpose of this paper is to develop a framework for reasoning about narratives that deals with inaccurate observations about properties of the world. It contributes to the study of action narratives in two aspects. First, it presents an integration of belief revision with action-occurrence-incomplete narratives. It focuses on narratives described in [5] but the proposed approach can be adapted to any other formalisms for reasoning about narratives. Second, it defines the notion of most preferred models of a narrative that takes into account the likelihood of action occurrences and a preferred relation among revisions.

The next section reviews the action language $\mathcal{L}$. Section 3 presents our formalization that integrates belief revision into $\mathcal{L}$ and two alternative characterizations of most preferred models of a narrative when observations might be imprecise. The paper concludes with a discussion on related work and some remarks on future work.

2   Background: Language $\mathcal{L}$ and Narratives

The language $\mathcal{L}$ reviewed in this paper is slightly different from the original version in [5]. It is proposed and used in [6]. $\mathcal{L}$ is defined by a domain description language $\mathcal{L}_D$ and an observation language $\mathcal{L}_O$.

2.1 $\mathcal{L}_D$: The Domain Description Language

The alphabet of $\mathcal{L}_D$ – a language that closely follows the language $\mathcal{A}$ from [15] – comprises two nonempty disjoint sets of symbols $\mathbf{F}$ (the set of fluents) and $\mathbf{A}$ (the set of actions). For $f \in \mathbf{F}$, f and $\neg f$ are *literals*. A *fluent formula* is a propositional formula constructed from literals; $\top$ and $\bot$ denote *true* and *false*, respectively. Propositions in $\mathcal{L}_D$ are of the following three forms:

$$a \textbf{ causes } \varphi \textbf{ if } \psi \tag{1}$$

$$\varphi \textbf{ if } \psi \tag{2}$$

$$\textbf{impossible } a \textbf{ if } \psi \tag{3}$$

where a is an action and φ and ψ are fluent formulas. Propositions of form (1) describe direct effects of actions on the world and are called *dynamic causal laws*. Propositions of form (2), called *static causal laws*, describe causal relation between fluents in a world. Propositions of form (3), called *executability conditions*, state when actions are not executable.

A *domain description* D is a set of propositions in $\mathcal{L}_D$. An *interpretation* I of the fluents in $\mathbf{F}$ is a maximal consistent set of fluent literals of $\mathcal{L}_D$. A fluent f is said to be true (resp. false) in I iff $f \in I$ (resp. $\neg f \in I$). The truth value of a fluent formula in I is defined recursively over the propositional connectives in the usual way. A set of formulas from $\mathcal{L}_D$ is *logically closed* if it is closed under propositional logic (wrt. $\mathcal{L}_D$). Let V be a set of formulas and K be a set of static causal laws of the form $\varphi \, \mathbf{if} \, \psi$. We say that V is closed under K if for every proposition $\varphi \, \mathbf{if} \, \psi$ in K, if ψ belongs to V, then so does φ. By $Cn(V \cup K)$ we denote[1] the least logically closed set of formulas from $\mathcal{L}_D$ that contains V and is also closed under K. A *state* of D is an interpretation that is closed under the set of static causal laws of D.

An action a is *not executable* in a state s if there exists an executability condition "**impossible** a **if** φ" in D such that φ holds in s. The *effect of a in s* is the set of formulas $e_a(s) = \{\varphi \mid D$ contains a law "a **causes** φ **if** ψ" and ψ holds in $s\}$. Given the domain description D containing a set of static causal laws K_D, we formally define $\Phi_D(a, s)$, the set of states that may be reached by executing a in s as follows.

- If a is executable in s, then $\Phi_D(a, s) = \{s' \mid Cn(s') = Cn((s \cap s') \cup e_a(s) \cup K_D)\}$;
- If a is not executable in s, then $\Phi_D(a, s)$ is $\emptyset$.

It is shown that every domain description D in a language $\mathcal{L}_D$ has a unique transition function that will be denoted with Φ_D.

The intuition behind the above formulation is as follows. The direct effects (due to the dynamic causal laws) of an action a in a state s are given by $e_a(s)$, and all formulas in $e_a(s)$ must hold in any resulting state. In addition, the static causal laws (the set K_D) dictate additional formulas that must hold in the resulting state. While the resulting state should satisfy these formulas, it must also be otherwise closed to s. These three aspects are captured by the definition above. For additional explanation and motivation behind the above definition please see [4,21,24]. In particular, it should be noted that when K_D is empty, $\Phi(a, s)$ for an action a that is executable in a state s, as defined above, is equivalent to the set of states that satisfy $e_a(s)$ and are closest to s using the symmetric difference[2] as the measure of closeness (see, e.g., [21]).

2.2 $\mathcal{L}_O$: The Observation Language

$\mathcal{L}_O$ assumes a set of *situation constants* $\mathbf{S}$ which contains a designated *initial situation* s_0 and a distinguished *current situation* s_c. Note that *situations* written as s (possibly with subscripts) are different from *states* which are written as s (possibly with subscripts). As with the situation calculus, the ontology of $\mathcal{L}$ differentiates between a situation, which is a history of the actions from the

---

[1] Note that a fluent formula φ can be equivalently represented as a static causal law $\varphi \mathbf{if} \top$.

[2] s_1 is strictly closer to s than s_2 if $s_1 \setminus s \cup s \setminus s_1 \subset s_2 \setminus s \cup s \setminus s_2$.

initial situation, and a state, which is the truth value of fluents at a particular situation. Observations in $\mathcal{L}_O$ are propositions of the following forms:

$$\varphi \text{ at } s \tag{4}$$

$$\alpha \text{ between } s_1, s_2 \tag{5}$$

$$\alpha \text{ occ\_at } s \tag{6}$$

$$s_1 < s_2 \tag{7}$$

where φ is a fluent formula such that $Cn(\varphi \cup K_D)$ is consistent, α is a (possibly empty) sequence of actions, and s, s_1, s_2 are situation constants which differ from s_c.

Observations of the forms (4) and (7) are called *fluent facts* and *precedence facts*, respectively. (4) states that φ is observed at situation s and (7) states that s_1 precedes s_2. Observations of the forms (5) and (6) are referred to as *occurrence facts*. These two types of observations are different in that (5) states exactly what happened between two situations s_1 and s_2, whereas (6) only says what occurred in the situation s.

For simplicity of the presentation in this paper, we will assume that the set of precedence facts creates a transitive, total order, and irreflexive relation satisfying that $s_0 < s$ for every $s \in \mathbf{S} \setminus \{s_0\}$ and $s < s_c$ for every $s \in \mathbf{S} \setminus \{s_c\}$.

2.3   Narratives in $\mathcal{L}$

A *narrative* is a pair (D, OBS) where D is a domain description and OBS is a finite set of observations of the form $(4)-(6)$. Without the loss of generality, we assume that for $s \neq s_c$, OBS contains exactly one observation of the form (4) per situation; and $\top \text{ at } s_c \in OBS$. $\alpha \circ \beta$ denotes the concatenation of two action sequences, α and β. Since the precedence facts create a total order between the situation constants, we will often use a sequence $\langle s_0, s_1, \ldots, s_n \rangle$ as the enumeration of situations in $\mathcal{L}_O$ such that $s_i < s_j$ for $0 \leq i < j \leq n$ is given. Using this convention, we will omit the precedence facts from the examples in this paper.

Example 2. The story in Scenario 1 of Example 1 can be represent by (D_1, OBS_1) where $D_1 = \emptyset$ and $OBS_1 = \{f \text{ at } s_0, \neg f \text{ at } s_1\}$.

We sometimes use a graphical representation to describe the set of situations and fluent facts of a narrative as follows (Figs. 1 and 2):

Let (D, OBS) be a narrative. A *causal interpretation* Ψ of (D, OBS) is a partial function from action sequences to states of D, whose domain is denoted by $Dom(\Psi)$, such that $[] \in Dom(\Psi)$ and for every action sequence α, if $\alpha \in Dom(\Psi)$, then $\beta \in Dom(\Psi)$ for every prefix of α.

A *causal model* of D is a causal interpretation Ψ such that for every $\alpha \circ a \in Dom(\Psi)$, $\Psi(\alpha \circ a) \in \Phi_D(a, \Psi(\alpha))$.

A *situation assignment* of $\mathbf{S}$ with respect to D is a mapping Σ from $\mathbf{S}$ into the set of action sequences of D that satisfy the following properties: (i) $\Sigma(s_0) = []$; (ii) for every pair of i, j such that $i < j$, $\Sigma(s_i)$ is a prefix of $\Sigma(s_j)$; and (iii) for every $s \in \mathbf{S}$, $\Sigma(s)$ is a prefix of $\Sigma(s_c)$.

Fig. 1. Narrative (D_1, OBS_1)

An *interpretation* M of (D, OBS) is a pair (Ψ, Σ), where Ψ is a causal model of D, Σ is a situation assignment of $\mathbf{S}$, and $\Sigma(\mathsf{s_c})$ belongs to the domain of Ψ. For an interpretation $M = (\Psi, \Sigma)$ of (D, OBS):

(i) $\alpha\,\mathbf{occ\_at}\,\mathsf{s}$ is true in M if the sequence $\Sigma(\mathsf{s}) \circ \alpha$ is a prefix of $\Sigma(\mathsf{s_c})$;
(ii) $\alpha\,\mathbf{between}\,\mathsf{s}_a, \mathsf{s}_b$ is true in M if $\Sigma(\mathsf{s}_a) \circ \alpha = \Sigma(\mathsf{s}_b)$; and
(iii) $\varphi\,\mathbf{at}\,\mathsf{s}$ is true in M if φ holds in $\Psi(\Sigma(\mathsf{s}))$.

Definition 1. An interpretation $M = (\Psi, \Sigma)$ is a *model* of a narrative (D, OBS) if:

(i) facts in OBS are true in M;
(ii) there is no other interpretation $M' = (\Psi, \Sigma')$ such that M' satisfies (i) and $\Sigma'(\mathsf{s_c})$ is a subsequence of $\Sigma(\mathsf{s_c})$.

A narrative is *consistent* if it has a model and *inconsistent* otherwise. Models of a narrative are used to answer questions about properties of the system after the execution of a sequence of actions in a given situation. As our focus in this paper is not about query answering, we omit the query language in $\mathcal{L}$ for brevity.

3   A Framework for Narratives with Revisions

It is easy to see that (D_1, OBS_1) has no model under Definition 1 because D_1 is empty and thus there is no action that can cause $\neg f$ to become true. As we have discussed earlier, it would be more intuitive to conclude that the observation at s_0 might have been wrong. Indeed, this is exactly what one can expect from a *belief revision* perspective. In order to address the issue, it is necessary to allow the agent to revise his/her observations. More specifically, if f **at** s_0 is "revised" to be $\neg f$ **at** s_0, then the narrative becomes consistent. This requires that the agent has the ability to revise his/her observations. In this section, we propose a framework for this purpose. Our framework will define the notion of a *revision* of a narrative. Our definition will allow fluent facts of a narrative to be revised following the two principles:

(P1) : newer observations are more accurate; and
(P2) : only observed information can be revised.

(P1) represents the fact that our ability (e.g., our sensor actions) to acquire the truth value of fluent formulas is getting better and so we would prefer to believe in the newer observations. **(P1)** also implies that we do not want to revise the latest observation. **(P2)** indicates that revision should be done on what has been observed. Observe that (**P2**) prevents the introduction of extraneous information to the narrative. The discussion following Definition 2 elaborates on this issue.

In the following, we us $\star$ to denote a generic belief revision operator satisfying the *AGM postulates* (see, e.g., [1]). Before introducing the framework, let us review the basic definition of a belief revision operator.

We assume a propositional language L with the usual consequence relation $\models$. As in the previous subsection, we use $Cn(K)$ to denote the set of all logical consequences of K, i.e., $Cn(K) = \{\varphi \mid K \models \varphi\}$. A theory K is any set of fluent formulas that is closed under $\models$, i.e., $K \equiv Cn(K)$. $K + \varphi$ denotes $Cn(K \cup \{\varphi\})$. A mapping $\star$ from pairs of theories and formulas into theories is called a *belief revision function*, i.e., given a theory K and a formula φ, $K \star \varphi$ is a new theory. It is generally agreed that $\star$ should satisfy the *AGM postulates*[3]. (see, e.g., [1]):

$(K \star 1)$ $K \star \varphi$ is a theory.
$(K \star 2)$ $\varphi \in K \star \varphi$.
$(K \star 3)$ $K \star \varphi \subseteq K + \varphi$.
$(K \star 4)$ If $\neg\varphi \notin K$, then $K + \varphi \subseteq K \star \varphi$.
$(K \star 5)$ If φ is consistent, then $K \star \varphi$ is also consistent.
$(K \star 6)$ If $\models \varphi \equiv \psi$, then $K \star \varphi = K \star \psi$.
$(K \star 7)$ $K \star (\varphi \wedge \psi) \subseteq (K \star \varphi) + \psi$.
$(K \star 8)$ If $\neg\psi \notin K \star \varphi$, then $(K \star \varphi) + \psi \subseteq K \star (\varphi \wedge \psi)$.

3.1   Narratives with Revisions

We next define the notion of a revision-candidate formula that can be used in the revision. Let (D, OBS) be a narrative. A *situation-stamped* formula in (D, OBS) (or *s-formula*, for short) is of the form $\varphi[\mathsf{s}]$ where φ is a fluent formula and s is a situation constant of (D, OBS). Recall that K_D denotes the set of static causal laws in D. For a formula φ, $\mathbf{f}(\varphi)$ denotes the set of fluents which occur in φ; $\mathbf{f}(X) = \bigcup_{\varphi \in X} \mathbf{f}(\varphi)$ for any set of formulas X.

Definition 2. Let (D, OBS) be a narrative. A s-formula $\varphi[\mathsf{s}_i]$ is said to be *revision-candidate* at s_i if OBS contains an observations ψ at s_j with $i < j$ such that $\mathbf{f}(\varphi) \subseteq \mathbf{f}(Cn(\psi \cup K_D))$ and $Cn(\varphi \cup K_D)$ is consistent.

The idea behinds the above definition is as follows. Assume that we have an inconsistent narrative (D, OBS) and the reason for this inconsistency is the existence of the observation ψ at s_j in OBS and revising this observation can help restoring the consistency of (D, OBS). To do so, we identify a formula φ at an earlier situation s_i such that if we revise the observation at s_i with φ, the narrative will become consistent.

This definition enforces the principles (**P1**)-(**P2**) in the following ways:

---

[3]   The discussion on whether these postulates need to be satisfied is outside the scope of this paper. The formalization in this paper is generic and can be used with any belief revision operator.

- First, the requirement that ψ at s_j exists implies that the latest observation of a narrative at s_n should not be revised; for example, we do not allow the revision of $\neg f$ at s_1 of the narrative (D_1, OBS_1). This is reasonable given the assumption that most recent observations are more accurate.
- $\mathbf{f}(\varphi) \subseteq \mathbf{f}(Cn(\psi \cup K_D))$ represents the requirement that φ and ψ should be relevant to each other[4]. By imposing this condition, we do not allow for the extraneous information to be added, e.g., no revision should add information about g at situation s_0 in Example 2 assuming that g is another fluent of D_1.
- The condition that $Cn(\varphi \cup K_D)$ is consistent is needed since (i) when $Cn(\varphi \cup K_D)$ is inconsistent, the narrative is definitely inconsistent; and (ii) the basic idea of a revision is to restoring consistency of a narrative and thus, if this condition were not satisfied, any revision operator would create an inconsistent state at s_i, rendering the revision useless.

Following the above definition, the only three possible revision-candidate s-formulas for (D_1, OBS_1) are: $f[s_0]$, $\neg f[s_0]$, and $\top[s_0]$. Of course, a narrative might need to be revised at multiple situations. For this reason, we define the notion of a revision of a narrative as follows.

Definition 3. A *revision* of (D, OBS) is a sequence Δ of revision-candidate formulas

$$\Delta = \langle \delta_0[s_0], \ldots, \delta_n[s_n] \rangle \tag{8}$$

Observe that because $\delta_i[s_i]$ is a revision-candidate formula, $Cn(\delta_i \cup K_D)$ is consistent for every i, i.e., Definitions 2 and 3 mean that we are only interested in revisions which do not contain inconsistent revision-candidate formulas. Observe that the condition imposed on revision-candidate formulas implies that $\delta_n = \top$ for any revision of a narrative[5]. Given a revision Δ of the form (8), we write $\delta_i[s] \in \Delta$ to denote that $\delta_i[s]$ occurs in Δ. The empty sequence $\langle \rangle$ denotes $\langle \top[s_0], \ldots, \top[s_n] \rangle$.

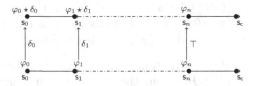

Fig. 2. Revising a Narrative (Assuming $\varphi_n \star \top = \varphi_n$)

Given a revision Δ of (D, OBS) as in (8), we define the *revision narrative* (D, OBS') of (D, OBS) w.r.t. Δ, written as $(D, OBS') = (D, OBS) \star \Delta$, is the narrative whose set of observations OBS' is obtained from OBS by replacing

---

4 Note that $\mathbf{f}(Cn(\psi \cup K_D))$ can be a proper subset of the set of fluents $\mathbf{F}$.
5 For simplicity of the representation, we still use formula (8) in our discussion.

every fluent fact φ_i at s_i in OBS with $\varphi_i \star \delta_i$ at s_i. Figure 3 illustrates this revision process.

Obviously, not all revisions are the same. Some might, for example, still be inconsistent. We introduce the notion of an acceptable revision of a narrative as follows.

Definition 4. Let (D, OBS) be a narrative. A revision Δ of (D, OBS) is an *acceptable revision* (or *a-revision*, for short) of (D, OBS) if $(D, OBS) \star \Delta$ is consistent.

Revising a narrative can help restoring its consistency.

Example 3. Consider (D_1, OBS_1) (Example 2). It is easy to see that $\langle \neg f[s_0] \rangle$ is an a-revision of (D_1, OBS_1) since $(D_1, OBS_1') = (D_1, OBS_1) \star \langle \neg f[s_0] \rangle$ has a unique model (Ψ_1, Σ_1) where $\Psi_1([]) = \{\neg f\}$ and $\Sigma_1(s) = []$ for every s (Assuming that $f \star \neg f = \neg f$). The two narratives are drawn in Fig. 2.

The next example shows that revision needs to take into consideration the set of static causal laws in the domain:

Example 4. Consider the narrative (D_2, OBS_2) where

- D_2 contains one static causal law $\bot$ **if** $f \wedge g$ and
- $OBS_2 = \{\neg f$ at $s_0, \quad f$ at $s_1, \quad g$ at $s_2\}$.

(D_2, OBS_2) is inconsistent and $\Delta = \langle \neg f[s_1] \rangle$ would restore its consistency. It is easy to see that $\Delta' = \langle f[s_0] \rangle$ is not a revision since $(D_2, OBS_2) \star \Delta'$ does not have a model. Observe that $\neg f \in Cn(g \wedge \{\bot$ **if** $f \wedge g\})$ and without considering the static causal law in D_2, $\neg f[s_1]$ is not a revision-candidate formula.

Revision can also be applied to consistent narratives as discussed in the introduction, detailed in the next example.

Example 5. Consider the narrative (D_3, OBS_3) where

- D_3 contains one dynamic law a **causes** $\neg f$ and
- $OBS_3 = \{f$ at $s_0, \quad \neg f$ at $s_1\}$.

(D_3, OBS_3) is consistent and has a model (Ψ_1, Σ_1) where $\Sigma_1(s_0) = []$, $\Sigma_1(s_1) = [a]$, $\Psi_1([]) = \{f\}$, $\Psi_1([a]) = \{\neg f\}$. Observe that this model *inserts* the action occurrence into the narrative whose occurrence is not observed. This is possible due to Definition 1.

Notice also that $\Delta = \langle \neg f[s_0], \top[s_1] \rangle$ is a revision of (D_3, OBS_3). The revision $(D_3, OBS_3) \star \Delta$ has a model (Ψ_2, Σ_2) where $\Psi_2([]) = \{\neg f\}$ and $\Sigma_2(s) = []$ for every s.

We define the notion of model of a narrative with revision.

Definition 5. Let (D, OBS) be a narrative. An interpretation (Ψ, Σ) is a *model* of (D, OBS) if there exists an a-revision Δ of (D, OBS) such that (Ψ, Σ) is a model of $(D, OBS) \star \Delta$ according to Definition 1.

Fig. 3. (D_1, OBS_1) (left) and $(D_1, OBS_1) \star \langle \neg f[s_0] \rangle$ (right)

From now on, whenever we refer to a model of a narrative, we mean a model according to Definition 5. Observe that Definition 5 might enlarge the set of models of a narrative (D, OBS) as an interpretation might not be a model of (D, OBS) according to Definition 1; yet still a model of (D, OBS) according to Definition 5 (see, e.g., Example 5).

3.2 Preferred Models

Examples 4–5 show that when observation facts can be revised then consistent narratives could also be revised, which produces new models. As we have alluded to it in the introduction, this also raises an interesting question on which model should be considered as the *true* model of the world given the narrative. This question has been investigated in the context of diagnosis (e.g., [2]) and in works integrating belief revision with action formalisms such as those discussed in Sect. 4. A possible way to address this issue is to define an ordering among the possible models of the narrative and then select the best models using this ordering. We next present a quantitative approach to identifying the most preferred models of a narrative. We assume that the set of actions **A** of D has a special action noop that is executable in any state s and does not change the state of the world.

Definition 6. For a domain description D, a mapping $P : \mathbf{A} \times \mathbf{States} \longrightarrow [0, 1]$, where **States** is the set of states in D and $[0, 1]$ denotes the real valued interval $[0, 1]$, is called a *likelihood function* of D if for every action a and every state s, $P(a|s) > 0$ if a is executable in s and $P(a|s) = 0$ otherwise; and for every state s, $\Sigma_{a \in \mathbf{A}} P(a|s) = 1$.

Each $P(a|s)$ represents the likelihood of a occurring in s. Observe that $P(\text{noop}|s)$ represents the likelihood of nothing happening in the state s.

Given a narrative (D, OBS), a likelihood function P of D, and a model (Ψ, Σ) of D, let $\gamma = \Sigma(s_c) = [a_1, \ldots, a_k]$. We say that the actions in $[a_i, \ldots, a_s]$ $(s \leq k)$ *must occur* in (Ψ, Σ) w.r.t. (D, OBS) if

- there exists an observation α at s in OBS and $\Sigma(s) = [a_1, \ldots, a_{i-1}]$ and $\alpha = [a_i, \ldots, a_s]$; or
- there exists an observation α between s_a, s_b in OBS and $\Sigma(s_a) = [a_1, \ldots, a_{i-1}]$, $\Sigma(s_b) = [a_1, \ldots, a_s]$, and $\alpha = [a_i, \ldots, a_s]$.

An action a_t in $\Sigma(s_c)$ is *exogenous* in (Ψ, Σ) w.r.t. (D, OBS) if it must not occur in (Ψ, Σ) w.r.t. (D, OBS). Let

$$E_{(\Psi, \Sigma)} = \begin{cases} \{a_i \mid a_i \text{ is } exogenous \text{ in } (\Psi, \Sigma) \text{ w.r.t } (D, OBS)\} & \text{if } \Sigma(s_c) \neq [] \\ \{\text{noop}\} \text{ otherwise} \end{cases}$$

The *likelihood* of (Ψ, Σ) w.r.t. P, denoted by $V(\Psi, \Sigma)$, is defined by

$$V(\Psi, \Sigma) = \begin{cases} \Pi_{i \in E_{(\Psi, \Sigma)}} P(a_i | \Psi([a_1, \ldots, a_{i-1}])) & \text{if } E_{(\Psi, \Sigma)} \neq \emptyset \\ 1 & \text{otherwise} \end{cases}$$

Intuitively, $V(\Psi, \Sigma)$ records the likelihood of the actions that are not observed (in OBS) and must occur in order to establish that (Ψ, Σ) is indeed a model of the narrative. An alternative is to define $V(\Psi, \Sigma) = \Pi_{i=1}^{k} P(a_i | \Psi([a_1, \ldots, a_{i-1}]))$. In our view, the first alternative is better under the assumption that occurrence facts are accurate. When occurrence facts might be inaccurate, the second option might be more appropriate.

Definition 7. Let (D, OBS) be a narrative, P be a likelihood function of D, and (Ψ_1, Σ_1) and (Ψ_2, Σ_2) be two models of (D, OBS). (Ψ_1, Σ_1) is *more preferred* than (Ψ_2, Σ_2) w.r.t. P, denoted by $(\Psi_1, \Sigma_1) \succ_P (\Psi_2, \Sigma_2)$, if $V(\Psi_1, \Sigma_1) > V(\Psi_2, \Sigma_2)$.

(Ψ, Σ) is *most preferred* w.r.t. P if there exists no other model that is more preferred than (Ψ, Σ) w.r.t. P.

It is easy to see that the following property holds.

Proposition 1. *Given a narrative (D, OBS) and a likelihood function P of D, $\succ_P$ is a transitive and irreflexive relation between models of (D, OBS).*

We note that the above definition and proposition provide a means for comparing different models of a narrative. One might question the applicability of Definition 7 and Proposition 1 as the likelihood function of D might not be available. As it turns out, we can easily define a *default* likelihood function that, given a state s, assigns the same likelihood for every executable action in s; more specifically, for every s, if $a \neq b$ and a, b executable in s, then $P(a|s) = P(b|s)$.

Example 6. Let us revisit Example 5. Consider the likelihood function P_λ with $P_\lambda(a|\{f\}) = P_\lambda(a|\{\neg f\}) = \lambda$ and $P_\lambda(noop|\{f\}) = P_\lambda(noop|\{\neg f\}) = 1 - \lambda$. We have that $E_{(\Psi_1, \Sigma_1)} = E_{(\Psi_2, \Sigma_2)} = \{noop\}$. As such, $(\Psi_1, \Sigma_1) \succ_{P_\lambda} (\Psi_2, \Sigma_2)$ if $\lambda > 0.5$ (or, (Ψ_1, Σ_1) is more preferred than (Ψ_2, Σ_2) w.r.t. P_λ); and $(\Psi_2, \Sigma_2) \succ_{P_\lambda} (\Psi_1, \Sigma_1)$ if $\lambda < 0.5$. Furthermore, (Ψ_1, Σ_1) is not more preferred than (Ψ_2, Σ_2) w.r.t. $P_{0.5}$ and vice versa.

3.3 Preferred Models with Preferred Revisions

Subsection 3.2 considers all revisions being equal and puts the emphasis on the likelihood of action occurrences. A disadvantage of this approach is that it does not take into consideration the revisions in its evaluation; sometimes it is desirable to prefer one revision over another. Let us consider the next examples.

Example 7. Consider the narrative (D_4, OBS_4) where

- D_4 contains one dynamic law b **causes** g and
- $OBS_4 = \{f$ **at** s_0, $\neg f \wedge g$ **at** $s_1\}$.

(D_4, OBS_4) is inconsistent and $\Delta_1 = \langle \neg f \wedge g[s_0] \rangle$ and $\Delta_2 = \langle \neg f[s_0] \rangle$ are two a-revisions of (D_4, OBS_4). The model of $(D_4, OBS_4) \star \Delta_1$ does not have any action occurrence and the model of $(D_4, OBS_4) \star \Delta_2$ requires that b occurs at s_0.

Although both revisions help restoring the consistency of (D_4, OBS_4), we believe that Δ_2 should be preferred over Δ_1. The reason is that Δ_2 only changes OBS_4 minimally in comparing with Δ_1, it does not require that g to be true at the initial situation as Δ_1 does.

The next example shows another possible preference.

Example 8. Consider the narrative (D_5, OBS_5) where

- D_5 contains one dynamic law b **causes** f and
- $OBS_5 = \{f \text{ at } s_0, \quad \neg f \text{ at } s_1, \quad f \text{ at } s_2\}$.

(D_5, OBS_5) is inconsistent since there exists no action that can cause $\neg f$ to be true. Furthermore, $\Gamma_1 = \langle \neg f[s_0] \rangle$ and $\Gamma_2 = \langle f[s_1] \rangle$ are two a-revisions of (D_5, OBS_5). The model of $(D_5, OBS_5) \star \Gamma_1$ requires that b occurs at s_1 and the model of $(D_5, OBS_5) \star \Gamma_2$ does not have any action occurrence.

In this case we believe that $(D_5, OBS_5) \star \Gamma_1$ should be preferred over $(D_5, OBS_5) \star \Gamma_2$. The reason is that Γ_1 revises (D_5, OBS_5) by modifying an older observation than Γ_2.

Examples 7 and 8 demonstrate that we might prefer a revision over another. To address this issue, we will define the notion called *preferred revision*. Intuitively, we would require that a revision be minimal with respect to some reasonable criteria. These criteria also need to enforce the two principles (**P1**) and (**P2**). Our definition of a revision already addresses one aspect of (**P2**). Example 7 shows that revision-candidate formulas should be minimal and Example 8 indicates that one should revise earlier observations before newer ones. Before precisely formalizing the criteria on a narrative revision, let us introduce some additional notation.

Definition 8. Let (D, OBS) be a narrative and $\Delta_1 = \langle \varphi_0[s_0], \ldots, \varphi_n[s_n] \rangle$ and $\Delta_2 = \langle \delta_0[s_0], \ldots, \delta_n[s_n] \rangle$ be two revisions of (D, OBS). We say that Δ_1 is *older* than Δ_2, written as $\Delta_1 <_O \Delta_2$, if there exist $0 \leq t_1 < t_2 < n$ such that

- $\varphi_j \equiv \delta_j$ for every $j = t_1 + 1, \ldots, n$ and $j \neq t_2$; and
- $k_1 < k_2$ where k_1 (resp. k_2) is the smallest index greater than t_1 (resp. t_2) such that $\psi_1 \text{ at } s_{k_1}$ (resp. $\psi_2 \text{ at } s_{k_2}$) belongs to OBS and $\varphi_{t_1}[s_{t_1}]$ is a revision-candidate of $\psi_1 \text{ at } s_{k_1}$ (resp. $\delta_{t_2}[s_{t_2}]$ is a revision-candidate of $\psi_2 \text{ at } s_{k_2}$).

The intuition behinds this notion is that if Δ_1 is older than Δ_2, then Δ_1 revises some older observation than Δ_2. By preferring older sequences, we can eliminate the issue raised in Example 8. The next notion will be used to address the issue raised in Example 7.

Definition 9. Let (D, OBS) be a narrative and $\Delta_1 = \langle \varphi_0[s_0], \ldots, \varphi_n[s_n] \rangle$ and $\Delta_2 = \langle \psi_0[s_0], \ldots, \psi_n[s_n] \rangle$ be two revisions of (D, OBS). We say that Δ_1 is *less informative* than Δ_2, written as $\Delta_1 <_I \Delta_2$, if there exists t, $0 \leq t \leq n$, such that

- for every $j = t + 1, \ldots, n$, $\varphi_j \equiv \psi_j$; and
- $\psi_t \models \varphi_t$ and $\varphi_t \not\equiv \psi_t$.

We next define the more preferred relation between revisions of a narrative.

Definition 10. Let (D, OBS) be a narrative and Δ_1 and Δ_2 be the two a-revisions of (D, OBS). We say that Δ_1 is *more preferred to* Δ_2, denoted by $\Delta_1 \prec \Delta_2$, if

- $\Delta_1 <_O \Delta_2$; or
- $\Delta_1 \not<_O \Delta_2$, $\Delta_2 \not<_O \Delta_1$, and $\Delta_1 <_I \Delta_2$.

An a-revision Δ' is a *most preferred revision* of (D, OBS) if there exists no a-revision Δ^* of (D, OBS) such that $\Delta^* \prec \Delta'$.

The more preferred relation among revisions is transitive:

Proposition 2. Let (D, OBS) be a narrative and Δ_i for $i = 1, 2, 3$ be a-revisions of (D, OBS). Furthermore $\Delta_1 \prec \Delta_2$ and $\Delta_2 \prec \Delta_3$ holds. Then, $\Delta_1 \prec \Delta_3$.

The proof of this property is done by considering the possible cases. It is easy to see that $(D_4, OBS_4) \star \Delta_2 \prec (D_4, OBS_4) \star \Delta_1$ (Example 7) because Δ_2 is less informative than Δ_1. On the other hand, $(D_5, OBS_5) \star \Gamma_1 \prec (D_5, OBS_5) \star \Gamma_2$ (Example 8) because Γ_1 is older than Γ_2. We next prove some important properties about most preferred revisions of a narrative.

Proposition 3. If a narrative (D, OBS) is consistent, then the empty revision $(D, OBS) \star \langle \rangle$ is the unique most preferred revision of (D, OBS).

The proof of this proposition relies on two facts: (i) $(D, OBS) \star \langle \rangle = (D, OBS)$ and is a revision of (D, OBS); and (ii) $\langle \rangle$ is both older and less informative than any revision sequence of (D, OBS).

Proposition 4. If a narrative (D, OBS) has a revision, then it has a most preferred revision.

Having defined the notion of a more preferred revision, we can extend the notion of a preferred model in Definition 7 by imposing an order among trajectories with the same likelihood using their corresponding preferred revisions. Since it is possible that a model (Ψ, Σ) of (D, OBS) can be a model of different a-revision of (D, OBS), we designate $\delta(\Psi, \Sigma)$ as the a-revision such that (i) (Ψ, Σ) is a model of $(D, OBS) \star \delta(\Psi, \Sigma)$; and (ii) there exists no a-revision $\Delta' \prec \delta(\Psi, \Sigma)$ such that (Ψ, Σ) is a model of $(D, OBS) \star \Delta'$. In other words, $\delta(\Psi, \Sigma)$ is the most preferred revision that can be used in justifying that (Ψ, Σ) is a model of (D, OBS).

Definition 11. Let (D, OBS) be a narrative, P be a likelihood function of D, and (Ψ_1, Σ_1) and (Ψ_2, Σ_2) be two models of (D, OBS). (Ψ_1, Σ_1) is *more preferred* than (Ψ_2, Σ_2) w.r.t. P, denoted by $(\Psi_1, \Sigma_1) \succ_P^r (\Psi_2, \Sigma_2)$, if

– either $V(\Psi_1, \Sigma_1) > V(\Psi_2, \Sigma_2)$;
– or $V(\Psi_1, \Sigma_1) = V(\Psi_2, \Sigma_2)$ and $\delta(\Psi_1, \Sigma_1) \prec \delta(\Psi_2, \Sigma_2)$.

A model (Ψ, Σ) of (D, OBS) is *most preferred* if there exists no model of (D, OBS) that is more preferred than (Ψ, Σ).

By Definiton 11 and given that $\lambda = 0.5$ in Example 6, we will show that $(\Psi_1, \Sigma_1) \succ^r_{P_{0.5}} (\Psi_2, \Sigma_2)$. Furthermore, $\delta(\Psi_1, \Sigma_1) = \langle \top[s_0], \top[s_1] \rangle$ because (Ψ_1, Σ_1) is the only model of $\delta(\Psi_1, \Sigma_1)$. Likewise, we can easily check that $\delta(\Psi_2, \Sigma_2) = \langle \neg f[s_0], \top[s_1] \rangle$. Furthermore, $\delta(\Psi_1, \Sigma_1) \prec \delta(\Psi_2, \Sigma_2)$ because $\delta(\Psi_1, \Sigma_1) <_O \delta(\Psi_2, \Sigma_2)$. Together with the fact that $V(\Psi_1, \Sigma_1) = V(\Psi_2, \Sigma_2)$, we can conclude that $(\Psi_1, \Sigma_1) \succ^r_{P_{0.5}} (\Psi_2, \Sigma_2)$.

Due to Propositions 1 and 2, we can prove the following proposition.

Proposition 5. *Given a narrative (D, OBS) and a likelihood function P of D, $\succ^r_P$ is a transitive and irreflexive relation between models of (D, OBS).*

4   Discussion and Related Work

There have been several attempts to integrate revision into an action formalism or combine revision and update. The focus has been to deal with the problem of wrong beliefs, inaccurate perceptions, failed actions, or exogenous actions. The key difference between our work and previous approaches lies in that we focus on the identification of models of action-occurrence-incomplete narratives while the majority of other work study the problem of belief change (of an agent) after an alternate sequence of actions and observations. We next discuss in detail some of the strongly related proposals which are not directly applicable to action-occurrence-incomplete narratives and thus differ significantly from the present work.

Using the notations presented in Sect. 2, the authors of [16] study the problem of belief change along the situations of the narrative (D, OBS) where D corresponds to the underlying transition system in their notation and OBS consists of φ_i **at** s_i $(i = 0, \ldots, n)$ and a_i **between** s_{i-1}, s_i $(i = 1, \ldots, n)$. They argued that the observations (φ_i) cannot simply be used to revise the current belief state (the beliefs at s_i) but should be used to revise the initial beliefs (φ_0) and specified a number of interaction properties that should hold whenever an update is followed by a revision. They defined a *belief evolution operator* that combines belief revision and belief update and studied various properties of the operator. This operation is then reformulated in [9] to remove the focus on the initial belief.

In [16], it is assumed that action occurrences are accurate, ontic actions never fail, and recent observations take precedence over earlier ones. These assumptions are then relaxed in [17] and the authors introduced a new approach to deal with the uncertainties of action occurrences and/or observations using ranking functions and defined the notion of most plausible histories given the observations.

We note that the assumptions in [16] are employed in our framework. Although we agree that there are situations in which these assumptions might be invalid, as discussed in [17], we leave the task of extending our framework to deal with these situations as a future work. It should be noted that the original approach in [5] already addressed the issue of exogenous actions; and our notion of most preferred model corresponds to that of the most plausible histories in [17].

Belief revision has also been integrated into situation calculus, a well-known formalism for reasoning about action and change, in [10,23] to address the problem of iterated belief change. Both of these works focus on answering the question about the beliefs of the agent at a situation which encodes the evolution of the world after a sequence of actions[6]. In [23], a plausibility function over situations is defined that is used in conjunction with the accessibility relation between situations to determine the *most plausible situations*. A formula is said to hold at a situation s if it holds at all most plausible situations accessible from s. In [10], the accessibility relation between situations has an extra parameter, the level of plausibility of the situation, which is updated by the successor state axiom for the fluent encoding the accessibility relation updates this number depending on the type of actions. Similar to [23], beliefs of an agent at a situation s are then defined as formulas that hold in situations accessible to s with the level of plausibility 0.

The proposed work is also related to formalisms suggesting an integration of belief update and belief revision [8,19,22]. Specifically, a generalized update model is proposed in [8]; belief extrapolation operators are developed in [22]; and revised belief update operators are proposed in [19]. The key distinction between these works and ours lies in the close connection of our formalism to action languages as in Examples 7 and 8 where explanations might require both revision and action occurrences.

Belief revision has also been investigated in the context of multi-agent systems (e.g., [3,7]) which focuses on defining a transition function between 'states' of the system that correctly captures the changes in the beliefs of agents when actions occur. The difference between our work and this line of research is similar to the ones mentioned above.

We next present a brief discussion on the general problem of finding a revision of a narrative. First, let us observe that a model of a narrative (D, OBS) could be viewed as alternate sequence of states and actions $s_0 a_0 s_1 \ldots a_{m-1} s_m$ where s_i's are states and a_i's are actions (or *trajectory*) satisfying that (i) there exists a sequence $i_0 = 0 < i_1 < \ldots < i_n \leq m$ such that φ_j is true in s_{i_j}, assuming that φ_j at s_j for $j = 0, \ldots, n$ are the fluent facts in OBS; (ii) $s_j \in \Phi(a_{j-1}, s_{j-1})$ for $0 < j < m$; and (iii) the mapping $\Sigma(s_j) = a_0 \ldots a_{i_j}$ and $\Sigma(s_c) = a_0 \ldots a_{m-1}$ satisfies the occurrence facts in OBS. Since the number of possible trajectories of bounded length and the number of all possible assignments of the sequence $i_0, i_1, \ldots, i_n$ are exponential in the size of the narrative, determining whether or not a narrative has a model is at least Σ_2^P-hard.

---

[6] In our notations, a situation represents a snapshot of the world rather than an action sequence.

Computing a trajectory of the above form can be implemented using answer set programming as shown in[7] [2]. Specifically, a narrative (D, OBS) can be represented as a logic program $P(D, OBS)$ whose answer sets correspond to models of (D, OBS) and the program is inconsistent whenever the narrative is inconsistent.

Assume that a concrete implementation of the operator $\star$ is available, a revision of a narrative (D, OBS) can be computed using a guess and check procedure: (i) guess a revision sequence Δ; (ii) check whether or not $(D, OBS) \star \Delta$ has a model (e.g., using the program $P((D, OBS) \star \Delta)$). This, however, depends on the concrete implementation of the operator $\star$ and is not our main focus of this paper. This investigation might benefit from the development of abductive reasoning systems. We leave this as a future work.

The present work is also somewhat related to the work in abductive reasoning (e.g., [20]) as a narrative (D, OBS) can be viewed as an abduction theory (T_D, OBS) whose set of abducibles is the set of revision sequences such that acceptable revisions of (D, OBS) are equivalent to models of its abduction theory. This provides another way for computing revisions of a narrative using procedures for abductive reasoning. Finally, it is worth mentioning that the proposed work is orthogonal to the research developed in [12–14, 25] in that it investigates the changes in the action theory, i.e., given that a narrative (D, OBS) is inconsistent, the research proposed in these papers focus on changing the action description D to restore the consistency of the narrative.

5   Conclusion

We study action narratives with imprecise observations about properties of the world and the problem of identifying the most preferred models of a narrative. We begin by proposing a framework that integrates belief revision with action narratives that assumes newer observations are more accurate than older ones. We define the notion of an acceptable revision of a narrative as well as the more preferred relation between revisions. We also define the notion of a more preferred model of a narrative with respect to a likelihood function of the domain description. We extend this notion to take into consideration the revisions of the narrative. We prove that the more preferred relation among models of a narrative is transitive and irreflexive. We relate our work to others and briefly discuss how revisions can be computed.

Our focus in this paper was the development of the theoretical foundation for the integration of belief revision in an action language. We therefore neglect the issue of how the proposed framework can be implemented. This will be the focus of our future work. We would like to note that an implementation of our framework needs to start with the selection of a concrete revision operator (e.g., [11]) and relies on a module that computes model(s) of a narrative (e.g., [2]).

---

[7]   We note that the definitions of action theories and narrative in [2] are slightly different from their counterparts in this paper.

Acknowledgement. We would like to thank the reviewers of the paper for their constructive comments and suggestions. The second author was partially supported by the NSF grant 1619273.

References

1. Alchourrón, C.E., Gärdenfors, P., Makinson, D.: On the logic of theory change: partial meet contraction and revision functions. J. Symb. Log. **50**(2), 510–530 (1985)
2. Balduccini, M., Gelfond, M.: Diagnostic reasoning with A-prolog. Theor. Pract. Log. Program. **3**(4–5), 425–461 (2003)
3. Baltag, A., Smets, S.: A qualitative theory of dynamic interactive belief revision. In: Proceedings of 7th LOFT. Texts in Logic and Games 3, pp. 13–60. Amsterdam University Press (2008)
4. Baral, C.: Reasoning about actions : non-deterministic effects, constraints and qualification. In: Proceedings of the 14th International Joint Conference on Artificial Intelligence, pp. 2017–2023. Morgan Kaufmann Publishers, San Francisco (1995)
5. Baral, C., Gelfond, M., Provetti, A.: Representing actions: laws, observations and hypothesis. J. Log. Program. **31**(1–3), 201–243 (1997)
6. Baral, C., McIlraith, S., Son, T.C.: Formulating diagnostic problem solving using an action language with narratives and sensing. In: Proceedings of the Seventh International Conference on Principles of Knowledge and Representation and Reasoning (KR 2000), pp. 311–322 (2000)
7. van Benthem, J.: Dynamic logic of belief revision. J. Appl. Non-Class. Log. **17**(2), 129–155 (2007)
8. Boutilier, C.: Generalized update: belief change in dynamic settings. In: Proceedings of the Fourteenth International Joint Conference on Artificial Intelligence - Volume 2, IJCAI 1995, Montréal, Québec, Canada, 20–25 August 1995, pp. 1550–1556. Morgan Kaufmann (1995)
9. Delgrande, J.P.: Considerations on belief revision in an action theory. In: Erdem, E., Lee, J., Lierler, Y., Pearce, D. (eds.) Correct Reasoning. LNCS, vol. 7265, pp. 164–177. Springer, Heidelberg (2012). doi:10.1007/978-3-642-30743-0_12
10. Delgrande, J.P., Levesque, H.J.: Belief revision with sensing and fallible actions. In: Brewka, G., Eiter, T., McIlraith, S.A. (eds.) Principles of Knowledge Representation and Reasoning: Proceedings of the Thirteenth International Conference, KR 2012, Rome, Italy, 10–14 June 2012. AAAI Press (2012)
11. Dixon, S., Wobcke, W.: The implementation of a first-order logic AGM belief revision system. In: Fifth International Conference on Tools with Artificial Intelligence, ICTAI 1993, Boston, Massachusetts, USA, 8–11 November 1993, pp. 40–47. IEEE Computer Society (1993)
12. Eiter, T., Erdem, E., Fink, M., Senko, J.: Resolving conflicts in action descriptions. In: ECAI (2006)
13. Eiter, T., Erdem, E., Fink, M., Senko, J.: Resolving conflicts in action descriptions. Artif. Intell. **174**(15), 1172–1221 (2010)
14. Erdem, E., Ferraris, P.: Forgetting actions in domain descriptions. In: AAAI (2007)
15. Gelfond, M., Lifschitz, V.: Representing actions and change by logic programs. J. Log. Program. **17**(2–4), 301–323 (1993)
16. Hunter, A., Delgrande, J.P.: Iterated belief change due to actions and observations. J. Artif. Intell. Res. (JAIR) **40**, 269–304 (2011)

17. Hunter, A., Delgrande, J.P.: Belief change with uncertain action histories. J. Artif. Intell. Res. (JAIR) **53**, 779–824 (2015)
18. Katsuno, H., Mendelzon, A.: On the difference between updating a knowledge base and revising it. In: Proceedings of KR 1992, pp. 387–394 (1992)
19. Lang, J.: Belief update revisited. In: Veloso, M.M. (ed.) IJCAI 2007, Proceedings of the 20th International Joint Conference on Artificial Intelligence, Hyderabad, India, 6–12 January 2007, pp. 2517–2522 (2007)
20. Lobo, J., Uzcátegui, C.: Abductive consequence relations. Artif. Intell. **89**(1–2), 149–171 (1997)
21. McCain, N., Turner, H.: A causal theory of ramifications and qualifications. In: Proceedings of the 14th International Joint Conference on Artificial Intelligence, pp. 1978–1984. Morgan Kaufmann Publishers, San Mateo (1995)
22. de Saint-Cyr, F.D., Lang, J.: Belief extrapolation (or how to reason about observations and unpredicted change). Artif. Intell. **175**(2), 760–790 (2011)
23. Shapiro, S., Pagnucco, M., Lespérance, Y., Levesque, H.J.: Iterated belief change in the situation calculus. Artif. Intell. **175**(1), 165–192 (2011)
24. Turner, H.: Representing actions in logic programs and default theories. J. Log. Program. **31**(1–3), 245–298 (1997)
25. Varzinczak, I.: On action theory change. J. Artif. Intell. Res. **37**, 189–246 (2010)

Reasoning About Belief, Evidence and Trust in a Multi-agent Setting

Fenrong Liu[1] and Emiliano Lorini[2(✉)]

[1] Tsinghua University, Beijing, China
[2] IRIT-CNRS, Toulouse University, Toulouse, France
lorini@irit.fr

Abstract. We present a logic for reasoning about the interplay between belief, evidence and trust in a multi-agent setting. We call this logic DL-BET which stands for "Dynamic Logic of Belief, Evidence and Trust". According to DL-BET, if the amount of evidence in support a given fact φ and the ratio of evidence in support of φ to the total amount of evidence in support of either φ or its negation are sufficient then, as a consequence, one should be willing to believe φ. We provide a sound and complete axiomatization for the logic and illustrate its expressive power with the aid of a concrete example.

1   Introduction

As emphasized by the philosopher A.J. Ayer, the connection between evidence and belief is an essential aspect of human rationality:

> "...A rational man is one who makes a proper use of reason: and this implies, among other things, that he correctly estimates the strength of evidence" [3, p. 3].

The connection between belief and evidence is also relevant for artificial intelligence (AI) and, in particular, for reasoning under uncertainty [32] and information fusion [17]. For instance, information fusion can be conceived as an aggregation process which aims to extract truthful knowledge from incomplete or uncertain information coming from various sources of evidence.

The aim of the present paper is to provide a logic of the interplay between evidence and trust, on the one hand, and between evidence and belief, on the other hand. We call this logic DL-BET which stands for "Dynamic Logic of Belief, Evidence and Trust". Specifically, DL-BET supports reasoning about an agent's belief formation and belief change due to evidence provided by reliable information sources.

The central idea of DL-BET is that an agent accumulates *evidence* in support of a given fact φ from other agents in the society and the body of evidence in support of φ can become a reason to *believe* φ. *Trust* is a necessary condition for an agent to accept the information provided by another agent and to integrate it as a new piece of evidence in support of a given fact.

© Springer International Publishing AG 2017
B. An et al. (Eds.): PRIMA 2017, LNAI 10621, pp. 71–89, 2017.
https://doi.org/10.1007/978-3-319-69131-2_5

A central assumption of the logic DL-BET is that, to form a belief that a certain fact φ is true, an agent is sensitive both (i) to the *amount* of evidence in support of φ, and (ii) to the *ratio* of evidence in support of φ to the total amount of evidence in support of either φ or its negation. The notion of "amount of evidence" is reminiscent of Keynes's well-known concept of "weight of argument", as clearly defined in the following paragraph from the famous treatise on probability:

> "...As the relevant evidence at our disposal increases, the magnitude of the probability of the argument may either decrease or increase, according as the new knowledge strengthens the unfavourable or the favourable evidence; but something seems to have increased in either case, - we have more substantial basis upon which to rest our conclusion. I express this by saying that an accession of new evidence increases the weight of argument" [25, p. 77].

The present work is mainly theoretical but, we believe, it can offer interesting insights for people working on multi-agent system (MAS) applications in which agents are supposed to be artificial entities such as a robot, a chatbot or a conversational agent interacting with a human user. Such agents may be endowed with the capability of forming beliefs on the basis of the collected evidence. By way of example, consider a chatbot similar to Apple's Siri or Microsoft's Cortana connected to the Internet who has to provide information to the human user about the quality of a certain movie. In particular, the human user wants to know whether a certain movie is good or bad. The chatbot has access to different recommendation systems about movies in the Internet which are more or less reliable (e.g., Netflix, Rotten Tomatoes, IMDb). The chatbot will form the belief that the movie is good and inform the human user about this, depending on the evidence it possesses in support of this fact.

The paper is organized as follows. In Sect. 2 we present the syntax and semantics of the logic DL-BET and discuss some of its general properties. The semantics of DL-BET combines a relational semantics for the concepts of knowledge and belief and a neighbourhood semantics for the concept of evidence. A sound and complete axiomatization for the logic is given in Sect. 3. The completeness proof is non-standard, given the interrelation between the concepts of belief and knowledge, on the one hand, and the concepts of trust and evidence, on the other hand. In Sect. 4 we discuss related work. Finally, in Sect. 5 we conclude.

2   Dynamic Logic of Belief, Evidence and Trust

In this section, we present the syntax and the semantics of the logic DL-BET and illustrate it on a concrete example.

The static component of DL-BET is called L-BET, which includes modal operators for beliefs, knowledge, trust and evidence sources *plus* special atomic formulas that allow us to represent an agent's disposition to form beliefs based on evidence, namely, how much evidence she needs to collect in support of a fact in order to have a sufficient reason to believe that the fact is true. DL-BET extends L-BET with four kinds of dynamic operators describing, respectively, (i) the consequences of an agent's public announcement, (ii) the consequences of an agent's mental operation of losing trust, (iii) the consequences of an agent's mental operation of relying on someone's judgment, and (iv) the consequences of an agent's mental operation of assessing whether a certain fact is true or false.

On the technical side, DL-BET combine methods from Dynamic Epistemic Logic (DEL) that has been developed in the past decades (cf. [5,9,16]), with those techniques from neighbourhood semantics for modal logic (cf. [12]).

2.1 Syntax

Assume a non-empty countable set of atomic propositions $Atm = \{p, q, \ldots\}$ and a non-empty finite set of agent names $Agt = \{i_1, \ldots, i_n\}$. Elements of 2^{Agt} are called groups (or coalitions) and are denoted by $J, J', \ldots$ For every $J \in 2^{Agt}$, $|J|$ denotes the cardinality of J.

The language of DL-BET, denoted by $\mathcal{L}_{\text{DL-BET}}$, is defined by the following grammar in Backus-Naur Form (BNF):

$$\alpha ::= !_i\varphi \mid -_{i,j}\varphi \mid +_{i,j}\varphi \mid ?_i\varphi$$
$$\varphi ::= p \mid \text{type}(i, x, y) \mid \neg\varphi \mid \varphi \wedge \psi \mid \mathsf{K}_i\varphi \mid \mathsf{B}_i\varphi \mid \mathsf{E}_{i,j}\varphi \mid \mathsf{T}_{i,j}\varphi \mid [\alpha]\varphi$$

where p ranges over Atm, i, j range over Agt, x ranges over $Evd = \{k \in \mathbb{N} : 0 \leq k \leq card(Agt)\}$ and y ranges over a finite chain $Qt \subseteq [\frac{1}{2}, 1]$ such that $1 \in Qt$. Sets Evd and Qt are, respectively, the set of possible numbers of collected evidence and the set of *quota* values. Evd and Qt are finite because an agent can have a number of different evidence in support of a given fact which is at most equal to the size of Agt.

The other Boolean constructions $\top, \bot, \vee, \rightarrow$ and $\leftrightarrow$ are defined from p, $\neg$ and $\wedge$ in the standard way.

The language of L-BET (Logic of Belief, Evidence and Trust), denoted by $\mathcal{L}_{\text{L-BET}}$, is defined by:

$$\varphi ::= p \mid \text{type}(i, x, y) \mid \neg\varphi \mid \varphi \wedge \psi \mid \mathsf{K}_i\varphi \mid \mathsf{B}_i\varphi \mid \mathsf{E}_{i,j}\varphi \mid \mathsf{T}_{i,j}\varphi$$

K_i is the standard modal operator of knowledge and $\mathsf{K}_i\varphi$ has to be read "agent i knows that φ is true". $\mathsf{B}_i\varphi$ has to be read "agent i believes that φ is true". The dual of the knowledge operator and the dual of the belief operator are defined as follows: $\widehat{\mathsf{K}}_i\varphi \stackrel{\text{def}}{=} \neg\mathsf{K}_i\neg\varphi$ and $\widehat{\mathsf{B}}_i\varphi \stackrel{\text{def}}{=} \neg\mathsf{B}_i\neg\varphi$.

$\mathsf{E}_{i,j}\varphi$ has to be read "agent i has evidence in support of φ based on the information provided by agent j".

$\mathsf{T}_{i,j}\varphi$ has to be read "agent i trusts agent j's judgement on φ". Note that, when $i = j$, the operator $\mathsf{T}_{i,j}\varphi$ captures a notion of self-trust (or self-confidence). As we mentioned earlier, since [27] similar modal operators for trust have been studied by [14,31,33]. In this paper, following [27], we use a neighbourhood semantics for interpreting the trust operators $\mathsf{T}_{i,j}$ because these modal operators are not normal. We want to allow situations in which, at the same time, agent i trusts agent j's judgement about φ and i trusts agent j's judgement about $\neg\varphi$, without inferring that i trusts agent j's judgement about $\bot$, that is, we want formula $\mathsf{T}_{i,j}\varphi \wedge \mathsf{T}_{i,j}\neg\varphi \wedge \neg\mathsf{T}_{i,j}\bot$ to be satisfiable. This means i has potential to access j's information some of which may support φ, some of which may reject φ. For example, Bill may trust Mary's judgement about the fact that a certain stock will go upward (i.e., $\mathsf{T}_{Bill,Mary}stockUp$) and, at the same time, trust Mary's judgement about the fact that the stock will not go upward (i.e., $\mathsf{T}_{Bill,Mary}\neg stockUp$), without trusting Mary's judgement about $\bot$ (i.e., $\mathsf{T}_{Bill,Mary}\bot$).[1]

type(i, x, y) is a constant which characterizes agent i's epistemic type. Specifically, type(i, x, y) has to be read as "agent i has a level of epistemic cautiousness equal to x and an acceptance *quota* equal to y". Agent i's acceptance *quota* corresponds to the *ratio* of evidence in support of a given fact to the total amount of evidence in support of either the fact or its negation, that is required for the agent to form the belief that the fact is true. A similar notion of *quota* is studied in the area of judgment aggregation [15]. Agent i's level of epistemic cautiousness corresponds to the *amount of evidence* in support of a given fact that agent i needs to collect before forming the belief that the fact is true. As we will show below, an agent's epistemic type characterizes the agent's disposition to change her beliefs on the basis of the evidence she collects.

We distinguish four types of events: $!_i\varphi$, $-_{i,j}\varphi$, $+_{i,j}\varphi$ and $?_i\varphi$. The symbol $!_i\varphi$ denotes the event of agent i publicly announcing that φ is true. $-_{i,j}\varphi$ denotes agent i's mental operation of losing trust in agent j about φ, while the symbol $+_{i,j}\varphi$ denotes agent i's mental operation of relying on agent j's judgment about φ. We assume that if an agent loses trust in someone or relies on someone, then this fact is public (i.e., it is common knowledge that the agent has lost trust in someone/has relied on someone's judgment). Note that our logic clearly distinguishes the concept of "trusting someone's judgment", denoted by formula $\mathsf{T}_{i,j}\varphi$, from the concept of "relying on someone's judgment", denoted by events $+_{i,j}\varphi$. The former is conceived as an agent's mental attitude, while the latter is conceived as an agent's mental operation affecting her mental attitudes. Finally, $?_i\varphi$ denotes agent i's mental operation assessing whether φ is true or false. As we will show in Sect. 2.2, the latter mental operation has different possible outcomes, depending on agent i's epistemic state. In particular, agent i will be prone to *expand* her set of beliefs by φ, if she does not believe the contrary and she has sufficient reason to believe φ. She will *revise* her set of beliefs by φ, if she has sufficient reason to believe φ and currently believes the contrary.

The formula $[\alpha]\varphi$ has to be read "φ will hold after the event α takes place".

---

[1] As we will show in Sect. 3, formula $\neg\mathsf{T}_{i,j}\bot$ is valid in the logic DL-BET. Thus, if $\mathsf{T}_{i,j}$ was a normal modal operator, $\neg(\mathsf{T}_{i,j}\varphi \wedge \mathsf{T}_{i,j}\neg\varphi)$ would have been valid, which is highly counter-intuitive.

Let us define the following abbreviations for every $i \in Agt$ and $x \in Evd$:

$$\mathsf{E}_i^{\geq x}\varphi \overset{\text{def}}{=} \bigvee_{J \in 2^{Agt} : |J|=x} \bigwedge_{j \in J} \mathsf{E}_{i,j}\varphi$$

$$\mathsf{E}_i^x\varphi \overset{\text{def}}{=} \mathsf{E}_i^{\geq x}\varphi \wedge \neg\mathsf{E}_i^{\geq x+1}\varphi$$

$$\mathsf{R}_i\varphi \overset{\text{def}}{=} \bigvee_{x,x',x''\in Evd, y\in Qt:x>x',\frac{x}{x+x'}\geq y \text{ and } x\geq x''} \left(\mathsf{E}_i^x\varphi \wedge \mathsf{E}_i^{x'}\neg\varphi \wedge \mathsf{type}(i,x'',y) \right)$$

We use the conventions $\mathsf{E}_i^{\geq 0}\varphi \overset{\text{def}}{=} \top$ and $\mathsf{E}_i^{\geq|Agt|+1}\varphi \overset{\text{def}}{=} \bot$.

$\mathsf{E}_i^{\geq x}\varphi$ has to be read "agent i has at least x pieces of evidence in support of φ", whereas $\mathsf{E}_i^x\varphi$ has to be read "agent i has exactly x pieces of evidence in support of φ".

$\mathsf{R}_i\varphi$ has to be read "agent i has a *sufficient* reason to believe that φ is true". According to our definition, an agent has a sufficient reason to believe that φ is true if and only if:

(i) she has more evidence in support of φ than evidence in support of $\neg\varphi$,
(ii) the ratio of evidence in support of φ to the total amount of evidence in support of either φ or $\neg\varphi$, is equal to or above her acceptance quota,[2]
(iii) the amount of evidence in support of φ is equal to or above her threshold of epistemic cautiousness.

As we will highlight in Sect. 2.2, a sufficient reason to believe that φ is true ensures that the mental operation of assessing whether φ is true will result in either the expansion or the revision of the agent's set of beliefs by formula φ.

2.2 Semantics

The main notion in the semantics is given by the following definition of evidence source model which provides the basic components for the interpretation of the logic DL-BET:

Definition 1 (Evidence Source Model). *An evidence source model (ESM) is a tuple $M = (W, E, D, S, C, T, V)$ where:*

- *W is a set of worlds or situations;*
- *$E : Agt \longrightarrow 2^{W \times W}$ s.t. for all $i \in Agt$, $E(i)$ is an epistemic relation on W;*
- *$D : Agt \longrightarrow 2^{W \times W}$ s.t. for all $i \in Agt$, $D(i)$ is a doxastic relation on W;*
- *$S : Agt \times Agt \times W \longrightarrow 2^{2^W}$ is an evidence source function;*
- *$C : Agt \times Agt \times W \longrightarrow 2^{2^W}$ is a confidence function;*
- *$T : Agt \times W \longrightarrow Evd \times Qt$ is an epistemic type function;*
- *$V : W \longrightarrow 2^{Atm}$ is a valuation function;*

---

[2] Note that this ratio can be conceived as the probability that φ is true, computed of the basis of the number of evidence supporting φ.

*and which satisfies the following conditions for all $i, j \in Agt$, for all $w, v \in W$
and for all $X \subseteq W$:*

(C1) $E(i)$ *is an equivalence relation;*
(C2) $D(i)$ *is a serial relation;*
(C3) $D(i) \subseteq E(i)$;
(C4) *if* $wE(i)v$ *then* $D(i)(w) = D(i)(v)$;
(C5) *if* $wE(i)v$ *then* $S(i,j,w) = S(i,j,v)$;
(C6) *if* $wE(i)v$ *then* $C(i,j,w) = C(i,j,v)$;
(C7) *if* $X \in C(i,j,v)$ *then* $X \subseteq E(i)(w)$;
(C8) $\emptyset \notin C(i,j,v)$;
(C9) *if* $X \in S(i,j,v)$ *then* $X \in C(i,j,v)$;
(C10) *if* $wE(i)v$ *then* $T(i,w) = T(i,v)$;

where, for any binary relation R on W, $R(w) = \{v \in W : wRv\}$.

For notational convenience, we write E_i instead of $E(i)$ and D_i instead of $D(i)$. For every $w \in W$, $E_i(w)$ and $D_i(w)$ are called, respectively, agent i's information set and belief set at w. Agent i's information set at w is the set of worlds that agent i envisages at world w, while agent i's belief set at w is the set of worlds that agent i thinks to be possible at world w.

Constraint C1 ensures that the epistemic relation $E(i)$ is nothing but the indistinguishability relation traditionally used to model a fully introspective and truthful notion of knowledge. Constraint C2 guarantees that an agent always considers possible at least one world. This guarantees consistency of beliefs.

Constraint C3 ensures that the set of possible worlds is included in the set of envisaged worlds. Indeed, following [26], a ESM requires that an agent is capable of assessing whether an envisaged situation is *possible* or not.[3]

Constraint C4 just means that if two worlds are in the same information set of agent i, then agent i has the same belief set at these two worlds. In other words, an agent knows her beliefs.

It is worth noting that Constraints C1, C2, C3 and C4 together imply that every relation D_i is transitive and Euclidean.

$S(i,j,w)$ is the set of evidence that agent j has provided to agent i where, following [10], a piece of evidence is identified with a set of worlds. Constraint C5 means that if two worlds are in the same information set of agent i, then agent i has the same evidence at these two worlds. In other words, an agent knows her evidence.

The confidence function C specifies an agent's trust in the judgments of other agents. In particular, since each set of possible worlds X is the semantic counterpart of a formula, the meaning of $X \in C(i,j,w)$ is that, at world w, agent i trusts agent j's judgment on the truth of the formula corresponding to

---

[3] Here we take the term "envisaged" to be synonymous of the term "imagined". Clearly, there are situations that one can imagine that she considers impossible. For example, a person can imagine a situation in which she is the president of French republic and, at the same time, considers this situation impossible.

X. Constraint C6 means that if two worlds are in the same information set of agent i, then agent i has the same trust at these two worlds. This corresponds to a property of positive introspection for trust, i.e., an agent knows whether she trusts someone.

Constraint C7 captures compatibility between knowledge and trust. Specifically, according to Constraint C7, an agent can trust someone only about facts which are compatible with her current information set. According to Constraint C8, an agent cannot trust someone about inconsistent facts.

Constraint C9 captures the basic relationship between evidence and trust: an agent i cannot receive a piece of evidence from another agent j, unless agent i trusts agent j's judgement. In other words, trust in the source is a necessary condition for making the information provided by the source a piece of evidence. It is worth noting that Constraints C7 and C9 together imply that an agent can have evidence only about facts which are compatible with her current information set, while Constraints C8 and C9 together imply that an agent cannot have evidence about inconsistent facts, that is:

- if $X \in S(i, j, v)$ then $X \subseteq E(i)(w)$, and
- $\emptyset \notin S(i, j, v)$.

$T(i, w)$ corresponds to agent i's epistemic type at world w. Constraint C10 just means that if two worlds are in the same information set of agent i, then agent i has the same epistemic type at these two worlds. In other words, an agent knows her epistemic type. As emphasized above, an agent's epistemic type is defined by the agent's level of epistemic cautiousness and the agent's acceptance *quota*.

Truth conditions of DL-BET formulas are inductively defined as follows.

Definition 2 (Truth conditions). *Let* $M = (W, E, D, S, C, T, V)$ *be a ESM and let* $w \in W$. *Then:*

$$M, w \models p \Longleftrightarrow p \in V(w)$$
$$M, w \models \mathsf{type}(i, x, y) \Longleftrightarrow T(i, w) = (x, y)$$
$$M, w \models \neg\varphi \Longleftrightarrow M, w \not\models \varphi$$
$$M, w \models \varphi \wedge \psi \Longleftrightarrow M, w \models \varphi \text{ and } M, w \models \psi$$
$$M, w \models \mathsf{K}_i\varphi \Longleftrightarrow \forall v \in E_i(w) : M, v \models \varphi$$
$$M, w \models \mathsf{B}_i\varphi \Longleftrightarrow \forall v \in D_i(w) : M, v \models \varphi$$
$$M, w \models \mathsf{E}_{i,j}\varphi \Longleftrightarrow \|\varphi\|_{i,w}^M \in S(i, j, w)$$
$$M, w \models \mathsf{T}_{i,j}\varphi \Longleftrightarrow \|\varphi\|_{i,w}^M \in C(i, j, w)$$
$$M, w \models [\alpha]\psi \Longleftrightarrow M^\alpha, w \models \psi$$

where

$$\|\varphi\|_{i,w}^M = \{v \in W : M, v \models \varphi\} \cap E_i(w),$$

$M^{!_i\varphi}$, $M^{-_{i,j}\varphi}$, $M^{+_{i,j}\varphi}$ *and* $M^{?_i\varphi}$ *are updated models defined according to the following Definitions 3, 4, 5 and 6.*

According to the truth conditions: agent i knows that φ at world w if and only if φ is true in all worlds that at w agent i envisages, and agent i believes that φ at world w if and only if φ is true in all worlds that at w agent i considers possible. Moreover, at world w agent j has provided evidence in support of φ to agent i if and only if, at w, agent i has the fact corresponding to the formula φ (i.e., $||\varphi||_{i,w}^{M}$) included in her evidence set $S(i,j,w)$. Finally, at world w agent i trusts agent j's judgment about φ if and only if, at w, the fact corresponding to the formula φ (i.e., $||\varphi||_{i,w}^{M}$) is included in agent i's confidence set $C(i,j,w)$. In what follows, we define the updated models triggered by the four kinds of events:

Definition 3 (Update via $!_i\varphi$). Let $M = (W,E,D,S,C,T,V)$ be a ESM. Then, $M^{!_i\varphi}$ is the tuple $(W,E,D,S^{!_i\varphi},C,T,V)$ such that, for all $j,k \in Agt$ and $w \in W$:

$$S^{!_i\varphi}(j,k,w) = \begin{cases} S(j,k,w) \cup \{||\varphi||_{j,w}^{M}\} & \text{if } k=i \text{ and } M,w \models \mathsf{T}_{j,i}\varphi \\ S(j,k,w) & \text{otherwise} \end{cases}$$

Definition 4 (Update via $-_{i,j}\varphi$). Let $M = (W,E,D,S,C,T,V)$ be a ESM. Then, $M^{-_{i,j}\varphi}$ is the tuple $(W,E,D,S^{-_{i,j}\varphi},C^{-_{i,j}\varphi},T,V)$ such that, for all $k,l \in Agt$ and $w \in W$:

$$S^{-_{i,j}\varphi}(k,l,w) = \begin{cases} S(k,l,w) \setminus \{||\varphi||_{k,w}^{M}\} & \text{if } k=i \text{ and } l=j \\ S(k,l,w) & \text{otherwise} \end{cases}$$

$$C^{-_{i,j}\varphi}(k,l,w) = \begin{cases} C(k,l,w) \setminus \{||\varphi||_{k,w}^{M}\} & \text{if } k=i \text{ and } l=j \\ C(k,l,w) & \text{otherwise} \end{cases}$$

Definition 5 (Update via $+_{i,j}\varphi$). Let $M = (W,E,D,S,C,T,V)$ be a ESM. Then, $M^{+_{i,j}\varphi}$ is the tuple $(W,E,D,S,C^{+_{i,j}\varphi},T,V)$ such that, for all $k,l \in Agt$ and $w \in W$:

$$C^{+_{i,j}\varphi}(k,l,w) = \begin{cases} C(k,l,w) \cup \{||\varphi||_{k,w}^{M}\} & \text{if } k=i \text{ and } l=j \text{ and } M,w \models \widehat{\mathsf{K}}_{i}\varphi \\ C(k,l,w) & \text{otherwise} \end{cases}$$

Definition 6 (Update via $?_i\varphi$). Let $M = (W,E,D,S,C,T,V)$ be a ESM. Then, $M^{?_i\varphi}$ is the tuple $(W,E,D^{?_i\varphi},S,C,T,V)$ such that, for all $j \in Agt$ and $w \in W$:

$$D_j^{?_i\varphi}(w) = \begin{cases} D_j(w) \cap ||\varphi||_{j,w}^M & \textit{if } j = i \textit{ and } M, w \models \mathsf{R}_i\varphi \wedge \neg \mathsf{B}_i\neg\varphi \\ D_j(w) \cap ||\neg\varphi||_{j,w}^M & \textit{if } j = i \textit{ and } M, w \models \mathsf{R}_i\neg\varphi \wedge \neg \mathsf{B}_i\varphi \\ ||\varphi||_{j,w}^M & \textit{if } j = i \textit{ and } M, w \models \mathsf{R}_i\varphi \wedge \mathsf{B}_i\neg\varphi \\ ||\neg\varphi||_{j,w}^M & \textit{if } j = i \textit{ and } M, w \models \mathsf{R}_i\neg\varphi \wedge \mathsf{B}_i\varphi \\ D_j(w) & \textit{otherwise} \end{cases}$$

As highlighted by Definition 3, if an agent announces that φ is true, then she will provide a piece of new evidence in support of φ only to the agents who trust her judgement about φ.

According to Definition 4, if an agent i loses trust in someone about a given fact, then this fact is removed from the set of facts for which i trusts j's judgment. To ensure that Constraint C9 in Definition 1 is preserved under this model update operation, the fact is also removed from the set of evidence provided by agent j to agent i.

Acccording to Definition 5, if agent i relies on agent j's judgment about a certain fact then, as a consequence, this fact is added to the set of facts for which i trusts j's judgment, under the condition that the fact is consistent with i's knowledge. The latter condition guarantees that Constraint C8 in Definition 1 is preserved under this model update operation.

According to Definition 6, the mental operation of assessing whether φ is true has five possible outcomes:

- if an agent has a sufficient reason to believe that φ is true and does not believe that φ is false, then she *expands* her beliefs by removing from her belief set the worlds in which φ is false,
- if an agent has a sufficient reason to believe that φ is false and does not believe that φ is true, then she *expands* her beliefs by removing from her belief set the worlds in which φ is true,
- if an agent has a sufficient reason to believe that φ is true and actually believes that φ is false, then she *revises* her beliefs by removing from her belief set the worlds in which φ is false and including all worlds of her information set in which φ is true,
- if an agent has a sufficient reason to believe that φ is false and actually believes that φ is true, then she *revises* her beliefs by removing from her belief set the worlds in which φ is true and including all worlds of her information set in which φ is false,
- if an agent has no sufficient reason to believe that φ is true and has no sufficient reason to believe that φ is false, then she *suspends her judgement* about φ and does not change her belief set.

This highlights the distinction between *expansion, revision* and *suspension of judgement*. Since [1], the former two mental operations have been extensively studied in the area of belief revision. While expansion captures the idea of increasing the set of facts that an agent believes, revision captures the idea of restoring consistency, after having added to the set of beliefs a new information that is inconsistent with the pre-existing information. The latter mental operation has been studied in the epistemological area (see, e.g., [20]). It captures the idea that an agent is not willing to integrate a new information in her set of beliefs, unless she has gathered enough evidence in support of it.

As the following proposition highlights, our model update operations are well-defined as they preserve the properties of evidence source models (ESMs) as defined in Definition 1.

Proposition 1. *If M is a ESM then $M^{!_i\varphi}$, $M^{-_{i,j}\varphi}$, $M^{+_{i,j}\varphi}$ and $M^{?_i\varphi}$ are ESMs too.*

For every $\varphi \in \mathcal{L}_{\text{DL-BET}}$, we write $\models \varphi$ to mean that φ is valid w.r.t. the class of ESMs, that is, for every $M = (W, E, D, S, C, T, V)$ and for every $w \in W$ we have $M, w \models \varphi$. We say that φ is satisfiable w.r.t. the class of ESMs if and only if $\neg\varphi$ is not valid w.r.t. the class of ESMs.

2.3 Some Properties

In this section we focus on some basic properties of the logic DL-BET. We start with the following static properties of evidence, trust and reason:

$$\models \mathsf{T}_{i,j}\varphi \rightarrow \widehat{\mathsf{K}}_i\varphi \tag{1}$$

$$\models \mathsf{E}_{i,j}\varphi \rightarrow \widehat{\mathsf{K}}_i\varphi \tag{2}$$

$$\models \mathsf{R}_i\varphi \rightarrow \widehat{\mathsf{K}}_i\varphi \tag{3}$$

$$\models \neg(\mathsf{R}_i\varphi \wedge \mathsf{R}_i\neg\varphi) \tag{4}$$

According to the validities (1), (2) and (3), trust, evidence and reason are always consistent with knowledge. The validity (4) highlights that an agent cannot have inconsistent reasons.

Let us now consider some dynamic properties that only apply to the propositional fragment of the logic DL-BET. Let $\mathcal{L}_{Atm}$ be the propositional language build out of the set of atoms Atm. Then, for $\varphi, \psi \in \mathcal{L}_{Atm}$ we have:

$$\models \mathsf{T}_{i,j}\varphi \rightarrow [!_j\varphi]\mathsf{E}_{i,j}\varphi \tag{5}$$

$$\models [-_{i,j}\varphi](\neg\mathsf{E}_{i,j}\varphi \wedge \neg\mathsf{T}_{i,j}\varphi) \tag{6}$$

$$\models \widehat{\mathsf{K}}_i\varphi \rightarrow [+_{i,j}\varphi]\mathsf{T}_{i,j}\varphi \tag{7}$$

$$\models \mathsf{R}_i\varphi \rightarrow [?_i\varphi]\mathsf{B}_i\varphi \tag{8}$$

$$\models \mathsf{R}_i\neg\varphi \rightarrow [?_i\varphi]\mathsf{B}_i\neg\varphi \tag{9}$$

$$\models ((\mathsf{R}_i\varphi \wedge \mathsf{K}_i(\varphi \rightarrow \psi)) \vee (\mathsf{R}_i\neg\varphi \wedge \mathsf{K}_i(\neg\varphi \rightarrow \psi))) \rightarrow [?_i\varphi]\mathsf{B}_i\psi \tag{10}$$

$$\models ((\mathsf{R}_i\varphi \wedge \neg\mathsf{B}_i\neg\varphi \wedge \mathsf{B}_i\psi) \vee (\mathsf{R}_i\neg\varphi \wedge \neg\mathsf{B}_i\varphi \wedge \mathsf{B}_i\psi)) \rightarrow [?_i\varphi]\mathsf{B}_i\psi \tag{11}$$

According to the validity (5), if an agent trusts the information source's judgment about φ, then she will have an additional evidence in support of φ after the information source has publicly announced that φ is true. Validities (6) and (7) highlight the basic properties of the mental operation of losing trust in someone's judgment and relying on someone's judgment. Specifically, after having lost trust in agent j's judgment about φ, i does not trust anymore j's judgment about φ and j cannot provide any more evidence in support of φ. Moreover, if φ is consistent with agent i's knowledge then, after having relied on agent j's judgment about φ, i does trusts j's judgment about φ. Validities (8) and (9) highlight the role of reason in the formation of belief: if agent i has a sufficient reason to believe $\varphi/\neg\varphi$ then, after having assessed whether φ is true, she will start to believe $\varphi/\neg\varphi$. Validity (10) highlights the role of knowledge in reason-based belief change: if an agent has a sufficient reason to believe $\varphi/\neg\varphi$ and knows that $\varphi/\neg\varphi$ implies ψ then, after having assessed whether φ is true, she will start to believe ψ. Validity (11) highlights the conservative aspect of reason-based belief expansion: if an agent has a sufficient reason to believe $\varphi/\neg\varphi$ without believing the contrary and believes ψ then, after having assessed whether φ is true, she will continue to believe ψ.

The reason why we need to impose that φ and ψ are propositional formulas is that there are DL-BET-formulas such as the Moore-like formula $p \wedge \neg B_i p$ for which the previous validities (5)–(11) do not hold. For instance, the following formula is not valid:

$$R_i(p \wedge \neg B_i p) \rightarrow [?_i(p \wedge \neg B_i p)]B_i(p \wedge \neg B_i p).$$

This is intuitive since if I have sufficient reason to believe that my uncertainty about p could be unjustified then, after assessing whether this is the case, I may start to believe that p and that I believe this (since I have introspection over my beliefs).

2.4   An Example

This section is devoted to illustrate the syntax and the semantics of the logic DL-BET with the aid of a concrete example of AI application.

Suppose a human user wants to know whether the movie The Tree of Life by Terrence Malick is a great movie or not and asks this to her chatbot. The chabot has access to four information sources in the Internet, namely, Wikipedia, IMDb, Amazon and Rotten Tomatoes (RT). The chatbot knows that if "The Tree of Life has won the Palm d'Or at the Cannes festival", denoted by proposition p, then "The Tree of Life is a great movie", denoted by proposition q:

$$Hyp1 \stackrel{\text{def}}{=} K_{chatbot}(p \rightarrow q)$$

Moreover, the chatbot trusts the judgments of both RT and Amazon about q and $\neg q$. This means that if either RT or Amazon says that The Tree of Life is a great movie/is not a great movive, then this counts as a piece of evidence in support of this fact. Finally, the chatbot trusts the judgments of both Wikipedia and IMDb about p and $\neg p$:

$$Hyp2 \stackrel{\text{def}}{=} \mathsf{T}_{chatbot,Wikipedia}p \wedge \mathsf{T}_{chatbot,IMDb}p \wedge$$
$$\mathsf{T}_{chatbot,Wikipedia}\neg p \wedge \mathsf{T}_{chatbot,IMDb}\neg p \wedge$$
$$\mathsf{T}_{chatbot,RT}q \wedge \mathsf{T}_{chatbot,Amazon}q \wedge$$
$$\mathsf{T}_{chatbot,RT}\neg q \wedge \mathsf{T}_{chatbot,Amazon}\neg q$$

Moreover, suppose that the chatbot (i) is uncertain whether p is true and is uncertain whether q is true, (ii) has no evidence in support of $p, \neg p, q$ and $\neg q$, and (iii) has a level of epistemic cautiousness equal to 2 and an acceptance *quota* equal to 1. That is:

$$Hyp3 \stackrel{\text{def}}{=} \neg\mathsf{B}_{chatbot}p \wedge \neg\mathsf{B}_{chatbot}\neg p \wedge \neg\mathsf{B}_{chatbot}q \wedge \neg\mathsf{B}_{chatbot}\neg q \wedge$$
$$\mathsf{E}^0_{chatbot}p \wedge \mathsf{E}^0_{chatbot}\neg p \wedge \mathsf{E}^0_{chatbot}q \wedge \mathsf{E}^0_{chatbot}\neg q \wedge \mathsf{type}(chatbot,2,1)$$

Thus, if the chatbot learns from Amazon that The Tree of Life is a great movie while it learns from RT that The Tree of Life is not a great movie, it will be unable to draw any conclusion about the fact that The Tree of Life is a great movie and keep its initial uncertainty. That is:

$$\models (Hyp1 \wedge Hyp2 \wedge Hyp3) \rightarrow | \, [!_{Amazon}q][!_{RT}\neg q][?_{chatbot}q](\neg\mathsf{B}_{chatbot}q \wedge \neg\mathsf{B}_{chatbot}\neg q)$$

On the contrary, if the chatbot learns both from Wikipedia and from IMDb that The Tree of Life has won the Palm d'Or at the Cannes festival, then it will be able to infer that The Tree of Life is a great movie. That is:

$$\models (Hyp1 \wedge Hyp2 \wedge Hyp3) \rightarrow [!_{Wikipedia}p][!_{IMDb}p][?_{chatbot}p]\mathsf{B}_{chatbot}q$$

3   Axiomatization

Let us now present sound and complete axiomatizations for the logic L-BET and its dynamic extension DL-BET. The completeness proof of L-BET is based on a canonical model construction.[4] All axioms of L-BET, except two, are used in the usual way to prove that the canonical model so constructed is a ESM. There are two special axioms of the logic L-BET, about the interrelation between knowledge and trust and between knowledge and evidence that are used in an unusual way to prove the truth lemma.

Definition 7 (L-BET). *We define L-BET to be the extension of classical propositional logic given by the following rules and axioms:*

---

[4] The proof can be found in the extended version of this paper [28].

$$(K_i\varphi \wedge K_i(\varphi \to \psi)) \to K_i\psi \qquad\qquad (\mathbf{K}_{K_i})$$

$$K_i\varphi \to \varphi \qquad\qquad (\mathbf{T}_{K_i})$$

$$K_i\varphi \to K_iK_i\varphi \qquad\qquad (\mathbf{4}_{K_i})$$

$$\neg K_i\varphi \to K_i\neg K_i\varphi \qquad\qquad (\mathbf{5}_{K_i})$$

$$(B_i\varphi \wedge B_i(\varphi \to \psi)) \to B_i\psi \qquad\qquad (\mathbf{K}_{B_i})$$

$$\neg(B_i\varphi \wedge B_i\neg\varphi) \qquad\qquad (\mathbf{D}_{B_i})$$

$$\neg T_{i,j}\bot \qquad\qquad (\mathbf{Cons}_{T_{i,j}})$$

$$\bigvee_{x \in Evd, y \in Qt} \text{type}(i, x, y) \qquad\qquad (\mathbf{AtLeast}_{\text{type}(i,x,y)})$$

$$\text{type}(i, x, y) \to \neg\text{type}(i, x', y') \text{ if } x \neq x' \text{ or } y \neq y' \qquad (\mathbf{AtMost}_{\text{type}(i,x,y)})$$

$$K_i\varphi \to B_i\varphi \qquad\qquad (\mathbf{Mix1}_{K_i, B_i})$$

$$B_i\varphi \to K_iB_i\varphi \qquad\qquad (\mathbf{Mix2}_{K_i, B_i})$$

$$\text{type}(i, x, y) \to K_i\text{type}(i, x, y) \qquad\qquad (\mathbf{Mix}_{K_i, \text{type}(i,x,y)})$$

$$E_{i,j}\varphi \to T_{i,j}\varphi \qquad\qquad (\mathbf{Mix}_{E_{i,j}, T_{i,j}})$$

$$E_{i,j}\varphi \to K_iE_{i,j}\varphi \qquad\qquad (\mathbf{Mix1}_{K_i, E_{i,j}})$$

$$T_{i,j}\varphi \to K_iT_{i,j}\varphi \qquad\qquad (\mathbf{Mix1}_{K_i, T_{i,j}})$$

$$(T_{i,j}\varphi \wedge K_i(\varphi \leftrightarrow \psi)) \to T_{i,j}\psi \qquad\qquad (\mathbf{Mix2}_{K_i, T_{i,j}})$$

$$(E_{i,j}\varphi \wedge K_i(\varphi \leftrightarrow \psi)) \to E_{i,j}\psi \qquad\qquad (\mathbf{Mix2}_{K_i, E_{i,j}})$$

$$\frac{\varphi}{K_i\varphi} \qquad\qquad (\mathbf{Nec}_{K_i})$$

Note that the rule of necessitation for B_i is provable by $(\mathbf{Nec}_{K_i})$ and $(\mathbf{Mix1}_{K_i, B_i})$. Moreover, Axiom 4 for B_i is provable by $(\mathbf{Mix1}_{K_i, B_i})$ and $(\mathbf{Mix2}_{K_i, B_i})$. Axiom 5 for B_i is provable by means of $(\mathbf{Mix1}_{K_i, B_i})$, $(\mathbf{Mix2}_{K_i, B_i})$, $\mathbf{K}_{K_i}$, $\mathbf{T}_{K_i}$, $\mathbf{4}_{K_i}$ and $\mathbf{5}_{K_i}$. A syntactic proof can be found in [30]. Finally, the following rules of equivalence for trust and evidence are provable by means of $(\mathbf{Nec}_{K_i})$, $(\mathbf{Mix2}_{K_i, T_{i,j}})$ and $(\mathbf{Mix2}_{K_i, E_{i,j}})$:

$$\frac{\varphi \leftrightarrow \psi}{T_{i,j}\varphi \leftrightarrow T_{i,j}\psi} \qquad\qquad (12)$$

$$\frac{\varphi \leftrightarrow \psi}{E_{i,j}\varphi \leftrightarrow E_{i,j}\psi} \qquad\qquad (13)$$

Theorem 1. *The logic L-BET is sound and complete for the class of ESMs.*

The axiomatics of the logic DL-BET includes all principles of the logic L-BET *plus* a set of reduction axioms and the rule of replacement of equivalents.

Definition 8. *We define DL-BET to be the extension of L-BET generated by the following reduction axioms for the dynamic operators $[!_i\varphi]$:*

$$[!_i\varphi]p \leftrightarrow p \qquad \qquad (\mathbf{Red}_{!_i\varphi,p})$$

$$[!_i\varphi]\mathsf{type}(k,x,y) \leftrightarrow \mathsf{type}(k,x,y) \qquad \qquad (\mathbf{Red}_{!_i\varphi,\mathsf{type}(l,x,y)})$$

$$[!_i\varphi]\neg\psi \leftrightarrow \neg[!_i\varphi]\psi \qquad \qquad (\mathbf{Red}_{!_i\varphi,\neg})$$

$$[!_i\varphi](\psi \wedge \chi) \leftrightarrow ([!_i\varphi]\psi \wedge [!_i\varphi]\chi) \qquad \qquad (\mathbf{Red}_{!_i\varphi,\wedge})$$

$$[!_i\varphi]\mathsf{K}_j\psi \leftrightarrow \mathsf{K}_j[!_i\varphi]\psi \qquad \qquad (\mathbf{Red}_{!_i\varphi,\mathsf{K}_j})$$

$$[!_i\varphi]\mathsf{B}_j\psi \leftrightarrow \mathsf{B}_j[!_i\varphi]\psi \qquad \qquad (\mathbf{Red}_{!_i\varphi,\mathsf{B}_j})$$

$$[!_i\varphi]\mathsf{E}_{j,k}\psi \leftrightarrow \mathsf{E}_{j,k}[!_i\varphi]\psi \text{ if } i \neq k \qquad \qquad (\mathbf{Red}_{!_i\varphi,\mathsf{E}_{j,k}})$$

$$[!_i\varphi]\mathsf{E}_{j,i}\psi \leftrightarrow \Big(\big(\mathsf{T}_{j,i}\varphi \rightarrow (\mathsf{E}_{j,i}[!_i\varphi]\psi \vee \mathsf{K}_j(\varphi \leftrightarrow [!_i\varphi]\psi))\big)\wedge$$

$$\big(\neg\mathsf{T}_{j,i}\varphi \rightarrow \mathsf{E}_{j,i}[!_i\varphi]\psi\big)\Big) \qquad \qquad (\mathbf{Red}_{!_i\varphi,\mathsf{E}_{j,i}})$$

$$[!_i\varphi]\mathsf{T}_{j,k}\psi \leftrightarrow \mathsf{T}_{j,k}[!_i\varphi]\psi \qquad \qquad (\mathbf{Red}_{!_i\varphi,\mathsf{T}_{j,k}})$$

the following ones for the dynamic operators $[-_{i,j}\varphi]$:

$$[-_{i,j}\varphi]p \leftrightarrow p \qquad \qquad (\mathbf{Red}_{-_{i,j}\varphi,p})$$

$$[-_{i,j}\varphi]\mathsf{type}(k,x,y) \leftrightarrow \mathsf{type}(k,x,y) \qquad \qquad (\mathbf{Red}_{-_{i,j}\varphi,\mathsf{type}(l,x,y)})$$

$$[-_{i,j}\varphi]\neg\psi \leftrightarrow \neg[-_{i,j}\varphi]\psi \qquad \qquad (\mathbf{Red}_{-_{i,j}\varphi,\neg})$$

$$[-_{i,j}\varphi](\psi \wedge \chi) \leftrightarrow ([-_{i,j}\varphi]\psi \wedge [-_{i,j}\varphi]\chi) \qquad \qquad (\mathbf{Red}_{-_{i,j}\varphi,\wedge})$$

$$[-_{i,j}\varphi]\mathsf{K}_k\psi \leftrightarrow \mathsf{K}_k[-_{i,j}\varphi]\psi \qquad \qquad (\mathbf{Red}_{-_{i,j}\varphi,\mathsf{K}_k})$$

$$[-_{i,j}\varphi]\mathsf{B}_k\psi \leftrightarrow \mathsf{B}_k[-_{i,j}\varphi]\psi \qquad \qquad (\mathbf{Red}_{-_{i,j}\varphi,\mathsf{B}_k})$$

$$[-_{i,j}\varphi]\mathsf{E}_{k,l}\psi \leftrightarrow \mathsf{E}_{k,l}[-_{i,j}\varphi]\psi \text{ if } i \neq k \text{ or } j \neq l \qquad (\mathbf{Red}_{-_{i,j}\varphi,\mathsf{E}_{k,l}})$$

$$[-_{i,j}\varphi]\mathsf{E}_{i,j}\psi \leftrightarrow (\mathsf{E}_{i,j}[-_{i,j}\varphi]\psi \vee \neg\mathsf{K}_i(\varphi \leftrightarrow [-_{i,j}\varphi]\psi)) \qquad (\mathbf{Red}_{-_{i,j}\varphi,\mathsf{E}_{i,j}})$$

$$[-_{i,j}\varphi]\mathsf{T}_{k,l}\psi \leftrightarrow \mathsf{T}_{k,l}[-_{i,j}\varphi]\psi \text{ if } i \neq k \text{ or } j \neq l \qquad (\mathbf{Red}_{-_{i,j}\varphi,\mathsf{T}_{k,l}})$$

$$[-_{i,j}\varphi]\mathsf{T}_{i,j}\psi \leftrightarrow (\mathsf{T}_{i,j}[-_{i,j}\varphi]\psi \vee \neg\mathsf{K}_i(\varphi \leftrightarrow [-_{i,j}\varphi]\psi)) \qquad (\mathbf{Red}_{-_{i,j}\varphi,\mathsf{T}_{i,j}})$$

the following ones for the dynamic operators $[+_{i,j}\varphi]$:

$$[+_{i,j}\varphi]p \leftrightarrow p \qquad \qquad (\mathbf{Red}_{+_{i,j}\varphi,p})$$

$$[+_{i,j}\varphi]\mathsf{type}(k,x,y) \leftrightarrow \mathsf{type}(k,x,y) \qquad \qquad (\mathbf{Red}_{+_{i,j}\varphi,\mathsf{type}(l,x,y)})$$

$$[+_{i,j}\varphi]\neg\psi \leftrightarrow \neg[+_{i,j}\varphi]\psi \qquad \qquad (\mathbf{Red}_{+_{i,j}\varphi,\neg})$$

$$[+_{i,j}\varphi](\psi \wedge \chi) \leftrightarrow ([+_{i,j}\varphi]\psi \wedge [+_{i,j}\varphi]\chi) \qquad \qquad (\mathbf{Red}_{+_{i,j}\varphi,\wedge})$$

$$[+_{i,j}\varphi]\mathsf{K}_k\psi \leftrightarrow \mathsf{K}_k[+_{i,j}\varphi]\psi \qquad \qquad (\mathbf{Red}_{+_{i,j}\varphi,\mathsf{K}_k})$$

$$[+_{i,j}\varphi]\mathsf{B}_k\psi \leftrightarrow \mathsf{B}_k[+_{i,j}\varphi]\psi \qquad \qquad (\mathbf{Red}_{+_{i,j}\varphi,\mathsf{B}_k})$$

$$[+_{i,j}\varphi]\mathsf{E}_{k,l}\psi \leftrightarrow \mathsf{E}_{k,l}[+_{i,j}\varphi]\psi \qquad \qquad (\mathbf{Red}_{+_{i,j}\varphi,\mathsf{E}_{k,l}})$$

$$[+_{i,j}\varphi]\mathsf{T}_{k,l}\psi \leftrightarrow \mathsf{T}_{k,l}[+_{i,j}\varphi]\psi \text{ if } i \neq k \text{ or } j \neq l \qquad (\mathbf{Red}_{+_{i,j}\varphi,\mathsf{T}_{k,l}})$$

$$[+_{i,j}\varphi]\mathsf{T}_{i,j}\psi \leftrightarrow \Big(\big(\hat{\mathsf{K}}_i\varphi \rightarrow (\mathsf{T}_{i,j}[+_{i,j}\varphi]\psi \vee \mathsf{K}_i(\varphi \leftrightarrow [+_{i,j}\varphi]\psi))\big)\wedge$$

$$\big(\mathsf{K}_i\neg\varphi \rightarrow \mathsf{T}_{i,j}[+_{i,j}\varphi]\psi\big)\Big) \qquad \qquad (\mathbf{Red}_{+_{i,j}\varphi,\mathsf{T}_{i,j}})$$

the following ones for the dynamic operators $[?_i\varphi]$:

$$[?_i\varphi]p \leftrightarrow p \qquad\qquad (\mathbf{Red}_{?_i\varphi,p})$$

$$[?_i\varphi]\mathsf{type}(k,x,y) \leftrightarrow \mathsf{type}(k,x,y) \qquad\qquad (\mathbf{Red}_{?_i\varphi,\mathsf{type}(l,x,y)})$$

$$[?_i\varphi]\neg\psi \leftrightarrow \neg[?_i\varphi]\psi \qquad\qquad (\mathbf{Red}_{?_i\varphi,\neg})$$

$$[?_i\varphi](\psi \wedge \chi) \leftrightarrow ([?_i\varphi]\psi \wedge [?_i\varphi]\chi) \qquad\qquad (\mathbf{Red}_{?_i\varphi,\wedge})$$

$$[?_i\varphi]\mathsf{K}_j\psi \leftrightarrow \mathsf{K}_j[?_i\varphi]\psi \qquad\qquad (\mathbf{Red}_{?_i\varphi,\mathsf{K}_j})$$

$$[?_i\varphi]\mathsf{B}_j\psi \leftrightarrow \mathsf{B}_j[?_i\varphi]\psi \ \ if\ i \neq j \qquad\qquad (\mathbf{Red}_{?_i\varphi,\mathsf{B}_j})$$

$$[?_i\varphi]\mathsf{B}_i\psi \leftrightarrow \Big(\big(\alpha_1 \to \mathsf{B}_i(\varphi \to [?_i\varphi]\psi)\big)\wedge \quad \big(\alpha_2 \to \mathsf{B}_i(\neg\varphi \to [?_i\varphi]\psi)\big)\wedge$$

$$\big(\alpha_3 \to \mathsf{K}_i(\varphi \to [?_i\varphi]\psi)\big)\wedge \quad \big(\alpha_4 \to \mathsf{K}_i(\neg\varphi \to [?_i\varphi]\psi)\big)\wedge$$

$$\big(\alpha_5 \to \mathsf{B}_i[?_i\varphi]\psi\big)\Big) \qquad\qquad (\mathbf{Red}_{?_i\varphi,\mathsf{B}_i})$$

$$[?_i\varphi]\mathsf{E}_{j,k}\psi \leftrightarrow \mathsf{E}_{j,k}[?_i\varphi]\psi \qquad\qquad (\mathbf{Red}_{?_i\varphi,\mathsf{E}_{j,k}})$$

$$[?_i\varphi]\mathsf{E}_{j,k}\psi \leftrightarrow \mathsf{E}_{j,k}[?_i\varphi]\psi \qquad\qquad (\mathbf{Red}_{?_i\varphi,\mathsf{E}_{j,k}})$$

$$[?_i\varphi]\mathsf{T}_{j,k}\psi \leftrightarrow \mathsf{T}_{j,k}[?_i\varphi]\psi \qquad\qquad (\mathbf{Red}_{?_i\varphi,\mathsf{T}_{j,k}})$$

and the following rule of inference:

$$\frac{\psi_1 \leftrightarrow \psi_2}{\varphi \leftrightarrow \varphi[\psi_1/\psi_2]} \qquad\qquad (\mathbf{RRE})$$

with:

$$\alpha_1 \stackrel{\text{def}}{=} \mathsf{R}_i\varphi \wedge \neg\mathsf{B}_i\neg\varphi$$

$$\alpha_2 \stackrel{\text{def}}{=} \mathsf{R}_i\neg\varphi \wedge \neg\mathsf{B}_i\varphi$$

$$\alpha_3 \stackrel{\text{def}}{=} \mathsf{R}_i\varphi \wedge \mathsf{B}_i\neg\varphi$$

$$\alpha_4 \stackrel{\text{def}}{=} \mathsf{R}_i\neg\varphi \wedge \mathsf{B}_i\varphi$$

$$\alpha_5 \stackrel{\text{def}}{=} \neg\alpha_1 \wedge \neg\alpha_2 \wedge \neg\alpha_3 \wedge \neg\alpha_4$$

The completeness of DL-BET follows from Theorem 1, in view of the fact that the reduction axioms and the rule (**RRE**) may be used to find, for any DL-BET formula, a provably equivalent L-BET formula.

Theorem 2. *DL-BET is sound and complete for the class of ESMs.*

4   Related Work

Artemov [2] proposes so-called justification logic in which evidence is expressed as a term, and possible manipulations of evidence are operations over terms. This framework has been further connected to the notion of explicit and implicit beliefs and belief revision in [6]. Differently, [10,11] adopts a neighbourhood semantics, adding evidence to the standard belief model in the form of families of sets of possible worlds, and studies evidence-based belief change. These approaches share with DL-BET the idea of modeling the relationship between evidence and belief.

Social influence in terms of individual's belief change has caught a lot of attention in recent years. Liu, Seligman and Girard [29] proposes a finite state automata model with a threshold to deal with social influence. As a simple case, agent i would change her belief from p to $\neg p$ if all her neighbors believe $\neg p$. This model can successfully explain social phenomena, like peer pressure, and behavior adoption. Christoff [13] further develops this model and investigates various features of social networks and their evolution over time, including information flow and spread of opinions. Xue and Parikh [34] looks at expert influence in social network, and show how an agent makes decisions when facing conflicting choices in belief update. These approaches share with DL-BET the idea of modeling belief change and belief formation due to the information received by, possibly conflicting, information sources.

When considering the relationship between agents in the context of information exchange, trust is the core notion in play. Early work [27] studies the influence of trust on agent's formation of beliefs with an axiom saying that if agent i believes that agent j has told her the truth about p, and she trusts the judgement of j about p, then she will also believe p. In the context of social influence, [4] introduces quantitative measurement on trust between agents and strength of evidence, and stipulates how these parameters influence one's valuation of new evidence. Lorini, Jiang and Perrussel [31] studies the phenomenon of trust-based belief change, that is, belief change that depends on the degree of trust the receiver has in the source of information. In a similar way, in [22] trust is conceived as a pre-processing step before belief revision. Viewed in line of social choice theory, one can also think of belief formation or change as a process of aggregating opinions from different reliable information sources, as in [21]. These approaches share with DL-BET the idea that trust in the information source plays a fundamental role in belief change and belief formation.

In the area of information fusion, a similar concern on belief, evidence and trust has led to number of proposals [18, 23, 24, 32]. However, these approaches lean heavily on the machinery of Bayesian probability theory. For instance, in so-called subjective logic, based on the Dempster-Shafer rule, Jøsang proposes a new Bayesian update function to study belief revision. In contrast, our main concern with DL-BET is the logical relationship between notions of knowledge, belief, evidence and trust, as well as the principles of reasoning about them, thus our work is qualitative in nature.

5 Conclusion

In this paper we have proposed a new logic, called "Dynamic Logic of Belief, Evidence and Trust" (DL-BET), which supports reasoning about evidence-based belief formation and belief change in a multi-agent setting. We have provided a complete axiomatization for both the static L-BET and its dynamic extension DL-BET. We have illustrated the expressive power of DL-BET with the aid of a concrete example involving a chatbot interacting with a human.

The logical account of belief revision we have provided (Definition 6) is radical: if an agent has a sufficient reason to believe a certain fact φ and currently believes the opposite then, after assessing whether φ is true, she will include in her belief set *all worlds* of her information set in which φ is true. In future work, we plan to extend the formal semantics of the logic DL-BET by a plausibility ordering over possible words for each agent, as traditionally used in modal logic analysis of belief revision (see, e.g., [7,8]). This extension will allow us to refine the belief revision operation by assuming that, after a revision by φ, an agent will include in her belief set only the *best worlds* (according to the plausibility ordering) of her information set in which φ is true.

We have emphasized that the epistemic cautiousness level and acceptance quota specify together how much evidence one needs to collect to form a belief, or change one's belief. Though our framework has worked with numerals already, we have managed to get a complete logic. In future work we would like to extend our model to handle uncertainties in evidence and belief as well as with degrees of trust or graded trust in information sources. It is our intention to explore how far we can go with such a still qualitative-oriented approach against a completely quantitative method.

Finally, an agent obtains information from trusted sources by social communication, and forms her beliefs on the basis of reasons. In this paper, we have investigated epistemic reasons. We plan to extend our logical framework with agents' goal and preferences in order to incorporate practical reasons in our analysis and to study their connection with epistemic reasons. This may also bring us closer to the cognitive trust model [19] where sentences like "i trusts j to do α in order to achieve φ" are dealt with.

References

1. Alchourrón, C.E., Gärdenfors, P., Makinson, D.: On the logic of theory change: partial meet contraction and revision functions. J. Symbo. Logic **50**, 510–530 (1985)
2. Artemov, S.N.: The logic of justification. Rev. Symb. Logic **1**(4), 477–513 (2001)
3. Ayer, A.J.: Probability and Evidence. Columbia University Press, New York City (1972)
4. Baltag, A., Liu, F., Smets, S.: Reason-based belief revision in social networks. In: Slides, KNAW-Workshp on the Logical Dynamics of Information, Agency and Interaction, Amsterdam (2014)
5. Baltag, A., Moss, L.S., Solecki, S.: The logic of common knowledge, public announcements, and private suspicions. In: Gilboa, I. (ed.) Proceedings of the 7th Conference on Theoretical Aspects of Rationality and Knowledge (TARK 1998), pp. 43–56 (1998)
6. Baltag, A., Renne, B., Smets, S.: The logic of justified belief, explicit knowledge, and conclusive evidence. Ann. Pure Appl. Logic **165**(1), 49–81 (2014)

7. Baltag, A., Smets, S.: A qualitative theory of dynamic interactive belief revision. In: Wooldridge, M., Bonanno, G., van der Hoek, W. (eds.) Logic and the Foundations of Game and Decision Theory. Texts in Logic and Games, vol. 3. Amsterdam University Press, Amsterdam (2008)
8. van Benthem, J.: Dynamic logic for belief revision. J. Appl. Non Class. Logic **17**, 129–156 (2007)
9. van Benthem, J.: Logical Dynamics of Information and Interaction. Cambridge University Press, Cambridge (2011)
10. van Benthem, J., Fernández-Duque, D., Pacuit, E.: Evidence logic: a new look at neighborhood structures. In: Bolander, T., Braüner, T., Ghilardi, S., Moss, L. (eds.) Proceedings of Advances in Modal Logic, vol. 9, pp. 97–118. King's College Press, London (2012)
11. van Benthem, J., Pacuit, E.: Dynamic logics of evidence-based beliefs. Studia Logica **99**(1–3), 61–92 (2011)
12. Chellas, B.F.: Modal Logic: An Introduction. Cambridge University Press, Cambridge (1980)
13. Christoff, Z.: Dynamic logics of networks. Information Flow and the Spread of Opinion. Ph.D. thesis, ILLC, University of Amsterdam (2016)
14. Dastani, M., Herzig, A., Hulstijn, J., van der Torre, L.: Inferring trust. In: Leite, J., Torroni, P. (eds.) CLIMA 2004. LNCS, vol. 3487, pp. 144–160. Springer, Heidelberg (2005). doi:10.1007/11533092_9
15. Dietrich, F., List, C.: Judgment aggregation by quota rules: majority voting generalized. J. Theor. Polit. **19**(4), 391–424 (2007)
16. Ditmarsch, H., van der Hoek, W., Kooi, B.: Dynamic Epistemic Logic. Springer, Berlin (2007)
17. Dubois, D., Liu, W., Ma, J., Prade, H.: The basic principles of uncertain information fusion. An organised review of merging rules in different representation frameworks. Inf. Fusion **32**, 12–39 (2016)
18. Dubois, D., Prade, H.: Representation and combination of uncertainty with belief functions and possibility measures. Comput. Intell. **4**(3), 244264 (1988)
19. Falcone, R., Castelfranchi, C.: Social trust: a cognitive approach. In: Tan, Y.-H., Castelfranchi, C. (eds.) Trust and Deception in Virtual Societies, pp. 55–90. Springer, Netherlands (2001). doi:10.1007/978-94-017-3614-5_3. Chap. 1
20. Friedman, J.: Suspended judgment. Philos. Stud. **162**(2), 165–181 (2013)
21. Grandi, U., Lorini, E., Perrussel, L.: Propositional opinion diffusion. In: Proceedings of the 14th International Conference on Autonomous Agents and Multiagent Systems (AAMAS 2015), pp. 989–997. ACM Press (2015)
22. Hunter, A., Booth, R.: Trust-sensitive belief revision. In: Proceedings of the Twenty-Fourth International Joint Conference on Artificial Intelligence (IJCAI 2015), pp. 3062–3068. AAAI Press (2015)
23. Jøsang, A.: A logic for uncertain probabilities. Int. J. Uncertain. Fuzziness Knowl. Based Syst. **9**(3), 279–311 (2016)
24. Jøsang, A.: Interpretation of fusion and hyper opinions in subjective logic. In: 15th International Conference on Information Fusion, Singapore, pp. 1225–1232 (2017)
25. Keynes, J.M.: A Treatise on Probability. The Collected Writings, vol. 8. Macmillan, Hampshire (1973)
26. Kraus, S., Lehmann, D.J.: Knowledge, belief and time. Theoret. Comput. Sci. **58**, 155–174 (1988)
27. Liau, C.-J.: Belief, information acquisition, and trust in multi-agent systems: a modal logic formulation. Artif. Intell. **149**(1), 31–60 (2003)

28. Liu, F., Lorini, E.: Reasoning about belief, evidence and trust in a multi-agent setting (extended version). Technical report, Institut de Recherche en Informatique de Toulouse (IRIT) (2017)
29. Liu, F., Seligman, J., Girard, P.: Logical dynamics of belief change in the community. Synthese **191**(11), 2403–2431 (2014)
30. Lorini, E.: A minimal logic for interactive epistemology. Synthese **193**(3), 725–755 (2016)
31. Lorini, E., Jiang, G., Perrussel, L.: Trust-based belief change. In: Proceedings of the 21st European Conference on Artificial Intelligence (ECAI 2014), pp. 549–554. IOS Press (2014)
32. Shafer, G.: A Mathematical Theory of Evidence. Princeton University Press, Princeton (1976)
33. Singh, M.: Trust as dependence: a logical approach. In: Proceedings of the 10th International Conference on Autonomous Agents and Multiagent Systems (AAMAS 2011), pp. 863–870. ACM (2011)
34. Xue, Y., Parikh, R.: Strategic belief updates through influence in a community. Stud. Logic **8**, 124–143 (2015)

Teamwork and Coordination
in Multiagent Systems

Reachability and Expectation in Gossiping

Hans van Ditmarsch[1], Ioannis Kokkinis[1(✉)], and Anders Stockmarr[2]

[1] LORIA, CNRS, University of Lorraine, Nancy, France
{hans.van-ditmarsch,ioannis.kokkinis}@loria.fr
[2] Technical University of Denmark, Kongens Lyngby, Denmark
anst@dtu.dk

Abstract. We give combinatorial, computational and simulation results for well-known distributed protocols for gossiping on completely connected networks. The protocols consist of: making any call (ANY), only calling agents whose secret you do not know ("learn new secrets" LNS), and never repeating calls ("call once" CO). First, we show that these protocols all differ in what distributions of secrets are reachable by their execution. Next, we formulate ANY and LNS as Markov chains. We present an algorithm that generates the states of these Markov chains and computes the exact value of the expected duration of the protocols. Finally, we study the asymptotic behaviour of LNS via simulations, and compare this to the known result for ANY.

Keywords: Gossip · Networks · Reachability · Expectation · Markov chain

1 Introduction

Let each of a set of agents $\{a, b, c, \ldots\}$ know a single secret $\{A, B, C, \ldots\}$, respectively. The agents can communicate via telephone calls. When they call, they share all the secrets they know. The goal is that all agents get to know all secrets. An agent who knows all secrets is an *expert*. A protocol achieving this is called a *gossip protocol* [13, 16]. Three protocols of a more epistemic nature [1–3, 6] are:

ANY Until all agents are experts, select two agents a and b, and let a call b.
CO   Until all agents are experts, select two agents a and b who did not call each other, and let a call b.
LNS Until all agents are experts, select two agents a and b such that a does not know b's secret, and let a call b.

For example, let there be three agents only. We represent a secret distribution by listing the secrets known/held by each agent. Given initial distribution (A, B, C), the call ab (the call from a to b) results in (AB, AB, C). (Strictly, we go from $(\{A\}, \{B\}, \{C\})$ to $(\{A, B\}, \{A, B\}, \{C\})$.) After the call sequence $ab; bc; ac$ all three agents are experts. This sequence is permitted in all three protocols, but already for three agents there is a difference between ANY, LNS, and

© Springer International Publishing AG 2017
B. An et al. (Eds.): PRIMA 2017, LNAI 10621, pp. 93–109, 2017.
https://doi.org/10.1007/978-3-319-69131-2_6

CO. The sequence $ab; bc; ca$ is ANY- and CO-permitted, but not LNS-permitted: as c already knows A, the call ca is not allowed in LNS. The sequence $ab; bc; ab$ is ANY-permitted, but it is not CO-permitted (repeating ab is not allowed); and clearly if a call is not CO-permitted it is also not LNS-permitted.

Apart from sequences of calls we can also imagine calls to be done in parallel; a *round* is a collection of simultaneous calls. This was already conceived at an early stage in the gossip community but in the sense that no agent can be involved in more than one telephone call (for example, for three agents, if a and b are selected to make call ab, then c cannot be matched with anyone to call and is 'idle' in that round). A well-known result is that n agents can become experts in $\lceil \log_2 n \rceil$ calls for even n (and $\lceil \log_2 n \rceil + 1$ for odd n) [17]. (For 3 agents we then still need 3 rounds/calls $\{ab, bc, ac\}$. But for 4 agents two rounds $\{ab; cd, ac; bd\}$ suffice.) The more recent distributed gossip literature allows a single agent to receive multiple calls [9]. For example, the round of calls $ab; cb; bc$ transforms (A, B, C) into (AB, ABC, BC). This distribution of secrets brings up the matter of *reachability*: (AB, ABC, BC) cannot be the result of a sequence of calls, only of a *round* of simultaneously processed calls. It is then unreachable. Reachability is not addressed in the gossip literature to our knowledge.

In this contribution we address the reachability of ANY, LNS, *and* CO.

If all agents can call each other, the *minimum number of calls* needed for all agents to become experts (for $n \geq 4$) is $2n - 4$ [23]. A simple sequence realizing that in ANY is: select four agents a, b, c, d, and select one among those, say a. Let a call all other agents. Then, execute $ab; cd; ac; bd$. Then, let a again call all other agents. All agents are now experts. This takes $(n - 4) + 4 + (n - 4) = 2n - 4$ calls. Similar executions are possible in LNS and CO. The *maximum number of calls*, where all calls are *informative* (either the caller or the callee learns a new secret) is $\binom{n}{2}$: if we order all pairs ab lexicographically, all calls are informative and everybody becomes an expert (and this is ANY-, LNS- and CO-permitted). Consider four agents, then the minimum is 4 and the maximum is 6. In distributed systems the minimum 4 cannot be guaranteed, because after the first call ab the second call *must* then be cd. But c cannot know that she must call d. She just calls any other agent. The question then comes up: what is the expected execution length of a given protocol?

When thus modelling a protocol consisting of sequences of calls we now face a choice. We can randomly select calls that are permitted according to the protocol. However, when modelling gossip as a distributed system, it seems natural to, firstly, randomly select an agent who can make a permitted call, and then, secondly, randomly select a call for that agent to make. As a simple example assume that we can choose only between the following 4 call sequences: $ad; ab$, $ad; ac$, $ad; bc; ca$ and bd. Their average length is $\frac{5}{3}$ under the former criterion but $\frac{7}{4}$ under the latter criterion. The well-known expectation of ANY is discussed below. We present novel expectation results on other protocols, namely:

In this contribution we address the expectation of LNS *and* CO.

In order to answer that question, we model a gossip protocol as a discrete-time random process. This strongly relates to older mathematical results for random graphs [8,18]. Landau [18] already studied a parallel gossip protocol where communications are made in rounds, modelled this by a discrete-time finite absorbing Markov chain with stationary transition probabilities, and calculated the exact value of the expected duration of his protocol for a small number of agents.

Gossip as a random and distributed process, typically using the ANY protocol, while varying network topology such as the number of neighbours (nodes with which there is a direct connection) and the network depth (the minimum number of links to connect any two nodes in the network), have resulted in many publications [9,13,16]. Of particular interest to us is the search in that community to reduce the expectation of gossip protocols. Parallel, distributed versions of LNS-like protocols are presented in [11] with an expectation (called *connection communication complexity*) of order $n \log^2 n$ (where log without subscript is the natural logarithm), and a version of CO (for a different communicative setting, not for sharing —so-called push-pull— but for *sending* —push— secrets) in [7]. Such results are highly dependent on network features (parametrizing the number of neighbours, network depth, etc.) and to a lesser extent seem to depend on the parallel execution of protocols. We are unaware of similar results for sequentially executed gossip protocols other than ANY, and this stimulated our research.

We study the expected duration of our protocols in complete graphs since in other graphs CO and LNS may not terminate, so that the expected duration of CO and LNS is then not defined. For example, if a and b can call each other, b can call c, and c can call a, then $bc; ca; ba$ is a terminating execution of LNS, but $ca; ab$ is a non-terminating halting execution. For the ANY protocol in a complete network the expectation is $\frac{3}{2} \cdot n \log n + \mathcal{O}(n)$ [4,12,20]. For the LNS protocol we obtain exact results for small numbers of agents, and simulation results for larger numbers of agents, approaching a complexity of $1.0976 \cdot n \log n - 1.1330$. This is lower than for ANY but only by a constant factor and not by an order of magnitude, the result that we had been hoping for. Also, this only marginally depends on scheduling calls randomly or first scheduling agents randomly, as we will discuss later. We do not see these results as the end of our efforts, and we wish to determine the expectation of epistemic gossip protocols and other recent variations, in order to push the expectation boundary lower.

Many parameters can be changed in gossip. If not all agents can call all other agents, we assume a network topology. Some or all executions of the protocol may then terminate (in all agents being experts), as above. Protocols may require more complex epistemic conditions for calls to be executed [1,2,6]. For example, a may only call b if a *knows* that b will learn a new secret in that call. Alternatively, protocols may require more complex epistemic termination criteria [14]. For example, the agents may not merely share secrets in a call, but also shared knowledge of those secrets. By iterating that, the agents can obtain concurrent common knowledge [22] of all secrets. Such variations may be interesting in order to reduce the expectation of gossip protocols, although possibly at the price of computationally more expensive calls. Our results should be seen as applicable to such more generalized settings.

This is an overview of our contribution. In Sect. 2 we define the state of a gossip protocol as a tuple of collections of secrets and the important notion of isomorphic tuple. In Sect. 3 we demonstrate that different states are reached by the protocols ANY, LNS, and CO. Section 4 contains an algorithm generating ANY- and LNS-reachable states. Section 5 contains our main results on the expectation of ANY and LNS for small numbers of agents, including Markov chain modelling, and an asymptotic expectation result for CO. Section 6 contains our other main results namely on the simulation-based expectation for LNS. Section 7 concludes the paper.

2   Protocol States

In this section we define the notion of a protocol state. The number of agents, the set of agents, and the set of secrets are represented by, respectively, n, Ag and S. We use the (possibly primed or subscripted) lower-case letters $a, b, c, d, \ldots$ for agents and the corresponding upper-case letters $A, B, C, D, \ldots$ for the relevant secrets. The symbol P represents ANY, CO or LNS unless stated otherwise.

Definition 1 (Secrets Tuple). *If $S_i \subseteq$ S then $(S_1, \ldots, S_n)$ and $\{S_1, \ldots, S_n\}$ are an **ordered secrets n-tuple** and an **unordered secrets n-tuple** respectively.*

We will write $\{ABC, AB, ABC, D\}$ instead of $\{\{A, B, C\}, \{A, B\}, \{A, B, C\}, \{D\}\}$ (and similarly for ordered tuples). We will simply refer to tuples (without the proper characterizations) if this causes no confusion. The **initial tuple** is $(A_1, \ldots, A_n)$ and the **final tuple** is $(S, \ldots, S)$. Intuitively, the ordered tuple $(S_1, \ldots, S_n)$ represents the distribution of secrets, where agent a_i knows the secrets in S_i. The unordered tuple $\{S_1, \ldots, S_n\}$ represents the distributions of secrets defined by all corresponding ordered tuples, i.e. $(S_1, S_2, \ldots, S_n)$, $(S_2, S_1, \ldots, S_n)$, etc.

Definition 2 (Calls). *A **call** is an ordered pair (a, b), for some $a, b \in$ Ag. We will write ab instead of (a, b). A **call sequence** is a (possibly empty) finite or infinite sequence of calls. We write $ab; cd; \ldots$ for a call sequence. Let $s = (S_1, \ldots, S_n)$ be a tuple and $a_i a_j$ be a call ($i < j$). The tuple obtained by applying $a_i a_j$ to $(S_1, \ldots, S_n)$ is:*

$$s^{a_i a_j} = (S_1, \ldots, S_{i-1}, S_i \cup S_j, S_{i+1}, \ldots, S_{j-1}, S_i \cup S_j, S_{j+1}, \ldots, S_n).$$

*We extend this definition for call sequences and unordered tuples naturally. A call sequence is called **successful** iff, when we apply it to the initial tuple we get the final tuple.*

Let P be ANY or LNS and let s be an ordered tuple. A call ab is P-**permitted** on s if a can call b on s under the restrictions of P. The empty call sequence is P-permitted on any tuple. Call sequence $ab; \sigma$ is P-permitted on s iff σ is P-permitted on s^{ab}. A P-permitted call sequence will also be called P-call sequence.

Definition 3. *A tuple s is* P-***reachable*** *if s can be obtained by applying a P-permitted call sequence on the initial tuple.*

Permitted calls on arbitrary tuples are defined only for ANY and LNS. However, slightly abusing notation, we may exceptionally speak of CO-reachable tuples since reachability implies application of a call sequence to the initial tuple only. We are interested in finding the reachable tuples of our protocols. For this purpose, the ordered tuples nicely describe the states of LNS and ANY, since they give an answer to the question "which agent knows which secret". However, in the case of ANY all the calls are permitted at any time, so it suffices to know that there is one agent who knows this set of secrets and there is another agent who knows the other set of secrets, etc. Therefore the unordered tuples are more succinct representatives of the states in ANY. The tuples (ordered or unordered) are not suitable representations for states in CO, since they cannot always provide all the necessary information about which calls have taken place. The states in CO can be nicely described by simple undirected graphs which have integers assigned to their edges (weighted graphs). The integers correspond to the time when a call takes place. This representation scheme was introduced by Bumby [5] and has been used several times in the gossip community [10, 24].

In order to reduce the set of reachable tuples it makes sense to understand the tuples as directed graphs and then consider tuples up to isomorphism only.

Definition 4 (Underlying Graph). *Let $t = (S_1, \ldots, S_n)$ be an ordered secrets tuple. The underlying graph of t is the directed graph $G = (\mathsf{Ag}, E)$ where $(a_i, a_j) \in E$ iff $A_j \in S_i$.*

Definition 5 (Isomorphic Tuples). *Two ordered tuples are called **isomorphic** iff their underlying graphs are isomorphic. Two unordered tuples, t and s, are called **isomorphic** iff there are isomorphic ordered tuples s' and t' that correspond to s and t, respectively.*

Definition 6 (Canonical Form). *Let G be a graph. The canonical form of G is a labelled graph $\mathsf{can}(G)$ such that $\mathsf{can}(G)$ is isomorphic to G and such that any graph isomorphic to G has $\mathsf{can}(G)$ as its canonical form.*

By Definitions 4 and 6 every ordered tuple t has a unique canonical form (which is a unique representative of the class of isomorphic tuples where t belongs). Therefore we may speak of canonical tuples. Observe that if we can find the canonical form of a tuple, then we can solve the famous graph isomorphism problem: two tuples (i.e. directed graphs) are isomorphic iff their canonical forms are identical. Thus, finding the canonical form of a tuple is a complicated procedure. Any ordered tuple corresponds to the adjacency matrix of its underlying graph. For example $(ABCD, ABD, ABC, ABCD)$ corresponds to $[1111, 1101, 1110, 1111]$. If we consider this adjacency matrix as a linear string then we can define a lexicographical order (represented by $<$) on tuples. For example we have that:

$$(ABCD, ABD, ABC, ABCD) < (ABCD, ABCD, ABC, ABD),$$

since $[1111, 1101, 1110, 1111] < [1111, 1111, 1110, 1101]$. Based on this order we can define a simple —but not computationally efficient— canonical form of a tuple. Given a tuple s, $\mathsf{can}(s)$ is the lexicographically smallest tuple in the isomorphism class of s.

Before studying reachability issues in our protocols we need the following theorem.

Theorem 1. *Let s be a P-reachable ordered tuple and let t be an ordered tuple that is isomorphic to s. Then s is also P-reachable.*

Proof. Assume that h is the isomorphism of s and t, and that σ is the P-call sequence that can be applied to the initial tuple in order to get s. $h(\sigma)$ is the sequence obtained by replacing every occurrence of a in σ by $h(a)$. A violation of P in $h(\sigma)$ implies a violation of P in σ. Hence $h(\sigma)$ is a P-call sequence. Further it is easy to show that isomorphism is preserved after a call application. Thus the application of $h(\sigma)$ to the initial tuple produces t.   □

By Theorem 1 we may consider only canonical tuples when we investigate reachability issues in our protocols.

3   Reachability

In this section we show that the sets of ordered tuples reachable by the protocols are not the same. We first determine what lengths of successful call sequences can be realized in CO and LNS. There are several proofs that the minimum length of a successful ANY-call sequence is $2n - 4$, and that such a call sequence can be realized in CO and LNS [13,15]. A maximal successful call sequence is realizable in CO and LNS by lexicographically ordering all $\binom{n}{2}$ calls. We show that in LNS (and thus in CO) it is possible to realize a successful call sequence of any length (between the minimum and the maximum).

Theorem 2. *For any k between and including $2n - 4$ and $\binom{n}{2}$, there is an LNS-permitted and successful call sequence of length k.*

Proof. In the lexicographically ordered call sequence, each agent a_i calls every agent from a_{i+1} to a_n ($1 \leq i \leq n - 1$). However, for all callers except a_1, the callee already knows the information given to him by the caller. In other words, for $i > 1$, any call made by a_i except $a_i a_n$ is "redundant" and can be removed in order to get a shorter successful call sequence. Obviously, these shorter sequences are still LNS-permitted, and after the last call $a_{n-1} a_n$ all agents are still experts. Without all redundant calls the remaining sequence has length $2n - 3$. We can therefore realize in LNS a successful call sequence of any length between $2n - 4$ and $\binom{n}{2}$.   □

Although a successful call sequence of any length between the minimum and the maximum is CO-realizable, ANY can reach more tuples than CO.

Theorem 3. *The 4-tuple* $t = (ABCD, ABCD, ABC, ABD)$ *is reachable in* ANY *but not in* CO.

Proof. We show that in order to reach t one has to choose the same call twice.

- The initial 4-tuple is (A, B, C, D).
- Since c and d must not learn each others secret, the first call cannot be cd. Furthermore, if the first call is ac then, when d learns a's secret, she will also learn c's secret. With similar arguments we can show that the first call cannot be ad, bc or bd. Thus in order to reach t we have to select ab which leads to (AB, AB, C, D).
- Now, d has to learn A and B. So, without loss of generality the next call is ad which leads to (ABD, AB, C, ABD).
- Now, c has to learn A and B. The only way of achieving this is by selecting bc which leads to (ABD, ABC, ABC, ABD).
- Until now we have made the CO-permitted call sequence: $ab; ad; bc$. The only way of reaching t is by selecting call ab again, which is a clear violation of CO. □

We continue by showing that CO can reach more tuples than LNS.

Theorem 4. *The following 6-tuple is reachable in* CO *but not in* LNS:

$$t = (ABCDEF, ABC, ABCDE, ABCDEF, DEF, ABDEF).$$

Proof. We will show that we can reach t without repeating calls, but at the price of having to make a call between agents that already know each other's secrets.

- The initial 6-tuple is (A, B, C, D, E, F).
- b has to learn A and C and nothing else and d has to learn e and f and nothing else. So, without loss of generality, the first four calls can be $ab; bc; de; ef$, which lead to:

$$(AB, ABC, ABC, DE, DEF, DEF).$$

- Now c has to learn everything but F. The only way of achieving this is by selecting the call cd. Similarly in order for f to learn everything but c we need to select call fa. So, until now we have made the LNS-permitted call sequence $ab; bc; de; ef; cd; fa$ which leads to

$$(ABDEF, ABC, ABCDE, ABCDE, DEF, ABDEF).$$

- Only the CO-permitted call ad (or da) will now lead to t. But neither ad nor da are LNS-permitted. □

4 Algorithm Generating ANY- and LNS-Reachable Canonical Tuples

In this section P is always ANY or LNS. For every $n \le i \le n^2$ we define $S_{n,i}$ as consisting of the canonical tuples $(X_1, X_2, \ldots, X_n)$ for which $\sum_{j=1}^{n} |X_j| = i$.

Table 1. Algorithm generating the P-reachable canonical tuples

For every $n \leq i \leq n^2$ do the following:

1. Let s be the next non-processed tuple in $H[i]$.
2. Let ab be the next non-processed P-permitted call on s.
3. Generate the tuple s^{ab}. Let j be the total number of known secrets in s^{ab}.
4. Search the sorted list $H[j]$ for $\mathsf{can}(s^{ab})$. If such a tuple does not exist, add $\mathsf{can}(s^{ab})$ in $H[j]$, keeping it sorted.
5. If there are more P-permitted calls in s go to step 2.
6. If there are more tuples in $H[i]$ go to step 1.

For example we have that the initial tuple belongs to $S_{n,n}$ and that the final tuple belongs to S_{n,n^2}.

Now we describe the algorithm generating the P-reachable canonical tuples. Initially we create an empty one-dimensional array H of size n^2. The purpose of the entry $H[i]$ is to store a lexicographically sorted list of the tuples in $S_{n,i}$. The first $n-1$ elements of H are not used, since $S_{n,i} = \emptyset$, for $1 \leq i \leq n-1$. The lexicographical sorting of the tuples serves in making the search in $H[i]$ faster.

In order to generate all the P-reachable canonical tuples we first add the canonical initial tuple in $H[n]$ and then we execute the algorithm in Table 1. The ANY-reachable canonical 4-tuples are presented in Table 2. Recall that states in ANY can be described by unordered tuples too. This representation of ANY-states rapidly reduces the search space, already for 4 agents, as we can see in Table 2: $(ABC, ABD, ABCD, ABCD)$ and $(ABCD, ABD, ABC, ABCD)$ are instances of $\{ABC, ABD, ABCD, ABCD\}$. So, by modifying the algorithm in Table 1 we can generate the ANY-reachable non-isomorphic unordered tuples. The code of our implementation is available at:

https://github.com/Jannis17/gossip_protocol_expectation.

For finding the canonical form of a tuple we used the software "nauty" [19]. Experiments made by the developers of "nauty" show that it is the fastest known software for finding the canonical forms of graphs. The results of our implementation are shown in Table 3. It shows that:

- The idea of using unordered tuples in ANY reduces the search space rapidly and therefore allows us to generate 8-tuples, which would otherwise be impossible.
- In order to generate n-tuples for $n > 8$, an important optimization is needed. An idea is to generate the lists of table H in parallel. We can assign the calculation of every entry of H to a different thread. For example, when processing an element of some $H[i]$ we will generate some elements of an $H[j]$ with $j > i$. Then the thread assigned to $H[j]$ can start processing its elements (and generating new tuples) before the thread assigned to $H[i]$ has finished.[1]

---

[1] This idea was presented to us by Dionysis Kakolyris.

Table 2. All the ANY-reachable canonical 4-tuples.

i (secrets):		$H[i]$:
16		$(ABCD, ABCD, ABCD, ABCD)$
15		$(ABCD, ABCD, ABCD, ABD)$
14	$(ABC, ABC, ABCD, ABCD)$	$(ABC, ABD, ABCD, ABCD)$
	$(ABCD, ABD, ABC, ABCD)$	$(ABCD, ABCD, ABC, ABD)$
		$(ABCD, ABCD, ABCD, CD)$
13	$(ABC, AB, ABCD, ABCD)$	$(ABCD, AB, ABC, ABCD)$
12	(ABC, ABD, ABC, ABD)	$(ABCD, AB, ABCD, CD)$
10		(ABC, ABC, ABC, D)
9		(ABC, AB, ABC, D)
8		(AB, AB, CD, CD)
6		(AB, AB, C, D)
4		(A, B, C, D)

Table 3. The numbers of LNS- and ANY-reachable non-isomorphic tuples. If it takes more than 1 second, the time needed for generating them (in an Intel 2.70 GHz processor with 3.7 GB RAM and 2 cores) is shown in parentheses.

n	Unordered tuples (ANY)	Ordered tuples (LNS)	Ordered tuples (ANY)
1	1	1	1
2	2	2	2
3	4	4	4
4	13	15	16
5	68	97	111
6	775	1,551	1,940
7	17,489 (6.9 s)	49,046 (48.6 s)	68,300 (196.9 s)
8	788,057 (9 h 09 min)		

5 Expectation of the Protocols

The number of P-permitted calls until all agents become experts is represented by T_n^{P}. If v is a fixed agent, then $T_{v,n}^{\mathsf{P}}$ represents the number of P-permitted calls until everybody learns v's secret. In this section we show how the exact value of $\mathbb{E}(T_n^{\mathsf{ANY}})$ and $\mathbb{E}(T_n^{\mathsf{LNS}})$ can be computed for small numbers and then we discuss the asymptotic behaviour of $\mathbb{E}(T_n^{\mathsf{ANY}})$ and $\mathbb{E}(T_n^{\mathsf{CO}})$.

5.1   Exact Value for Small Numbers

Protocol LNS describes a random process for generating ordered tuples. Since an ordered tuple provides all the necessary information for selecting the available LNS-calls, this random process is a Markov process on the set of ordered tuples. The same holds for ANY and the set of unordered tuples. Of course for every number of agents we have a different Markov chain.

In this subsection we assume that P represents ANY or LNS and that the number of agents n is fixed. If we assume that in each tuple calls are selected uniformly at random, then the transition matrix of the Markov chain corresponding to the execution of P can be generated by a simple modification of the algorithm in Table 1. Assume that the tuple t is reachable from the tuple s via r different calls. (Since t might belong to an isomorphism class of many tuples reachable from s, or since t might be an instance of an unordered tuple that has other instances reachable from s, t might be reachable from s via several calls.) Then the transition probability from s to t is:

$$p_{st} = \frac{r}{|\#\text{P-available calls in } s|}.$$

Remark 1 ([18]). Let P be the transition matrix of some Markov chain that describes an execution of P. Since the total number of secrets known is non-decreasing, a state $s \in S_{n,i}$ can only access states belonging to $S_{n,j}$ with $j > i$ and possibly s. Now if we assign indices to the states in an increasing order according to the states $S_{n,i}$ we have that every state can only access states with greater or equal index. *Thus P is upper triangular.* (All the elements below the largest diagonal of P are equal to 0.) In addition to that, any tuple can reach at most $\binom{n}{2}$ tuples. Since $\binom{n}{2}$ is significantly smaller compared to the number of total states (see Table 3), P is *sparse* (most of P's elements are equal to 0).

Now the algorithm for computing the expected duration of P should be clear: we compute the canonical P-reachable tuples using the algorithm in Table 1. These are the states of the corresponding Markov chain. Since the final tuple is unique, this Markov chain has only one absorption state. We index the states in H increasingly as follows: we assign the index 1 in $H[n]$, then the next indices to states in $H[n+1]$, ..., and finally the biggest index, N, to the absorption state in $H[n^2]$. We compute the transition probabilities and then we create the transition matrix, P_N (because of Remark 1 the transition matrix can be easily stored in the memory despite its large size). Let $\boldsymbol{E_N}$ be a vector, such that the i-th entry of $\boldsymbol{E_N}$ is equal to the average time that the Markov chain needs to reach the absorption state when it starts from state i. It is well known (see for example [21, Sect. 1.3]) that E_N has to satisfy the following linear system:

$$\boldsymbol{1_N} = (I_N - P_N) \cdot \boldsymbol{E_N}.$$

where I_N is the identity matrix of dimension $N \times N$ and $\boldsymbol{1_N}$ is an N-vector of all 1's. From the above linear system we can compute E_1, i.e. the exact value of the expected duration of P for n agents. As we can see from Table 3 the transition matrix in our Markov chains will have a very big dimension. At first sight, solving a linear system with a matrix of this dimension seems impossible. However, since the matrix is upper triangular (Remark 1), the linear system can be solved without inverting the transition matrix. We can calculate the entries of E_N immediately in linear time with respect to the non-zero values of P_N. The results from our implementation are presented in Table 4.

Table 4. The exact value of $\mathbb{E}(T_n^{\text{ANY}})$ and $\mathbb{E}(T_n^{\text{LNS}})$.

n	$\mathbb{E}(T_n^{\text{ANY}})$	$\mathbb{E}(T_n^{\text{LNS}})$
1	0	0
2	1	1
3	4	3
4	7.588001	5.261905
5	11.703006	7.860293
6	16.186623	10.711012
7	20.966995	13.770599
8	25.994711	

Example 1. For 3 agents, the Markov chain for the execution of ANY is presented in Fig. 1. We index the states from bottom to top as in the picture (1 is the initial state and 4 the final, absorbing state). The transition matrix then is:

$$P_4 = \begin{bmatrix} 0 & 1 & 0 & 0 \\ 0 & \frac{1}{3} & \frac{2}{3} & 0 \\ 0 & 0 & \frac{1}{3} & \frac{2}{3} \\ 0 & 0 & 0 & 0 \end{bmatrix}$$

Let E_i be the average number of steps needed to hit state 4 when we are in state i, $1 \leq i \leq 4$. We now have the linear system

$$(I_4 - P_4) \cdot E = 1_4$$

Since P_4 is upper triangular we immediately get (since by definition $E_4 = 0$) that $E_3 = \frac{3}{2}$, that $E_2 = 3$, and that $E_1 = 4$. So, the expected duration of ANY with 3 agents is 4.

5.2   Asymptotic Behaviour

Some bounds on $\mathbb{E}(T_n^{\text{ANY}})$ were first proved by Moon [20]. These bounds were later sharpened by Boyd and Steele [4], and subsequently by Haigh [12], who showed that:

$$\mathbb{E}(T_n^{\text{ANY}}) = \frac{3}{2} \cdot n \log n + \mathcal{O}(n).$$

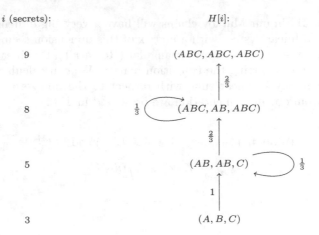

Fig. 1. The Markov chain corresponding to the execution of ANY with 3 agents.

Let us think of the weighted graph that describes the execution of CO. Before any call has taken place this graph is empty, and as the execution of CO proceeds, edges are randomly added to it. This process generates random graphs according to the model of Erdős and Rényi [8]. In [8] it is shown that, for $n \to \infty$, when a random graph contains at most $\frac{1}{2} \cdot n \log n + \mathcal{O}(n)$ edges, then this graph will contain isolated nodes with probability 1. The isolated nodes correspond to agents that have not communicated with anyone. In order for a single secret to be communicated the weighted graph has to be connected. Hence we obtain the following lower bound for $\mathbb{E}(T_{v,n}^{\mathsf{CO}})$:

$$\lim_{n \to \infty} \mathbb{E}(T_{v,n}^{\mathsf{CO}}) \geq \frac{1}{2} \cdot n \log n + \mathcal{O}(n),$$

from which we trivially get:

$$\lim_{n \to \infty} \mathbb{E}(T_n^{\mathsf{CO}}) \geq \frac{1}{2} \cdot n \log n + \mathcal{O}(n).$$

6   Approximating the Distribution of LNS

Let us first assume that all calls (but not all agents who make a call) in LNS are randomly selected. Since in LNS the length of a call sequence is between $2 \cdot n - 4$ and $\binom{n}{2}$, we have that $\Pr(T_n^{\mathsf{LNS}} = k) > 0$ only if k is between (and including) the previous values. These probabilities can be calculated using the transition matrix of the Markov chain that corresponds to the execution of LNS with n agents. Let P_N be the transition matrix of this Markov Chain. For every $1 \leq k \leq \binom{n}{2}$ let P_N^k be the k-th power of P_N. It is well known that the element $(P_N^k)_{ij}$ is equal to the probability of going from state i to state j in at most k steps. So, if the index of the initial state is 1 and the index of the final (absorbing) state

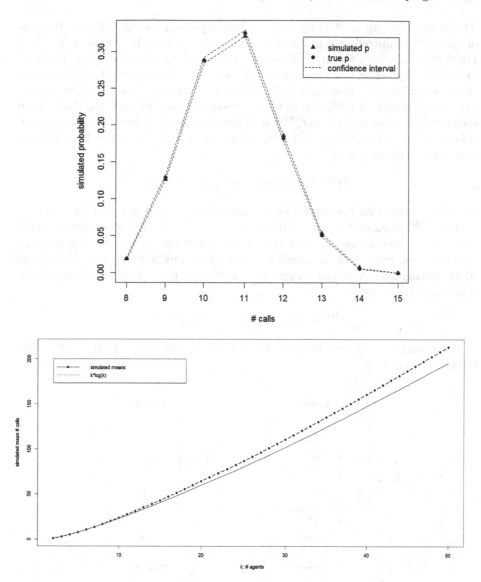

Fig. 2. Top: True and Simulated values for $\Pr(T_n^{\mathsf{LNS}})$. **Bottom:** Simulated values for $\mathbb{E}(T_n^{\mathsf{LNS}})$. The reference line is $n \log n$.

is N then the element $(P_N^k)_{1N}$ is equal to the probability of LNS terminating in at most k steps. The probability of LNS terminating in k steps is equal to $(P_N^k)_{1N} - (P_N^{k-1})_{1N}$, where $2n - 4 \leq k \leq \binom{n}{2}$.

We were only able to calculate the values for these probabilities for up to 6 agents, due to the large number of LNS-states. To obtain approximate figures for the distribution of LNS for larger numbers of agents we resorted to simulations.

This is easily set up by starting at the initial tuple and successively selecting one of the LNS-permitted calls uniformly at random until the final tuple is reached. For 6 agents, a comparison of the simulated and the real probabilities is shown in Fig. 2 (top). The confidence intervals are ±1.96 standard deviations from the binomial distribution. In Fig. 2 (bottom) we also present the values of the expected duration of LNS according to our simulations. From Fig. 2 (bottom) it seems safe to assume that $\mathbb{E}(T_n^{\mathsf{LNS}})$ is of the magnitude $n \log n$ and also that it takes off from this reference with an estimated 9.76%. Using the least squares method we obtain that:

$$\mathbb{E}(T_n^{\mathsf{LNS}}) \approx 1.0976 \cdot n \log n - 1.1330.$$

We also observe that the simulations indicate a fast convergence of the distribution of T_n^{LNS} towards the normal distribution. In Fig. 3 histograms are depicted for 4, 6, 10 and 50 agents. Our observations can also be verified by quantile normal plots. Studies of the development of the empirical variance of the simulations suggest a variance structure of the form $\theta_0 + \theta_2 k^2$, resulting in the following conjecture:

$$T_n^{\mathsf{LNS}} \sim N(\alpha \cdot n \log n + \beta, \theta_0 + \theta_2 k^2).$$

Provisionary estimates for α, β, θ_0 and θ_2 are 1.0976, -1.1330, 10.3675 and 0.0304, respectively.

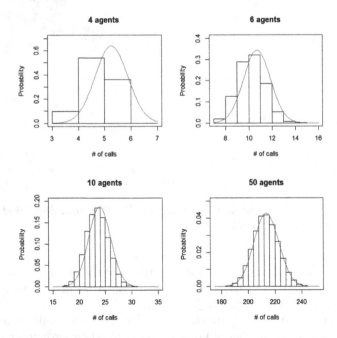

Fig. 3. Histograms of simulations for 4, 6, 10 and 50 agents, with corresponding normal density curves (50,000 simulations).

So far, we assumed that the calls are selected with uniform probability. As said, for distributed systems modelling it is justifiable that agents who can make a call are selected with uniform probability, and that subsequently for such an agent a call that this agent can make is selected with uniform probability. Transitions between tuples have different probabilities with the two methods. Let $s = (ABC, AB, ABC, D)$ and $t = (ABC, ABC, ABC, D)$. The only LNS-permitted call that leads from s to t is bc. If all the calls have the same probability of being chosen, then we have that the probability of going from s to t is $p_{st} = \frac{1}{7}$. However, the probability of selecting b is $\frac{1}{4}$ (since all 4 agents can make a call) and then the probability of b selecting call bc is $\frac{1}{2}$ (since b can make two calls). With this method of selecting call we get that $p_{st} = \frac{1}{8}$.

The exact values of the expectation and the probability distributions do not differ much when first the agents and then the calls are selected. By repeating our previous analysis with the new method for selecting calls we get the following estimation for the new expected duration of LNS:

$$\mathbb{E}(T_n^{\mathsf{LNS}}) \approx 1.0986 \cdot n \log n - 1.3113$$

This is only marginally different from our previous figure ($1.0976 \cdot n \log n - 1.1330$), which was not what we expected.

7   Conclusions, Applications, and Further Research

We gave results for reachability and expectation of three distributed protocols for gossiping on completely connected networks, ANY (making any call), LNS (only calling agents whose secret you do not know), and CO (agents who have been in a call may not call each other again). We showed that more distributions of secrets are reachable by ANY than by CO, and more are reachable by CO than by LNS. We modelled ANY and LNS as discrete time Markov processes and presented an algorithm generating the states of these Markov chains. We also determined the asymptotic behaviour of LNS via simulations. This value $\mathbb{E}(T_n^{\mathsf{LNS}})$ differs by a constant factor only from the known results for ANY (50% more calls are expected), and not by an order of magnitude.

Open problems are to additionally obtain asymptotic (not approximate, simulation-based) results for $\mathbb{E}(T_n^{\mathsf{LNS}})$ and asymptotic results for $\mathbb{E}(T_n^{\mathsf{CO}})$, where we expect that $\mathbb{E}(T_n^{\mathsf{ANY}}) \geq \mathbb{E}(T_n^{\mathsf{CO}}) \geq \mathbb{E}(T_n^{\mathsf{LNS}})$. It seems that the methods of [4,12,20] cannot be directly applied to CO and LNS since they heavily depend on any call being available at any moment. We note that in the case of ANY the two different models for selecting calls (i.e. uniform selection of calls and uniform selection of an agent a followed by a uniform selection of a call for a to make) do not make any difference in the probability distribution: each call will have the same probability under any of the two models. However in CO and LNS the calls will no longer have the same probabilities under the different models. The first model seems easier for asymptotic analysis of CO and LNS since, as we noted before, it resembles traditional random graph generation [8].

We hope that our results may contribute to further efforts to determine the expectation of sequential and parallel gossip algorithms, and in particular, as mentioned, those for *epistemic* gossip algorithms, in view of practical applications of gossip in multi-agent systems. The most ambitious goal there is to 'beat' the gossip community at their own game, by producing faster gossip algorithms (than currently known) for very specific network topologies or with very specific epistemic conditions for executing calls in distributed protocols, or with epistemic goals.

Acknowledgements. We are grateful to Christophe Chareton, George Giakkoupis, Dionysis Kakolyris, and Aris Pagourtzis for useful discussions and to the anonymous reviewers for many useful comments and suggestions. We acknowledge financial support from ERC project EPS 313360. Hans van Ditmarsch is also affiliated to IMSc, Chennai, as research associate.

References

1. Apt, K.R., Grossi, D., van der Hoek, W.: Epistemic protocols for distributed gossiping. In: Proceedings of 15th TARK (2015)
2. Attamah, M., van Ditmarsch, H., Grossi, D., van der Hoek, W.: Knowledge and gossip. In: Proceedings of the 21st ECAI, pp. 21–26. IOS Press (2014)
3. Attamah, M., van Ditmarsch, H., Grossi, D., van der Hoek, W.: The pleasure of gossip. In: Başkent, C., Moss, L.S., Ramanujam, R. (eds.) Rohit Parikh on Logic, Language and Society. OCL, vol. 11, pp. 145–163. Springer, Cham (2017). doi:10.1007/978-3-319-47843-2_9
4. Boyd, D.W., Steele, J.M.: Random exchanges of information. J. Appl. Probab. **16**, 657–661 (1979)
5. Bumby, R.T.: A problem with telephones. SIAM J. Algebr. Discrete Methods **2**(1), 13–18 (1981)
6. van Ditmarsch, H., van Eijck, J., Pardo, P., Ramezanian, R., Schwarzentruber, F.: Epistemic protocols for dynamic gossip. J. Appl. Log. **20**, 1–31 (2017)
7. Doerr, B., Friedrich, T., Sauerwald, T.: Quasirandom rumor spreading. ACM Trans. Algorithms **11**(2), 1–35 (2014)
8. Erdös, P., Rényi, A.: On random graphs I. Publ. Math. (Debrecen) **6**, 290–297 (1959)
9. Eugster, P.T., Guerraoui, R., Kermarrec, A., Massoulié, L.: Epidemic information dissemination in distributed systems. IEEE Comput. **37**(5), 60–67 (2004)
10. Göbel, F., Cerdeira, J.O., Veldman, H.J.: Label-connected graphs and the gossip problem. Discrete Math. **87**(1), 29–40 (1991)
11. Haeupler, B.: Simple, fast and deterministic gossip and rumor spreading. J. ACM **62**(6), 47 (2015)
12. Haigh, J.: Random exchanges of information. J. Appl. Probab. **18**, 743–746 (1981)
13. Hedetniemi, S., Hedetniemi, S., Liestman, A.: A survey of gossiping and broadcasting in communication networks. Networks **18**, 319–349 (1988)
14. Herzig, A., Maffre, F.: How to share knowledge by gossiping. AI Commun. **30**(1), 1–17 (2017)
15. Hurkens, C.: Spreading gossip efficiently. Nieuw Archief voor Wiskunde **5/1**(2), 208–210 (2000)

16. Kermarrec, A.M., van Steen, M.: Gossiping in distributed systems. SIGOPS Oper. Syst. Rev. **41**(5), 2–7 (2007)
17. Knödel, W.: New gossips and telephones. Discrete Math. **13**, 95 (1975)
18. Landau, H.: The distribution of completion times for random communication in a task-oriented group. Bull. Math. Biophys. **16**(3), 187–201 (1954)
19. McKay, B.D., Piperno, A.: Practical graph isomorphism II. J. Symb. Comput. **60**, 94–112 (2014)
20. Moon, J.: Random exchanges of information. Nieuw Archief voor Wiskunde **20**, 246–249 (1972)
21. Norris, J.R.: Markov Chains. Cambridge University Press, Cambridge (1998)
22. Panangaden, P., Taylor, K.: Concurrent common knowledge: defining agreement for asynchronous systems. Distrib. Comput. **6**, 73–93 (1992)
23. Tijdeman, R.: On a telephone problem. Nieuw Archief voor Wiskunde **3**(19), 188–192 (1971)
24. West, D.B.: A class of solutions to the gossip problem, part I. Discrete Math. **39**(3), 307–326 (1982)

Optimising Social Welfare in Multi-Resource Threshold Task Games

Fatma R. Habib[1,2]([✉]), Maria Polukarov[3], and Enrico H. Gerding[1]

[1] University of Southampton, Southampton SO17 1BJ, UK
{fh5g11,eg}@ecs.soton.ac.uk, fhabib@kau.edu.sa
[2] King Abdulaziz University, Jeddah 21589, Kingdom of Saudi Arabia
[3] King's College London, Strand, London WC2R 2LS, UK
maria.polukarov@kcl.ac.uk

Abstract. In this paper, we introduce a discrete model for overlapping coalition formation called the multi-resource threshold task game (MR-TTG), which generalises the model introduced in [6]. Furthermore, we define the coalition structure generation (CSG) Problem for MR-TTGs. Towards the efficient solution of CSG problems for MR-TTGs, we provide two reductions to the well-known knapsack problems: the bounded multidimensional knapsack problem and the multiple-choice multidimensional knapsack problem. We then propose two branch and bound algorithms to compare between these reductions. Empirical evaluation shows that the latter reduction is more efficient in solving difficult instances of the problem.

Keywords: Cooperative games · Overlapping coalitions · Coalition formation

1 Introduction

The majority of research in cooperative game theory assume that an agent can take part in only one coalition. This assumption is too restrictive and cannot be applicable to many real-world settings. In particular, an agent can utilise the surplus from their resources by joining another coalition, e.g., investing in multiple businesses. This motivates the need for a more general model that captures this behaviour of agents. In this view, Shehory and Kraus [18,19] introduced the concept of overlapping coalitions. Overlapping coalition formation games (OCF-Gs) were formally introduced by Chalkiadakis et al. [6] along with threshold task games (TTGs), a subclass of OCF-Gs where a coalition's value depends on the tasks it completed. These models assume that agents are endowed with a single resource. In this work, we extend the TTG model to consider multiple resource types. This is a natural scenario where agents could distribute their computational resources and memory among different activities. Consider a task defined in a wireless sensor network environment. Here, a task may require a number of sensors and sufficient memory to log the readings from the sensors. In particular, we consider resources

© Springer International Publishing AG 2017
B. An et al. (Eds.): PRIMA 2017, LNAI 10621, pp. 110–126, 2017.
https://doi.org/10.1007/978-3-319-69131-2_7

divisible into integral parts. I.e., resources cannot be divided into fractions such as sensors and bytes of memory.

Two central problems studied in cooperative games are payoff distribution and coalition structure generation (CSG). The objective of payoff distribution is to divide the payoff of a coalition in a stable and/or fair way. These aims are addressed through the core [12] and the Shapley value [17] respectively. In contrast, CSG is concerned with increasing the overall value of coalitions, which is our focus here. Overlapping coalition formation has been effective in solving networked multi-agent systems problems. For instance, [7] investigated the problem of widearea surveillance in multi-sensor networks. Similarly, [10] investigated overlapping coalition formation for collaborative smartphone sensing. Moreover, OCF-Gs had an improved performance over non-overlapping coalition structures in the problems of cooperative interference management in small cell networks [24] and collaborative spectrum sensing in cognitive networks [21].

1.1   Contributions

We propose a discrete model that extends TTGs to multi-resource threshold task games (MR-TTGs) that can handle multiple resource types. In addition, we formulate the CSG problem for MR-TTGs and show that it is $\mathcal{NP}$-hard (Theorem 1). Furthermore, we address the CSG problem of MR-TTGs by reducing it to two well-known knapsack problems: The bounded multi-dimensional knapsack problem (Theorem 2) and the multiple-choice multi-dimensional knapsack problem (Theorem 3). We develop algorithms for the reduced problems, in which the complexity is independent of the number of agents. Finally, we empirically evaluate the proposed reductions and algorithms.

1.2   Related Work

As mentioned earlier, [18,19] introduced the concept of overlapping coalitions and applied it in distributed task-based environments, in particular, tasks with precedence order. Furthermore, they presented simple, distributed approximation algorithms for task execution via overlapping coalitions. OCF-Gs were formally introduced in 2010. However, most of the research in this domain has focused on the distribution of payoff among agents in a coalition and stability, e.g., [25,26]. In regards to fairness of distribution, [26] extended the Shapley value for OCF-G. In regards to stability, [26] introduced arbitrators to OCF-Gs that allocate payoffs to deviating agents to produce stable outcomes. In addition, [25] studied the algorithmic complexity of finding stable and socially optimal outcomes for a discrete model of OCF-G. Moreover, they identify computationally tractable subclasses of the model and provide efficient algorithms and hardness results for games belonging to these subclasses.

Researchers have introduced interesting models of coalitional games in the non-overlapping setting. Some of these models are similar to MR-TTGs, in particular, the ones which represent resource-based and task-based environments. The coalitional resource games (CRG) model [22] is similar to the MR-TTG model for which agents possess an amount of different resources. However, in those games, agents are associated with a set of goals and supposed to achieve one of them. The set of goals might overlap and agents are indifferent between the goals available to them, while in the TTG setting we consider here, the available tasks and their valuations are the same for all agents. In CRGs, as in TTGs, the ability of a coalition to achieve a set of goals depends on the collective sum of the agents' resources. In contrast to our work, the researchers considered the complexity of solving CRGs in environments comprising self-oriented agents.

One of the early models of coalitional games in a task-based environment was introduced by [8]. They approached a very general model making no assumptions about the coalition value, or restrictions on the number of agents in a coalition. Therefore, the problem addressed is harder than the CSG problem in characteristic function games. The value of a coalition depends on the agents' identities and completed tasks. Contributions of this work include a CSG algorithm for the model and lower bound for the problem.

Another class of coalitional games defined in a task-based environment is the coalitional skill game introduced by [4]. Here, agents posses a set of skills and are expected to complete some tasks that require several skills. I.e., a coalition completes a set of tasks if the required skills can be covered by its members. In their model, skills are not quantified. Furthermore, to determine the value of a coalition, two games were defined. Firstly, the task count skill game, where the value of a coalition is defined as the number of tasks it can accomplish. Secondly, the weighted task skill game that, as in TTGs, assigns a weight to each task and a coalition's value is defined as the sum of the weights of the tasks it accomplished. This work focused on questions related to stability and fairness.

The complexity of finding the optimal coalition structure in coalitional skill games was studied by [3]. They proved hardness results for single-task skill games. However, they give positive results when reformulating the problem as constraint satisfaction on a hypergraph. Moreover, they provide a polynomial time CSG algorithm for instances with bounded tree width and number of tasks.

In coalitional skill vectors [20], an extension of coalitional skill games, an agent's set of skills is represented as a vector to encompass the agent's level in each skill. Similarly, in order to complete a task, agents are required to satisfy a certain minimum threshold represented by the aggregate level of agents in a skill. The vector representation of skills is similar to ours of resources. It is expressive and concise since a coalition's value does not depend on the agents' identity. Moreover, it is efficient to compute the upper bound for problems of up to 500 agents.

2   Preliminaries

For completeness, we define preliminaries of CSG in classical and overlapping coalitional games.

2.1   Coalitional Games and Coalition Structure Generation

A cooperative or coalitional game $\langle A, v \rangle$ is defined by a set of players and a valuation function. The valuation function, $v : 2^A \to \mathbb{R}$, defines the worth of each coalition; denoted as $v(\mathcal{C})$. A coalition $\mathcal{C}$ is a set of agents such that $\mathcal{C} \subseteq A$. Cooperative settings typically focus on the social welfare, i.e., the overall value of coalitions, as opposed to the utilities of individual agents. The CSG problem addresses this objective by finding a coalition structure, i.e., a partition of agents, of maximal value. In a coalition structure [2], agents are divided into disjoint coalitions; a coalition structure CS is feasible if and only if $\cup_{\mathcal{C} \in CS}\, \mathcal{C} = |A|$ and $\forall \mathcal{C}, \mathcal{C}' \in CS$ s.t. $\mathcal{C} \neq \mathcal{C}', \mathcal{C} \cap \mathcal{C}' = \phi$. The value of a CS is the sum of all the values of its coalitions. Therefore, $v(CS) = \sum_{\mathcal{C} \in CS} v(\mathcal{C})$.

2.2   Overlapping Coalition Formation Games

In OCF-Gs [6], it is assumed that agents possess a certain amount of resources. Furthermore, in order to fulfil their goals, agents are expected to distribute their resources among several coalitions. In general, the overlapping setting allows agents to join as many coalitions as they wish. In some scenarios though, the agents' participation in coalitions depend on the resources they possess. For simplicity, the OCF-G model considers a single divisible resource and it is assumed that agents have one unit of that resource. As agents partially contribute to coalitions, the notion of 'coalition' is replaced by 'partial coalition' in the non-overlapping setting. A coalition structure is a list[1] (or a multiset) of partial coalitions. In addition, the sum of an agent's contribution across all partial coalitions should not exceed 1.

Threshold task games (TTGs), introduced by [6], provide a simple, yet, expressive representation for OCF-Gs. Here, agents in a partial coalition aggregate their resources in order to accomplish a task. A TTG is defined considering a single-resource environment, however, as opposed to the OCF-G model described above, every agent has a specific resource weight. A task type is defined by a resource threshold and a value. The threshold specifies the minimum resource amount needed to complete the task and the value is the gain obtained upon completing a task copy of that type. It is assumed that there is an infinite number of copies of every task type and agents working on completing a certain task can contribute any amount of the resource they possess.

Considering the above specifications of OCF-Gs and TTGs, there may be an infinite number of feasible partial coalitions. Hence, it might not be possible to define the CSG problem for these models. However, we could define the CSG problem for MR-TTGs since we consider indivisible resources.

3   Model

In this work, we introduce the MR-TTG model, which is a discretised extension of the TTG model that can capture multiple resources. Furthermore, we

---

[1] A coalition structure is defined as a list rather than a set because different partial coalitions can have the same weights of agents' contributions.

formulate the associated CSG problem for that model. Finally, we provide two knapsack reductions for the CSG problem on MR-TTGs.

3.1 Multi-resource Threshold Task Games

An MR-TTG is defined by a set of agents $A = \{1, \ldots, n\}$, a set of resource types $R = \{1, \ldots, m\}$ and a set of task types $T = \{1, \ldots, q\}$. For each task type $k \in T$, its demand $d_k \in \mathbb{N}$, indicates the number of copies available of task type k. Each agent $i \in A$ is associated with a vector of resources $r^i = (r_1^i, \ldots, r_m^i)$, where $r_j^i \in \mathbb{N}_0$ is the integer weight that agent i possesses of each resource $j \in R$. Each task type $k \in T$ is described by a value $v_k \in \mathbb{N}$ and a vector of thresholds $\tau_k = (\tau_{1k}, \ldots, \tau_{mk})$, where $\tau_{jk} \in \mathbb{N}_0$ denotes the weight of resource j needed to complete a task of type k. For a copy $l = 1, \ldots, d_k$ of a task type $k = 1, \ldots, q$, a partial coalition C_{kl} is given by an m vector — indicating the amount of each resource that the agents contribute towards the task kl. $C_{kl} = (\bar{w}_{1kl}, \ldots, \bar{w}_{mkl})$, where $\bar{w}_{jkl} = (w_{jkl}^1, \ldots, w_{jkl}^n)$; w_{jkl}^i is the integer weight that agent i allotted of his resource j to C_{kl}. If this amount meets the requirement given by the threshold τ_k, the value of the coalition is v_k, and is 0 otherwise. Thus, $v(C_{kl}) = v_k$ if $\sum_{i=1}^{n} w_{jkl}^i \geq \tau_{jk}, \forall j \in R$ and $v(C_{kl}) = 0$ otherwise.

3.2 Coalition Structure Generation in MR-TTGs

We now formulate the CSG problem for MR-TTGs. In addition, to utilise existing knapsack algorithms, we reduce the CSG problem to two knapsack problems.

A coalition structure CS for an MR-TTG is defined as a multiset of partial coalitions. Let $CS_k \subseteq CS$ be a multiset that contains all the partial coalitions working on task type k, then $\cup_{k=1}^{q} CS_k = CS$ and $|CS_k| \leq d_k$, implying $|CS| \leq \sum_{k=1}^{q} d_k$. The set of feasible coalition structures is denoted by $\mathcal{CS}$. For an MR-TTG, a coalition structure CS is feasible, i.e., $CS \in \mathcal{CS}$ if and only if it satisfies the agent's resource constraints $\sum_{C_{kl} \in CS} w_{jkl}^i \leq r_j^i, \forall i \in A, j \in R, k \in T$ and task demands $|CS_k| \leq d_k$. The coalition structure generation problem for an MR-TTG is the problem of finding the coalition structure $CS^* \in \mathcal{CS}$ which maximises the sum of the values of all partial coalitions $C_{kl} \in CS^*$. Hence, $CS^* \in max_{CS \in \mathcal{CS}} \sum_{C_{kl} \in CS} v(C_{kl})$.

Having formulated the CSG problem on MR-TTGs, we now look at its complexity.

Theorem 1. *The CSG problem on MR-TTGs is $\mathcal{NP}$-hard.*

The full proof can be found in [13]. Briefly, we prove that it is $\mathcal{NP}$-hard by reduction from the bounded multidimensional knapsack problem (BMKP). The BMKP is known to be strongly $\mathcal{NP}$-hard when the number of dimensions is greater than 1. It is defined as: There is a knapsack with m dimensions and a set of q item types. Each item type $k = 1, \ldots, q$ is characterised by a profit p_k and a vector of weights w_k to specify its dimensions, where $w_{jk}, j = 1, \ldots, m$ is the weight of the of j'th dimension of item type k. Besides, there is a limited number of copies of each item type k, denoted by b_k, the bound of k. The problem is to maximise the profit of items to be packed in the knapsack by packing at most b_k copies of item type k while adhering to the capacity constraints $c_j, j = 1, \ldots, m$.

The remaining of this section shows two reductions of the CSG problem into two variants of the knapsack problem.

Reduction to BMKP. The following theorem shows the reduction of the CSG problem for an MR-TTG into a BMKP.

Theorem 2. *The Coalition Structure Generation problem for an MR-TTG can be reduced in a polynomial time to a BMKP.*

The formal proof can be found in [13]. Briefly, the proof works as follows. The task types are mapped directly to item types along with their attributes: the resource thresholds, demand and value correspond to the weight vector of an item, its value and bound consecutively. Although, in our model, each agent has his own possession of the various resources, the value gained by completing a task is independent of the contributing agents. The only constraint enforced on resource consumption is the sum of all agents' possessions of that certain resource. This sum is mapped to the knapsack capacity so that each resource type corresponds to one of the dimensions. When inferring the partial coalitions in the optimal coalition structure from the solution of the BMKP, we directly re-map the packed items' copies to successful tasks. However, that gives us no information regarding the identity of the agents involved in each task. In order to satisfy the definition of a partial coalition, we need to re-distribute the agents' resources among completed tasks.

The BMKP reduction can be used to transform the CSG problem to a multiple-choice multidimensional knapsack problem (MMKP).

Reduction to MMKP. An MMKP is defined as follows. There is a knapsack with m dimensions and a number of classes, each of which corresponds to a set of items. Each item is associated with a profit and a vector of m weights to specify the item's dimensions. The problem is to maximise the values of items to be packed in the knapsack by choosing exactly one item from each class while adhering to the knapsack constraints. An MMKP can be constructed from a given BMKP. In the context of our problem, the MMKP is constructed from the BMKP reduction in Theorem 2.

Theorem 3. *A bounded multi-dimensional knapsack problem can be reduced to a multiple-choice multi-dimensional knapsack problem.*

The proof can be found in [13]. The MMKP reduction is demonstrated in the following example:

Example 1. Given a BMKP with two item types, where $w_1 = (2, 3), p_1 = 2, b_1 = 3$ and $w_2 = (4, 1), p_2 = 3, b_2 = 2$, we construct 2 different MMKPs. The multiset

$C = \{1, 1, 1, 2, 2\}$ can be partitioned in different ways. We construct the MMKPs of 2 of these partitions, where ϕ denotes the empty set:

First partition: $C^1 = \{1, 1, 1\}$ and $C^2 = \{2, 2\}$. It results in the power sets $\mathcal{P}(C^1) = \{\{1, 1, 1\}, \{1, 1\}, \{1\}, \phi\}$ and $\mathcal{P}(C^2) = \{\{2, 2\}, \{2\}, \phi\}$, and MMKP:

Class 1	Class 2
$w_1^1 = (6, 9), p_1^1 = 6$	$w_1^2 = (8, 2), p_1^2 = 6$
$w_2^1 = (4, 6), p_2^1 = 4$	$w_2^2 = (4, 1), p_2^2 = 3$
$w_3^1 = (2, 3), p_3^1 = 2$	
$w_4^1 = (0, 0), p_4^1 = 0$	

Second partition: $C^1 = \{1, 2\}$, $C^2 = \{1, 2\}$ and $C^3 = \{1\}$. It results in the power sets $\mathcal{P}(C^1) = \mathcal{P}(C^2) = \{\{1, 2\}, \{1\}, \{2\}, \phi\}$ and $\mathcal{P}(C^3) = \{\{1\}, \phi\}$, and MMKP:

Class 1	Class 2	Class 3
$w_1^1 = (6, 4), p_1^1 = 5$	$w_1^2 = (6, 4), p_1^2 = 5$	$w_1^3 = (2, 3), p_1^3 = 2$
$w_2^1 = (2, 3), p_2^1 = 2$	$w_2^2 = (2, 3), p_2^2 = 2$	$w_2^3 = (0, 0), p_2^3 = 0$
$w_3^1 = (4, 1), p_3^1 = 3$	$w_3^2 = (4, 1), p_3^2 = 3$	
$w_4^1 = (0, 0), p_4^1 = 0$	$w_4^2 = (0, 0), p_4^2 = 0$	

4   Algorithms

In this section, we propose two branch and bound algorithms to solve the knapsack problems resulting from the reductions in the previous section. The purpose of the algorithms is to analyse these reductions and determine which one is best used depending on the problem instance.

4.1   Solving the BMKP

We propose a branch and bound algorithm based on a best first search to solve the MR-TTG CSG problem as a BMKP.

The Search Tree. A search tree is constructed to explore all the possible solutions for the reduced problem. The number of levels of the tree is equal to the number of item types q. Each developed node in the tree corresponds to a partial solution. A node is identified by its level and x_k, $k = 1, \ldots, q$; the number of copies packed of item k. Also, at a given level λ, a node cannot have any items packed of the next levels. Thus, $x_k = 0, \ldots, d_k, \forall k = 1, \ldots, \lambda$ and $x_k = 0, \forall k = \lambda + 1, \ldots, q$. A node is feasible if $c_j \geq \sum_{k=1}^{q} x_k \cdot w_{jk}, \forall j = 1, \ldots, m$ and it is infeasible otherwise. Furthermore, the value of a feasible node is calculated as $\sum_{k=1}^{q} x_k \cdot p_k$, and in any given set L, the best node $\in L$, is the node with the greatest value. A son of a node at a given level is a node, in the next level, with x_k equal to its father $\forall k = 1, \ldots, \lambda, \lambda + 2, \ldots, q$ and $x_k = 0, \ldots, b_k$, $k = \lambda + 1$.

Lower and Upper Bounds. No lower bound is calculated before running the algorithm. Since a best first search approach is adopted, the quality of the solution rapidly improves during the early steps. Moreover, because the number of tree levels is limited a reasonable lower bound is reached once a leaf node is developed; in $\sum_{k=1}^{q} d_k$ steps maximum. However, an upper bound is calculated for each developed node in order to prune the search space. The dimensions of the BMKP are aggregated into a single dimension as in [11] and the integrality constraints are removed. The resultant problem is a bounded knapsack problem (BKP) with the capacity $\sum_{j=1}^{m} c_j$ and each item $k = 1, \ldots, q$ has the dimension $\sum_{j=1}^{m} w_{jk}$ and the bound b_k.

The linear programme outcome serves as an upper bound to the BMKP and it can be solved using Dantzig's approach described in [9]. The approach consists of two steps. Firstly, items are ordered descendingly with respect to their efficiency; the efficiency of an item k is calculated by $e_k = \frac{p_k}{\sum_{j=1}^{m} w_{jk}}$. Secondly, items are packed into the knapsack, in the order generated by the first step, until the capacity $\sum_{j=1}^{m} c_j$ is reached.

In order to calculate the upper bound for any node at a given level λ, a subproblem of the BMKP is considered with the items $k = \lambda + 1, \ldots, q$ and the corresponding bounds $(b_{\lambda+1}, \ldots, b_q)$. The capacity of each dimension is calculated as $c_j = \sum_{i=1}^{n} r_j^i - \sum_{k=1}^{q} x_k \cdot w_{jk}, \forall j \in m$. Afterwards, the subproblem is mapped to a LP BKP and solved using Dantzig's approach described above.

A psuedocode of the algorithm is given in Algorithm 1. Furthermore, the algorithm is summarised in the following steps:

Initialisation. The root node is developed (a node at level 0 with $x_k = 0, \forall k = 1, \ldots, q$), and the solution is set to the root node. Throughout the algorithm, the list L is used to keep track of the nodes whose sons are to be developed; leaf nodes are not added to the list (line 13). To start with, the root node is added to L.

Branching. The best node in L is selected and all its feasible sons are developed in the order $x_k = 0, \ldots, b_k$ (lines 8, 17 & 18), where k is the level of the son nodes in the tree. The best node is discarded (line 19) afterwards. For each developed node, its value is calculated and the solution is updated accordingly (lines 11 & 12). Furthermore, the upper bound (UB) is calculated and only the nodes whose upper bound is greater than the incumbent solution are added to the list (lines 13 to 16).

Termination. The algorithm terminates once there are no further nodes to be developed and the solution is returned, this is achieved when L is empty.

Algorithm 1. Solving the reduced BMKP

```
1: node = root node
2: solution = node
3: L = node
4: while L ≠ φ do
5:    best = best(L)
6:    repeat
7:       k = level(best) + 1
8:       x_k = 0
9:       node = son(best,k) {develop son of best with x_k copies of item k}
10:      if feasible(node) then
11:         if value(node) > value(solution) then
12:            update solution
13:         if level(node) < q then
14:            calculate UB(node)
15:            if UB(node) > value(solution) then
16:               L = L ∪ node
17:      x_k = x_k + 1
18:   until x_k > b_k or not feasible(node)
19:   L = L \ best
20: return  solution
```

4.2 Solving the MMKP

We first present the EMKP, exact algorithm for the MMKP, proposed by [16] and highlight some problems regarding it. Later on, we provide our modified version of the EMKP algorithm to optimally solve the MMKP.

The Original EMKP Algorithm. The EMKP algorithm is based on branch and bound best first search approach as summarised in the following steps:

Initialisation. The lower bound is calculated using a heuristic algorithm. The items of each class are sorted in decreasing order of their corresponding profits. The root node, consisting of the first item in the first class, is developed.

Branching. The best node in the tree is selected, and a son node is developed if the best node was feasible. Also, if exists, the brother of the best node is developed and added to the tree. The son node is only added to the tree if its upper bound was greater than the lower bound.

Termination. If the developed son node is a leaf node and is feasible.

Two problems with the EMKP algorithm were pointed out in [5]; the ineffectiveness of the pruning and elimination strategies. As a result, the algorithm might omit the subspace that contains the optimal solution from the search and unnecessarily compute upper bound of infeasible nodes. Two additional problems, we point out here, are the order of developed nodes and the optimality of the solution found at the proposed stopping condition. Proposition 3 in [16] proves that the first obtained feasible solution is the optimal solution. It is based on Lemma 1 [16] which states that the solutions obtained by the EMKP are developed in decreasing order of their profit regardless of their feasibility state. Here, we give a counter example to falsify the proposition.

Example 2. For simplicity we give an example of a multiple-choice knapsack problem (MCKP), which has one dimension, and assume that the weight of each item is equal to its profit. Consider the following MCKP, with capacity 38.

Class 1	Class 2	Class 3
$w_1^1 = (20), p_1^1 = 20$	$w_1^2 = (12), p_1^2 = 12$	$w_1^3 = (10), p_1^3 = 10$
$w_2^1 = (17), p_2^1 = 17$	$w_2^2 = (7), p_2^2 = 7$	$w_2^3 = (3), p_2^3 = 3$
$w_3^1 = (16), p_3^1 = 16$		

For clarity, we write the nodes in terms of their profits when tracing the algorithm. Initially, the list L will include the first item of the first class, $L = \{(20)\}$. At each step, we develop a son and a brother for the item with the highest value. Upon the first iteration, $L = \{(20, 12), (17)\}$. Upon the second iteration, $L = \{(20, 12, 10), (20, 7), (17)\}$. Now, we could develop a brother for, $(20, 12, 10)$, the best node in L. The brother of the best node, $(20,12,3)$, is the first feasible solution, we could stop now according to the claim that nodes are developed in decreasing order of profit. We skip this node since it is not clear from the algorithm that we could exit even if the last item in the node is not the first item of the last class. Now, $L = \{(20, 7), (17)\}$. In the next iteration, the node $(20, 7, 10)$ is developed. According to the algorithm, $(20, 7, 10)$ is the optimal solution. However, it is clear that $(16, 12, 10)$ is the optimal solution. In fact, in this example, the optimal solution is developed lastly.

The Modified EMKP. Here, we present our new version of the EMKP algorithm. To reduce the execution time, we added two preprocessing steps before running the algorithm. Furthermore, we address the problems in the EMKP algorithm. A pseudocode of the modified algorithm is given in Algorithm 2.

Removing Dominated Items. As a preprocessing step, dominated items are removed from each class $y = 1, \ldots, v$. An item is dominated if there is another item in the same class that yields a greater profit while having less (or equal) weight for each dimension.

Reducing Duplicate States. Another preprocessing step is to reduce the number of items in each class due to the special structure of the MMKP constructed. Since classes are created by deriving power sets and the original set we partition is a multiset, many of the classes in the MMKP might be identical. Due to that, identical nodes might be developed in the search process. In addition, in each class, there is an item which corresponds to the element $\phi \in \mathcal{P}(C^y)$. We refer to this item as the fictitious item. The existence of the fictitious items adds to the number of duplicate states that can be derived. As a result, the processing time of the algorithm would be adversely affected. This situation can be demonstrated by the following MMKP:

Consider the second partition in Example 1, in the resulting MMKP, selecting $\{1, 2, \}$ from $\mathcal{P}(C^1)$ and ϕ from $\mathcal{P}(C^2)$ is identical to selecting $\{1\}$ from $\mathcal{P}(C^1)$ and $\{2\}$ from $\mathcal{P}(C^2)$.

Storing all the developed nodes in a list and searching through the list to determine if a developed node has a duplicate is expensive. However, we reduce the effect of duplicates by eliminating some of the sets in classes which has duplicates. If the multiset C was partitioned, such that there are partitions which are identical. Then for every partition $C^{y'}$ which is identical to C^y, we can safely eliminate the sets with cardinality $|C^{y'}|$ from the power set of $C^{y'}$. As a result, in Example 1, the MMKP formed by the set Y is identical to: $Y' = \{\{\{1, 2, \}, \{1\}, \{2\}, \phi\}, \{\{1, 2, \}, \phi\}, \{\{1\}, \phi\}\}$.

Pruning the Search Space. No lower bound is calculated prior to running the modified algorithm since the tree nodes can serve as an incumbent solution. For feasible nodes, the upper bound is calculated as in the EMKP algorithm. In the modified algorithm, if a node is infeasible then its upper bound is set to its father's upper bound.

A brother node is only developed if the upper bound of its father is greater than the incumbent solution. When developing a brother, instead of keeping infeasible nodes in the tree, we keep on developing brother of a brother nodes until a feasible one is encountered. A feasible brother is added to the search space of it does not have an item if the class v. As in the EMKP algorithm, a son node is developed for nodes whose upper bounds are greater than the incumbent solution.

Termination Condition. The algorithm terminates when the search space is empty.

5   Empirical Evaluation

We evaluate the performance of Algorithms 1 and 2 to solve different instances of the BMKP and their corresponding MMKP reductions. For the purpose of testing the algorithms, we considered BMKP instances, instead of MR-TTG, since the hardness of solving BMKPs depends on some factors that we consider in generating the data sets. The algorithms were programmed in C++ and run on a Mac 2.9 GHz Intel Core i5 processor and 8 GB memory.

5.1   Instance Generation

Two types of BMKP data sets were generated: uncorrelated and strongly correlated data sets with the latter being considered hard to solve [15]. In uncorrelated instances, the profit of an item is independent of its dimensions, and the profits

Algorithm 2. The Modified EMKP

```
1:  node = item 1 in class 1
2:  father_UB(node) = ∑ᵤ₌₁ᵛ pᵧᵧ, g = 1
3:  value(solution) = 0
4:  L = node
5:  while L ≠ φ do
6:      best = best(L)
7:      L = L \ best
8:      if last_class(best) ≠ v and feasible(best) and UB(best) ≥ value(solution) then
9:          son = son(best)
10:         L = L ∪ son
11:     if feasible(son) then
12:         if value(son) > value(solution) then
13:             solution=son
14:         if last_class(son) = v then
15:             return solution
16:     if father_UB(best) ≥ value(solution) and has_brother(best) then
17:         brother=brother(best)
18:         while not feasible(brother) do
19:             brother=brother(brother) {there will always exist a feasible brother due to the
                fictitious item}
20:         if feasible(brother) and value(brother) > value(solution) then
21:             solution=brother
22:         if not (feasible(brother) and last_class(brother) = v) then
23:             L = L ∪ brother
```

were drawn randomly from the interval $[1, 100]$. On the other hand, in strongly correlated instances, the profit of an item is a linear function of its weight [14] and these were calculated by $p_k = \sum_{j=1}^{m} w_{jk} + 10$. The number of item types was fixed throughout the experiments ($q = 6$), and the number of dimensions of the knapsacks was varied twice in the BMKP and fixed in the MMKP ($m = 5$, $m = 10$). For each item, the weight of each dimension was drawn randomly from the interval $[0, 10]$. The bound b_k of item types $k = 1, \ldots, 6$ was randomly drawn in the BMKP experiments and fixed in the MMKP experiments. The random intervals and bounds are discussed in each experiment.

The generated items sets were tested for knapsacks with different capacities. [23] introduced the term, the degree of constraint slackness. We used the formula $s_j = c_j / \sum_{k=1}^{q} w_{jk} \cdot b_k$, where, s_j is the slackness ratio of the constraint j from [1]. The slackness $s_j, \forall j = 1, \ldots, m$ was drawn from the intervals $[0.40, 0.60]$, $[0.60, 0.80]$, $[0.80, 1]$ and $[0.40, 1]$.

5.2 BMKP

Due to the relatively long running time of the algorithm, the number of instances tested of each set is considered small. The bound b_k was drawn randomly in these experiments from the intervals $[1, 20]$ and $[1, 50]$. As a result, the total number of items was not determined earlier. Figure 1a through Fig. 5b shows the correlation between the run time and the total number of items, the box plots show the run time distribution. We can observe the following from the experiments:

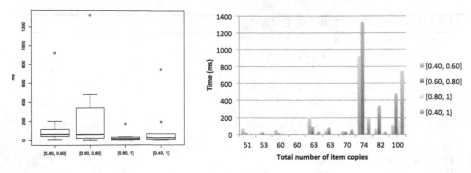

(a) Distribution of run times.   (b) Run time vs. total number of item copies.

Fig. 1. Run time of 10 uncorrelated BMKP instances, $m = 5$, $b_k = [1, 20]$.

1. From Fig. 1a through Fig. 5a we can observe that instances with constraint slackness ratios in the interval [0.80, 1] are generally easier to solve.
2. There is a sharp rise in the execution time of the algorithm, when the number of total item copies is around 200. See Figs. 2b, 4b and 5b.
3. The execution time of uncorrelated problems is greater than the execution time of strongly correlated problems when the number of constraints is 5, as shown in Figs. 2a and 3a.
4. The execution time of strongly correlated problems is greater than the execution time of uncorrelated problems when the number of constraints is 10, as shown in Figs. 4a and 5a.
5. In correlated instances with slackness ratios drawn from the interval [0.40, 1], the increase in the number of constraints make the problem significantly harder to solve, see Figs. 3a and 5a.

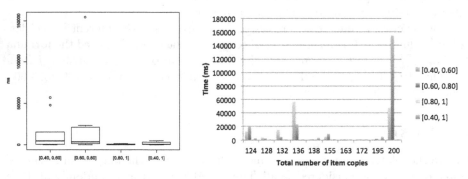

(a) Distribution of run times.   (b) Run time vs. total number of item copies.

Fig. 2. Run time of 10 uncorrelated BMKP instances, $m = 5$, $b_k = [1, 50]$.

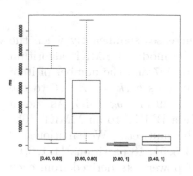
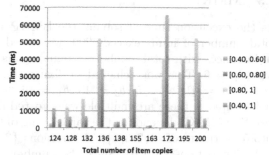

(a) Distribution of run times.   (b) Run time vs. total number of item copies.

Fig. 3. Run time of 10 strongly correlated BMKP instances, $m = 5$, $b_k = [1, 50]$.

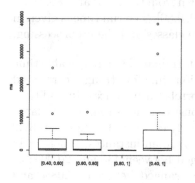
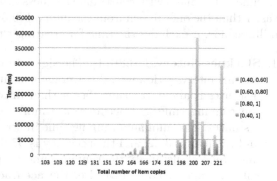

(a) Distribution of run times.   (b) Run time vs. total number of item copies.

Fig. 4. Run time of 15 uncorrelated BMKP instances, $m = 10$, $b_k = [1, 50]$.

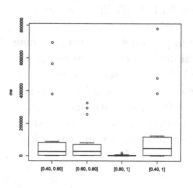
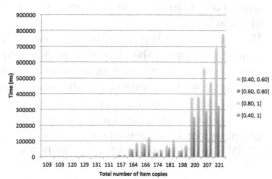

(a) Distribution of run times.   (b) Run time vs. total number of item copies.

Fig. 5. Run time of 15 strongly correlated BMKP instances, $m = 10$, $b_k = [1, 50]$.

5.3   MMKP

As the execution time of solving the BMKP increases significantly when the total number of items exceeds 200, we tested the modified EMKP algorithm on instances with total number of items equals to 207 and the number of item types $q = 6$. This was achieved by fixing the bounds $b_k, k = 1, \ldots, 6$ to the values: $b_1 = 41$, $b_2 = 5$, $b_3 = 43$, $b_4 = 16$, $b_5 = 49$ and $b_6 = 53$. As shown in Example 1, there are multiple ways to reduce a BMKP to an MMKP. The resulting MMKP depends on the partitioning of the multiset C. We partitioned C into 5 partitions of $\{1, 2, 3, 3\}$, 16 partitions $\{3, 4, 5, 5\}$, 18 partitions $\{1, 1, 6, 6\}$ and 17 partitions $\{3, 5, 6\}$. Since the number of power sets derived from each partition is exponential to the number of elements, we reduced the number of power sets by repeating elements in partitions. As an example, $|\mathcal{P}\{1, 2, 3, 3\}| = 12$ while $|\mathcal{P}\{1, 2, 3, 4\}| = 16$.

The results of the experiments can be grouped depending on the knapsack slackness. Instances with constraint slackness drawn from the interval $[0.80, 1]$ are easier than the ones drawn from the interval $[0.60, 0.80]$. The run time is given in milliseconds, it excludes the time for creating the classes and the preprocessing.

1. **Slackness interval $[0.80, 1]$.** The algorithm terminated in a reasonable time for this interval. However, the average execution time for strongly correlated instances is about 150 times faster than uncorrelated instances. In addition, the running time and accuracy are more consistent in strongly correlated instances. The minimum running time in strongly correlated instances is 37.2 and the max is 38.2, and the accuracy is 97.06% in all instances. Whereas, in uncorrelated instances, the running time ranged between 435 and 20,995 ms, with average $5, 557.4$. Likewise, the accuracy ranged between 86.08% and 98.84% with average 94.45%.
2. **Slackness interval $[0.60, 0.80]$.** The running time was considerably large in most instances. As with the slackness interval $[0.80, 1]$, the algorithm is more consistent when ran on strongly correlated instances. The average run time was 1,035,985 ms and the accuracy ranged from 93.15% 95.83% with average of 95.56%.

We ran the experiments again to measure the improvement in accuracy over time. By stopping the algorithm at different times, we can make use of the existence of the fictitous item in the unassigned classes. In strongly correlated instances, we were able to get the same approximations for all instances in 0.5 ms, while in uncorrelated instances, at 1,000 ms, the average accuracy was 85.55%. This figure improved by 0.40% at time 20,000 ms. was a slight improvement in some of the instances. The average accuracy increased from 85.55% at 1,000 ms to 85.95% at 20, 000 ms.

5.4   Summary

We evaluated two reductions of the CSG problem for MR-TTGs, the BMKP and MMKP. We found that the run time of solving the BMKP depends on three factors: the correlation of the value of task types with the resource requirements, the total number of tasks and the slackness of the resources available in the environment compared to the ones required by all tasks. When evaluating the MMKP reduction, we aimed to address instances with total number of tasks greater than 200. The algorithm's accuracy and running time were consistent for the strongly correlated instances, which are considered harder to solve [15]. Moreover, the run time for instances with slackness drawn from the interval [0.80, 1] was significantly less than the running time for the slackness interval [0.6, 0.8] and the accuracy was about 10% higher. We obtained better results when running the modified EMKP algorithm on instances with slackness interval drawn from [0.60, 0.80]. The strongly correlated instances needed 0.5 ms to reach average accuracy of 95% while the uncorrelated instances needed 1,000 ms to reach average accuracy of 86%.

6   Conclusions and Future Work

We proposed the MR-TTG model and studied the problem of maximising the social welfare in settings allowing overlapping coalitions. Our model is capable of handling multiple resource types divisible into integral units. In addition, two knapsack reductions of the problem were proposed and evaluated; the BMKP and the MMKP. Empirical evaluation showed that the MMKP reduction is more efficient in solving particular instances of the problem than the BMKP. However, as shown in Sect. 5.3, the MMKP reduction was tested using one possible partition. In our future work, we will further analyse the reduction to determine the characteristics of partitions effective in solving specific instances of the problem. To this end, we will run experiments to solve multiple MMKP reductions using more advanced algorithms and ILP solvers.

References

1. Akçay, Y., Li, H., Xu, S.H.: Greedy algorithm for the general multidimensional knapsack problem. Ann. Oper. Res. **150**(1), 17–29 (2007)
2. Aumann, R.J., Dreze, J.H.: Cooperative games with coalition structures. Int. J. Game Theor. **3**(4), 217–237 (1974)
3. Bachrach, Y., Meir, R., Jung, K., Kohli, P.: Coalitional structure generation in skill games. In: AAAI, vol. 10, pp. 703–708 (2010)
4. Bachrach, Y., Rosenschein, J.S.: Coalitional skill games. In: AAMAS, vol. 2, 1023–1030 (2008)
5. Bing, H., Leblet, J., Simon, G.: Hard multidimensional multiple choice knapsack problems, an empirical study. Comput. Oper. Res. **37**(1), 172–181 (2010)
6. Chalkiadakis, G., Elkind, E., Markakis, E., Polukarov, M., Jennings, N.R.: Cooperative games with overlapping coalitions. JAIR **39**(1), 179–216 (2010)
7. Dang, V.D., Dash, R.K., Rogers, A., Jennings, N.R.: Overlapping coalition formation for efficient data fusion in multi-sensor networks. In: AAAI, pp. 635–640 (2006)

8. Dang, V.D., Jennings, N.R.: Coalition structure generation in task-based settings. In: ECAI, pp. 210–214 (2006)
9. Dantzig, G.B.: Discrete-variable extremum problems. Oper. Res. **5**(2), 266–288 (1957)
10. Di, B., Wang, T., Song, L., Han, Z.: Incentive mechanism for collaborative smartphone sensing using overlapping coalition formation games. In: GLOBECOM, pp. 1705–1710 (2013)
11. Dobson, G.: Worst-case analysis of greedy heuristics for integer programming with nonnegative data. Math. Oper. Res. **7**(4), 515–531 (1982)
12. Gillies, D.B.: Solutions to general non-zero-sum games. In: Tucker, A.W., Luce, R.D. (eds.) Contributions to the Theory of Games, vol. 4, pp. 47–85. Princeton University Press, Princeton (1959)
13. Habib, F.R., Polukarov, M., Gerding, E.H.: Optimising social welfare in multi-resource threshold task games: Appendix (2017). https://eprints.soton.ac.uk/413650/
14. Pisinger, D.: A fast algorithm for strongly correlated knapsack problems. Discrete Appl. Math. **89**(1–3), 197–212 (1998)
15. Pisinger, D.: Where are the hard knapsack problems? Comput. Oper. Res. **32**(9), 2271–2284 (2005)
16. Sbihi, A.: A best first search exact algorithm for the multiple-choice multidimensional knapsack problem. J. Comb. Optim. **13**(4), 337–351 (2007)
17. Shapley, L.S.: A value for n-person games. In: Tucker, A.W., Kuhn, H.W. (eds.) Contributions to the Theory of Games, vol. 2, pp. 307–317. Princeton University Press, Princeton (1953)
18. Shehory, O., Kraus, S.: Formation of overlapping coalitions for precedence-ordered task-execution among autonomous agents. In: ICMAS, pp. 330–337 (1996)
19. Shehory, O., Kraus, S.: Methods for task allocation via agent coalition formation. Artif. Intell. **101**(1–2), 165–200 (1998)
20. Tran-Thanh, L., Nguyen, T.D., Rahwan, T., Rogers, A., Jennings, N.R.: An efficient vector-based representation for coalitional games. In: AAAI, pp. 383–389 (2013)
21. Wang, T., Song, L., Han, Z., Saad, W.: Overlapping coalitional games for collaborative sensing in cognitive radio networks. In: WCNC, pp. 4118–4123. IEEE (2013)
22. Wooldridge, M., Dunne, P.E.: On the computational complexity of coalitional resource games. J. Artif. Intell. **170**(10), 835–871 (2006)
23. Zanakis, S.H.: Heuristic 0–1 linear programming: an experimental comparison of three methods. Manag. Sci. **24**(1), 91–104 (1977)
24. Zhang, Z., Song, L., Han, Z., Saad, W.: Coalitional games with overlapping coalitions for interference management in small cell networks. IEEE Trans. Wirel. Commun. **13**(5), 2659–2669 (2014)
25. Zick, Y., Chalkiadakis, G., Elkind, E.: Overlapping coalition formation games: charting the tractability frontier. In: AAMAS, vol. 2, pp. 787–794 (2012)
26. Zick, Y., Elkind, E.: Arbitrators in overlapping coalition formation games. In: AAMAS, vol. 1, pp. 55–62 (2011)

Speed up Automated Mechanism Design by Sampling Worst-Case Profiles: An Application to Competitive VCG Redistribution Mechanism for Public Project Problem

Mingyu Guo[1]([✉]) and Hong Shen[1,2]

[1] School of Computer Science, University of Adelaide, Adelaide, Australia
{mingyu.guo,hong.shen}@adelaide.edu.au
[2] School of Data and Computer Science, Sun Yat-Sen University, Guangzhou, China

Abstract. Computationally Feasible Automated Mechanism Design (CFAMD) combines manual mechanism design and optimization.

In CFAMD, we focus on a parameterized family of strategy-proof mechanisms, and then optimize within the family by adjusting the parameters. This transforms mechanism design (functional optimization) into value optimization, as we only need to optimize over the parameters.

Under CFAMD, given a mechanism (characterized by a list of parameters), we need to be able to efficiently evaluate the mechanism's performance. Otherwise, parameter optimization is computationally impractical when the number of parameters is large.

We propose a new technique for speeding up CFAMD for worst-case objectives. Our technique builds up a set of worst-case type profiles, with which we can efficiently approximate a mechanism's worst-case performance. The new technique allows us to apply CFAMD to cases where mechanism performance evaluation is computationally expensive.

We demonstrate the effectiveness of our approach by applying it to the design of competitive VCG redistribution mechanism for public project problem. This is a well studied mechanism design problem. Several competitive mechanisms have already been proposed. With our new technique, we are able to achieve better competitive ratios than previous results.

Keywords: Automated mechanism design · VCG redistribution mechanisms · Dominant strategy implementation · Groves mechanisms · Public good provision

1 Introduction

1.1 Automated Mechanism Design

Automated Mechanism Design (AMD) [1] studies how to use computational techniques to design new mechanisms. AMD is a core topic of algorithmic game

© Springer International Publishing AG 2017
B. An et al. (Eds.): PRIMA 2017, LNAI 10621, pp. 127–142, 2017.
https://doi.org/10.1007/978-3-319-69131-2_8

theory and has attracted significant attention from both computer science and economics community. It has also helped deliver many successes on a variety of mechanism design topics.

AMD can incorporate different computational approaches. One naive form of AMD simply discretizes the type space, and solves the mechanism design problem as a linear program (LP) or as a mixed-integer program (MIP). Under this naive approach, mechanism properties are enforced by creating inequalities for *every possible type profile*. For example, let us consider a single-item auction with 3 agents, where every agent's type space is $[0, 1]$. We can discretize the type space into $D = \{0, 0.1, \ldots, 0.9, 1\}$. The set of all possible type profiles is then

$$\{(x, y, z)|(x, y, z) \in D^3\}$$

For every type profile, we use $o_{i,x,y,z}$ to denote agent i's chance for winning the item when the type profile is (x, y, z). We use $p_{i,x,y,z}$ to denote agent i's payment when the type profile is (x, y, z). The $o_{i,x,y,z}$ and the $p_{i,x,y,z}$ are the variables of the optimization model. The $o_{i,x,y,z}$ may be continuous or integer variables, which depends on the problem setting. With the above characterization, many mechanism properties can then be expressed using *exponential number*[1] of linear inequalities. For example, the *non-deficit* property states that the agents' total payment should always be nonnegative, which is then

$$\forall(x, y, z) \in D^3, \sum_i p_{i,x,y,z} \geq 0$$

The *strategy-proofness* property states that under the mechanism, an agent can never benefit by misreporting. For agent 1, this is then

$$\forall x' \in D, (x, y, z) \in D^3, xo_{1,x,y,z} - p_{1,x,y,z} \geq xo_{1,x',y,z} - p_{1,x',y,z}$$

Often, the above naive approach is only realistic for tiny problem instances, as dealing with exponential number of constraints is too expensive. Nevertheless, even in this naive form, AMD can be useful, as good mechanisms discovered for tiny instances can help provide insight for more general cases. *Our paper is not based on the aforementioned naive approach, we take on a computationally feasible approach as detailed below.*

1.2   Computationally Feasible Automated Mechanism Design

One particular approach of AMD is Computationally Feasible Automated Mechanism Design (CFAMD) [5], which reduces the computational cost of AMD by combining computation and manual mechanism design. CFAMD works as follows:

- Manually select a parameterized family of strategy-proof mechanisms. Every mechanism inside the family is characterized by t parameters. We use $M(p_1, p_2, \ldots, p_t)$ to denote the mechanism characterized by the parameters p_1 to p_t.

---

[1] In terms of the number of agents.

- Given a setting, the task of optimizing over all mechanisms is often an impossible task, as we often cannot even characterize all feasible mechanisms.[2] Under CFAMD, we focus on the parameterized family and optimize by adjusting the parameters. This is computationally much easier as we are no longer dealing with a functional optimization problem. We only need to solve a value optimization problem where we optimize over the parameters.
- If the parameterized family is selected to be general enough, then the *locally* optimal mechanism within the parameterized family can perform close to (or is competitive against) the *globally* optimal mechanism over all possible mechanisms.
- There is often a trade-off between mechanism performance[3] and computational cost. It is easy to see that a more general parameterized family leads to better performance for the resulting mechanism. Meanwhile, it is also often the case that a more general parameterized family makes the optimization process computationally more expensive.

Guo and Conitzer [5] summarized many successful applications of CFAMD, including Likhodedov and Sandholm [12,13] for revenue-maximizing combinatorial auctions, Guo and Conitzer [4,8] for optimal VCG redistribution mechanisms for multi-unit auctions, and Guo and Conitzer [7] for mechanism design without payments.

One crucial presumption of CFAMD is that given the p_i, we are able to evaluate the performance of the corresponding mechanism $M(p_1, p_2, \ldots, p_t)$. Without this presumption, we have no clue on how to adjust the parameters. Furthermore, in practise, we need to be able to evaluate the performance of a mechanism *fast*. For example, if every mechanism is characterized by 20 parameters and we need $O(n^5)$ time complexity to evaluate one mechanism (characterized by one set of parameters), then parameter optimization is too expensive to be practical.

We use PE to denote the task of performance evaluation: given a set of parameters, evaluate the performance of the corresponding mechanism. To apply CFAMD, we need to pick a parameterized family of mechanisms that is general enough for achieving reasonable mechanism performance. Meanwhile, the family needs to be restrictive enough to ensure that PE is efficient.

1.3   Speed up CFAMD by Sampling Worst-Case Profiles

This paper proposes a new technique for speeding up CFAMD. We will demonstrate the effectiveness of our new technique by applying it to the design of competitive VCG redistribution mechanisms for the public project problem. VCG

---

[2] For example, when it comes to revenue-maximizing combinatorial auction design, we do not have an easy-to-work-with characterization of all combinatorial auctions that are strategy-proof and individually rational.

[3] By performance, we mean how well the mechanism performs with respect to the mechanism design objective. For example, if our objective is to maximize the expected revenue, then a mechanism's performance is the expected revenue under it.

redistribution mechanism for public project problem was first studied in Guo et al. [9]. Naroditskiy et al. [18] and Guo [3] later studied competitive VCG redistribution mechanism for public project problem. Our new technique is able to achieve more competitive mechanisms than previously proposed competitive mechanisms.

Below we summarize our new technique. We focus on mechanism design with worst-case objectives (e.g., maximizing competitive ratios).

- Our new technique aims to speed up CFAMD. We still need to manually select a parameterized family of strategy-proof mechanisms.

  Like under CFAMD, given a set of parameters, we need to be able to evaluate the performance of the corresponding mechanism, using a calculation process called PE. In this paper, performance of a mechanism refers to its competitive ratio (to be formally defined later).

  Under classic CFAMD, PE needs to be fast because we have to frequently call it whenever we change the mechanism parameters. For example, if we use a simple hill-climbing algorithm for adjusting the mechanism parameters, then we need to call PE to re-evaluate the mechanism performance every time we move the parameters.

  Under our new technique, PE is allowed to be computationally expensive, as we only need to call it infrequently. It should be noted that by allowing PE to be expensive, we are essentially allowing the parameterized mechanism family to be more general than before, which then means that we are able to achieve better mechanism objectives.

- Under CFAMD, we optimize over the mechanism parameters and solve for the optimal mechanism (the optimal set of parameters). For example, we may start from some parameter values, and run a hill-climbing process to obtain a final set of parameter values.

  We observe that we do not need to calculate the *exact* performance of the "intermediate" mechanisms during the optimization process. It is much faster to rely on *performance estimation* during optimization.

  For worst-case objectives (e.g., maximizing competitive ratios), to calculate a mechanism's exact worst-case performance, we either need to go over all possible type profiles, which gets very expensive (there are usually exponential number of type profiles), or we need to rely on complex analysis to pinpoint the worst cases, which is not always achievable.[4]

  One the other hand, it is much easier to *estimate* a mechanism's worst-case performance instead: we focus our attention to a set of *profile samples*, by assuming that the mechanism's worst-case performance (among all type profiles) is close to the worst-case (among only the profile samples).

- The larger the set of profile samples gets, the more accurate our estimation becomes. On the other hand, the larger the set gets, the more expensive is the estimation process. We want to keep the set small, to ensure fast computation. As a result, we need to carefully select a small set of "useful" profile samples that makes the estimation accurate.

---

[4] Even if it is achievable, the overall process may still be computationally expensive.

We start from an initial set of profile samples S. The initial value of S is not important. We can randomly generate a small set of type profiles to be S. Based on S, we can estimate a mechanism's worst-case performance (by assuming that the worst-case among S is close to the worst-case among all type profiles). We denote the estimation process by PE(S). Using PE(S), we solve for the optimal $M(p_1, p_2, \ldots, p_t)$ that has the best worst-case performance considering only type profiles in S. Let $M(p_1, p_2, \ldots, p_t)$'s worst-case performance be α_S. We keep in mind that α_S is obtained via estimation, by only considering type profiles among S. This optimization process is easier because we resort to performance estimation instead of exact performance evaluation. We then run exact performance evaluation (PE) on the resulting mechanism $M(p_1, p_2, \ldots, p_t)$ to calculate its exact worst-case performance α and the worst-case type profile θ.

If α and α_S are very close, then we stop our algorithm and consider α to be the resulting performance. The reason is that α_S is obtained by only considering the profile samples, so α_S can serve as an upperbound on the actual worst-case performance. If α is close to the upperbound, then it is already accurate.

α_S may also be quite off from α, because α_S was obtained via estimation, and in our estimation, we failed to consider θ. That is, the type profile θ is an important extreme point that we should consider. We keep a record of the best α achieved and denote it as α^*. We add θ into S and repeat the parameter optimization until we cannot improve α^* any further.

Our new technique speeds up the original CFAMD approach for two reasons. One reason already mentioned above is that, for the most part, we replaced the expensive PE process by the cheaper PE(S) process. Another equally import reason is that if we focus on type profiles from a small set S, it is also much easier to solve for the optimal mechanism parameters. For the mechanism design problem studied in this paper, without the new technique, parameter optimization is an unstructured multi-dimensional optimization problem, which requires methods such as hill-climbing. With the new technique, we can use a linear program to help obtain the optimal parameters. (To optimize a list of parameters, LP is much easier than less-structured methods such as hill-climbing.)

2   Model Description

For the rest of this paper, we focus on designing competitive VCG redistribution mechanism for public project problem. With the help of our new technique, we are able to discover mechanisms with better competitive ratios compared to previous results.

2.1   VCG Redistribution Mechanism for Public Project Problem

The public project problem is a classic mechanism design model [14–16]. In this model, n agents need to decide whether or not to build a public project (*e.g.*, a new airport). There are only two outcomes: *build* or *not build*. The cost of the project is 1. If the agents decide to build, then everyone benefits from the project. We use θ_i ($0 \leq \theta_i \leq 1$) to denote agent i's valuation for the project (if it is built).[5] If the agents decide not to build, then everyone saves her share of the cost, which equals $1/n$. In summary, for agent i, her valuation is either θ_i (if the project is built) or $1/n$ (if the project is not built).

Ideally, an efficient decision for the public project problem is that we should build if and only if the agents' total valuation for the project exceeds the total cost (*e.g.*, $\sum \theta_i \geq 1$). Of course, in order to calculate the agents' total valuation, we need the agents to truthfully reveal their private types. For the above reasoning, we focus on mechanisms that are efficient and strategy-proof. It turns out that for the public project problem, a mechanism is efficient and strategy-proof if and only if it is a Groves mechanism [11].

For the public project problem, Groves mechanisms[6] work as follows:

- Build if and only if $\sum_i \theta_i \geq 1$.
- Agent i receives $\sum_{j \neq i} \theta_j - h(\theta_{-i})$ (payment) if the decision is to build. Agent i receives $(n-1)/n - h(\theta_{-i})$ if the decision is not to build. Here, h is an arbitrary function and θ_{-i} refers to the types from the agents other than i herself.

A Groves mechanism is characterized by the function h. Every Groves mechanism is efficient and strategy-proof. Another mechanism property that we wish to enforce in this paper is the non-deficit property. That is, we do not require external funding to run the mechanism. A Groves mechanism is non-deficit if and only if the total payment received is non-positive, that is:

If the decision is to build ($\sum_i \theta_i \geq 1$), then

$$\sum_i \sum_{j \neq i} \theta_j - \sum_i h(\theta_{-i}) = (n-1) \sum_i \theta_i - \sum_i h(\theta_{-i}) \leq 0$$

If the decision is not to build ($\sum_i \theta_i \leq 1$), then

$$\sum_i (n-1)/n - \sum_i h(\theta_{-i}) = (n-1) - \sum_i h(\theta_{-i}) \leq 0$$

Combining the above, we have that a Groves mechanism is non-deficit if and only if for all type profiles

$$(n-1) \max\{\sum_i \theta_i, 1\} \leq \sum_i h(\theta_{-i})$$

---

[5] Naroditskiy *et al.* [18] proved that it is without loss of generality to assume that every agent's type is bounded above by the project cost, as any competitive mechanism can be easily generalized to cases without this constraint, and still keeps the same competitive ratio.

[6] For our setting, it is without loss of generality to focus on anonymous mechanisms [9].

We adopt the notation from Naroditskiy *et al.* [18]. Given a type profile θ, we use $S(\theta)$ to denote $\max\{\sum_i \theta_i, 1\}$. The non-deficit property is then

$$\forall \theta, (n-1)S(\theta) \leq \sum_i h(\theta_{-i})$$

Under the Groves mechanism, agent i's utility equals $\sum_i \theta_i - h(\theta_{-i})$ if the decision is to build, and her utility equals $1 - h(\theta_{-i})$ if the decision is not to build. That is, agent i's utility equals $S(\theta) - h(\theta_{-i})$. The social welfare (total utility considering payments) is then

$$nS(\theta) - \sum_i h(\theta_{-i})$$

Non-deficit Groves mechanisms are sometimes also called the VCG redistribution mechanisms. In this paper, we focus on non-deficit mechanisms, so we will use the two terms ("VCG redistribution mechanisms" and "Groves mechanisms") interchangeably.[7]

Even though every VCG redistribution mechanism is efficient, the agents' social welfare under a VCG redistribution mechanism can be very low due to the high payments. For example, the VCG mechanism (*aka*, the Clarke mechanism) itself is a VCG redistribution mechanism, characterized by $h(\theta_{-i}) = \max\{\sum_{j \neq i} \theta_j, (n-1)/n\}$. Let us consider the type profile $(1, 0, \ldots, 0)$. The social welfare under this type profile equals

$$nS(\theta) - \sum_i h(\theta_{-i}) = n - (n-1)/n - \sum_{i>1} 1 = 1/n$$

That is, the social welfare approaches 0 as n approaches infinity. In this paper, we aim to find VCG redistribution mechanisms that maximize social welfare for the public project problem.

2.2 Competitive VCG Redistribution Mechanism for Public Project Problem

VCG redistribution mechanisms have been widely studied for various resource allocation settings, such as multi-unit auctions and heterogeneous-item auctions [2,4,6,8,9,17]. They have also been studied for the public project problem [3,9,10,18]. Among the previous studies, Naroditskiy *et al.* [18] and Guo [3]

---

[7] The name "VCG redistribution mechanisms" emphasizes on the fact that a non-deficit Groves mechanism can be interpreted as a two step process, where we first allocate and charge payments according to the VCG mechanism (*aka*, the Clarke mechanism), and then we redistribute the VCG payments back to the agents. An agent's redistribution does not depend on her own bid, which ensures that the redistribution amount does not affect an agent's incentives. We also need to ensure that the agents' total redistribution received is never more than the total VCG payment collected, which is to ensure the non-deficit property.

are the closest related to this paper. Naroditskiy *et al.* [18] first studied "competitive" VCG redistribution mechanisms for public project problem, by borrowing the definition of competitive VCG redistribution mechanism from Moulin [17]. Moulin [17] observes that the notion of maximizing social welfare is not a well-defined one, as social welfare depends on the agents' type profile. A mechanism may achieve high social welfare for some type profiles, but not for the others. This leads to the study of competitive VCG redistribution mechanisms.

Definition 1 *(Due to Moulin [17]).* A VCG redistribution mechanism is competitive if its achieved social welfare guarantees a constant fraction of the first-best social welfare, no matter what the actual type profile is. The constant fraction is called the mechanism's *competitive ratio*.

The first-best social welfare is defined as the optimal social welfare assuming that the agents act unselfishly.

Under the public project problem, if the agents act unselfishly, then the first-best social welfare is achieved by the following mechanism:[8]

- Build the project if and only if the agents' total valuation exceeds the total cost.
- The agents don't have to pay any payments because no payments are needed to enforce strategy-proofness for unselfish agents.

As a result, the first-best social welfare under a type profile θ is simply $S(\theta)$. A VCG redistribution mechanism characterized by function h is α-competitive if and only if

$$\forall \theta, nS(\theta) - \sum_i h(\theta_{-i}) \geq \alpha S(\theta)$$

Combining the non-deficit constraint, we have

$$\forall \theta, (n-1)S(\theta) \leq \sum_i h(\theta_{-i}) \leq (n-\alpha)S(\theta) \tag{1}$$

We focus on mechanisms that are strategy-proof, efficient, and non-deficit, which implies that we are focusing on the VCG redistribution mechanisms. Since every VCG redistribution mechanism is characterized by a h function, our problem is then to design h that satisfies Inequality 1 and maximizes the competitive ratio α.

Naroditskiy *et al.* [18] derived the optimal VCG redistribution mechanism for the case of 3 agents. The optimal mechanism is characterized by the following h function, and the optimal competitive ratio is $\alpha = 2/3$.

$$h(\theta_{-i}) = \frac{5}{6}T(\theta_{-i}, 1) + \frac{2}{3}T(\theta_{-i}, \frac{1}{2}) - \frac{1}{3}T(\theta^1_{-i}, \frac{1}{2}) - \frac{1}{3}$$

---

[8] It should be noted that this mechanism is only used as a benchmark. The competitive ratio can be interpreted as the ratio between "best social welfare for selfish agents" and "best social welfare for unselfish agents".

Here, $T(\theta_{-i}, b)$ is defined as the maximum between "the sum of the types among θ_{-i}" and constant b. $T(\theta^1_{-i}, b)$ is defined as the maximum between "the highest type among θ_{-i}" and constant b.

Unfortunately, the technique used for deriving the above does not generalize to cases with more than three agents. For more than three agents, Naroditskiy *et al.* [18] proposed a *conjectured* upper bound on the optimal competitive ratio. Naroditskiy *et al.* [18] also proposed heuristic-based mechanisms. These mechanisms were *conjectured* to be competitive for *4 to 6 agents*.

Guo [3] proposed a VCG redistribution mechanism that is proven to be competitive. When n approaches infinity, the competitive ratio is at least

$$\lim_{n \to \infty} (1 - U(n) + L(n)) = 0.102$$

where

$$U(n) = \frac{1}{n-1} + \frac{n-1}{4n} + \frac{4(n+1)^3}{27n(n-1)^2}$$

$$L(n) = \min\{\frac{1}{n-1} - \frac{1}{n} - \frac{(n-1)^2}{4n^2}, \frac{1}{n-1} + \frac{1}{2n} - \frac{1}{2}\} - \frac{n-2}{n(n-1)}$$

It should be noted that the above bound is only useful for large n. When $n = 3$, $1 - U(n) + L(n)$ is negative. Nevertheless, for small n, the mechanism proposed by Guo [3] can be evaluated numerically to show that they have positive competitive ratios.

Using our new technique, we find another optimal mechanism for the case of three agents. That is, we discover that the optimal mechanism is not unique when $n = 3$. For $n > 3$, we found competitive VCG redistribution mechanisms with better competitive ratios. We leave the details to Sect. 4.

3   Technical Details

In this section, we present all technique details for solving for competitive VCG redistribution mechanisms for the public project problem. We will make use of our new technique for speeding up CFAMD by sampling worst-case type profiles.

3.1   Parameterized Family

We recall that for three agents, Naroditskiy *et al.* [18] showed that the following mechanism has the optimal competitive ratio:

$$h(\theta_{-i}) = \frac{5}{6}T(\theta_{-i}, 1) + \frac{2}{3}T(\theta_{-i}, \frac{1}{2}) - \frac{1}{3}T(\theta^1_{-i}, \frac{1}{2}) - \frac{1}{3}$$

$T(\theta_{-i}, b)$ is defined as the maximum between "the sum of the types among θ_{-i}" and constant b. $T(\theta^1_{-i}, b)$ is defined as the maximum between "the highest type among θ_{-i}" and constant b.

We introduce a slightly modified notation $T(\theta^a_{-i}, b)$, which is defined as the maximum between "the sum of the a highest types among θ_{-i}" and constant b. Here, a is an integer between 1 and $n-1$. Obviously, $T(\theta_{-i}, b)$ is just $T(\theta^{n-1}_{-i}, b)$.

We introduce the following parameterized family of mechanisms:

$$h(\theta_{-i}) = \sum_{t=1}^{k} c_t T(\theta^{a_t}_{-i}, b_t) + c_0$$

As shown above, a mechanism is characterized by $3k+1$ parameters: the c_t, the a_t, and the b_t. The a_t are integers between 0 and $n-1$. The b_t are nonnegative. It is obvious to see that the aforementioned optimal mechanism for three agents belongs to this family. As will be demonstrated in Sect. 4, we are able to identify mechanisms with good competitive ratios by focusing on this family. The family also satisfies the presumption that given a mechanism inside the family, we are able to evaluate its competitive ratio.

3.2   Performance Evaluation

In this subsection, we discuss how to evaluate the performance of a mechanism, given its parameters.

Let M be the mechanism to be evaluated. Let M's parameters be as follows

$$h(\theta_{-i}) = \sum_{t=1}^{k} c_t T(\theta^{a_t}_{-i}, b_t) + c_0$$

According to Inequality 1, h must satisfy

$$\forall \theta, (n-1)S(\theta) \leq \sum_i h(\theta_{-i}) \leq (n-\alpha)S(\theta)$$

We define value Δ_L as follows:

$$\Delta_L = \max_\theta \left((n-1)S(\theta) - \sum_i h(\theta_{-i}) \right) \tag{2}$$

Δ_L is M's maximum deficit. If $\Delta_L > 0$, then it means that sometimes M incurs deficit. To remedy this, we can increase the constant payment term c_0 by Δ_L/n and focus on the new mechanism instead. Similarly, if $\Delta_L < 0$, then it means that there is always positive surplus. To maximize social welfare, we could decrease c_0 by $|\Delta_L|/n$. That is, it never hurts to replace c_0 by $c_0 + \frac{\Delta_L}{n}$. So for any M, before evaluating its competitive ratio, we first calculate Δ_L and then update the constant term of h. After the update, the maximum deficit is exactly 0. That is, after the update, the mechanism is sure to be non-deficit.

Of course, evaluating Δ_L is not an easy task. We use Θ to denote the set of all type profiles. Without loss of generality, we assume $1 \geq \theta_1 \geq \theta_2 \geq \ldots \geq \theta_n \geq 0$.

$$\Theta = \{(\theta_1, \theta_2, \ldots, \theta_n) | 1 \geq \theta_1 \geq \theta_2 \geq \ldots \geq \theta_n \geq 0\}$$

Define

$$\theta^L = \arg\max_{\theta \in \Theta} \left((n-1)S(\theta) - \sum_i h(\theta_{-i}) \right)$$

Define B to be whether or not the project is built under θ^L. That is, B is True if $\sum_i \theta_i^L \geq 1$. B is False otherwise.

Besides the constant term c_0, h contains k terms. For agent i, the t-th term is $c_t T(\theta_{-i}^{a_t}, b_t)$. We observe that $\theta_{-i}^{a_t}$ is nondecreasing in i. Define G_t to be the following:

$$G_t = \left| \{i | T(\theta_{-i}^{a_t}, b_t) = b_t, i \in \{1, 2, \cdots, n\}\} \right|$$

G_t is an integer. For i from 1 to G_t, $T(\theta_{-i}^{a_t}, b_t)$ is simply b_t. For i from $G_t + 1$ to n, $T(\theta_{-i}^{a_t}, b_t)$ is just the sum of the a_t highest types among θ_{-i}.

Given θ^L, it is easy to calculate $(B, G_1, G_2, \ldots, G_k)$. On the other hand, given $(B, G_1, G_2, \ldots, G_k)$, we can also calculate θ^L using the following linear program.

Variables: $1 \geq \theta_1 \geq \theta_2 \geq \ldots \geq \theta_n \geq 0$
Maximize: $(n-1)S(\theta) - \sum_i h(\theta_{-i})$
Subject to:
If B is True, then $\sum_i \theta_i \geq 1$.
If B is False, then $\sum_i \theta_i \leq 1$.
For all t, $\sum \theta_{-G_t}^{a_t} \leq b_t$ and $\sum \theta_{-(G_t+1)}^{a_t} \geq b_t$

The above is a linear program with n variables. The objective function involves S and h. Since we assume $(B, G_1, G_2, \ldots, G_k)$ is known. Both S and h can be rewritten as linear functions. The constraints are for ensuring that the assumed values of $(B, G_1, G_2, \ldots, G_k)$ are not violated. There are $2k + 1$ constraints, besides the constraints on the range and relative order of the θ_i.

We showed how to calculate θ^L given $(B, G_1, G_2, \ldots, G_k)$. But how do we calculate θ^L without the values of B and the G_t?

B can take two possible values. G_t can take $n + 1$ possible values (0 to n). The total possible values for $(B, G_1, G_2, \ldots, G_k)$ is $2(n+1)^k$. We can go over all possible values of $(B, G_1, G_2, \ldots, G_k)$ in order to find θ^L. Solving one linear program takes $O(poly(n))$ complexity. We need to solve $O(n^k)$ linear programs. Altogether, the complexity is $O(n^k poly(n))$, which is feasible when k is small.

We then define function Δ_R to be as follows:

$$\Delta_R(\alpha) = \max_\theta \left(\sum_i h(\theta_{-i}) - (n - \alpha)S(\theta) \right) \tag{3}$$

Given a mechanism M (updated according to the calculation of Δ_L), if $\Delta_R(\alpha) \leq 0$, then we can claim that M's competitive ratio is at least α. Since $\Delta_R(\alpha)$ is a monotone function and $0 \leq \alpha \leq 1$, we can use binary search to solve the equation $\Delta_R(\alpha) = 0$. Binary search only needs ten iterations to ensure an error of at most one tenth of one percent ($\frac{1}{2^{10}}$). We can reapply our method for calculating Δ_L to the calculation of $\Delta_R(\alpha)$. Suppose we only run ten iterations of binary search, the complexity of this step is still $O(n^k poly(n))$. We use θ^R to denote the worst-case type profile when we stop the algorithm for calculating $\Delta_R(\alpha)$.

In summary, given a mechanism, we are able to calculate its competitive ratio. The time complexity is $O(n^k poly(n))$. If k is slightly large, then the process becomes very expensive. Fortunately, as mentioned in Subsect. 1.3, we only need to call this process infrequently during the whole algorithm. As a side product of the optimization process, we identified two worst-case type profiles θ^L and θ^R. In the next subsection, we describe how we can use these worst-case type profiles to estimate mechanism performance, which is for speeding up CFAMD.

3.3   Performance Estimation and Parameter Optimization

Due to the fact that PE (evaluating a mechanism's competitive ratio) takes $O(n^k poly(n))$ complexity, we resort to estimation when optimizing over the parameters, to avoid calling PE frequently.

To optimize within the parameterized family, we break down our whole task into two subtasks.

- Task 1: Choose k terms of form $T(\theta_{-i}^{a_t}, b_t)$. Each term is characterized by an integer a_t and a nonnegative real value b_t.
- Task 2: Choose k coefficients (the c_t) for combining these terms, and also choose c_0.

We first focus on Task 2. We assume we have already completed Task 1. That is, given k terms, we want to set the c_t only. This again can be done via a linear program.

As mentioned in Subsect. 1.3, we initialize our algorithm with a set of profile samples. We will use these profile samples to optimize over the mechanism parameters. Once we find an optimal mechanism, which is based estimation, we evaluate its exact competitive ratio using the expensive process described in the previous subsection. If the estimated competitive ratio is quite off from the actual competitive ratio, then we add the corresponding worst-case type profiles (θ^L and θ^R) into our samples. Overtime, we have better and better estimations (and as a result, better and better competitive ratios).

For our problem, we start with only $n + 1$ type profiles:

$$S = \{(\underbrace{1, \ldots, 1}_{x}, 0, \ldots, 0) | x \in \{0, 1, \ldots, n\}\}$$

Given a set of profile samples S and k terms, to set the c_i, we use the following linear program:

Variables: $c_0, \ldots, c_k$ and α
Maximize: α
Subject to:
For every $\theta \in S$,

$$(n-1)S(\theta) \leq \sum_i \left(\sum_{t=1}^{k} c_t T(\theta_{-i}^{a_t}, b_t) + c_0 \right) \leq (n-\alpha)S(\theta)$$

The above is a linear program because for every $\theta \in S$, $S(\theta)$ is a constant. For all i, all t, all $\theta \in S$, $T(\theta_{-i}^{a_t}, b_t)$ is also a constant. The above linear program involves only $k+1$ variables, but it has a lot of constraints if S is large. To keep the size of S small, when we add type profile θ_{new} to S, we remove all profiles in S that are close to θ_{new}. Two type profiles' difference is defined as $Diff(\theta, \theta') = \sum_i |\theta_i - \theta_i'|$. We will show in Sect. 4 that in our experiments, the size of S is usually only a few hundred before the algorithm terminates. So it is generally quite cheap to solve the above linear program.

Above we showed how to carry out Task 2 given the result of Task 1. Next, we go back to Task 1. We approach Task 1 as follows:

- **Expansion and Consolidation:** We randomly generate $2k$ terms and use the above linear program to set the optimal coefficients $(c_1, c_2, \ldots, c_{2k})$. We sort the c_i according to their absolute values. We drop terms with low absolute values. The rationale is that if $|c_t|$ is small, then the t-th term is not playing an important role in our mechanism. We repeat this process: expand the list of terms by adding randomly generated ones and then drop those less important terms determined by the linear program. The end result is a list of k "important" terms.
- **Hill Climbing:** After the above expansion and consolidation process, we end up with k terms. We perform "final touch" by running hill climbing on these terms' parameters (namely, the a_t and the b_t).

4   Numerical Results

For three agents, using our technique, besides the optimal mechanism described in Naroditskiy et al. [18]. We identified another optimal mechanism:

$$h(\theta_{-i}) = T(\theta_{-i}, \frac{2}{3}) + \frac{1}{2}T(\theta_{-i}, 1) - \frac{1}{2}T(\theta_{-i}^1, \frac{2}{3}) - \frac{1}{6}$$

For four or more agents, we compare our mechanism to the following previous results:

- The heuristic-based SBR mechanism [18]: This mechanism's competitive ratio was numerically calculated for four to six agents. The authors discretized an agent's type space into $\{0, 1/N, 2/N, \ldots, 1\}$, and examined all type profiles in order to calculate a mechanism's competitive ratio. For at most six agents, the authors were able to push N large enough for the resulting competitive ratio to be numerically stable.

- The ABR[9] mechanism [3]: This mechanism's competitive ratio was proven to be above 0.102 when n goes to infinity. For small n, we can numerically calculate its competitive ratio.
- The *conjectured* optimal upper bound on a mechanism's competitive ratio, proposed in [18]: It should be noted that the upper bound has been proven to be valid. The authors conjectured that it is strict.

We present the competitive ratios of different mechanisms in the following table. It should be noted that for our mechanism, the competitive ratios presented are the ratios we have achieved after running our algorithm for a reasonable amount of time. When presenting our mechanisms, the integer inside the parenthesis is the number of samples in S when the algorithm first identifies the first two significant digits of the competitive ratio.[10] In our simulation, we picked $k = 5$.

n	SBR	ABR	Our mechanism	Upper bound
3	0.333	0.334	0.667 (38)	0.667
4	0.354	0.459	0.600 (603)	0.666
5	0.360	0.402	0.545 (298)	0.714
6	0.394	0.386	0.497 (444)	0.868
7	n too large	0.360	0.465 (514)	0.748
8	n too large	0.352	0.444 (276)	0.755
9	n too large	0.339	0.422 (621)	0.772
10	n too large	0.336	0.405 (184)	0.882

5   Conclusion

We proposed a new technique for speeding up Computationally Feasible Automated Mechanism Design (CFAMD) for worst-case objectives. We demonstrated the effectiveness of our approach by applying it to the design of competitive VCG redistribution mechanism for public project problem. With our new technique, we achieved better competitive ratios than previous results.

---

[9] Guo [3] proposed only one mechanism, which is based on averaging the VCG payments. Therefore, we call the proposed mechanism average-based redistribution (ABR) mechanism.

[10] For example, on a i7-4770 desktop, for $n = 3$, it takes a few seconds to obtain a mechanism with competitive ratio at least 0.66, but it takes a lot longer to push for more significant digits.

Acknowledgment. This work is supported by Research Initiative Grant of Sun Yat-Sen University under Project 985 and Australian Research Council Discovery Project DP150104871.

References

1. Conitzer, V., Sandholm, T.: Complexity of mechanism design. In: Proceedings of the 18th Annual Conference on Uncertainty in Artificial Intelligence (UAI), Edmonton, Canada, pp. 103–110 (2002)
2. Gujar, S., Narahari, Y.: Redistribution mechanisms for assignment of heterogeneous objects. J. Artif. Intell. Res. **41**, 131–154 (2011)
3. Guo, M.: Competitive VCG redistribution mechanism for public project problem. In: Baldoni, M., Chopra, A.K., Son, T.C., Hirayama, K., Torroni, P. (eds.) PRIMA 2016. LNCS, vol. 9862, pp. 279–294. Springer, Cham (2016). doi:10.1007/978-3-319-44832-9_17
4. Guo, M., Conitzer, V.: Worst-case optimal redistribution of VCG payments in multi-unit auctions. Games Econ. Behav. **67**(1), 69–98 (2009)
5. Guo, M., Conitzer, V.: Computationally feasible automated mechanism design: General approach and case studies. In: Proceedings of the National Conference on Artificial Intelligence (AAAI), Atlanta, GA, USA, pp. 1676–1679 (2010). NECTAR track
6. Guo, M., Conitzer, V.: Optimal-in-expectation redistribution mechanisms. Artif. Intell. **174**(5–6), 363–381 (2010)
7. Guo, M., Conitzer, V.: Strategy-proof allocation of multiple items between two agents without payments or priors. In: Proceedings of the Ninth International Joint Conference on Autonomous Agents and Multi-Agent Systems (AAMAS), Toronto, Canada, pp. 881–888 (2010)
8. Guo, M., Conitzer, V.: Better redistribution with inefficient allocation in multi-unit auctions. Artif. Intell. **216**, 287–308 (2014)
9. Guo, M., Markakis, E., Apt, K.R., Conitzer, V.: Undominated groves mechanisms. J. Artif. Intell. Res. **46**, 129–163 (2013)
10. Guo, M., Naroditskiy, V., Conitzer, V., Greenwald, A., Jennings, N.R.: Budget-balanced and nearly efficient randomized mechanisms: Public goods and beyond. In: Proceedings of the Seventh Workshop on Internet and Network Economics (WINE), Singapore (2011)
11. Holmström, B.: Groves' scheme on restricted domains. Econometrica **47**(5), 1137–1144 (1979)
12. Likhodedov, A., Sandholm, T.: Methods for boosting revenue in combinatorial auctions. In: Proceedings of the National Conference on Artificial Intelligence (AAAI), San Jose, CA, USA, pp. 232–237 (2004)
13. Likhodedov, A., Sandholm, T.: Approximating revenue-maximizing combinatorial auctions. In: Proceedings of the National Conference on Artificial Intelligence (AAAI), Pittsburgh, PA, USA (2005)
14. Mas-Colell, A., Whinston, M., Green, J.R.: Microeconomic Theory. Oxford University Press, New York (1995)
15. Moore, J.: General Equilibrium and Welfare Economics: An Introduction. Springer, Heidelberg (2006). doi:10.1007/978-3-540-32223-8
16. Moulin, H.: Axioms of Cooperative Decision Making. Cambridge University Press, Cambridge (1988)

17. Moulin, H.: Almost budget-balanced VCG mechanisms to assign multiple objects. J. Econ. Theor. **144**(1), 96–119 (2009)
18. Naroditskiy, V., Guo, M., Dufton, L., Polukarov, M., Jennings, N.R.: Redistribution of VCG payments in public project problems. In: Proceedings of the Eighth Workshop on Internet and Network Economics (WINE), Liverpool (2012)

Coalition Structure Generation for Partition Function Games Utilizing a Concise Graphical Representation

Aolong Zha[1](✉), Kazuki Nomoto[1], Suguru Ueda[2], Miyuki Koshimura[1], Yuko Sakurai[3], and Makoto Yokoo[1]

[1] Kyushu University, Fukuoka, Japan
{aolong.zha,koshi,yokoo}@inf.kyushu-u.ac.jp,
nomoto@agent.inf.kyushu-u.ac.jp
[2] Saga University, Saga, Japan
sgrueda@cc.saga-u.ac.jp
[3] National Institute of Advanced Industrial Science and Technology, Tokyo, Japan
yuko.sakurai@aist.go.jp

Abstract. Coalition Structure Generation (CSG), a main research issue in the domain of coalition games, involves partitioning agents into exhaustive and disjoint coalitions to optimize the social welfare. The advent of compact representation schemes, such as Partition Decision Trees (PDTs), promotes the efficiency of solving CSG problems.

This paper studies the CSG problem for partition function games (PFGs) which are coalitional games with externalities. In PFGs, each value of a coalition depends on how the other agents are partitioned. We apply PDTs to represent PFGs and present two methods to solve CSG problems: a depth-first branch-and-bound algorithm and MaxSAT encoding.

Keywords: Coalition structure generation · Partition function game · Depth-first branch-and-bound · Maximum satisfiability

1 Introduction

Coalitional games are abstract models of cooperation that have been scrutinized in AI and multi-agent systems (MAS) research communities. A coalition of agents can sometimes accomplish things that individual agents cannot do or perhaps do them more efficiently. The Coalition Structure Generation (CSG) problem is one major research topic in coalitional games. The CSG problem involves partitioning a set of agents into coalitions to maximize social surplus, that is, the sum of the rewards of all coalitions [1]. There are various real CSG applications, such as distributed vehicle routing [15], multi-sensor networks [3], and so on. The CSG problem is equivalent to a complete set partition problem [19], and many MAS researchers have developed efficient algorithms to solve it.

© Springer International Publishing AG 2017
B. An et al. (Eds.): PRIMA 2017, LNAI 10621, pp. 143–159, 2017.
https://doi.org/10.1007/978-3-319-69131-2_9

There are two major types of the coalitional games: characteristic function games (CFGs) and partition function games (PFGs). CFGs are coalitional games with no externalities in which the value of a coalition is determined based on its members. On the other hand, PFGs are coalitional games with externalities in which the value of a coalition in partition function games depends on how the other agents are partitioned.

In this paper, we study CSG problems in PFGs. While various CSG algorithms for CFGs have been developed by many MAS researchers, there are few CSG algorithms for PFGs. However, in practice, CSG problems for coalitional games with externalities have been receiving greater attention. For example, consider restructuring and consolidating multiple companies in a market. If several competitors are merged into a single entity, the competitors of this new large company might lose sales. The market must consider the best way of restructuring the merged companies to maximize expected sales. Such a problem is represented as a PFG.

In PFGs, the input of a coalitional game is a black-box function called a partition function that maps an embedded coalition (a coalition and a coalition structure containing the coalition) to its value. Representing an arbitrary partition function explicitly requires $\Theta(n^n)$ numbers, which are prohibitive for a large n. Recently, several concise representation schemes for a partition function have been proposed [11,13,16].

In this paper, we utilize a graphical representation of PFGs called partition decision trees (PDTs) proposed by Skibski *et al.* [16]. In PDTs, multiple rules are graphically represented using rooted directed trees. Each rule consists of a condition for the partitioning agents and their positive/negative values. We propose the following new methods to solve CSG problems by PDTs representations: (1) a depth-first branch-and-bound (DFBnB) algorithm for PDTs, (2) a DFBnB algorithm for modified PDTs, and (3) MaxSAT encoding. We experimentally show that our algorithm can reasonably solve CSG problems.

The rest of this paper is organized as follows. Related works are introduced in Sect. 2. CSG definitions and notations are given in Sect. 3. In Sect. 4, we overview PDTs. In Sects. 5 and 6, we respectively propose our DFBnB algorithm and MaxSAT encoding for PDTs, followed by an empirical evaluation in Sect. 7. Some final conclusions are presented in Sect. 8.

2   Related Works

In this section, we briefly introduce works related to this paper.

The model of coalitional games with externalities, called *partition function games* (PFGs) [17], faces many computational challenges. PFGs require prohibitive time and space to represent the game. Since a coalition's value depends on the coalition structure to which it belongs, thus we must take into account all possible coalition structures. So the complexity of representing PFGs is $\omega(n^{\frac{n}{2}})$ and $O(n^n)$, where n is the number of agents [14].

For concise representation, Michalak *et al.* [11] proposed embedded marginal contribution nets (embedded MC-nets) by extending marginal contribution nets

(MC-nets) [4], which represent characteristic function games (CFGs) to handle externalities. Michalak *et al.* [10] developed a concise representation called Weighted MC-Nets, which was also an extension of MC-nets. Recently, Skibski *et al.* [16] proposed another representation called Partition Decision Trees (PDTs) and developed efficient algorithms that compute the extensions of the Shapley value in polynomial time. In Sect. 4, we precisely explain PDTs.

Rahwan *et al.* [13] first considered the CSG problem in PFGs, but their problem settings were the restricted classes of PFGs, where only positive or negative externalities exist. Ueda *et al.* [18] developed MIP formulations for CSG problems in PFGs, which were represented by embedded MC-nets. In their settings, the number of agents equaled the number of rules, which was at most 150. Thus, their experimental setting was sparse in terms of the number of embedded MC-nets rules to evaluate against the number of all possible rules.

Liao *et al.* presented two MaxSAT encodings for CSGs represented by MC-nets or embedded MC-nets: agent-based and rule-based [7–9]. The former encodes agent relations into propositional logic while the latter encodes a rule relation-based approach [12,18]. Their experimental results show that agent-based encoding is more time efficient than a relation-based approach. In this paper, we present MaxSAT encoding with the agent-based approach.

3   Preliminaries

Let $N = \{1, 2, \ldots, n\}$ be a set of agents. Coalition structure CS is defined as a partition of N into disjoint and exhaustive coalitions.

Definition 1 (Coalition Structure). *Coalition structure $CS = \{S_1, S_2, \ldots\}$ satisfies the following conditions:*

$$\forall i, j \ (i \neq j), \ S_i \cap S_j = \emptyset, \ \bigcup_{S_i \in CS} S_i = N.$$

Denote the set of all coalition structures as $\Pi(N)$.

In this paper, we study coalitional games with externalities, which are called *partition function games*. In partition function games, the value of a coalition depends on how other agents have been partitioned.

Definition 2 (Embedded Coalition). *An embedded coalition consists of a pair of (S, CS), where $S \in CS \in \Pi(N)$. The set of all embedded coalitions over N is denoted by $M(N)$, i.e., $M := \{(S, CS) : CS \in \Pi(N), S \in CS\}$.*

Next we define a partition function.

Definition 3 (Partition Function). *A partition function assigns a real-valued payoff to every embedded coalition: $w : M \to \mathbb{R}$, where $w(\emptyset, CS) = 0$ for all CS.*

For any coalition structure $CS \in \Pi(N)$, the value of CS is calculated by

$$W(CS) = \sum_{S_i \in CS} w(S_i, CS).$$

In general, a grand coalition that contains every agent in a single coalition is not always an optimal coalition structure. Thus, we have to find the optimal coalition structure that maximizes the sum of the values of partition functions. We define a coalition structure generation (CSG) problem in partition function games as follows.

Definition 4 (Coalition Structure Generation (CSG) problem). *For set of agents N, a coalition structure generation problem is to find optimal coalition structure CS^* such that*

$$CS^* \in \arg \max_{CS \in \Pi(N)} W(CS).$$

Here we show an example of partition function games.

Example 1. Assume four agents, $N = \{a_1, a_2, a_3, a_4\}$. A partition function is given as follows:

$w(\{a_1\}, \{\{a_1\}, \{a_2\}, \{a_3\}, \{a_4\}\}) = 1,$ $w(\{a_2\}, \{\{a_1\}, \{a_2\}, \{a_3\}, \{a_4\}\}) = 1,$
$w(\{a_3\}, \{\{a_1\}, \{a_2\}, \{a_3\}, \{a_4\}\}) = 0,$ $w(\{a_4\}, \{\{a_1\}, \{a_2\}, \{a_3\}, \{a_4\}\}) = 1,$
$w(\{a_1, a_2\}, \{\{a_1, a_2\}, \{a_3\}, \{a_4\}\}) = 0,$ $w(\{a_3\}, \{\{a_1, a_2\}, \{a_3\}, \{a_4\}\}) = 0,$
$w(\{a_4\}, \{\{a_1, a_2\}, \{a_3\}, \{a_4\}\}) = 0,$ $w(\{a_1\}, \{\{a_1\}, \{a_2, a_4\}, \{a_3\}\}) = 0,$
$w(\{a_2, a_4\}, \{\{a_1\}, \{a_2, a_4\}, \{a_3\}\}) = 0,$ $w(\{a_3\}, \{\{a_1\}, \{a_2, a_4\}, \{a_3\}\}) = 0,$
$w(\{a_1\}, \{\{a_1\}, \{a_2\}, \{a_3, a_4\}\}) = 1,$ $w(\{a_2\}, \{\{a_1\}, \{a_2\}, \{a_3, a_4\}\}) = 1,$
$w(\{a_3, a_4\}, \{\{a_1\}, \{a_2\}, \{a_3, a_4\}\}) = 3,$ $w(\{a_1, a_3\}, \{\{a_1, a_3\}, \{a_2\}, \{a_4\}\}) = 1,$
$w(\{a_2\}, \{\{a_1, a_3\}, \{a_2\}, \{a_4\}\}) = 1,$ $w(\{a_4\}, \{\{a_1, a_3\}, \{a_2\}, \{a_4\}\}) = 1,$
$w(\{a_1\}, \{\{a_1\}, \{a_2, a_3\}, \{a_4\}\}) = 1,$ $w(\{a_2, a_3\}, \{\{a_1\}, \{a_2, a_3\}, \{a_4\}\}) = 1,$
$w(\{a_4\}, \{\{a_1\}, \{a_2, a_3\}, \{a_4\}\}) = 1,$ $w(\{a_1, a_4\}, \{\{a_1, a_4\}, \{a_2\}, \{a_3\}\}) = 2,$
$w(\{a_2\}, \{\{a_1, a_4\}, \{a_2\}, \{a_3\}\}) = -1,$ $w(\{a_3\}, \{\{a_1, a_4\}, \{a_2\}, \{a_3\}\}) = 3,$
$w(\{a_1\}, \{\{a_1\}, \{a_2, a_3, a_4\}\}) = 0,$ $w(\{a_2, a_3, a_4\}, \{\{a_1\}, \{a_2, a_3, a_4\}\}) = 2,$
$w(\{a_2\}, \{\{a_2\}, \{a_1, a_3, a_4\}\}) = -1,$ $w(\{a_1, a_3, a_4\}, \{\{a_2\}, \{a_1, a_3, a_4\}\}) = 0,$
$w(\{a_3\}, \{\{a_3\}, \{a_1, a_2, a_4\}\}) = 3,$ $w(\{a_1, a_2, a_4\}, \{\{a_3\}, \{a_1, a_2, a_4\}\}) = 4,$
$w(\{a_4\}, \{\{a_4\}, \{a_1, a_2, a_3\}\}) = 0,$ $w(\{a_1, a_2, a_3\}, \{\{a_4\}, \{a_1, a_2, a_3\}\}) = 4,$
$w(\{a_1, a_2\}, \{\{a_1, a_2\}, \{a_3, a_4\}\}) = 0,$ $w(\{a_3, a_4\}, \{\{a_1, a_2\}, \{a_3, a_4\}\}) = 2,$
$w(\{a_1, a_3\}, \{\{a_1, a_3\}, \{a_2, a_4\}\}) = 0,$ $w(\{a_2, a_4\}, \{\{a_1, a_3\}, \{a_2, a_4\}\}) = 0,$
$w(\{a_1, a_4\}, \{\{a_1, a_4\}, \{a_2, a_3\}\}) = 2,$ $w(\{a_2, a_3\}, \{\{a_1, a_4\}, \{a_2, a_3\}\}) = 2,$
$w(\{a_1, a_2, a_3, a_4\}, \{\{a_1, a_2, a_3, a_4\}\}) = 6.$

In this example, optimal coalition structure CS^* is $\{\{a_1, a_2, a_4\}, \{a_3\}\}$, and its value is 7.

4   Partition Decision Trees (PDT)

In this section, we introduce Partition Decision Trees (PDT), which were proposed by Skibski *et al.* (2015) [16].

In PDT, the game is represented by a set of PDT rules. A single PDT rule consists of a rooted directed tree, where non-leaf nodes are labeled with agent names, leaf nodes are labeled with payoff vectors, and edges are labeled with numbers that correspond to coalitions. Formally, PDT rule T is tuple $T = \langle V, E, x, f_V, f_E \rangle$, where

- (V, E) is a directed tree with root x;
- $f_V : V \to N \cup \mathbb{R}^{|N|}$ is a label function for nodes;
- $f_E : E \to \{1, 2, \ldots, |N|\}$ is a label function for edges, assuming that $f_V(v) \in N$ for every non-leaf v and $f_V(v) \in \mathbb{R}^N$ for every leaf v.

Given rule T, let $P(T)$ be the set of paths from the root to any leaf and let $last(p)$ denote the last leaf node in any $p \in P(T)$. Now, every path $p = (v_1, v_2, \ldots, v_k) \in P(T)$ represents a partition of agents, where $f_E(v_i, v_{i+1})$ is the number of the coalition to which agent $f_V(v_i)$ belongs. Thus, for every such path,

- all non-leaf nodes on the path are labeled with different agents:

$$|\{f_V(v_1), f_V(v_2), \ldots, f_V(v_{k-1})\}| = k - 1;$$

- for every path from x to v_i, the set of labels on the edges is the set of consecutive natural numbers beginning with 1. Thus, $f_E(v_1, v_2) = 1$, and a label of an edge is not bigger than the maximal label used earlier on this path plus one: $f_E(v_i, v_{i+1}) \leq max_{1 \leq j < i} f_E(v_j, v_{j+1}) + 1$ for $1 \leq i < k$;
- the label of a leaf node is exactly the same size as the number of coalitions: $|f_V(v_k)| = max_{1 \leq j < k} f_E(v_j, v_{j+1})$.

Coalition structure (partition) $CS \in \Pi(N)$ satisfies $p \in P(T)$ denoted by $CS \sim p$, if it covers the partition described by this path. Thus, for any two members of the same coalition that appear on the path, the labels of the outgoing edges are identical. Since paths describe different partitions, no more than one path exists in one PDT rule satisfied by partition CS. If $CS \sim p$, a mapping exists from the coalitions in partition CS to the set of labels of edges with zero: $g_p^{CS} : CS \to \{1, 2, \ldots, max_{1 \leq j < k} f_E(v_j, v_{j+1})\} \cup \{0\}$, where 0 is assigned to coalitions whose agents do not appear on the path.

From mapping g_p^{CS} for $CS \sim p$, for every coalition S embedded in coalition structure CS such that the agents in S appear on path p, there exists a unique value in a payoff node: $f_V(last(p))[g_p^{CS}(S)]$. For $\forall \, CS \sim p, \, \forall \, S \in CS$,

$$\delta_p^{CS}(S) = \begin{cases} f_V(last(p))[g_p^{CS}(S)] & \text{if } g_p^{CS}(S) > 0, \\ 0 & \text{otherwise} \end{cases} \tag{1}$$

The value of coalition S embedded in CS in game v^T, described by PDT rule T, is the value from the path satisfied by P:

$$w^T(S, CS) := \sum_{\substack{p \in \Pi(T), \\ P \sim p}} \delta_p^{CS}(S). \tag{2}$$

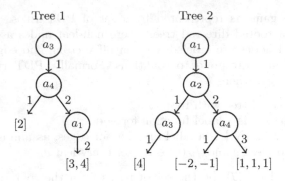

Fig. 1. PDTs of coalitional game given in Example 1

In every PDT rule, at most one path exists that is satisfied by particular coalition structure CS. If $\mathcal{T} = \{T_1, T_2, \ldots\}$ is the set of PDT rules, then game $v^{\mathcal{T}}$, described by set of rules $\mathcal{T}$, is the sum of games described by each of the following rules:

$$w^{\mathcal{T}}(S, CS) := \sum_{T \in \mathcal{T}} w^{T}(S, CS) = \sum_{T \in \mathcal{T}} \sum_{\substack{p \in \Pi(T), \\ CS \sim p}} \delta_p^{CS}(S). \tag{3}$$

Example 2. Figure 1 shows the PDTs of the game given in Example 1. The left-hand rule in Tree 1 indicates that when agents a_3 and a_4 belong to an identical coalition, 2 is added to the value of the coalition that includes a_3 and a_4. The right-hand rule in Tree 1 indicates that when a_3 and a_4 are in different coalitions, but a_4 and a_1 are in an identical coalition, 3 is added to the value of the coalition that includes a_3 and 4 is added to the value of the coalition that includes a_4 and a_1.

The value of coalition structure $W(CS)$ is calculated as the sum of the values of the compatible rules to CS. When CS is $\{\{a_1, a_2, a_3, a_4\}\}$, $W(CS)$ becomes $2 + 4 = 6$ by applying the rules indicated by the right-hand path in Tree 1 and the left-hand path in Tree 2.

PDT representations can be more concise than the existing representations. To represent the same game, Weighted MC-Nets [10] have a rule for every path of the PDT tree (whose size equals the size of the path), and Embedded MC-Nets need a rule for every value in the leaf of every path.

5   Branch-and-Bound Algorithm

In this section, we introduce a depth-first branch-and-bound (DFBnB) algorithm for PDTs and a DFBnB algorithm for modified PDTs.

For an optimization/maximization problem, we must carefully consider how to deal with negative rules. If no negative rule exists, we can straightforwardly solve a CSG problem.

5.1   Naive Algorithm for Positive Rules

When all of the rules are positive, we seek as many compatible rules as possible. Thus, a CSG problem's dilemma is finding a set of compatible rules that maximizes the sum of the values by selecting at most a rule from each tree.

Due to space limitations, we show the outline of our depth-first branch-and-bound (DFBnB) algorithm, which is guaranteed to obtain the optimal coalition structure:

(1) We make a search tree by combining multiple PDTs. We first sort the PDTs by decreasing the average number of coalitions in their rules. In a search tree, a node indicates a rule. All of the rules exist in a single PDT at the same depth. Each rule in the i-th PDT appears at the i-th depth in the search tree. Then we sort the nodes by decreasing their value, i.e., the rule value at each depth. Here we add an empty node with 0-value as the last sibling node. Selecting the empty node indicates that no rule in the PDT is selected during the search.

(2) We apply a depth-first branch-and-bound algorithm to a search tree. Here we restrict the search space with a heuristic function and also check the compatibility among rules on the path. Whenever we go down to a child node, we examine the compatibility between the obtained nodes on a path and the child node. If they are compatible, we expand one grandchild node. Otherwise, we move to a sibling node next to the child node. If there is no sibling node, we expand the sibling node next to the current node. If we reach a leaf node, the rules on the path imply a condition satisfied by the optimal coalition structure.

(3) The obtained result does not imply a concrete coalition structure, since some agents might not appear in the set of rules. Such non-appeared agents do not affect the coalition's values in the result because the agents affecting the result must be examined in the search and appear in the set of rules. Therefore, we can add these non-appeared agents to any coalitions without changing their values. Currently, we add each of them to a coalition selected randomly to generate a concrete coalition structure.

Concerning compatibility between nodes, if we obtain $\{\{a_1, a_4\}, \{a_2\}, \{a_3\}\}$ at the i-th deepest node and the node of the $i+1$-st deepest node is $\{\{a_1, a_2, a_3\}\}$, we cannot combine $\{\{a_1, a_4\}, \{a_2\}, \{a_3\}\}$ with $\{\{a_1, a_2, a_3\}\}$.

5.2   Algorithm Using Modified PDTs

When a negative rule exists in PDTs, finding an optimal coalition structure is not straightforward. When a PDT has a negative rule, we need to examine whether the negative rule is incompatible with the other obtained rules. As a naive method, we first find an optimal set of rules that maximizes the sum of the values by ignoring the existence of the negative rules. If there exists a tree with negative rules in which a positive rule is not selected in an optimal set of rules, we examine whether the obtained rules are incompatible with every

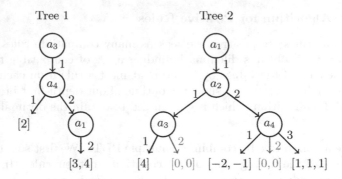

Fig. 2. Modified partition decision trees

negative rule in the tree. Thus, we examine whether the set of obtained rules is compatible with all possible negations of the negative rules. This operation is very complicated, since its computational complexity depends on the number of agents included in the negative rules.

To solve the above difficulty, we modify the description of the PDTs and explicitly represent the rules with a value of 0 when a tree has a negative rule. If the original PDT is concisely represented, the negations of the negative rules are also concisely represented. For modified PDTs, we apply the same search algorithm proposed for the original PDTs in the previous subsection without adding an empty set in procedure (1).

Example 3. Figure 2 shows our modified PDTs. In tree 2, since negative rules exist, we add two rules with the values of 0.

Figure 3 shows a search tree generated by the modified PDTs in Fig. 2. Since Tree 1 has only positive rules, we add an empty node that indicates a set of rules with a value of 0. In a search tree, a node indicates a rule. We sort the nodes by decreasing the node value. For this search tree, we apply a depth-first branch-and-bound algorithm. Whenever we go down to a child node, we examine

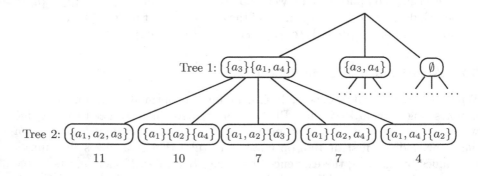

Fig. 3. Search tree

the compatibility between the obtained nodes on a path and the child node. If they are compatible, we expand the grandchild node. Otherwise, we move to a sibling node next to the child node. If no sibling node exits, we expand the sibling node next to the node. If we reach the leaf node, the rules on the path imply a condition satisfied by the optimal coalition structure.

6 MaxSAT Encoding

The Boolean Satisfiability Problem (SAT) was the first problem shown to be NP-complete [2]. SAT is represented by a Boolean formula. Typically, a Boolean formula is expressed in a *Conjunctive Normal Form (CNF)*, which consists of a conjunction (logic *and*) of one or more clauses. A *clause* is a disjunction (logic *or*) of one or more literals, and a *literal* is an occurrence of a Boolean variable or its negation. In this paper, a set of clauses is regarded as a conjunction of all the clauses in the set.

SAT determines whether there exists a variable assignment that satisfies all clauses. Maximum Satisfiability (MaxSAT) is an optimal version of SAT [6]. Also, in practice, the problem instance is typically expressed as a set of hard and soft clauses where each soft clause has a bounded positive numerical *weight*. The problem is to find an assignment that satisfies all the hard clauses and maximizes the sum of the weights of the satisfied soft clauses.

Formally, we denote a MaxSAT formula by $\phi = \{(C_1, w_1), \ldots, (C_m, w_m), C_{m+1}, \ldots, C_{m+m'}\}$ where the first m clauses are soft and the rest are hard. With each soft clause C_i, Boolean variable b_i is associated such that $b_i = 1$ if clause C_i is satisfied and otherwise $b_i = 0$. Solving MaxSAT instance ϕ amounts to finding an assignment that satisfies all $C_{m+1}, \ldots, C_{m+m'}$ and maximizes $\sum_{i=1}^{m} w_i b_i$.

To deal with a relation where two agents are in the same coalition, we introduce Boolean variable $C(i, j)$ for a pair of agents i and j where $i < j$. If i and j are in the same coalition, $C(i, j) = 1$, and otherwise, $C(i, j) = 0$. It is apparent that the relation is transitive, because any three agents, i, j, and k ($1 \leq i < j < k \leq n$), satisfy the following transitive laws: $\neg C(i, j) \vee \neg C(j, k) \vee C(i, k)$, $\neg C(i, j) \vee \neg C(i, k) \vee C(j, k)$, and $\neg C(i, k) \vee \neg C(j, k) \vee C(i, j)$, where n is the number of agents. The number of hard clauses for representing the transitive laws is $n \cdot (n - 1) \cdot (n - 2)/2$.

In MaxSAT encoding, we introduce a soft clause for a leaf in PDT rule T. Let $\pi \in P(T)$ be a path from the root to a leaf in T:

$$\pi : x_1 \xrightarrow{n_1} x_2 \xrightarrow{n_2} \ldots x_{k-1} \xrightarrow{n_{k-1}} [r_1, r_2, \ldots, r_m]$$

where x_i represents an agent, n_i is the coalition number to which x_i belongs, and $[r_1, r_2, \ldots, r_m]$ represents a payoff vector. From π, we build set Ls^π of literals as a minimum set satisfying the following conditions (1) and (2), where $first(n_i)$ denotes the first agent on π belonging to n_i:

(1) When $first(n_i) = x_i$, for all coalition numbers j in π satisfying $1 \leq j < n_i$, $\neg C(first(j), x_i) \in Ls^\pi$ if $first(j) < x_i$, $\neg C(x_i, first(j)) \in Ls^\pi$ if $first(j) > x_i$.

(2) When $first(n_i) \neq x_i$, $C(first(n_i), x_i) \in Ls^\pi$ if $first(n_i) < x_i$, $C(x_i, first(n_i)) \in Ls^\pi$ if $first(n_i) > x_i$.

(1) indicates that if x_i is the first agent belonging to n_i then x_i must not be in any coalition before n_i. (2) indicates that if x_i is not the first agent belonging to n_i then x_i must be in the same coalition as the first agent. Thus, Ls^π denotes a set of literals that hold in any partition satisfying π.

Example 4. Consider Tree 1 in Fig. 1. For left path π_1, $first(1) = a_3$ and $Ls^{\pi_1} = \{C(a_3, a_4)\}$. For right path π_2, $first(1) = a_3$, $first(2) = a_4$, and $Ls^{\pi_2} = \{\neg C(a_3, a_4), C(a_1, a_4)\}$.

Next, consider Tree 2. For left path π_3, $first(1) = a_1$, and $Ls^{\pi_3} = \{C(a_1, a_2), C(a_1, a_3)\}$. For middle path π_4, $first(1) = a_1$, $first(2) = a_2$, and $Ls^{\pi_4} = \{\neg C(a_1, a_2), C(a_1, a_4)\}$. For right path π_5, $first(1) = a_1$, $first(2) = a_2$, $first(3) = a_4$, and $Ls^{\pi_5} = \{\neg C(a_1, a_2), \neg C(a_1, a_4), \neg C(a_2, a_4)\}$.

A soft clause and several hard clauses for path π are introduced with $Ls^\pi = \{L_1, L_2, \ldots, L_l\}$ as follows where $R = \sum_{i=1}^{m} r_i$:

(1) When $R > 0$, a soft clause (b_π, R) is introduced with a newly created variable b_π, and l hard clauses $\neg b_\pi \vee L_i$ $(1 \leq i \leq l)$ are introduced.

(2) When $R < 0$, a soft clause $(\neg L_1 \vee \neg L_2 \vee \cdots \vee \neg L_l, -R)$ is introduced.

(3) When $R = 0$, no clause is introduced.

(1) indicates that we obtain surplus R from a partition satisfying π in which each literal in Ls^π must hold. (2) indicates that we obtain surplus $-R$ from a partition that does not satisfy π. In other words, we do not obtain $-R$ from a partition that satisfies π. That is, we lose when the partition satisfies π. In this way, all negative values Rs in PDT rules are negated. Therefore, after encoding, the final social surplus is $-W_{neg}$ larger than the original one, where W_{neg} is the sum of all negative values.

Example 5. Consider an identical example as Example 4. From the five paths, the following five soft clauses and eight hard clauses are introduced:

	Soft clause	Hard clause
π_1	$(b_{\pi_1}, 2)$	$\neg b_{\pi_1} \vee C(a_3, a_4)$
π_2	$(b_{\pi_2}, 7)$	$\neg b_{\pi_2} \vee \neg C(a_3, a_4)$, $\neg b_{\pi_2} \vee C(a_1, a_4)$
π_3	$(b_{\pi_3}, 4)$	$\neg b_{\pi_3} \vee C(a_1, a_2)$, $\neg b_{\pi_3} \vee C(a_1, a_3)$
π_4	$(C(a_1, a_2) \vee \neg C(a_1, a_4), 3)$	-
π_5	$(b_{\pi_5}, 3)$	$\neg b_{\pi_5} \vee \neg C(a_1, a_2)$, $\neg b_{\pi_5} \vee \neg C(a_1, a_4)$, $\neg b_{\pi_5} \vee \neg C(a_2, a_4)$

7   Experimental Results

We experimentally evaluated the DFBnB performance for modified PDTs (MPDT) and MaxSAT encoding on an Intel Xeon E5 Quad-Core 3.7 GHz processor (with 64 GB RAM) running a Mac OS X 10.10.5 with a 300-second timeout. MPDT is implemented in Java and runs on Java 1.8.0_40. We used a MaxSAT solver QMaxSAT [5] written in C++ and compiled with gcc 5.0.0.

We used randomly generated instances for our evaluation. Problem instances were generated in the following manner. First, make m subsets A_i $(i = 1, \ldots, m)$ of agents randomly to satisfy $\forall i \forall j (i \neq j)(A_i \nsubseteq A_j)$. Second, randomly generate l_i distinct partitions $p_1, \ldots, p_{l_i}$ of A_i, and make PDT rule T_i to represent them. Thus, we obtain m PDT rules whose leaves remained unlabeled. Last, label each leaf of T_i with a payoff vector. Each value in the vector follows two distributions: normal or Normally Distribution Coalition Structures (NDCS). For normal distribution, we uniformly chose a value from $[0, |C|]$ at random, where C is the set of agents corresponding to the value. For NDCS, we chose a value based on the following distribution. Its average is $|C|$, and its standard deviation is $\sqrt{|C|}$. We convert the value to be negative with probability q.

The experiment was performed with the following parameter settings: number (#agents) of agents was 100 or 200 and number (#rules) of PDT rules was 10 or 20. The number (#leaves) of leaves in each rule was chosen from $[15, 25]$ or $[25, 35]$ so that their average was either 20 or 30, respectively. The number of agents in each rule was uniformly chosen from $[7, 13]$ at random. Probability q was 0, 0.2, or 0.4. Thus, we have 24 $(= 2 \times 2 \times 2 \times 3)$ combinations of settings. For each setting, we generated 100 instances.

Tables 1 and 2 respectively show the experimental results with 100 and 200 agents. Notation "TnLl-m" in the first row denotes that the number of PDT rules is n and the number of leaves in each rule is chosen from $[l, m]$. Five numbers are written in each cell. The bottom number surrounded by round brackets indicates the number of instances solved within 300 s. The number in the upper left indicates the average CPU time in seconds. The underlined number in the middle left indicates the standard deviation of the CPU time. The number surrounded by square brackets in the upper right indicates the number of nodes searched by MPDT or the number of unit propagations[1] by MaxSAT. The underlined number surrounded by square brackets in the middle right indicates the standard deviation of the number of nodes for MPDT or the number of unit propagations for MaxSAT.

The CSG problems become more difficult when #rules or #leaves increases in Tables 1 and 2. This is natural. If #rules or #leaves increase, the number of possible combinations of leaves in the PDT rules increases for MPDT, and the number of soft clauses increases for MaxSAT.

We also expected that the problems would become more difficult when #agents increase. But the experimental results indicate that this does not necessarily hold. Look at columns "T10L15-25" and "T10L25-35" in Tables 1 and 2.

---

[1] This corresponds to the space searched for by the solver.

Table 1. {MPDT, MaxSAT} for {uniform, NDCS} distribution with 100 agents

Value distrib.	Solvers	Prob. of neg. value	T10L15-25	T10L25-35	T20L15-25	T20L25-35
uniform	MPDT	$q = 0.0$	1.26 [$6.3E^5$] 2.78 [$1.4E^6$] (100)	2.81 [$1.5E^6$] 7.32 [$4.5E^6$] (100)	119.30 [$7.0E^7$] 75.34 [$4.4E^7$] (35)	144.54 [$8.4E^7$] 48.76 [$3.0E^7$] (4)
		$q = 0.2$	33.46 [$2.4E^7$] 60.33 [$4.3E^7$] (84)	21.14 [$1.4E^7$] 40.38 [$2.8E^7$] (93)	− [−] − [−] (0)	− [−] − [−] (0)
		$q = 0.4$	40.14 [$3.0E^7$] 57.16 [$4.4E^7$] (87)	31.92 [$2.2E^7$] 53.24 [$3.8E^7$] (85)	− [−] − [−] (0)	− [−] − [−] (0)
	MaxSAT	$q = 0.0$	6.41 [$2.1E^7$] 2.42 [$6.7E^6$] (100)	15.51 [$5.4E^7$] 6.92 [$2.0E^7$] (100)	175.85 [$3.3E^8$] 65.90 [$1.1E^8$] (46)	255.18 [$5.2E^8$] 0 [0] (1)
		$q = 0.2$	5.11 [$1.7E^7$] 2.29 [$5.8E^6$] (100)	10.99 [$3.9E^7$] 4.66 [$1.3E^7$] (100)	189.38 [$3.4E^8$] 65.90 [$1.0E^8$] (45)	241.22 [$4.9E^8$] 32.18 [$3.7E^7$] (3)
		$q = 0.4$	3.36 [$1.2E^7$] 1.40 [$3.7E^6$] (100)	7.96 [$2.9E^7$] 2.94 [$8.7E^6$] (100)	161.98 [$2.9E^8$] 65.54 [$1.0E^8$] (80)	228.77 [$4.6E^8$] 54.19 [$9.2E^7$] (9)
NDCS	MPDT	$q = 0.0$	2.69 [$1.5E^6$] 4.67 [$2.9E^6$] (100)	7.50 [$4.1E^6$] 23.40 [$1.4E^7$] (100)	173.48 [$1.1E^8$] 84.50 [$5.5E^7$] (11)	− [−] − [−] (0)
		$q = 0.2$	50.13 [$3.6E^7$] 71.95 [$5.3E^7$] (79)	42.85 [$2.9E^7$] 69.36 [$4.7E^7$] (88)	− [−] − [−] (0)	− [−] − [−] (0)
		$q = 0.4$	33.46 [$2.4E^7$] 54.54 [$3.9E^7$] (83)	39.05 [$2.6E^7$] 63.25 [$4.3E^7$] (80)	− [−] − [−] (0)	− [−] − [−] (0)
	MaxSAT	$q = 0.0$	8.01 [$2.6E^7$] 2.79 [$7.6E^6$] (100)	19.36 [$6.6E^7$] 8.79 [$2.4E^7$] (100)	185.96 [$3.3E^8$] 52.70 [$7.8E^7$] (17)	− [−] − [−] (0)
		$q = 0.2$	6.17 [$2.0E^7$] 2.68 [$7.2E^6$] (100)	13.88 [$4.9E^7$] 5.57 [$1.6E^7$] (100)	206.98 [$3.4E^8$] 66.14 [$9.1E^7$] (24)	− [−] − [−] (0)
		$q = 0.4$	4.20 [$1.4E^7$] 1.74 [$5.0E^6$] (100)	9.70 [$3.5E^7$] 3.39 [$9.7E^6$] (100)	194.99 [$3.2E^8$] 55.73 [$7.5E^7$] (51)	269.95 [$4.9E^8$] 7.17 [$4.3E^7$] (2)

Table 2. {MPDT, MaxSAT} for {uniform, NDCS} distribution with 200 agents

Value distrib.	Solvers	Prob. of neg. value	T10L15-25	T10L25-35	T20L15-25	T20L25-35
uniform	MPDT	$q = 0.0$	0.71 [$1.9E^5$] 2.60 [$7.7E^5$] (100)	0.46 [$1.1E^5$] 2.03 [$5.9E^5$] (100)	173.46 [$5.3E^7$] 87.91 [$2.8E^7$] (5)	63.04 [$1.8E^7$] 9.20 [$1.6E^6$] (3)
		$q = 0.2$	4.46 [$1.5E^6$] 24.36 [$8.5E^6$] (100)	1.54 [$5.0E^5$] 5.88 [$2.2E^6$] (100)	− [−] − [−] (0)	− [−] − [−] (0)
		$q = 0.4$	3.66 [$1.3E^6$] 11.17 [$4.1E^6$] (100)	1.05 [$3.2E^5$] 3.32 [$1.1E^6$] (98)	− [−] − [−] (0)	− [−] − [−] (0)
	MaxSAT	$q = 0.0$	6.32 [$1.3E^7$] 2.51 [$4.8E^6$] (100)	11.21 [$2.9E^7$] 4.67 [$9.8E^6$] (100)	207.39 [$2.7E^8$] 62.27 [$8.1E^7$] (14)	241.87 [$4.0E^8$] 14.76 [$1.9E^7$] (3)
		$q = 0.2$	5.47 [$1.0E^7$] 1.94 [$3.4E^6$] (100)	8.84 [$2.3E^7$] 3.60 [$7.7E^6$] (100)	186.50 [$2.3E^8$] 64.67 [$7.3E^7$] (19)	283.64 [$4.4E^8$] 2.72 [$7.0E^6$] (3)
		$q = 0.4$	4.35 [$7.7E^6$] 2.00 [$3.0E^6$] (100)	6.71 [$1.7E^7$] 2.38 [$5.1E^6$] (100)	198.23 [$2.3E^8$] 59.42 [$6.9E^7$] (46)	213.27 [$3.0E^8$] 51.37 [$6.1E^7$] (12)
NDCS	MPDT	$q = 0.0$	0.78 [$2.2E^5$] 2.93 [$9.5E^5$] (100)	1.76 [$5.4E^5$] 7.83 [$2.5E^6$] (100)	282.63 [$7.8E^7$] 0.90 [$3.5E^6$] (2)	− [−] − [−] (0)
		$q = 0.2$	4.67 [$1.6E^6$] 24.78 [$9.0E^6$] (100)	1.82 [$6.1E^5$] 6.17 [$2.4E^6$] (100)	− [−] − [−] (0)	− [−] − [−] (0)
		$q = 0.4$	2.86 [$9.4E^5$] 12.42 [$4.3E^6$] (100)	2.30 [$7.6E^5$] 8.26 [$3.1E^6$] (99)	− [−] − [−] (0)	− [−] − [−] (0)
	MaxSAT	$q = 0.0$	6.87 [$1.5E^7$] 2.80 [$5.6E^6$] (100)	12.06 [$3.2E^7$] 5.60 [$1.2E^7$] (100)	262.42 [$3.6E^8$] 44.78 [$4.2E^7$] (6)	297.02 [$5.2E^8$] 0 [0] (1)
		$q = 0.2$	5.63 [$1.1E^7$] 2.23 [$4.1E^6$] (100)	9.17 [$2.5E^7$] 3.38 [$7.7E^6$] (100)	240.50 [$3.0E^8$] 46.53 [$6.1E^7$] (7)	280.82 [$4.3E^8$] 10.80 [$1.5E^7$] (2)
		$q = 0.4$	4.31 [$8.2E^6$] 1.56 [$2.8E^6$] (100)	7.11 [$1.8E^7$] 3.18 [$7.0E^6$] (100)	199.66 [$2.3E^8$] 65.25 [$6.2E^7$] (38)	210.04 [$3.1E^8$] 47.32 [$5.9E^7$] (8)

The problems for #agents = 200 are easier than those for #agents = 100 for the following reason. There are 200 agents and 10 PDT rules in this setting. Since the number of agents in each rule is chosen between 7 and 13, approximately half of 200 agents (100 agents) are irrelevant for solving the CSG. This means that solving CSG for the setting is substantially the same as that for 100 agents. Furthermore, quite a few agents belong to more than one rule. This implies that a conflict between the rule combinations rarely happens. Thus, the problems are simplified.

As probability q increases, the CPU time increases for MPDT, but it decreases for MaxSAT. In MPDT, several 0-valued leaves are explicitly added to the PDT rule for its negative valued leaves. This increases the number of combinations to be examined and consumes CPU. On the other hand, for MaxSAT only one soft clause is generated for a negative valued leaf while a soft clause and several hard clauses are generated for a positive valued leaf. This means that MaxSAT solvers generally have to perform fewer inferences for negative valued leaves than those for the positive valued leaves. Thus, the CPU time for MaxSAT decreases as q increases.

Comparing MPDT and MaxSAT, MPDT outperforms MaxSAT when the problem only has positive values ($q = 0$), but MaxSAT outperforms MPDT, and otherwise ($q > 0$). For a PDT rule, the path from the root to a leaf is considered a partial coalition structure. MPDT takes these partial coalition structures one by one from each PDT rule and combines them to make a whole coalition structure. On the other hand, MaxSAT builds such a coalition structure from scratch, which explains why MPDT outperforms MaxSAT when $q = 0$.

Comparing the standard deviations of MPDT and MaxSAT, MPDT is unstable while MaxSAT is stable for solving the CSG. The DFBnB performance heavily depends on the order in which the rules are generally searched. The sorting works well on average but worse in some cases. These worse cases seem to increase the deviations.

Figures 4 and 5 compare two distributions for MPDT and MaxSAT, uniform and NDCS. Each point in the graphs represents a problem instance. Let its coordinate be (x, y). Recall that each leaf in the PDT rule is labeled with a payoff vector whose values follow a normal distribution or NDCS. x indicates the CPU time in seconds for an instance with a normal distribution while y indicates that with NDCS. Therefore, if a point is above the diagonal line, the corresponding instance with NDCS is more difficult than that with a normal distribution.

The instances become more difficult when their leaves are labeled with payoff vectors following NDCS as a whole. This coincides with the comparison between the corresponding average CPU times in Tables 1 and 2. The MPDT points are scattered while those of MaxSAT are gathered. This means that MaxSAT is stable for solving the CSG, as we have already have seen.

We studied a formulation using mixed integer programming. The formulation is basically identical as previous research [18]. Even though we preliminarily

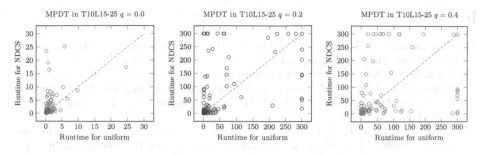

Fig. 4. Uniform vs. NDCS in MPDT

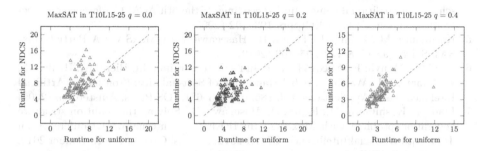

Fig. 5. Uniform vs. NDCS in MaxSAT

evaluated the formulation, we cannot solve any tiny instances that have only five PDT rules within ten minutes.

8   Conclusion

In this paper, we proposed two methods to solve the CSG problem represented by PDTs. One is a DFBnB algorithm (MPDT), and the other is MaxSAT encoding. When PDT rules have negative valued leaves, the MPDT inserts several 0-valued nodes into the PDT rules, while MaxSAT negates both the constraints and the leaf values. In this respect, MaxSAT is probably superior to MPDT when the rules are negative. The experimental results support this superiority: MPDT outperforms MaxSAT when the problem has only positive values, but otherwise MaxSAT outperforms MPDT. Furthermore, MaxSAT is more stable than MPDT for solving the CSG problem.

Future works will do the following: (1) perform more experiments to analyze the features of the methods, (2) improve the MPDT's stableness, and (3) further study the mixed integer programming for CSG.

Acknowledgment. This work was supported by JSPS KAKENHI Grant Numbers JP16K00304, JP17K00307, JP17H00761, JP15H02751.

References

1. Chalkiadakis, G., Elkind, E., Wooldridge, M.: Computational Aspects of Cooperative Game Theory. Morgan and Claypool Publishers, San Rafael (2011)
2. Cook, S.A.: The Complexity of theorem-proving procedures. In: Harrison, M.A., Banerji, R.B., Ullman, J.D. (eds.) Proceedings of the 3rd Annual ACM Symposium on Theory of Computing, 3–5 May 1971, Shaker Heights, Ohio, USA, pp. 151–158. ACM (1971)
3. Dang, V.D., Dash, R.K., Rogers, A., Jennings, N.R.: Overlapping coalition formation for efficient data fusion in multi-sensor networks. In: Proceedings of the 21st National Conference on Artificial Intelligence (AAAI), pp. 635–640 (2006)
4. Ieong, S., Shoham, Y.: Marginal contribution nets: a compact representation scheme for coalitional games. In: Proceedings of the 6th ACM Conference on Electronic Commerce (ACM EC), pp. 193–202 (2005)
5. Koshimura, M., Zhang, T., Fujita, H., Hasegawa, R.: QMaxSAT: A Partial MaxSAT Solver. JSAT 8(1/2), 95–100 (2012)
6. Li, C.M., Manyà, F.: MaxSAT, hard and soft constraints. In: Biere, A., Heule, M., van Maaren, H., Walsh, T. (eds.) Handbook of Satisfiability: Frontiers in Artificial Intelligence and Applications, vol. 185, pp. 613–631. IOS Press, Amsterdam (2009)
7. Liao, X., Koshimura, M., Fujita, H., Hasegawa, R.: Solving the coalition structure generation problem with MaxSAT. In: IEEE 24th International Conference on Tools with Artificial Intelligence, ICTAI 2012, Athens, Greece, 7–9 November 2012, pp. 910–915. IEEE Computer Society (2012)
8. Liao, X., Koshimura, M., Fujita, H., Hasegawa, R.: Extending MaxSAT to solve the coalition structure generation problem with externalities based on agent relations. IEICE Trans. 97–D(7), 1812–1821 (2014)
9. Liao, X., Koshimura, M., Fujita, H., Hasegawa, R.: MaxSAT encoding for MC-net-based coalition structure generation problem with externalities. IEICE Trans. 97–D(7), 1781–1789 (2014)
10. Michalak, T., Rahwan, T., Marciniak, D., Szamotulski, M., Jennings, N.: Computational aspects of extending the shapley value to coalitional games with externalities. In: ECAI, pp. 197–202 (2010)
11. Michalak, T.P., Marciniak, D., Szamotulski, M., Rahwan, T., Wooldridge, M., McBurney, P., Jennings, N.R.: A logic-based representation for coalitional games with externalities. In: Proceedings of the 9th International Conference on Autonomous Agents and Multiagent Systems (AAMAS), pp. 125–132 (2010)
12. Ohta, N., Conitzer, V., Ichimura, R., Sakurai, Y., Iwasaki, A., Yokoo, M.: Coalition structure generation utilizing compact characteristic function representations. In: Gent, I.P. (ed.) CP 2009. LNCS, vol. 5732, pp. 623–638. Springer, Heidelberg (2009). doi:10.1007/978-3-642-04244-7_49
13. Rahwan, T., Michalak, T.P., Jennings, N.R., Wooldridge, M., McBurney, P.: Coalition structure generation in multi-agent systems with positive and negative externalities. In: Proceedings of the 21st International Joint Conference on Artificial Intelligence (IJCAI), pp. 257–263 (2009)
14. Sandholm, T., Larson, K., Andersson, M., Shehory, O., Tohmé, F.: Coalition structure generation with worst case guarantees. Artif. Intell. 111(1–2), 209–238 (1999)
15. Sandholm, T., Lesser, V.R.: Coalitions among computationally bounded agents. Artif. Intell. 94(1–2), 99–137 (1997)
16. Skibski, O., Michalak, T., Sakurai, Y., Wooldridge, M., Yokoo, M.: A Graphical Representation for Games in Partition Function Form. In: Proceedings of the Twenty-Ninth AAAI Conference on Artificial Intelligence, pp. 1036–1042 (2015)

17. Thrall, R.M., Lucas, W.F.: N-Person games in partition function form. Naval Res. Logistics Q. **10**(1), 281–298 (1963)
18. Ueda, S., Hasegawa, T., Hashimoto, N., Ohta, N., Iwasaki, A., Yokoo, M.: Handling negative value rules in mc-net-based coalition structure generation. In: Proceedings of the 11th International Conference on Autonomous Agents and Multiagent Systems (AAMAS), pp. 795–804 (2012)
19. Yeh, D.Y.: A dynamic programming approach to the complete set partitioning problem. BIT Numer. Math. **26**(4), 467–474 (1986)

Applications of Agents
and Multiagent Systems

Rename and False-Name Manipulations in Discrete Facility Location with Optional Preferences

Tomohiro Ono[✉], Taiki Todo, and Makoto Yokoo

Graduate School of Information Science and Electrical Engineering,
Kyushu University, Fukuoka, Japan
t-ono@agent.inf.kyushu-u.ac.jp, {todo,yokoo}@inf.kyushu-u.ac.jp

Abstract. We consider the problem of locating facilities on a discrete acyclic graph, where agents' locations are publicly known and the agents are requested to report their demands, i.e., which facilities they want to access. In this paper, we study the effect of manipulations by agents that utilize vacant vertices. Such manipulations are called rename or false-name manipulations in game theory and mechanism design literature. For locating one facility on a path, we carefully compare our model with traditional ones and clarify their differences by pointing out that some existing results in the traditional model do not carry over to our model. For locating two facilities, we analyze the existing and new mechanisms from a perspective of approximation ratio and provide non-trivial lower bounds. Finally, we introduce a new mechanism design model where richer information is available to the mechanism designer and show that under the new model false-name-proofness does not always imply population monotonicity.

1 Introduction

Designing mechanisms that achieve desirable properties is a central research topic in the literature of mechanism design and social choice theory, and recently has also attracted considerable attention from AI researchers and computer scientists. Several papers published in top-tier AI venues over the past decades have studied various mechanism design problems, such as voting, auctions, and matching.

The facility location problem is one special case of voting, where agents' preferences are restricted so that well-known impossibility results do not hold. For example, in the traditional model of locating one facility on a continuous line, there is a class of strategy-proof and anonymous mechanisms [6], while in general voting contexts, any strategy-proof mechanism must be dictatorial, under some natural assumptions. Various facility location models have also been studied from the perspective of approximation algorithms [3,4,8,10,15].

The facility location model we study in this paper is inspired by the one proposed by Serafino et al. [9]. In their model, the mechanism designer is trying

© Springer International Publishing AG 2017
B. An et al. (Eds.): PRIMA 2017, LNAI 10621, pp. 163–179, 2017.
https://doi.org/10.1007/978-3-319-69131-2_10

to build two heterogeneous facilities on discrete acyclic graphs. The mechanism designer knows the locations of the agents, but she does not know their *demands*, i.e., which facilities they want to use. A facility location mechanism for such a model is thus a function to decide the locations of two facilities based on agents' demands.

Since the mechanism designer only knows the agents' locations In other words, the agents' demands are private information, and they are allowed to misreport their demands if they want to do so. A mechanism is said to be *strategy-proof* if truthfully reporting their demands to it is a dominant strategy equilibrium, i.e., the best response for every agent, regardless of the other agents' behavior.

Misreporting one's demand is just a simple kind of manipulation. In the literature of game theory and mechanism design, various manipulations have been studied, some of which remain meaningful in this facility location model. For example, *rename* is a manipulation that changes one's identity and behaves as a different individual [7], such as creating a different e-mail account or asking a colleague to participate on one's behalf. *False-name manipulations*, which are a bit more powerful, use more than one identity and behave as multiple individuals [1,2,5,11,13,14].

In this paper, we investigate the mechanism design for a facility location model where agents are on a discrete acyclic graph and their locations are public and study the effect of both rename and false-name manipulations. To the best of our knowledge, this is the first work that deals with these manipulations in discrete models. We also consider both situations of one facility and two heterogeneous facilities. The former resembles traditional social choice settings, while the latter has been actively studied in combinatorial optimization.

Our Contribution. Our contribution is threefold. First, for the case of locating one facility, we clarify the differences between our model and traditional ones, and show that the existing characterization of strategy-proofness by Dokow et al. [3] does not apply to rename-proofness in our model, although these properties look quite similar. We then show that the existing equivalence result for false-name-proofness and population monotonicity by Todo et al. [13] does not carry over to our discrete model.

Second, for the problem of locating two heterogeneous facilities on a discrete path, we analyze the approximation ratios of several new/existing mechanisms, as well as a non-trivial lower bound for maximum cost. We also propose a false-name-proof and Pareto-efficient mechanism. Furthermore, we propose a deterministic false-name-proof mechanism on general discrete acyclic graphs and analyze its approximation ratio.

Finally, we introduce a new model, where the mechanism designer observes under which vertex a fake identity can appear. Under this new model, false-name-proofness does not imply population monotonicity, while in various mechanism design situations the former implies the latter [1,12].

2 Model

In this section, we introduce the facility location model considered in our paper. Let $G = (V, E)$ be an underlying undirected acyclic graph, where V is the set of vertices and E is the set of edges. Let $\mathcal{N} := V$ be the set of potential agents, and let $\mathcal{F} := (F_j)_{1 \leq j \leq k}$ denote the set of k heterogeneous facilities. In this paper, we focus only on $k = 1$ and $k = 2$. The distance function $d : V \times V \to \mathbb{N}_{\geq 0}$ is such that for any $v, w \in V$, $d(v, w) := \#\{e \in E | e \in s(v, w)\}$, where $s(v, w)$ is the shortest path between v and w in G.

Let $N \subseteq \mathcal{N}$ be a set of participating agents, where each agent $i \in N$ has a *demand*, i.e., a set of facilities requested by agent i. Let $T_i \in \mathcal{T} := 2^{\mathcal{F}}$ denote agent i's demand, let $T := (T_i)_{i \in N} \in \mathcal{T}^{|N|}$ denote a profile of the agents' demands, and let $T_{-i} := (T_{i'})_{i' \neq i}$ denote a profile of them without i's. Given N, T, and j ($1 \leq j \leq k$), let $N_j[T]$ be the set of agents who request the j-th facility, i.e., $N_j[T] := \{i \in N \mid F_j \in T_i\}$. For simplicity, we use N_j instead of $N_j[T]$ if it is obvious from the context. Let $n_j := |N_j|$ be the number of agents who request F_j.

We sometimes restrict G to path graphs, under which the vertices are labeled as $\{1, 2, ..., |V|\}$, so that $E = \{(i, i+1) \mid 1 \leq i \leq |V| - 1\}$. For a path graph G, and given N and T, let $\min N_j := \min\{i \in N \mid T_i \ni F_j\}$, $\max N_j := \max\{i \in N \mid T_i \ni F_j\}$, and $\mu_j := (\min N_j + \max N_j)/2$. Furthermore, $d([v, w], x) := \min_{y \in [v, w]} d(y, x)$ for any $v, w, x \in V$.

Given G, N, T, and j, let $\pi(N_j)$ denote the convex subset of vertices V in G consisting of the minimum spanning tree that involves all the vertices $i \in N_j$. Moreover, given a convex set $D \subseteq V$ in G and a vertex $v \in V$, $\tau_v(D) := \arg\min_{w \in D} d(v, w)$. This vertex w is unique since D is convex and G is restricted to acyclic graphs. For example, consider the graph $G(V, E)$ such that $V = \{1, \ldots, 5\}$, $E = \{(1, 2), (1, 3), (1, 4), (1, 5)\}$. If $N_j = \{2, 3\}$ then $\pi(N_j) = \{1, 2, 3\}$ and $\tau_4(\pi(N_j)) = \arg\min_{w \in \{1,2,3\}} d(w, 4) = 1$.

A profile of the locations of k facilities $l = (l_j)_{1 \leq j \leq k} \in V^k$ is a *feasible outcome* if $l_j \neq l_{j'}$ for all $j, j' \neq j$, where l_j is the location of F_j under l. Let $\mathcal{L}$ denote the set of all feasible outcomes. Given i, T_i, and l, let $c_i(T_i, l)$ denote the cost of agent i who has true demand T_i, defined as the sum of distances to the facilities she requests, i.e., $c_i(T_i, l) := \sum_{j | F_j \in T_i} d(i, l_j)$. If $T_i = \emptyset$, then $c_i(T_i, l) = 0$ for any $l \in \mathcal{L}$. Let $\Delta(\mathcal{L})$ be the set of possible probability distributions over $\mathcal{L}$. Given $i \in N$, $T_i \in \mathcal{T}$, and distribution $P \in \Delta(\mathcal{L})$, let $c_i(T_i, P) := \mathbb{E}_{l \sim P}[c_i(T_i, l)]$.

In this paper, we consider both deterministic and randomized mechanisms. A deterministic mechanism maps a profile of agents' demands to an outcome, while a randomized mechanism maps a profile of agents' demands to a probability distribution over the outcomes. A mechanism f is *strategy-proof* if $\forall N \subseteq \mathcal{N}$, $\forall i \in N$, $\forall T = (T_i, T_{-i}) \in \mathcal{T}^{|N|}$, $\forall T_i' \in \mathcal{T}$, $c_i(T_i, f(T)) \leq c_i(T_i, f(T_i', T_{-i}))$. Note that strategy-proofness implies *participation*, which requires that participating by reporting one's true demand is weakly better than not participating. We next define *rename-proofness* and *false-name-proofness* as a generalization of strategy-proofness.

Definition 1 (Rename-Proofness). *A mechanism f is* rename-proof *if* $\forall N \subseteq \mathcal{N}$, $\forall i \in N$, $\forall \mathcal{T} \in \mathscr{T}^{|N|}$, $\forall i' \in \{i\} \cup (\mathcal{N} \setminus N)$, *and* $\forall T_{i'} \in \mathscr{T}$,

$$c_i(T_i, f(\mathcal{T})) \leq c_i(T_i, f(T_{i'}, \mathcal{T}_{-i})).$$

Definition 2 (False-Name-Proofness). *A mechanism f is* false-name-proof *if* $\forall N \subseteq \mathcal{N}$, $\forall i \in N$, $\forall \mathcal{T} \in \mathscr{T}^{|N|}$, $\forall S \subseteq \{i\} \cup (\mathcal{N} \setminus N)$, *and* $\forall T'_S = (T'_{i'})_{i' \in S} \in \mathscr{T}^{|S|}$,

$$c_i(T_i, f(\mathcal{T})) \leq c_i(T_i, f(T'_S, \mathcal{T}_{-i})).$$

For evaluating mechanisms, we introduce some efficiency criteria. *Pareto efficiency* is one of the most popular properties of efficiency in economics literature. An outcome l is *Pareto undominated* if no outcome l' exists s.t. $c_i(T_i, l') \leq c_i(T_i, l)$ for every $i \in N$ and $c_{i'}(T_{i'}, l') < c_{i'}(T_{i'}, l)$ for at least one $i' \in N$. A mechanism f is *Pareto efficient* (PE) if $f(\mathcal{T})$ is Pareto undominated for any N and $\mathcal{T}$.

Approximation ratio is another well-known measure. Given N, $\mathcal{T}$, and l, the maximum cost (MC) is defined as $MC(N, \mathcal{T}, l) := \max_{i \in N} c_i(T_i, l)$. Analogously, the social cost (SC) is defined as $SC(N, \mathcal{T}, l) = \sum_{i \in N} c_i(T_i, l)$.

Definition 3. *A mechanism f is α-approximation (shortly, approx.) for MC if α is the minimum real number such that $\forall N, \forall \mathcal{T}, MC(N, \mathcal{T}, f(\mathcal{T})) \leq \alpha \cdot \min_{l \in \mathscr{L}} MC(N, \mathcal{T}, l)$. Analogously, a mechanism f is α-approx. for SC if α is the minimum real number such that $\forall N, \forall \mathcal{T}, SC(N, \mathcal{T}, f(\mathcal{T})) \leq \alpha \cdot \min_{l \in \mathscr{L}} SC(N, \mathcal{T}, l)$.*

3   Locating One Facility ($k = 1$)

In this section, we consider general undirected acyclic graph G and randomized mechanisms. The main purpose of this section is clarifying how our model considered in this paper differs from previously established ones. Indeed, we present the following new findings: (a) rename-proofness in our model is less demanding than strategy-proofness in the traditional discrete facility location model, and (b) false-name-proofness in our model is less demanding than false-name-proofness in the traditional continuous facility location model. Both are shown by the existence of rules that were not included in the previously known characterization results.

3.1   Rename-Proofness

Let us first briefly introduce the relation between rename-proofness in our model and strategy-proofness in the traditional discrete model by Dokow et al. [3]. In that model, agents can misreport their *locations* (instead of their demands), and strategy-proofness requires that no agent benefits by misreporting her location. Dokow et al. characterized strategy-proof mechanisms on path graphs by three properties. A mechanism is strategy-proof if and only if it satisfies monotonicity (MON), disjoint-independence (DI), and 1-step-independence (1-SI). Intuitively, 1-SI means that a deviation that occurs in an interval sufficiently far from the original outcome does not affect the outcome.

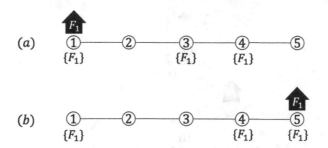

Fig. 1. Instance used in Theorem 1: (a) $N_1 = \{1,3,4\}$ and (b) $N_1 = \{1,4,5\}$

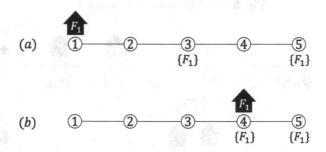

Fig. 2. Instance used in Example 1: (a) $N_1 = \{3,5\}$ and (b) agent 3 uses vertex 4 instead of 3

Definition 4 (Dokow et al. [3]). *A deterministic mechanism f satisfies* 1-step-independence *(1-SI) if $\forall N \subseteq \mathcal{N}$, $\forall \mathcal{T} \in \mathcal{T}^{|N|}$, $\forall i \in N$, $\forall i' \in \mathcal{N} \setminus N$, and $\forall T_{i'} \in \mathcal{T} \setminus \emptyset$,*

$$[d([\min(i,i'),\max(i,i')], f(\mathcal{T})) > 1]$$
$$\Rightarrow [f(\mathcal{T}) = f(T_{i'}, \mathcal{T}_{-i})].$$

Definition 5 (Dokow et al. [3]). *A deterministic mechanism f satisfies* disjoint independence *(DI) if $\forall N \subseteq \mathcal{N}$, $\forall \mathcal{T} \in \mathcal{T}^{|N|}$, $\forall i \in N$, $\forall i' \in \mathcal{N} \setminus N$, and $\forall T_{i'} \in \mathcal{T} \setminus \emptyset$,*

$$[f(\mathcal{T}) = l \neq l' = f(T_{i'}, \mathcal{T}_{-i})]$$
$$\Rightarrow [|[\min(i,i'),\max(i,i')] \cap [\min(l,l'),\max(l,l')]| \geq 2].$$

Definition 6 (Dokow et al. [3]). *A deterministic mechanism f satisfies* monotonicity *(MON) if $\forall N \subseteq \mathcal{N}$, $\forall \mathcal{T} \in \mathcal{T}^{|N|}$, $\forall i \in N$, $\forall i' \in \mathcal{N} \setminus N$, and $\forall T_{i'} \in \mathcal{T} \setminus \emptyset$,*

$$i > i' \Rightarrow f(\mathcal{T}) \geq f(T_{i'}, \mathcal{T}_{-i}).$$

In our model where at most one agent can appear in a vertex, however, the 1-SI condition is not necessary for rename-proofness, while the other two remain necessary.

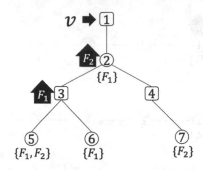

Fig. 3. Instance used in Example 4

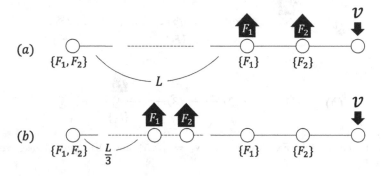

Fig. 4. Worst case for MC: the top figure (a) represents the location that TREE-TARGET returns, while the bottom (b) represents the optimal location for MC.

Theorem 1. *There exists a deterministic RP mechanism that violates 1-SI. On the other hand, any deterministic RP mechanism also satisfies both DI and MON.*

Proof. Since the second sentence can be easily proved by a similar argument with the proof of Theorem 3.4 in Dokow et al. [3], we focus on the first sentence. Consider a path graph with $V = \{1, 2, 3, 4, 5\}$ and a mechanism f that returns 5 if $N_1 \supseteq \{4, 5\}$ and $\tau_1(\pi(N_1))$ otherwise. It is obviously RP. Let us then see that it violates 1-SI. When $N_1 = \{1, 3, 4\}$ and $T_1 = T_3 = T_4 = \{F_1\}$, f returns $\tau_1(\{1, 2, 3, 4\}) = 1$. On the other hand, when $N' = \{1, 4, 5\}$, and $T_1' = T_4' = T_5' = \{F_1\}$, f returns 5. Since $d([3, 5], 1) = 2 > 1$ and $f(T) = 1 \neq 5 = f(T')$, f violates 1-SI. $\qquad\square$

3.2   False-Name-Proofness

We next investigate the effect of false-name manipulations by characterizing false-name-proof mechanisms based on their very local behavior, under the assumption of Pareto efficiency. More precisely, we show that a Pareto efficient mechanism is false-name-proof if and only if the arrival of a new agent increases the cost of every other agent. This solidarity condition is known as *population monotonicity* in social choice literature.

Definition 7. *A randomized mechanism f is* population monotonic *if* $\forall N$, $\forall i \in N$, $\forall \mathcal{T}$, $\forall i' \in \mathcal{N} \setminus N$, *and* $\forall T_{i'}$, $c_i(T_i, f(\mathcal{T})) \leq c_i(T_i, f(\mathcal{T}_{i'}, \mathcal{T}))$ *holds.*

Theorem 2. *Assume that a randomized mechanism f is Pareto efficient. Then f is false-name-proof if and only if it is population monotonic.*

Proof Sketch. For the only if part, assume that there exists N, $\mathcal{T}$, i, i', and $T_{i'}$ such that $c_i(T_i, f(\mathcal{T})) > c_i(T_i, f(\mathcal{T}, T_{i'}))$ under a Pareto efficient and false-name-proof mechanism f. This means that agent i can reduce her cost by adding a fake identity to vertex i', which violates false-name-proofness.

For the if part, we first observe that any Pareto efficient and population monotonic mechanism f also satisfies participation, i.e., $c_i(T_i, f(\mathcal{T})) \leq c_i(T_i, f(\mathcal{T}_{-i}))$ holds for any N, $\mathcal{T}$, and i. Otherwise, $f(\mathcal{T})$ must differ from $f(\mathcal{T}_{-i})$. Since $f(\mathcal{T}_{-i}) \in \pi(N_1[\mathcal{T}_{-i}])$ holds from the assumption of Pareto efficiency, there exists some $i' \in N \setminus \{i\}$ such that $c_{i'}(T_{i'}, f(\mathcal{T})) < c_{i'}(T_{i'}, f(\mathcal{T}_{-i}))$. This implies that i''s cost is reduced when a new agent i joins, which violates population monotonicity. Furthermore, population monotonicity implies that agent i's cost never decreases when she adds a fake identity i'; formally, $c_i(T_i, f(\mathcal{T})) \leq c_i(T_i, f(\mathcal{T}, T_{i'}))$ holds for any N, $\mathcal{T}$, $i \in N$, $i' \in \mathcal{N} \setminus N$, and $T_{i'}$. We can simulate any false-name manipulation by adding and removing identities one by one. Therefore, these two inequalities guarantee false-name-proofness. $\square$

Note that the following example shows the necessity of Pareto efficiency, i.e., a mechanism exists that is population monotonic, but neither false-name-proof nor Pareto efficient, although any false-name-proof mechanism is population monotonic.

Example 1. Consider a path graph with $V = \{1, 2, 3, 4, 5\}$ and a mechanism that returns min N_1 if $N_1 \subseteq \{4, 5\}$ and 1 otherwise. We can easily verify that it is population monotonic but not Pareto efficient. Let us now verify that it is not rename-proof, and thus not false-name-proof. When $N = \{3, 5\}$ and $T_3 = T_5 = \{F_1\}$, F_1 is built at 1. If agent 3 uses vertex 4, instead of vertex 3, and reports $T_4 = \{F_1\}$, F_1 moves to 4, which reduces her cost from 2 to 1.

In a continuous model, a quite similar statement with Theorem 2 was shown by Todo et al. [13]. Under the assumptions of Pareto efficiency and strategy-proofness, a mechanism is false-name-proof if and only if it is also population monotonic. Furthermore, such a mechanism is characterized by the target rule, which is defined by a target function τ_v associated with a parameter v on a continuous line. In our discrete model, however, we found a Pareto efficient and false-name-proof mechanism that is not described as a target rule, while any target rule still satisfies both properties.

Example 2. Consider a path graph with $V = \{1, 2, 3, 4, 5\}$ and a mechanism that returns $\tau_2(\pi(N_1))$ if $N_1 \subseteq \{1, 2, 3\}$ and $\tau_5(\pi(N_1))$ otherwise. This is obviously not a target rule, since its behavior is described as a combination of two different target rules. We can easily verify, however, that it is false-name-proof and Pareto efficient.

Note that our model differs from the traditional continuous model in two points: (i) the set of outcomes is restricted to be discrete, and (ii) at most one agent can appear in each vertex. The characterization of false-name-proof mechanisms in models where only one of the restrictions applies remains an open question.

4 Locating Two Facilities ($k = 2$)

In this section, we consider $k = 2$ and investigate rename-proof and false-name-proof mechanisms on path graphs G. For rename-proofness, we propose a randomized mechanism that is optimal for SC. On the other hand, since there is no mechanism that is false-name-proof and 1-approx. for SC, we also propose approximation mechanisms.

We first introduce additional notations. Given N, $\mathcal{T}$, and j, let $m_j \in V$ be the location of the median agent among N_j, if n_j is odd. If n_j is even, let m_j^L and m_j^R respectively be the location of the left- and right-median agents among N_j. Given N, $\mathcal{T}$, and $j \in \{1, 2\}$, let $\mathrm{Opt}(N_j)$ denote the set $\{m_j\}$ if n_j is odd, and $\{m_j^L, m_j^R\}$ if n_j is even. Note that since we focus on $k = 2$ in this section, the subscript numbers in the algorithms are modulo 2, e.g., N_3, n_3, and S_3 denote N_1, n_1, and S_1, respectively.

To describe the mechanisms, we introduce three functions: COMPUTESUP-PORT [10], COMPUTESUPPORT2, and COMPUTESUPPORT3, each of which returns a probability distribution. Given (μ_1, μ_2), COMPUTESUPPORT returns a feasible probability distribution P such that for each $j \in \{1, 2\}$, the expected position of F_j becomes μ_j. COMPUTESUPPORT2 is given as Algorithm 1, which generalizes COMPUTESUPPORT to weaken the agents' incentives for rename manipulations. For example, assume that an even number of agents requests F_j. Under the probability distribution returned by COMPUTESUPPORT, F_j is most likely located at vertices near μ_j, which may incentivize agents to change μ_j using a different vertex. Under COMPUTESUPPORT2, on the other hand, F_j is located at m_j^L and m_j^R uniformly at random, which never gives such an incentive to agents. COMPUTE-SUPPORT3 returns, for given (N_1, N_2), an arbitrary probability distribution such that for each $j \in \{1, 2\}$, F_j is located at $\min N_j$, $\lfloor \mu_j \rfloor$, $\lceil \mu_j \rceil$, and $\max N_j$ uniformly at random, if $n_j > 1$. If $n_j = 1$, F_j is located at μ_j and $\mu_j - 1$ (or $\mu_j + 1$ if $\mu_j - 1 \leq 0$) uniformly at random. The marginal distribution for F_j in COMPUTE-SUPPORT3 guarantees the existence of such a distribution.

4.1 Rename-Proof Mechanisms

For a one-facility situation, choosing the median location is rename-proof and optimal for social cost. We now extend this observation to a two-facility situation.

Algorithm 1. COMPUTESUPPORT2

Require: N_1, N_2
Ensure: $P \in \Delta(\mathscr{L})$
 1: **if** both n_1 and n_2 are odd **then**
 2:    **if** $m_1 \neq m_2$ **then**
 3:       **return** (m_1, m_2) w.p. 1
 4:    **else**
 5:       **return** $(m_1, m_2 - 1)$ w.p. $\frac{1}{2}$, $(m_1, m_2 + 1)$ w.p. $\frac{1}{2}$
 6:    **end if**
 7: **else if** $\exists j \in \{1, 2\}$ s.t. $[n_j$ is even $\wedge n_{j+1}$ is odd$]$ **then**
 8:    $p := (m_1^R - m_1^L)/(2 \cdot (m_1^R - m_1^L - 1))$
 9:    **if** $m_j^L = m_{j+1}$ **then**
10:       **return** $(m_j^L + 1, m_{j+1})$ w.p. p,
                     (m_j^R, m_{j+1}) w.p. $1 - p$
11:    **else if** $m_j^R = m_{j+1}$ **then**
12:       **return** (m_j^L, m_{j+1}) w.p. $(1 - p)$,
                     $(m_j^R - 1, m_{j+1})$ w.p. p
13:    **else**
14:       **return** (m_j^L, m_{j+1}) w.p. $\frac{1}{2}$, (m_j^R, m_{j+1}) w.p. $\frac{1}{2}$
15:    **end if**
16: **else**
17:    **if** $m_1^L \neq m_2^R$ **then**
18:       **return** (m_1^L, m_2^R) w.p. $\frac{1}{2}$, (m_1^R, m_2^L) w.p. $\frac{1}{2}$
19:    **else**
20:       **return** (m_1^L, m_2^L) w.p. $\frac{1}{2}$, (m_1^R, m_2^R) w.p. $\frac{1}{2}$
21:    **end if**
22: **end if**

Indeed, we modify the RANDOPT [9] mechanism for our model, which we call RANDOPT-FOR-RP (Mechanism 1), and show that it is rename-proof. Note that RANDOPT-FOR-RP only differs from RANDOPT in line 13.

Theorem 3. RANDOPT-FOR-RP *is rename-proof and 1-approx. for SC.*

Proof Sketch. The proof for optimality is an analogy from Theorem 10 in a previous work [9]. We now verify rename-proofness. Since the mechanism is symmetric between F_1 and F_2 in expectation, we focus on an agent i with $T_i \ni F_1$ w.l.o.g. and show that for any i' and $T_{i'}$, either the expected cost for F_1 never decreases or the expected loss for F_2 exceeds the expected gain for F_1.

Consider the case where n_1 is even. If $i \in \text{Opt}(N_1) = \{m_1^L, m_1^R\}$, assume $i = m_1^L$ w.l.o.g. Since n_1 is even and $i = m_1^L$, choosing $T_{i'} = \{F_2\}$ changes the location of F_1 to m_1^R w.p. 1, which never decreases the expected cost for F_1. Thus, it suffices to consider $T_{i'} \ni F_1$ in the following.

There are two possible marginal distributions of the location of F_1: (i) built at $m_1^L = i$ w.p. 1/2 and at m_1^R w.p. 1/2, and (ii) built at $m_1^L + 1$ w.p. p and at m_1^R w.p. $1 - p$, where p is s.t. $p \cdot (m_1^L + 1) + (1 - p) \cdot m_1^R = (m_1^L + m_1^R)/2$ by the definition of COMPUTESUPPORT2. Note that (ii) occurs if and only if

Mechanism 1. RANDOPT-FOR-RP

Require: $N \subseteq \mathcal{N}, T \in \mathcal{T}^{|N|}$
Ensure: $P \in \Delta(\mathcal{L})$
1: $S_1 := \mathrm{Opt}(N_1),\ S_2 := \mathrm{Opt}(N_2)$
2: **if** $\exists j \in \{1, 2\}$ s.t. $[|S_j| = 2 \wedge |S_j \cap S_{j+1}| \leq 1]$ **then**
3:      $d'_v := \min_{s \in S_{j+1}} d(v, s)$ for each $v \in S_j$
4:      $l_j := \arg\max_{v \in S_j} d'_v$
5:      **if** $|S_{j+1}| = 2$ **then**
6:          $d''_v := \min_{s \in S_j} d(v, s)$ for each $v \in S_{j+1}$
7:          $l_{j+1} := \arg\max_{v \in S_{j+1}} d''_v$
8:          **return** (l_j, l_{j+1}) w.p. 1
9:      **else**
10:         **return** (l_j, m^L_{j+1}) w.p. $\frac{1}{2}$, (l_j, m^R_{j+1}) w.p. $\frac{1}{2}$
11:     **end if**
12: **else**
13:     **return** $P := \mathrm{COMPUTESUPPORT2}(N_1, N_2)$
14: **end if**

$m_2 = m^L_1$ (lines 9–11 in COMPUTESUPPORT2), and therefore it must be the case that $T_i = \{F_1, F_2\}$.

When (i) occurs, by any $T_{i'} \ni F_1$, F_1 is built at m^R_1 w.p. 1/2 and another $v \neq m^R_1$ w.p. 1/2, whose expected cost is minimized under $i' = i$. The expected cost for F_1 therefore never decreases. When (ii) occurs, it must hold that $T_i = \{F_1, F_2\}$, as we already observed. She can get an expected gain for F_1 of at most 1/2 only when she uses $i' = i - 1$ with $T_{i'} \ni F_1$. However, this also incurs an expected loss for F_2 of at least 1, where the expected loss exceeds the expected gain.

For $i \notin \mathrm{Opt}(N_1)$, assume $i < m^L_1$ w.l.o.g. The possible marginal distributions for F_1 are exactly the same, i.e., (i) and (ii), and choosing $T_{i'} = \{F_2\}$ moves F_1 to the original m^R_1 w.p. 1, which never decreases the expected cost for F_1. Furthermore, choosing $i' < m^L_1$ s.t. $T_{i'} \ni F_1$ does not affect the marginal distribution for F_1. Finally, choosing $i' > m^L_1$ s.t. $T_{i'} \ni F_1$ increases the expected cost for F_1 to $(m^R_1 + v)/2 - i$, where m^R_1 and v are now the two medians.

These arguments guarantee that no rename manipulation is beneficial for any even n_1. Since the case where n_1 is odd is much easier, it is omitted. □

4.2   False-Name-Proof Deterministic Mechanisms

We next investigate false-name-proof mechanisms for two facilities. As a first step, we study an existing deterministic mechanism called TWOEXTREMES, which is 3-approx. for MC [10]. and $(|N| - 1)$-approx. for SC [9]. We now show that it is also false-name-proof.

Theorem 4. TwoExtremes f *is false-name-proof:*

$$f(\mathcal{T}) = \begin{cases} (\min N_1, \max N_2) & \textit{if } \min N_1 \neq \max N_2, \\ (\min N_1, \max N_2 - 1) & \textit{if } [\min N_1 = \max N_2] \\ & \quad \wedge [\max N_2 \geq 2], \\ (\min N_1 + 1, \max N_2) & \textit{otherwise.} \end{cases}$$

Proof Sketch. Since TwoExtremes is a natural extension of the well-known leftmost and rightmost mechanisms for one facility, it is not difficult to show that there is no beneficial false-name manipulation for agents who require only one facility. Let us then focus on a false-name manipulation by an agent i with $T_i = \{F_1, F_2\}$. Since $T_i = \{F_1, F_2\}$, $\min N_1 \leq i \leq \max N_2$ also obviously holds. Therefore, if a beneficial manipulation exists, it must be the case that either $i = \min N_1$ or $i = \max N_2$ exclusively holds. However, when $i = \min N_1$, agent i can bring F_2 closer to her only if she changes the location of F_1, and such a manipulation always moves the location of F_1 more to the left from the original location of F_2, which does not reduce her total cost. From symmetry, a similar argument applies for $i = \max N_2$. □

We then show a lower bound of the approx. ratio for MC.

Theorem 5. *Any deterministic false-name-proof mechanism has an approx. ratio of at least 2 for MC.*

Proof. Consider the path graph with $V = \{1, 2, 3, 4, 5\}$, and the case where $N = \{2, 3, 4\}$, $T_2 = \{F_1\}$, $T_3 = \{F_1, F_2\}$, and $T_4 = \{F_2\}$. The optimal outcomes for MC are $(2, 3)$ and $(3, 4)$, which cause a maximum cost of 1. Any other outcome produces a maximum cost of at least 2, and thus any $(2 - \epsilon)$-approx. mechanism f must return either of them. W.l.o.g., assume that f returns $(3, 4)$, under which agent 2's cost is 1. Then consider another case where $N' = \{1, 2, 3, 4\}$, $T_1 = T_2 = \{F_1\}$, $T_3 = \{F_1, F_2\}$, and $T_4 = \{F_2\}$. The unique optimal outcome is now $(2, 3)$, and any other outcome produces a maximum cost of at least 2. Therefore, f must return $(2, 3)$, under which agent 2 incurs a cost of 0. Thus, agent 2 in the first case is better off by adding a fake identity to vertex 1. □

4.3 False-Name-Proof Randomized Mechanisms

In this subsection, we first provide lower bounds for both MC and SC. The proofs are inspired by Theorem 3.4 in Procaccia et al. [8] and Theorem 7 in Todo et al. [13]. Actually, although we consider locating two facilities, the proofs focus on cases where all the agents request the same single facility. Due to space limitations, we omit them.

Theorem 6. *Any randomized false-name-proof mechanism has an approx. ratio of at least 3/2 for MC and $\Omega(|N|)$ for SC.*

We then propose a randomized false-name-proof mechanism, defined as Mechanism2, which has a better approx. ratio for MC than TwoExtremes.

Mechanism 2. LRM-FOR-TWOFACILITIES

Require: $N \subseteq \mathcal{N}, \mathcal{T} \in \mathcal{T}^{|N|}$
Ensure: $P \in \Delta(\mathcal{L})$
 1: **if** $n_1 = 1 \wedge n_2 = 1$ **then**
 2:     **return** (μ_1, μ_2) w.p. 1
 3: **end if**
 4: **return** $P := $COMPUTESUPPORT3$(N_1, N_2)$

Theorem 7. LRM-FOR-TWOFACILITIES *is false-name-proof, 2-approx. for MC, and $O(|N|)$-approx. for SC.*

Proof. The $O(|N|)$-approx. for SC is very obvious. We next briefly explain the intuition of false-name-proofness. From the definition of COMPUTESUPPORT3, the two marginal distributions are independent, i.e., a change on one marginal distribution does not affect the other. Therefore, if a beneficial manipulation exists, the expected cost for at least one facility must decrease. Here, for the case of $n_j > 1$, the behavior is almost the same with as the *left-right-middle* mechanism [8] for one facility, which is false-name-proof [13]. Also, for the case of $n_j = 1$, such that $N_j = \{i\}$, the expected cost of the agent i is $1/2$, which never decreases by any manipulation.

Finally, let us give an intuition of 2-approx. for MC. As mentioned above, the marginal distribution for each F_j is almost the same as *left-right-middle*, which is 3/2-approx. for MC. Consider the case where $n_1 = 1$ and $n_2 > 1$. The expected cost for F_2 is thus 3/2. On the other hand, F_1 is located at $\mu_1 - 1$ w.p. 1/2, where the expected cost is 1/2.

Consider the case where $n_1 > 1$ and $n_2 > 1$. Let $l^* = (l_1^*, l_2^*)$ be the optimal outcome, and let $l = (l_1, l_2)$ be the outcome returned by LRM-FOR-TWOFACILITIES. Let i be the agent with maximum cost under l, let $\Delta c := c_i(T_i, l) - c_i(T_i, l^*)$, and let OPT be the maximum cost under l^*. Then it holds that $c_i(T_i, l) \leq OPT + \Delta c \leq$ OPT $+ \Sigma_{k \in \{1,2\}} d(i, l_k) - d(i, l_k^*) \leq OPT + \Sigma_{k \in \{1,2\}} d(l_k, l_k^*)$. F_k is located at $\min N_k$ with probability $\frac{1}{4}$, $\max N_k$ with probability $\frac{1}{4}$, and μ_k with probability $\frac{1}{2}$, so it holds that $E[d(l_k, l_k^*)] = \frac{1}{4} \cdot d(\min N_k, l_k^*) + \frac{1}{4} \cdot d(\max N_k, l_k^*) + \frac{1}{2} \cdot d(\mu_k, l_k^*)$. Let MEC be the expected maximum cost for LRM-FOR-TWOFACILITIES then it holds that MEC $\leq E[OPT + \Sigma_{k \in \{1,2\}} d(l_k, l_k^*)] \leq$ OPT $+ \Sigma_{k \in \{1,2\}} \frac{1}{2} \cdot (\frac{d(\min N_k, \max N_k)}{2} + d(\mu_k, l_k^*))$. It obviously holds that $\frac{d(\min N_k, \max N_k)}{2} + d(\mu_k, l_k^*) \leq$ OPT. Therefore MEC $\leq 2 \cdot$ OPT holds. As a result, the expected maximum cost is 2.   □

4.4   Further Discussion on Two-Facilities on a Path

It is worth mentioning that a good approx. mechanism may result in Pareto dominated outcomes. We now propose a false-name-proof and Pareto efficient mechanism for two facilities. This is a slight modification of the well-known left-most mechanism, which is false-name-proof and Pareto efficient for one facility.

Mechanism 3. RANDAVG

Require: $N \subseteq \mathcal{N}, \mathcal{T} \in \mathcal{T}^{|N|}$
Ensure: $P \in \Delta(\mathcal{L})$
1: **if** $[\exists j \in \{1,2\} \text{ s.t. } \mu_j = |V|] \wedge [|\mu_1 - \mu_2| < 1]$ **then**
2:      **return** $(l_j = \mu_j, l_{j+1} = \lceil \mu_{j+1} - 1 \rceil)$ w.p. 1
3: **end if**
4: **if** $[\exists j \in \{1,2\} \text{ s.t. } \mu_j = 1] \wedge [|\mu_1 - \mu_2| < 1]$ **then**
5:      **return** $(l_j = \mu_j, l_{j+1} = \lfloor \mu_{j+1} + 1 \rfloor)$ w.p. 1
6: **end if**
7: **return** $P := \text{COMPUTESUPPORT}(\mu_1, \mu_2)$

Theorem 8. *Consider a mechanism that returns* $(\min N_1, \min N_2)$ *if* $\min N_1 \neq \min N_2$, $(\min N_1, \min N_2 + 1)$ *if* $\min N_1 = \min N_2 \wedge (\min N_1, \min N_2 + 1)$ *is Pareto undominated, and* $(\min N_1 + 1, \min N_2)$ *otherwise. It is false-name-proof and Pareto efficient.*

Proof. This mechanism is obviously false-name-proof. We now show that it is also Pareto efficient. Consider the case where $\min N_1 \neq \min N_2$. In this case, mechanism returns $l = (\min N_1, \max N_2)$. For any $l' \in \mathcal{L} \setminus \{l\}$, there exists $i \in \{\min N_1, \min N_2\}$ that holds $c_i(T_i, l) < c_i(T_i, l')$. Thus l is Pareto optimal. Consider the case where $\min N_1 = \min N_2$. In this case, mechanism returns $l = (\min N_1, \max N_2 + 1)$ or $(\min N_1 + 1, \min N_2)$. It is obvious that l is Pareto undominated by $(\min N_1 - 1, \min N_2), (\min N_1, \min N_2 - 1)$. For agent $i (= \min N_1 = \min N_2)$, her cost under l is 1. Therefore for any $l' \in \mathcal{L} \setminus \{(\min N_1, \min N_2 + 1), (\min N_1 + 1, \min N_2), (\min N_1 - 1, \min N_2), (\min N_1, \min N_2 - 1)\}$ i's cost under l' is 2, so l is Pareto undominated by l'. If $l = (\min N_1, \max N_2 + 1)$ then l is Pareto undominated by $(\min N_1 + 1, \max N_2)$ and if $l = (\min N_1 + 1, \max N_2)$ then l is Pareto undominated by $(\min N_1, \max N_2 + 1)$. Therefore the mechanism is Pareto efficient. □

Note that (i) RANDAVG [9] is strategy-proof but not rename-proof, and (ii) RANDOPT-FOR-RP is rename-proof but not false-name-proof. Combined with Theorem 4, the existence of these mechanisms implies the strictness of inclusion relations among these three properties. Due to space limitations, we only show that RANDAVG is not rename-proof.

Example 3. Consider a path graph with $V = \{1, 2, 3, 4\}$ and a case where $N = \{1, 2, 3\}$, $T_1 = \{F_1, F_2\}$, and $T_2 = T_3 = \{F_1\}$. RANDAVG returns $(2, 1)$ w.p. 1, and thus agent 3 has an expected cost of 1. When agent 3 uses a fake identity at vertex 4, instead of her true identity 3, and reports $T_4' = \{F_1\}$, RANDAVG returns $(2, 1)$ w.p. $\frac{1}{2}$ and $(3, 1)$ w.p. $\frac{1}{2}$ for (T_1, T_2, T_4'). The expected cost of agent 3 then decreases to $\frac{1}{2}$, which violates rename-proofness.

5 False-Name-Proof Location on a Tree

In this section, we propose a deterministic false-name-proof mechanism for two facilities on general acyclic graph G, which is called TREE-TARGET.

Mechanism 4. TREE-TARGET

Require: G, $N \subseteq \mathcal{N}$, $T \in \mathcal{T}^{|N|}$, and arbitrary $v \in V$
Ensure: $(l_1, l_2) \in \mathcal{L}$
 1: $V_1 := \{w \mid d(w, v) \text{ is even}\}$, $V_2 := \{w \mid d(w, v) \text{ is odd}\}$
 2: **for each** $j \in \{1, 2\}$ **do**
 3:    **if** $V_j \cap \pi(N_j) = \emptyset$ **then**
 4:       $l_j :=$ an arbitrary neighbor of unique $\pi(N_j)$
 5:    **else**
 6:       $M_j := \arg\min_{x \in V_j \cap \pi(N_j)} d(x, v)$
 7:       $l_j := \min M_j$
 8:    **end if**
 9: **end for**
10: **return** (l_1, l_2)

For general acyclic graph G, assume that each vertex has a label, say 1, 2, ..., $|V|$, in some order, so that for any $M \subseteq V$, $\min M$ is defined as the vertex in M with the smallest label. TREE-TARGET first categorizes all the vertices into two groups V_1 and V_2, (line 1 in the mechanism), so that in any path, the vertices from these two groups appear one after the other. After this preprocessing, the mechanism deterministically locates F_1 on a vertex in V_1 and F_2 on a vertex in V_2 to guarantee feasibility. The following example illustrates the behavior of TREE-TARGET.

Example 4. We consider the graph $G(V, E)$ depicted in Fig. 5. In the instance, $N = \{2, 5, 6, 7\}$, $T_2 = \{F_1\}$, $T_5 = \{F_1, F_2\}$, $T_6 = \{F_1\}$, $T_7 = \{F_2\}$, $v = 1$. Then $V_1 = \{1, 3, 4\}$, $V_2 = \{2, 5, 6, 7\}$. Since $\arg\min_{x \in V_1 \cap \pi(N_1)} d(x, 1) = 3$ and $\arg\min_{x \in V_2 \cap \pi(N_2)} d(x, 1) = 2$, TREE-TARGET locates F_1 on vertex 3 and F_2 on vertex 2.

Theorem 9. TREE-TARGET *is false-name-proof, 3-approx. for MC, and* $(max(n_1, n_2) - 1)$-*approx. for SC.*

Proof. We first show that TREE-TARGET is $(\max(n_1, n_2) - 1)$-approx. for SC. Let $l^* = (l_1^*, l_2^*)$ be the optimal outcome, and let $\text{OPT} = \text{OPT}_1 + \text{OPT}_2$ be the social cost under l^*, where OPT_j is the social cost for F_j. Let L_j be the length of the longest path in $\pi(N_j)$, and let v, w be its extreme points. Then, it obviously holds that $c_v(\{F_j\}, l^*) + c_w(\{F_j\}, l^*) \geq L_j$, which implies $\text{OPT}_j \geq L_j$.

On the other hand, let $l = (l_1, l_2)$ be the outcome by TREE-TARGET, and let $\text{MEC} = \text{MEC}_1 + \text{MEC}_2$ be the social cost under l, where MEC_j is the social cost for F_j. Let x, y be a pair of agents such that l_j is located on a path between x and y, i.e., $c_x(\{F_j\}, l) + c_y(\{F_j\}, l) = d(x, y)$ holds. By the definition of L_k, $c_x(\{F_j\}, l) + c_y(\{F_j\}, l) \leq L_j$. Moreover, each agent except x, y has a cost of at most L_j. Thus, $\text{MEC}_j \leq L_j + (n_j - 2) \cdot L_j = (n_j - 1) \cdot L_j$. As a result, the ratio MEC/OPT is bounded from above by $\frac{n_1 L_1 + n_2 L_2}{L_1 + L_2} - 1$. Since $n_1 L_1 + n_2 L_2 \leq \max(n_1, n_2)(L_1 + L_2)$, the approximation ratio is $\max(n_1, n_2) - 1$.

We next show that TREE-TARGET is 3-approx. for MC, by a similar argument with the proof of Theorem 4.4 in a previous work [10]. Let l be the location that TREE-TARGET returns, and MEC be the maximum cost under l. Let i be the agent that has maximum cost under l, let l^* be the optimal outcome for MC, and let OPT be the maximum cost under l^*. For any $F_k \in T_i$ it holds that $\Delta l := d(i, l_k) - d(i, l_k^*) \leq d(l_k, l_k^*)$. Because $l_k \in \pi(N_k)$, there exists agent x that $d(l_k, l_k^*) \leq d(x, l_k^*)$. It obviously holds that $d(x, l_k^*) \leq$ OPT. Therefore (i) if $|T_i| = 1$ $(T_i = \{F_k\})$ then $c_i(T_i, l) = $ MEC $ = $ OPT $+ \Delta l_k \leq 2 \cdot$ OPT, (ii) if $|T_i| = 2$ $(T_i = \{F_1, F_2\})$ then $c_i(T_i, l) = $ MEC $ = $ OPT $+ \Delta l_1 + \Delta l_2 \leq 3 \cdot$ OPT. $\square$

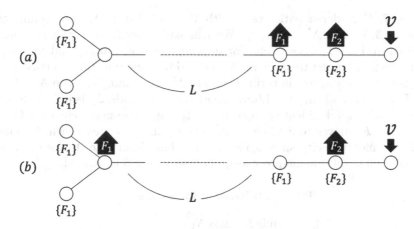

Fig. 5. Worst case for SC: the top figure (a) represents the location that TREE-TARGET returns, while the bottom (b) represents the optimal location for SC.

Actually, the following two examples shows that these two bounds are tight, i.e., there exists a profile under which the approximation ratio matches the bound.

Example 5. Let us consider the instance in Fig. 5. In case (a), the maximum cost is $2L+1$. In case (b), on the other hand, the maximum cost is $\frac{2L}{3} + 1$. Therefore, the approximation ratio is $\frac{2L+1}{\frac{2L}{3}+1}$, which converges to 3 when L is large enough.

Example 6. Let us consider the instance in Fig. 5. In case (a), the social cost is $2L + 2$. In case (b), on the other hand, the social cost is $L + 2$. Therefore, the approximation ratio is $\frac{2L+2}{L+2}$, which converges to 2 $(= \max(n_1, n_2) - 1)$ when L is large enough.

6   Location with Richer Information

We show in this section that the equivalence between false-name-proofness and population monotonicity does not hold when richer information is available to the mechanism designer. More precisely, when the mechanism designer knows the vertices in which fake accounts can/cannot appear, there exists a mechanism that is Pareto efficient and false-name-proof, but not population monotonic. Intuitively, under this new model with richer information, the definition of false-name-proofness is slightly weakened, so that the mechanism can ignore false-name manipulations that use any of the vertices in which fake identities cannot appear.

Let $\mathcal{N}_v$ be the set of verified potential agents, on which no fake identities appear, and let $\mathcal{N}_u$ be the set of unverified potential agents, on which fake identities may appear. Assume that $\mathcal{N} = \mathcal{N}_v \cup \mathcal{N}_u$ and that $\mathcal{N}_v \cap \mathcal{N}_u = \emptyset$. The following example shows that there exists a mechanism that is false-name-proof but not population monotonic.

Example 7. Consider a path graph with $V = \{1,2,3,4,5\}$, and assume that $\mathcal{N}_v = \{2,3,5\}$ and $\mathcal{N}_u = \{1,4\}$. We can easily verify that the mechanism described in Table 1, whose behavior depends only on $\min N_1$ and $\max N_1$, is false-name-proof under this new model, i.e., adding any unverified vertices in $\mathcal{N}_u$ is not beneficial for agents in verified vertices $\mathcal{N}_v$. For example, when $N = \{1,3\}$, $T_1 = T_3 = \{F_1\}$, and they truthfully report their demands, F_1 is built at 2. Even if agent 3 adds a fake identity to vertex 4, the outcome never changes. On the other hand, F_1 moves to 3 when a new agent joins at vertex 5, which violates population monotonicity since agent 3's cost falls from 1 to 0. Note that this does not violate false-name-proofness, because vertex 5 is verified.

Table 1. Behavior of the mechanism

$\min N_1$	$\max N_1$				
	1	2	3	4	5
1	1	2	2	2	3
2	–	2	2	2	3
3	–	–	3	4	4
4	–	–	–	4	4
5	–	–	–	–	5

7   Concluding Remarks

This paper initiates the mechanism design for a discrete version of facility location problems where agents' power of manipulation is rather strong, but the mechanism designer simultaneously might have some information to verify agents' manipulations. Such a verification-based approach looks quite promising, in the sense that so far many negative results have been presented in works on false-name-proofness. As well as filling the gaps between the upper and lower bounds, our future work will also characterize the rename-proof/false-name-proof mechanisms for two facilities. Based on the discussion in Sect. 6, seeking a necessary and sufficient condition on available information under which false-name-proofness and population monotonicity coincide is another interesting open question.

Acknowledgement. This work was partially supported by JSPS KAKENHI Grants Number 17H00761 and 17H04695.

References

1. Bu, N.: Unfolding the mystery of false-name-proofness. Econ. Lett. **120**(3), 559–561 (2013)
2. Conitzer, V.: Anonymity-proof voting rules. In: Papadimitriou, C., Zhang, S. (eds.) WINE 2008. LNCS, vol. 5385, pp. 295–306. Springer, Heidelberg (2008). doi:10.1007/978-3-540-92185-1_36
3. Dokow, E., Feldman, M., Meir, R., Nehama, I.: Mechanism design on discrete lines and cycles. In: ACM Conference on Electronic Commerce, EC 2012, Valencia, Spain, 4–8 June 2012, pp. 423–440 (2012)
4. Feldman, M., Fiat, A., Golomb, I.: On voting and facility location. In: Proceedings of the 2016 ACM Conference on Economics and Computation, EC 2016, Maastricht, The Netherlands, 24–28 July 2016, pp. 269–286 (2016)
5. Lesca, J., Todo, T., Yokoo, M.: Coexistence of utilitarian efficiency and false-name-proofness in social choice. In: International Conference on Autonomous Agents and Multi-agent Systems, AAMAS 2014, Paris, France, 5–9 May 2014, pp. 1201–1208 (2014)
6. Moulin, H.: On strategy-proofness and single peakedness. Public Choice **35**(4), 437–455 (1980)
7. Penna, P., Schoppmann, F., Silvestri, R., Widmayer, P.: Pseudonyms in cost-sharing games. In: Leonardi, S. (ed.) WINE 2009. LNCS, vol. 5929, pp. 256–267. Springer, Heidelberg (2009). doi:10.1007/978-3-642-10841-9_24
8. Procaccia, A.D., Tennenholtz, M.: Approximate mechanism design without money. ACM Trans. Econ. Comput. **1**(4), 18 (2013)
9. Serafino, P., Ventre, C.: Heterogeneous facility location without money on the line. In: 21st European Conference on Artificial Intelligence, ECAI 2014, 18–22 August 2014, Prague, Czech Republic - Including Prestigious Applications of Intelligent Systems PAIS 2014, pp. 807–812 (2014)
10. Serafino, P., Ventre, C.: Truthful mechanisms without money for non-utilitarian heterogeneous facility location. In: Proceedings of the 29th AAAI Conference on Artificial Intelligence, 25–30 January 2015, Austin, Texas, USA, pp. 1029–1035 (2015)
11. Sonoda, A., Todo, T., Yokoo, M.: False-name-proof locations of two facilities: economic and algorithmic approaches. In: Proceedings of the 30th AAAI Conference on Artificial Intelligence, Phoenix, Arizona, USA, 12–17 February 2016, pp. 615–621 (2016)
12. Todo, T., Conitzer, V.: False-name-proof matching. In: International Conference on Autonomous Agents and Multi-Agent Systems, AAMAS 2013, Saint Paul, MN, USA, 6–10 May 2013, pp. 311–318 (2013)
13. Todo, T., Iwasaki, A., Yokoo, M.: False-name-proof mechanism design without money. In: 10th International Conference on Autonomous Agents and Multiagent Systems AAMAS 2011, Taipei, Taiwan, 2–6 May 2011, vol. 1–3, pp. 651–658 (2011)
14. Wagman, L., Conitzer, V.: False-name-proof voting with costs over two alternatives. Int. J. Game Theor. **43**(3), 599–618 (2014)
15. Zou, S., Li, M.: Facility location games with dual preference. In: Proceedings of the 2015 International Conference on Autonomous Agents and Multiagent Systems, AAMAS 2015, Istanbul, Turkey, 4–8 May 2015, pp. 615–623 (2015)

An Agent-Based System
for Printed/Handwritten Text Discrimination

Florence Cloppet$^{(\boxtimes)}$, Pavlos Moraitis, and Nicole Vincent

LIPADE, Paris Descartes University, Paris, France
{florence.cloppet,pavlos,nicole.vincent}@mi.parisdescartes.fr

Abstract. The handwritten/printed text discrimination problem is a
decision problem usually solved after a binarization of grey level or color
images. The decision is usually made at the connected component level
of a filtered image. These image components are labeled as *printed* or
handwritten. Each component is represented as a point in a n dimensional
space based on the use of n different features. In this paper we present
the transformation of a (state of the art) traditional system dealing with
the handwritten/printed text discrimination problem to an agent-based
system. In this system we associate two different agents with the two
different points of view (i.e. linearity and regularity) considered in the
baseline system for discriminating a text, based on four (two for each
agent) different features. We are also using argumentation for modeling
the decision making mechanisms of the agents. We then present experimental results that compare the two systems by using images of the
IAM handwriting database. These results empirically prove the significant improvement we can have by using the agent-based system.

1 Introduction

Automated image analysis is an important topic in artificial intelligence. The
handwritten/printed text discrimination problem is a specific problem in the
field of image analysis. Several systems in the literature (see e.g. [8,10,11]) have
proposed different solutions for this particular problem. The main idea is to
consider only small elements of the document image such as textual parts that
form a *connected component (CC)*. Such elements are the characters in printed
texts and the words in cursive handwritten texts. The connected components are
labeled using three labels namely "printed", "handwritten" or "other", depending on the type of the document being processed (e.g. document with or without
images). Usually CCs are extracted from a binarized image. The labeling process
may be applied at different levels according to the statistical approach used. Thus
some systems are considering a block of text, a paragraph, a whole page or few
lines to make the measurements statistically consistent. The characterization of
these components is based on several features (e.g. size, density, Gabor filters,
Run-length, SIFT, bag of visual words, etc.) and therefore a high dimensional
space is needed for their representation. Then, a two class classifier is learnt.

© Springer International Publishing AG 2017
B. An et al. (Eds.): PRIMA 2017, LNAI 10621, pp. 180–197, 2017.
https://doi.org/10.1007/978-3-319-69131-2_11

Sometimes, a post processing phase is considered using a more global view. In that case the labeled components' positioning in the space may be modeled by using for example a Markov random field.

In [6] we have presented one of those systems. The specificity of the developed approach relies on a small number of features considered as meaningful and a quantization of their evolution . The features are related to the description of a written text style (i.e. aspect of the trace of the writing stroke on the sheet of paper) and can be divided in two classes namely features linked to the (more or less) *linear aspect* of the strokes and features linked to the (more or less) *regular aspect* of the components. Both points of view give hints on the nature of a text.

In this paper, we first present the *handwritten/printed text* discrimination problem and we analyze the system proposed in [6]. We then motivate our decision to use agent technology for solving the above problem and we prove the added value of our approach by presenting an agent-based approach of the handwritten/printed text discrimination problem as formulated in [6]. More particularly we show that this problem can be modeled as a *distributed decision making problem* by presenting a detailed description of the agents' architecture, the way the agents reason for making individual decisions by using argumentation and finally the way they interact through a bilateral dialogue for solving collectively the given problem. Finally we present experimental results that empirically prove that our agent-based approach significantly improves the performances of the traditional system proposed in [6]. For this reason we have compared both systems based on 2138 connected components extracted from 25 randomly chosen images from the IAM handwriting database[1].

2 Basics

2.1 Argumentation

Argumentation (see e.g. [2]) can be abstractly defined as the formal interaction of different conflicting arguments for and against some conclusion due to different reasons and provides the appropriate semantics (see e.g. [5]) for resolving such conflicts and determining which are the winning arguments. Thus, it is very well suited for implementing decision making mechanisms. Moreover when the decisions are involving dynamic preferences we need a specific type of argumentation frameworks. For this reason we have chosen the framework proposed in [7]. This framework has been applied in a successful way in different applications[2] involving dynamic preferences and it is supported by an open source software called Gorgias[3].

In this framework the argumentation theories are represented at three levels. The *object level arguments* representing the decisions (or the actions) an agent can undertake in a specific domain of application and *priority arguments*

---

[1] http://www.iam.unibe.ch/fki/databases/iam-handwriting-database.
[2] http://gorgiasb.tuc.gr/.
[3] http://www.cs.ucy.ac.cy/~nkd/gorgias/.

expressing preferences on the object level arguments in order to resolve possible conflicts. *Higher order priority arguments* are also used in order to resolve potential conflicts between priority arguments of the previous level. This framework allows for the representation of dynamic preferences under the form of dynamic priorities over arguments and uses Dung semantics [5].

An argumentation theory is a pair $(\mathcal{T}, \mathcal{P})$ whose sentences are formulas in the background monotonic logic $(\mathcal{L}, \vdash)$ of the form $L \leftarrow L_1, \ldots, L_n$, where $L, L_1, \ldots, L_n$ are positive or negative ground literals. Rules in $\mathcal{T}$ represent the object level arguments. Rules in $\mathcal{P}$ represent priority arguments where the head L refers to an (irreflexive) *higher priority* relation. L has the general form $L = h\_p(rule1, rule2)$ where h_p stands for higher priority. The derivability relation, $\vdash$, of the background logic is given by the simple inference rule of modus ponens. Thus, more formally we have:

Definition 1 *[7]. An agent's* **argumentative policy theory or theory,** T, *is a triple* $T = (\mathcal{T}, \mathcal{P}_R, \mathcal{P}_C)$ *where the rules in* $\mathcal{T}$ *do not refer to* h_p, *all the rules in* $\mathcal{P}_R$ *are priority rules with head* $h\_p(r_1, r_2)$ *s.t.* $r_1, r_2 \in \mathcal{T}$ *and all rules in* $\mathcal{P}_C$ *are priority rules with head* $h\_p(R_1, R_2)$ *s.t.* $R_1, R_2 \in \mathcal{P}_R \cup \mathcal{P}_C$.

2.2 Image Analysis

In this section we discuss basic concepts related to the image analysis problem. An image is composed of a set of pixels each of them having a different luminance level that corresponds to a particular color (i.e. from 0 for black color to 255 for white). Their spatial distribution is represented in a matrix. An image is then represented as a rectangular array where the indexes refer to the spatial location of a pixel while the elements' values refer to the color of the pixels. A document image is a specific type of image, representing a paper document through an array structure. A binary image is characterized by the use of only two luminance levels. This limitation is quite convenient when studying document images where the text appears in black and the background in white. Then a binary image corresponds to a set of objects that are the connected components of the black pixels. In printed texts, connected components are basically the characters. Nevertheless, an "i" letter comprises two connected components as the dot is a connected component by itself.

3   The Handwritten/Printed Text Discrimination Problem

A document is a juxtaposition of different media (i.e. text or image for instance) that have different appearances. Thus automatization of a document image processing greatly depends on the content of these media. In the field of document image analysis, the different parts of a document are not processed in the same way. For example illustrative figures are not processed as are texts or tables [9]. Herein we are interested in the discrimination between printed and handwritten texts. Although they are both texts, they refer to different sources of knowledge. To overcome the semantic gap between a word image and its meaning, an optical character recognition software (OCR) is used. However, we cannot use the same OCR software for both types of texts (i.e. printed and handwritten). Current electronic document management systems (EDMS) don't apply for hybrid documents (e.g. printed documents with handwritten annotations). Thus, adding an automated printed/handwritten discrimination step in the management of electronic documents would allow processing such hybrid documents.

3.1   The Baseline System

The handwritten/printed text discrimination is a problem involving two possible decisions (or two-class problem) usually solved after a binarization of grey level images. The decision is usually made at the *connected component* (CC) level of a binarised image (see Fig. 1) and they are labeled as *printed* or *handwritten*. n features are computed enabling the representation of each CC as a point in a n dimensional space. These features refer to the texture or the shape of the CCs and are computed through image transformations (e.g. wavelets, Haralick features). The vectors of features' values are the input of a classifier. Then classifiers such as Support Vector Machine (SVM, see e.g. [8]), k nearest neighbors (see e.g. [4]), or naive Bayes classifier (see e.g. [4]) can be built, during a training step.

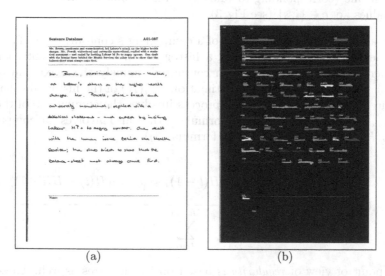

(a)   (b)

Fig. 1. *Working Connected Components* (WCCs) of the image iam087: (a) Binarized document image (image 087 of the IAM database) (b) Its WCCs.

As previously said, in our work we use as baseline system the framework we proposed in [6]. This framework uses a small number of features that may refer to two different points of view, namely *regularity* and *linearity*. Indeed, a printed text is more regular than a handwritten one. The characters of the printed text have all the same height and are well aligned along a straight line. Then regularity can be computed as the variance of the upper or lower profile of the text. The more regular the profile, the higher the probability of being a printed text. Besides, straight segments are drawn with more or less accuracy in handwritten texts, whereas the linearity is perfect in printed texts. We then estimate linearity by measuring the degradation of the approximation of straight segments at different levels (see Fig. 2). The labeling process is applied on *CCs* extracted from the binarized image on which a Run Length Smoothing Algorithm (*RLSA*) transformation has been applied in order to have *Working CCs* (or *WCCs*) with a significant area (see Fig. 1). Moreover in this work we have shown that although the number of features we use is very small, the obtained results are competitive with the results of systems using several hundreds of features. For helping the reader we will explain here these two points of view.

Linearity is computed on *CCs* using two parameters:

1. a parameter denoted a representing the error level of the polygonal approximation of a CC's contour (see Fig. 2). This parameter takes two values i.e. $a \in \{1, 5\}$;
2. a parameter denoted c comparing the value of a feature related to a component with the value of the same feature related to the union of the component itself (corresponding to value i) and its symmetrical one wrt a horizontal straight line (corresponding to value s). This parameter takes therefore also two values i.e. $c \in \{i, s\}$ (see Fig. 3).

From a polygonal approximation of a component's contour, a set of straight line segments is extracted and then a histogram H of the segments' lengths is considered. Two features are then computed, namely the maximum of the segment lengths $SM_{a,c}(H)$ and an estimation $L_{a,i}(H)$ of the histogram shape as defined in formula (1). The decision process involves the comparison of the two values $L_{5,i}(H)$ and $L_{1,i}(H)$ (used in formula (2)). It also involves the comparison of $SM_{5,i}(H)$ and $SM_{5,s}(H)$ (used in formula (3)).

$$L_{a,i}(H) = \frac{\sum_{l=1}^{SM_{a,i}(H)} l \cdot (H(l) - H(l-1)) \cdot \chi_{[0,+\infty[}(H(l) - H(l-1))}{\sum_{l=0}^{SM_{a,i}(H)} H(l)} \tag{1}$$

The point of view of *regularity* is based on two features as well. These features are computed from the upper and lower profile of a component and are called *upper regularity* R_U and *lower regularity* R_L. Each profile is a sequence of points characterized by their vertical position. R_U and R_L are defined as the standard deviation of the points' vertical positions in the upper and lower profile respectively (used in formulas (4) and (5)). In the current work we consider

(a)   (b)   (c)

Fig. 2. Two different polygonal approximations: (a) original images, (b) accurate polygonal approximation (a = 1), (c) less accurate polygonal approximation (a = 5) from [6]

Fig. 3. The zone of interest i (left) and its union with its symmetrical part s (right)

the same definition of features as in [6]. More precisely the evolution of the L value relies on the values of parameter a which correspond to the values of the *precision* parameter in the Wall algorithm [12]. We also consider the evolution of SM when using i and s (see above).

$$L_{5,i}(H) > LT_1 \cdot L_{1,i}(H) \tag{2}$$

$$SM_{5,i}(H) > LT_2 \cdot SM_{5,s}(H) \tag{3}$$

$$R_U > RT_1 \tag{4}$$

$$R_L > RT_2 \tag{5}$$

The decision making is achieved after a learning step providing four threshold values i.e. $LT_1 = 3$, $LT_2 = 1.5$, $RT_1 = 0.02$, $RT_2 = 0.0045$. The decision function based on those values is a piecewise linear function. Once the four previous boolean values have been computed (see above formulas (2)–(5)), the decision is taken according to the following rule (see formula (6)).

A component is labeled as handwritten if (2) AND (3) AND ((4) OR (5))   (6)

3.2   The Baseline System Vs. State of the Art

The comparison between different methods is difficult as the used databases are not public and therefore they may differ from one study to another. The evaluation can be done at word, pseudo-word or pixel level. Furthermore the results depend on the sets used for the learning and validation steps. The system we presented in [6] was developed in an industrial environment and it has been evaluated on a large dataset of real documents used by the company. The system was run by the company and evaluated at pixel level. It has been also compared to another system [1] chosen by the same company and the results are presented in Table 1.

Table 1. Comparison of systems proposed in [1,6] (presented in [6])

	Baseline system [6]	Belaid et al. system [1]
Text entity	Pseudo-word	Pseudo-word
Descriptors	4	137
Classifiers	Decision rules	SVM
Regularization	kNN	kNN
Database	Industrial dataset	Industrial dataset
Recognition rate (%)	90.15	89.05

As we can see in the above table, the baseline system slightly outperforms the system proposed in [1] although it uses far fewer features than this system. That means that the features considered in [6] are very meaningful.

4   Why Using Agent Technology?

4.1   Motivation

Our motivation for using agent technology is based on four drawbacks we have observed regarding the baseline system we proposed in [6] (and discussed in the previous section) but also other traditional systems (see e.g. [1,8,10,11]) using several points of view:

1. The different points of view (e.g. regularity and linearity in our case) are not independently represented. This is what is happening in other approaches such as machine learning-based approaches where different points of view are merged from the beginning as the learning is based on a unique data set. So possible optimal solutions, that could be found considering each point of view independently before looking for solutions that correspond to a compromise between them, can be missed.
2. The parameters of the decision functions associated with these points of view cannot change after the learning phase.
3. There is a need for dynamic decision making by adapting the decisions to the particular contexts.
4. There is a lack of explanation of the decisions taken by the system.

In this paper we propose a novel approach which takes into consideration the four aforementioned drawbacks. More precisely, by associating an agent (as autonomous decision maker) with a point of view, we are able to look initially for optimal solutions wrt each point of view independently and then to detect situations where the decisions do not coincide (i.e. the agents have an initial disagreement). This is an important information as it can trigger in both agents a fine tuning of their initial decision models. In that case the discrimination problem is transformed into a *distributed decision making* problem where agents are looking for an agreement (i.e. by proposing the same decision namely "printed" or "handwritten") through a bilateral dialogue. During this dialogue their initial decision models are evolving when a (transitory) disagreement occurs at the end of a round. Finally, the last two drawbacks are taken into consideration by using argumentation for modeling the decision making mechanisms of the agents. The framework we are using [7] allows for the modeling of generic but also context dependent decisions when this is needed. Argumentation also allows for decisions explanation as the framework we are using can present a trace of the reasoning that agents have followed for making a decision.

4.2 Our Approach

For illustrating how our system works we will consider the decision making problem considered in [6] where two different decisions (or opinions), referring to two different points of view, have to be reconciliated. We may consider that each decision is based on different numerical features (e.g. presence of straight line segments on the contour of the writing, upper and lower regularity profiles of the writing, etc.) extracted from an image. Each decision is made by using a decision function. In our case the representation space for both points of view is a two dimensional space and thus the decision function can be represented by a curve in a two dimensional space. This function is built by using a learning technique. The image under analysis is represented by a point in this space. A decision is therefore depending on the position of this point wrt to the curve (see Fig. 4(a)). The initial situation is represented by a solid line (see Fig. 4(a)). We have two possible decisions, decision D_1 (i.e. the image represents a printed text) and decision D_2 (i.e. the image represents a handwritten text).

Let's now describe our approach where we associate an agent with a point of view. We consider two agents α and β associated with the initial decisions D_1 and D_2 respectively. As these decisions are different, the agents will enter into a dialogue. In [6] these decisions cannot change during the process but in our approach they can. More particularly, the agents cannot challenge the structure of the decision function but they can move the curve in one direction so that the point representing the image gets closer to the curve. As the curve's shifting cannot be done in a continuous way, we consider a *unit measure* representing the "distance" between two successive curve's positions. Every shifting of a curve corresponds to an action undertaken by each agent when a disagreement is detected after the exchange of their individual decisions. This action refers to the change of some parameters of the decision function within the chosen family of functions used. As the iso-decision curves are not regularly positioned in the space, we have decided to model the shifting of the decision curves by using two different parameters. Each exchange of the individual decisions is considered as a dialogue round. This process continues until a consensus is reached. An agent changes his opinion/decision when the image representation is found on the other side of the moving curve.

As we can see in Fig. 4(a), agent α needs three steps for changing his decision (illustrated by the dotted line curves) while agent β needs only two. In the

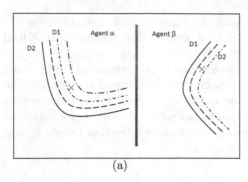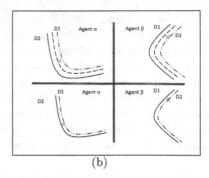

(a)   (b)

Fig. 4. (a) Initial position (solid line) and shifting (dotted lines) of the decision function for α and β during the dialogue (b) Change of the unit measure value when agents change decision simultaneously in a dialogue round

current example we can observe that agent β has changed his decision after two dialogue rounds. The final decision will therefore be decision D_1 which is the initial decision of agent α. We therefore associate more confidence to the agent who has more resisted to a change of his decision.

However, we can have situations where both agents might change their decisions in the same dialogue round. In that case our approach proposes the adaptation of the unit measure in a recursive way. This case is illustrated in the upper part of the Fig. 4(b) where both agents change their decisions after the second round of the dialogue. In this situation agents have to get back to the previous state of the dialogue and to decrease the unit measure before starting a new dialogue round as illustrated in the bottom of Fig. 4(b). The dialogue terminates either with an agreement (i.e. when one of the agents changes his decision and agrees with the other) or with a final disagreement (i.e. when the unit measure attains a minimum value without an agreement to be found). In that case, the decision is taken randomly. The overall architecture of our agent-based approach can be represented as in Fig. 5(a).

5   The Agent-Based System

In this section we will present the agent-based system we have designed for implementing the approach we have proposed in Sect. 4.2.

5.1   Decision Theories of Agents

In this section we present the transformation of the baseline system presented in [6] into a multi-agent system involving two autonomous agents associated with the two different points of view presented in Sect. 3.1, namely *linearity* and *regularity*. We will call the agents, *Linearity* Agent and *Regularity* Agent, respectively. For representing the knowledge of these agents we have used the formulas (2)–(5) and the decision rule (6). As presented in Sect. 3.1, the first two conditions (i.e. (2) and (3)) are referring to the linearity point of view, while the last two conditions (i.e. (4) and (5)) to the regularity point of view. Thus the decisions (i.e. "printed" or "handwritten") taken in the baseline system by using the decision rule (6), will, in our approach, be taken through a bilateral dialogue between Linearity Agent (LA) and Regularity Agent (RA). The final decision will thus be corresponding to an agreement between the two agents reached after one or several rounds of dialogue.

For representing the decision theories of the two agents we translated the corresponding formulas into argumentation theories by using the argumentation framework proposed in [7] (and discussed in Sect. 2.1). The use of argumentation allows to represent in a more explicit way the different scenarios that are generated when the features $L_{5,i}(H)$, $L_{1,i}(H)$, $SM_{5,i}(H)$ and $SM_{5,s}(H)$ are taking specific values wrt the thresholds LT_1 and LT_2 for Linearity Agent. The same holds for the scenarios that are generated when the features R_U and R_L are taking specific values wrt the thresholds RT_1 and RT_2 for Regularity Agent. This representation puts explicitly in evidence the possible dilemmas of the agents by detecting conflicting situations (i.e. when both decisions namely "handwritten" and "printed" are possible) and allows to use default (or generic) and contextual knowledge for solving these conflicts.

The *Linearity* agent theory is as follows. The two possible decisions are $d_1^{Lin} = $ "*Printed*" and $d_2^{Lin} = $ "*Handwritten*".

$$r_1 : d_1^{Lin} \leftarrow (SM_{5,s}(H)/SM_{5,i}(H)) > LT_1$$
$$r_2 : d_2^{Lin} \leftarrow (L_{5,i}(H)/L_{1,i}(H)) > LT_2$$
$$r_3 : d_2^{Lin} \leftarrow (SM_{5,s}(H)/SM_{5,i}(H)) \leq LT_1$$
$$r_4 : d_1^{Lin} \leftarrow (L_{5,i}(H)/L_{1,i}(H)) \leq LT_2$$
$$R_1 : h\_p(r_1, r_2) \leftarrow true$$
$$R_2 : h\_p(r_4, r_3) \leftarrow true$$

The *Regularity* agent theory is as follows. The two possible decisions are $d_1^{Reg} = $ "*Printed*" and $d_2^{Reg} = $ "*Handwritten*".

$$r_1 : d_1^{Reg} \leftarrow R_U \leq RT_1$$
$$r_2 : d_1^{Reg} \leftarrow R_L \leq RT_2$$
$$r_3 : d_2^{Reg} \leftarrow R_L > RT_2$$
$$r_4 : d_2^{Reg} \leftarrow R_U > RT_1$$
$$R_1 : h\_p(r_3, r_1) \leftarrow true$$
$$R_2 : h\_p(r_4, r_2) \leftarrow true$$
$$R_3 : h\_p(r_1, r_3) \leftarrow H_{CC} \leq HT, W_{CC} > 20 * HT$$
$$R_4 : h\_p(r_2, r_4) \leftarrow H_{CC} \leq HT, W_{CC} > 20 * HT$$
$$C_1 : h\_p(R_3, R_1) \leftarrow true$$
$$C_2 : h\_p(R_4, R_2) \leftarrow true$$

The above theories show how we can represent the conflicting knowledge associated with each point of view (i.e. linearity and regularity) and how we can put in evidence the contradictory decisions that can be taken when some situations may arrive simultaneously. These conflicting situations are described by rules r_1 and r_2 and rules r_3 and r_4 in the linearity theory and also by rules r_1 and r_3 and rules r_2 and r_4 in the regularity theory. However, we note that the experts are able to prioritize these conflicting situations and to solve the generated conflicts. This is done with rules R_1 and R_2 in the linearity theory where the priority is given to the decision "printed" and the rules R_1 and R_2 in the regularity theory where the priority is given to the decision "handwritten". This information is hidden in the decision making models of traditional systems but it can be captured and exploited in our system due to the use of argumentation. This is one of the added values of our approach. Moreover the use of this particular argumentation framework (i.e. [7]) allows for the contextualization and the resolution of conflicts at different hierarchical levels. This case is presented in the regularity theory. As we said before, rules R_1 and R_2 are indicating that, when both decisions (i.e. "handwritten" and "printed") can be simultaneously taken, the priority is usually given to the decision "handwritten" (see that r_3 is preferred over r_1 and r_4 is preferred over r_2). However, when some specific conditions (described in the premises of rules R_3 and R_4) are satisfied, then the priority must be given to the decision "printed" (see that r_1 is preferred over r_3 and r_2 is preferred over r_4). Indeed, these conditions are based on contextual knowledge and indicate that when the height of a connected component H_{CC}, is less or equal to a threshold HT and its width W_{CC}, is greater than 20 times the threshold HT, then the decision for this connected component should be rather "printed" than "handwritten". As we will then show in Sect. 5.4, the contextualization of the decisions allowed to sensibly improve the recognition of "printed" components (see Table 3) by the agent-based system and consists in one of the added values of our approach. So for giving the priority to the decisions based on the contextual knowledge (rules R_3 and R_4) over the decisions based on the generic knowledge (rules R_1 and R_2), we use the rules C_1 (i.e. R_3 is preferred over R_1) and C_2 (i.e. R_4 is preferred over R_2) at a higher level of the theory. With this framework we can also keep a trace of the reasoning made by the agents and more particularly we can have an explanation concerning the arguments (i.e. rules r, R and C) that have been used for making a decision and the facts (i.e. the domain knowledge) that have been considered (i.e. the values of the different parameters) as supporting information of these arguments. This allows to take into consideration one of the observations we highlighted in Sect. 4.1 namely the need of explanation for the users.

5.2   The Agent Architecture

In this section we will describe and discuss the Linearity and Regularity Agents' architecture (see Fig. 5(b)). Indeed, the two types of agents have exactly the same architecture. Their only difference is the specific knowledge (e.g. argumentative decision theories presented above, features involved, etc.) related to the linearity and regularity points of view that instantiates the different modules of their architectural structures.

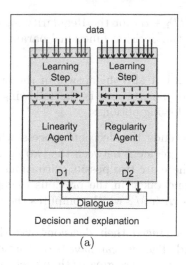
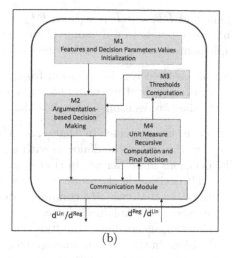

(a)   (b)

Fig. 5. (a) Representative architecture of our proposal (b) Architecture of Linearity/Regularity Agent

Module $M2$ contains the argumentation theories presented above. It provides the decision (d^{Lin} or d^{Reg}) based on the information (i.e. initial values of parameters) coming from module $M1$ at the beginning of the analysis process or from module $M3$ (concerning the new values of the thresholds) after the first round of the dialogue. This decision is sent to the *communication module*. $M2$ sends also the decision to the module $M4$.

Communication modules are responsible for the communication and the implementation of the dialogue between the two agents. The communication module sends the decision to the other agent and waits for the answer. Then it informs the module $M4$.

Module $M3$ updates the decision surface in the representation space. In our case this corresponds to the computation of the new thresholds LT_1, LT_2, RT_1, RT_2 based on:

- Two parameters namely α_1, associated with LT_1 and RT_1, and α_2, associated with LT_2 and RT_2. These parameters allow to manage the shifting of the decision function and are chosen for guaranteeing a balance between the possible change of opinion of both agents. According to the shape of the decision functions in the baseline system and the nature of the features we are using, the shifting is not regular and that is why these two parameters have been introduced. Their values need to be fixed according to a validation set.
- The current decision i.e. "handwritten" or "printed". The decision curve is always moved towards the position of the representation point in the working space. More particularly if the current decision is "printed" then $LT_1 = LT_1 - \alpha_1$ and $LT_2 = LT_2 + \alpha_2$ for the Linearity Agent and $RT_1 = RT_1 - \alpha_1$ and $RT_2 = RT_2 - \alpha_2$ for the Regularity Agent. Otherwise, if the current decision is "handwritten" then $LT_1 = LT_1 + \alpha_1$ and $LT_2 = LT_2 - \alpha_2$ for the Linearity

Agent and $RT_1 = RT_1 + \alpha_1$ and $RT_2 = RT_2 + \alpha_2$ for the Regularity Agent. This corresponds to a dynamic change of the decision functions' parameters implemented as argumentation theories.

Module $M4$ receives information from $M2$ but also the answer of the other agent transferred by the communication module. Its role is the following. It compares the two decisions and it has the following options:

- The decisions coincide. In that case $M4$ ends the decision process which provokes the end of the dialogue with an agreement between the two agents.
- The decisions are different. In that case there are two possible situations:
  1. Each decision is the same with the one taken in the previous dialogue round. In that case $M4$ communicates with $M3$ which computes the new thresholds as explained above.
  2. The two agents have simultaneously changed their decisions wrt their decisions in the previous dialogue round. Then we can have two situations:
     (a) the values of the unit measures α_1 and α_2 are greater than their minimal values in which case $M4$ decreases the values of unit measures. In the current implementation we have defined empirically the initial values of α_1 and α_2 and the decrease of their values is defined as follows: $\alpha_1 = \alpha_1 \div 5$ and $\alpha_2 = \alpha_2 \div 5$. This information is sent to $M3$. This is a recursive procedure as explained in Sect. 4.2.
     (b) the values of the unit measures are lower than their minimal values in which case $M4$ ends the decision process. This provokes the end of the dialogue with a final disagreement between the two agents. In that case $M4$ returns a random decision.

The agent-based system has been implemented by using the well known agent development platform JADE[4]. However, we had also to implement an interface with SWI-Prolog[5] for running the Gorgias system that we have used for implementing the argumentation-based reasoning of the agents (i.e. module $M2$).

5.3   How the Dialogue Evolves?

In Fig. 6 we show a trace of a dialogue between a Regularity Agent and a Linearity Agent concerning a working connected component (i.e. number 63 of image 087 of the IAM database).
In this figure we may see several elements:

1. The predicates we have defined for representing the features, the thresholds and the dimensions of the components used in the argumentation theories presented in Sect. 5.1 as well as the implementation of those theories with Gorgias (i.e. in regularity theory the rules named "hp" implement the rules named "R" and the rules named "hphp" implement the rules named "C"; in linearity theory the rules named "hp" implement the rules named "R");

---

[4] http://jade.tilab.com/.
[5] www.swi-prolog.org.

```
CC n°: 63
....
Printed-Handwritten

Dialogue Round REGULARITY AGENT  :2
Dialogue Round LINEARITY AGENT:2

#### alpha1 REGULARITY AGENT: 0.001
#### alpha2 REGULARITY AGENT: 5.0E-4
#### alpha1 LINEARITY AGENT: 0.1
#### alpha2 LINEARITY AGENT: 0.05

***** LINEARITY DATA *********
:- compile('gorgias-src-0.6d/lib/gorgias').
:- compile('gorgias-src-0.6d/ext/lpwnf').
rule(r1(X1,Y1,T1), pr(X1,Y1,T1), [hs(X1),  hi(Y1),  thr1(T1),
X1>(T1*Y1)]).
rule(r2(X2,Y2,T2), hw(X2,Y2,T2), [linA1(X2), linA2(Y2),  thr2(T2),
Y2>(T2*X2)]).
rule(r3(X1,Y1,T1), hw(X1,Y1,T1), [hs(X1),  hi(Y1),  thr1(T1),
X1=<(T1*Y1)]).
rule(r4(X2,Y2,T2), pr(X2,Y2,T2), [linA1(X2), linA2(Y2),  thr2(T2),
Y2=<(T2*X2)]).
rule(hp1, prefer(r1(X1,Y1,T1), r2(X2,Y2,T2)), [ ]).
rule(hp2, prefer(r4(X2,Y2,T2), r3(X1,Y1,T1)), [ ]).
rule(f1, hs(60.0), [ ]).
rule(f2, hi(86.0), [ ]).
rule(f3, linA1(3.6969696969696697), [ ]).
rule(f4, linA2(10.64), [ ]).
rule(f5, thr1(1.6), [ ]).
rule(f6, thr2(2.8), [ ]).
conflict(r1(X1,Y1,T1), r2(X2,Y2,T2)).
conflict(r3(X1,Y1,T1), r4(X2,Y2,T2)).
conflict(r2(X2,Y2,T2), r1(X1,Y1,T1)).
conflict(r4(X2,Y2,T2), r3(X1,Y1,T1)).
```

```
******* REGULARITY DATA ********
:- compile('gorgias-src-0.6d/lib/gorgias').
:- compile('gorgias-src-0.6d/ext/lpwnf').
rule(r1(X1,T1,X3,X4,T3),pr(X1,T1,X3,X4,T3),[ru(X1),thr1(T1),X1=<T
1]).
rule(r2(X2,T2,X3,X4,T3),pr(X2,T2,X3,X4,T3),[r1(X2),thr2(T2),X2=<T
2]).
rule(r3(X2,T2,X3,X4,T3),hw(X2,T2,X3,X4,T3),[ru(X2),thr2(T2),X2>T2
]).
rule(r4(X1,T1,X3,X4,T3),hw(X1,T1,X3,X4,T3),[r1(X1),thr1(T1),X1>T1
]).
rule(hp1, prefer(r3(X2,T2,X3,X4,T3),r1(X1,T1,X3,X4,T3)), []).
rule(hp2, prefer(r4(X1,T1,X3,X4,T3),r2(X2,T2,X3,X4,T3)), []).
rule(hp3, prefer(r1(X1,T1,X3,X4,T3),r3(X2,T2,X3,X4,T3)),
[hcc(X3),wcc(X4),ht(T3),X3=<T3,X4>20*X3]).
rule(hp4, prefer(r2(X2,T2,X3,X4,T3),r4(X1,T1,X3,X4,T3)),
[hcc(X3),wcc(X4),ht(T3),X3=<T3,X4>20*X3]).
rule(hphp31, prefer(hp3,hp1),[]).
rule(hphp42, prefer(hp4,hp2),[]).
rule(f1,ru(0.036110187766118164),[]).
rule(f2,r1(0.006284141516083502),[]).
rule(f3,thr1(0.022000000000000002),[]).
rule(f4,thr2(0.0055),[]).
rule(f5,hcc(36.0),[]).
rule(f6,wcc(204.0),[]).
rule(f7,ht(50),[]).
conflict(r1(X1,T1,X3,X4,T3),r3(X2,T2,X3,X4,T3)).
conflict(r2(X2,T2,X3,X4,T3),r4(X1,T1,X3,X4,T3)).
conflict(r3(X2,T2,X3,X4,T3),r1(X1,T1,X3,X4,T3)).
conflict(r4(X1,T1,X3,X4,T3),r2(X2,T2,X3,X4,T3)).

Handwritten-Handwritten
Dialogue Round LINEARITY AGENT: 3
Dialogue Round REGULARITY AGENT: 3

LINEARITY AGENT: Agreement with final decision:
Handwritten
REGULARITY AGENT: Agreement with final decision:
Handwritten

Agreement-Handwritten-Handwritten
```

(a)   (b)

Fig. 6. Part of a trace of a dialogue on working connected component number 63 of image 087 of IAM database: Agents LA (a) and RA (b) enter in round 3 with a disagreement and end up their dialogue on component 63, in round 3 with an agreement by both proposing "handwritten" as final decision.

2. The evolution of the values of those features during the dialogue. For example the initial values of the thresholds presented in Sect. 3.1 are $LT_1 = 3$, $LT_2 = 1.5$, $RT_1 = 0.02$, $RT_2 = 0.0045$ while at the end of the dialogue they are $LT_1 = 1.6$ (see f_5), $LT_2 = 2.8$ (see f_6), $RT_1 = 0.022$ (see f_3), $RT_2 = 0.0055$ (see f_4) respectively;

3. The initial values for α_1 (i.e. "alpha1") and α_2 (i.e. "alpha2");

4. We note that the agents had an initial disagreement (i.e. Regularity Agent has proposed "printed" and Linearity Agent "handwritten") which has persisted during the round 2 but they finally terminated this dialogue by reaching an agreement after the end of round 3 by both proposing "handwritten" as final decision (see rules r_2, r_3 and facts f_1, f_2, f_3, f_4, f_5, f_6 in Regularity Agent (see Fig. 6(b)) and rules r_3, r_4 and facts f_1, f_2, f_3, f_4, f_5, f_6 in Linearity Agent (see Fig. 6(a))). That means that Regularity Agent has changed his opinion in round 3.

5.4 Experimental Results

The Datasets. The aim of our experiments was to test the capability of our system to improve the final decisions proposed by the baseline system [6]. For our experiments we have chosen a public database that contains the same number of handwritten and printed words. This is the well known IAM handwriting database[6] that consists of a number of pages containing printed texts reproduced by different writers. The comparison of the two systems (i.e. the baseline system [6] and the agent-based system) has been done at the WCC level. Comparison at WCC level (see Fig. 1) is more appropriate than at word or pixel level, as the agents are taking decisions at that level. As IAM database does not contain the ground truth (GT) (i.e. set of pairs (WCC, label)) at WCC level, we built a GT by doing a manual labeling on 25 images. These 25 pages are written by various writers. This set of images contains 3347 words and among them 1591 are handwritten and 1756 are printed. It corresponds to 2138 $WCCs$ where 1771 are handwritten and 367 are printed (see Table 2). We consider that this is the best option for evaluating the contribution of the dialogue between the two agents on the final decision (i.e. "printed" or "handwritten"). All the results concerning the 25 images are available here[7].

Evaluation. In Table 2 we present the confusion matrices (i.e. number of correct and false labels wrt GT) of the baseline and agent-based system respectively. The best results for handwritten and printed $WCCs$ appear in bold. We can observe that the agent-based system has clearly improved the results concerning the handwritten $WCCs$.

Table 2. Confusion matrices for baseline [6] and agent-based system at WCC level

		GT handwritten	GT Printed
Baseline system	Handwritten	1147	43
	Printed	624	**324**
Agent system	Handwritten	**1656**	54
	Printed	115	313
Total GT		1771	367

Indeed, as seen in Table 3, the agent-based system outperforms the baseline system as far as the handwritten $WCCs$ recognition is concerned, with a reduction of 81.67% of the error rate. Moreover, we note a real improvement of the global recognition rate as it has increased from 68.80% to 92.1%. This means that we have a reduction of 74.66% of the global error rate.

As far as the printed $WCCs$ recognition is concerned, Table 2 shows that our system is slightly dominated by the baseline system (i.e. 313/367 correct results for the agent-based system vs. 324/367 for the baseline system). This is basically due to the fact that our system fails labeling as "printed" the component on the

---

[6] http://www.iam.unibe.ch/fki/databases/iam-handwriting-database.
[7] http://www.math-info.univ-paris5.fr/~cloppet/PRIMA/ResultsIamPRIMA2017.pdf.

Table 3. Handwritten Recognition Rate (HRR), Printed Recognition Rate (PRR) and Global Recognition Rate (GRR) at working connected component (WCC) level.

	HRR (%)	PRR (%)	GRR (%)
Baseline system [6]	64.77	88.28	68.80
Agent system without contextualization	93.45	82.02	91.49
Agent system with contextualization	93.51	85.29	92.10
Final % of change	28.74	−3.01	23.29
Final % of change of error rate	−81.57	+25.58	−74.66

Table 4. Dialogues between Linearity and Regularity Agents

Total number of CC	Number of dialogues terminating with an agreement (right or wrong decision)	Average number of dialogue rounds
2138	2137	3.90

top right of the images including numbers. It is however worth noting that the agent-based system attains a score of 93.51% of correct decisions concerning the handwritten $WCCs$ while simultaneously it attains a high score (i.e. 85.29%) of correct decisions concerning the printed $WCCs$. During the processing, the agents start a dialogue only when they disagree during the initial round. In our experiments this happened in 92.32% of the cases. As shown in Table 4, the average number of dialogue rounds is 3.90, and only one dialogue out of 2138 ended up with a final disagreement (i.e. a random decision was taken). This illustrates the very good convergence of the system. Finally, concerning the total computation time for processing a single image, the average time cost is 10196 ms on a laptop equipped with a 1.3 GHz IntelCore i5 processor and 4 GB RAM (1600 MHz), where only 595 ms are dedicated to the processing involving the two agents.

6   Conclusion and Future Work

In this paper we have presented an agent-based approach for solving an important problem in the field of image analysis namely the automated discrimination of handwritten/printed texts. Agent technology has already been used in the domain of image processing (see e.g. [3]) but never for dealing with this particular problem. More precisely we have shown that this problem can be transformed in a distributed decision making problem where the decision about the labeling (i.e. "handwritten" or "printed") of a text is made through a dialogue between autonomous agents. We also showed that computational argumentation (and more particularly a structured argumentation framework [7] and its associated development tool) is very well suited for implementing the decision making mechanisms of such agents. Our system can be easily extended by adding much more features (if necessary) through the insertion of additional rules in the argumentation theories. Our experimental results have proven that our solution considerably improves the performance of a (state of the art) traditional system [6]. It therefore contributes to the opening of new directions towards an increased use of agent technology (and argumentation) in the important domain of document analysis. Our system can be used in several real world applications related to this domain such as printed text detection and extraction for Optical Character Recognition (OCR), handwritten text extraction from filled up printed forms, automated detection of manually annotated printed documents. Moreover, as current electronic document management systems (EDMS) don't apply for hybrid documents (e.g. printed documents with handwritten annotations), adding an automated printed/handwritten discrimination step in these systems, would allow processing such documents in an automated way.

References

1. Belaïd, A., Santosh, K.C., Poulain D'Andecy, V.: Handwritten and printed text separation in real document. In: Proceedings of the 13th IAPR International Conference on Machine Vision Applications, MVA 2013, Kyoto, Japan, pp. 218–221, 20–23 May 2013
2. Bench-Capon, T.J.M., Dunne, P.E.: Argumentation in artificial intelligence. Artif. Intell. **171**(10–15), 619–641 (2007)
3. Bovenkamp, E.G.P., Dijkstra, J., Bosch, J.G., Reiber, J.H.C.: Multi-agent segmentation of IVUS images. Pattern Recogn. **37**(4), 647–663 (2004)
4. Duda, R.O., Hart, P.E., Stork, D.G.: Pattern Classification, 2nd edn. Wiley-Interscience, New York (2000)
5. Dung, P.M.: On the acceptability of arguments and its fundamental role in nonmonotonic reasoning, logic programming and n-person games. Artif. Intell. **77**, 321–357 (1995)
6. Hamrouni, S., Cloppet, F., Vincent, N.: Handwritten and printed text separation: linearity and regularity assessment. In: Campilho, A., Kamel, M. (eds.) ICIAR 2014. LNCS, vol. 8814, pp. 387–394. Springer, Cham (2014). doi:10.1007/978-3-319-11758-4_42
7. Kakas, A., Moraitis, P.: Argumentation based decision making for autonomous agents. In: Proceedings of the 2nd International Joint Conference on Autonomous Agents and Multi-Agents Systems, pp. 883–890 (2003)
8. Kumar, J., Prasad, R., Cao, H., Abd-Almageed, W., Doermann, D., Natarajan, P.: Shape codebook based handwritten and machine printed text zone extraction. In: Document Recognition and Retrieval, San Francisco, vol. 7874, pp. 1–8, January 2011
9. Lins, R.D.: Meeting new challenges in document engineering. J. UCS **17**(1), 1–2 (2011)
10. Peng, X., Setlur, S., Govindaraju, V., Sitaram, R.: Handwritten text separation from annotated machine printed documents using Markov random fields. IJDAR **16**(1), 1–16 (2013)

11. Ricquebourg, Y., Raymond, C., Poirriez, B., Lemaitre, A., Coüasnon, B.: Boosting bonsai trees for handwritten/printed text discrimination. In: Document Recognition and Retrieval XXI, San Francisco, California, USA, pp. 902105–902105-12, 5–6 February 2014
12. Wall, K., Danielsson, P.E.: A fast sequential method for polygonal approximation of digitized curves. Comput. Vis. Graph. Image Process. **28**(3), 220–227 (1984)

Towards a Generic Multi-agent Approach for Medical Image Segmentation

Mohamed T. Bennai[1,2], Zahia Guessoum[1,3(✉)], Smaine Mazouzi[4],
Stéphane Cormier[1], and Mohamed Mezghiche[2]

[1] CReSTIC, Université de Reims Champagne Ardenne, Reims, France
[2] LIMOSE Laboratory, Computer Science Department, Faculty of Sciences,
University M'Hamed Bougara, Independency Avenue, 35000 Boumerdès, Algeria
[3] LIP6, Université Paris-Sorbonne, Paris, France
Zahia.guessoum@lip6.fr
[4] Department of Computer Science, Univsersité 20 Août 1955, Skikda, Algeria

Abstract. Medical image segmentation is a difficult task, essentially due to the inherent complexity of human body structures and the acquisition methods of this kind of images. Manual segmentation of medical images requires advance radiological expertize and is also very time-consuming. Several methods have been developed to automatize medical image segmentation, including multi-agent approaches. In this paper, we propose a new multi-agent approach based on a set of autonomous and interactive agents that integrates an enhanced region growing algorithm. It does not require any prior knowledge. This approach was implemented and experiments were performed on brain MRI simulated images and the obtained results are promising.

Keywords: Medical images · Segmentation · Multi-agent systems · Interaction · Region growing algorithm

1 Introduction

Image segmentation has been a very active research field for the last decades and has been successfully applied to several application domains such as manufacture [23], face recognition [15], object tracking [34], human interaction [27], bio-metric identification [8], text recognition [24] and medical imaging [29].

The medical images, due to their nature, are one of the most challenging application domains of segmentation. The medical image segmentation, when it is manually performed, requires a high-level expertize. To acquire such expertize human experts spend several years on learning and practicing. So, the elaboration of an automated and efficient system that gives equivalent results remains a challenging issue.

Several approaches have thus been proposed to address the problem of medical image segmentation. The first category of approaches is based on centralized algorithms such as statistical approaches, genetic algorithms and quantum evolutionary algorithms [29]. The second category of approaches is based on swarm

© Springer International Publishing AG 2017
B. An et al. (Eds.): PRIMA 2017, LNAI 10621, pp. 198–211, 2017.
https://doi.org/10.1007/978-3-319-69131-2_12

and collective intelligence [28]. The aim of this last category is to improve the efficiency of the first category by distributing the segmentation process. The so proposed approaches have thus provided promising results. However, they are specific to some types of images and require a high expertize to fix the parameters.

This paper introduces a generic approach for medical image segmentation. That approach does not require any prior knowledge and can be applied to several types of medical images. It is based on a set of interactive and autonomous agents. Each agent explores the image to find a region and uses a growing algorithm to extract a part of this region. In a second phase, the agents use a coordination mechanism to explore and realize the possible merging of their regions and those of their neighbors. Finally, each agent removes noise and refines its borders. To validate this multi-agent approach we carry out several experiments and compare the obtained results to the most efficient approaches of the literature.

The paper is organized as follows. Section 2 analyzes the related work and motivates the proposed approach. Section 3 describes the proposed approach. Section 4 presents the implementation of that approach and analyzes the different experiments. Section 5 gives an overview of the proposed approach and highlights some future work.

2 Related Work

This section gives an overview of medical image segmentation issue and analyzes the related work.

2.1 Medical Image Segmentation

Image segmentation is the partitioning of an image into no-overlapping, constituent regions which are homogeneous with respect to some characteristics such as intensity or texture [29]. It is used in image processing to isolate the objects of interest from the rest of the image. It is also a critical step in machine vision because the whole process of extracting information from the image is mainly based on its segmentation. Any small variation in the results of the segmentation process can produce a significant difference in the image interpretation.

In medical imaging, it is not easy to provide a partition that matches as close as possible the anatomical or functional structures of an explored organ, even with regularly the use of different modalities. Medical image segmentation is a key technique in providing complementary information to visualize and study anatomical or functional structures. The aim of segmentation is to help the clinicians for different purposes like pathologies diagnostic pre-operative planning or image guided surgical procedure, disease tracking, treatment planning [12], etc.

An accurate segmentation is therefore vital in medical imaging, but it is a very difficult task and remains an open issue. The difficulty of segmenting these images comes from different factors, inherent to medical images. Different characteristics (with respect to image modalities) must be taken into account to segment this kind of images:

- anatomical information (MRI, Computed tomography, Ultrasonology, etc.) and functional information (PET, fMRI, CEUS, etc.);
- intra-patient or inter-patient variability;
- specific characteristics and pathology of the explored organs or tissues such as the tissues intensity in-homogeneity, the closeness in gray level of different soft tissues or complexity of human body anatomical structures;
- specific acquisition protocols or acquisition techniques generating noise and/or artifacts such as partial volume effect in Computed Tomography scans or speckle noise in ultrasound images.

So, image segmentation is a very active field and a wide range of segmentation approaches were introduced for segmenting different modalities and pathologies. Those approaches use different techniques such as threshold [35], region growing [1,18], Markov Random Fields [16], Fuzzy and Hard Clustering [2,11], and Deformable Models [21]. They are often coupled with pre-processing techniques to reduce noise or artifacts, or with manual initialization [5]. All those approaches employ monolithic, sequential and centralized systems to perform complex tasks [3]. To improve segmentation efficiency, some approaches use multi-agent systems. Those approaches are summarized in the next section.

2.2   Multi-agent Segmentation Approaches

In recent years, multi-agent paradigm has been used to develop significant applications in different fields of the health care domain [4] among which medical image segmentation.

Several multi-agent approaches have been proposed to deal with medical image segmentation. We distinguish two categories of approaches. In the first category, the agents encapsulate one of the existing algorithms. The agents are thus used to distribute and improve classical segmentation algorithms (Edge detection [25], region fusion [10], genetic algorithms [22] ...). Some systems use RGM (Region Growing Method) on images sub parts, to label pixels from a set of known classes. Richard et al. [31] use this approach for MR brain image segmentation while Chitsaz and Woo [6] use it for CT image scan segmentation. Other multi-agent approaches associate RGM with other segmentation methods, such as Haroun et al. [14]. The latter uses both RGM and Fuzzy C-Mean in a multi-agent system applied to brain MR image. Moreover, Benamrane and Nassane [3] apply RGM and region fusion in the MAS segmentation of the same type of images. Furthermore, Pereira et al. [28] use also the region fusion and RGM in the process of microaneurysm detection in fundus images. Also, Germond et al. [13] propose a modular system that combines an agent based system (using RGM), a deformable model and an edge detector for the segmentation of MRI brain scans.

The second category exploits all the potential of the multi-agent paradigm. The proposed solutions rely on social coordination mechanisms such as ant colonies and social spider colonies [26]. For instance, Djemame et al. [9] use self-organization and adaptation of social spiders to extract homogeneous regions of an image. Liu et al. [19] use agents with living beings' behavior to extract brain structures in a scan image. Richard et al. [32] use cooperative and interactive behaviors to respectively distribute the work and propagate information among agents of their MAS to segment medical images.

2.3 Discussion

The previous sub-sections describe interesting and innovative approaches. Most of those approaches provide promising results. However, they often suffer from one or several drawbacks:

- each approach is specific to the type of images that was designed for and does not support generalization;
- each approach is based on a prior knowledge or a training data set that affects the segmentation results;
- each approach requires a user intervention for setting up parameters or thresholds.

In the aim of overcoming some of these disadvantages, we developed an adaptive multi-agent approach for medical image segmentation. This approach is described in the next section.

3 An Adaptive Agent-Based Medical Image Segmentation

Our approach is based on a set of agents situated in an environment. The latter is defined as a two-dimensional matrix of pixels. Each pixel contains two types of information: the scalar gray level intensity of the corresponding pixel in the processed image, and a vector value of the gradient on this pixel. This gradient value is obtained by the application of a Sobel filter on the initial image. During a multi-agent system execution, several generations of agents are successively created on the unexplored areas of the image. The different generations of agents have the same behavior but they may have different parameters. The agents of those generations have the following life cycle:

- When activated, an agent starts exploring its environment looking for a seed pixel to initialize a region. It then begins growing this region by using a new version of the adaptive region growing algorithm proposed in [30].
- When the region becomes sufficiently large, the associated agent use a coordination mechanism to explore possible merging with its neighbors. This coordination mechanism is based on the contract net protocol.
- Finally, the agent improves its region by removing noise.

These different activities are described in the following sections.

3.1 Environment Exploration

Each agent uses a random walk to explore the environment and find a seed pixel.
The latter satisfies the following condition:

$$E_{V(P)}(\|\mathbf{\nabla}\|) < E_A(\|\mathbf{\nabla}\|) \times \alpha \tag{1}$$

where:

- P is the visited pixel.
- $E_{V(P)}(\|\mathbf{\nabla}\|)$ is the average value of the gradient in the neighborhood of P.
- $E_A(\|\mathbf{\nabla}\|)$ is the average value of the gradient in the whole image.
- α is a parameter that evolves from one generation of agents to another.

This condition allows selecting seed pixels as possibly distant from contour pixels
in the beginning of the process. Then, this distance is decreased at each new
generation of agents, using the α parameter. When an agent detects a pixel that
satisfies the condition (1), that pixel is considered as a seed of a new region and
the agent switches then to the Region Growing behavior and it creates another
agent to continue the exploration of the Neighborhood. This agent belongs to
another generation.

3.2 Region Growing

The agents use an improved version of the region growing approach proposed
by Pohle and Toennies [30]. This approach is suitable to medical images, the
obtained results are promising. However, it relies only on image intensity information. This characteristic can lead to region leakage due to partial volume
effects and the low contrast between adjacent regions [20]. To avoid this leakage,
we propose to simultaneously perform the growing of the different regions. We
also add a condition for pixel assimilation that considers the value of the gradient at the pixel position. As the initial growing approach, our agents perform
two phases: initial and final region growing.

Initial Region Growing. This first phase is used to determine the characteristics of the region. Starting from the seed pixel, an agent uses a random walk and
adds to its initial region R_{init} any pixel P that satisfies the following condition:

$$G(P) \in [T_{upper}, T_{lower}] \quad \bigwedge \quad \|\mathbf{\nabla}(P)\| < E_{R_{init}}(\|\mathbf{\nabla}\|) + \beta \tag{2}$$

with

$$T_{upper} = Md(R_{init}) + (\sigma_u(R_{init}) \times w) + c(R_{init}) \tag{3}$$

and

$$T_{lower} = Md(R_{init}) - ((\sigma_l(R_{init}) \times w) + c(R_{init})) \tag{4}$$

where $G(P)$ is the gray level of P, $\|\mathbf{\nabla}(p)\|$ is the value of the gradient at P,
$E_{R_{init}}(\|\mathbf{\nabla}\|)$ is the mean value of the gradient in the initialization region(R_{init})

and β is a parameter. $Md(R_{init})$ is the median gray level value of R_{init}, $\sigma_l(R_{init})$ and $\sigma_u(R_{init})$ respectively lower and upper standard derivations of R_{init}, w and $c(R_{init})$ allow adjusting the homogeneity of R_{init} .

The first term of Eq. (2) was proposed in [30] and we add the second term to take into account both the intensity and the gradient of the pixel. This new information allows avoiding the situations where an agent crosses a contour and overflows to another region during this initial step. The agent stops its random walk when it performs several walks without adding any pixel. It then goes back to the initial pixel (seed) and starts the next phase.

Final Region Growing. In this phase, the agent exploits the information collected during the previous phase. It calculates the mean gray level $E_{R_{init}}(G)$ and standard derivation $\sigma(R_{init})$ of the pixels of the initial region. Those two values are then used to evaluate the predicate of pixel assimilation during this region growing phase as follows:

$$Predicate(P) = \begin{cases} true \;\; if \; G(P) \in [E_{R_{init}}(G) \pm (\sigma(R_{init}) \times 2.5)] \\ \\ false \; otherwise \end{cases} \qquad (5)$$

Starting from the seed pixel, the agent creates its final region, and its neighbors' pixels are considered as the contours of that region. Thus, at each step of execution, the agent browses the list of its contour pixels, assimilates all of those pixels that satisfy its predicate, and updates then its contours. This growing process is repeated while some contour pixels satisfy the agent predicate.

3.3 Merging

The previous steps generate several regions, each region is managed by an agent. The regions may be neighbor. Two regions are considered as neighbor if they share borders. In this step, agents choose the best merging by interacting with their neighbors. They use the contract net protocol [33] (See Fig. 1). The main steps of this protocol are:

- **CFP:** Firstly, each agent defines its standard deviation and sends a merging request with a Call for Proposal message with this value and a timeout to all its neighbors.
- **Refuse/Propose:** When receiving a merging request, an agent analyzes the standard derivation of its region when merging with that of the sender. If this merging increases its standard deviation, it then sends a propose message otherwise it sends a refuse message to the sender.
- **Accept/Reject:** After the time out, the initiator analyzes the proposals. It selects the one that maximizes it standard deviation. It then sends an accept message to the associated agent and sends a reject to the others.
- **Failure/Confirm:** When receiving an accept message, an agent sends a confirm message if it has not accepted another merging request otherwise it sends a failure message. In the farmer case, the agent disappears after sending the message.

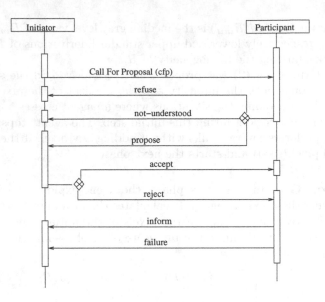

Fig. 1. Contract net protocol

– **Merging:** When receiving a confirm message, the agent merges its region with that of the sender.

This behavior is repeated by each agent while it has neighbors and while it receives accept messages.

3.4 Border Refining and Noise Removing

The purpose of this behavior is to define the final borders of the regions and to remove any eventual noise in two steps:

1. Each agent launches another region growing process, assimilating pixels according to the following condition :

$$G(P) \in [E_{R_{final}}(G) \pm (\sigma(R_{final}) \times 2.5)] \tag{6}$$

The agent uses the final mean gray level and standard derivation of its region. Thanks to the previous steps (final region growing and merging), those values give a good description of the characteristics of the agent region. The agent uses $E_{R_{final}}(G)$ and $\sigma(R_{final})$ instead of $E_{R_{init}}(G)$ and $\sigma(R_{init})$ because only isolated pixels remain unassimilated, allowing the assimilation of the pixels situated at the limits of regions (generally affected by the partial volume effect) without leakage.

2. Finally, the agent tries to assimilate all the pixels that actually belong to its region but they are affected by a noise due to the acquisition method. While avoiding the real-contour pixels, an agent A assimilates thus any pixel P that verifies the following conditions:

- $\forall P_x \in V(P)$, $P_x \in R_A$
- $\|\nabla(P)\| < E_{RC_A}(\|\nabla\|)$

Explicitly, all isolated remaining pixels that are inside the region R_A with a gradient value lower than the average gradient value of its contours are absorbed.

When the agent cannot add pixels to its region anymore, it marks the remaining pixels as contours and self-deactivates. The whole system stops when all agents are deactivated.

4   Implementation and Experiments

The segmentation process is time-consuming. The efficiency of our multi-agent approach is thus an important criteria. Our MAS consists of a population of agents with simple behavior and limited communication. The implementation of those agents with an existing environment such as JADE or MADKIT does not guarantee the required performances. We therefore implemented our multi-agent approach with C# language and MS.Net framework. Agents are implemented as generic classes.

To validate the implemented approach, we use bi-dimensional slices extracted from 3D phantom brain MR Image volumes with T1 ponderation. Segmentation tests were performed on a PC with an I7 1.9 GHz processor and 8 GB RAM.

4.1   Image Dataset

Brainweb phantom database is a MRI dataset produced by McConnell Brain Imaging Center at Montreal Neurological Institute [7]. It provides different simulated brain phantom volumes, with different simulation options among which values of noise and intensity non-uniformity. In our experiments, we used bidimensional slices extracted from T1 MRI with an image size 181×217, and a pixel size of $1\,mm \times 1\,mm$. These images were generated in 18 versions by variating the level of noise (0%, 1%, 3%, 5%, 7%, 9%) and the level of intensity non-uniformity (0%, 20%, 40%) called INU. The segmentation results were compared to Brain web discrete anatomical ground truth model.

4.2   Experimental Evaluation

In our experiments, we considered the extraction of the white matter (WM) and the gray matter (GM) in MRI brain slices extracted from a normal MRI brain volume. The parameters α and β (used in the environment exploration and region growing) were experimentally set to respectively $0, 5$ and $1, 5$. Also, the initial number of agents was set to 10, and it evolves during the system runtime.

Obtained results were used to elaborate quantitative and qualitative evaluation of the proposed multi-agent system. For this purpose, we adopted as our evaluation metric the κ-coefficient (kappa), also known as Dice similarity coefficient [37]. This coefficient is commonly used in the medical image processing to evaluate the performance of segmentation algorithms which has a predefined ground truth information or dataset. It is calculated using the following formula:

$$\kappa = \frac{2 * TP}{(2 * TP) + FP + FN} \tag{7}$$

where TP, FP and FN are the numbers respectively of True Positives, False Positives and False Negatives instances of pixel labeling. The value of the κ coefficient well expresses the segmentation quality.

For the quantitative evaluation, our system was tested on MRI brain slice with different conditions of noise and intensity non-uniformity, and previously processed the brain extraction tool of Fsl [17] to extract the brain tissues from the image. The results are presented in Table 1.

Table 1. κ coefficient for GM and WM extraction with different noise and INU levels

Noise level	Gray matter						White matter					
	0%	1%	3%	5%	7%	9%	0%	1%	3%	5%	7%	9%
κ for 0% INU	96	94	89	89	90	88	98	88	95	95	94	92
κ for 20% INU	83	90	94	89	87	88	93	93	89	92	94	93
κ for 40% INU	88	87	86	87	88	86	96	92	94	95	90	91

Table 1 and Fig. 2 present the variation of the segmentation results according to the noise level and the intensity non-uniformity. We can note that our approach gives promising results for GM and WM extraction for the used test images. Figure 2 also shows the robustness of the proposed approach against MRI images artifacts.

Figure 3 presents the obtained segmentation results of a bi-dimensional slice from the test dataset. Figure 3a is the original image, Fig. 3c and 3d illustrate

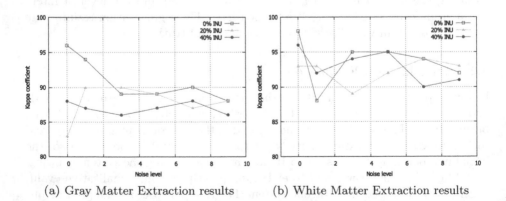

(a) Gray Matter Extraction results   (b) White Matter Extraction results

Fig. 2. κ coefficient results depending on noise and INU levels

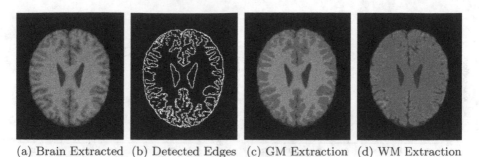

(a) Brain Extracted (b) Detected Edges (c) GM Extraction (d) WM Extraction

Fig. 3. Segmentation example of a brain slice with 20% INU level and 7% of noise

respectively gray matter and white matter regions. Figure 2 represents the contours obtained by the edge detection process. Those illustrations allow a visual appreciation of the system efficiency.

To evaluate the quality of our results, we compared them to the ones obtained from other segmentation methods published in the literature. For this purpose, we used the comparison data provided by Yazdani et al. [36] instead of re-implementing several segmentation algorithms. The results introduced in [36] concern volumic data, while ours are obtained from 2D slices. Nevertheless, this does not significantly affect the κ coefficient in our case because it is based on ratios of large sets of pixels or voxels.

Table 2. K coefficient calculated for images with 20% INU level

Noise level	Gray matter					White matter				
	0%	1%	5%	7%	9%	0%	1%	5%	7%	9%
Our system	83,0	90,0	89,0	87,0	88,0	93,0	93,0	92,0	94,0	93,0
EM	83,1	90,8	92,0	89,1	84,2	86,1	91,5	92,2	90,1	86,4
PM 5	91,2	93,4	92,1	90,0	86,6	91,1	94,2	93,6	90,2	86,3
HMC	97,0	96,5	93,7	91,6	90,3	97,8	97,7	93,9	92,3	91,7
Fast	96,0	95,8	93,8	91,5	91,1	97,4	96,8	94,8	94,3	91,9
FCM	97,0	96,0	91,0	87,0	83,0	97,0	96,0	92,0	88,0	84,0
NL-FCM	95,40	94,1	92,9	89,9	79,3	95,6	94,2	91,5	89,8	83,2
UFBSMRI	95,9	95,7	93,8	92,1	91,2	97,0	95,0	94,9	94,4	92,2

In Table 2 and Fig. 4, we can note that our multi-agent system has acceptable results and gas a good robustness to increasing noise, compared to the cited methods. We also notice that the extraction of the white matter gives better results than that of the gray matter. This is due to the fact that GM has a complex tortuous shape, more difficult to detect for agents. Those results are encouraging, knowing the fact that our approach does not require any learning

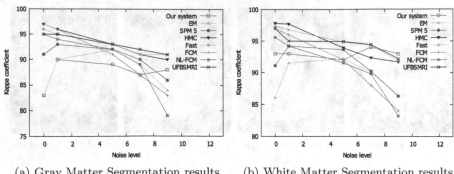

(a) Gray Matter Segmentation results   (b) White Matter Segmentation results

Fig. 4. Kappa coefficient calculated for images with 20% INU level

dataset or thresholds, but only few calibration parameters (α, β and agent initial number). It infer the needed information from the local characteristics of agent's neighborhood and it does not need any pre-treatment such as noise removing or smoothing.

5   Conclusion and Future Work

In this paper, we introduced a new multi-agent approach for medical image segmentation. This approach allows the simultaneous detection of different regions without any input of the user such as the region number, or some characteristics pre-defined with a learning phase or a prior knowledge.

Our approach relies on a set of interactive agents and a modified adaptive region growing algorithm. The agents explore the environment (the image) looking for homogeneous regions. This exploration stops when an agent detects a pixel satisfying the seed condition. The agent creates then a new region and starts a growing process. When the evolution of the region becomes not possible, the agent starts a coordination process with its neighbors to determine the best merging.

The proposed approach was implemented and validated on simulated T1 MR Images with different levels of noise and intensity non-uniformity. The obtained results were compared to the other segmentation methods that were proposed for this type of medical images, permitting an evaluation of proposed system accuracy. This evaluation highlighted promising performances and robustness to image artifacts (noise...). Note that our approach is generic, it was not specifically designed for this sort of images, it was only calibrated. The experiments showed some limits of our approach. For instance, we noticed that segmentation results are correlated with agents' initial positions and movements. These parameters were chosen randomly. Our approach also requires an experimental calibration of the α and β parameters. However, it is not specific to a type of medical images and it does not use any prior knowledge or learning phase.

In our future work, our efforts will be focused on the elaboration of an automatic mechanism that does not require the use of the previously cited parameters to deal with image properties. Moreover, we aim extending our experiments to other types of medical images and improving agent postponement and exploration. Another future work is the extension of our approach to consider volumic segmentation and the extension of the proposed multi-agent approach to make it self-adaptive to automatically consider the processed image type without any help of the user.

References

1. Adams, R., Bischof, L.: Seeded region growing. IEEE Trans. Pattern Anal. Mach. Intell. **16**(6), 641–647 (1994)
2. Albouy-Kissi, A., Cormier, S., Tranquart, F.: Perfusion quantification of contrast-enhanced ultrasound images based on coherence enhancing diffusion and competitive clustering. In: 2012 19th IEEE International Conference on Image Processing (ICIP), pp. 2321–2324. IEEE (2012)
3. Benamrane, N., Nassane, S.: Medical image segmentation by a multi-agent system approach. In: Petta, P., Müller, J.P., Klusch, M., Georgeff, M. (eds.) MATES 2007. LNCS, vol. 4687, pp. 49–60. Springer, Heidelberg (2007). doi:10.1007/978-3-540-74949-3_5
4. Chakraborty, S., Gupta, S.: Medical application using multi agent system-a literature survey. J. Eng. Res. Appl. **4**(2), 528–546 (2014)
5. Chen, C.H.: Handbook of Pattern Recognition and Computer Vision. World Scientific, Singapore (2015)
6. Chitsaz, M., Woo, C.S.: Medical image segmentation using a multi-agent system approach. Int. Arab J. Inf. Technol. **10**(3), 222–229 (2013)
7. Collins, D.L., Zijdenbos, A.P., Kollokian, V., Sled, J.G., Kabani, N.J., Holmes, C.J., Evans, A.C.: Design and construction of a realistic digital brain phantom. IEEE Trans. Med. Imaging **17**(3), 463–468 (1998)
8. Daugman, J.: How iris recognition works. IEEE Trans. Circ. Syst. Video Technol. **14**(1), 21–30 (2004)
9. Djemame, S., Nekkache, M., Batouche, M.: A multi-agent system for image segmentation a bio-inpired approach. In: Proceedings of the Third international conference on Innovation and Information and Communication Technology, p. 17. British Computer Society (2009)
10. Duchesnay, E., Montois, J.J., Jacquelet, Y.: Cooperative agents society organized as an irregular pyramid: a mammography segmentation application. Pattern Recogn. Lett. **24**(14), 2435–2445 (2003)
11. Duncan, J.S., Ayache, N.: Medical image analysis: progress over two decades and the challenges ahead. IEEE Trans. Pattern Anal. Mach. Intell. **22**(1), 85–106 (2000)
12. Elnakib, A., Gimel'farb, G., Suri, J.S., El-Baz, A.: Medical image segmentation: a brief survey. In: El-Baz, A., Acharya, U.R., Laine, A., Suri, J. (eds.) Multi Modality State-of-the-Art Medical Image Segmentation and Registration Methodologies, pp. 1–39. Springer, New York (2011). doi:10.1007/978-1-4419-8204-9_1
13. Germond, L., Dojat, M., Taylor, C., Garbay, C.: A cooperative framework for segmentation of MRI brain scans. Artif. Intell. Med. **20**(1), 77–93 (2000)

14. Haroun, R., Boumghar, F., Hassas, S., Hamami, L.: A massive multi-agent system for brain mri segmentation. In: Ishida, T., Gasser, L., Nakashima, H. (eds.) MMAS 2004. LNCS, vol. 3446, pp. 174–186. Springer, Heidelberg (2005). doi:10.1007/11512073_13

15. He, X., Yan, S., Hu, Y., Niyogi, P., Zhang, H.J.: Face recognition using laplacian-faces. IEEE Trans. Pattern Anal. Mach. Intell. **27**(3), 328–340 (2005)

16. Held, K., Kops, E.R., Krause, B.J., Wells, W.M., Kikinis, R., Muller-Gartner, H.W.: Markov random field segmentation of brain mr images. IEEE Trans. Med. Imaging **16**(6), 878–886 (1997)

17. Jenkinson, M., Pechaud, M., Smith, S.: Bet2: Mr-based estimation of brain, skull and scalp surfaces. In: Eleventh annual meeting of the organization for human brain mapping, Toronto, vol. 17, p. 167 (2005)

18. Kupinski, M.A., Giger, M.L.: Automated seeded lesion segmentation on digital mammograms. IEEE Trans. Med. Imaging **17**(4), 510–517 (1998)

19. Liu, J., Tang, Y.Y.: Adaptive image segmentation with distributed behavior-based agents. IEEE Trans. Pattern Anal. Mach. Intell. **21**(6), 544–551 (2002)

20. Ma, Z., Tavares, J.M.R., Renato, M., Jorge, N.: A review on the current segmentation algorithms for medical images. In: IMAGAPP, pp. 135–140 (2009)

21. McInerney, T., Terzopoulos, D.: Deformable models in medical image analysis: a survey. Med. Image Anal. **1**(2), 91–108 (1996)

22. Melkemi, K.E., Foufou, S.: Fuzzy distributed genetic approaches for image segmentation. CIT. J. Comput. Inf. Technol. **18**(3), 221–231 (2010)

23. Mery, D., Filbert, D.: Automated flaw detection in aluminum castings based on the tracking of potential defects in a radioscopic image sequence. IEEE Trans. Robot. Autom. **18**(6), 890–901 (2002)

24. Mohamed, M., Gader, P.: Handwritten word recognition using segmentation-free hidden Markov modeling and segmentation-based dynamic programming techniques. IEEE Trans. Pattern Anal. Mach. Intell. **18**(5), 548–554 (1996)

25. Mohammed, R., Said, A.: An adaptative multi-agent system approach for image segmentation. Int. J. Comput. Appl. **51**(12), 21–26 (2012)

26. Moussa, R., Beurton-Aimar, M., Desbarats, P.: On the use of social agents for image segmentation. In: International Conference on complex systems and applications (ICCSA) (2009)

27. Oliver, N.M., Rosario, B., Pentland, A.P.: A Bayesian computer vision system for modeling human interactions. IEEE Trans. Pattern Anal. Mach. Intell. **22**(8), 831–843 (2000)

28. Pereira, C., Veiga, D., Mahdjoub, J., Guessoum, Z., Gonçalves, L., Ferreira, M., Monteiro, J.: Using a multi-agent system approach for microaneurysm detection in fundus images. Artif. Intell. Med. **60**(3), 179–188 (2014)

29. Pham, D.L., Xu, C., Prince, J.L.: Current methods in medical image segmentation 1. Annual Rev. Biomed. Eng. **2**(1), 315–337 (2000)

30. Pohle, R., Toennies, K.D.: Segmentation of medical images using adaptive region growing. In: Proceedings of International Society for Optics and Photonics, Medical Imaging, pp. 1337–1346 (2001)

31. Richard, N., Dojat, M., Garbay, C.: Automated segmentation of human brain MR images using a multi-agent approach. Artif. Intell. Med. **30**(2), 153–176 (2004)

32. Richard, N., Dojat, M., Garbay, C.: Distributed Markovian segmentation: Application to mr brain scans. Pattern Recogn. **40**(12), 3467–3480 (2007)

33. Smith, R.G.: The contract net protocol: high-level communication and control in a distributed problem solver. IEEE Trans. Comput. **29**(12), 1104–1113 (1980)

34. Stauffer, C., Grimson, W.E.L.: Adaptive background mixture models for real-time tracking. In: 1999 IEEE Computer Society Conference on Computer Vision and Pattern Recognition, vol. 2, pp. 246–252. IEEE (1999)
35. Xu, M., Luk, W., Cutler, P., Digby, W.: Local threshold for segmented attenuation correction of pet imaging of the thorax. IEEE Trans. Nucl. Sci. **41**(4), 1532–1537 (1994)
36. Yazdani, S., Yusof, R., Karimian, A., Riazi, A.H., Bennamoun, M.: a unified framework for brain segmentation in MR images. Comput. Math. Methods Med. **2015**, 1–17 (2015). doi:10.1155/2015/829893. Article ID 829893
37. Zijdenbos, A.P., Dawant, B.M., Margolin, R.A., Palmer, A.C.: Morphometric analysis of white matter lesions in MR images: method and validation. IEEE Trans. Med. Imaging **13**(4), 716–724 (1994)

A Balking Queue Approach for Modeling Human-Multi-Robot Interaction for Water Monitoring

Masoume M. Raeissi[1(✉)], Nathan Brooks[2], and Alessandro Farinelli[1]

[1] University of Verona, 37134 Verona, VR, Italy
{masoume.raeissi,alessandro.farinelli}@univr.it
[2] Carnegie Mellon University, Pittsburgh, PA 15213, USA
nbb@andrew.cmu.edu

Abstract. We consider multi-robot scenarios where robots ask for operator interventions when facing difficulties. As the number of robots increases, the operator quickly becomes a bottleneck for the system. Queue theory can be effectively used to optimize the scheduling of the robots' requests. Here we focus on a specific queuing model in which the robots decide whether to join the queue or balk based on a threshold value. Those thresholds are a trade-off between the reward earned by joining the queue and cost of waiting in the queue. Though such queuing models reduce the system's waiting time, the cost of balking usually is not considered. Our aim is thus to find appropriate balking strategies for a robotic application to reduce the waiting time considering the expected balking costs. We propose using a Q-learning approach to compute balking thresholds and experimentally demonstrate the improvement of team performance compared to previous queuing models.

Keywords: Multi-robot systems · Human-robot interaction · Balking queue · Reinforcement learning

1 Introduction

The increasing use of multi-robot systems in real world applications, makes the supervisory role of human operators a key task. In many scenarios (such as rescue robotics, manufacturing and environmental monitoring), one or more operators are required to interact with teams of robots to achieve flexible and robust behavior, particularly when the environment is dynamic and action execution is non deterministic.

As the size of the team grows or the demands of the environment increase (e.g. several robots need the operator's attention at the same time), the operator's monitoring and supervisory role can become very difficult. In these cases to decrease the operator's workload and increase the overall team performance, several approaches have considered the concept of self-assessment where robots initiate an interaction with the operator when needed [1-3].

© Springer International Publishing AG 2017
B. An et al. (Eds.): PRIMA 2017, LNAI 10621, pp. 212–223, 2017.
https://doi.org/10.1007/978-3-319-69131-2_13

Since the operator cannot handle all requests at the same time, the requests will be queued and addressed sequentially. The idea of applying queue theory to multi-agent systems to improve the supervisory role of operators has been studied in the literature [4,5]. However, most previous work did not consider the fact that autonomous agents can assess whether to wait for the human intervention (i.e., join the queue) or try to act autonomously based on some key information, such as the severity of the request. Consequently, the focus of such previous works was on investigating different queue disciplines (i.e. the order in which the requests should be processed by the operator). For example, [1,4] examine and compare FIFO and SJF[1] queuing models where the requests will be queued according to their arrival time and shortest service time respectively, while [5] proposes using a priority queue in which an assistant agent rearranges the requests and offers the highest priority task to the operator. Since the queue-related autonomy of robots was not addressed in those work, the queue size may grow indefinitely as no robot will leave the queue before receiving the operator's attention. This will impact team performance, since it can significantly delay the operations of robots waiting in the queue.

To deal with this problem, we focus on a specific queuing model with a balking property in which the robot can decide according to a threshold value either to join the queue or balk [6][2]. For computing the threshold value, the model in [6] assigns a generic reward associated with receiving the service and a cost for waiting in the queue to each robot, but there is no gain or loss associated with the balking action. The robot is willing to join the queue if it expects that the cost of waiting for service will be no more than the value obtained from service. When applying this model to a robotic application, there is no clear indication how such a threshold can be computed and essentially this model does not consider the cost of balking.

In this work, we are looking at a domain where teams of robotic boats collect information in bodies of water and a human operator monitors and controls the team behavior. While performing their tasks, these robotic boats may face several difficulties such as running out of battery, facing obstacles, navigating water phenomena (e.g. waves) and so on. In these cases, the operator should manage the situation by interrupting, teleoperating, or directly going to the field to resolve the problem. Our aim is investigating how the elements of balking strategy should be computed according to this practical robotic scenario and precisely identifying under which conditions such a model can improve performance. The contributions of this work are as follows:

- First, we compute a threshold policy which is based on the dynamic features (i.e. the reward of finishing a service and the cost of waiting) of our robotic application domain in contrast to the static threshold value used in [6].
- Second, we use a single robot reinforcement learning approach to learn the optimal balking strategy of one robot while all other team members follow the

---

[1] SJF stands for Shortest Job First.

[2] In this model, the arrivals to the system are customers. However our work applies this model into a robotic application, so the arrivals are robots with different requests.

previously computed threshold. The goal is to optimize the objective function that is a trade-off between lower waiting time and fewer failures.

- Third, the learned values of the previous step are used as new threshold strategies for all robots in the system. We assume this learning approach fits well to our application for two main reasons. First, because robots in our model are doing their tasks independently so there is no communication or information sharing among them and the decision making steps are independent for each robot. Second, the main parameter that impact robots' decision is the probability of failure and since the robots are homogeneous, the same requests from different robots have the same probability of failure. For example when the waiting time for a request is high and the probability of failure for that request is low, the corresponding robot by balking the queue will increase its rewards (self-performance) and prevent congestion in the queue (team-performance). The same strategy works for other members as well.

- Finally, we compare the team performance of our model to the queues without balking property (e.g. FIFO and SJF). Overall, the experimental results show that the use of dynamic threshold model decreases the total waiting time up to 45% over SJF and 60% over FIFO model. Furthermore we compare the dynamic threshold to the trained threshold values (computed by Q-learning approach). As the results show, in addition to a significant reduction in the percentage of failures compared to the dynamic threshold, the reduction in total waiting time is better than SJF and FIFO.

The rest of the paper is organized as follows, Sect. 2 provides background on several important and recent human-multi-robot interaction approaches. Section 3 describes the the application domain and formalization of the problem. Section 4 details the empirical methodology discussing obtained results. Finally, Sect. 5 concludes the paper.

2 Related Work

The goal of this paper is to investigate how to improve the interaction between humans and a multi-robot team to increase the performance of both humans and team members. According to this goal, previous works in this area can be categorized into three groups.

In the first group, the autonomy of the robots was not considered, so the operators should monitor the team behavior and interact with members whenever they see abnormal situations in order to help the team members to solve the problems. For example, [7] proposes a mechanism which helps the operator interrupting an individual member of a multi-robot team without disrupting the other robots' activity.

While in the second group, researchers assume that agents can perceive their situations and inform or ask the operator for help. In these works, after sending the request, robots will wait for the operator's reply (usually in a passive mode). For example the work by [2] uses this idea in interaction between a single service robot and humans. Considering larger multi-robot teams with small number of operators, several robots may need the operator's attention at the same time or when the operator is busy, so the requests must be queued for being processed later on. Authors in [4] explore different queue disciplines for solving the reported errors by robots and compare the performance of operators with respect to each type of queue. The work in [8] proposes the idea of providing suggestions to an operator in order to assist him or her choosing an action, but the operator is not forced to follow the suggestions. In their model, assuming that an operator has other tasks to do rather than only monitoring, an advisory agent will prioritize these tasks (according to domain specific heuristics) for the operator.

On the other hand, the third category investigates the idea of adjustable autonomy or transfer of control. In these lines of research, the autonomy of the agents allows them to decide (after noticing an abnormal situation) whether to ask for help or not. Authors in [3] propose the use of transfer of control strategies which are conditional sequences of two types of actions: transfer of decision making control (e.g., an agent giving control to a user) and coordination changes (e.g., an agent delaying the execution of a joint task). The authors evaluate their method in a deployed multi-agent system where autonomous agents assist a group of people in daily activities (e.g., scheduling and re-scheduling meetings, ordering meals, and so forth).

Our work also belongs to the latter category in the sense that the robots decide whether to wait for the operator or not. More specifically, we applied a queuing model supporting the balking property which was first introduced by Naor [6]. In his paper, the individual's optimizing strategy is straightforward, a customer will join the queue while n other customers are already in the system if $R - nC\frac{1}{\mu} \geq 0$ where a uniform cost C for staying in the queue and a similar reward R for receiving service are assigned to each customer and μ is the intensity parameter of exponentially distributed service time. Thus, n serves as an equilibrium threshold for balking strategy, in other words, if the number of customers waiting in the queue is greater than n, the newly arrived customer will not join the queue.

The most closely related work to our approach is [9], where authors consider and analyze a queuing model (with decision point of joining or balking) within a game theoretic framework. In particular, they propose a model to characterize the rational equilibrium decisions where both agents and the operator(s) aim at maximizing their expected net utility. The agent's net payoff should be more than its waiting time to join the queue and the goal of the operator is to reduce the queue's congestion. Hence, the main focus of their work is to compute the optimal equilibrium outcomes such as the service time selected by the operator or the optimal arrival rate under different circumstances, e.g. different operator's skills, different task types, etc. In contrast, our focus is on showing how the elements (i.e. reward and cost) of balking strategy should be adjusted according to a practical robotics scenario. In other words, to apply this model to a robotic application, different rewards and costs for each type of request should be considered. For example, a robot with a high severity request cannot balk the queue only because the queue is too long. Moreover, an equilibrium strategy is not our focus as we consider robots to be fully cooperative. So we compute the balking threshold parameters with respect to our application domain and try to improve the system performance.

In addition, balking has a cost for the team since the robot that balks a request may not be able to accomplish its assigned task(s). In this case the remaining task(s) of that robot should be reassigned to the other robots which brings an extra load to both the operator and other team members. In order to adjust our balking model to work with a real environment considering all above elements, one convenient and practical technique is reinforcement learning where the robots can learn through direct interaction with the environment. Many different reinforcement learning approaches for both single and multi-robot systems have been discussed in literature [10–12]. In this paper, we use a single robot Q-learning approach and then extend the results to the whole multi-robot team. We can do this because of the following assumptions of our domain:

- The robots work on independent tasks (e.g. each robot should visit different locations) and the decision making steps are discrete for each robot.
- The robots are homogeneous i.e. they all have the same state and action space.

Next section details the application domain and the formalization of threshold value under the balking queue model.

3   Problem Definition

This section first provides a brief description of our application domain then the formalization of the problem will be explained.

3.1   Water Monitoring Scenario

We consider a multi-robot system including a human operator and several robotic boats which perform environmental monitoring. The operator controls team behavior by interrupting and teleoperating through a user interface or directly going to the field to resolve the problem. Figure 1 shows different components of the operators' user interface, which help them achieve their supervisory role.

Here, we consider a specific team mission where, after a set up phase (e.g. switching on the system and connecting all elements), the robotic platforms will start a team mission in which each boat is assigned to visit some locations (e.g. in a river or lake) and measure specific parameters, such as temperature, electro conductivity or dissolved oxygen. During a mission, a boat might face several difficulties that require the operator's attention or permission. For example, there are areas which are hard to traverse without being teleoperated (e.g. the water is too shallow, the current is too strong, etc.) or they need the operator's permission to enter specific areas because those areas are beyond the communication range.

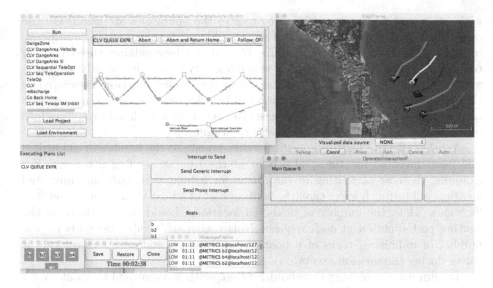

Fig. 1. Different components of the Cooperative Robotic Watercraft system

Previously in this application framework, the operator has to monitor the team behavior through a graphical monitoring tool and proactively intervene when these situations might arise. For example, if the operator sees that a boat is getting into an area which is hard to traverse, he/she will interrupt (through an interrupt interface) the boat's current action and teleoperates it passing over that area. But when the number of boats grows, the operator will be overwhelmed by this monitoring task which will affect on both the quantity and quality of his/her role.

3.2   Balking Queue Model

Adding self-awareness to boats (e.g. by warning the operator or asking his/her permission) may help the operator to be more focused on his/her controlling role. However, keeping boats idle until the operator is available might decrease the overall team efficiency. For example, using a FIFO or SJF or any other types of queue without balking causes a boat with a request to wait in the queue and this waiting can reduce the team performance when time is a critical element.

To deal with this issue, under the same problem settings as in [6] (e.g. FIFO queue discipline, single server/one operator, etc.), we map the human-multi-robot interaction part of our application into a balking queue structure in which the boats can choose to join the queue or balk according to a threshold value. However instead of assuming a static threshold value as it is usually done in the literature [6], each boat computes its own threshold dynamically based on its current state and the state of the queue.

In our water monitoring application domain, there are different types of requests, each with a different severity or importance. This means that, requests with lower severity are less critical to receive the operator's attention. On the other hand, requests with higher severity should wait for the operator's response because there is a higher probability of failure when balking these kind of requests. So we consider the severity of a request type (or equivalently the probability of failure) as an important feature in the reward function associated to that request thus a higher reward value will be achieved when receiving a service in response to a higher severity request. In Sect. 4 we will classify requests into different groups based on their probability of failure.

Another effective feature, specific for this domain, is the number of unfinished tasks (or unvisited locations) of a boat at the time of sending a request. For example, the cost of waiting in the queue for a boat with only one unvisited location will be much lower than the waiting cost of a boat with several unvisited locations. Thus, the number of unvisited locations should be considered in the waiting cost function of each request. Notice that, this value depends on the number of unfinished tasks of a boat at the time of sending a request (i.e. it varies during the mission execution).

To sum up, the balking threshold for $boat_i$ with k unfinished tasks at time t with a request type $type_j$ will be as follows:

$$n_{threshold} \leq \frac{R(type_j)\mu}{C(k)}. \tag{1}$$

where $R(type_j)$ is the reward function associated with the request $type_j$ and $C(k)$ is the cost function of $boat_i$ with k unfinished tasks. Equation (1) indicates that $boat_i$ at time t joins the queue if and only if the number of requests inside the queue is not more than $n_{threshold}$. As you can see $n_{threshold}$ is a dynamic value including the state of the queue and the state of a boat (i.e. type of the request and number of unvisited locations). Two functions $R(type_j)$ and $C(k)$ are adjusted based on the designer experience considering the average arrival rate, average service rate and the probability of failures.

Even though we show the benefit of using this model through experiments, see Sect. 3.2, we investigate the use of reinforcement learning to devise a balking strategy that can result in better overall team performance.

3.3 Learning the Balking Strategy

In this section, we formulate our water monitoring application with reinforcement learning approach, specifically we use Q-learning [13], an off-policy reinforcement learning method, to find the optimal balking strategies. As discussed earlier, this application scenario has specific attributes including homogeneous robots with highly independent tasks. Considering these properties, we can use the single-robot setting to learn the Q-values for one boat while the others use the threshold values in Eq. (1).

In Q-learning, considering a single-robot and fully-observable[3] setting, the robot will select its action according to a potential stochastic policy and will

---

[3] Assuming a fully-observable setting works for this application, since the only global state variable is the queue size, which can be obtained easily.

update its policy by greedily maximizing the Q-values. The Q-value at each time-step, will be updated according to (2):

$$Q(s,a) \leftarrow Q(s,a) + \alpha(r + \gamma(\max_{a'} Q(s',a') - Q(s,a))). \tag{2}$$

where r and s' are respectively the reward and the state observed after performing action a in state s; a' is the action in state s' that maximizes the future expected rewards; α is the learning rate and γ is the discount factor.

According to our application, action and state spaces are defined as follows:

– The action space A includes $\langle Join, Balk \rangle$;
– The state space S of the learner boat is a tuple $\langle N_q, N_{tasks}, S_b \rangle$ where:
  • N_q represents the number of requests inside the Queue
  • N_{tasks} shows the number of remaining tasks of the boat
  • S_b is the current internal state of the boat (e.g. whether it has a request (which type), if it is waiting for the operator (in the queue), etc.). More specifically $S_b \in \{R_j, Waiting, Failed, Normal\}$ where $j = 1, 2, ..., n$ is the cardinality of request types. In our model, R_j refers to one of the types in Table 1 where $n = 3$. For example, the state tuple of a boat when the current length of the queue is 2, it has 3 tasks to finish and it comes up with a request type of *Battery Recharge*, would be $s = \langle 2, 3, R_1 \rangle$

The general rule for immediate reward r in our model is the following: when a boat joins the queue with length N_q, it receives $\frac{1}{N_q}$ reward. When it balks, it may end up in a failure where in this case it receives -2 reward. However if the failure does not happen a reward 0.3 would be assigned to the boat. In general for action selection (i.e. to balance exploration/exploitation) in Q-learning there are different methods such as ϵ_greedy and $softmax$. In our model, ϵ_greedy method works better with parameter $\epsilon = 0.1$ that determines the randomness in action selections. Our algorithm uses the learning rate $\alpha = 0.1$ and discount factor $\gamma = 0.9$ throughout the experiments.

Notice that, all the above elements such as ϵ, α, γ and the reward values have been determined by a tuning process[4]. As mentioned before, we also apply a multi-robot Q-learning approach where, the results learned by this boat will be used by other boats as well. In the next section, we will examine several configurations for evaluating of our model in the above multi-robot application scenario.

4   Empirical Results

In this section, we evaluate the use of our balking queue model within a simulation of the water monitoring application. A central queue is provided to both the operator and the boats where operator can select one request at a time and

---

[4] We estimate the dynamic variables of the domain such as the average arrival rate, average service time, probability of failures, etc. based on some the data from field.

assign a specific submission to resolve that request. Submissions are a set of recovery plans provided to the operators (i.e. he/she knows which submission should be selected for each request type) and they range from giving permission to a boat entering a specific area to ones that need teleoperating a boat. For example, in our experiments we used three different submissions, one for each class of requests as following:

- **Recharge** sends a boat to the closest station to change/charge its battery.
- **Permission** allows/not-allows a boat to go further (to the area that it might loose connection).
- **Teleoperation** gives control to the operator to teleoperate the boat traversing a specific area.

The size of the queue is accessible to all boats and they can send a request to the queue.

Our aim is to decrease both the overall team waiting time and the total number of failures. A large number of failures shows that boats' balking decisions are not reasonable even if these decisions decrease the waiting time. In other words, as mentioned before, the remaining tasks of the failed boat(s) should be reassigned to other boats, which decrease the performance of both the operator and the team. For this purpose, we run two different sets of experiments with the following setups:

- In all cases we consider a single operator (server) responding to different requests from boats.
- The mission of the team is generated by the operator where the operator assigns a list of locations to be visited to each boat. Five boats and thirty tasks are considered for each mission and all experiments.
- For our experiments, three types of request each with different severity has been considered as Table 1 shows. The service time and arrival rate of each kind of request are assumed to be independent and exponentially distributed.
- A mission finishes either when all locations have been visited or after a fixed amount of time (since there is some probability that some boats cannot finish all their tasks)

Table 1. Different request types considered in the experiments

Request type (R_j)	Severity	Probability of failure
Battery recharge (R_1)	High	0.9
Traversing dangerous area (R_2)	Med	0.4
Risk of loosing connection (R_3)	Low	0.2

In the first set of experiments, we programmed all the boats to follow the dynamic threshold computed in Eq. (1). For each set of configurations, we run

20 trials and we report the average over all such runs. Both the service times and arrival times are independent and exponentially distributed with rate parameter μ and λ respectively, which are estimated from field data[5].

We compared the behavior of the proposed model to FIFO and SJF without balking strategy.

Table 2 shows the results for 5 boats and 30 tasks. As the results show, the waiting times for the dynamic threshold approach are less than FIFO and SJF model since in the former all requests do not join the queue and this obviously decreases the total waiting time.

Table 2. Results for 5 boats, 30 tasks, $\lambda = 0.25$ and $\mu = 0.27$. Each column shows the average value over 20 simulation runs. All times are in minutes. Results are statistically significant according to a t-test with alpha = 0.05.

Queue model	#Req	Total w.t.	%Balking
Dynamic thresh.	30	139	34%
SJF	30	256	0
FIFO	30	356	0

In the second set of experiments, we used Q-learning approach for one boat to learn the threshold policies while others follow the dynamic threshold policy.

For training one boat, we run a set of tests considering different number of requests (i.e. different arrival rate for each request type) and different period of time in a mission (i.e. very close to the beginning, close to the end and in the middle). Each episode[6] stops, if the learner boat ends up to a failure (because of balking a request)[7] or it finishes all assigned tasks respected to its mission. Figure 2 plots the mean cumulative rewards at each episode of these experiments where you can see the convergence of our Q-learning approach.

Finally, we use the same Q-values computed by one boat, for all boats to see how the behavior of the system changes. Table 3 shows the result of Q-learning for one boat (QL-Single Boat) and Q-learning for all boats (QL-All Boats) where we used the same simulation setup as the first experiment. As the results show the percentage of balking in QL-All Boats is less than the other methods, thus the waiting time in the queue increases. However, the percentage of failures has fallen substantially in QL-All Boats in comparison to dynamic threshold and QL-Single Boat. Since the waiting time is still better than approaches without

---

[5] During the training phase in Q-learning approach, we used a small range around the estimated values for each of the arrival and service rate.

[6] In reinforcement learning, an episode means a run of the algorithm beginning from a start state to a final state.

[7] In our model, failures only happen for balking. This assumption is in favor of non-balking models. For example, if a boat waits too long for the operator the battery might run out, thus the mission fails just because time passes. Hence, in practice the results will probably be even more in favor of our approach.

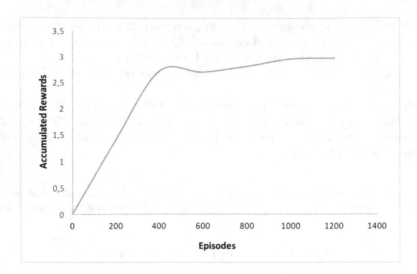

Fig. 2. Learning curve of a single robotic boat.

Table 3. Results for 5 boats, 30 tasks, $\lambda = 0.25$ and $\mu = 0.27$. Each column shows the average value over 20 simulation runs. All times are in minutes. Results are statistically significant according to a t-test with alpha $= 0.05$.

Queue model	#Req	Total w.t.	%Balking	%Failure
Dynamic thresh.	30	139	34%	14%
QL–Single Boat	30	163	28%	9%
QL–All Boats	30	209	10%	1%

balking, our results suggest that QL-All Boats is the most promising approach for this scenario.

5   Conclusion

This paper investigates the use of a queue with balking property to model human-multi-robot interaction in a water monitoring scenario. Two different approaches for computing the balking strategy have been discussed. First, we introduced a dynamic threshold policy by defining the reward and costs associated to the balking model for our specific water monitoring scenario. The empirical results show that by using this dynamic threshold values, the waiting times decrease significantly compared to the queuing models such as FIFO and SJF. Furthermore, we apply Q-learning approach to improve the balking strategies of the boats. The experimental results show that our Q-learning approach compares favorably with FIFO and SJF queue models (in terms of waiting time) and it results in a lower percentage of failures with respect to the dynamic threshold model.

An interesting direction for future work is to consider the operator behavior in the learning process of the robots, because the actual service time is related to the operators' skills and speed. In addition, a human study can illustrate how much the length of the queue affects the operator's efficiency. Another promising direction for future work is to investigate and model the situations where the boats can decide to leave the queue when the expected waiting time, after joining the queue, does not meet their requirements.

References

1. Chien, S.Y., Lewis, M., Mehrotra, S., Brooks, N., Sycara, K.: Scheduling operator attention for multi-robot control. In: Intelligent Robots and Systems (IROS), pp. 473–479. IEEE (2012)
2. Rosenthal, S., Veloso, M.: Using symbiotic relationships with humans to help robots overcome limitations. In: Workshop for Collaborative Human/AI Control for Interactive Experiences (2010)
3. Scerri, P., Pynadath, D.V., Tambe, M.: Towards adjustable autonomy for the real world. J. Artif. Intell. Res. 17(1), 171–228 (2002)
4. Chien, S.Y., Lewis, M., Mehrotra, S., Han, S., Brooks, N., Wang, H., Sycara, K.: Task switching for supervisory control of multi-robot teams. IEEE Trans. Hum. Mach. Syst. (2016)
5. Rosenfeld, A.: Human-multi-robot team collaboration using advising agents: (doctoral consortium). In: Proceeding of the International Conference on Autonomous Agents and Multiagent Systems, pp. 1516–1517 (2016)
6. Naor, P.: The regulation of queue size by levying tolls. J. Econom. Soc. 37(1), 15–24 (1969)
7. Farinelli, A., Raeissi, M.M., Brooks, N., Scerri, P.: Interacting with team oriented plans in multi-robot systems. J. Auton. Agents Multi-Agent Syst. 31(2), 332–361 (2017)
8. Rosenfeld, A., Agmon, N., Maksimov, O., Azaria, A., Kraus, S.: Intelligent agent supporting human-multi-robot team collaboration. In: IJCAI, pp. 1902–1908 (2015)
9. Dai, T., Sycara, K., Lewis, M.: A game theoretic queueing approach to self-assessment in human-robot interaction systems. In: IEEE International Conference on Robotics and Automation, Shanghai, pp. 58–63 (2011)
10. Buşoniu, L., Babuška, R., De Schutter, B.: Multi-agent reinforcement learning: an overview. In: Srinivasan, D., Jain, L.C. (eds.) Innovations in Multi-Agent Systems and Applications-1, pp. 183–221. Springer, Heidelberg (2010). doi:10.1007/978-3-642-14435-6_7
11. Hu, Y., Gao, Y., An, B.: Multiagent reinforcement learning with unshared value functions. IEEE Trans. Cybern. 45(4), 647–662 (2015)
12. Tan, M.: Multi-agent reinforcement learning: independent vs. cooperative agents. In: Proceedings of the Tenth International Conference on Machine Learning, pp. 330–337 (1993)
13. Sutton, R.S., Barto, A.G.: Reinforcement Learning: An Introduction, vol. 1. MIT press, Cambridge (1998). No. 1

Cooperation and Negotiation
in Multiagent Systems

Specifications for Peer-to-Peer Argumentation Dialogues

Bas Testerink$^{(\boxtimes)}$ and Floris J. Bex

Department of Information and Computing Sciences,
Utrecht University, Utrecht, The Netherlands
B.J.G.Testerink@uu.nl

Abstract. In this paper, we propose a generic specification framework for argumentation dialogue protocols in an open multi-agent system. The specification framework is based on reusable elements – *dialogue templates* – which are realized as an open-source implementation. We provide operational semantics and show formally how templates can be used to determine the possible dialogues. Furthermore, for open multi-agent systems we need to be able to specify *peer-to-peer dialogues*, where the agents themselves are in a position to know whether their dialogue actions are legal according to the protocol without relying on central entities, institutes or middleware. We prove that all protocols that can be specified in our framework are peer-to-peer suitable.

1 Introduction

Dialogue games attempt to capture aspects of structured, mixed-initiative communication with the aim of understanding, improving, and automatically recreating such communication. Particularly for more complex tasks such as software design discussions [7], argument-based negotiation [23], collaborative learning [17] or legal argument [22], it is imperative that the agents' behaviour is constrained by so-called dialogue protocols, so that the agents can argue, inform, investigate and negotiate in a regulated way. We believe that argumentation dialogue games [15] are particularly suited for more complex dialogues, as they nicely straddle the divide between the naturalistic dialogues from the intelligent user interface community [12] and the more rigid multi-agent communication protocols [18]. Furthermore, argumentation dialogue games allow for many features of realistic dialogues, such as agent dialogue strategies and the construction of underlying argument structures, to be captured.

There are several protocol proposals for argumentation dialogue games, many of which have been analysed for their formal properties (see e.g. [1,9,21]). The wide range of possible dialogue protocols has given rise to an effort to define generic, executable specification languages for notating protocols [5,6,25]. The motivation behind these generic specification languages is twofold. First, these specification languages allow us to represent the syntax and update semantics of any arbitrary dialogue game we care to define in a common language. This allows us to move away from the case-by-case approach common in the literature on

© Springer International Publishing AG 2017
B. An et al. (Eds.): PRIMA 2017, LNAI 10621, pp. 227–244, 2017.
https://doi.org/10.1007/978-3-319-69131-2_14

computational argumentation and move towards a class-of-systems approach. Second, generic specification languages allow for the development of general purpose execution engines for dialogue games (such as DGEP [3], which has been proposed as an execution engine for DGDL [25]). Such execution engines not only allow us to empirically analyse and compare different protocols, but also take dialogue games out of the academic lab and deploy them in realistic, large-scale settings. Unfortunately, existing specification languages either have no formal operational semantics that allow us to formally study protocols [5,25], or they lack an implemented execution engine for handling protocol execution [6].

A more general problem of existing argumentation dialogue games in the literature is that, from the perspective of open multi-agent systems, dialogue games are too rigid: dialogues are mostly one-on-one where it is assumed that the participants see all the communication, there is a strict turntaking order and communication is instantaneous, agents are assumed to never fail and always behave according to the protocol, and it is assumed that the internal states of the agents participating in the dialogues is known. These assumptions do not hold in realistic systems, where different dialogues may run in parallel, agents can only be assumed to observe the messages that they themselves send and receive and communication is peer-to-peer rather than governed by a central entity, institute or middleware [3,8,10,16].

As a case-in-point, consider the prototype multi-agent system for the Dutch National Police that we are currently developing [4]. In this system, various agents work together to build a case regarding internet trade fraud (e.g. scammers on eBay or fake online stores). We have agents that interact with human users (victims, police detectives), agents that exchange information with external services (banks, trade sites) and agents that automatically combine and reason with information from these different sources. This distributed, open, peer-to-peer multi-agent system is needed because (i) the police uses strict privacy policies that make it undesirable to centrally gather and reason with data; and (ii) not all participating agents in the system are known beforehand: for instance, the human users that file online complaints are initially unknown.

Removing the usual assumptions of argumentation dialogue games brings extra challenges in the design of these games. Because individual agents each have their view on a dialogue that only includes the messages they themselves sent or received, and because the agents cannot rely on a third-party or control mechanism to determine which dialogue moves are legal, the agent itself then needs to be in a position to know whether its actions break protocol in order to plan a dialogue or formulate strategies. In order for this to work, the protocols need to be *peer-to-peer suitable*. Take, as an example from our implementation domain, the situation where two software agents, A and B, are talking to a human user about one or more criminal complaints. What we do not want is for A to make claims that contradict something B has said, as this would make the police, as an organization, to come across as inconsistent to the human user. If we simply specify the protocol to be 'A may not contradict a claim that B made towards the user and vice versa', then this is not peer-to-peer suitable. When

A wants to make a claim, then it is not guaranteed to know which messages B sent to the user, and hence whether A's claim contradicts an earlier claim from B. For the protocol regulating the communication between A, B and the user to be peer-to-peer suitable it would need to include explicit mechanisms to ensure that A and B are consistent (e.g. only allow a claim to be made in the dialogue with the user of which one agent is certain that the other agent agrees). Note that peer-to-peer suitability of a protocol implies that the protocol can be followed without violations by agents, but does not guarantee that there will be no violations. Hence in open multi-agent systems where some agents are not trusted, we may still want to realize a controlling proxy interface to check those untrusted agents.

To summarize, we need a generic, formally underpinned framework for expressing dialogues, protocols and the ways in which those protocols update dialogue structures. Importantly, the protocols expressed in this framework need to be peer-to-peer suitable, that is, the protocols should allow agents to, given their view on a dialogue, determine their legal actions themselves. Inspired by [5], we propose a specification framework for dialogue protocols based on reusable elements called *dialogue templates*[1], and we show formally how templates can be used to determine the possible dialogues. We furthermore define peer-to-peer suitable protocols for dialogues between individual agents, and show that all protocols that can be specified using dialogue templates are in fact peer-to-peer suitable. Our framework includes an execution engine and is part of an open-source multi-agent system.

The rest of this paper is organized as follows. Section 2 discusses related research. In Sect. 3.1 we formalize the notion of protocol and peer-to-peer suitability. Our specification framework itself is presented in Sect. 3.2. Finally, in Sect. 4 we provide conclusions and future work.

2 Related Work

Conversational agents have experienced a resurgence as of late, with much of the work focusing on (spoken) language interpretation issues [12] or on dialogue learning policies for more simple recommendation or negotiation tasks [24]. However, these dialogues are lacking in formal (logical) semantics, which is needed if we want to regulate and formally verify the behaviour of agents in dialogues about more complex and information-rich tasks.

Among the most prominent proposals for the specification of formal protocols for multi-agent systems is Agent UML [2,18] which has been formally analysed with coloured petri-nets [14,20]. Formal semantics for these protocols investigate the properties of protocols when they are followed or how agents can interpret locutions, but to our knowledge have not been analysed for determining whether agents are guaranteed to know whether their own behaviour violates a protocol.

---

[1] Black and Hunter [6] use a similar concept which they call action rules.

The work by Pitt and Mamdani [19] focuses on the agent perspective of communication and specifies protocols using finite state machines, but does not address and analyse the protocol specifications directly.

There have recently been various proposals for generic specification languages for argumentation dialogue protocols, such as Dialogue Interaction Diagrams (DID) [13], which can be verified with coloured Petri nets, and the Framework for Dialogical Argumentation (FDA) [6], which defines protocols in an executable logic and simulates dialogues using finite state machines. Whilst these approaches thus allow for the specification and theoretical analysis of different argumentation dialogue protocols, they are not suitable for peer-to-peer argumentation dialogue specifications in implemented open multi-agent systems, for various reasons. First, no mention is made of peer-to-peer suitability in either approach, and hence they cannot guarantee that for a protocol designed in their respective specification language an agent can determine what the legal moves are given its view on the dialogue. Second, both DID and FDA lack implemented engines for execution protocols, and do not concern themselves with apects such as, for example, connections to software agents and human-computer interfaces.

Recent work that does provide an execution engine for argumentation dialogues is the Dialogue Game Execution Platform (DGEP) [3]. However, this execution platform is not suited for peer-to-peer dialogues in open multi-agent systems, as it uses middleware to provide the agents participating in a dialogue the next possible legal moves, from which the agents have to pick a choice. This 'black box' approach makes it hard for an individual agent to plan ahead: it has to learn a model of the black box or it has to run 'simulations' of dialogues on the black box (if possible) to see possible outcomes of certain strategies. The first option requires a learning phase and offers no guarantees whereas the second option will likely have to deal with an exponential blow-up of simulations. Furthermore, DGEP uses a central knowledge base, the AIFdb [11], and provides the agents with arguments from this central knowledge base; an agent thus cannot use its own private knowledge base to determine which types of utterances can be made in a dialogue. A second shortcoming of DGEP is that as its specification language, DGEP uses the dialogue game description language DGDL [25] and DGDL+ [3], the latter of which is based on the dialogue templates of [5]. While DGDL(+) is very rich and allows for the specification of many different types of dialogue protocols, it has no formal operational semantics. Hence, the outcomes of executing a dialogue protocol with certain knowledge bases and parameters cannot be formally checked or analysed. In this paper we present a template-based protocol specification language inspired by [5], provide operational semantics, and show that all protocols that can be specified in this language allow agents to determine their legal actions themselves.

3   Protocol Specification

In this section we specify our framework. We first model dialogue systems and protocols, and then define the specification of protocols through reusable dialogue templates.

3.1 Peer-to-Peer Protocols

A dialogue system is an abstract description of agents, modelled by atoms, and the locutions, also modelled by atoms, that they may utter.

Definition 1 (Dialogue System, D). *A dialogue system* D *is specified by* (A, L), *where* A *and* L *are sets of agent and locution atoms, respectively.*

Example 1 (Dialogue System). We will use the same dialogue system throughout our examples. The example scenario is an interaction between some user and expert agent. We will make the scenario quite simple in order to not over complicate full formal specifications of all the aspects of the scenario. We have made a demonstration of a more advanced example publicly available[2]. This demonstration contains implementation examples of the proposed framework, a dialogue among nine different agents, visual representations, and more expanded argumentation-specific aspects of dialogues such as commitments and book-keeping of arguments that were made. For the remainder of this paper, our example dialogue system D is specified by (A, L) where $A = \{user, expert\}$ and $L = \{claim(x)|x \in P\} \cup \{why(x)|x \in P\} \cup \{support(x,y)|x,y \in P\}$ such that $P = \{p, q, r, s\}$. The elements of P are logical atoms, $claim(x)$ can be read as that x is stated to be true, $why(x)$ can be read as a question why x was stated to be true and finally $support(x, y)$ can be read that x follows from y and y is true.

A dialogue system allows for dialogue events, which are the events of sending or receiving a message. An event is specified by its type (sending/receiving), the subject (the sender/recipient), the message (a locution) and the object (the recipient/sender).

Definition 2 (Dialogue Event, e). *Let* D = (A, L) *be a dialogue system. A dialogue event* e *is specified by either* s(a, l, a′) *or* r(a, l, a′), *where* a, a′ ∈ A *and* l ∈ L.

Example 2 (Dialogue Event). An example event for our scenario is s(*expert, claim(p), user*) which can be read as "The expert sends locution *claim(p)* to the user". Similarly, r(*user, claim(p), expert*) can be read as "The user receives the locution *claim(p)* from the expert".

Dialogue events do not need to occur in sequential order, because agents may reason and communicate in parallel with other agents. We model a dialogue as a sequence of sets of events (we name these sets moments). If multiple events are in the same moment, then we interpret this as those events happening simultaneously. Non-instantaneous communication is captured by the constraint that a moment in which a message is received has to be preceded by some moment in the past where the message was sent. The constraint takes into account that a message might be sent at different moments. Therefore, a message should not be received more often than that it was sent.

---

[2] https://git.science.uu.nl/B.J.G.Testerink/OO2APL-P2PArgumentationDialog Demo.

Definition 3 (Dialogue, d). *Let* $D = (A, L)$ *be a dialogue system and* $\mathbb{E}$ *be all possible dialogue events given* D. *A dialogue* $d = M_1...M_k$ *is a finite sequence of sets of events, referred to as moments, such that for each moment* $M_i \subseteq \mathbb{E}$, $i \in [1, k]$, *if* $r(a, l, a') \in M_i$ *then the number of moments* M_j, $j \in [1, i-1]$, *such that* $r(a, l, a') \in M_j$ *is less than the number of moments* M_n, $n \in [1, i-1]$, *such that* $s(a', l, a) \in M_n$.

Example 3 (Dialogue). Consider a dialogue where the expert claims p, the user asks why the expert thinks p is true, and the expert responds with a support for p by arguing that "p because q". This dialogue could be captured by the moments/dialogue: $M_1 M_2 M_3$ where $M_1 = \{s(expert, claim(p), user)\}$, $M_2 = \{r(user, claim(p), expert), s(user, why(p), expert)\}$, $M_3 = \{r(expert, why(p), user), s(expert, support(p, q), user)\}$.

Consider an alternative sequence of moments $M_1' M_2'$ where $M_1' = \{s(expert, claim(p), user), r(user, claim(p), expert)\}$, $M_2' = \{r(user, claim(p), expert)\}$. This is not a dialogue for two reasons: (1) the send action in moment one was simultaneously received, and (2) the second moment contains a receive event without there being a message that still had to be received.

A protocol specifies how a dialogue ought to be conducted. Hence we can view a protocol as a specification that divides a set of dialogues into those dialogues that follow the protocol and those dialogues that violate it. We note that a protocol violation in a dialogue means that any extension of that dialogue is also a dialogue with a protocol violation. This constraint is captured by requiring that if a dialogue obeys a protocol then all its prefixes do so too (item one in Definition 4). Finally, we add a constraint that receiving a message never violates the protocol. An agent has no control over the messages that it receives, and no control over when a sent message is received. If receiving a message would violate the protocol then the sending agent therefore potentially cannot determine beforehand whether the arrival of the message will break protocol, and the receiving agent cannot avoid the protocol violation since it cannot prevent the message from being received. Hence allowing the receipt of messages to break protocol can bring about situations where the legality of actions is uncertain. If a dialogue violates the protocol, then it must have a smallest prefix (possibly the dialogue itself) that violates the protocol. The final moment of that prefix contains the dialogue events that brought about the violation. If receiving a message cannot violate a protocol, then removing all the send actions from that final moment should give us a dialogue which does not violate the protocol (item two in Definition 4).

Definition 4 (Protocol, P). *Let* $\mathbb{D}$ *be all possible dialogues given a dialogue system* D. *A protocol* $P \subseteq \mathbb{D}$ *for* D *is a set of dialogues, such that:*

1. $\forall M_1...M_k \in P, i \in [1, k] : M_1...M_i \in P$.
2. *For each* $d \in \mathbb{D}$ *if* $d \notin P$ *and* $M_1...M_k$ *is the shortest prefix of* d *that is not in* P, *then* $d' \in P$ *where* $d' = M_1...M_{k-1}M_k'$ *such that* $M_k' = \{r(a, l, a') \in M_k\}$.

Example 4 (Protocol). As an example protocol we want to specify that a $why(x)$-locution for some propositional atom $x \in \{p, q, r, s\}$ can only be uttered by the user and only as a response to some earlier claim or support that involved x. Similarly, the protocol also specifies that support locutions can only be uttered for supporting earlier claim or support locutions (which in turn are only allowed for the expert). Our example protocol P therefore contains a dialogue d iff for each agent a, a' $\in$ A: (a) each send action s(a, $why(x)$, a') in the dialogue is preceded by some previous moment in which r(a, $claim(x)$, a') or r(a, $support(y, x)$, a') is contained and a = *user* and (b) each send action s(a, $support(x, y)$, a') in the dialogue is preceded by some previous moment in which s(a, $claim(x)$, a') or s(a, $support(z, x)$, a') is contained, where $x, y, z \in \{p, q, r, s\}$ and a = *expert*. In summary, protocol P allows the expert to make claims at any time, the user to request support of previously made claims and the expert to support past claims/supports of itself.

To illustrate the second item of Definition 4, consider the dialogue $M_1 M_2$ such that $M_1 = \{s(expert, claim(p), user)\}$ and $M_2 = \{r(user, claim(p), expert), s(user, claim(r), expert)\}$. This dialogue is illegal because the user may not send the claim. The shortest prefix of this dialogue that is not in the protocol is $M_1 M_2$ itself. Let M_2' be M_2, except that we remove the send actions (i.e., s($user, claim(r), expert$)). Clearly $M_1 M_2'$ satisfies the protocol.

Agents do not have a total view of the dialogue. In fact, only those events where they send or receive a message can be assumed to be observable by them. We model this view of an agent on a dialogue as a function that filters the moments of the dialogue to those events that concern that agent. Hence, the view of an agent on a dialogue is a sequence of moments where each event has that agent as the subject.

Definition 5 (View, v_a). *Let* $\mathbb{D}$ *be all possible dialogues given a dialogue system* D = (A, L), a $\in$ A *be an agent and* d = $M_1 ... M_k \in \mathbb{D}$ *be a dialogue. For a moment M and agent* a *let* $M \downarrow_a = \{x(a, l, a') \in M | x \in \{s, r\}\}$. *The view of* a *on a moment M in* d*, notated* $v_a(M)$*, is the single-moment sequence* $M \downarrow_a$ *if* $M \downarrow_a \neq \emptyset$ *and the empty sequence* ε *otherwise. The view of* a *on* d*, notated* $v_a(d)$*, is the concatenation of the views of each moment:* $v_a(d) = v_a(M_1) ... v_a(M_k)$.

Example 5 (View). The view of the user on the dialogue $M_1 M_2 M_3$ from Example 3 is $v_{user}(M_1) v_{user}(M_2) v_{user}(M_3) = \varepsilon M_2' \varepsilon = M_2'$, where $M_2' = \{r(user, claim(p), expert), s(user, why(p), expert)\}$. Hence, from the user's point of view only one moment has passed in the dialogue, where it responded to a claim with a why question.

We will next specify the class of peer-to-peer suitable protocols. These protocols guarantee that an agent is always in a position to know that its send actions are not violating the protocol. If an agent wants to check whether a dialogue is violating the protocol, then it has to do this using its view on the dialogue. Many different dialogues will look the same to an agent given its view. For each specific agent we want to specify a personal set of dialogues such that the agent can distinguish with its view whether a dialogue is in or out of that set. If a dialogue is out of an agent's dialogue set, then the dialogue violates the protocol (but not necessarily the other way around). A protocol is peer-to-peer suitable if we can define such a set for each agent and furthermore, if a dialogue violates the protocol then there must be at least one agent that can detect this (i.e. the dialogue falls out of that agent's personal set). The latter constraint is captured by requiring that the intersection of all the personal dialogue sets is the protocol itself.

Definition 6 (Peer-to-Peer Suitable). *Let* $\mathbb{D}$ *be all possible dialogues given a dialogue system* $D = (A, L)$ *and* P *be a protocol for* D. P *is peer-to-peer suitable iff for each agent* $a \in A$ *there exists a subset* $P_a \subseteq \mathbb{D}$ *such that* $P = \bigcap_{a \in A} P_a$ *and for each* $d, d' \in \mathbb{D}$ *if* $v_a(d) = v_a(d')$ *then* $d, d' \in P_a$ *or* $d, d' \notin P_a$.

Example 6 (Peer-to-Peer Suitable). Our example protocol P from Example 4 is peer-to-peer suitable. We can make P_{user} such that a dialogue is in P_{user} iff each send action $s(user, why(x), a)$ in the dialogue is preceded by some previous moment in which $r(user, claim(x), a)$ or $r(user, support(y, x), a)$ is contained, and there is no occurence of $s(user, claim(x), a)$ or $s(user, support(x, y), a)$, for $a \in \{user, expert\}$. We can make P_{expert} such that a dialogue is in P_{expert} iff each send action $s(expert, support(x, z), a)$ in the dialogue is preceded by some previous moment in which $s(expert, claim(x), a)$ or $s(expert, support(y, x), a)$ is contained, and there is no occurence of $r(expert, why(x), a)$, for $a \in \{user, expert\}$. The intersection $P_{user} \cap P_{expert}$ forms the protocol. A violation is detected when either agent sends illegally a message. For instance, if the sender violates a protocol, then it sent a why question, which clearly is not allowed by P_{expert}.

Consider another protocol in which the agents must take turns but there are no further restrictions. This protocol could be defined by specifying that each dialogue in the protocol contains only moments where at most one agent sends messages. This protocol is not peer-to-peer suitable. Intuitively, the view of an agent does not allow the agent to distinguish between moments where it alone sends a message and moments where others send messages as well. Therefore, no agent can detect a violation. A solution would be to introduce a special turn-yielding locution in the dialogue system, and specify that (a) an agent may only send messages if it has received the yield-turn locution and has not yet send it after the last time that the locution was received (or if the agent is the starting agent and no messages have been sent yet), (b) sending the yield-turn locution is only allowed if the agent has not sent it since the last time the locution was received (note that this implies that the agent can only yield the turn to a single peer, and it is not restricted which peer this is). We note that turn taking brings with it the risk of agents not yielding their turn and thereby threatening the liveness of a dialogue application. Hence, unlike many protocol specification frameworks for argumentation, we do not assume that turn taking is always part of the protocol.

We show that a peer-to-peer suitable protocol violation can always be detected by one of the agents, that is, one of the agents can, given its view on the violating dialogue, determine that the protocol is violated. At the same time, if the dialogue is not violated, then it is not violated given the views of all the agents. We show this by constructing a set of views per agent that is based on the personal set of dialogues in the definition of peer-to-peer suitability. Given that the protocol is the intersection of the personal sets, we know that a violating dialogue is outside of at least one personal dialogue set. Given further that the personal sets of dialogues are closed under the views of agents, we know that at least one agent can distinguish a bad dialogue from the good ones. If a dialogue is not violating the protocol then it is contained in each personal dialogue set. If we define the set of views per agent as the views on the dialogues in the personal sets, then it follows immediately that a correct dialogue is always in all the sets of views per agent.

Proposition 1. *Let $\mathbb{D}$ be all possible dialogues given a dialogue system $\mathsf{D} = (\mathsf{A}, \mathsf{L})$ and P be a peer-to-peer suitable protocol for D. For each agent $a \in \mathsf{A}$ there exists a set of views $\mathsf{V_a} \subseteq \{v_a(d) | d \in \mathbb{D}\}$ such that (a) if $d \notin \mathsf{P}$ then there is an agent $a' \in \mathsf{A}$ and $v_{a'}(d) \notin \mathsf{V}_{a'}$ and (b) if $d \in \mathsf{P}$ then for each agent $a \in \mathsf{A} : v_a(d) \in \mathsf{V_a}$.*

Proof. From the definition of peer-to-peer suitable we know that for each agent $a \in \mathsf{A}$ there exists a subset $\mathsf{P_a} \subseteq \mathbb{D}$ such that $\mathsf{P} = \bigcap_{a \in \mathsf{A}} \mathsf{P_a}$ and for each $d, d' \in \mathbb{D}$ if $v_a(d) = v_a(d')$ then $d, d' \in \mathsf{P_a}$ or $d, d' \notin \mathsf{P_a}$. Let for each agent $a \in \mathsf{A}$ the set $\mathsf{V_a}$ be defined as $\{v_a(d) | d \in \mathsf{P_a}\}$. For a dialogue $d \in \mathbb{D}$ if $d \notin \mathsf{P}$ and there is no agent $a \in \mathsf{A}$ such that $d \notin \mathsf{P_a}$, then it means that d is in each $\mathsf{P}_{a'}$, $a' \in \mathsf{A}$, i.e., $d \in \bigcap_{a \in \mathsf{A}} \mathsf{P_a}$ (d would be deemed legal by all agents). This cannot be the case as $\mathsf{P} = \bigcap_{a \in \mathsf{A}} \mathsf{P_a}$. Therefore, if $d \notin \mathsf{P}$ then there is an agent $a \in \mathsf{A}$ such that $d \notin \mathsf{P_a}$. From the peer-to-peer suitability definition we also know that there cannot be a dialogue $d' \in \mathsf{P_a}$ such that $v(d) = v(d')$ if $d \notin \mathsf{P_a}$. Therefore if $d \notin \mathsf{P_a}$ then $v_a(d) \notin \mathsf{V_a}$, thus proving (a). If $d \in \mathsf{P}$, then $d \in \mathsf{P_a}$ for each agent $a \in \mathsf{A}$, and therefore $v_a(d) \in \mathsf{V_a}$ for each agent $a \in \mathsf{A}$, thus proving (b).

We note that there exist peer-to-peer suitable protocols where only the agent that causes the violation can see the violation. The notion of peer-to-peer suitability could be expanded such that it guarantees that if some send action causes a violation that then the receipt of that message allows the recipient to determine the protocol violation as well. Such an expansion falls out of the scope of this paper.

3.2 Templates for Argumentation Dialogues

We observe that most dialogue systems, such as argumentation dialogue systems, require information about whether a received locution is a response to some past locution. This is not always as straightforward as saying that the last locution is a response to the penultimate locution. In an argumentation dialogue an agent can, for instance, utter an extra support locution in a response to some past question.

Since the coherence relation among locutions cannot be derived solely from the legality conditions of a protocol, we include the coherence relation as part of our protocol specification framework. We opt to capture dialogue coherence with graphs in order to accommodate a wide variety of coherence structures (linear lists, trees, and arbitrary graphs). We refer to such a graph as a dialogue graph and assume that a dialogue graph is what agents use to decide upon their next locution(s). As always, a graph consists of nodes and edges. We do not assume any structure on nodes. We add the agent that belongs to a graph to the graph's specification.

Definition 7 (Dialogue Graph, g). *Let* A *be a set of agents. A dialogue graph* g *is specified by* (a, N, E), *where* $a \in A$, N *is a set of nodes and* $E \subseteq N \times N$ *are the edges. We use* $g_a^\emptyset$ *for the empty graph* (a, ∅, ∅).

Example 7 (Dialogue Graph). For our example scenario we use dialogue events as nodes in dialogue graphs. As an example graph consider g = (*user*, N, E) where $N = \{e_1, e_2, e_3, e_4\}$ and $E = \{(e_1, e_3), (e_3, e_4)\}$ such that $e_1 = r(user, claim(p), expert)$, $e_2 = r(user, claim(q), expert)$, $e_3 = s(user, why(p), expert)$, $e_4 = r(user, support(p,q), expert)$. This graph represents the user's view on a dialogue where the expert has claimed both p and q in the dialogue. The user has also asked why p is the case, which is why this event is connected to the claim of p. Then, the answer of the expert, that q supports p, is connected to the why question.

As reusable high-level elements for dialogue system specifications we propose dialogue templates [5]. A dialogue template tells for a specific locution under which circumstances it might be sent or received and how this updates the dialogue graph of the sender (or receiver, respectively). The condition of a template is specified by a function that takes a dialogue graph and returns the agents to which the locution might be sent (or from whom it might be received, respectively). The update of a graph is conditioned on the graph that is being updated

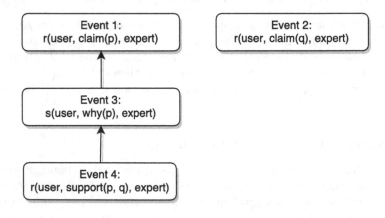

Fig. 1. Example dialogue graph. See Example 7.

and the agent to which the locution is sent (or from whom it is received). An update must furthermore produce a graph for the same agent that belongs to the input graph of the function. We can interpret the update function as a specification for how new locutions are related to previous locutions in a dialogue (Fig. 1).

Definition 8 (Dialogue Template, t). *Let* L *be a set of locutions,* A *be a set of agent atoms, and* G *be a set of dialogue graphs. A dialogue template* t *for* L, A *and* G *is specified by either* $t_s(l, c, u)$ *or* $t_r(l, c, u)$, *where* $l \in$ L, $c :$ G $\rightarrow 2^A$ *returns to which agents* I *might be sent (or received, respectively) and* $u :$ G $\times$ A $\rightarrow$ G *specifies a dialogue graph update given a dialogue graph and recipient (or sender, respectively) such that* $u((a, N, E)) = (a, N', E')$.

Example 8 (Dialogue Templates). For all possible dialogue events $\mathbb{E}$ given our example scenario we define the set of all dialogue graphs G to be G $=$ $\{(a, N, E) | a \in$ A $\wedge$ N $\subseteq \mathbb{E} \wedge$ E $\subseteq$ N $\times$ N$\}$. In the following we use x and y as placeholders for values in $\{p, q, r, s\}$. We also abbreviate the expert and user to e and u, respectively.

For our example scenario we specify the protocol from Example 4 with a set of six dialogue templates. We specify a receive and a send template for each of the locutions. In general there can be multiple templates for receiving/sending the same locution. The templates T for our example scenario are given by:

- $t_s(claim(x), c^4, u_{s,claim(x)})$, $t_r(claim(x), c^3, u_{r,claim(x)})$
- $t_s(why(x), c_x^1, u_{s,why(x)})$, $t_r(why(x), c^4, u_{r,why(x)})$
- $t_s(support(x, y), c_{x,y}^2, u_{s,support(x,y)})$, $t_r(support(x, y), c^3, u_{r,support(x,y)})$

Formally, for a graph $g = (a, N, E)$ the condition functions are defined as:

$$c_x^1(g) = \begin{cases} \{e\} & \exists r(u, claim(x), e) \in N \\ \{e\} & \exists r(u, support(y, x), e) \in N \\ \emptyset & \text{otherwise} \end{cases}$$

$$c_{x,y}^2(g) = \begin{cases} \{u\} & \exists s(e, claim(x), u) \in N \\ \emptyset & \text{otherwise} \end{cases}$$

$$c^3(g) = \{e\}$$

$$c^4(g) = \{u\}$$

So for instance $t_r(support(x, y), c^3, u_{r,support(x,y)})$ says that $support(x, y)$ can be received from the expert and if it is received, then the update function $u_{r,support(x,y)}$ is applied to the agent's dialogue graph (specified below). Intuitively, for a specific agent the update functions specify that sending a why question is a response to either an earlier received claim or received support utterance, receiving a why question is a response to an earlier sent claim or sent support utterance, sending a support utterance is a response to a received why question and receiving a support utterance is a response to an earlier sent why question. We parametrize the update functions with a communication mode (send or receive) and a locution. Formally, for a locution l, a graph $\mathsf{g} = (\mathsf{a}, \mathsf{N}, \mathsf{E})$ and an agent a' the update functions are defined as:

$$u_{\mathsf{s},\mathsf{l}}(\mathsf{g}, \mathsf{a}') = (\mathsf{a}, \mathsf{N} \cup \{\mathsf{s}(\mathsf{a}, \mathsf{l}, \mathsf{a}')\}, \mathsf{E}')$$
$$u_{\mathsf{r},\mathsf{l}}(\mathsf{g}, \mathsf{a}') = (\mathsf{a}, \mathsf{N} \cup \{\mathsf{r}(\mathsf{a}, \mathsf{l}, \mathsf{a}')\}, \mathsf{E}')$$

such that $(\mathsf{e}_1, \mathsf{e}_2) \in \mathsf{E}'$ iff:

$\mathsf{e}_1 = \mathsf{r}(\mathsf{a}, claim(x), \mathsf{a}') \in \mathsf{N}$ and $\mathsf{e}_2 = \mathsf{s}(\mathsf{a}, why(x), \mathsf{a}') \in \mathsf{N}$,

or $\mathsf{e}_1 = \mathsf{r}(\mathsf{a}, support(y, x), \mathsf{a}') \in \mathsf{N}$ and $\mathsf{e}_2 = \mathsf{s}(\mathsf{a}, why(x), \mathsf{a}') \in \mathsf{N}$,

or $\mathsf{e}_1 = \mathsf{s}(\mathsf{a}, claim(x), \mathsf{a}') \in \mathsf{N}$ and $\mathsf{e}_2 = \mathsf{r}(\mathsf{a}, why(x), \mathsf{a}') \in \mathsf{N}$,

or $\mathsf{e}_1 = \mathsf{s}(\mathsf{a}, support(y, x), \mathsf{a}') \in \mathsf{N}$ and $\mathsf{e}_2 = \mathsf{r}(\mathsf{a}, why(x), \mathsf{a}') \in \mathsf{N}$,

or $\mathsf{e}_1 = \mathsf{r}(\mathsf{a}, why(x), \mathsf{a}') \in \mathsf{N}$ and $\mathsf{e}_2 = \mathsf{s}(\mathsf{a}, support(x, y), \mathsf{a}') \in \mathsf{N}$,

or $\mathsf{e}_1 = \mathsf{s}(\mathsf{a}, why(x), \mathsf{a}') \in \mathsf{N}$ and $\mathsf{e}_2 = \mathsf{r}(\mathsf{a}, support(x, y), \mathsf{a}') \in \mathsf{N}$.

A template-based dialogue system is a dialogue system that is extended with possible dialogue graphs and templates.

Definition 9 (Template-Based System, D^+). *A template-based dialogue system D^+ is specified by $(\mathsf{A}, \mathsf{L}, \mathsf{G}, \mathsf{T})$ where A and L are sets of agent and locution atoms, respectively, G is a set of dialogue graphs such that $\mathsf{g}_{\mathsf{a}}^{\emptyset} \in \mathsf{G}$ for each $\mathsf{a} \in \mathsf{A}$ and T is a set of dialogue templates for L, A and G.*

We will next specify the operational semantics of a template-based dialogue system with Plotkin style transition rules. These rules give insight in how exactly a dialogue system can transition and help us and agents to reason about possible dialogues that may result from the specification. The runtime configuration of a dialogue system consists of the history of moments that have already passed, the messages that are to be received now or in the future (notated τ_1, these messages were sent in earlier moments), the messages that are to be received in the future (notated τ_2, these messages are being sent in the current moment) and the dialogue graphs of each agent. There are four possible transition rules that apply for a transition: an agent receives a message for which a template is specified, an agent receives a message for which no template is specified (in which case the message has no effect), an agent sends a message or the moment passes. An agent can receive a message if that message was sent in an earlier moment. If there is a template specified for the reception of the message, then this template is used to update the dialogue graph. An agent can only send a message if there is a template that allows this. Finally, if the current moment passes, then all sent messages of the current moment can be received during the following moments.

Definition 10 (Dialogue Operational Semantics, c_{D^+}). *Let $\mathsf{D}^+ = (\mathsf{A}, \mathsf{L}, \mathsf{G}, \mathsf{T})$ be a template-based dialogue system where $\mathsf{A} = \{\mathsf{a}_1, ..., \mathsf{a}_k\}$. A runtime configuration of D^+ is specified by $c_{\mathsf{D}^+} = (d, M, \tau_1, \tau_2, \mathsf{g}_1...\mathsf{g}_k)$, where $d \in (2^{\mathbb{E}})^*$ is a sequence of sets of dialogue events, $M \subseteq \mathbb{E}$ is a set of dialogue events, τ_1 and τ_2 are sets of receive events and g_i, $i \in [1, k]$, is a dialogue graph $(\mathsf{a}_i, \mathsf{N}_i, \mathsf{E}_i)$. The initial runtime configuration of D^+ is $(\varepsilon, \emptyset, \emptyset, \emptyset, \mathsf{g}_{\mathsf{a}_1}^{\emptyset}...\mathsf{g}_{\mathsf{a}_k}^{\emptyset})$. The operational semantics of D^+ is given by:*

$$\frac{r(a_i, l, a') \in \tau_1 \ \& \ \exists t_r(l, c, u) \in T : a' \in c(g_i) \ \& \ u(g_i, a') = g'_i}{(d, M, \tau_1, \tau_2, g_1 \ldots g_i \ldots g_k) \xrightarrow{r(a_i, l, a')}_d (d, M', \tau'_1, \tau_2, g_1 \ldots g'_i \ldots g_k)} \quad (\textit{Dialogue Receive 1})$$

where $M' = M \cup \{r(a_i, l, a')\}$ *and* $\tau'_1 = \tau_1 \setminus \{r(a_i, l, a')\}$

$$\frac{r(a_i, l, a') \in \tau_1 \ \& \ \not\exists t_r(l, c, u) \in T : a' \in c(g_i)}{(d, M, \tau_1, \tau_2, g_1 \ldots g_i \ldots g_k) \xrightarrow{r(a_i, l, a')}_d (d, M', \tau'_1, \tau_2, g_1 \ldots g_i \ldots g_k)} \quad (\textit{Dialogue Receive 2})$$

where $M' = M \cup \{r(a_i, l, a')\}$ *and* $\tau'_1 = \tau_1 \setminus \{r(a_i, l, a')\}$

$$\frac{\exists t_s(l, c, u) \in T : a' \in c(g_i) \ \& \ u(g_i, a') = g'_i}{(d, M, \tau_1, \tau_2, g_1 \ldots g_i \ldots g_k) \xrightarrow{s(a_i, l, a')}_d (d, M', \tau_1, \tau'_2, g_1 \ldots g'_i \ldots g_k)} \quad (\textit{Dialogue Send})$$

where $M' = M \cup \{s(a_i, l, a')\}$ *and* $\tau'_2 = \tau_2 \cup \{r(a'_i, l, a_i)\}$

$$\frac{\tau'_1 = \tau_1 \cup \tau_2}{(d, M, \tau_1, \tau_2, g_1 \ldots g_k) \xrightarrow{moment}_d (dM, \emptyset, \tau'_1, \emptyset, g_1 \ldots g_k)} \quad (\textit{Dialogue Moment})$$

Example 9 (Operational Semantics). For our scenario we specify D^+ as (A, L, G, T), where the elements are drawn from the previous examples. In Table 1 we show the transitions that take place in the dialogue $M_1 M_2 M_3$ such that $M_1 = \{s(e, claim(p), u)\}$, $M_2 = \{r(u, claim(p), e), s(u, why(p), e)\}$, $M_3 = \{r(e, why(p), u), s(e, support(p, q), u)\}$. The transitions are enabled by the dialogue templates T. In the initial state the graphs of the expert and user are their empty graphs (g_e^0 and g_u^0). Then the sender sends a claim to the user. This causes its graph to be updated with the $u_{s,claim(x)}$ function, resulting in g_e^1 (where the locution is added to its nodes). The send event is added to the current moment and the corresponding receive event to τ_2. This means that somewhere in the future the message will be received. The second transition passes the moment. The receive event switches to τ_1, meaning that the message can be received in the current moment. The other transitions further handle the other messages and moments. The result is intuitively that the operational semantics allow for a dialogue to take place. In the rest of this section we show that the transitions indeed allow for dialogues and that the set of all possible allowed dialogues specifies a peer-to-peer suitable protocol.

Given the operational semantics of a template-based dialogue system we may specify the set of sequences of sets of dialogue events that may result from those transitions, which is called the language of that template-based dialogue system. A sequence of sets of dialogue events d is in the language of a template-based dialogue system if and only if from the initial runtime configuration we can make transitions such that we reach a runtime configuration where d is the first argument of the state.

Definition 11 (Dialogue Language, $\mathcal{L}_{D^+}$). *Let* $D^+ = (A, L, G, T)$ *be a template-based dialogue system. The language of* D^+, *notated* $\mathcal{L}_{D^+}$ *are all sequences of sets of dialogue events* d *such that there is a sequence of transitions* $c_{D^+} \to_d \ldots \to_d c'_{D^+}$ *possible where* c_{D^+} *is the initial runtime configuration of* D^+ *and* $c'_{D^+} = (d, M, \tau_1, \tau_2, g_1 \ldots g_k)$.

Table 1. Example transitions (see Example 9). A row indicates the left hand side state of a transition and ends with the name of the transition rule that is used to transition to the next row. The events are $e_1 = s(e, l_1, u)$, $e_2 = r(u, l_1, e)$, $e_3 = s(u, l_2, e)$, $e_4 = r(e, l_2, u)$, $e_5 = s(e, l_3, u)$, $e_6 = r(u, l_3, e)$, where the locutions are $l_1 = claim(p)$, $l_2 = why(p)$ and $l_3 = support(p, q)$.

D	M	τ_1	τ_2	g_e	g_u	Transition
ε	$\emptyset$	$\emptyset$	$\emptyset$	g_e^0	g_u^0	Send
ε	$\{e_1\}$	$\emptyset$	$\{e_2\}$	g_e^1	g_u^0	Moment
M_1	$\emptyset$	$\{e_2\}$	$\emptyset$	g_e^1	g_u^0	Receive 1
M_1	$\{e_2\}$	$\emptyset$	$\emptyset$	g_e^1	g_u^1	Send
M_1	$\{e_2, e_3\}$	$\emptyset$	$\{e_4\}$	g_e^1	g_u^2	Moment
$M_1 M_2$	$\emptyset$	$\{e_4\}$	$\emptyset$	g_e^1	g_u^2	Receive 1
$M_1 M_2$	$\{e_4\}$	$\emptyset$	$\emptyset$	g_e^2	g_u^2	Send
$M_1 M_2$	$\{e_4, e_5\}$	$\emptyset$	$\{e_6\}$	g_e^3	g_u^2	Moment
$M_1 M_2 M_3$	$\emptyset$	$\{e_6\}$	$\emptyset$	g_e^3	g_u^2	-

As intended, each element in the language of a template-based dialogue system is a dialogue.

Proposition 2. *Let* $D^+ = (A, L, G, T)$ *be a template-based dialogue system. Each element in* $\mathcal{L}_{D^+}$ *is a dialogue.*

Proof. By Definition 3, a sequence of sets of dialogue events $d = M_1...M_k$ is a dialogue iff for each moment M_i, $i \in [1, k]$, if $r(a, l, a') \in M_i$ then the number of moments M_j, $j \in [1, i-1]$, such that $r(a, l, a') \in M_j$ is less than the number of moments M_n, $n \in [1, i-1]$, such that $s(a', l, a) \in M_n$. The operational semantics only allow a receive transition for an event $r(a, l, a')$ if a corresponding send transition took place for the event $s(a', l, a)$ in a previous moment. Furthermore, if a receive transition takes place, then the event is removed from the runtime configuration. Hence for a new receive event it is required that first a new send transition for that event takes place. This means that a receive event $r(a, l, a')$ can only be in the current moment M_i if the corresponding send event $s(a', l, a)$ is in a past moment M_j, $j < i$, and in between those two moments no receive event took place: $\forall n \in [j+1, i-1] : r(a, l, a') \notin M'_n$. Hence any possible sequence of sets of dialogue events of role based dialogue system fits the definition of a dialogue, and therefore the language of a role based dialogue system is a set of dialogues.

The language of a template-based dialogue system is a protocol. This means that a template-based dialogue system can be seen as a protocol specification.

Proposition 3. *Let* $D^+ = (A, L, G, T)$ *be a template-based dialogue system.* $\mathcal{L}_{D^+}$ *is a protocol.*

Proof. By Definition 4, $\mathcal{L}_{D+}$ is a protocol iff:

1. $\forall M_1...M_k \in \mathcal{L}_{D+}$, $i \in [1, k]$: $M_1...M_i \in \mathcal{L}_{D+}$.
2. For each $d \in \mathbb{D}$ if $d \notin \mathcal{L}_{D+}$ and $M_1...M_k$ is the shortest prefix of d that is not in $\mathcal{L}_{D+}$, then $d' \in \mathcal{L}_{D+}$ where $d' = M_1...M_{k-1}M_k'$ such that $M_k' = \{r(a, l, a') \in M_k\}$.

Point 1 is easily verifiable; a dialogue $d \in \mathcal{L}_{D+}$ is possible due to a number of consecutive transitions. Hence, all prefixes of d are also in $\mathcal{L}_{D+}$ since we can obtain each prefix by executing only an initial segment of the consecutive transitions that create the prefix.

Point 2 follows from the fact that a receive transition can always be made, even if there is no template specified (rule Dialogue Receive 2). The transitions that create $M_1...M_{k-1}$ result in a configuration $c_{D+} = (M_1...M_{k-1}, M, \tau_1, \tau_2, g_1...g_k)$ where necessarily all the receive events from M_k are in τ_1. Therefore, we can make receive transitions until a configuration $c_{D+}' = (M_1...M_{k-1}, M', \tau_1', \tau_2, g_1'...g_k')$ is reached such that $M' = \{r(a, l, a') \in M_k\}$. If we follow this transition with a moment transition, then $M_1...M_{k-1}M'$ is created, which is thus in $\mathcal{L}_{D+}$, which proves point 2.

Finally our main theorem formulates the goal of this paper: the language of a template-based dialogue system is a peer-to-peer suitable protocol. This means that we can use a specification of a template-based dialogue system as a protocol specification that is suitable for open multi-agent systems.

Theorem 1. *Let* $D^+ = (A, L, G, T)$ *be a template-based dialogue system.* $\mathcal{L}_{D+}$ *is a peer-to-peer suitable protocol.*

Proof. $\mathcal{L}_{D+}$ is a protocol, hence we only need to prove that we can make for each agent $a \in A$ a set of dialogues $P_a \subseteq \mathbb{D}$ such that $\mathcal{L}_{D+} = \bigcap_{a \in A} P_a$ and for each $d, d' \in \mathbb{D}$ if $v_a(d) = v_a(d')$ then $d, d' \in P_a$ or $d, d' \notin P_a$. First, let P_a for each agent $a \in A$ be defined as $P_a = \{d \in \mathbb{D} | \exists d' \in \mathcal{L}_{D+} : v_a(d) = v_a(d')\}$. By this construction it follows immediately that for each agent $a \in A$ if $v_a(d) = v_a(d')$ then $d, d' \in P_a$ or $d, d' \notin P_a$.

A dialogue d is not in $\mathcal{L}_{D+}$ iff there is no sequence of transitions $c_{D+} \rightarrow_d$ ... $\rightarrow_d c_{D+}'$ where c_{D+} is the initial runtime configuration of D^+ and $c_{D+}' = (d, M, \tau_1, \tau_2, g_1...g_k)$. Necessarily at least one unallowed send transition for some event $s(a, l, a')$ is required to make d (receive and moment transitions are always possible). This means that given the view of a there cannot be a dialogue $d' \in \mathcal{L}_{D+}$ such that $v_a(d) = v_a(d')$. And thus if $d \notin \mathcal{L}_{D+}$ then there is an agent $a \in A$ such that $d \notin P_a$. Furthermore, for each $d \in \mathcal{L}_{D+}$ and agent $a \in A$ it holds that $v_a(d) = v_a(d)$, hence if $d \in \mathcal{L}_{D+}$ then $d \in P_a$ for each $a \in A$. Therefore $\mathcal{L}_{D+} = \bigcap_{a \in A} P_a$.

We can see a template-based dialogue system as a protocol specification because the language of a template-based dialogue system is a peer-to-peer suitable protocol. The protocol handles the legality of locutions, but does not address the 'low-level' concerns such as ensuring that messages will arrive. The templates ought to be notated in a human/machine readable format in order to make them interpretable for the agents. An agent can, given the protocol, determine all the views on all the dialogues that are allowed by the protocol and use this to strategise. For instance, in a strict turn-based dialogue system it may build a game tree and apply classic decision mechanisms for deciding upon a locution. We note that the templates can formally be quite involved, but at the same time might be quite straightforward in their manifestation as programs. Similarly, the maintenance of dialogue graphs in the formal semantics implies that the graph can grow indefinitely as the dialogue grows, but in an implementation this might not always be the case.

4   Conclusion

In this paper we have presented a formal framework for specifying communication protocols for open multi-agent systems. Our main reusable building blocks for specifying protocols are dialogue templates, which we have provided with a formal operational semantics. In open multi-agent systems we cannot assume that agents have knowledge about the messages that are exchanged among other agents, and an agent can also not assume any order on which messages are received when it sends messages. We formalised such concerns as peer-to-peer dialogues and presented a specification method to specify protocols that guarantee that each agent is in a position to know whether an action from itself causes a protocol violation.

With respect to argumentation, future work consists of further developing the framework to specify argumentation dialogue protocols which specify illocutionary force, that is, how argumentation dialogues can be used to build and analyse logical argument structures. Further work includes adapting the multitude of dialogue protocols specified in DGDL [25] to the current specification framework, representing common elements such as turntaking, commitments, and so on in our framework.

Not enforcing a protocol through a proxy agent or middleware brings up numerous interesting situations for argumentation dialogue systems. In this paper we focus on ensuring that agents can determine whether their own behaviour causes a violation of a protocol. In the future we want to investigate under which conditions it can be guaranteed that an agent can determine that another agent violated the protocol. The current work also assumes that agents adhere to the same protocol, but how does an agent determine the protocol under which it is communicating with other agents when there is no middleware? For which types of protocols/moves and under which conditions are agents guaranteed to pick up protocol violations from other agents? Is it possible to induce which protocols other agents are using from their behaviour? These are all questions we want to answer in future research.

Acknowledgements. This research is part of the project *Intelligence Amplification for Cybercrime* which has been funded by the Dutch National Police Innovation Programme.

References

1. Amgoud, L., Maudet, N., Parsons, S.: Modelling dialogues using argumentation. In: Proceedings of the 4th Conference on Multi-Agent Systems, pp. 31–38. IEEE (2000)
2. Bauer, B., Müller, J.P., Odell, J.: Agent UML: a formalism for specifying multi-agent software systems. Int. J. Softw. Eng. Knowl. Eng. **11**(03), 207–230 (2001)
3. Bex, F., Lawrence, J., Reed, C.: Generalising argument dialogue with the dialogue game execution platform. In: Proceedings of COMMA 2014. Frontiers in Artificial Intelligence and Applications, vol. 266, pp. 141–152. IOS Press (2014)
4. Bex, F., Peters, J., Testerink, B.: A.I. for online criminal complaints: from natural dialogues to structured scenarios. In: Workshop A.I. for Justice - Proceedings of ECAI 2016, pp. 22–29 (2016)
5. Bex, F., Reed, C.: Dialogue templates for automatic argument processing. In: Proceedings of COMMA 2012. Frontiers in Artificial Intelligence and Applications, vol. 245, pp. 366–377. IOS Press (2012)
6. Black, E., Hunter, A.: Executable logic for dialogical argumentation. In: Proceedings of ECAI, pp. 15–20. IOS Press (2012)
7. Black, E., McBurney, P., Zschaler, S.: Towards agent dialogue as a tool for capturing software design discussions. In: Black, E., Modgil, S., Oren, N. (eds.) TAFA 2013. LNCS, vol. 8306, pp. 95–110. Springer, Heidelberg (2014). doi:10.1007/978-3-642-54373-9_7
8. Dastani, M., Grossi, D., Meyer, J.-J.C., Tinnemeier, N.A.M.: Normative multi-agent programs and their logics. In: Meyer, J.-J.C., Broersen, J. (eds.) KRAMAS 2008. LNCS, vol. 5605, pp. 16–31. Springer, Heidelberg (2009). doi:10.1007/978-3-642-05301-6_2
9. Fan, X., Toni, F.: A general framework for sound assumption-based argumentation dialogues. Artif. Intell. **216**, 20–54 (2014)
10. Hannoun, M., Boissier, O., Sichman, J.S., Sayettat, C.: MOISE: an organizational model for multi-agent systems. In: Monard, M.C., Sichman, J.S. (eds.) IBERAMIA/SBIA -2000. LNCS, vol. 1952, pp. 156–165. Springer, Heidelberg (2000). doi:10.1007/3-540-44399-1_17
11. Lawrence, J., Bex, F., Reed, C., Snaith, M.: AIFdb: infrastructure for the argument web. In: Proceedings of COMMA 2012, pp. 515–516 (2012)
12. Lemon, O., Pietquin, O. (eds.): Data-Driven Methods for Adaptive Spoken Dialogue Systems: Computational Learning for Conversational Interfaces. Springer, New York (2012)
13. Maghraby, A., Robertson, D., Grando, A., Rovatsos, M.: Automated deployment of argumentation protocols. In: Proceedings of COMMA 2012. Frontiers in Artificial Intelligence and Applications, vol. 245, pp. 197–204 (2012)
14. Mazouzi, H., Seghrouchni, A.E.F., Haddad, S.: Open protocol design for complex interactions in multi-agent systems. In: Proceedings of the First International Joint Conference on Autonomous Agents and Multi-Agent Systems: Part 2, pp. 517–526. ACM (2002)
15. McBurney, P., Parsons, S.: Dialogue games for agent argumentation. In: Simari, G., Rahwan, I. (eds.) Argumentation in Artificial Intelligence, pp. 261–280. Springer, Boston (2009). doi:10.1007/978-0-387-98197-0_13
16. Minsky, N., Ungureanu, V.: Law-governed interaction: a coordination and control mechanism for heterogeneous distributed systems. TOSEM, ACM Trans. Softw. Eng. Methodol. **9**, 273–305 (2000)

17. Noroozi, O., Weinberger, A., Biemans, H.J., Mulder, M., Chizari, M.: Argumentation-based computer supported collaborative learning (ABCSCL): a synthesis of 15 years of research. Educ. Res. Rev. **7**(2), 79–106 (2012)
18. Odell, J.J., Van Dyke Parunak, H., Bauer, B.: Representing agent interaction protocols in UML. In: Ciancarini, P., Wooldridge, M.J. (eds.) AOSE 2000. LNCS, vol. 1957, pp. 121–140. Springer, Heidelberg (2001). doi:10.1007/3-540-44564-1_8
19. Pitt, J., Mamdani, A.: A protocol-based semantics for an agent communication language. In: Proceedings of IJCAI 1999, pp. 486–491 (1999)
20. Poutakidis, D., Padgham, L., Winikoff, M.: Debugging multi-agent systems using design artifacts: the case of interaction protocols. In: Proceedings of the First International Joint Conference on Autonomous Agents and Multiagent Systems: Part 2, pp. 960–967. ACM (2002)
21. Prakken, H.: Coherence and flexibility in dialogue games for argumentation. J. Log. Comput. **15**(6), 1009–1040 (2005)
22. Prakken, H.: A formal model of adjudication dialogues. Artif. Intell. Law **16**(3), 305–328 (2008)
23. Rahwan, I., Ramchurn, S.D., Jennings, N.R., Mcburney, P., Parsons, S., Sonenberg, L.: Argumentation-based negotiation. Knowl. Eng. Rev. **18**(4), 343–375 (2003)
24. Schatzmann, J., Weilhammer, K., Stuttle, M., Young, S.: A survey of statistical user simulation techniques for reinforcement-learning of dialogue management strategies. Knowl. Eng. Rev. **21**(2), 97–126 (2006)
25. Wells, S., Reed, C.: A domain specific language for describing diverse systems of dialogue. J. Appl. Log. **10**(4), 309–329 (2012)

Crafting Ontology Alignments from Scratch Through Agent Communication

Jérôme Euzenat[✉]

Univ. Grenoble Alpes, Inria, CNRS, Grenoble INP, LIG, 38000 Grenoble, France
Jerome.Euzenat@inria.fr
http://mOeX.inria.fr

Abstract. Agents may use different ontologies for representing knowledge and take advantage of alignments between ontologies in order to communicate. Such alignments may be provided by dedicated algorithms, but their accuracy is far from satisfying. We already explored operators allowing agents to repair such alignments while using them for communicating. The question remained of the capability of agents to craft alignments from scratch in the same way. Here we explore the use of expanding repair operators for that purpose. When starting from empty alignments, agents fails to create them as they have nothing to repair. Hence, we introduce the capability for agents to risk adding new correspondences when no existing one is useful. We compare and discuss the results provided by this modality and show that, due to this generative capability, agents reach better results than without it in terms of the accuracy of their alignments. When starting with empty alignments, alignments reach the same quality level as when starting with random alignments, thus providing a reliable way for agents to build alignment from scratch through communication.

1 Introduction

We usually develop a representation of the world we live in from a combination of experience and education. Artificial agents may be designed along the same principles. Experience is gathered through the interaction with their environment and education through the interaction with their peers.

Various experiments have been developed concerning how interaction with peers can shape agents knowledge. In particular, we dealt with situations in which agents have correct but not complete description of their environments as ontologies and they use alignments between each others ontologies to interact. Alignments between two ontologies are made of correspondences which express the (subsumption) relation between different concepts of these ontologies.

For instance, agents may classify the objects of their environment through a collection of features: size, colour, ability to move, dangerousness, etc. They may however classify such objects differently: first by colour, then by dangerousness or first by mobility, then by size. In such conditions, it can be difficult to communicate. Agents may use alignments between their ontologies expressing

© Springer International Publishing AG 2017
B. An et al. (Eds.): PRIMA 2017, LNAI 10621, pp. 245–262, 2017.
https://doi.org/10.1007/978-3-319-69131-2_15

that all purple dangerous objects are mobile or that static objects are yellow and harmless. The question we explore is how such alignments may be elaborated.

We have developed experiments in which agents can repair random alignments through playing some interaction game [7]. For that purpose, agents would use adaptation operators to alter the alignments when their use causes errors. For instance, discovering an object which is yellow, harmful, static and small would invalidate the second correspondence. An operator may thus discard it and replace it by a weaker correspondence such as static and large objects are yellow and harmless. However, the experimental protocol was relying on random initial alignments that agents would only correct.

Recently, such operators have been improved by providing agents with the opportunity to go beyond repairing existing alignments by introducing new tentative correspondences when necessary [8]. This was shown to improve results measured as the proximity of the resulting alignments with those known as correct. It remained unclear whether agents could build correspondences *ex nihilo* through communication. However, the newly introduced modalities open the possibility to test agents starting with no alignment and generating tentative (random) correspondences when they do not know any.

Here, we show how such a function can be implemented in artificial agents and observe the way such agents behave. We first consider what it means to start with no alignments for communicating and find that, in such a case, agents make no progress as they do not have an occasion to discover errors to correct. Hence, we introduce a new variation in which agents having no non-trivial correspondence to use would generate one tentatively useful one on the spot.

We compare results obtained with this new modality when agents are provided with random correspondences or not. It happens that, already if agents are provided with random initial correspondences, this new modality improves the results. Moreover, agents without alignments can develop them from scratch through interacting and reach results with the same quality as agents provided with random alignments (and the same modalities).

The paper is organised as follows. After reviewing related work (Sect. 2), we recall the settings previously developed for studying alignment evolution (Sect. 3). We then report on starting with empty networks of ontologies (Sect. 4), using the new generative modality (Sect. 5) and combining both approaches (Sect. 6).

2   Related Work

Interacting agents need a way to understand each others to some degree. They can all use the same ontology or preserve heterogeneous ontologies. In the latter case, heterogeneity is often reduced by using alignments between these ontologies [13]. However, because matching systems are not always correct or because agents change their ontologies, alignments may become incorrect. There have been various ways to solve this problem independently of agent tasks: gossiping to ensure a global coherence of the networks of ontologies [1], arguing over correspondences to select the relevant ones [13,17], logical repair to enforce consistency [9,11,14] or conservativity [10] constraints. Such approaches have been integrated within agent systems through specific protocols [1,13,18].

Cultural language evolution [16] showed how a particular culture can be shared by a population of agents through communication. This work offers an experimental methodology: a population of agents has to play randomly an "interaction game" with precise rules. The outcome of the game is clearly identified as a success or a failure. In function of the outcome, agents adapt their language. The state of the system is monitored and especially the success rate which measures the convergence of agents to a stable state. This approach may be applied to language [16] or ontologies [15].

In this paper, we are considering approaches in which agents elaborate and repair alignments, playing such interaction games, achieving global repair through local action.

This approach has been applied to agent-based data interlinking where agents would exchange graph patterns assumed to characterise entities to be identified [2]. They compared several ways to select the graph patterns to be exchanged in order to maximise the recognition. It has also been considered in the context of more elaborate games. Interaction-situated semantic alignment [3] considers ontology matching as framed by interaction protocols that agents use to communicate. Agents induce alignments between the different ontologies that they use depending on the success expectation of each correspondence with respect to the protocol. Failing dialogues lead them to revise their expectations and associated correspondences.

Cultural evolution has been adapted to the evolution of ontology alignments: agents have their own ontologies related by public ontology alignments (network of ontologies). They play simple reclassification games involving the alignments. The games allow agents to detect incorrect correspondences through their use and to locally repair the alignment with adaptation operators. Several operators were compared and were shown to converge towards fully correct alignments [7,8]. The evolutionary approach has also been combined with classical matching, but can be interpreted as a way to repair alignments through their use [4]. This has recently been generalised to less constrained declarative protocols with isomorphic alignments [5].

Anemone [18] is a comprehensive framework with the same goal: matching ontologies opportunistically at run time. It provides a protocol allowing agents to negotiate the relation between concepts of their ontologies when they cannot express a message they know the interlocutor will understand. Agents can then communicate a definition of the concept or, if this is not possible, provide examples of concept instance.

In spite of superficial differences —we repair alignments, Anemone extends ontologies—, both approaches may be considered as achieving the same tasks, in a lazy way, and they share their inspiration from cultural evolution for the assertional aspect. However, there are also notable differences in the proposed concepts and the methodology. Regarding concepts, our agents never exchange concept definitions, nor rely on negotiation. They operate at a lower level in which they apply corrective operations based on simple failure detection. As a consequence, communication is sound but not lossless: agents usually end up in a more general concept than what can be expressed. Concerning methodology, some theoretical properties (sound and lossless communication) of Anemone have been established and the system has been illustrated on a use case [18]. Here, we provide randomised experimental results comparing various operators and modalities which may be considered as variants of the Anemone protocol. Hence these work may be seen as complementary.

The work considered here is an extension of [7,8] to the case where agents starts with empty alignments. It can be thus considered as another instance of ontology matching through interaction [3,4]. However, instead of being guided by the interaction protocol, it is guided by the more expressive ontology structure.

3   Experimental Setting and Background

The experimental method and software used in this work is directly derived from [7]. The setting is deliberately abstract. This allows to control experiment variables, as our goal is to understand better which factors, in the setting and adaptation operators, influence the properties of the result. These experiments are randomised, which would be difficult with real-world data.

3.1   Setting

Objects in the world are described by a finite set of Boolean features (named a, b, c, etc.). Each object is described by the presence or absence of each feature, e.g., $a \land \neg b \land \neg c \land d$.

Objects, also called instances, are classified in ontologies which are strict hierarchies. Each class in the hierarchy corresponds to the conjunction of the features of its ancestors. For instance, the bottom-leftmost class in Fig. 1 is defined by $\neg c \land \neg d \land \neg a$. Each level in these hierarchies adds one constraint (positive or negative) related to exactly one feature. This means that classes not in subsumption relation are disjoint. Ontologies are incomplete since they have one level less than the environment has features (d for the middle ontology of Fig. 1). Ontologies, expressed in OWL, only use a very simple description logic. The boolean separation, may seem universal and/or artificial, it is simply a minimal language that features subsumption and disjointness.

An alignment is a set of correspondences between two ontologies. A correspondence is an expression like $\langle C, r, C' \rangle$ in which C and C' identify classes of the two ontologies and r is the relation between these classes. We use relation symbols $\leq, \geq$ and $=$ denoting subsumption and equivalence relations between classes. Figure 1 shows a fragment of the correct alignments, called reference, between one ontology and two others. Alignments are required to be functional —a class is subsumed by at most one more specific class in each alignment, but one class may subsume several classes— so as to be able to use them to reclassify instances.

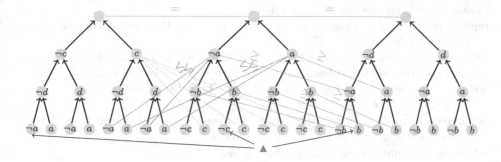

Fig. 1. One central ontology and fragments of the correct alignments to two other ontologies.

The instance ▲ featured in Fig. 1 is characterised by features $\neg a \wedge b \wedge \neg c \wedge \neg d$. Knowing this, each agent can classify it in its own ontology under the adequate most specific class. By using the expressed alignments, agents with the right most ontology, can reclassify this instance in the class $\neg a \wedge b$ in the middle ontology.

3.2   Games

There are as many agents as ontologies (each agent has a different ontology). Agents do not have access to the ontologies of other agents —they know the class names but not their definitions— nor to the reference alignments. They are instead provided with random alignments with the constraint that the topmost classes of each ontology are equivalent and alignments are functional.

Agents are no other goal than continuously playing an interaction game. In each game, two agents are chosen at random, one agent (A) picks up an instance (▲) at random and asks the other one (A') in which class it would classify the instance in its own ontology (O) using the public alignment between O and O'. A' determines which correspondence is applicable and communicates both the correspondence ($\langle C, r, C' \rangle$) and the class (C). A considers the relations between C and the class D in which it would classify ▲.

If C is compatible with D (C subsumes D, noted $D \sqsubseteq C$) the interaction is considered successful, otherwise (C is disjoint from D, noted $C \perp D$) it is a failure. A and A' then use an adaptation operator to adapt the alignment (in this case, they only do it in case of failure). Various adaptation operators may be used.

3.3   Adaptation Operators

The way agents play the game is built into their design. They use a specific adaptation operator to adapt their alignments. We consider six operators [8]: delete, replace, refine, add, addjoin and refadd. Assuming that the faulty correspondence $\langle C, r, C' \rangle$ has been crossed by the object from C' to C:

delete simply removes the correspondence;

replace in case r is =, then, in addition to delete, adds the same correspondence with a $\leq$ relation ($\langle C, \leq, C' \rangle$);

refine extends replace by adding a correspondence between C and the subclasses C'' of C' that do not subsume the actual class of the object ($\langle C, \geq, C'' \rangle$);

add extends replace by adding a correspondence between C' and the direct superclass C'' of C ($\langle C'', \geq, C' \rangle$);

addjoin is a variation of add which adds a correspondence between C' and the lowest superclass C'' of C compatible with D ($\langle C'', \geq, C' \rangle$);

refadd is the combination of addjoin and refine.

Figure 2 illustrates these operators. It shows two ontology fragments, left and right, with some assertions of disjointness (edges labelled $\perp$) and subsumption (unlabelled edges). Disjointness assertions simply materialises what can be deduced from class definitions by agents knowing them. During a game, the orange triangle instance is drawn and each agent knows to which class it belongs in its ontology (orange arrows). They identify the red correspondence (marked =) as erroneous: it leads to the conclusion that this instance belongs to a class which is disjoint from the identified class. delete removes this correspondence. replace replaces it with the subsumption part of the correspondence ($\leq$) that has not been proved incorrect. add (addjoin) will add a ($\geq$) correspondence from a (the common) subsumer of C (and D). The refine operator will add ($\geq$) correspondences to the subsumees of C' not subsuming D'.

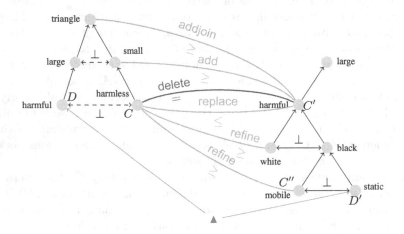

Fig. 2. Illustration on two ontology fragments of the effect of the various operators on the correspondence $\langle C, =, C' \rangle$ (adapted from [8]). $\perp$ denotes class disjointness. The displayed object is characterised by the features: triangle, large, harmful, black and static. (Color figure online)

3.4 Expansion and Relaxation

We introduced two different modalities further refining agent behaviour [8]. In particular, the expansion modality permits agents to go beyond the initially provided alignments.

The **expansion** modality, when an operator removes a correspondence and is not able to replace it by another correspondence, adds a new random correspondence. This modality can be associated with any operator above.

Agents rely on random correspondences in the sense that there is nothing which guides them towards a particular correspondence. This modality is associated with a memory recording discarded correspondences so as to avoid regenerating them [8].

Moreover, correspondences that the agent can find entailed by its ontology and the current alignment or by a recorded correspondence will not be added.

The **relaxation** modality makes agents more curious: Agent A' has the opportunity to not use the most specific correspondence when answering to A, but to chose a more general one. This is alike someone answering a question with a general statement and not the most specific answer she knows (this is Latin music vs. this is Brazilian bossa nova vs. this is a Luiz Bonfá tune).

With relaxation, when encountering a correspondence that applies to the current instance, agents use this correspondence only with a specific probability, called immediate consumption probability, which also applies to the shadowed correspondences. As in [8], we use 80% immediate consumption probability (in 20% of the cases agents try to answer with less specific correspondences). Relaxation permits to detect incorrect correspondences that otherwise would never be detected because they are shadowed by more specific correct correspondences. This modality allows agents to reach 100% precision. In case there is no shadowed correspondence but the topmost one, agents use the applicable correspondence.

3.5 Measures

As agents play games, measures may be applied to the resulting situation (the current network of ontologies) and the evolution of the game. We use the same measures as in the initial experiments [7]:

- **Success rate** [16] characterised by the ratio of success over games played is the main measure.
- **Semantic precision and recall** [6] measures the degree of correctness and completeness of the resulting alignments with respect to the known correct reference alignments.[1]
- **Incoherence rate** [12] measures the proportion of incoherent correspondences in alignments taken one by one.
- **Convergence** is the number of games taken to converge in all cases (it is an observed maximum, not an average) when the process converges.

---

[1] Contrary to classical precision and recall, it is not possible to deduce them from the numbers given hereafter.

The quality of an alignment is thus measured through its precision and recall, usually aggregated as F-measure. The incoherence rate is also a quality measure but it is negatively correlated with precision.

In [7], results were also compared with those of logical repair systems. Since, agents are allowed to generate new correspondences not entailed by the initial alignments, the comparison would not be meaningful any more. What would be relevant is to compare the agent results with that of ontology matching systems. However, this is more difficult to achieve than with logical repair systems which were relying on logic only. Indeed, ontology matching can take advantage of various features found in real-world ontologies that are not available in our synthetic ontologies.

In the following, we will test hypotheses by performing experiments on our *Lazy lavender* platform[2]. We use only 4 agents to be able to compare with previous result and due to the complexity incurred in our setting by multiplying agents: this also increases ontology complexity. Experiments are run over 10000 random games. All results are the average of 10 runs (usually not the same ones).

The experiments are run with all six presented operators. We only deal with them under the expansion modality which is the only one generating correspondences. Hence, we compare with both expansion and expansion+relaxation modalities (see summary in Fig. 7).

4   Starting Empty

The expansion modality enables agents to introduce new correspondences. The question arises of whether this is sufficient to create the alignments in the first place. It is our first hypothesis (H1), that agents with expansion modality can reach the same quality if they start with an empty network of alignments.

4.1   Experimental Setting: Empty Network

To test this, we experiment with agents starting with empty alignments. These alignments are not truly empty, they contain an equivalence correspondence between the topmost class of both ontologies. This materialises the idea that agents model the same domain. This is not a particularly strong assumption.

4.2   Results and Discussion

The results are found in the third section (empty) of Table 1.

The exact same result is actually obtained by all adaptation operators, independently from the use of expansion and relaxation. This explains why the third section of Table 1 is simply reduced to one line. The resulting network is made of the initial empty alignments, which provides a coherent (incoherence = 0.) and correct (precision = 100%) alignment which is far from complete (recall = 7%).

---

[2] http://lazylav.gforge.inria.fr.

Table 1. Measures with the reference and initial network of ontologies, and those obtained by the 6 adaptation operators (delete, replace, refine, add, addjoin, refadd) with expansion, relaxation and generative modalities starting with random or empty networks of alignments [4 agents; 10 runs; 10000 games].

| | | Network and Success | | Incoherence | Semantic | Semantic | Semantic | |
		operator	rate	Size	degree	Precision	F-measure	Recall	Convergence
		reference	1.0	86	0.0	1.0	1.0	1.0	-
		initial	0.24	54	0.34	0.11	0.20	0.89	-
plain	expansion	delete	0.98	14	0.03	0.94	0.26	0.15	2003
		replace	0.97	25	0.06	0.90	0.40	0.26	1664
		refine	0.96	36	0.10	0.85	0.56	0.42	2798
		add	0.96	59	0.23	0.69	0.67	0.65	4209
		addjoin	0.98	51	0.20	0.74	0.65	0.57	2029
		refadd	0.97	63	0.20	0.75	0.74	0.72	3203
	exp+rel	delete	0.98	14	0.00	1.00	0.26	0.15	2851
		replace	0.97	23	0.00	1.00	0.33	0.19	2916
		refine	0.96	37	0.00	1.00	0.56	0.38	2610
		add	0.95	49	0.00	1.00	0.64	0.47	7202
		addjoin	0.97	42	0.00	1.00	0.58	0.41	3393
		refadd	0.96	64	0.00	1.00	0.82	0.70	6002
empty	*any*		1.0	12	0.0	1.0	0.13	0.07	
generative	expansion	delete	0.94	61	0.12	0.84	0.70	0.59	9099
		replace	0.94	63	0.12	0.84	0.70	0.59	8857
		refine	0.94	71	0.15	0.81	0.78	0.75	7063
		add	0.91	75	0.22	0.71	0.76	0.82	9344
		addjoin	0.95	75	0.21	0.75	0.78	0.81	6230
		refadd	0.95	78	0.21	0.73	0.79	0.86	5840
	exp+rel	delete	0.94	52	0.00	1.00	0.60	0.43	8973
		replace	0.94	57	0.00	1.00	0.65	0.48	6782
		refine	0.93	63	0.00	1.00	0.77	0.62	6092
		add	0.91	68	0.00	1.00	0.78	0.64	9907
		addjoin	0.95	68	0.00	1.00	0.79	0.65	9501
		refadd	0.94	74	0.00	1.00	0.87	0.76	8495
generative+empty	expansion	delete	0.94	72	0.13	0.85	0.71	0.61	9199
		replace	0.94	71	0.12	0.84	0.70	0.59	7305
		refine	0.94	78	0.15	0.82	0.77	0.72	7458
		add	0.94	83	0.16	0.82	0.77	0.72	9173
		addjoin	0.96	80	0.16	0.81	0.78	0.74	5910
		refadd	0.95	82	0.18	0.80	0.80	0.80	7391
	exp+rel	delete	0.94	61	0.00	1.00	0.64	0.47	9504
		replace	0.94	62	0.00	1.00	0.63	0.46	6997
		refine	0.94	72	0.00	1.00	0.76	0.61	6798
		add	0.93	76	0.00	1.00	0.78	0.63	8562
		addjoin	0.95	75	0.00	1.00	0.78	0.64	9412
		refadd	0.94	79	0.00	1.00	0.84	0.73	7078

If agents start with empty alignments, then communication never fails —it can use the correspondence between the topmost classes which are correct— and the operators are never triggered, leading to no generation of new correspondences. So, agents are not able to evolve their knowledge.

This shows that Hypothesis H1 is not valid.

5 Generative Modality: Trying Useful Correspondences

To address this problem it is necessary to enhance agent behaviours. We achieve this by introducing a new modality, called generative, which allows agents, when they realise that they do not have a correspondence for a given object, to generate and immediately use a new correspondence that can apply to this object.

Because this changes the behaviour of the agents, we first run the modality under the same condition as the initial experiments (Sect. 3, [8]), i.e., starting with random alignments. This allows to be able to compare the impact of starting with empty correspondences (Sect. 6) on the same basis.

Our hypothesis is that (H2) the generative modality should not bring different results than the expansion modality which is already able to generate correspondences.

5.1 Generative Modality

The generative modality applies when the only applicable correspondence for a given instance (▲) is one of the topmost correspondence. Then the agent will generate a new correspondence that applies to this object. For that purpose, it will pick up at random a class (D) subsuming or equal to the class (C) of the instance and create a correspondences $\langle D, \leq, C' \rangle$ in which C' is taken randomly in the other ontology.

Figure 3 shows this situation highlighting the areas from which the correspondence is taken at random.

This modality applies before any failure occurs. It injects correspondences which are immediately consumed. During the game, three situations may happen:

- the correspondence is correct: then communication will succeed and the correspondence will be preserved;
- the correspondence is incorrect and communication fails: then the correspondence is discarded immediately;
- the correspondence is incorrect and communication succeeds: then the correspondence is preserved and may be detected as incorrect later on (this is the case of Fig. 3).

As in the expansion modality, agents record discarded correspondences so that they do not generate them again.

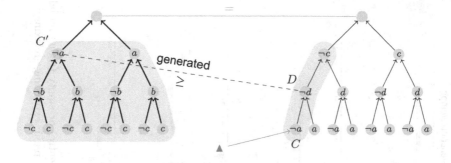

Fig. 3. Generative modality. Because no correspondences but the topmost one is applicable for ▲, a new one (in red, dashed) is drawn at random between the two gray areas of the ontologies. (Color figure online)

5.2 Experimental Setting

We run the experiments comparing the results obtained by starting with random alignments and using or not using the new generative modality.

5.3 Results

The final results are found in the second (non generative) and fourth (generative) sections of Table 1 as well as the centre plots of Fig. 5.

The resulting network features higher size when using the generative modality (see Fig. 4). This is particularly relevant with the operators not allowed to add many correspondences (delete, replace and refine).

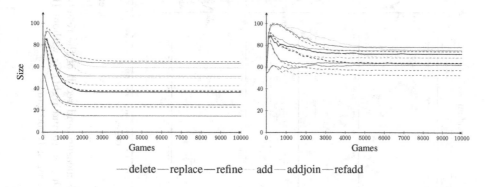

Fig. 4. Size of the resulting networks of ontologies without (left) and with (right) the generative modality. Expanding modality is in plain; expanding+relaxing in dashed [4 agents; 10 runs; 10000 games].

The generative modality is slower to converge: this is quite natural as it tries more correspondences.

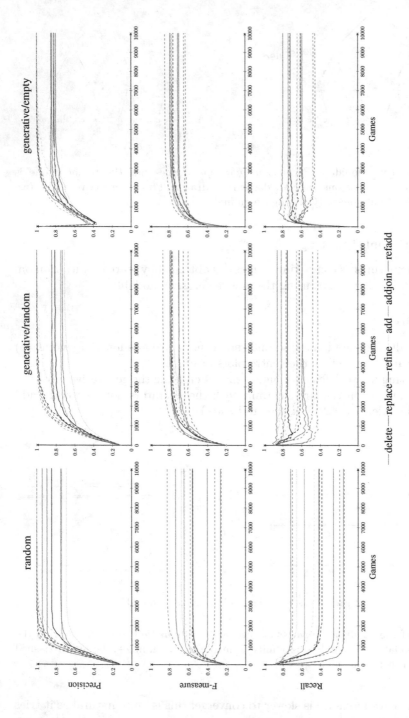

Fig. 5. Precision, F-measure and recall of the resulting networks of ontologies with random (left and centre) or empty (right) initial alignments and with (centre and right) or without (left) generative modality. Expanding modality is in plain; expanding+relaxing in dashed [4 agents; 10 runs; 10000 games].

Precision still reaches 100% when using relaxation. It however decreases (and inconsistency increases) when not using it. This is especially true for (delete and replace). This can be related to more correspondences generated which end up shadowed by other correspondences.

Recall is definitively higher for all operators causing higher F-measure for all conditions.

5.4 Analysis

Contrary to our expectation (H2), the generative modality allows agents to achieve better results than plain operators with expansion.

It is especially better in terms of recall. This is due to its capability to test correspondences even when the expansion modality would not have been applied: the expansion modality adds correspondences, if possible, when the number of correspondences decreases, while the generative modality generates correspondences a priory and where they would be needed. This is especially visible for the worst operators (delete and replace), that had not many opportunities to remove correspondences.

The generative modality reaches a slightly lower precision and a far higher recall, which largely improves F-measure.

6 Generating from Scratch

Results of Sect. 5 provide a new baseline: it is now possible to compare the behaviour of agents when they start with random or empty networks.

In this third experiment, the hypothesis (H3) is that agents starting from scratch are able to build alignments just like agents starting with random alignments.

6.1 Experimental Setting

The experimental setting here is very simple as it combines the two previous ones: agents starts with empty alignments and they use the generative modality. Experiments are run in the same conditions as before.

6.2 Results

The final results are found in the last section (generative+empty) of Table 1 and the right-hand side of Fig. 5.

The size of the resulting networks follow the same curves after 500 games. Success rate are the same passed 200 games.

F-measure values seem even more concentrated than with random alignments.

6.3   Analysis

When using the generative modality, if agents start with empty alignments, they reach the same level of precision, recall and F-measure than if they would start with random alignments. We are talking of levels here because results are not exactly the same, but there is a lot of randomisation in these experiments. Looking at the raw figures of Table 1, there seems to be a slight increase of precision (except of course when relaxing is used) and a slight decrease in recall leading to an overall stable F-measure.

Hence, we do not think that this is strong enough to refute H3.

This means that the generation of initial random alignments is not necessary for agents to reach interoperability, they are able to generate tentative alignments and to discard them if they are wrong. Moreover, they will produce alignments with a commensurate quality, measured through F-measure, as if they were starting with a random network.

The centre and right curves of Fig. 5 clearly differs as starting with empty alignments makes precision starting at 1 and steeply dropping, while recall starts near 0 and sharply rises. On the contrary, starting with random alignments, precision is very low and rises steadily while recall is quite high and drops steeply before stabilising.

Figure 6 superimposes these curves to better assess their relations. It shows that after a few hundred games, the curves tend to have the same shape, though not exactly superimposed—again, keep in mind that the experiments are random.

Results could be further decomposed between the three first modalities (delete, replace, refine) and the three last ones (add, addjoin, refadd) which seems to benefit differently from the generative modality. For the three former ones, curves are very close indeed. This is different for the three latter ones: in case of relaxation, the curves are again nearly the same. However, without it, precision remains at a higher level and recall at a lower level when starting empty. This may be explained by the shadowing effect [8] which prevents from discarding incorrect correspondences that relaxation can debunk. Correspondences generated by the generative modality are never shadowed correspondences. Recall is higher because shadowed incorrect correspondences may entail correct correspondences accounted for by *semantic* precision and recall [6]. Both effects seems to compensate when computing F-measure which is globally the same.

Starting empty with the generative modality, agents achieve networks of alignments with more correspondences. It is not fully clear why this is the case.

Finally, although it seems that agents are actually traversing the whole search space, this is not the case. Indeed, they do not reach full recall and their networks of alignments are smaller than the reference network. This has been explained in [8] by the reverse shadowing effect which can clearly be observed in the case of relaxation: the size of alignments increases slightly, and they are 100% correct. However, their recall is lower. This counter-intuitive observation is related to enforcing functionality and preserving correct but not the most general correspondences.

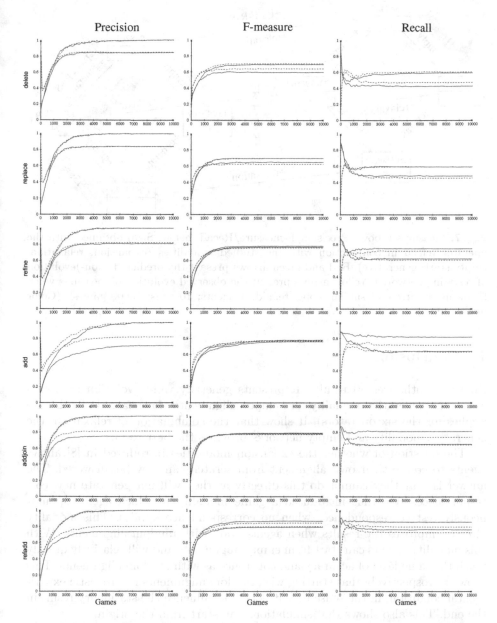

Fig. 6. Superimposition of the precision (left), F-measure (centre) and recall (right) curves for operators with expansion (red) and expansion+relaxation (blue) starting with random alignments (plain) and empty ones (dashed) [generative; 4 agents; 10 runs; 10000 games]. (Color figure online)

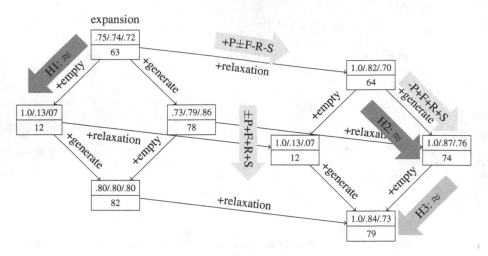

Fig. 7. Measures (above: Precision/F-measure/Recall; below: Size) obtained with the operator refadd in conjunction with the studied modalities (expansion, relaxation, empty start, generative). Red and green arrows present the predicted (non-)evolution of resulting networks. Yellow arrows present the observed evolution of measures when following an arrow of similar slope [refadd; 4 agents; 10 runs; 10000 games]. (Color figure online)

7   Conclusion

Figure 7 synthesises all results. It presents generally valid evolution for relaxation, the generative modality and empty alignments (for refadd, but this also applies for the six operators). It show that the combination of relaxation, the generative modality and empty networks provides the best results.

The question of whether the expansion modalities introduced in [8] allows agents to create their own alignment from scratch can now be answered. The answer is that they cannot do this directly as they will not generate new correspondences. We thus introduced a game modality in which agents spontaneously test correspondences when no correspondence applies. This modality already improves the results when agents start with random alignments. With this modality, agents can start from empty alignments and will relatively quickly reach the same level of accuracy and coherence as with random alignments. This shows retrospectively that starting with random alignments is a realistic experimental condition, in the sense that it does not influence the stationary result in the end. This also shows that simulations can start from the origin.

This work is part of a wider investigation on experimental cultural knowledge evolution. Our first experiments aimed at developing local adaptation operators. We have demonstrated that agents are able to acquire alignments from scratch through communication. We will now investigate how this can be achieved by a population of agents and to what extent they reach common knowledge that can be qualified of culture. We could then expose such populations of agents to changes in their environments and encountered population showing how adaptation turns into evolution.

Experiment Material

Experiment records are available under the *Lazy lavender* (see Footnote 2) logbook at entries: [20170529-NOOR] [20170530-NOOR] [20170531-NOOR] [20170607-NOOR].

References

1. Aberer, K., Cudré-Mauroux, P., Hauswirth, M.: Start making sense: the Chatty Web approach for global semantic agreements. J. Web Semant. **1**(1), 89–114 (2003)
2. Anslow, M., Rovatsos, M.: Aligning experientially grounded ontologies using language games. In: Croitoru, M., Marquis, P., Rudolph, S., Stapleton, G. (eds.) GKR 2015. LNCS, vol. 9501, pp. 15–31. Springer, Cham (2015). doi:10.1007/978-3-319-28702-7_2
3. Atencia, M., Schorlemmer, M.: An interaction-based approach to semantic alignment. J. Web Semant. **13**(1), 131–147 (2012)
4. Chocron, P., Schorlemmer, M.: Attuning ontology alignments to semantically heterogeneous multi-agent interactions. In: Proceedings of the 22nd European Conference on Artificial Intelligence (ECAI), The Hague, Netherlands, pp. 871–879 (2016)
5. Chocron, P., Schorlemmer, M.: Vocabulary alignment in openly specified interactions. In: Proceedings of the 16th International Conference on Autonomous Agents and Multi-agent Systems (AAMAS), Saõ Paolo, Brazil, pp. 1064–1072 (2017)
6. Euzenat, J.: Semantic precision and recall for ontology alignment evaluation. In: Proceedings of the 20th International Joint Conference on Artificial Intelligence (IJCAI), pp. 348–353 (2007)
7. Euzenat, J.: First experiments in cultural alignment repair (Extended Version). In: Presutti, V., Blomqvist, E., Troncy, R., Sack, H., Papadakis, I., Tordai, A. (eds.) ESWC 2014. LNCS, vol. 8798, pp. 115–130. Springer, Cham (2014). doi:10.1007/978-3-319-11955-7_10
8. Euzenat, J.: Interaction-based ontology alignment repair with expansion and relaxation. In: Proceedings of the 26th International Joint Conference on Artificial Intelligence (IJCAI), Melbourne, VIC, Australia, pp. 185–191 (2017)
9. Jiménez-Ruiz, E., Meilicke, C., Grau, B.C., Horrocks, I.: Evaluating mapping repair systems with large biomedical ontologies. In: Proceedings of the 26th Description logics workshop, Ulm, Germany, pp. 246–257 (2013)
10. Jiménez-Ruiz, E., Payne, T., Solimando, A., Tamma, V.: Limiting logical violations in ontology alignnment through negotiation. In: Proceedings of the 15th Conference on Principles of Knowledge Representation and Reasoning (KR), Cape Town, South Africa, pp. 217–226 (2016)
11. Meilicke, C.: Alignment incoherence in ontology matching. Ph.D. thesis, Universität Mannhein (2011)
12. Meilicke, C., Stuckenschmidt, H.: Incoherence as a basis for measuring the quality of ontology mappings. In: Proceedings of the 3rd ISWC International Workshop on Ontology Matching, pp. 1–12 (2008)

13. Payne, T., Tamma, V.: Negotiating over ontological correspondences with asymmetric and incomplete knowledge. In: Proceedings of the 14th International Conference on Autonomous Agents and Multi-agent Systems (AAMAS), pp. 517–524 (2014)
14. Santos, E., Faria, D., Pesquita, C., Couto, F.: Ontology alignment repair through modularization and confidence-based heuristics. PLoS ONE **10**(12), 1–19 (2015)
15. Steels, L.: The origins of ontologies and communication conventions in multi-agent systems. Auton. Agent. Multi Agent Syst. **1**(2), 169–194 (1998)
16. Steels, L. (ed.): Experiments in Cultural Language Evolution. John Benjamins, Amsterdam (2012)
17. Trojahn, C., Euzenat, J., Tamma, V., Payne, T.: Argumentation for reconciling agent ontologies. In: Elai, A., Kona, M., Orgun, M. (eds.) Semantic Agent Systems, vol. 344, pp. 89–111. Springer, New-York (2011). doi:10.1007/978-3-642-18308-9_5
18. van Diggelen, J., Beun, R.-J., Dignum, F., van Eijk, R., Meyer, J.-J.: Ontology negotiation in heterogeneous multi-agent systems: the ANEMONE system. Appl. Ontol. **2**(3–4), 267–303 (2007)

Rethinking Frequency Opponent Modeling in Automated Negotiation

Okan Tunalı[1]([⊠]), Reyhan Aydoğan[1,2], and Victor Sanchez-Anguix[3]

[1] Department of Computer Science, Özyeğin University, Istanbul, Turkey
okan.tunali@ozu.edu.tr
[2] Interactive Intelligence Group, Delft University of Technology,
Delft, The Netherlands
R.Aydogan@tudelft.nl
[3] Coventry University, Coventry, UK
ac0872@coventry.ac.uk

Abstract. Frequency opponent modeling is one of the most widely used opponent modeling techniques in automated negotiation, due to its simplicity and its good performance. In fact, it outperforms even more complex mechanisms like Bayesian models. Nevertheless, the classical frequency model does not come without its own assumptions, some of which may not always hold in many realistic settings. This paper advances the state of the art in opponent modeling in automated negotiation by introducing a novel frequency opponent modeling mechanism, which soothes some of the assumptions introduced by classical frequency approaches. The experiments show that our proposed approach outperforms the classic frequency model in terms of evaluation of the outcome space, estimation of the Pareto frontier, and accuracy of both issue value evaluation estimation and issue weight estimation.

Keywords: Agreement technologies · Automated negotiation · Opponent modeling · Multi-agent systems

1 Introduction

In the last few years, we have seen an increasing interest on the study of agreement technologies [27]. This increasing interest goes hand in hand with an incipient acceptance of autonomy and delegation in technology, with some technologies such as self-driven cars [19] being the prime example of this trend. As delegation and autonomous systems become the norm, so will agreement technologies. The reason is simple: autonomous agents are driven by real users' preferences, and, as we all know, conflict is inherent in our world. As a consequence, we need technologies that allow autonomous agents to solve preferential conflicts and, hence, make delegation and autonomy as transparent for the user as possible. Automated negotiation [16,23,29] is considered as one of the core technologies in agreement technologies, as it provides autonomous entities with protocols and algorithms to reach agreements in a distributed way.

© Springer International Publishing AG 2017
B. An et al. (Eds.): PRIMA 2017, LNAI 10621, pp. 263–279, 2017.
https://doi.org/10.1007/978-3-319-69131-2_16

Despite this recent and increasing interest in automated negotiation, research has been carried out for decades. Researchers have proposed a number of negotiation protocols [3,5] and negotiation strategies that guide autonomous agents on how to act in a distributed negotiation process [4,17,26,28]. There are two main families of strategies in automated negotiation process: game theoretic and heuristic approaches. On the one hand, the former focuses on achieving optimal negotiation results under the assumption of full rationality, unbounded computational resources, and, often, full disclosure of preferences. On the other hand, heuristic approaches assume that agents' resources are limited and partial or nil knowledge about the others' preferences, precluding agents from guaranteeing optimal results. This present work is categorized as a heuristic approach.

While optimal negotiation outcomes cannot be guaranteed, it is still crucial for agents to reach outcomes that are as close as possible to the optimal outcomes. There are several ways that agents can resort to optimizing the resulting negotiation outcomes, but perhaps opponent modeling is one of the most important mechanisms. Opponent modeling [9] allows us to build an approximate model of the opponents' preferences, which can be used to propose outcomes that result in win-win situations for involved parties. Hence, making outcomes more appealing and maximizing the odds of reaching an agreement.

One of the most popular opponent modeling mechanisms in automated negotiation is the frequency model [25]. The frequency model aims to build a model of the opponents' preferences assuming linear additive utility functions and steady concession towards lower utilities. For that, the frequency model uses the frequency of negotiation issue values as an indicator of both negotiation issue and value importance. Due to its simplicity and wide acceptance, the frequency model has been used in a myriad of scenarios [1,2,7,18,25]

Despite its popularity, there is no informed research on the robustness of the frequency model in a wide variety of scenarios. Most of the work in this field focuses only on the quality of the agreements and/or percentage of successful negotiations when the given negotiation strategy uses this model as opponent modeling. However, there are a number of factors having a significant impact on the negotiation outcome such as bidding strategy, acceptance strategy, how the estimated opponent's preference model is used in the underlying negotiation strategy, and so on. Therefore, gaining high utility agreements does not indicate by itself how good the opponent model is. Accordingly, this study analyzes how well the frequency model predicts opponent's preferences elaborately by comparing the estimated opponent model with the real preferences. The contributions of this paper are twofold. Firstly, we pose the problems faced by the frequency model in realistic scenarios. Secondly, we propose a new opponent modeling mechanism that deals with some of these problems and outperforms the classic frequency model mechanism.

The rest of this paper is structured as follows: Sect. 2 provides an overview of related work and Sect. 3 addresses the potential problems with the frequency model. The proposed opponent model is explained in Sect. 4. Section 5 provides a detailed analysis of the frequency model as well as the proposed opponent model empirically. Finally, Sect. 6 concludes the paper.

2   Related Work

A variety of opponent modeling mechanisms have been proposed in the automated negotiation literature. Some opponent modeling mechanisms aim to provide an educated guess over the opponents' reservation value or the opponent's concession strategy, while other opponent modeling approaches take an educated guess on the opponents' preferences with respect to outcomes. This paper is enclosed in the latter family. As far as learning techniques for opponent's preferences are concerned, two main approaches namely, probabilistic models (e.g. Bayesian) and frequency approaches, come to the forefront.

Bayesian approaches [10,11,21,28] usually employ Bayes' update rule and a set of hypotheses to model the opponents' preferences. For instance, Bui *et al.* [11] propose a multi-party cooperative negotiation mechanism for the distributed meeting scheduling domain. Agents follow an iterative process that gradually partitions the negotiation space into acceptable areas by expressing their preferences on suggested partitions. In order to speed up the negotiation process, the agents employ Bayesian classifiers to learn other agents' preferences according to the information gathered from the current and past negotiations. Another example of the use of Bayesian learning in negotiation is presented by Buffett *et al.* [10]. In the proposed model, agents negotiate over a set of limited objects that can either be included or excluded from the final deal. Bayesian classifiers are employed to classify opponent's preferences into classes of preference relations over the objects in the negotiation domain. Bayesian learning was also used by Hindriks and Tykhonov [21] in order to predict the shape of the opponent's utility function (i.e., downhill, uphill and triangular), as well as the corresponding rank of issue values and issue weights. Sanchez-Anguix *et al.* [28] used Bayesian classifiers to learn the acceptability of partial offers for each team member in a negotiation team, and their opponent.

On the other hand, frequency approaches [1,2,7,18,25] usually model opponents' preferences by counting the frequency of issue values and the frequency of changes in negotiation issues of the given bids, without considering an explicit set of initial hypotheses in mind. The most popular frequency model was introduced by the HardHeaded agent [25], whereby issue weights are updated when issue values do not change in consecutive pairs of opponent offers, and issue value weights are estimated by counting the occurrences of values in opponent's offers. A more detailed description of this model can be found in Sect. 3. In [18], the authors propose a frequency model similar to HardHeaded's frequency model. The main difference between those approaches is how they estimate the issue weights. The approach in [18] estimates the issue weights based on the relative frequency of the most offered values. Afiouni [1] adapted the classic frequency model to a real-time strategy for a video game (i.e., Civilization IV) where bilateral negotiation is used to exchange resources between parties. The frequency model showed to be applicable in real time, while also shortening the negotiation time/interactions between parties. HardHeaded agent, and thus the frequency opponent modeling, was also employed in [2] to study the efficiency of different agents in cloud computing negotiations. Furthermore, Ikarashi and Fujita proposed a weighted counting method, which aims to learn opponent's preferences by taking what time the bids made by the opponent into account [22]. That study focuses on learning from past negotiations so that the proposed approach was applied on the history of their opponent's bids in the previous negotiation.

There are also other remarkable approaches that are not classified under those two families. Aydoğan *et al.* proposed a concept based learning algorithm to figure out what offers are more likely acceptable for the opponent during the negotiation [6]. Kernel density function was used to predict issue weights of the opponent's preferences by Coehoorn and Jennings [12].

Recently, Baarslag [7–9] showed that, despite their simplicity, frequency models tend to outperform in practice more complex approaches like Bayesian opponent models. Part of this success can be attributed to the fact that frequency approaches tend to make less assumptions about the opponent behavior, and the fact that frequency models allow for more exploration of the negotiation space due to its quicker computation with respect to Bayesian approaches. In this paper, we further study how to improve the efficiency of the classic frequency model by alleviating the effect of some of its assumptions.

3   The Classical Frequency Model

As mentioned in the previous sections, frequency models have been widely used as opponent modeling mechanisms in automated negotiation [1,2,7,18,25]. Apart from being reported as one of the most effective families of opponent modeling techniques, frequency approaches have the advantage of being simple and offering a good balance of time/exploration [7].

There have been multiple implementations and variations of frequency models in the automated negotiation literature, but perhaps the most popular implementation is the frequency model in HardHeaded's agent [25]. The model was proposed with the following assumptions in mind: (1) the opponent steadily restricts the offers proposed to a possibly moving and decreasing utility range; (2) the opponent prefers to explore the negotiation space rather than repeating the same offer(s) over and over; (3) Opponents tend to concede less on the most preferred issues, keeping them unchanged.

Briefly, this model works as follows. To estimate the weight of an issue value (e.g. Dell, HP, MAC for "laptop brand"), the frequency model computes how often each issue value appears in the opponent's bids. The weight of the issue value is then normalized by the most repeated issue value. For instance, consider that Dell, HP and MAC appear 20 times, 10 times and 15 times respectively. In that case, the model estimates the issue value weights as $V(\text{Dell}) = \frac{20}{20}$, $V(\text{HP}) = \frac{10}{20}$ and $V(\text{MAC}) = \frac{15}{20}$. The frequency model analyzes how often the value of an issue changes. At the beginning, the assumption is that each issue has the same importance. For example, if we have four issues, the weight of each issue is set as 0.25. For each successive pair of offers made by the opponent, if the value of an issue did not change, then the model increases the weight of that issue.

While these assumptions may sound appropriate for some scenarios, the truth is that many state of the art agents do not fully comply with those assumptions. Firstly, agents may prefer to follow a more flexible concession and bidding strategy that allows them to stochastically explore a wide portion of the negotiation space. Despite the fact that the general trend for the opponent is conceding, consecutive offers may not reflect this general trend due to the stochastic and flexible nature of agents. As a consequence, opponents may make a range of negotiation steps (e.g., concession, trade-off, unfortunate move, etc.), misleading the learning mechanism in the classic frequency model.

Secondly, another common behavior of the state-of-the-art agents is repeating the same set of offers for a long period of time. This is true for those agents that try to avoid exploitation by not leaking significant and full information about their utility functions. This goes against the classic frequency's assumptions and the original model is not ready for dealing with these cases. In fact, we experimentally found that, when the same bid is repeated for a significant number of rounds, the update and normalization rules in the classic frequency implementation presents a convergence problem: all the issue weights converge towards $\frac{1}{n}$, where n is the number of issues in the negotiation. Being hard headed and repeating the same offer does not mean that all of the issues are equally valued. Hence, other mechanisms are necessary to tackle these situations.

Last, but not least important, it is true that in the first negotiation rounds most agents do not tend to vary the value for those issues that are the most important. The reason for this is because most agents start by demanding the best offers for themselves, and these offers entail very little changes in the most important issues. However, as the negotiation proceeds, opponents may concede. At some point, it is possible to reach one's own aspirations by varying the values for the most important issues and maximizing less important issues. In fact, this behavior can be observed in many state of the art agents who trade-off issues to achieve one's own aspirations. Therefore, the assumption that opponents tend to concede less on the most preferred issues may hold for hardheaded agents or agents that do not steadily concede, but it may result fruitless in other scenarios.

4   Distribution-Based Frequency Model

Our proposed frequency model relies on the comparison of frequency distributions across negotiation windows. Hence, we have taken the liberty of naming it *distribution-based frequency model*. Next, we describe the details of our opponent modeling mechanism.

4.1   Negotiation Setting

For the sake of simplicity we assume that two agents negotiate following the alternating offers protocol. Nevertheless, the model can also be extrapolated to other protocols, including multilateral scenarios. The agents negotiate in a time-bounded scenario where T delimits the end of the negotiation. If the deadline is reached without any agreement, the agents get their reservation utility.

The negotiation scenario consists of $\mathcal{AI} = \{1, 2, \ldots, n\}$ negotiation issues whose domain values are represented by $\mathcal{D} = \{D_1, \ldots, D_n\}$. An offer is represented by o, while $\mathcal{O}^*$ represents the set of all the offers in the negotiation domain. The agents' preferences are represented by means of linear additive utility functions in the form of $\mathcal{U}(o) = \sum_{i \in \mathcal{AI}} w_i \times V_i(o_i)$, where w_i represents the importance of the negotiation issue i, o_i represents the value for issue i in offer o, and $V_i(.)$ is the valuation function for issue i, which returns the desirability of the issue value. Without losing generality, it is assumed that $\sum_{i \in \mathcal{AI}} w_i = 1$ and the domain of $V_i(.)$ is (0,1) for any i.

There are two main components that an opponent model should estimate in a linear additive function scenario: a vector of weights $\hat{\mathcal{W}} = (\hat{w}_1, \ldots, \hat{w}_n)$ representing the estimation of the importance given by the opponent to the different negotiation issues, and an estimation for every possible valuation function $\hat{V}_i(.)$. Thus, our model defines update mechanisms for both.

4.2 Value Function Estimation

Firstly, we describe how the the valuation functions $\hat{V}_i(.)$ are estimated. It should be highlighted that we employ a similar strategy to the one outlined in [25]. The rationale behind our estimation is that, in opponents' offers, the most preferred issue values should appear more frequently than less preferred issue values. Hence, a frequency count of the issue values should provide an educated guess on the real valuation functions $V_i(.)$. We define the estimation of the valuation functions as:

$$\hat{V}_i(j) = \frac{(1 + \sum_{o \in \mathcal{O}_{1 \to t}} \delta_i(j, o))^\gamma}{max_{k \in \mathcal{AI}}(1 + \sum_{o \in \mathcal{O}_{1 \to t}} \delta_i(k, o))^\gamma} \tag{1}$$

where $\delta_i(j, o)$ is 1 if the value j is used for issue i in offer o and 0 otherwise. Please note that the frequency count is smoothed by using a Laplace approach. The rationale behind the smoothing is avoiding crisp distributions and giving importance to issue values that do not appear in $\mathcal{O}$, as they may not appear due to the limited nature of $\mathcal{O}$. On the other hand, both denominator and numerator are passed by an exponential filter with $0 < \gamma \leq 1$ exponential filter. The idea is that of slowing the growth of unbalanced value distributions when opponents send the same offer over and over for a significant part of the negotiation. When $\gamma = 1$ the value estimation is equivalent to the value estimation proposed in the classic frequency model plus a Laplace smooth.

4.3 Issue Weight Estimation

The main differences between our opponent modeling technique and that described in [25] resides in the estimation of the issue weights $\hat{\mathcal{W}}$. In order to provide a more robust estimation of the issue weights, our strategy analyzes consecutive and disjoint windows of the negotiation history instead of individual offers. As mentioned, many of the most popular negotiating agents do not steadily concede but often fluctuate in the demanded utility, even though as a general trend they may concede. By analyzing pairs of offers, the agent may be misled by such stochastic fluctuations and it may end up updating the model incorrectly. However, when analyzing disjoints windows of the negotiation history the effect of such stochastic fluctuations should be alleviated, and general trends better observed.

We divide the current negotiation history into consecutive and disjoint windows of k offers received from the opponent, as it can be observed in Fig. 1. The rationale behind our strategy is comparing the offers in the last window with the offers in the previous window[1]. If the distribution of offers is different between both windows, then it suggests that the opponent has moved its negotiation strategy (e.g., concession, trade-off, etc.). By comparing distributions of offers, one alleviates the problem of stochastic variations between pairs of offers in the strategy of opponents, and it also helps to observe general trends and changes in the opponent strategy.

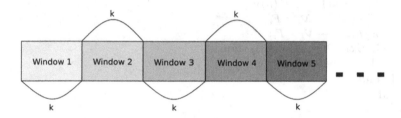

Fig. 1. The negotiation history divided into disjoint windows of offers, each containing k offers sent by the opponent

The classic frequency approach considers that negotiation issues that remain the same between pairs of offers are normally those that are the most relevant. Despite the fact that this may be true in the initial rounds of the negotiation, as the negotiation proceeds opponents may decide to concede on the most preferred issues and achieve its aspirations with less important issues. A classic frequency approach can be misled by this type of behavior, which is not so uncommon in many state of the art agents. As a countermeasure to this behavior, we introduce an issue weight update rule whose effect decays over time. The update rule can be observed in Eq. 2. This update rule will be used to update weights whose value distribution did not change over consecutive windows.

$$\Delta(t) = \alpha \times (1 - t^{\beta}) \tag{2}$$

The issue weight estimation is triggered whenever a new window of k disjoint opponent offers is completed. The outline of the mechanism can be observed in Algorithm 1. As mentioned, the algorithm takes the two latest consecutive and disjoint windows of k offers ($\mathcal{O}$, $\mathcal{O}'$), the current negotiation time t, and the current estimation of the issue weights $\mathcal{W}'$. Before explaining the algorithm in

---

[1] Please note that windows are not overlapping and not sliding.

Data: t: The current time in the negotiation, $\mathcal{O}'$: The previous partition of k offers, $\mathcal{O}$: The current partition of k offers, $\mathcal{O}_{1\to t}$: All the offers received so far, $\mathcal{W}' = \{w'_1, \ldots, w'_n\}$: The current weights for the opponent model

Result: $\mathcal{W} = \{w_1, \ldots, w_n\}$: The new weights for the opponent model

1 $e \leftarrow \emptyset$;
2 concession$\leftarrow$ *False*;
3 **foreach** $i \in \mathcal{N}$ **do**
4 $\quad\mid\quad w_i \leftarrow w'_i$
   end
5 **foreach** $i \in \mathcal{AT}$ **do**
6 $\quad\mid\quad F'_i \leftarrow (Fr_i(1, \mathcal{O}'), \ldots, Fr_i(n, \mathcal{O}'))$;
7 $\quad\mid\quad F_i \leftarrow (Fr_i(1, \mathcal{O}), \ldots, Fr_i(n, \mathcal{O}))$;
8 $\quad\mid\quad p_{val} \leftarrow \mathcal{X}^2\text{-test}(F_i = F'_i)$;
9 $\quad\mid\quad$ **if** $p_{val} > 0.05$ **then**
10 $\quad\mid\quad\mid\quad e \leftarrow e \cup \{i\}$;
   $\quad\mid\quad$ **else**
11 $\quad\mid\quad\mid\quad \mathcal{V}_i \leftarrow (\hat{V}_i(1), \ldots, \hat{V}_i(n))$;
12 $\quad\mid\quad\mid\quad E[\mathcal{U}_i(\mathcal{O}')] \leftarrow \mathcal{V}_i \times F'_i$;
13 $\quad\mid\quad\mid\quad E[\mathcal{U}_i(\mathcal{O})] \leftarrow \mathcal{V}_i \times F_i$;
14 $\quad\mid\quad\mid\quad$ **if** $E[\mathcal{U}_i(\mathcal{O})] < E[\mathcal{U}_i(\mathcal{O}')]$ **then**
15 $\quad\mid\quad\mid\quad\mid\quad$ concession $\leftarrow$ *True*;
   $\quad\mid\quad\mid\quad$ **end**
   $\quad\mid\quad$ **end**
   end
16 **if** $|e| \neq n$ **and** *concession*$=$ *True* **then**
17 $\quad\mid\quad$ **foreach** $i \in e$ **do**
18 $\quad\mid\quad\mid\quad w_i \leftarrow w'_i + \Delta(t)$
   $\quad\mid\quad$ **end**
   end

Algorithm 1. The issue weight update mechanism

detail, we need to define the following equation that defines the frequency of a negotiation value j of issue i in a window of offers $\mathcal{O}$:

$$Fr_i(j, \mathcal{O}) = \frac{1 + \sum_{o \in \mathcal{O}} \delta_i(j, o)}{n + |\mathcal{O}|} \quad (3)$$

The equation above counts the number of times that a value j appears in a window of offers, and divides by the total number of offers in the window. Again, the count is smoothed using Laplacian smoothing. This formula will be used in Algorithm 1 to provide a frequency distribution for issue values given a window of offers. Next, we explain the algorithm for updating issue weights in detail.

Initially, the new estimation for the weights $\mathcal{W}$ takes the value of the current estimation $\mathcal{W}'$ in lines 3 and 4. Then, the algorithm iterates over every single negotiation issue i from lines 5 to 15. In this loop, we calculate the frequency distribution of the issue values in the previous window $\mathcal{F}'_i$ and the frequency distribution of the issue values in the current window $\mathcal{F}_i$. Both frequency distributions are calculated by applying the expression in Eq. 3 to every single possible value in the domain of issue i. Then, a Chi-squared test is carried out with the null hypothesis being that both frequency distributions, $\mathcal{F}_i$ and $\mathcal{F}'_i$, are statistically equivalent. The main goal behind this test is checking whether or not the distribution of issue values for i has changed from the previous window of offers to the current one. This information will help us to determine if, overall, the opponent has changed the type of offers sent. In the case that the null hypothesis cannot be rejected (lines 9 and 10), we add the issue i to the set of issues e whose distribution did not change from the previous to the current window.

When the null hypothesis is rejected (lines 11 to 15), it means that the frequency distribution for issue i has been different from the past to the current window. The question is in what direction the change points for that issue (e.g., concession, increase of utility). More specifically, inspired by classic frequency approaches, we are interested in checking if the opponent has conceded in the issue, because then we can update the weights for those issues that remained the same. Again, the assumption is that opponents tend not to change the most important issues more often than less preferred issues. In order to estimate if the opponent has conceded in the issue, we employ the frequency distribution for issue i during the whole negotiation $\mathcal{V}_i$ as an approximation of the real valuations, as specified in Eq. 1. Then, the expected utility obtained in issue i for the previous window of opponent offers $E[\mathcal{U}_i(\mathcal{O}')]$ is calculated in line 12. The same procedure is applied to obtain the expected utility obtained in issue i for the current window $E[\mathcal{U}_i(\mathcal{O})]$. Then, both expected utilities are compared to assess if a concession has been carried out in the issue i.

We take an agressive strategy to detecting overall concessions over two consecutive windows of opponent offers. We consider that there is a concession as long as the opponent has conceded in one of the issues (line 16). In that case, we update the importance for those issues that stayed in the same frequency distribution (lines 17 and 18). We understand that there are other strategies to detect an overall concession, and we are currently exploring the performance of more conservative approaches and probabilistic approaches.

5   Experiments

In this section we evaluate the performance of the proposed frequency mechanism, the distribution-based frequency model, and compare it with the classic frequency opponent modeling mechanism. The goal of this section is assessing whether or not the proposed strategy is capable of overcoming the shortcomings highlighted in the previous sections. First, we describe how the experiments were designed, and then we analyze the results gathered.

5.1   Experimental Design

Given the fact that the goal of this paper is comparing the performance of two learning mechanisms (classic frequency model, and distribution-based frequency model), we decided to use the same bidding and concession strategies for both strategies. This setting allows us to study both learning mechanisms in fair and equal conditions. More specifically, we chose HardHeaded's concession and bidding strategy. The rationale for selecting this strategy is twofold. First, as the agent employs a Boulware strategy [15], it guarantees that the agent will not rapidly end the negotiation. A quick and abrupt end of the negotiation would preclude learning mechanisms from being studied effectively, as they have not been exposed to sufficient bids. Second, the HardHeaded's bidding strategy actively employs the opponent model to propose bids to the opponent. This is important, as many times opponent modeling will have an impact on the opponent's actions and bidding steps. By taking this realistic setting, we are also able to observe whether or not one's opponent model influences the negotiation towards actions that further improve one's opponent model. For the sake of simplicity, we decided to employ the alternating offers protocol although the opponent modeling mechanism should be applicable to other settings as long as multiple offers are exchanged between parties over time. Accordingly, we employed bilateral negotiation domains to experimentally test the performance of our opponent modeling mechanism. More specifically, we decided to test our modeling mechanism under a wide range of domain characteristics. These characteristics include different domain sizes (i.e., number of possible outcomes) and different degrees of competition between agents, measured by the distance from the Kalai point to the complete satisfaction point (1,1) [9]. The list of domains can be found in Table 1. Discount factors were ignored (i.e., removed) in this experimental setting and they are regarded as a matter of future study.

Table 1. The domains chosen for testing our opponent modeling mechanism

	Laptop	CypressI.	EngvsZim.	Grocery	Amsterdam	Camera	S.market	Travel
Size	Small	Small	Medium	Medium	Medium	Large	Large	Large
Conflict	Low	High	Medium	Low	Low	Low	High	Medium

Another important decision to take for the experimental setting was deciding on the opponent agents to negotiate with. There were some factors that influenced our decision in this matter. First of all, any agent with offline opponent modeling was discarded as these may introduce interdependences between the outcomes of different negotiations, leading to effects in our opponent model that may be the by-product of past negotiation interactions. Second, we wanted to expose our opponent modeling mechanism to a variety of concession behaviors and bidding strategies representing the state of the art in negotiation. For that, we employed the following opponent agents:

– AgentK [24]: This agent was the winning agent of the 2010 ANAC negotiation competition. It is a conceder agent whose concession speed is regulated by the average utility of all received bids and its standard deviation. In terms of bid proposal, it just selects any offer from above the current aspiration. Hence, pairs of consecutive offers may not present an obvious decreasing trend. This behavior is in conflict with assumption 1 in Sect. 3.

- IAmHaggler2011 [30]: A negotiating agent that uses Gaussian processes to predict the future concession of its opponent, and then adjust its concession rate accordingly to get the most from the negotiation. The goal of this agent is that of optimizing one's own utility while also trying to reduce the utility received by the opponent. Bids are only selected from a small range around the target utility. This aggressive stance usually results in the agent repeating the same offers. This is contradiction with assumption 2 in Sect. 3.

- TheNegotiatorReloaded [13]: This agent was the best performing agent in undiscounted domains for the ANAC 2012 agent competition. The agent divides the negotiation into non-sliding windows, similarly to our approach. For each window, the agent estimates the type of agent behavior that it is facing and adjusts its concession rate accordingly. The most similar bids to the current target utility are sent back to the opponent. This agent was selected for the experiment for similar reasons to IAmHaggler2011.

- Boulware agent [15]: A classic negotiation agent that adjusts its aspiration levels according to time, only conceding in the later stages of the negotiation. Bids close to the target utility are selected and sent to the opponent. This agent was included as an example of scenarios where none of the aforementioned assumptions are strictly violated.

- Conceder agent [15]: A classic negotiation agent that adjusts its aspiration levels according to time. However, concessions are carried out early on in the negotiation process. Bid are randomly selected from above the threshold defined by the concession strategy. Due to the rapid concessions at the start of the negotiation, assumption 3 in Sect. 3 may be invalid very quickly.

The platform that supported our experiments was Genius [20]. We compared our opponent modeling with the performance of the classic frequency model. For that, both opponent models faced all of the opponents in every single domain, which included two preference profiles per domain. In order to capture stochastic variations in negotiations, each possible case was repeated a total of 20 times. This gives a total of 3200 negotiations[2].

In order to assess the quality of our opponent modeling mechanism, we employed the following quality metrics:

- Pearson correlation of bids: It aims to compare the estimated outcome space with the real outcome space. For that, the Pearson correlation of bids is calculated and averaged. This metric is employed due to the fact that it has a strong correlation with overall opponent modeling performance [7,8].

- Difference in surface of Pareto frontiers: Another metric that is employed to assess the overall performance of an opponent modeling mechanism is the absolute difference between the area under the real Pareto optimal curve and the area under the estimated Pareto optimal curve. The rationale behind this metric is that some claim that it is enough to accurately estimate the

---

[2] 2 models × 5 opponents × 8 domains × 2 profiles × 20 repetitions.

Pareto optimal frontier for succesful negotiations with the opponent. Again, this metric was shown to have a strong correlation with overall opponent modeling performance [7,8].
- Spearman rank correlation of the issue weights: The previous two metrics offer an insight into how the opponent modeling performs overall. However, both our opponent modeling mechanism and the classic frequency model have two components: the weight and the issue value update mechanisms. Therefore we decided to include extra metrics to assess the performance of each of these individual components. This metric compares the rank correlation between the issue weights learned by an opponent modeling mechanism and the target issue weights. The value is between -1 and 1, with 1 being used for a perfect ranking of the issue weights and -1 for a completely opposite ranking. The rationale for selecting a ranking metric is that a ranking of the issues is normally enough to trade-off [14,21].
- Weighted Root Mean Squared Error of the issue values: Given an estimated model and the target model, this metric computes a weighted version of the root mean squared error (RMSE) per issue. Predicted issue values are compared against the target issue values and weighted according to the importance of the issue value. This can be observed in Eq. 4

$$\text{WRMSE}(i) = \sqrt{\sum_{j \in D_i} w_j \times (\hat{V}_i(j) - V_i(j))^2} \tag{4}$$

In our case, the weights for issue values w_j were set to $\frac{V_i(j)}{max_{k \in D_i} V_i(k)}$ so that more weight is given to those issue values that provide more utility to the opponent. Then, after each negotiation, the metric is averaged with all the issues. In this case we employed a metric that both captures ranking and value accuracy. Although a ranking of issues is enough for carrying out trade-offs, one needs to have an accurate estimation of values for successfully providing appealing offers to the opponent.

As for the parameters of our model, we set $\alpha = 10$ and $\beta = 5$ in Eq. 2. This means that weight updates will have a greater magnitude at the start of the negotiation, and they will gradually be reduced as the negotiation finishes. This type of update is meant to avoid incorrect updates when the opponent starts changing the most important issues relatively soon in the negotiation. With regards to Eq. 1, γ was set to 0.25 to slow the growth of value importance when the opponent tends to repeat the same offer repeatedly. These values were found as good in a previous experimental setup. However, no exhaustive search was carried out over them. Therefore, the performance depicted in these experiments should be considered as a lower bound for the best achievable performance with this opponent modeling mechanism.

5.2 Results

In this section we analyze the performance of our opponent modeling mechanism with respect to the classic frequency model. As mentioned we employ four

Table 2. Results obtained for the Pearson correlation of bids (Prs. B.), the difference in surface of the Pareto optimal frontier (Par. Fr. D.), the Spearman rank correlation of the issue weights (Spr. W.), and the weighted root mean squared error of the issue values (WRMSE), aggregated by domain.

	Distribution-based frequency model				Frequency model			
	Prs. B.	Par. Fr. D.	Spr. W.	WRMSE	Prs. B.	Par. Fr. D.	Spr. W.	WRMSE
EngZimb	**0.91**	**0.003**	**0.35**	**0.053**	0.80	0.007	0.32	0.080
Cypress	**0.83**	**0.043**	**0.46**	**0.042**	0.60	0.092	0.30	0.063
Travel	**0.85**	**0.015**	**0.73**	**0.043**	0.70	0.019	0.21	0.057
Amst.	**0.91**	**0.004**	**0.61**	**0.044**	0.86	0.015	0.31	0.072
Grocery	**0.90**	**0.005**	**0.96**	**0.041**	0.86	0.010	0.54	0.046
Laptop	0.87	0.006	**0.84**	0.094	**0.89**	0.006	0.59	0.10
Camera	**0.89**	0.006	**0.77**	**0.035**	0.86	0.005	0.57	0.041
S.Market	**0.87**	**0.044**	**0.93**	**0.030**	0.69	0.067	0.59	0.050

Table 3. Results obtained for aforementioned metrics, aggregated by opponent.

	Distribution-based frequency model				Frequency model			
	Prs. B.	Par. Fr. Dis.	Spr. W.	WRMSE	Prs. B.	Par. Fr. Dis.	Spr. W.	WRMSE
AgentK	**0.91**	**0.007**	**0.76**	**0.040**	0.83	0.019	0.58	0.065
Haggler	**0.93**	**0.005**	**0.78**	0.035	0.88	0.014	0.32	0.036
TNR	**0.79**	0.024	**0.63**	**0.079**	0.74	0.018	0.50	0.092
Boulw.	**0.91**	**0.007**	**0.70**	**0.033**	0.78	0.017	0.35	0.072
Conc.	**0.84**	**0.035**	**0.67**	0.050	0.68	0.070	0.38	0.053

metrics: two that measure the overall quality of the model (i.e., Pearson correlation of bids, and the difference between the surfaces defined by the Pareto optimal frontiers) and two other metrics that assess the quality of the two individual components of the opponent modeling (i.e., Spearman rank correlation of the issue weights, and the weighted root mean squared error). Table 2 aggregates the results obtained by domain, while Table 3 aggregates the results obtained by opponent. Those results that are statistically better than its counterpart are highlighted with a bold font. For statistical significance, a one-tailed Mann-Whitney test was carried out with $\alpha = 0.05$.

First, we will analyze the results per domain. Both the Pearson correlation of bids, and the difference between Pareto optimal frontiers tend to indicate that our opponent modeling provides a more accurate and overall estimation of the opponent's preferences. In the case of the Pearson correlation of bids, our approach is statistically better for all domains except for the Laptop domain, where the classic frequency model obtains a better estimation. However, the difference between both metrics is small for that domain. Similarly, our model outperforms when it comes to estimating the Pareto optimal frontier in all domains except for the Laptop and Camera domain, where there is no difference between our and the classic frequency model. Both the Laptop and the Camera domain are two of the less competitive domains. This may suggest that our opponent modeling may not necessarily outperform the classic frequency model for domains with low conflict. However, further experiments will be needed to make that conclusion. In this very same table, we can also observe that both our weight and issue value estimation are statistically more accurate than the classic frequency model. This is supported by statistically better results in both the Spearman rank correlation of issue weights and the weighted root mean squared error for issue values. Only in the Laptop domain the issue value estimation is no better, but also no worse, than the classic frequency model.

We can observe very similar results if we focus on the results aggregated by opponent. Overall, our opponent model produces a statistically better and more accurate model of the opponent's preferences (i.e., Pearson correlation of bids, and Pareto frontier estimation). Only in the case of The Negotiation Reloaded (TNR) the estimation of the Pareto optimal frontier is no better, but also no worse than the classic frequency model. Component by component, we can appreciate that our weight update mechanism is consistently more accurate at detecting the relative importance of issues (i.e., Spearman rank correlation of weights). We also tend to produce a better value estimation for issue values for most opponent agents (i.e., WRMSE). Only we produce a statistically equivalent estimation against IAmHaggler2011 and the Conceder agent.

Overall, it can be appreciated that our opponent modeling mechanism tends to produce more accurate models of the opponent's preferences, regardless of opponent and domain. The differences tend to be more acute in the weight update mechanisms (i.e., Spearman rank correlation of weights) than in the issue value update mechanism (i.e., WRMSE). This suggests that, most likely, an important part of our improvement is due to the weight update mechanism. Other issue value update mechanisms may be necessary to further improve the classic frequency model. Further exploring other issue value update mechanism is highlighted as future areas of improvement for our current opponent modeling.

6   Conclusions

In the last few years, frequency modeling has been shown to outperform more sophisticated opponent modeling techniques like Bayesian approaches. The reason for this result is, among others, weaker assumptions on the opponent's behavior. Nevertheless, frequency models still rely on some underlying assumptions that may not be fully realistic in many scenarios. In this paper we have presented a new frequency approach to opponent modeling in automated negotiation. This new approach, which we named as distribution-based frequency model, soothes the effect of some of the assumptions in the classic frequency model. More specifically, the main characteristics of our opponent modeling are: (i) comparison of windows of offers instead of consecutive pairs of offers, offering a more robust estimation on the opponent's behavior; (ii) decayed weight update to avoid incorrect updates when the opponent starts conceding on the most important issues; and (iii) slow growth of issue values importance, avoiding unbalanced issue value distributions when the opponent offers the same offer repeatedly.

This paper advances the state of the art in frequency approaches to opponent modeling in automated negotiation by showing that the model proposed in this work outperforms the accuracy of the opponent obtained by the classic frequency model. The increased accuracy is observable in the learned outcome space, the estimated Pareto optimal frontier, and both in the learned issue weights and issue values. The difference in accuracy is specially acute in estimated issue weights, where our approach produces more accurate rankings of issues.

References

1. Afiouni, E.N., Øvrelid, L.J.: Negotiation for strategic video games. Master's thesis, NTNU (2013)
2. Alsrheed, F., El Rhalibi, A., Randles, M., Merabti, M.: Intelligent agents for automated cloud computing negotiation. In: IEEE International Conference on Multimedia Computing and Systems, pp. 1169–1174. IEEE (2014)
3. An, B., Gatti, N., Lesser, V.: Extending alternating-offers bargaining in one-to-many and many-to-many settings. In: Proceedings of the 2009 IEEE/WIC/ACM International Conference on Intelligent Agent Technology, vol. 2, pp. 423–426 (2009)
4. Aydoğan, R., Baarslag, T., Hindriks, K.V., Jonker, C.M., Yolum, P.: Heuristics for using cp-nets in utility-based negotiation without knowing utilities. Knowl. Inf. Syst. 45(2), 357–388 (2015)
5. Aydoğan, R., Festen, D., Hindriks, K.V., Jonker, C.M.: Alternating offers protocols for multilateral negotiation. In: Fujita, K., Bai, Q., Ito, T., Zhang, M., Ren, F., Aydoğan, R., Hadfi, R. (eds.) Modern Approaches to Agent-based Complex Automated Negotiation. SCI, vol. 674, pp. 153–167. Springer, Cham (2017). doi:10.1007/978-3-319-51563-2_10
6. Aydoğan, R., Yolum, P.: Ontology-based learning for negotiation. In: IEEE/WIC/ACM International Conference on Intelligent Agent Technology, pp. 177–184 (2009)
7. Baarslag, T.: Measuring the performance of online opponent models. In: Exploring the Strategy Space of Negotiating Agents. ST, pp. 111–127. Springer, Cham (2016). doi:10.1007/978-3-319-28243-5_6
8. Baarslag, T., Hendrikx, M., Hindriks, K., Jonker, C.: Predicting the performance of opponent models in automated negotiation. In: International Joint Conference on Web Intelligence and Intelligent Agent Technologies, vol. 2, pp. 59–66. IEEE (2013)
9. Baarslag, T., Hendrikx, M.J., Hindriks, K.V., Jonker, C.M.: Learning about the opponent in automated bilateral negotiation: a comprehensive survey of opponent modeling techniques. Auton. Agent Multi Agent Syst. 30, 849–898 (2016)
10. Buffett, S., Spencer, B.: Learning opponents' preferences in multi-object automated negotiation. In: Proceedings of the 7th International Conference on Electronic Commerce, pp. 300–305 (2005)
11. Bui, H.H., Kieronska, D., Venkatesh, S.: Learning other agents' preferences in multiagent negotiation. In: Proceedings of the National Conference on Artificial Intelligence, pp. 114–119 (1996)
12. Coehoorn, R.M., Jennings, N.R.: Learning an opponent's preferences to make effective multi-issue negotiation tradeoffs. In: The 6th International Conference on E-Commerce, pp. 59–68 (2004)

13. Dirkzwager, A., Hendrikx, M.: An adaptive negotiation strategy for real-time bilateral negotiations. In: Marsa-Maestre, I., Lopez-Carmona, M.A., Ito, T., Zhang, M., Bai, Q., Fujita, K. (eds.) Novel Insights in Agent-based Complex Automated Negotiation. SCI, vol. 535, pp. 163–170. Springer, Tokyo (2014). doi:10.1007/978-4-431-54758-7_10

14. Faratin, P., Sierra, C., Jennings, N.R.: Using similarity criteria to make issue trade-offs in automated negotiations. Artif. Intell. **142**(2), 205–237 (2002)

15. Faratin, P., Sierra, C., Jennings, N.R.: Negotiation decision functions for autonomous agents. Robot. Auton. Syst. **24**(3–4), 159–182 (1998)

16. Fatima, S., Kraus, S., Wooldridge, M.: Principles of Automated Negotiation. Cambridge University Press, Cambridge (2014)

17. Fatima, S.S., Wooldridge, M., Jennings, N.R.: An agenda-based framework for multi-issue negotiation. Artif. Intell. **152**(1), 1–45 (2004)

18. van Galen, L.N.: Agent smith: opponent model estimation in bilateral multi-issue negotiation. In: Ito, T., Zhang, M., Robu, V., Fatima, S., Matsuo, T. (eds.) New Trends in Agent-Based Complex Automated Negotiations. SCI, vol. 383, pp. 167–174. Springer, Heidelberg (2012). doi:10.1007/978-3-642-24696-8_12

19. Gerla, M., Lee, E.K., Pau, G., Lee, U.: Internet of vehicles: from intelligent grid to autonomous cars and vehicular clouds. In: IEEE World Forum on Internet of Things, pp. 241–246 (2014)

20. Hindriks, K., Jonker, C.M., Kraus, S., Lin, R., Tykhonov, D.: Genius: negotiation environment for heterogeneous agents. In: Proceedings of the 8th International Conference on Autonomous Agents and Multiagent Systems. pp. 1397–1398 (2009)

21. Hindriks, K., Tykhonov, D.: Opponent modelling in automated multi-issue negotiation using bayesian learning. In: 7th International Joint Conference on Autonomous Agents and Multiagent Systems, pp. 331–338 (2008)

22. Ikarashi, M., Fujita, K.: Compromising strategy using weighted counting in multi-times negotiations. In: Proceedings of the 3rd International Conference on Advanced Applied Informatics, pp. 453–458 (2014)

23. Jennings, N.R., Faratin, P., Lomuscio, A.R., Parsons, S., Wooldridge, M.J., Sierra, C.: Automated negotiation: prospects, methods and challenges. Group Decis. Negot. **10**, 199–215 (2001)

24. Kawaguchi, S., Fujita, K., Ito, T.: AgentK: Compromising strategy based on estimated maximum utility for automated negotiating agents. In: Ito, T., Zhang, M., Robu, V., Fatima, S., Matsuo, T. (eds.) New Trends in Agent-Based Complex Automated Negotiations. SCI, vol. 383, pp. 137–144. Springer, Heidelberg (2012). doi:10.1007/978-3-642-24696-8_8

25. van Krimpen, T., Looije, D., Hajizadeh, S.: HardHeaded. In: Ito, T., Zhang, M., Robu, V., Matsuo, T. (eds.) Complex Automated Negotiations: Theories, Models, and Software Competitions. SCI, vol. 435, pp. 223–227. Springer, Heidelberg (2013). doi:10.1007/978-3-642-30737-9_17

26. Luo, X., Jennings, N.R., Shadbolt, N., Leung, H.F., Lee, J.H.M.: A fuzzy constraint based model for bilateral, multi-issue negotiations in semi-competitive environments. Artif. Intell. **148**(1), 53–102 (2003)

27. Ossowski, S., Sierra, C., Botti, V.: Agreement technologies: a computing perspective. In: Ossowski, S. (ed.) Agreement Technologies. LGTS, vol. 8, pp. 3–16. Springer, Dordrecht (2013). doi:10.1007/978-94-007-5583-3_1

28. Sanchez-Anguix, V., Aydogan, R., Julian, V., Jonker, C.: Unanimously acceptable agreements for negotiation teams in unpredictable domains. Electron. Commer. Res. Appl. **13**(4), 243–265 (2014)

29. Sanchez-Anguix, V., Julian, V., Botti, V., García-Fornes, A.: Tasks for agent-based negotiation teams: analysis, review, and challenges. Eng. Appl. Artif. Intel. **26**(10), 2480–2494 (2013)
30. Williams, C.R., Robu, V., Gerding, E.H., Jennings, N.R.: IAMhaggler2011: a gaussian process regression based negotiation agent. In: Ito, T., Zhang, M., Robu, V., Matsuo, T. (eds.) Complex Automated Negotiations: Theories, Models, and Software Competitions. SCI, vol. 435, pp. 209–212. Springer, Heidelberg (2013). doi:10.1007/978-3-642-30737-9_14

Optimizing Affine Maximizer Auctions via Linear Programming: An Application to Revenue Maximizing Mechanism Design for Zero-Day Exploits Markets

Mingyu Guo[1]($\boxtimes$), Hideaki Hata[2], and Ali Babar[1]

[1] School of Computer Science, University of Adelaide, Adelaide, Australia
{mingyu.guo,ali.babar}@adelaide.edu.au
[2] Graduate School of Information Science,
Nara Institute of Science and Technology, Ikoma, Japan
hata@is.naist.jp

Abstract. Optimizing within the affine maximizer auctions (AMA) is an effective approach for revenue maximizing mechanism design. The AMA mechanisms are strategy-proof and individually rational (if the agents' valuations for the outcomes are nonnegative). Every AMA mechanism is characterized by a list of parameters. By focusing on the AMA mechanisms, we turn mechanism design into a value optimization problem, where we only need to adjust the parameters. We propose a linear programming based heuristic for optimizing within the AMA family. We apply our technique to revenue maximizing mechanism design for zero-day exploit markets. We show that due to the nature of the zero-day exploit markets, if there are only two agents (one offender and one defender), then our technique generally produces a near optimal mechanism: the mechanism's expected revenue is close to the optimal revenue achieved by the optimal strategy-proof and individually rational mechanism (not necessarily an AMA mechanism).

Keywords: Automated mechanism design · Revenue maximization · Mechanism design · Security economics · Bug bounty

1 Introduction

Revenue maximizing mechanism design is a fundamental topic in algorithmic game theory. Myerson [17] solved for the revenue maximizing mechanism for selling a single item, subject to a technical condition called the *monotone hazard rate* condition. Myerson's optimal auction is surprisingly elegant. For example, if every agent's type is drawn from an identical and independent distribution, then the optimal mechanism is simply the Vickrey auction [20] with a reserve price. Unfortunately, Myerson's technique does not generalize to more complex settings. For example, when it comes to combinatorial auctions (auctions where multiple items are for sale, and the agents bid on bundles of items), revenue

© Springer International Publishing AG 2017
B. An et al. (Eds.): PRIMA 2017, LNAI 10621, pp. 280–292, 2017.
https://doi.org/10.1007/978-3-319-69131-2_17

maximizing mechanism design remains an open problem. Another notable application domain of revenue maximizing mechanism design is the sponsored search auctions [13], where the search engines sell advertisement slots to advertisers, aiming to maximize revenue besides other objectives. Even though no optimal mechanisms have been derived for general combinatorial auctions or sponsored search auctions, for restricted domains, well performing mechanisms have been obtained based on a variety of revenue-boosting techniques [6,10,11,15,16].

There are several general revenue-boosting techniques. For example, we may artificially increase the winning chance of lower bidders, in order to drive up the competition faced by the higher bidders. As another example, we may artificially discourage or outright ban certain outcomes, in order to prevent low-revenue outcomes or force the agents to pay more to achieve the discouraged outcomes. The above techniques form the basis of a family of mechanisms called the *affine maximizer auctions (AMA)*. Lavi *et al.* [14] conjectured that a combinatorial auction is truthful if and only if it is an AMA mechanism, subject to technical conditions. Likhodedov and Sandholm [15,16] studied revenue maximizing combinatorial auction design by optimizing within the family of AMA mechanisms. The idea of optimizing within the AMA family is a general approach that can be applied to many different mechanism design settings, because generally the AMA mechanisms are well defined and the family contains a large number of mechanisms. By optimizing within the AMA family, there is a good chance of reaching a well-performing mechanism in terms of revenue. However, the issue with optimizing within the AMA family is that every AMA mechanism is characterized by $|O| + n$ parameters, where $|O|$ is the size of the outcome space O, and n is the number of agents. For combinatorial auctions, $|O|$ is exponential in the number of items, which makes it computationally impractical to optimize within the AMA family for this setting. Due to this, Likhodedov and Sandholm only studied the AMA family for the case of selling two items. When there are only two items, the number of parameters is small enough for the authors to conduct optimization via grid-based gradient descent.[1]

In this paper, we propose a linear programming based technique for optimizing within the AMA family. Every outcome corresponds to one variable in our LP model. As a result, our technique can handle reasonably large number of outcomes. For example, let us consider the case where $|O|$ is a few hundred. Running a LP with a few hundred variables is computationally tractable. On the other hand, methods such as grid-based gradient descent are impractical.

We apply our new technique to a specific mechanism design problem. Our paper focuses on revenue maximizing mechanism design for zero-day exploit markets [12]. Zero-day exploits refer to software vulnerabilities that are not known to the software vendor. Trading zero-day exploits as legitimate business

---

[1] The authors also proposed a restricted version of AMA called the VVCA mechanisms. A VVCA mechanism is only characterized by $2n$ parameters, which makes it much easier to optimize over. On the other hand, due to the fact that the VVCA family is only a tiny subset of the whole AMA family, we lose revenue by focusing only on it.

is a recent trend in the security industry [5]. According to a price list collected by Greenberg [9], the price of a zero-day exploit is between $5000 to $250,000. There are venture capital backed security consulting companies whose business model is selling zero-day exploits [7]. One of the companies mentioned in [7] even offered one point five million US dollars for one new iOS exploit. The reason an exploit can be priced so high is that generally it can stay alive for a long period of time [2]. Unless the software vendor is informed about an exploit, there is very low chance for an exploit to be discovered independently. To remedy this, software vendors often run bug bounty programs, which are markets where the software vendors buy exploits from security researchers [1,19].

Guo *et al.* [12] proposed a formal mechanism design model for zero-day exploit markets. In the authors' model, one exploit is being sold to multiple buyers over a period of time [0, 1]. The model is different from the classic single-item auction for the following reasons:

- There are two categories of buyers. The *defenders* buy exploits to fix them. Typically there is only one defender, which is the software vendor. The *offenders* buy exploits to utilize them. National security agencies and police are example offenders. For example, Zerodium [7] is a consulting company that buys zero-day exploits and resells them to mostly government agencies. The offenders wish to utilize an exploit for as long as possible. Once an exploit is obtained by a defender, the exploit becomes worthless. Using mechanism design terminologies, the buyers have *externalities*.
- The item being sold is an informational item, which means that we can sell the same item multiple times (*e.g.*, to multiple offenders). Of course, once an exploit is sold to a defender, we cannot sell it to any offenders *afterwards*, because it has become worthless.
- Because the item being sold is a piece of information, we cannot simply describe it in full details to the buyers without some kind of payment enforcing mechanism, because otherwise the buyers can walk away with the exploit for free. Furthermore, we cannot ask the buyers to bid on an exploit that carries no description, because the buyers cannot come up with their private valuations if no description is given.

Guo *et al.* [12] proposed a mechanism property called *straight-forwardness*: a mechanism is straight-forward if it describes the exploit in full details to the offenders, before they submit their bids. This is required because typically offenders already have many exploits in their arsenals. With full description, they can evaluate whether the exploit being sold is original, and to what extent the exploit helps them. Straight-forwardness does not require the mechanism to describe the exploit to the defenders before they bid (otherwise, the exploit gets fixed). Straight-forwardness only describes to the defenders how severe the exploit is: *e.g.*, this exploit allows anyone to remotely control an iOS device. From the perspective of a defender, every exploit is new (otherwise, it wouldn't be an exploit). We ask the defenders to come up with their private valuations based on the exploit's severity, which is exactly how bug bounty markets operate (in bug bounty markets, bugs are priced according to their severity levels [19]).

Guo *et al.* [12] showed that if straightforwardness is required together with strategy-proofness and individual rationality, then one revenue-maximizing mechanism must work as follows: we describe the exploit in full details to all offenders at time 0. We also describe the exploit's severity level to the defenders at time 0. The offenders and defenders submit their bids. The offenders bid to keep the exploit alive for as long as possible. The defenders bid to kill off the exploit as early as possible. In some sense, the model is similar to the *cake-cutting* problem [3,4] and the *single facility location* problem [8,18].[2] For this model, the authors proposed one heuristic-based randomized AMA mechanism.

In this paper, for the above model, we use our new technique to optimize within the AMA family. We also show that if there are only two agents (one offender and one defender), and if the defender's valuation is much lower than the offender's (typically true for zero-day exploit markets), the optimal AMA mechanism's revenue is close to the optimal revenue. For demonstrating this result, we propose and study a family of mechanisms called the *posted-price* mechanisms for our model.

2   Model Description

We use O to denote the outcome space. We use Θ_i to denote agent i's type space. We use $v_i(\theta_i, o)$ to denote agent i's valuation for outcome $o \in O$ when her type is $\theta_i \in \Theta_i$.

For the zero-day exploit mechanism design model proposed in Guo *et al.* [12], the outcome space is $[0, 1]$. An outcome $o \in [0, 1]$ represents when the exploit is killed off (revealed to the defenders).[3] In order to run the technique proposed in this paper, we require the outcome space to be finite. So for this technical reason, we set the outcome space to be $\{0, \frac{1}{k}, \frac{2}{k}, \ldots, 1\}$. That is, we will only reveal the exploit at these discrete moments. The size of the outcome space $|O| = k + 1$.

The family of AMA mechanisms is defined as follows:

- Given a type profile θ, the outcome picked is the following:

$$o^* = \arg\max_{o \in O} \left(\sum_{i=1}^{n} u_i v_i(\theta_i, o) + a_o \right)$$

- Agent i's payment equals:

$$\frac{\max_{o \in O} \left(\sum_{j \neq i} u_j v_j(\theta_j, o) + a_o \right) - \sum_{j \neq i} u_j v_j(\theta_j, o^*) - a_{o^*}}{u_i}$$

---

[2] In our model, we allow payments. After all, the objective is to maximize revenue.

[3] If we allow randomized mechanisms, then an outcome is a nonincreasing function $o(t)$, with $o(0) = 1$ and $o(1) = 0$. $o(t)$ represents the probability for the exploit to be alive at time t.

In the above description, the u_i and the a_o are constant parameters. $u_i \geq 1$ for all i. The a_o are unrestricted. In total, there are $n + |O|$ parameters. Every AMA mechanism is characterized by these many parameters. For any assignments of the parameters, the corresponding AMA mechanism is strategy-proof. However, not every AMA mechanism is individually rational. If we further assume that $\forall i, \theta_i, o, \ v_i(\theta_i, o) \geq 0$, then every AMA mechanism is individually rational. To show this, we only need to show that an agent's valuation is always at least her payment. That is,

$$v_i(\theta_i, o^*) \geq \frac{\max_{o \in O}\left(\sum_{j \neq i} u_j v_j(\theta_j, o) + a_o\right) - \sum_{j \neq i} u_j v_j(\theta_j, o^*) - a_{o^*}}{u_i}$$

$$\iff \sum_j u_j v_j(\theta_j, o^*) + a_{o^*} \geq \max_{o \in O}\left(\sum_{j \neq i} u_j v_j(\theta_j, o) + a_o\right)$$

The right-hand side is less than or equal to the left-hand side if every agent's valuation for every outcome is nonnegative.

In our model, an outcome represents when the exploit is killed off. For presentation purpose, we sometimes use t to refer to an outcome.

An offender's valuation is defined as:

$$v_i(\theta_i, t) = \int_0^t f_{\theta_i}(x)dx$$

A defender's valuation is defined as:

$$v_i(\theta_i, t) = \int_t^1 f_{\theta_i}(x)dx$$

An offender "enjoys" the exploit from time 0 to t, and a defender values the safe period from time t to 1. $f_{\theta_i}(x)$ represents agent i's instantaneous value (nonnegative) at time x, when her type is θ_i. Based on the above definitions of the agents' valuations, we have that every AMA mechanism is individually rational for our model.

3   Optimizing Affine Maximizer Auctions

We recall that an AMA mechanism is characterized by $n + |O|$ parameters (u_i for every agent i, and a_o for every outcome o). For presentation purpose, we define $Z = n + |O|$ and use $p_1, p_2, \ldots, p_Z$ to refer to the parameters. Let $M(p_1, p_2, \ldots, p_Z)$ be the AMA mechanism characterized by p_1 to p_Z. The task of optimizing within the AMA family is simply to optimize over the parameters:

$$\max_{p_1, p_2, \ldots, p_Z} ER(M(p_1, p_2, \ldots, p_Z))$$

Here, $ER(M)$ represents mechanism M's expected revenue. We have analytical characterization of the AMA payments, so the revenue of M given a specific type profile can be calculated accordingly. Unfortunately, there is no known short-cut for calculating the expected revenue. Given a prior distribution of the θ_i, we need to draw large amount of sample profiles to calculate the expected revenue. For example, if for every agent i, we draw 100 samples for θ_i, then altogether the number of type profiles is 100^n. For this reason, in this paper, we focus on cases where n is small.[4]

Likhodedov and Sandholm [15,16] used a grid-based gradient descent approach for optimizing the parameters. Under this approach, suppose we start from a grid point $(p_1, p_2, \ldots, p_Z)$, we have to examine all neighbouring points $(p_1 + \delta_1 h, p_2 + \delta_2 h, \ldots, p_Z + \delta_Z h)$, where $\delta_i \in \{-1, 0, 1\}$ and h is the grid size. We need to examine 3^Z points. So this approach requires that both n and $|O|$ be tiny. For example, if $Z = 100$, then the approach is impractical. For our technique, Z is allowed to be large: our technique involves a LP model with Z variables, which takes polynomial time in Z.

A high-level description of our optimizing technique is as follows:

- We initialize the algorithm with an AMA mechanism: *e.g.*, one based on random parameters, or the VCG mechanism.
- Given M_0 characterized by $p_1^0, p_2^0, \ldots, p_Z^0$, we use a heuristic to approximate the optimal AMA mechanism near this starting point, using a linear program. A mechanism M (characterized by $p_1, p_2, \ldots, p_Z$) is near M_0 if $\max_i |p_i - p_i^0| \leq \epsilon$ for a threshold ϵ. We repeat this step using the new mechanism as the starting point.

The above algorithm may end with a locally optimal mechanism, which means that we may need to repeat the algorithm using different initial points.

Now we present the details of the linear program. We index the outcomes using $0, 1, \ldots, k$. We denote the initial mechanism as $M(u_1^0, u_2^0, \ldots, u_n^0, a_0^0, a_1^0, \ldots, a_k^0)$.

The following optimization model solves for the optimal AMA mechanism near this starting point:

Model 1
Variables: $u_1, u_2, \ldots, u_n, a_0, a_1, \ldots, a_k$
Maximize: $ER(M(u_1, u_2, \ldots, u_n, a_0, a_1, \ldots, a_k))$
Subject to:
For all i, $u_i \geq 1$ and $u_i^0 - \epsilon \leq u_i \leq u_i^0 + \epsilon$
For all t, $a_i^0 - \epsilon \leq a_i \leq a_i^0 + \epsilon$

Of course, the above model is not a linear program, as $ER(M)$ is not a linear combination of the variables. *We will approximate $ER(M)$ using a linear combination of the variables.*

---

[4] We have to emphasize that this is not an uncommon constraint when it comes to using numerical methods for maximizing mechanism revenue.

Let S be a large set of type profiles, we will approximate $ER(M)$ as follows:

$$ER(M) \approx \sum_{\theta \in S} P(\theta) \sum_i C_i(M, \theta)$$

Here, $C_i(M, \theta)$ is agent i's payment under M when the type profile is θ. One way to pick S is to discretize the type space and let S be the set of all grid points. Now what remains to be done is to approximate $C_i(M, \theta)$ using a linear combination of the variables.

$$C_i(M, \theta) = \frac{\max_{o \in O}\left(\sum_{j \neq i} u_j v_j(\theta_j, o) + a_o\right) - \sum_{j \neq i} u_j v_j(\theta_j, o^*) - a_{o^*}}{u_i}$$

Here, o^* is defined as

$$o^* = \arg\max_{o \in O}\left(\sum_{i=1}^n u_i v_i(\theta_i, o) + a_o\right)$$

We use the following heuristic to approximate $C_i(M, \theta)$: because the u_i and the a_o are close to the u_i^0 and the a_o^0, we will use the u_i^0 and the a_o^0 to calculate the outcomes mentioned in the above expressions. That is, we assume that for most type profiles, small perturbation in the parameters will not change the mechanism outcomes.

$$o^{*0} = \arg\max_{o \in O}\left(\sum_{i=1}^n u_i^0 v_i(\theta_i, o) + a_o^0\right)$$

$$o^0 = \arg\max_{o \in O}\left(\sum_{j \neq i} u_i^0 v_i(\theta_i, o) + a_o^0\right)$$

We replace o^* and o using o^{*0} and o^0, we have that

$$C_i(M, \theta) \approx \frac{\sum_{j \neq i} u_j v_j(\theta_j, o^0) + a_{o^0} - \sum_{j \neq i} u_j v_j(\theta_j, o^{*0}) - a_{o^{*0}}}{u_i}$$

We use c_j to denote $v_j(\theta_j, o^0)$ and c_j^* to denote $v_j(\theta_j, o^{*0})$. Both the c_j and the c_j^* are *constants*.

$$C_i(M, \theta) \approx \frac{\sum_{j \neq i} c_j u_j + a_{o^0} - \sum_{j \neq i} c_j^* u_j - a_{o^{*0}}}{u_i}$$

We then observe that for any x, $\frac{x}{u_i} = \frac{x}{u_i^0} - \frac{x(u_i - u_i^0)}{u_i u_i^0}$.
We can then rewrite $C_i(M, \theta)$ into:

$$\frac{\sum_{j \neq i} c_j u_j + a_{o^0} - \sum_{j \neq i} c_j^* u_j - a_{o^{*0}}}{u_i^0} - \frac{\left(\sum_{j \neq i} c_j u_j + a_{o^0} - \sum_{j \neq i} c_j^* u_j - a_{o^{*0}}\right)(u_i - u_i^0)}{u_i u_i^0}$$

The first term is a linear combination of the variables, as u_i^0, the c_j, and the c_j^* are all constants.

The second term can be approximated as follows:

$$\frac{(\sum_{j\neq i} c_j u_j^0 + a_{o^0}^0 - \sum_{j\neq i} c_j^* u_j^0 - a_{o*0}^0)(u_i - u_i^0)}{u_i^0 u_i^0}$$

The above is a linear function involving one variable (u_i).

Using the above heuristic method, we are able to turn Model 1 into a linear program involving $n + |O|$ variables. The number of constraints is $n + |O| + |S|$. Therefore, we can afford reasonable large n and $|O|$, as long as $|S|$ is not too large.

4   Zero-Day Exploit Mechanism Design Model

In this section, we focus on a specific mechanism design setting for the zero-day exploit model: there are only two agents: one offender and one defender.

We use $EPO(M)$ to denote the offender's expected payment under mechanism M. We use $EPD(M)$ to denote the defender's expected payment under mechanism M.

Let F be the set of all strategy-proof and individually rational mechanisms.

Let M^* be the optimal mechanism that maximizes the expected revenue. We recall that $ER(M)$ denotes M's expected revenue.

$$M^* = \arg\max_{M\in F} (EPO(M) + EPD(M)) = \arg\max_{M\in F} ER(M)$$

Let MO^* be the optimal mechanism that maximizes the expected payment collected from the offender.

$$MO^* = \arg\max_{M\in F} EPO(M)$$

Let MD^* be the optimal mechanism that maximizes the expected payment collected from the defender.

$$MD^* = \arg\max_{M\in F} EPD(M)$$

Obviously, we have

$$ER(M^*) = EPO(M^*) + EPD(M^*) \leq EPO(MO^*) + EPD(MD^*)$$

We introduce the following *posted-price* mechanisms. These mechanisms allow only one agent to make decisions.

- Every outcome o is associated with a price a_o.
- One agent picks the outcome that maximizes her own utility.
- The other agent makes no decisions and pays 0.

It is without loss of generality to assume that both MO^* and MD^* are posted price mechanisms. Let MO^* be the mechanism that maximizes the offender's expected payment. Let $EPO(M, \theta_D)$ be the offender's expected payment under M when the defender bids θ_D. Because $EPO(MO^*) = \sum_{\theta_D} P(\theta_D) EPO(MO^*, \theta_D)$, there must exist one θ_D so that $EPO(MO^*, \theta_D) \geq EPO(MO^*)$. If we fix the defender's type to be the said θ_D, then the mechanism faced by the offender is exactly a posted-price mechanism, and the expected payment of the offender is at least $EPO(MO^*)$.

For zero-day exploit market, typically the defender has much lower valuation than the offender. For example, according to [9], an exploit that attacks the Chrome browser sells between 80k and 200k for offensive clients (USD). According to Google's official bug bounty reward program for the Chrome browser [19], a serious exploit is priced between 0.5k and 15k. Therefore, $EPD(MD^*)$ is generally much smaller than $EPO(MO^*)$.

We use $PP(a_0, a_1, \ldots, a_k)$ to denote the posted-price mechanism with the parameters a_0 to a_k. We use $M(u_O, u_D, a_0, a_1, \ldots, a_k)$ to denote the AMA mechanism with the parameters u_O (for offender), u_D (for defender), and the a_t. If the deciding agent under $PP(a_0, a_1, \ldots, a_k)$ is the offender, then $PP(a_0, a_1, \ldots, a_k)$ approaches $M(u_O, 1, 0, -a_1 u_O, \ldots, -a_k u_O)$, when u_O approaches infinity. If the deciding agent under $PP(a_0, a_1, \ldots, a_k)$ is the defender, then $PP(a_0, a_1, \ldots, a_k)$ approaches $M(1, u_D, -a_0 u_D, \ldots, -a_{k-1} u_D, 0)$, when u_D approaches infinity. For any posted-price mechanism, there exists an AMA mechanism whose expected performance is arbitrary close to it. That is, the optimal AMA mechanism's expected revenue is at least the optimal expected revenue of posted-price mechanisms.

We solve for the optimal posted-price mechanism for the offender, denoted as PP^*.

$$ER(PP^*) = EPO(M^*) \geq ER(M^*) - EPD(MD^*)$$

Because the optimal AMA mechanism outperforms PP^* (or they have the same expected revenue), when $EPD(MD^*)$ is small, we have that the optimal AMA mechanism's expected revenue is close to the expected revenue of the optimal mechanism M^*.

4.1 Optimal Posted-Price Mechanism

In this subsection, we discuss how to solve for the optimal posted-price mechanism.

First of all, we focus on the single-parameter setting [12]. For presentation purpose, we focus on solving for the optimal posted-price mechanism where the offender makes decisions.

In a single-parameter setting, an offender's valuation is defined as follows, assuming her type is θ_O:

$$v(\theta_O, t) = \int_0^t \theta_O c(x) dx$$

$c(x)$ is a fixed function that characterizes the instantaneous valuation of the exploit by the agent. At time x, the instantaneous valuation is $\theta_O c(x)$.

We use Myerson's standard technique. We assume $\theta_O \in [0, H]$, where H is a fixed upper bound. We assume θ_O's pdf and cdf are f and F, respectively. We also assume the following expression is monotone nondecreasing. This is called the *monotone hazard rate* condition, which is satisfied by many common distributions.

$$\phi(\theta_O) = \theta_O - \frac{1 - F(\theta_O)}{f(\theta_O)}$$

It turns out that if the above all hold, then the optimal post-price mechanism simply sells the whole time interval $[0, 1]$ as a bundle, with a fixed take-it-or-leave-it price p. If the agent is willing to afford p to buy the whole interval, then she gets it. Otherwise, she gets nothing and pays nothing. The optimal mechanism $PP^* = PP(0, \infty, \infty, \dots, \infty, p)$.

When k is small, we have another algorithm for solving for the optimal posted-price mechanism, and under this algorithm, we can drop the single-parameter assumption.

Let $PP(a_0, a_1, \dots, a_k)$ be the optimal posted-price mechanism. It is without loss of generality to assume that for any $i < j$, if both a_i and a_j are finite, then $a_i < a_j$. Otherwise, the outcome i is never chosen, and we can set a_i to be infinite. It is also without loss of generality to assume that for any a_i, either it is infinite (meaning that this outcome is not allowed), or it must satisfy the following condition:

$$\exists \theta_O, v(i, \theta_O) - a_i = \max_{j < i} v(j, \theta_O) - a_j$$

Here, $v(t, \theta_O)$ is the offender's valuation for outcome t when her type is θ_O. The above condition basically says that there exists a type for the offender, if we increase a_i just a bit, then it would force the offender to choose an earlier outcome than i. If the condition is not true, then we can safely increase a_j. By doing so, we can charge more for those types that choose j. We can also charge more if under some types, the offender chooses a later outcome, which also means that more payment will be collected.

Based on the above condition, if we know the a_j for $j < i$ and θ_O, then we can calculate a_i. We already know that $a_0 = 0$. To calculate a_1, we can go over all θ_O, possibly by discretizing the offender's type space. Then, to calculate a_2, we can go over all θ_O again. We do this for every i. Let N be the number of types in Θ_O after the discretization. The total number of iterations is then N^k.

5 Evaluation

As mentioned earlier, according to [9], an exploit that attacks the Chrome browser sells for at most 200k for offensive clients (USD). According to Google's official bug bounty reward program for the Chrome browser [19], a serious exploit is priced for at most 15k.

We start with the following setting, which is based on the numbers above. There are two agents. The offender's valuation function is

$$v(\theta_O, t) = \int_0^t \theta_O(1-x)dx$$

θ_O is drawn uniformly at random from $U(0, 400)$. That is, the offender's valuation for the whole time interval $[0, 1]$ is at most 200.

The defender's valuation function is

$$v(\theta_D, t) = \int_t^1 \theta_D x \, dx$$

θ_D is drawn uniformly at random from $U(0, 15)$. That is, the defender's valuation for the whole time interval $[0, 1]$ is at most 15.

The above valuation functions satisfy all the conditions needed for the single-parameter model. So MO^* simply sells the whole interval to the offender for a fixed price p_O, and MD^* simply sells the whole interval to the defender for a fixed price p_D.

$$p_O = \arg\max_{p \le 200} pP(v(\theta_O, 1) \ge p) = \arg\max_{p \le 200} p\frac{200 - p}{200} = 100$$

$$EPO(MO^*) = 50$$

$$p_D = \arg\max_{p \le 15} pP(v(\theta_D, 1) \ge p) = \arg\max_{p \le 15} p\frac{15 - p}{15} = 7.5$$

$$EPD(MD^*) = 3.75$$

Therefore, $ER(M^*)$ is at most 53.75. We pick $k = 10$ and $\epsilon = 0.01$. We use the VCG mechanism as the initial solution. The VCG mechanism's expected revenue is 6.9, which is very far away from the upper bound. Our technique starts from the VCG mechanism, and at the end produces a mechanism whose expected revenue equals 50.6, which is very close to the upper bound 53.75. That is, in this case, the optimal AMA mechanism's expected revenue is close to the optimal mechanism's expected revenue.

As demonstrated in our analysis, we have the above phenomenon if the defender's valuation is insignificant compared to the valuation of the offender. We then investigate an example where the defender's valuation is much higher. We change it so that the defender's type is drawn from $U(0, 150)$ instead of $U(0, 15)$. Now the upper bound for $ER(M^*)$ is 87.5. Our technique produces a mechanism whose expected revenue equals 57.9. This time, the achieved value is not close to the upper bound.

6   Conclusion

Optimizing within the affine maximizer auctions (AMA) is an effective approach for revenue maximizing mechanism design. We proposed a linear programming based heuristic for optimizing within the AMA family. We applied our technique to revenue maximizing mechanism design for zero-day exploit markets. We showed that due to the nature of the zero-day exploit markets, with one offender and one defender, our technique generally produces a near optimal mechanism.

References

1. Algarni, A.M., Malaiya, Y.K.: Software vulnerability markets: discoverers and buyers. Int. J. Comput. Electr. Autom. Control Inf. Eng. **8**(3), 71–81 (2014)
2. Bilge, L., Dumitras, T.: Before we knew it: an empirical study of zero-day attacks in the real world. In: Proceedings of 2012 ACM Conference on Computer and Communications Security, CCS 2012, pp. 833–844. ACM, New York (2012). http://doi.acm.org/10.1145/2382196.2382284
3. Brams, S.J., Jones, M.A., Klamler, C.: Better ways to cut a cake - revisited. In: Brams, S., Pruhs, K., Woeginger, G. (eds.) Fair Division. Dagstuhl Seminar Proceedings, No. 07261. Internationales Begegnungs- und Forschungszentrum für Informatik (IBFI), Schloss Dagstuhl, Germany (2007)
4. Chen, Y., Lai, J., Parkes, D., Procaccia, A.: Truth, justice, and cake cutting. In: Proceedings of the National Conference on Artificial Intelligence (AAAI), Atlanta, GA, USA (2010)
5. Egelman, S., Herley, C., van Oorschot, P.C.: Markets for zero-day exploits: ethics and implications. In: Proceedings of 2013 Workshop on New Security Paradigms Workshop, NSPW 2013, pp. 41–46. ACM, New York (2013). http://doi.acm.org/10.1145/2535813.2535818
6. Emek, Y., Feldman, M., Gamzu, I., Paes Leme, R., Tennenholtz, M.: Signaling schemes for revenue maximization. In: Proceedings of the ACM Conference on Electronic Commerce (EC), Valencia, Spain (2012)
7. Fisher, D.: Vupen founder launches new zero-day acquisition firm zerodium (2015). https://threatpost.com/vupen-launches-new-zero-day-acquisition-firm-zerodium/113933/. Accessed 25 July 2012
8. Goemans, M., Skutella, M.: Cooperative facility location games. J. Algorithms **50**, 194–214 (2004). Early version: SODA 2000, pp. 76–85
9. Greenberg, A.: Shopping for zero-days: a price list for hackers' secret software exploits (2012). http://www.forbes.com/sites/andygreenberg/2012/03/23/shopping-for-zero-days-an-price-list-for-hackers-secret-software-exploits/. Accessed 23 Mar 2012
10. Guo, M., Deligkas, A.: Revenue maximization via hiding item attributes. In: Proceedings of the Twenty-Third International Joint Conference on Artificial Intelligence (IJCAI), Beijing, China (2013)
11. Guo, M., Deligkas, A., Savani, R.: Increasing VCG revenue by decreasing the quality of items. In: Proceedings of the National Conference on Artificial Intelligence (AAAI), Quebec, Canada (2014)
12. Guo, M., Hata, H., Babar, A.: Revenue maximizing markets for zero-day exploits. In: Baldoni, M., Chopra, A.K., Son, T.C., Hirayama, K., Torroni, P. (eds.) PRIMA 2016. LNCS (LNAI), vol. 9862, pp. 247–260. Springer, Cham (2016). doi:10.1007/978-3-319-44832-9_15

13. Lahaie, S., Pennock, D.M., Saberi, A., Vohra, R.V.: Sponsored search auctions. In: Nisan, N., Roughgarden, T., Tardos, E., Vazirani, V. (eds.) Algorithmic Game Theory, Chap. 28. Cambridge University Press, Cambridge (2007)
14. Lavi, R., Mu'alem, A., Nisan, N.: Towards a characterization of truthful combinatorial auctions. In: Proceedings of the Annual Symposium on Foundations of Computer Science (FOCS), pp. 574–583 (2003)
15. Likhodedov, A., Sandholm, T.: Methods for boosting revenue in combinatorial auctions. In: Proceedings of the National Conference on Artificial Intelligence (AAAI), San Jose, CA, USA, pp. 232–237 (2004)
16. Likhodedov, A., Sandholm, T.: Approximating revenue-maximizing combinatorial auctions. In: Proceedings of the National Conference on Artificial Intelligence (AAAI), Pittsburgh, PA, USA (2005)
17. Myerson, R.: Optimal auction design. Math. Oper. Res. **6**, 58–73 (1981)
18. Procaccia, A.D., Tennenholtz, M.: Approximate mechanism design without money. In: Proceedings of the ACM Conference on Electronic Commerce (EC), Stanford, CA, USA, pp. 177–186 (2009)
19. TC Projects: Severity guidelines for security issues (2015). https://www.chromium. org/developers/severity-guidelines. Accessed 15 Sept 2015
20. Vickrey, W.: Counterspeculation, auctions, and competitive sealed tenders. J. Financ. **16**, 8–37 (1961)

Organizations, Institutions and Norms in Multiagent Systems

ADOPT JaCaMo: Accountability-Driven Organization Programming Technique for JaCaMo

Matteo Baldoni[1(✉)], Cristina Baroglio[1], Katherine M. May[2],
Roberto Micalizio[1], and Stefano Tedeschi[2]

[1] Dipartimento di Informatica, Università degli Studi di Torino, Turin, Italy
{matteo.baldoni,cristina.baroglio,roberto.micalizio}@unito.it
[2] Università degli Studi di Torino, Turin, Italy
{katherine.m.may,stefano.tedeschi}@edu.unito.it

Abstract. This work concerns the challenge of computational accountability in a multiagent setting where agents interact inside organizations. We illustrate the requirements to realize accountability with the help of a scenario. Then, we provide a characterization of computational accountability in terms of a few general principles. We introduce and explain the ADOPT accountability protocol and show how it satisfies these principles with the help of model checking.

Keywords: Computational ethics · Accountability · Multiagent systems · Sociotechnical systems

1 Introduction

JaCaMo [6] is a conceptual model and programming platform that integrates agents, environments, and organizations. It is built on the top of three platforms: Jason [7] for programming agents, CArtAgO [22] for programming environments, and Moise [19] for programming organizations. The aim of the framework is both to integrate the cited platforms and to integrate the related programming meta-models to simplify the development of complex multiagent systems. The presence of an actual programming platform fills the gap between the modeling level and the implementation level.

According to [18], the Moise+ organizational model, adopted in JaCaMo, explicitly decomposes the specification of an organization into three different dimensions. The *structural* dimension specifies roles, groups, and links between roles in the organization. The *functional* dimension is composed of one (or more) scheme(s) that elicits how the global organizational goal(s) is (are) decomposed into sub-goals and how these sub-goals are grouped in coherent sets, called missions, to be distributed to the agents. Finally, the *normative* dimension binds the two previous dimensions by specifying the roles' permissions and obligations for missions. One important feature of Moise+ [19] is to avoid a direct link between

© Springer International Publishing AG 2017
B. An et al. (Eds.): PRIMA 2017, LNAI 10621, pp. 295–312, 2017.
https://doi.org/10.1007/978-3-319-69131-2_18

roles and goals. Correspondingly, roles are linked to missions by means of per-missions and obligations, which consequently maintain an independence between the functional and structural specifications.

In the field of multiagent systems, individual and organizational actions have social consequences, which require the development of tools to trace and evaluate principles' behaviors and to communicate good conduct. This concerns the value of *accountability*. The independence between roles and goals in JaCaMo creates difficulties when reasoning about accountability. Namely, problems result from a scheme's dynamic creation and group assignment that can happen when agents are already playing associated roles. This means that agents, *when entering into an organization* by adopting an organizational role, *have no information about what they could be obliged to do in the future* because this information, related to a specific scheme, may be not available or even not yet present. The aim of this paper is to present an Accountability-Driven Organization Programming Technique (ADOPT) that attempts to face the challenges of handling account-ability computationally in an organization of agents. The main contribution is to provide a notion of when accountability can be ascribed in an organization by investigating the organization-construction process as well as to define a protocol that ensures the design and construction of an accountability-supporting organi-zation. The core of the analysis is the notion of role and the action of role adop-tion (or enactment). With some conceptual modifications, we believe JaCaMo [6] a particularly suitable platform for building in an accountability mechanism. On the other hand, the principles by which we characterize accountability provide a general account of accountability in organizational settings. The paper begins with a scenario that explains in a practical way the lack of accountability and its origin in systems realized by means of JaCaMo. Then, it provides a charac-terization of computational accountability including five founding principles. It describes ADOPT, an accountability protocol, and shows how it satisfies these principles with the help of model checking.

2   Lack of Accountability: A Scenario in JaCaMo

In order to illustrate the accountability problem, we use, as a reference scenario, an excerpt of the *building-a-house* example presented in [6]. An agent, called Gia-como, wants to build a house on a plot. In order to achieve this goal, Giacomo will have to hire some specialized companies and then ensure that the contrac-tors coordinate and execute in the right order the various tasks and subgoals. Each hired company must adopt a corresponding role in the organization. Roles are gathered in a group that is responsible for the house construction. After goal adoption, a company agent could be asked (through an obligation issued by the organization) to commit to some "missions". Now, let's suppose that Giacomo is a dishonest agent and wants to exploit the contracted companies in order to achieve some purposes that are unrelated to the house construction. In particu-lar, let's suppose he wants to delegate a `do_a_very_strange_thing` goal to the agent playing the `plumber` role. Giacomo's exploitive plan would work because when an agent adopts a role in a group, that agent has no information about the kind of tasks it could be assigned. Tasks are rather created independently of roles, and are only subsequently associated with them.

In the example, the `plumber` agent reasonably will not have a plan to achieve the `do_a_very_strange_thing` goal. Consequently, when the corresponding obligation is created, it will not be fulfilled.

Given the above scenario, who could we consider accountable for the inevitable goal failure of `do_a_very_strange_thing`? Should the agent playing the `plumber` role be held accountable? The agent violated its obligation but could not have reasonably anticipated the goal's introduction, which effectively made achievement impossible. Should Giacomo be held accountable since he introduced an unachievable goal, however licit? Perhaps the system itself ought to bear the brunt of accountability since it permits such unfair behavior? The system, however, doesn't know agent capabilities and cannot consequently make a fair/unfair judgment call.

Listing 1.1 shows how the organization for the building-a-house scenario is defined in Moise. The file contains: the structural, functional, and normative specification.

Listing 1.1. Excerpt of the organization for building-a-house.

```
1  <organisational-specification id="house_contruction"
2  ...
3  <structural-specification>
4    <role-definitions>
5      <role id="house_owner" />
6      <role id="building_company" />
7      <role id="plumber" >
8        <extends role="building_company"/>
9      </role>
10     ...
11   </role-definitions>
12   <group-specification id="house_group">
13     <roles>
14       <role id="house_owner" min="1" max="1"/>
15       <role id="plumber"     min="1" max="1"/>
16       ...
17     </roles>
18     ...
19   </group-specification>
20  </structural-specification>
21  <functional-specification>
22    <scheme id="build_house_sch">
23      <goal id="house_built">
24        <plan operator="sequence">
25          <goal id="site_prepared" ttf="20 minutes" />
26          ...
27          <goal id="plumbing_installed" ttf="20 minutes" />
28          ...
29        </plan>
30      </goal>
31      <mission id="management" min="1" max="1">
32        <goal id="house_built"/>
33      </mission>
34      <mission id="prepare_site" min="1" max="1">
35        <goal id="site_prepared" />
36      </mission>
37      <mission id="install_plumbing" min="1" max="1">
38        <goal id="plumbing_installed" />
39      </mission>
```

```
40     ...
41     </scheme>
42   </functional-specification>
43   <normative-specification>
44     <norm id="n1" type="obligation" role="house_owner"
45           mission="management" time-constraint="2 minutes" />
46     ...
47     <norm id="n8" type="obligation" role="plumber"
48           mission="install_plumbing" />
49     ...
50   </normative-specification>
51 </organisational-specification>
```

Line 7, for instance, defines a `plumber` role that is included in the `house_group` group at line 15. After the structural specification, we find the functional specification with a `build_house_sch` scheme. Line 37 defines an `install_plumbing` mission composed of the `plumbing_installed` goal. Finally, in the normative specification, norm `n8` binds the `plumber` role to the previously described mission. It's important to notice that this definition could change at runtime; in particular new schemes could be dynamically generated and, for instance, associated with the `house_group` that will become responsible for them.

Once the building phase is started, Giacomo creates a GroupBoard artifact, called `hsh_group`, following the XML specification of the `house_group`. GroupBoard artifacts are used to manage the lifecycle of specific group of agents. After that it adopts the role `house_owner`, and asks the auction winners (see [6] for explanations about the auction) to adopt the corresponding roles (`!contract_winners`). Finally, after all agents have adopted their roles and the group is ready, a SchemeBoard artifact called `bhsch` is created to manage the execution of the `build_house_sch` social scheme.

When the company agents receive the request sent by Giacomo, they adopt the roles by acting on the group artifact. From that moment on they could be asked (i.e. obliged) to commit to some missions according to the normative specification. This phase is needed in order to form the group which will become responsible of the scheme. For instance, agent `companyA` could be asked to commit to `install_plumbing` with an obligation of the form `obligation(companyA, n8 , committed(companyA, install_plumbing, bhsch), ...)`. Norm `n8` is, indeed, the norm that binds the `plumber` role with `install_plumbing` in the normative specification. When the group is well-formed, agents inside it can be obliged to achieve the related goals. Indeed, the main purpose of the `SchemeBoard` artifact is to keep track of which goals are ready to be pursued and create obligations for the agents accordingly. For instance, let's assume the `plumbing_installed` goal is ready to be pursued; an obligation `obligation(companyA, ..., achieved(bhsch, plumbing_installed, companyA),...)` will be generated, provided that the `companyA` agent is playing the `plumber` role. Such obligations are observed by the agents and the corresponding goals are automatically created. Listing 1.2 shows an excerpt of the `companyA` agent. The obligation creates the goal which is then achieved following the plan of line 20. As soon as other goals are ready to be pursued, new obligations are created.

Listing 1.2. Excerpt of code of the `companyA` agent.

```
1  ...
2  task_roles("Plumbing", [plumber]).
3  +!contract(Task,GroupName)
4    : task_roles(Task,Roles) <-
5    ...
6    lookupArtifact(GroupName, GroupId);
7    for (.member(Role, Roles)) {
8      adoptRole(Role)[artifact_id(GroupId)];
9      focus(GroupId)
10   }.
11 +obligation(Ag,Norm,committed(Ag,Mission,Scheme),Deadline)
12   : .my_name(Ag) <-
13   commitMission(Mission)[artifact_name(Scheme)].
14 +obligation(Ag,Norm,achieved(Scheme,Goal,Ag),Deadline)
15   : .my_name(Ag) <-
16   ...
17   !Goal[scheme(Scheme)];
18   ...
19   goalAchieved(Goal)[artifact_name(Scheme)].
20 +!plumbing_installed    // the organisational goal
21                         (created from an obligation)
22   <- installPlumbing. // simulates the action
```

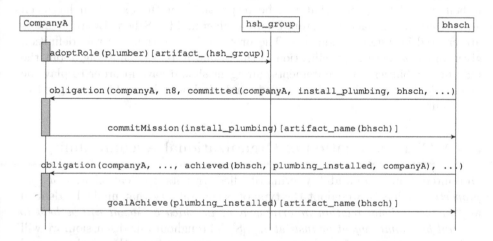

Fig. 1. Interaction between the `companyA` agent and the organization in the *building-a-house* example.

Figure 1 reports the general interaction pattern, concerning role adoption and mission distribution, instantiated on the `companyA` agent and plumbing. As underlined by the authors, *"[a] main advantage of this approach is that by simply changing the scheme specification (which can be done by the designer or by the agents themselves) at very high level, [...] we will change the overall behavior of the agent team without changing a single line of their code. [...] This artifact also manages the state of the obligations, checking, for instance, their fulfillment or violations. This feature is very useful for Giacomo who wants to monitor the execution of the scheme to ensure the house is built correctly and on time"*. Now, let's suppose Giacomo is dishonest and wants to achieve some tasks, that are not related to house construction, by assigning them to the player of plumber role. In particular, let's suppose he wants to delegate a do_a_very_strange_thing goal to the agent who is playing the plumber role (see Listing 1.3).

Listing 1.3. Organization specification involving do_a_very_strange_thing.

```
1  <functional-specification>
2    <scheme id="build_house_sch">
3      <goal id="house_built">
4        <plan operator="sequence">
5          ...
6          <goal id="do_a_very_strange_thing" ... />
7          ...
8        </plan>
9      </goal>
10     ...
11     <mission id="install_plumbing" min="1" max="1">
12       <goal id="do_a_very_strange_thing" />
13     </mission>
14     ...
15   </scheme>
16 </functional-specification>
```

The only two lines that have been modified are Lines 6 and 12. This modification is licit even if the group that will be responsible for the execution has been already created. In fact, the GroupBoard artifact and the SchemeBoard artifacts are created in different moments. The problem here is that the role definition given in the structural specification of the organization says nothing about the kind of capabilities (or requirements) an agent should have in order to play the given role. Similarly, it is not specified what kind of tasks could be assigned to the agent.

3   A Characterization of Organizational Accountability

Our interest in accountability primarily lies with its application as a *design property* [3]; that is, we adopt the type of accountability that might be defined as *"an institutional relation or arrangement in which an agent can be held to account by another agent or institution"* [8]. Throughout our discussion, we will make use of the term, *forum*, which is an investigative body that evaluates and passes judgment on agents. As a design property, we consider integral the various steps to an accountability-as-a-mechanism relationship as described in [8]: a forum must receive all information, including all causal actions, regarding a given situation under scrutiny, the forum must be able to contextualize actions to understand their adequacy and legitimacy, and finally the forum must be able to pass judgment on agents. Our goal lies in automating the entire process, that is, to create a structure that creates and collects contextualized, integral information so that accountability can be determined from any future institutional state.

One of the key difficulties in realizing our goal lies with the tricky notion of *contextualized action*. In our own societies, contextualizing might entail an examination of circumstances: for example, what should have a person done, why didn't she/he do that, what impact did her/his actions have, and given what the person had to work with, did she/he act in an exemplary fashion? The same process in a MAS would be guided by the same type of questions, though in order to facilitate their answers, we need to make use of different structures. In particular, we need structures that allow assessing who is accountable without actually infringing on the individual and private nature of agents. We can determine action impact or *significance* by identifying the amount of disruption it causes in terms of other agents and/or work affected.

We identify the following necessary-but-not-sufficient principles a MAS must exhibit in order to support accountability determinations.

Principle 1. *All collaborations and communications subject to considerations of accountability among the agents occur within a single scope that we call organization.*

In a word, situatedness. Accountability must operate in a specific context because individual actions take on their significance only in the presence of the larger whole. What constitutes a highly objectionable action in one context could instead be worthy of praise in another. Correspondingly, a forum can only operate in context and an agent's actions must always be contextualized. The same role in different contexts can have radically diverse impacts on the organization and consequently on accountability attribution. When determining attribution, thus, an organization will only take into account interactions that took place inside its boundaries.

Placing an organizational based limit on accountability determinations serves multiple purposes. It isolates events and actors into more manageable pieces so that when searching for causes/effects, one need not consider all actions from the beginning of time nor actions from other organizations. Agents are reassured that only for actions within an organization will they potentially be held accountable. Actions, thanks to agent roles, also always happen in context.

As illustrated in [10], accountability attribution consists in a rather complex process involving an investigative forum to assess the situation and evaluate who is accountable for what and to what degree[1]. The indispensability of the forum becomes clear in our societies in which intrigue and complex motivations come to bear. Luckily, a MAS greatly simplifies the matter, and our task takes the form of ensuring all possible actions are accounted for and categorized with respect to accountability, whose attribution will occur post-execution. The influence of an unrealized goal on its resulting mission failure determine the degree of accountability. For instance, should two agents fail to bring about their goals, leading to the failure of another, both agents would bear half the accountability for the consequent failure. Should only one agent cause the failure of a goal, that agent would bear the full brunt of the accountability.

To adequately account for accountability by categorizing action, we must deal with two properties within a given organization: (1) an agent properly completes its tasks and (2) an agent does not interfere with the tasks of others. The principles below deal more explicitly with the first property; that is, how to

---

[1] In the present proposal accountability is crisp and either holds or does not hold.

ensure that agents complete their tasks in a manner fair for both the agents and the organization. The second property is also partially satisfied in our discussion by ensuring that, in the presence of goal dependencies, the first agent in sequence not to complete its goal will bear accountability, not only for its incomplete goal, but for all dependent goals that will consequently remain incomplete. That is, should an agent be responsible for a goal on whose completion other agents wait, and should that agent not complete its goal, then it will be accountable for its incomplete goal and for that goal's dependents as well.

Principle 2. *An agent can enroll in an organization only by playing a role that is defined inside the organization.*

As an organizational and contextual aid to accountability, roles attribute social significance to an agent's actions and can, therefore, provide a guide to the severity of non-adherence.

Principle 3. *An agent willing to play a role in an organization must be aware of all the powers associated with such a role before adopting it.*

Following the tradition initiated by Hohfeld [17], a power is "one's affirmative 'control' over a given legal relation as against another." The relationship between powers and roles has long been studied in fields like social theory, artificial intelligence, and law. Here we invoke a knowledge condition for an organization's agents, and stipulate that an agent can only be accountable for exercising the powers that are publicly given to it by the roles it plays. Such powers are, indeed, the means through which agents affect their organizational setting. An agent cannot be held accountable for unknown effects of its actions but, rather, only for consequences related to an agent's known place in sequences of goals. On the other hand, an agent cannot be held accountable for an unknown goal that the organization attaches to its role, and this leads us to the next principle.

Principle 4. *An agent is only accountable, towards the organization or another agent, for those goals it has explicitly accepted to bring about.*

An organization may not obligate agents to complete goals without prior agreement otherwise we find ourselves in the unfortunate previously discussed scenario in which an organization can insert goals irrelevant to a given role like do_a_very_strange_thing in an agent's obligations. In other words, an organization must always communicate to each agent the goals it would like the agent to pursue.

Principle 5. *An agent must have the leeway for putting before the organization the provisions it needs for achieving the goal to which it is committing. The organization has the capability of reasoning about the requested provisions and can accept or reject them.*

Notice that with this principle we diverge from considerations in the field of ethics regarding accountability in the presence of causal determinism [9,15], where even in the absence of alternate possibilities humans can be morally responsible thanks to the significance of the choice to act. Finding the conversation fundamentally shifts when speaking of software agents, we consequently conclude that accountability is not attributable in the presence of impossibilities. Correspondingly, agents must be able to stipulate the *conditions* under which a given goal's achievement becomes possible, i.e. the agent's requested *provisions*. The burden of discovery for impossibilities, therefore, rests upon an agent collective who announce them by their combined silence for a given goal. That is, a goal becomes effectively impossible for a group of agents should no agent stipulate a method of achievement. Conversely, an agent also declares a goal possible the moment it provides provisions to that goal. Should an uniformed agent stipulate insufficient provisions for an impossible goal that is then accepted by an organization, that agent will be held accountable because by voicing its provisions, it declared an impossible goal possible. The opportunity to specify provisions, therefore, is fundamental in differentiating between impossibilities and possibilities.

To illustrate the need for provisions to model accountability, we can imagine an organization consisting of two members: one to prepare a wall, *wall-preparer*, and another who paints the wall, *painter*. Their organization would give both access rights to the wall and attribute to *wall-preparer* the goal of prepping the wall, and to *painter* the goal of painting the wall. Without the possibility of stipulating when goals are possible, perhaps *wall-preparer* fulfills its goal but whimsically paints a black stripe down the middle. Unfortunately, now *painter* has inadequate materials and cannot realize its goal. *Wall-preparer* made *painter's* goal impossible. The impossibility, however, only came about at runtime. Should *painter* stipulate provisions for its goal, it effectively qualifies possibility, permitting accountability to work by guaranteeing an absence of impossibilities.

4   The ADOPT Accountability Protocol

We turn now to a MAS design-phase application of the above-mentioned accountability principles. Chopra and Singh explored a similar approach of design-phase accountability in [12]. In their work, Chopra and Singh suggest that an actor can legitimately depend on another to make a condition become true only when such a dependency is formalized in an *institutionalized expectation*, whose structure describes expectations one actor has of another and whose inherently public nature exerts normative power. To tackle accountability as a design property, Chopra and Singh introduce the notion of *accountability requirement* as a special case of institutionalized expectation. An accountability requirement is a relation involving two principals, an account giver (a-giver) and an account taker (a-taker). The a-giver is accountable to the a-taker regarding some conditional expectation; namely, the expectation involves an antecedent condition and a consequent condition. Usually, the consequent condition is pursued only when the antecedent condition is true. In principle, if an accountability requirement is violated, the a-taker has a legitimate reason for complaint. The notion of accountability requirement can be further refined in terms of *commitments*, *authorizations*, *prohibitions*, and *empowerments* [12]. Each of these relations has specific implications in terms of who is accountable and for what reason. It is worth noting that an a-giver is normally accountable for a specific condition towards the whole group of agents in a MAS. That is, in an agent society, agents are accountable for their actions towards the society as a whole. Rather than creating an accountability requirement between each possible pairs of a-giver and a-taker, it is convenient to adopt the perspective by Chopra and Singh; namely, considering both the agents and the organization as principals, between which mutual expectations can be defined.

In other words, an organization is considered as a *persona iuris* [12], a legal person that can be the a-giver or a-taker of an accountability requirement, as any other principal represented by an agent. In addition, an organization will also be the conceptual means through which complex goals are articulated in terms of subgoals and distributed among a set of *roles*. An organization is, therefore, a design element that allows one to specify: (1) what should be achieved by the MAS (i.e., the organizational goals) and (2) what roles are included in the organization and with what (sub)goals. As far as accountability is concerned, an organization that shows the above features naturally satisfies Principles 1–3.

Our intuition is that in order to obtain accountability as a design property of a MAS, the agents who are willing to be members of an organization enroll in the organization by following a precise *accountability protocol*. The organization provides the context in which accountability requirements are defined. To define such an accountability protocol, we rely on the broad literature about commitment-based protocols and focus our attention on the accountability requirements that can be expressed as (practical) commitments. Commitments have been studied at least since the seminal works by Castelfranchi [11] and Singh [23]. A social commitment is formally represented as $C(x, y, p, q)$, where x is the debtor (a-giver, in our case), that commits to the creditor y (a-taker) to bring about the consequent condition q should the antecedent condition p hold. From the accountability point of view, the a-giver is accountable when the antecedent becomes true, but the consequent is false.

The gist of the accountability protocol is to make explicit the legal relationships between the agent and the organization. These are expressed as a set of (abstract) commitments, directed from organizational roles towards the organization itself, and vice versa. The first step captures the adoption of a role by an agent. Let $pwr_{i,1}, \ldots, pwr_{i,m}$ be the powers that agent Ag_i, willing to play role R_i, will get. Ag_i will commit towards the organization to exercise the powers, given to it by the role, when this will be requested by the legal relationships it will create towards other agents. In this way, the agent stipulates awareness of the powers it is endowed with, becoming accountable, not only towards some other agent in the same organization but also towards the organization itself, of its behavior:

$$cpwr_{i,1} \; :: \; C(Ag_i, Org, C(Ag_i, Z_1, pwr_{i,1}), pwr_{i,1})$$
$$\cdots$$
$$cpwr_{i,m} \; :: \; C(Ag_i, Org, C(Ag_i, Z_m, pwr_{i,m}), pwr_{i,m})$$

above Z_j, $j = 1, \ldots, m$ represent some roles or some (not necessarily different) agents in the organization. These commitments represent the fact that, from an accountability-based point of view, an agent, when exercising a power because of a social relationship with some other agents, has some duties towards the social institution which provides that power, too. Indeed, when an employee is empowered by a manager to perform a given task on behalf of the company, the result is not only a commitment of the employee with the manager, but also a commitment of the employee with the company. An agent willing to play a role is expected to create a commitment that takes the form:

$$cpwr_{R_i} :: \mathsf{C}(Ag_i, Org, \mathsf{accept\_player}_{Org}(Ag_i, R_i), cpwr_{i,1} \wedge \cdots \wedge cpwr_{i,m})$$

where $\mathsf{accept\_player}_{Org}(Ag_i, R_i)$ is a power of the organization to accept agent, Ag_i, as a player of role R_i.

Org, then, has the power to assign goals to the agents playing the various roles through $assign_{Org}$. This is done through the creation of commitments by which the organization promises to assign some goal to some agent should the agent accept to commit to pursue the goal:

$$cass_{i,1} :: \mathsf{C}(Org, Ag_i, cg_{i,1}, \mathsf{prov}_{i,1} \wedge \mathsf{assign}_{Org}(Ag_i, goal_{i,1}))$$
$$\ldots$$
$$cass_{i,n} :: \mathsf{C}(Org, Ag_i, cg_{i,n}, \mathsf{prov}_{i,n} \wedge \mathsf{assign}_{Org}(Ag_i, goal_{i,n}))$$

Above, $cg_{i,k=1,\ldots,n}$ denote the commitments by whose creation the agent explicitly accepts the goals and possibly asks for provisions $\mathsf{prov}_{i,k=1,\ldots,n}$. Here, $goal_{i,k}$ is a goal the organization would like to assign to the agent Ag_i. The antecedent condition of $cg_{i,k}$ has the shape $prov_{i,k} \wedge assign_{Org}(Ag_i, goal_{i,k})$, where $prov_{i,k}$ stands, as said, for a provision the agent requires for accomplishing the task, and the consequent condition has the shape $achieve_{Ag_i}(goal_{i,k})$:

$$cg_{i,1} :: \mathsf{C}(Ag_i, Org, \mathsf{prov}_{i,1} \wedge \mathsf{assign}_{Org}(Ag_i, goal_{i,1}), \mathsf{achieve}_{Ag_i}(goal_{i,1}))$$
$$\ldots$$
$$cg_{i,n} :: \mathsf{C}(Ag_i, Org, \mathsf{prov}_{i,n} \wedge \mathsf{assign}_{Org}(Ag_i, goal_{i,n}), \mathsf{achieve}_{Ag_i}(goal_{i,n}))$$

Provisions are to be instantiated with those prerequisites that Ag_i discloses as necessary for it to complete its job and that Org is expected to provide. On the agent side, these commitments are the means through which the agent arranges the boundaries of its accountability within the organization. For instance, *painter*, in our example above, is an agent hired in a painting organization including also *wall-preparer*. A provision for *painter* to paint a wall could be *wall-prepared*, a condition that is to be achieved by another agent from the same organization, and that appears in the accountability requirements of its role. Should *wall-preparer* behave maliciously (as in our example), *painter* would not be accountable for not painting the wall as provision *wall-prepared* would be missing. On the organization side, provisions are part of the information used to decide whether to assign the goal to the agent (the internal decision processes of an organization are outside the scope of the paper). An agent becomes obliged to achieve a goal only after this assignment so as to not violate the accountability requirement. Finally, $achieve_{Ag_i}(g_{i,j})$ denotes that goal $goal_{i,j}$ is achieved.

After these premises, we can now introduce the protocol that regulates the enrollment of an agent, Ag_i, in an organization, Org, as a player of role, R_i, and the subsequent assignment of goals to Ag_i carried out by Org.

(1) create($cpwr_{R_i}$)
(2) accept_player$_{Org}(Ag_i, R_i)$
(3) create($cpwr_{i,1}$), ..., create($cpwr_{i,m}$)
(4) create($cass_{i,k}$), $k = 1, \ldots, n$
(5) create($cg_{i,k}$), $k = 1, \ldots, n$
(6) assign$_{Org}(Ag_i, goal_{i,k})$, $k = 1, \ldots, n$
(7) prov$_{i,k}$, $k = 1, \ldots, n$
(8) achieve$_{Ag_i}(goal_{i,k})$, $k = 1, \ldots, n$

An agent Ag_i, willing to play role R_i, makes the first step by creating the commitment, $cpwr_{R_i}$ (1). By doing so it proposes itself as role player. It is worth noting that the creation of $cpwr_{R_i}$ is possible only as a consequence of Principle 3, by which an organization must disclose the powers associated with its roles. The organization is free to decide whether to accept an agent as role player (2). In case of acceptance the agent creates the commitments by which it becomes accountable with the organization of the use of its powers (3). Step (4) allows the organization to communicate the goals it wishes to assign to the agents. The agents are expected to accept them by creating the corresponding commitments of Step (5), thereby knowing which goals it may be asked to achieve at Step (6). Steps (7) and (8) respectively allow the organization to satisfy the provisions, and the agent to communicate goal achievement.

Principle 1 finds an actualization in the fact that all the mentioned commitments are created within a precise organization instance. When Org accepts Ag_i as a player for role R_i, the enrollment of the agent is successfully completed. After this step, the agent operates in the organization as one of its members. This satisfies Principle 2, for which an agent is a member of an organization only when it plays an organizational role. Principles 4 and 5 find their actualization in terms of the commitments $cg_{i,k}$'s. Principle 4 demands that an agent is accountable only for those goals it has explicitly accepted to bring about. The creation of one of the commitments $cg_{i,k}$ represents the acceptance of being responsible, and hence accountable, for the goal occurring in the commitment consequent condition. Principle 5 states that an agent must have the leeway to negotiate its own duties, which we obtain in two ways. First, the agent creates its own commitments, which means that the mission commitments might cover just a subset of the goals. Second, the agent can make explicit provisions for each role goal.

4.1 Verifying ADOPT

Driven by the five fundamental principles we have identified, we have proposed an accountability protocol to achieve accountability as a design property in a

MAS. We now wish to verify that the proposed protocol actually adheres to the five principles. Notably, in this paper we have used commitments as a means for specifying *accountability requirements*; that is, for specifying what a principal (either an agent or the whole organization) can legitimately expect from others, and vice versa. This choice has some important design consequences. In order to create the commitment $cpwr_{R_i}$, an agent willing to play role R_i must be aware both of the organization Org and of the role itself within Org together with the powers $pwr_{i,1}, \ldots, pwr_{i,n}$ associated with R_i. This means that: (1) the organization must exist, (2) roles must be defined in the context of an organization, and (3) powers associated with roles must be known at the time of role enactment. When these elements are all known to an agent before joining an organization, the system implicitly satisfies the accountability Principles 1, 2, 3, and 5. In other words, these principles are structurally satisfied by the adoption of commitments as a means to represent accountability requirements. The only principle that is still to be verified is Principle 4: an agent is only accountable for those goals for which it has taken an explicit commitment. The verification of this principle demands consideration of the dynamics of the accountability protocol in order to check whether such a principle is ever violated. We do this by translating Principle 4 into a set of CTL formulae and by verifying with a model checker whether the protocol satisfies these properties.

For the sake of discussion, we present here the CTL formulae in an abstract way, assuming the existence of only one agent willing to play the unique role, which can exert only one power, in a given organization. Provisions are not addressed explicitly, but the following discussion can be extended to treat them as well. Let us assume that the agent has already created the commitment, $cpwr_{R_i}$. As noted above, this is only the first step of enactment. In fact, to complete the enactment phase, the organization has to accept the agent. Only after this second step is the agent obliged to commit to the powers associated with the role. The following two properties capture this aspect of Principle 4.

$$\mathsf{AG}(enactment \rightarrow \mathsf{AF}(commit\_pwr)) \qquad (1)$$

$$\mathsf{A}(\neg commit\_pwr \ \mathsf{U} \ enactment) \qquad (2)$$

$$\mathsf{AG}(enactment \rightarrow \mathsf{AF}(\mathsf{A}(commit\_pwr \ \mathsf{U} \ exert\_goal))) \qquad (3)$$

Formula (1) specifies that whenever the enactment occurs (*enactment*) the agent will create the commitment to exert the power *pwr* as and when it will be expected by another principal Z (i.e., either another agent in the organization, or the organization itself). Formula (2), on the other hand, specifies that the agent will not commit to a exert a power until the organization completes enactment through acceptance. The second formula is required because we want to avoid situations in which an agent commits to use a power until it is endowed with the power itself. Finally, Formula (3), means that an agent remains committed to use the powers until it will actually need to use them.

So far, we have just modeled the properties that a proper role enactment phase must satisfy. The key aspect of Principle 4, however, is about the actual achievement of an organizational goal. Goals are issued by Org dynamically according policies which fall outside the scope of our discussion. What we want to verify is that an agent commits to goals that, although assigned by Org, have been previously accepted by the agent and are achievable with the powers that Org endows the agent with. This is expressed by the following CTL formulae.

$$A(\neg commit\_goal \text{ U } publish\_goal) \tag{4}$$

$$AG(commit\_goal \rightarrow AF \ assign\_goal) \tag{5}$$

$$AG(assign\_goal \rightarrow AF(exert\_pwr)) \tag{6}$$

Formula (4) means that an agent will not commit to a goal until it is published by the organization. Note, however, that when the organization publishes a goal, the agent has the free choice of accepting the goal. However, when the agent commits to a goal previously published by the organization, the organization is then obliged to assign the goal to the agent, this is modeled in Formula (5). Finally, Formula (6) means that whenever a goal is assigned to an agent, the agent will attempt to achieve the goal by exerting the power it has previously committed to. Of course, in practical situations, the agent may fail to achieve the goal, but from the point of view of ADOPT, and of Principle 4, the agent has done its job if it has, at least, tried to achieve the goal by using its powers. Determining the causes of a failed goal could involve various forms diagnostic reasoning, such as [20,21], which, although relevant for the accountability point of view, are left to future work. It is possible to show that our accountability protocol satisfies these CTL properties.

4.2 Applying ADOPT to the Building-a-House Scenario

We now show how the ADOPT protocol can be applied to the *building-a-house* example introduced above. First of all, ADOPT requires the existence of an organization where roles and powers associated with roles are disclosed. Here we focus on the role plumber and on its power *install_plumbing*. Then, an agent, here companyA, willing to play the role at issue should create the following two commitments, as a first step of the enactment phase:

$cpwr_p ::$ C$(companyA, Org,$ accept_player$_{Org}(companyA, plumber), cpwr_{inst\_p})$
$cpwr_{inst\_p} ::$ C$(companyA, Org, c_p, install\_plumbing)$

By creating the nested commitment on top, $cpwr_p$, the company accepts to be accountable with the organization for the power to install the plumbing within the organization itself, if it is accepted as plumber. Acceptance is completed by the creation of a set of specific commitments, each one concerning a single power. Here we have only one such commitment ($cpwr_{inst\_p}$) because the role gives the agent only one power. The antecedent condition c_p of such a commitment amounts to C$(companyA, Owner, install\_plumbing)$ that binds the company towards a role $Owner$ (of the future house) in the same organization. Thus, the nested commitment raises accountability for installing the plumbing to the organizational level.

Then, the organization dynamically assigns goals to its members; i.e., agents who were accepted as role players. In particular, ADOPT assumes that an organization will assign a goal to an agent only if the agent is aware of the goal and accepted it. Also in this case, we use commitments to formalize the relationship between the organization and the agent. Specifically, in our example Org assigns the goal to perform *install_plumbing* by means of the commitment $cass_{ip}$:

$cass_{ip} :: \mathsf{C}(Org, companyA, cg_{g\_ip},$
$\qquad \mathsf{prov}_{g\_ip} \wedge \mathsf{assign}_{Org}(companyA, install\_plumbing))$
$cg_{g\_ip} :: \mathsf{C}(companyA, Org, \mathsf{prov}_{g\_ip} \wedge \mathsf{assign}_{Org}(companyA, install\_plumbing),$
$\qquad \mathsf{achieve}_{companyA}(install\_plumbing)$

In words, Org commits to assign the goal to companyA and to supply the related provisions (prov_{g_ip}) if the agent takes a commitment (cg_{g_ip}) to pursue the goal, given those provisions and if the goal is assigned to it. Here provisions are assumed to be the result of a negotiation phase which is outside the scope of the paper; of course, it may be possible that no provision is requested. If companyA accepts the mission (i.e., goal and provisions), it creates commitment cg_{g_ip}, and this will detach commitment $cass_{ip}$. This is the pivotal aspect of the ADOPT proposal: companyA becomes accountable towards Org because it assumes voluntarily the responsibility of bringing about a goal in case that goal will ever be assigned to it. Org is now expected to assign companyA goal *install_plumbing* for discharging its commitment. In the example, Org will also have to bring about provisions in order to discharge its commitment towards companyA.

Now, companyA is obliged by the detached commitment cg_{g_ip} to bring about the goal *install_plumbing*. This goal can be achieved by using the power companyA has acquired, and has committed to use, when it joined the organization by issuing the commitments $cpwr_p$ and $cpwr_{inst\_p}$ during the enactment phase. If the goal is not achieved because power *install_plumbing* is not exerted, companyA can be held accountable for the violation of $cpwr_{inst\_p}$ and cg_{g_ip}. Namely, companyA can be held accountable because it didn't even attempt to bring about a task it had committed to when it had adopted the role. On the other hand, if the organization assigns an unexpected goal to companyA, let us say goal, *do_a_very_strange_thing*, this does not detach any commitment and, consequently, companyA is not obliged to do anything. It is worth noting that thanks to the ADOPT protocol we can immediately identify the behavior of the organization as a violation of the accountability property. In fact, because of Principle 4, the organization is not authorized to issue goals to agents that are not committed to bring about those goals.

5 Discussion

Our work with JaCaMo highlights a conceptual challenge in the concept of role and a role's central place in responsibility and accountability (in the form of "role-following responsibility") as illustrated by [13]. To a certain degree, decoupling a role from an organizational execution essentially negates the role's function to limit its operational domain. As illustrated with building-a-house, without prior agreement of what exactly a role means in a particular organizational context, we can force a role to mean whatever we want so long as the language matches. The consequent dynamism of roles makes automatic considerations of accountability impossible to conclude. In our construction of computational accountability, roles represent a division of responsibility and pattern of interaction that serve the investigative forum to assign accountability.

The accountability protocol allows design-phase incorporation of accountability (1) by excluding that the organization changes the goals assigned to roles after agents enacted them and (2) by allowing agents to make their provisions explicit. As one way to enforce a behavior that respects the protocol, one could modify JaCaMo's conceptual model and implementation so that it follows the five principles. The modification would be possible since JaCaMo relies on obligations, which can be used to represent detached commitments. Another way is to introduce proper monitors that, if needed, can check protocol adherence. This calls for the realization of a kind of artifact that can monitor the interaction, represent the social state (made of the existing commitments), and track its evolution. This kind of system could be realized by means of 2COMM [1,2].

The resulting accountability-supporting organization has affinities with the model of social structures defined in [14], which describe a *whole* made up of *parts* that are organized by specific relationships. Wholes and parts are all entities, and parts can be wholes themselves. The social structure has *causal properties* (that is, it can affect the world) in its own right. Such properties (also known as powers), synchronically emerge only with the constitution of a social structure. Even in the presence of all individual members, if the structure's characterizing relationships are absent, so too are the previously mentioned properties. In this framework, it is easy to see that accountability is, indeed, an emergent property of a social structure (organization). Like all emergent causal properties of a social structure, it co-exists with the causal powers of its parts (the agents), whose acts are affected by the ways in which they are organized, so generally events are multiply determined.

If we adapt the approach to roles developed in [4,5] in which roles essentially define an organization, accountability takes on functional implications for the very definitional existence of the organization. Should some roles remain unfulfilled, an organization would correspondingly find itself in definitional crisis. As illustrated in [16], role fulfillment means continual realization of role relationships, that is, a role's duties and obligations. Accountability allows an organization some recourse in crisis and a method of expressing the relative importance its roles play. Armed with the knowledge of relative responsibility and therefore importance in the collective, an organization enables role-playing agents to make informed decisions should conflicts arise and to make their own cost/benefit analysis should an agent not wish to not perform its function.

A mechanism based on commitments presents numerous conceptual advantages for accountability. An agent is able to specify the exact social context in which it can fulfill the specified goal, g. It effectively announces to the organization,

Org, that should its requirements become true, it will be accountable for fulfilling g. Essentially the commitments require pre-execution knowledge of expectations and requirements both on the part of the organization and of the agent, which satisfies accountability's foreknowledge requirement. Commitments can therefore provide indications of responsibility, as a pre-execution assignment, which will then, thanks to the exhaustive definitions of pre and post conditions, provide a direct mapping to accountability post execution. Since the agent, Ag, by design creates the commitment to the organization, the agent, not the organization, specifies its requirements to satisfy the goal, g. Casual determinism consequently cannot manifest because agent Ag stipulates the exact social circumstances in which it can operate and realize g. Moreover, role relationships become explicit through the provision stipulation, which will later provide a basis for role-adherence determination. The commitment structure therefore provides the necessary characteristics for beginning to speak of accountability.

Acknowledgments. This work was partially supported by the *Accountable Trustworthy Organizations and Systems (AThOS)* project, funded by Università degli Studi di Torino and Compagnia di San Paolo (CSP 2014). The authors warmly thank the reviewers for their constructive and helpful comments which helped revising the paper.

References

1. Baldoni, M., Baroglio, C., Capuzzimati, F.: A commitment-based infrastructure for programming socio-technical systems. ACM Trans. Internet Technol. **14**(4), 23:1–23:23 (2014)
2. Baldoni, M., Baroglio, C., Capuzzimati, F., Micalizio, R.: Commitment-based agent interaction in JaCaMo+. Fundamenta Informaticae (2017, to appear). http://www.di.unito.it/~argo/papers/2017_FundamentaInformaticae.pdf
3. Baldoni, M., Baroglio, C., May, K.M., Micalizio, R., Tedeschi, S.: Computational accountability. In: Proceedings of the AI*IA Workshop on Deep Understanding and Reasoning: A Challenge for Next-generation Intelligent Agents 2016. CEUR Workshop Proceedings, vol. 1802, pp. 56–62. CEUR-WS.org (2017)
4. Baldoni, M., Boella, G., van der Torre, L.W.N.: Interaction between objects in powerJava. J. Object Technol. **6**(2), 5–30 (2007)
5. Boella, G., van der Torre, L.: The ontological properties of social roles in multi-agent systems: definitional dependence, powers and roles playing roles. Artif. Intell. Law **15**, 201–221 (2007)
6. Boissier, O., Bordini, R.H., Hübner, J.F., Ricci, A., Santi, A.: Multi-agent oriented programming with JaCaMo. Sci. Comput. Program. **78**(6), 747–761 (2013)
7. Bordini, R.H., Hübner, J.F., Wooldridge, M.: Programming Multi-agent Systems in AgentSpeak Using Jason, vol. 8. Wiley, Hoboken (2007)
8. Bovens, M., Goodin, R.E., Schillemans, T. (eds.): The Oxford Handbook of Public Accountability. Oxford University Press, Oxford (2014)
9. Braham, M., van Hees, M.: An anatomy of moral responsibility. Mind **121**(483), 601–634 (2012)

10. Burgemeestre, B., Hulstijn, J.: Design for the values of accountability and transparency: a value-based argumentation approach. In: van den Hoven, J., Vermaas, P.E., van de Poel, I. (eds.) Handbook of Ethics, Values, and Technological Design: Sources, Theory Values and Application Domains. Springer, Netherlands (2015). doi:10.1007/978-94-007-6994-6_12-1
11. Castelfranchi, C.: Commitments: from individual intentions to groups and organizations. In: ICMAS, pp. 41–48. The MIT Press (1995)
12. Chopra, A.K., Singh, M.P.: The thing itself speaks: accountability as a foundation for requirements in sociotechnical systems. In: IEEE 7th International Workshop RELAW, p. 22. IEEE Computer Society (2014)
13. Conte, R., Paolucci, M.: Responsibility for societies of agents. J. Artif. Soc. Soc. Simul. 7(4) (2004). http://jasss.soc.surrey.ac.uk/7/4/3.html
14. Vass, D.E.: The Causal Power of Social Structures: Emergence Structure and Agency. Cambridge Univ Press, Cambridge (2010)
15. Frankfurt, H.G.: Alternate possibilities and moral responsibility. J. Philos. 66(23), 829–839 (1969)
16. Guarino, N., Welty, C.: Evaluating ontological decisions with OntoClean. Commun. ACM 45(2), 61–65 (2002)
17. Hohfeld, W.N.: Some fundamental legal conceptions as applied in judicial reasoning. Yale Law J. 23(1), 16–59 (1913)
18. Hübner, J.F., Boissier, O., Kitio, R., Ricci, A.: Instrumenting multi-agent organisations with organisational artifacts and agents. Auton. Agent. Multi Agent Syst. 20(3), 369–400 (2010)
19. Hubner, J.F., Sichman, J.S., Boissier, O.: Developing organised multiagent systems using the MOISE+ model: programming issues at the system and agent levels. Int. J. Agent Oriented Softw. Eng. 1(3/4), 370–395 (2007)
20. Micalizio, R., Torasso, P.: Agent cooperation for monitoring and diagnosing a MAP. In: Braubach, L., Hoek, W., Petta, P., Pokahr, A. (eds.) MATES 2009. LNCS (LNAI), vol. 5774, pp. 66–78. Springer, Heidelberg (2009). doi:10.1007/978-3-642-04143-3_7
21. Micalizio, R., Torasso, P.: Cooperative monitoring to diagnose multiagent plans. J. Artif. Intell. Res. 51, 1–70 (2014)
22. Ricci, A., Piunti, M., Viroli, M., Omicini, A.: Environment programming in CArtAgO. In: El Fallah Seghrouchni, A., Dix, J., Dastani, M., Bordini, R. (eds.) Multi-Agent Programming, pp. 259–288. Springer, Boston (2009). doi:10.1007/978-0-387-89299-3_8
23. Singh, M.P.: An ontology for commitments in multiagent systems. Artif. Intell. Law 7(1), 97–113 (1999)

Architecture of an Institutional Platform for Multi-Agent Systems

Maiquel de Brito[1]([⊠]), Jomi F. Hübner[2], and Olivier Boissier[3]

[1] Federal Institute of Education, Science and Technology of Rio Grande do Sul,
Rolante, RS, Brazil
maiquel.brito@rolante.ifrs.edu.br
[2] Federal University of Santa Catarina, Florianópolis, SC, Brazil
jomi.hubner@ufsc.br
[3] Laboratoire Hubert Curien UMR CNRS 5516, Institut Henri Fayol,
MINES Saint-Etienne, Saint-Etienne, France
Olivier.Boissier@emse.fr

Abstract. Artificial institutions usually consider that the regulation of
the behaviour of the agents is expressed by norms that refer to an institutional reality, that is an institutional interpretation of the environment in
which the agents are situated. To be applied on real systems, however,
artificial institutions need to advance from the theory to the practice.
Such step requires to conceive the institutional platform components
that are in charge of building the institutional reality used in the normative regulation of the system. Such components must be connectable to
the heterogeneous elements composing the environment and must also
be able to accommodate the different normative platforms that regulate the system. This paper proposes the architecture of an institutional
platform having these features. It is shown also how the proposed institutional platform can be linked to environmental and normative ones.

Keywords: Institutions · Constitutive rules · Situatedness · Norms

1 Introduction

In Multi-Agent Systems (MAS), norms are a usual way to express the agents'
expected behaviour, conciliating their autonomy with the system's goals [6].
Norms usually abstract from the shared physical or digital resources (referred
hereafter as *environment*) that support the activities of the agents [1,32]. For
example, while it makes sense for an auction to have a norm stating that "the
winner is obliged to pay its offer", it is not explicit neither who must pay nor
what must be done to comply with that expectation. We can say that norms refer
to an *institutional reality*, composed of elements such as *winners* and *payments*,
that are *constituted* from environmental elements [26,27]. For example, the agent
that utters the highest bid may constitute the *winner* and a credit card operation
may constitute a *payment*.

© Springer International Publishing AG 2017
B. An et al. (Eds.): PRIMA 2017, LNAI 10621, pp. 313–329, 2017.
https://doi.org/10.1007/978-3-319-69131-2_19

From a practical point of view, grounding the normative regulation on the institutional reality requires to instrument the system with the components[1] that operationalize the constitution of this institutional reality. In existing approaches, such components are usually mixed with the normative engines [1,10,29]. Since constitution is intimately coupled with regulation, it is not easy to change the constitution without changing the regulation or inversely. Moreover, normative regulation and institutional reality cover different social aspects in MAS: while norms prescribe the expected agents' behaviour, institutional reality is the social interpretation about the environment. For this reason, in this paper, we look for instrumenting MAS with components that, on the one hand, build an institutional reality independent of the normative platform in charge of the regulation and, on the other hand, make possible for different normative platforms to base their regulation on the institutional reality that they build. Conceiving independent constitutive components enables the developer to build the institutional reality from heterogeneous environmental elements and to open the regulation of this institutional reality to different normative models as proposed in the literature.

To build such components, we turn to the *Situated Artificial Institutions* model (SAI) [14]. In this model, institutions represent and manage the institutional reality built from the environment. Norms then refer to such institutional reality and, thus, the normative regulation is grounded on the environment in which the agents act. For example, the norm stating that "the winner is obliged to pay its offer" defines an obligation for the agent that counts as the winner in the institutional reality. Current works on SAI have been mainly theoretical, defining the representations of artificial institutions [14], the dynamics of constitution within them [15], and the coupling of the normative regulation on the institutional reality produced by the constitution process [16]. This paper advances on practical aspects of SAI proposing (i) the architecture of an institutional platform, i.e. a set of components that interpret institutional specifications and build the institutional reality following the SAI model, (ii) the means to connect the heterogeneous components from the environment to the institutional infrastructure and (iii) the required machinery to connect normative engines into the institutional platform s.t. the normative regulation based on different normative models follows the built institutional reality. In the following, Sect. 2 briefly describes the SAI model, Sect. 3 describes the proposed architecture, Sect. 4 describes insertion of the proposed architecture in an MAS infrastructure, Sect. 5 relates this work with other existing ones, and Sect. 6, describes future work and some final remarks.

2   Situated Artificial Institutions

The Situated Artificial Institutions (SAI) model is inspired by the theory of the philosopher John Searle [14–16,26,27]. SAI assumes that the expected agents'

---

[1] In this paper, *component* means a software element that encapsulates a set of functions and that can interact with other components in a broader system [21].

behaviour is given by a *normative state*, built from the interpretation of norms that define obligations, prohibitions, and permissions to be followed. Different normative models can express the expected agents' behaviour in different ways and even norms based on different models may take part in the same MAS [13].[2] SAI assumes that the norms regulating a system refer to an abstract level that is not directly related to the environment. For example, the norm stating that *"the winner of an auction is obliged to pay its offer"* does not specify neither who is the winner that is obliged to fulfil the norm nor what the winner must concretely do to fulfil it. To be effective, norms take part in *institutions* that ground the abstract concepts in the environment. In the SAI model, such grounding is based on the constitution of *status functions*, that are status, assigned by the institution to the environmental elements, that impose functions to these elements. In the previous auction example, *winner* and *payment* are *status functions*.[3] The *constitution* of the status functions, i.e. the assignment of status functions to environmental elements, is specified through *constitutive rules*, that define, for example, that the agent that utters the highest bid counts as the auction winner. The constituted status functions compose the *constitutive state*, that is the SAI representation of what Searle calls *institutional reality*, being the institutional interpretation of the current environmental state (Fig. 1).

The SAI model defines thus the elements to represent, specify, and animate the constitutive state within artificial institutions [14–16]. In the following, Sect. 2.1 explains how the constitutive rules specify the constitution of the constitutive state while Sect. 2.2 describes the dynamics of such constitution.

2.1 Constitutive Specification

The constitutive specification defines how the elements that *may* be part of the environment, defined below, are viewed from the institutional perspective.

Definition 1 (Environmental elements). *The environmental elements are represented by* $\mathcal{X} = \mathcal{A}_\mathcal{X} \cup \mathcal{E}_\mathcal{X} \cup \mathcal{S}_\mathcal{X}$ *where* $\mathcal{A}_\mathcal{X}$ *is the set of agents possibly acting in the system,* $\mathcal{E}_\mathcal{X}$ *is the set of events that may happen in the environment, and* $\mathcal{S}_\mathcal{X}$ *is the set of properties used to describe the possible states of the environment.*

Agents in $\mathcal{A}_\mathcal{X}$ are represented by atoms (e.g. *bob*). Events in $\mathcal{E}_\mathcal{X}$ are pairs (e, a) where e is a first-order logic predicate identifying the event with its possible arguments and a identifies the element that has triggered the event e. Properties in $\mathcal{S}_\mathcal{X}$ are represented by first-order logic predicates. From the institutional point of view, the environmental elements may carry some *status functions* [27].

---

[2] Among the huge literature in the field, details on norms can be found in [2,4,7] and in the COIN series of workshops (http://www.pcs.usp.br/~coin/).

[3] In SAI, as in Searle's work, the expression *"status function"* means both the *status* and the corresponding *function* assigned by the institution to the environmental elements. For example, the agent *bob* carrying the status function *auction winner* means that *bob* has both the status of *auction winner* and the functions corresponding to such status.

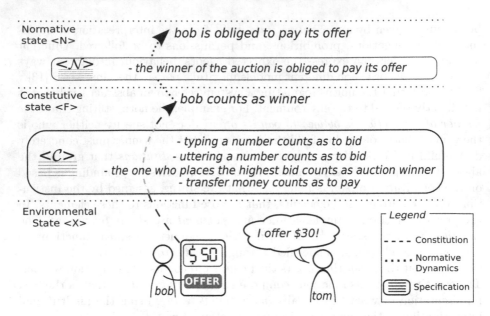

Fig. 1. In the current environmental state, agents are uttering numbers and also typing numbers in electronic devices. In the constitutive state, these actions count as bids, and the agent that places the highest bid is the winner of the auction, that, according to the normative state, becomes obliged to pay the offer. This obligation can be fulfilled through a money transfer, that, according to a constitutive rule, counts as a payment.

Definition 2 (Status function). *The status functions of a SAI are represented by $\mathcal{F} = \mathcal{A}_{\mathcal{F}} \cup \mathcal{E}_{\mathcal{F}} \cup \mathcal{S}_{\mathcal{F}}$ where $\mathcal{A}_{\mathcal{F}}$ is the set of agent-status functions (i.e. status functions assignable to agents), $\mathcal{E}_{\mathcal{F}}$ is the set of event-status functions (i.e. status functions assignable to events), and $\mathcal{S}_{\mathcal{F}}$ is the set of state-status functions (i.e. status functions assignable to states).*

For example, in an auction, an agent may have the agent-status function of *winner*, the utterance "I offer \$100" may have the event-status function of *bid*, and "more than 20 people placed in a room at Friday 10am" may have the state-status function of *minimum quorum* for its realization. Agent-status functions are represented by atoms. Event- and state-status functions are represented by first-order logic predicates. The assignment of status functions of $\mathcal{F}$ to the environment elements of $\mathcal{X}$ is specified through *constitutive rules*.

Definition 3 (Constitutive rule). *A constitutive rule $c \in \mathcal{C}$ is a tuple $\langle x, y, t, m \rangle$ where $x \in \mathcal{F} \cup \mathcal{X} \cup \{\varepsilon\}$, $y \in \mathcal{F}$, $t \in \mathcal{E}_{\mathcal{F}} \cup \mathcal{E}_{\mathcal{X}} \cup \top$, $m \in W$, and $W = W_{\mathcal{F}} \cup W_{\mathcal{X}}$.*

A constitutive rule $\langle x, y, t, m \rangle$ specifies that x counts as y when t has happened while m holds. If $x = \varepsilon$, then there is a *freestanding assignment* of the status function y, i.e. an assignment where there is not a concrete environmental element carrying y [14,27]. When x actually counts as y (i.e. when the conditions

t and m declared in the constitutive rule are true), we say that there is a *status function assignment* (SFA) of the status function y to the element x. The establishment of a SFA of y to some x is the *constitution* of y.

Example of SAI Constitutive Specification. A language to specify the constitution of status functions is proposed in [14]. Figure 2 shows the constitutive specification for the use case addressed in [17], where agents collaborate to manage crisis such as floodings, car crashes, etc. Such collaboration is regulated by norms (e.g. *firefighters are obliged to evacuate insecure zones*). The agents act in an environment composed of geographic information systems (GIS) and of tangible tables [23] where they put objects equipped with RFID tags on to signal their intended actions. For example, if an agent intends to command the evacuation of an area, it puts the proper object on the proper position of the table. The actions of the agents upon the tables, as well as the informations from the GIS, do not have themselves any meaning in the crisis scenario and, thus, they cannot ground, by themselves, the checking of the norm compliance. For instance, an agent putting an object on a specific point of the table does not mean, by itself, a command for the evacuation of a zone and the GIS information of a zone having a certain number of inhabitants does not mean, by itself, that such zone is insecure. Such informations become meaningful in the crisis scenario through the interpretation of constitutive rules. For example, agents are recognized as *mayor* and *firefighter* according to the table where they are acting in (constitutive rules 1 and 2), a zone is considered insecure when it has over than 500 inhabitants (constitutive rule 5), and putting a *launch_object* on the coordinates (15,20) of a table signals the evacuation of the downtown (constitutive rule 3).

```
status_functions:
  agents: mayor, firefighter.
  events: evacuate(Zone).
  states: secure(Zone), insecure(Zone).
constitutive_rules:
              /*** Agent-Status Functions constitutive rules ***/
  /*Actors carry the status functions according to their check in the tables*/
  1: Actor count-as mayor
         when checkin(table_mayor,Actor) while not(Other is mayor)|Other==Actor.
  2: Actor count-as firefighter
         when checkin(table_fire_brigade,Actor).
              /*** Event-Status Functions constitutive rules ***/
  /*Putting a ``launch_object'' on (15,20) means the evacuation of the downtown*/
  3: put_tangible(launch_object,15,20,Actor) count-as evacuate(downtown).
  /*A zone is secure if it has at most 500 inhabitants
   (nb_inhabit(Zone,X) is an information coming from GIS)*/
  4: nb_inhabit(Zone,X) count-as secure(Zone)
         while X<=500
  /*A zone is insecure if it is over than 500 inhabitants*/
  5: nb_inhabit(Zone,X) count-as insecure(Zone)
         while X>500
```

Fig. 2. Example of constitutive specification

2.2   Constitutive Dynamics

Status functions are dynamically assigned to the actual environmental elements by the interpretation of constitutive specifications, building thus the *constitutive state* [15]. This section describes the basic elements involved on this dynamics.

Definition 4 (Environmental state). *The environmental state is represented by* $X = A_X \cup E_X \cup S_X$ *where (i)* A_X *is the set of agents currently participating in the system, (ii)* E_X *is the set of events currently occurring in the environment and (iii)* S_X *is the set of environmental properties describing the current environmental state.*

Agents in A_X are represented by their names. States in S_X are represented by first order logic atomic formulae. Events in E_X are represented by pairs (e, a) where e is the event, represented by a first order logic atomic formula, triggered by the agent a. Events can be triggered by actions of the agents (e.g. the utterance of a bid in an auction, the handling of an environmental artifact, etc.) but can be also produced by the environment itself (e.g. a clock tick). In this case, events are represented by pairs (e, ε).

Definition 5 (Constitutive state). *The constitutive state of a SAI is represented by* $F = A_F \cup E_F \cup S_F$ *where (i)* $A_F \subseteq A_X \times \mathcal{A}_{\mathcal{F}}$ *is the set of agent-status function assignments, (ii)* $E_F \subseteq E_X \times \mathcal{E}_{\mathcal{F}} \times A_X$ *is the set of event-status function assignments and (iii)* $S_F \subseteq S_X \times \mathcal{S}_{\mathcal{F}}$ *is the set of state-status function assignments.*

Elements of F are *status-function assignments* (SFA), i.e. relations between environmental elements and status functions. Elements of A_F are pairs $\langle a_X, a_{\mathcal{F}} \rangle$ meaning that the agent a_X has the status function $a_{\mathcal{F}}$. Elements of E_F are triples $\langle e_X, e_{\mathcal{F}}, a_X \rangle$ meaning that the event-status function $e_{\mathcal{F}}$ is assigned to the event e_X produced by the agent a_X.[4] Elements of S_F are pairs $\langle s_X, s_{\mathcal{F}} \rangle$ meaning that the state s_X carries the status function $s_{\mathcal{F}}$. The process of interpretation of constitutive rules that builds the constitutive state is detailed in [15]. Briefly, if the actual environment matches with the elements t and m of a constitutive rule $\langle x, y, t, m \rangle$, then the environmental element x constitutes the status function y, producing an SFA. On the other hand, if the environment is no longer matching the conditions that lead to the production of an existing SFA, then such SFA is dropped from the constitutive state.

3   Architecture of the Institutional Platform

According to the SAI model, norms, maybe following different models, take part in the institution, basing their regulation on the constitutive state. Such constitutive state is built from an environment composed of heterogeneous environmental

---

[4] As events are supposed to be considered at the individual agent level in normative systems (i.e. they can be related to a triggering agent) [31], it is important to record the agent that causes an event-status function assignment.

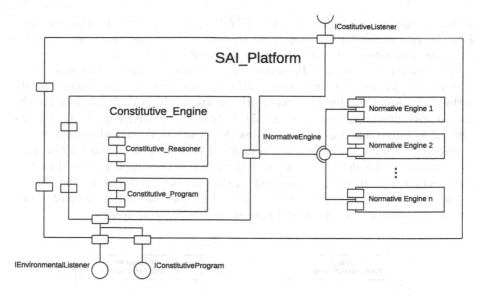

Fig. 3. Component diagram of the SAI platform

elements. From these considerations, it is possible to see that deploying SAI in MAS requires to conceive institutional infrastructures able to be coupled with (i) different normative components to situate their regulation, and (ii) different environmental components to provide different physical reality so that both constitutive and normative states are animated. Following these requirements, this section proposes the architecture of the corresponding institutional platform, defining its components, the relations among them, and its interaction with the components that are external to the institution (environmental and normative ones).

The general view of the proposed architecture is shown in the component diagram of Fig. 3, that follows the UML notation [8]. The institutional platform is, itself, conceived as a component to be inserted into a broader system. It is represented in Fig. 3 by the component *SAI_Platform*. In SAI, an institution is conceived to animate both the institutional reality and the normative regulation. This feature is captured by the *SAI_Platform*, that is composed of two kinds of components: the *Constitutive_Engine* and some *Normative_Engine*, presented in Sects. 3.1 and 3.2 respectively.

3.1 Managing the Constitutive State: The *Constitutive_Engine*

The *Constitutive_Engine* is responsible for managing the constitutive state by interpreting constitutive specifications. It encloses a *Constitutive_Program* component, responsible for storing and managing a constitutive specification. Following the SAI model, the *Constitutive_Program* component incorporates the elements described in Sect. 2.1. The elements of a constitutive specification are added by components external to the *SAI_Platform* through the *IConstitutive-Program* provided interface (Fig. 4(a)). Parsers for the constitutive specification language illustrated in Fig. 2 are among these external elements.

Besides the *Constitutive_Program*, the *Constitutive_Engine* contains also a *Constitutive_Reasoner*, that is responsible for interpreting constitutive specifications and for managing the constitutive state of the SAI. It implements the constitutive dynamics conceived in [15]. Following the SAI model, the *Constitutive_Reasoner* component incorporates the elements described in Sect. 2.2. It is responsible, first, to keep a representation of the actual environment, that corresponds to the element X of the SAI state (cf. Definition 4). Based on this representation of the environment and on the constitutive program, the *Constitutive_Reasoner* is responsible for checking the SFAs that must be created and dropped, building then the constitutive state F (cf. Definition 5).

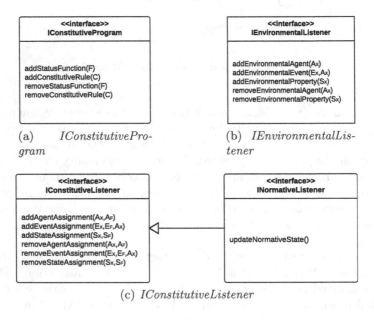

(a)   *IConstitutivePro-gram*

(b)   *IEnvironmentalLis-tener*

(c) *IConstitutiveListener*

Fig. 4. Interfaces of the *SAI_Platform*

The integration between the *SAI_Platform* and the components external to the institution is done through two interfaces:

– *IEnvironmentalListerner* (cf. Fig. 4(b)): this provided interface is used by environmental components to provide informations about the environmental state into the *SAI_Platform*. Following the SAI model, these informations are about the agents participating/leaving the system, about occurring events, and about properties starting/ceasing to hold in the environment. Implementing the SAI model, through this interface, the environmental components lead the *SAI_Platform* to keep a consistent representation of the environmental state (cf. Definition 4).

- *IConstitutiveListener* (cf Fig. 4(c)): this required interface enables external components to be informed about the constitutive state. External components implementing this interface can be plugged in the *SAI_Platform*. They are informed about SFAs that are added to and removed from the constitutive state. In relation with the SAI model, through this interface, external components can keep a consistent representation of the constitutive state of the institution (cf. Definition 5).

The dynamics involving the *IEnvironmentalListener* and the *IConstitutiveListener* evolves as follows: the environmental components use the methods provided by the *IEnvironmentalListener* to inform the *SAI_Platform* about changes in the environmental state. The *Constitutive_Reasoner* then checks whether the new environmental state implies changes in the constitutive state. If this is the case, the constitutive listeners are informed about the SFAs that have been added and removed. This dynamics is illustrated in the sequence diagram shown in Fig. 5. Notice that, while the constitutive engine is informed about agents leaving the system and about environmental properties ceasing to hold, informations about environmental events are added but are not removed. This is because the SAI model considers that events do not have a fluent nature. Rather, they just occur in the environment and this atomic nature must be reproduced in the constitutive level by the constitutive engine [15]. On the other hand, the constitutive engine explicitly removes the event status function assignments from the constitutive listeners because the constitutive listeners are not supposed to implement the semantics of event-status functions and their implicit atomic nature.

3.2 Adding Norms to the Institutional Platform: The *Normative_Engine*

The normative regulation in SAI may be provided by norms following different models, having thus, different implementations. For this reason, the proposed architecture allows to integrate different normative engines in the institution. To this end, the different normative engines must implement (or be embedded in some implementation of) the required interface *INormativeListener*. This interface is a specialization of *IConstitutiveListener* and, for this reason, the normative engines are informed about changes in the constitutive state when they occur. It is up to each normative engine to properly manage such information. In addition to the behaviour of a *IConstitutiveListener*, the components implementing *INormativeListener* have the operation *updateNormativeState*. The *Constitutive_Engine* triggers this operation when a new constitutive state is achieved. The different normative engines are expected, through the operation *updateNormativeState*, to evaluate the normative state based on the new constitutive state. Thus, facing a new constitutive state, the normative engines check whether new normative states are also achieved. This dynamics is illustrated in the UML

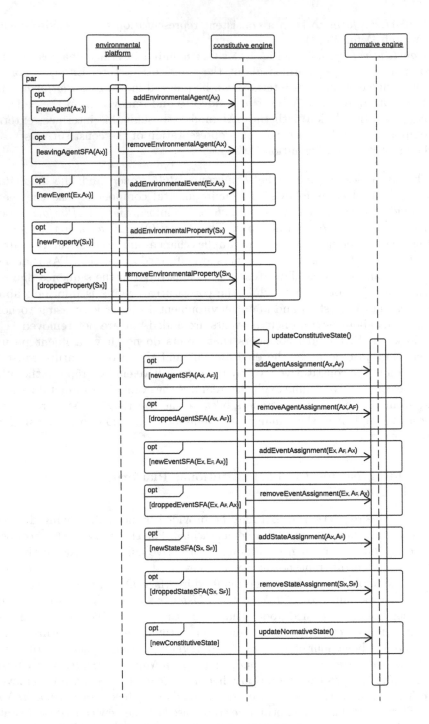

Fig. 5. Dynamics of the *SAI_Platform*

sequence diagram shown in Fig. 5. At this point, two remarks are important. First, different engines may contain norms that produce conflicting normative states for the same constitutive one. Analysing and solving such conflicts are beyond the scope of this paper. Second, the proposed architecture does not consider any kind of feedback from the normative engine neither to the environment nor to the constitutive state. The SAI model indeed considers that these are not the norms but the agents who have the power to impose changes in the environment that may count as new constitutive states.

4   Connecting the Institutional Platform to Environment and Norms

This section describes the coupling of the proposed architecture with existing environmental and normative implementations. More precisely, it describes *SAI_Platform* as an institutional platform where (i) the environment is based on the CArtAgO platform [24] (ii) the regulation is provided by a normative engine based on NPL norms [22]. Section 4.1 describes the connection of the *SAI_ platform* with CArtAgO environments. Section 4.2 describes the coupling of a NPL engine with the *SAI_platform*.

4.1   Connecting the *SAI_Platform* to CArtAgO Environments

Environments running on top of CArtAgO platform[5] are composed of *artifacts*, that represent the different environmental elements that can be perceived and acted upon by the agents. The agents act upon the artifacts through available *operations* and perceive the state of the artifacts through their *observable properties*. Thus, in CArtAgO environments, the environmental events to be considered by SAI are produced when operations are performed on the artifacts. The agents acting upon the artifacts are the environmental agents considered by SAI. The observable properties of the artifacts compose the environmental state to be considered by SAI.

CArtAgO environments are composed of one or more *workspaces*, that are logical places collecting the artifacts. Events occurring in the workspaces, triggered when operations are performed, as well as the changes in the observable properties, are caught by specializations of the *AbstractRuleEngine* class available in the CArtAgO machinery. In our proposed integration between SAI and CArtAgO, such specialization is called *SAIRuleEngine*. It is responsible to get the elements from the environment and to put them into the *SAI_Platform* (Fig. 6). In practical applications, it is possible to have several workspaces, each one with their corresponding *SAIRuleEngine* connected to the same *SAI_Platform*.

By having such connection, the *SAI_Platform* can compute the constitutive state based on the dynamics of CArtAgO environments. Information about the current constitutive state is available to the agents as observable properties of the artifact *ConstitutiveArt*. When a new constitutive state is achieved,

---

[5] An implementation of CArtAgO is available at cartago.sf.net.

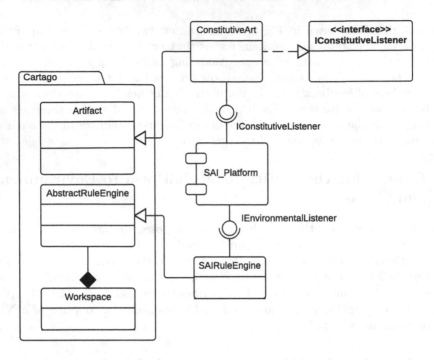

Fig. 6. Connecting the *SAI_Platform* with CArtAgO

the *SAI_Platform* informs the *ConstitutiveArt*, as well as every other *IConstitutiveListener*, about the new constitutive state.

4.2   Inserting a NPL Engine Within the Institution

As described in Sect. 3.2, normative engines are connected to the constitutive engine through the interface *INormativeListener* (cf. Fig. 3). To connect the NPL engine introduced in [22][6] to the *SAI_Platform*, we conceive the class *Npl2Sai* (Fig. 7). This class implements the behaviour of a *INormativeListener*, being thus informed about changes in the constitutive state and having also the method *updateNormativeState()* triggered by the constitutive engine.

Npl2Sai objects have access to the NPL machinery. The *NPLInterpreter* is responsible for interpreting NPL programs, managing the normative state based on a set of facts that, in this case, is the SAI constitutive state. These facts are stored in a *BeliefBase*. As soon as the *Npl2Sai* is informed about changes in the constitutive state, these changes are added to this *BeliefBase*. The NPL engine has, thus, a consistent view about the current constitutive state to evaluate the norms. The *Constitutive_Engine* then triggers the operation *updateNormativeState* in the normative listeners when the a new constitutive state is achieved (cf. Sect. 3.2). This method thus is triggered in the *Npl2Sai* objects connected to

---

[6] An implementation of NPL is available at http://github.com/moise-lang/npl.

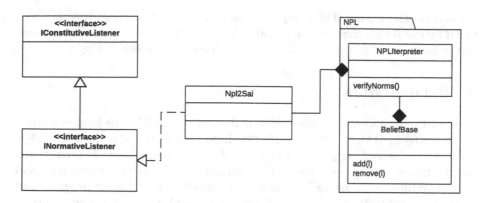

Fig. 7. The *Npl2Sai* class implements the behaviour of a *INormativeListener* and contains a *NPLInterpreter*

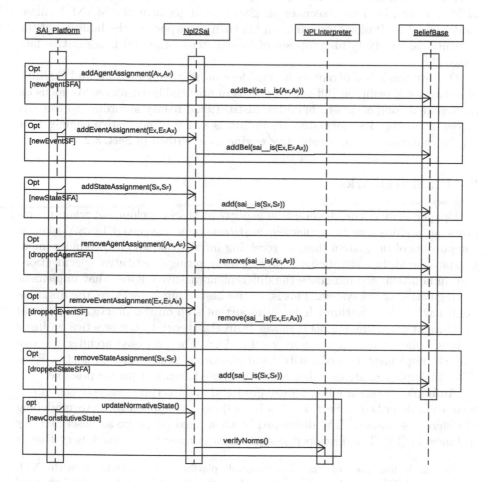

Fig. 8. Dynamics of the NPL interpreter inserted in the *SAI_Platform*

the constitutive engine. These objects then call the method *verifyNorms()*, provided by the *NPLInterpreter*, that make the norms to be evaluated with respect to the facts stored in the *BeliefBase*. This dynamics is shown in Fig. 8.

5   Related Work

Although several works propose theoretical models to build some kind of institutional reality in MAS [1,5,9,10,12,19,30], there are a few ones, to our knowledge, that have advanced on practical aspects of having some kind of institutional interpretation of the environment. They consider that both the constitutive and regulative dimensions of the institutions are specified in the same program and operationalized by the same engine. While Aldewereld et al. [1] propose to specify both constitution and normative regulation as DROOLS programs [25], similar directions are taken by Cardoso et al. [10,11] with an implementation based on JESS [20], and by Tampitsikas et al. [28], that implement the MANET metamodel based on Prolog. Testerink, on his turn, incorporates the building of the institutional reality in his proposal of interpreter of the 2OPL normative language [29].

Our approach is different as it considers normative regulation and building of institutional reality as different concerns of artificial institutions. We focus on the required components to build the institutional reality according to the SAI model, assuming that normative regulation is a task of normative engines that can be connected to the constitutive engine as described in Sect. 3.2.

6   Final Remarks

This paper advances on the practical aspects of MAS development when it proposes an architecture to implement *institutions* as conceived by SAI, i.e. as components of the system that, by receiving information about the environmental state, build the institutional reality by interpreting constitutive specifications and, in addition, accommodate the different normative engines that implement the regulation of the system. This is, to the best of our knowledge, the first proposal having these features. It is an important step on the practical aspects of multi-agent programming, as it moves from the theory to the practice on institutions – more than just on norms – in MAS. The proposed architecture can base the implementation of institutional platforms, as described in Sect. 4. Even different implementations following the proposed architecture are possible.

An implementation following the proposed architecture – namely the implementation described in Sect. 4 – has been done and applied to MAS modelling of different scenarios.[7] The developed MAS worked properly, as described, for instance, in [18]. The developed systems have a constitutive machinery that is

---

[7] The implementation of the institutional platform, its interfaces with NPL and CArtAgO, as well as some examples, are available at http://github.com/artificial-institutions/sai.

independent but connectable to the environmental components as well as to different normative engines. It is possible to see, thus, that the proposed architecture is suitable to develop institutional infrastructures to take part in MAS. Thus, from the proposed architecture and from the resulting implementations, it has been possible not just to project but also to implement MAS applying the notion of a normative regulation based on the institutional reality. In such MAS, the agents are aware not only about what they must do but also about how they can use the environmental resources to do that [3]. Building real applications using the SAI approach requires, however, to consider how complex data provided by the environment are managed in the constitutive state (e.g three financial operations of $3 count as a payment of $9). The handling of complex data in the constitutive state is a future work. Future works include also to integrate the described implementation of proposed architecture with other environmental and normative platforms. Analysing the performance of the SAI machinery is also planned.

References

1. Aldewereld, H., Álvarez Napagao, S., Dignum, F., Vázquez-Salceda, J.: Making norms concrete. In: van der Hoek, W., Kaminka, G.A., Lespérance, Y., Luck, M., Sen, S. (eds.) Proceedings of the 9th International Conference on Autonomous Agents and Multiagent Systems (AAMAS 2010): Volume 1–3, pp. 807–814. IFAAMAS, Richland (2010)
2. Andrighetto, G., Governatori, G., Noriega, P., van der Torre, L.W.N. (eds.) Normative Multi-Agent Systems, Dagstuhl, Germany. Dagstuhl Follow-Ups, vol. 4. Schloss Dagstuhl - Leibniz-Zentrum fuer Informatik (2013)
3. Baldoni, M., Baroglio, C., Calvanese, D., Micalizio, R., Montali, M.: Towards data- and norm-aware multiagent systems. In: Baldoni, M., Müller, J.P., Nunes, I., Zalila-Wenkstern, R. (eds.) EMAS 2016. LNCS, vol. 10093, pp. 22–38. Springer, Cham (2016). doi:10.1007/978-3-319-50983-9_2
4. Boella, G., Noriega, P., Pigozzi, G., Verhagen, H. (eds.) Normative Multi-Agent Systems, 15.03. - 20.03.2009, Dagstuhl, Germany. Dagstuhl Seminar Proceedings, vol. 09121. Schloss Dagstuhl - Leibniz-Zentrum für Informatik, Germany (2009)
5. Boella, G., van der Torre, L.: Constitutive norms in the design of normative multi-agent systems. In: Toni, F., Torroni, P. (eds.) CLIMA 2005. LNCS, vol. 3900, pp. 303–319. Springer, Heidelberg (2006). doi:10.1007/11750734_17
6. Boella, G., van der Torre, L., Verhagen, H.: Introduction to the special issue on normative multiagent systems. Auton. Agents Multi-Agent Syst. 17(1), 1–10 (2008)
7. Boella, G., van der Torre, L.W.N., Verhagen, H. (eds.) Normative Multi-agent Systems, 18.03. - 23.03.2007, Dagstuhl, Germany. Dagstuhl Seminar Proceedings, vol. 07122. Internationales Begegnungs- und Forschungszentrum für Informatik (IBFI), Schloss Dagstuhl, Germany (2007)
8. Booch, G., Rumbaugh, J., Jacobson, I.: The Unified Modeling Language User Guide. Object Technology Series. Addison-Wesley, Reading (2005)
9. Campos, J., López-Sánchez, M., Rodríguez-Aguilar, J.A., Esteva, M.: Formalising situatedness and adaptation in electronic institutions. In: Hübner, J.F., Matson, E., Boissier, O., Dignum, V. (eds.) COIN -2008. LNCS, vol. 5428, pp. 126–139. Springer, Heidelberg (2009). doi:10.1007/978-3-642-00443-8_9

10. Cardoso, H.L., Oliveira, E.C.: Institutional reality and norms: specifying and monitoring agent organizations. Int. J. Coop. Inf. Syst. **16**(1), 67–95 (2007)
11. Cardoso, H.L., Oliveira, E.C.: Electronic institutions for B2B: dynamic normative environments. Artif. Intell. Law **16**(1), 107–128 (2008)
12. Cliffe, O., De Vos, M., Padget, J.: Answer set programming for representing and reasoning about virtual institutions. In: Inoue, K., Satoh, K., Toni, F. (eds.) CLIMA 2006. LNCS, vol. 4371, pp. 60–79. Springer, Heidelberg (2007). doi:10. 1007/978-3-540-69619-3_4
13. Criado, N., Argente, E., Botti, V.J.: Open issues for normative multi-agent systems. AI Commun. **24**(3), 233–264 (2011)
14. de Brito, M., Hübner, J.F., Boissier, O.: A conceptual model for situated artificial institutions. In: Bulling, N., van der Torre, L., Villata, S., Jamroga, W., Vasconcelos, W. (eds.) CLIMA 2014. LNCS, vol. 8624, pp. 35–51. Springer, Cham (2014). doi:10.1007/978-3-319-09764-0_3
15. de Brito, M., Hübner, J.F., Boissier, O.: Bringing constitutive dynamics to situated artificial institutions. In: Pereira, F., Machado, P., Costa, E., Cardoso, A. (eds.) EPIA 2015. LNCS, vol. 9273, pp. 624–637. Springer, Cham (2015). doi:10.1007/ 978-3-319-23485-4_63
16. de Brito, M., Hübner, J.F., Boissier, O.: Coupling regulative and constitutive dimensions in situated artificial institutions. In: Rovatsos, M., Vouros, G.A., Julian, V. (eds.) EUMAS/AT -2015. LNCS, vol. 9571, pp. 318–334. Springer, Cham (2016). doi:10.1007/978-3-319-33509-4_25
17. De Brito, M., Thevin, L., Garbay, C., Boissier, O., Hübner, J.F.: Situated artificial institution to support advanced regulation in the field of crisis management. In: Demazeau, Y., Decker, K.S., Bajo Pérez, J., de la Prieta, F. (eds.) PAAMS 2015. LNCS, vol. 9086, pp. 66–79. Springer, Cham (2015). doi:10.1007/ 978-3-319-18944-4_6
18. De Brito, M., Thevin, L., Garbay, C., Boissier, O., Hübner, J.F.: Situated regulation on a crisis management collaboration platform. In: Demazeau, Y., Decker, K.S., Bajo Pérez, J., de la Prieta, F. (eds.) PAAMS 2015. LNCS, vol. 9086, pp. 267–270. Springer, Cham (2015). doi:10.1007/978-3-319-18944-4_24
19. Fornara, N., Viganò, F., Verdicchio, M., Colombetti, M.: Artificial institutions: a model of institutional reality for open multiagent systems. Artif. Intell. Law **16**(1), 89–105 (2008)
20. Friedman-Hill, E.: Jess in Action: Rule-Based Systems in Java. Action Series. Manning, Greenwich (2003)
21. Heineman, G.T., Councill, W.T.: Component-Based Software Engineering: Putting the Pieces Together. ACM Press Series. Addison-Wesley, Boston (2001)
22. Hübner, J.F., Boissier, O., Bordini, R.H.: A normative programming language for multi-agent organisations. Ann. Math. Artif. Intell. **62**(1–2), 27–53 (2011)
23. Kubicki, S., Lepreux, S., Kolski, C.: RFID-driven situation awareness on TangiSense, a table interacting with tangible objects. Pers. Ubiquit. Comput. **16**(8), 1079–1094 (2012)
24. Ricci, A., Piunti, M., Viroli, M.: Environment programming in multi-agent systems: an artifact-based perspective. Auton. Agents Multi-Agent Syst. **23**(2), 158–192 (2011)
25. Salatino, M., De Maio, M., Aliverti, E.: Mastering JBoss Drools 6. Community Experience Distilled. Packt Publishing, Birmingham (2016)
26. Searle, J.: The Construction of Social Reality. Free Press, New York (1995)
27. Searle, J.: Making the Social World: The Structure of Human Civilization. Oxford University Press, Oxford (2009)

28. Tampitsikas, C., Bromuri, S., Schumacher, M.I.: MANET: a model for first-class electronic institutions. In: Cranefield, S., van Riemsdijk, M.B., Vázquez-Salceda, J., Noriega, P. (eds.) COIN -2011. LNCS, vol. 7254, pp. 75–92. Springer, Heidelberg (2012). doi:10.1007/978-3-642-35545-5_5

29. Testerink, B.: Norms for Distributed Organizations - Syntax, Semantics and Interpreter. Master's thesis, Faculty of Science - Utrecht University, Utrecht, The Netherlands (2012)

30. Viganò, F., Colombetti, M.: Specification and verification of institutions through status functions. In: Noriega, P., Vázquez-Salceda, J., Boella, G., Boissier, O., Dignum, V., Fornara, N., Matson, E. (eds.) COIN -2006. LNCS, vol. 4386, pp. 115–129. Springer, Heidelberg (2007). doi:10.1007/978-3-540-74459-7_8

31. De Vos, M., Balke, T., Satoh, K.: Combining event-and state-based norms. In: Gini, M.L., Shehory, O., Ito, T., Jonker, C.M. (eds.) International Conference on Autonomous Agents and Multi-Agent Systems, AAMAS 2013, Saint Paul, MN, USA, 6–10 May 2013, pp. 1157–1158. International Foundation for Autonomous Agents and Multiagent Systems, Richland (2013)

32. Weyns, D., Omicini, A., Odell, J.: Environment as a first-class abstraction in multiagent systems. Auton. Agents Multi-Agent Syst. **14**(1), 5–30 (2007)

Norm Enforcement as Supervisory Control

Mehdi Dastani[1], Sebastian Sardina[2], and Vahid Yazdanpanah[3(✉)]

[1] Utrecht University, Utrecht, The Netherlands
m.m.dastani@uu.nl
[2] RMIT University, Melbourne, Australia
sebastian.sardina@rmit.edu.au
[3] University of Twente, Enschede, The Netherlands
v.yazdanpanah@utwente.nl

Abstract. In this paper, we study normative multi-agent systems from a supervisory control theory perspective. Concretely, we show how to model three well-known types of norm enforcement mechanisms by adopting well-studied supervisory control theory techniques for discrete event systems. Doing so provides a semantics for normative multi-agent systems rooted in formal languages and the ability to automatically synthesize SCT-based norm enforcement mechanisms for special, but still fairly expressive, type of systems and properties.

1 Introduction

In multi-agent systems literature, norms are proposed as a flexible means to regulate and control the behavior of autonomous agents in multi-agent settings [5]. Norms, for example, may indicate that certain states or actions are obligatory (obligation norms) or prohibited (prohibition norms) [15,19]. There are various ways to enforce norms on a multi-agent system. For example, norms can be enforced by means of regimentation (i.e., by preventing violating behaviors), sanctioning (i.e., by allowing but sanctioning violating behaviors), or reparation (i.e., by allowing violating behaviors if some external repair event is expected). We emphasize that this paper merely focuses on regulative norms and dismiss constitutive norms [10]. Multi-agent systems that are controlled by means of norms are called *normative multi-agent systems*. In such systems, norms are often represented by logical formulas, which specify good or bad behaviors, while norm enforcement mechanisms are explained by means of model update, i.e., enforcing a norm on a multi-agent system is seen as updating the multi-agent model with the norm. Although these approaches contribute to the formal understanding and analysis of crucial concepts in normative multi-agent systems, they are less concerned with the implementability and complexity issues that are involved in synthesizing norm enforcement mechanisms.

In this paper, we consider norm enforcement as a "controllability" problem. Controlling autonomous processes has been the focus of extensive studies in *Supervisory Control Theory (SCT)* for (physical) Discrete Event Systems (DESs), with applications in a wide spectrum of (physical) systems, including manufacturing,

B. An et al. (Eds.): PRIMA 2017, LNAI 10621, pp. 330–348, 2017.
https://doi.org/10.1007/978-3-319-69131-2_20

traffic, logistics, and communication systems [13]. The general goal in SCT is to control the system at hand by restricting its behavior as little as possible so that undesirable sequences of (discrete) events are prevented [21]. The significant advantage of SCT is its reliance on standard formal language theory, one of the most well known and accessible areas in Computer Science. This enables us to come-up with rigorous and implementable semantics for control mechanisms [9]. Indeed, the attractive computational properties in SCT have led to the development of various tools to synthesize control mechanisms (e.g., TCT/STCT [27], GRAIL [23], DESUMA [24], and SUPREMICA [20]).

In order to adopt techniques from SCT to synthesize norm-based enforcement mechanisms, we need to bridge the two mature fields of normative multi-agent systems and discrete event systems. To that end, we start by considering a multi-agent system as a plant and use in the rest of the paper the terms "plant" and "multi-agent systems" interchangeably. In our formalization, all possible behaviors of a plant can be generated by a finite state automaton; in case of a multi-agent system the automaton's transitions represent joint actions. In SCT, the behavior of a plant is meant to be controlled—restricted—by a so-called *supervisor*. We assume perfect observability but limited control for plant supervisors. Plant supervisors have partial control in the sense that they can prevent/allow some but not all events. Using results and models from SCT, we propose regimentation, sanctioning, and repairing supervisors to model the corresponding forms of norm enforcement. We stress that it is *not* the objective of this work to claim that an SCT approach to norm modeling and reasoning is "better" than existing norm enforcement approaches. The novelty and significance of our contribution comes from connecting SCT and normative systems, two otherwise unrelated fields/problems, which has the potential of opening the door for synergies between the two.

The text is structured as follows. Section 2 provides some background on norms and norm enforcement mechanisms in multi-agent systems and Sect. 3 introduces a normative framework rooted in discrete event systems and supervisory control theory. Sections 4, 5, and 6 present formal models for regimentation, sanctioning, and repairing supervisors. Finally, Sects. 7 and 8 review related studies and conclude the paper.

2   Norms and Norm Enforcement

Imagine a computer system of a university that provides access to an intranet network. Students can log-in the computer system to browse material provided by the university. Via this account, students can also log-in to the Internet after which they are enabled to either watch some study-relevant tutorials or enjoy watching some study-irrelevant movies. The purpose of giving access to the Internet is to enable students to watch study-relevant tutorials, not to watch study-irrelevant movies. So, through the eyes of the system designer, it is not *normal* to watch movies using the provided Internet access. Any sequence of events that ends with a *movie watching* event (and all its extensions) is thus seen as a *violating* behavior. For example, if a student logs into the university intranet and thereafter to the Internet, and then watches a movie followed by a tutorial, the behavior is considered as a violating one too. In our approach, a norm can be specified as a set of *event strings* that represent violating behaviors, i.e., a norm can be seen as a (possibly infinite) set of event sequences that are interpreted as "bad" behaviors. Note that this interpretation of norms is in line with the general idea that norms distinguish good and bad behaviors [8]. In our approach, a norm is specified by the bad behaviors; all other behaviors are considered to be good behaviors.

In order to avoid or suppress violating behaviors, various mechanisms have been proposed to enforce norms. For example, one may want to regiment norms in the sense that all violating behaviors are prevented. In our running example, regimentation would amount to blocking Internet access to students. This is based on the assumption that the designer of the system has control over students' log-in access. Norm regimentation has some drawbacks, such as limiting the autonomy of students and preventing some compliant/good behaviors. For example, blocking the Internet access prevents students from watching study-relevant tutorials. An alternative approach would be to allow violating behaviors, but to impose *sanctions* on violating behaviors. In our scenario, this amounts to giving students free Internet access, but sanction the violating behaviors by closing the Internet access after some occurrences of watch-movie events, or to charge students the cost of the Internet access. In general, a sanction can either be modeled as an obligation for agents (in our case to oblige the student to pay the cost of Internet access) or forced by a controller/supervisor (in our case the supervisor withdraws money from the student's deposit). The former type of sanctioning may result in multiple sanctioning rounds, as the agent may not comply to her obligations (e.g. to pay). In this paper, we follow the latter approach. Although norm sanctioning does not guarantee the prevention of norm-violating behaviors, it does not restrict the autonomy of agents nor prevents any norm-compliant behavior. Finally, a third approach is to allow norm violations if these are expected to be "repaired" by some other external events. In our scenario, students may be allowed to watch a movie if they watch a tutorial thereafter. This mechanism requires the possibility to predict the behavior of agents.

3 Preliminaries

In this section we develop a normative framework rooted in Discrete Event Systems (DESs) and Supervisory Control Theory (SCT) [13,21]. This will allow us to take advantage of the existing models and results from the respective communities and transfer them to norm-based multi-agent systems. Generally speaking, SCT is concerned with *imposing control* on the sequences of events (or strings/words) that such processes/systems -commonly referred to as the plant- may generate [21]. The techniques used by SCT are based on standard formal language theory [17].

We start by assuming a set of events Σ that can be generated by the multi-agent systems considered as the plant. A *language* L over the set of events Σ is any set of finite sequences (strings/words) of events from Σ, i.e., $L \subseteq \Sigma^*$. We use $\epsilon \in \Sigma^*$ to denote the empty string. We assume the set of events to consist of disjoint sets of controllable Σ_c and uncontrollable events Σ_u, i.e., $\Sigma = \Sigma_c \cup \Sigma_u$. The *prefix-closure* of a language L, denoted by $\overline{L}$, is the language of all prefixes of words in L, that is, $w \in \overline{L}$ if and only if $w.w' \in L$, for some $w' \in \Sigma^*$ ($w.w'$ denotes the concatenation of words w and w'). A language L is *prefix-closed* if $L = \overline{L}$.

A multi-agent system is viewed then as a "generator" of the language of string of events. We note here that for multi-agent systems, an event may be an action profile in case we consider synchronized models or a single action of an individual agent in case of a turn-based multi-agent system. Formally, a *generator* is a deterministic finite-state machine $\mathcal{G} = \langle \Sigma, G, g_0, \gamma, G_m \rangle$, where Σ is the finite alphabet of events; G is a finite set of states; $g_0 \in G$ is the initial state; $\gamma : G \times \Sigma \mapsto G$ is the transition function; and $G_m \subseteq G$ is the set of marked states. We generalize the transition function γ to words as follows: $\gamma : G \times \Sigma^* \mapsto G$ is such that $\gamma(g, \epsilon) = g$ and $\gamma(g, w.\sigma) = \gamma(\gamma(g, w), \sigma)$, with $w \in \Sigma^*$ and $\sigma \in \Sigma$. We say that a state $g \in G$ is *reachable* iff $g = \gamma(g_0, w)$ for some word $w \in \Sigma^*$. Finally, given two words $w_1, w_2 \in \Sigma^*$, $w_1 \sqsubseteq w_2$ iff $w_2 = w_1.w$ for some $w \in \Sigma^*$. Moreover, $w_1 \sqsubset w_2$ iff $w_2 = w_1.w$ for some $w \in \Sigma^* \setminus \{\epsilon\}$.

The *language* generated by generator $\mathcal{G}$ is $L(\mathcal{G}) = \{w \in \Sigma^* \mid \gamma(g_0, w)$ is defined$\}$, where the *marked* language of $\mathcal{G}$ is $L_m(\mathcal{G}) = \{w \in L(\mathcal{G}) \mid \gamma(g_0, w) \in G_m\}$. Words in the former language stand for, possibly partial, operations or tasks, while words in the marked language represent the completion of some operations or tasks. Note that $L_m(\mathcal{G}) \subseteq L(\mathcal{G})$ and that $L(\mathcal{G})$ is always prefix closed, while $L_m(\mathcal{G})$ may not be.

A *norm* n is specified by a set of (finite) words, i.e., $n \subseteq \Sigma^*$. An element of n is interpreted as a sequence of events that causes a violation. In case $w_1, w_2 \in n$ such that $w_1 \sqsubset w_2$, we interpret w_2 as a word causing more than one violation. Note that we take a semantic approach to norms and norm enforcement by focusing on agents' (norm-compliant/-violating) behaviors. The language itself for describing such behaviors is out of the scope of this paper. The following example illustrates our formal framework by means of the running scenario.

Example 1. **Norm Enforcement Mechanisms.** Our running student scenario can be formally represented as $\mathcal{S} = \langle \Sigma, G, g_0, \gamma \rangle$, where $\Sigma_c = \{I_u, I_i, O_u, O_i\}$ is the set of controllable events, $\Sigma_u = \{W_t, W_m, B\}$ is the set of uncontrollable events, and $\Sigma = \Sigma_u \cup \Sigma_c$. The controllable events I_u and I_i stand for logging-in for *the University intranet* and *the Internet*, respectively; O_u and O_i stand for logging-out from *the university intranet* and *the Internet*, respectively. Moreover, the uncontrollable events W_t and W_m stand for *watching tutorial* and *watching movie*, respectively, and B for *browsing in the university intranet*. The set of states G consists of three possible states S, U, and I, representing the states where (1) the student is neither logged-in for the university intranet nor for the Internet, (2) the student is logged-in for the university intranet and has access only to the provided university material, and (3) the student is logged-in for the Internet and has access to both tutorials and movies on the Internet. The initial state of this plant is state S (i.e., $g_0 = \{S\}$) and the transition function γ is represented by the following graph.

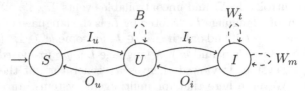

In this scenario, we consider the norm of not watching a movie on the Internet to be specified by $n = \Sigma^*.W_m$. Note that all the members of norm n in this example end with a specific event W_m, suggesting that W_m is in fact the event that causes the violation. This is not the case in general as we do not use the concept of violating events in our framework. For instance, under an alternative norm $n' = \Sigma^*.W_m e$, with $e \in \Sigma \setminus \{W_t\}$, there is no single event causing the violation: watching a movie *and* not watching a tutorial immediately afterwards is the problem. While there are sequences of events containing W_m that are a case of violation (e.g. $I_u I_i W_m O_i O_u$), there are also sequences of events containing W_m but that are not a case of violation (e.g. $I_u I_i W_m W_t O_i O_u$). It follows then that, given a sequence of events ξ, verifying the occurrence of violation with respect to an arbitrary norm n is not, in general, reducible to syntactically checking whether ξ contains (or ends with) a specific class of violating events. This highlights our semantic approach to norms, as we focus on sequences of events (*system behaviors*) and see them as (potential) norm violations. Such view intrinsically contrasts to syntactic ones that are sensitive to the incidence of so called "violating events". In further sections, we present a formal account of normative behaviors and illustrate how norm-violating/-compliant behaviors can be expressed in our SCT-based setting.

Given a multi-agent system and a norm specification, we aim at modeling the enforcement of the norm on the multi-agent system by means of a system supervisor. There are various forms of norm enforcement. In the following sections we model three well-known forms of norm enforcement in multi-agent systems using the concept of supervisory control in DESs. These three forms of norm enforcement are called regimentation, sanctioning and reparation. We say a supervisor enforces a norm on a multi-agent system by means of regimentation if norm violations are prevented. A norm is said to be enforced by means of sanctions if norm violations are allowed (not prevented), but compensated by some sanctions. Finally, a norm is said to be enforced by means of reparation if norm violations are followed by some reparation events generated by the multi-agent system itself. Norm sanctioning and norm reparation are similar in the sense that the system supervisor allows norms to be violated. However, they differ as norm sanctioning responds to norm violations by adding an external sanction event to repair the violations, while the reparation mechanism considers some system events as reparation events and allows norm violations when they are followed by reparation events. These forms of norm enforcement will be formally modeled in the following three sections.

4 Regiment-Based Supervision

In order to enforce a norm $n \subseteq \Sigma^*$ on a multi-agent system by means of regimentation, we first identify norm violating and norm compliant behaviors under the regimentation mechanism. Given a norm specification containing all words that causes violations, the set of all "bad/undesired" behaviors (norm-violating behaviors) under regimentation consists of all words that simply extend a word from the norm specification. The set of "good/desired" behaviors (norm-compliant behaviors) under regimentation consists of all other behaviors.

Definition 1. Norm Violating and Compliant behaviors. *Let $n \subseteq \Sigma^*$ be a norm. The set of n-violating behaviors under regimentation, denoted as $Viol_n$, is the set of suffixes of n, i.e., $Viol_n = n.\Sigma^*$. The set of n-compliant behaviors under regimentation, denoted as K_n, is the complement of n-violating behaviors, i.e., $K_n = \Sigma^* \setminus Viol_n$.*

In our running example, I_uBB, I_uBBI_i, $I_uI_iW_t \in K_n$. It should be clear that the concepts of norm specification, norm violating, and norm compliant behaviors are defined independent of a plant $\mathcal{G}$. Moreover, the set of norm violating behaviors and the set of norm compliant behaviors depend on the form of norm enforcement that we consider, which is regimentation in this case. Note that K_n is prefix-closed, i.e., if $w.w' \in K_n$ then $w \in K_n$.

Since events that are involved in a system can be uncontrollable, it may not always be possible for the system supervisor to regiment a norm in order to prevent norm violating behaviors. For example, consider uncontrollable event $u \in \Sigma_u$ and suppose $u \in n$. If the system generates a behavior that starts with event u, then the system supervisor cannot regiment the norm specified by n since u is an uncontrollable event. Therefore, given a system we identify which norms can be regimented by the system supervisor. A norm is said to be regimentable on a system if the occurrences of uncontrollable events in the system directly after n-compliant behaviors are n-compliant as well.

Definition 2. Regimentability. *A norm specified by n is regimentable in $\mathcal{G}$ if $\overline{K_n}.\Sigma_u \cap L(\mathcal{G}) \subseteq \overline{K_n}$.*

Since K_n is prefix-closed, i.e., $\overline{K_n} = K_n$, norm n is regimentable if $K_n.\Sigma_u \cap L(\mathcal{G}) \subseteq K_n$. Note that every norm is regimentable when the system does not involve uncontrollable events, i.e., $\Sigma_u = \emptyset$. Also observe that the norm of our running example is *not* regimentable since $I_uI_iW_t \in K_n$, but $I_uI_iW_tW_m \notin K_n$. The non-regimentability of norms does not mean that bad behaviors cannot be prevented, it just states that not all good behaviors (which are also specified by norms) can be guaranteed if all bad behaviors are to be prevented. This is because, technically, the regimentability of a norm n is defined in terms of the good behaviors K_n. So, as we have seen, regimentability is, in some sense, a very demanding property. Then, given a norm n, one will generally be interested in the *largest subset* of good behaviors of K_n that can be allowed, if all bad behaviors are prevented. The following definition captures this.

Definition 3. Supremal Regimentability. *Let $\mathcal{G}$ be a multi-agent system and $n \subseteq \Sigma^*$ a norm such that $K_n \neq \emptyset$. The supremally regimentable n-compliant behavior in $\mathcal{G}$ is defined as $K_n\!\uparrow = \bigcup\limits_{K \in R(K_n)} K$ where $R(K_n) = \{K \subseteq K_n :$ $\overline{K}.\Sigma_u \cap L(\mathcal{G}) \subseteq \overline{K}\}$.*

That is, $K_n\!\uparrow$ represents the largest sublanguage of K_n that satisfies the regimentability condition (Definition 2). Clearly, $K_n\!\uparrow$ only includes good behaviors, but maybe not all: some have to be sacrificed so as to guarantee the norm. Obviously, if the norm is (perfectly) regimentable, then the supremal is the whole K_n. Importantly, the supremal for a given norm is unique.

Corollary 1. *For any norm $n \subseteq \Sigma^*$, we have that $K_n\!\uparrow$ is unique. Moreover, if n is regimentable, then $K_n\!\uparrow = K_n$.*

Next, we discuss the concrete mechanism used to regiment a multi-agent system so that violating behaviors are prevented. For this, we define a so-called *regimentation-based supervisor*, which intuitively speaking, controls a system by *enabling/disabling* controllable events at each execution moment.

Definition 4. Regiment-Based Supervisor. *A regiment-based supervisor for a multi-agent system $\mathcal{G}$ is a function of the form $V_r : L(\mathcal{G}) \mapsto \{\Sigma_e \mid \Sigma_e \in 2^{\Sigma}, \Sigma_u \subseteq \Sigma_e\}$, where $V_r(w)$ denotes the set of events that are enabled (i.e., allowed) next.*

Observe that supervisors must enable all uncontrollable events (i.e., $\Sigma_u \subseteq \Sigma_e$)—they cannot be disabled. However, a supervisor may decide to disable—block—some controllable events (i.e., events in Σ_c). The following definition captures what it means to supervise a multi-agent system.

Definition 5. Regimentation-Based Supervision. *Let $\mathcal{G}$ be a multi-agent system and V_r a regimentation-based supervisor for $\mathcal{G}$. The supervised language of $\mathcal{G}$ under V_r is defined as $L(V_r/\mathcal{G}) = \{w.\sigma \in L(\mathcal{G}) \mid w \in L(V_r/\mathcal{G}), \sigma \in V_r(w)\} \cup \{\epsilon\}$.*

That is, $L(V_r/\mathcal{G})$ represents all behaviors that the multi-agent system $\mathcal{G}$ may yield when supervised by V_r. Note that while recursively defined, the set $L(V_r/\mathcal{G})$ is well-defined. Importing results from classical controllability [21], this supervision is a sufficient mechanism for regimentability of norms (if at all possible).

Theorem 1. *Let $\mathcal{G}$ be a multi-agent system and $n \subseteq \Sigma^*$ a norm such that $K_n \neq \emptyset$. There exists a regiment-based norm supervisor V_r such that $L(V_r/\mathcal{G}) = \overline{K_n}$ iff norm n is regimentable in $\mathcal{G}$.*

Proof. We directly import the Controllability Theorem (CT) as presented in [13] (Page 145). According to CT, having a plant G that generates $L(G)$ and a nonempty $K \subseteq L(G)$, there exists a supervisor S such that $L(S/G) = \overline{K}$ iff $\overline{K}.\Sigma_u \cap L(G) \subseteq \overline{K}$. By considering our Definition 2 (Regimentability), we have Theorem 1.

For our running example, this theorem implies the non-existence of regimentation-based norm supervisor: norm $n = \Sigma^*.W_m$ is *not* (perfectly) regimentable. Indeed, any supervisor should disable controllable event I_i in state U so as to prevent a behavior involving non-controllable event W_m happening (thus producing a norm violating behavior). However, doing so, will inevitably exclude norm-compliant behaviors that choose W_t in state I. Nonetheless, the next proposition shows that for any norm and plant, regardless of its regimentability, there exists a regiment-based supervisor that guarantees the supremally regimentable n-compliant behavior.

Proposition 1. *Let $\mathcal{G}$ be a multi-agent system and $n \subseteq \Sigma^*$ a norm such that $K_n \neq \emptyset$. Then, there exists a regiment-based supervisor V_r^* such that $L(V_r^*/\mathcal{G}) = K_n\!\uparrow$.*

Proof. $K_n\!\uparrow$ satisfies the regimentability condition. The rest follows the proof of Theorem 1.

For our running example, this proposition ensures that there exists indeed a supervisor that can prevent all norm violating behaviors. Importantly, such a supervisor is *maximally permissive*: it is not possible to cater for more "good" behaviors without running the risk of violating some norm. An important result from SCT is that when both the plant and the specification are regular languages, and hence representable via finite automata (i.e., generators), the supervisor realizing the supremal realizable language can be finitely represented and in fact computed in polynomial time (w.r.t. the automata for the plant and specification) [26]. We can import such results as follows.

Proposition 2. *Let $\mathcal{G}$ be a multi-agent system and $n \subseteq \Sigma^*$ a norm for which there exists a generator $\mathcal{G}_n$ such that $L(\mathcal{G}_n) = n$. Suppose further that $K_n \neq \emptyset$. Then, a generator $\mathcal{R}$ such that $L(\mathcal{R}) = K_n\!\uparrow$ can be computed in polynomial time w.r.t. $\mathcal{G}$ and $\mathcal{G}_n$.*

Proof. Because norm specification n is regular and implemented with $\mathcal{G}_n$, languages $Viol_n$ and K_n are regular as well (and implementable with a generator that has one more state than $\mathcal{G}_n$). Since $\mathcal{G}$ is a generator, we can directly apply the results in [26] and the thesis follows.

We close by pointing out that besides leveraging on the solid theoretical foundations of SCT, the development above allows us to apply the existing tools for supervisor synthesis, such as TCT/STCT [27], GRAIL [23], DESUMA [24], and SUPREMICA [20], to automatically compute norm regimentation policies.

5   Sanction-Based Supervision

For many applications, norm regimentation is too restrictive, limiting the autonomy of agents. In such applications it is more desirable to allow agent to violate norms, but to compensate the violations with *sanctions*. In this section and without loss of generality, we assume a single sanction event s to keep the presentation simple. We also assume that the unique sanction event does not appear in the behavior of the plant and that it is added to (imposed on) the plant by the supervisor after any norm-violating event. Finally, for $w \in (\Sigma \cup \{s\})^*$ we use $\hat{w}$ to denote w from which all occurrences of s are removed, e.g., if $w = e_1 e_2 s e_3 s e_4 s$, we have $\hat{w} = e_1 e_2 e_3 e_4$. As before we assume a norm specification $n \subseteq \Sigma^*$ and interpret its elements as sequences of events that cause a violation. We also assume the set of violating behaviors as extensions of norms, i.e., $Viol_n = n.\Sigma^*$. Given a norm specification, we first define what it means to add sanctions after norm-violating event sequences in the norm specification.

Definition 6. Sanctioned Norm. *Let $n \subseteq \Sigma^*$ be a norm, s be the sanction event, and $w \in (\Sigma \cup \{s\})^*$. The set of the sanctioned event sequences from n, denoted as $San(n)$ and called sanctioned norm, is inductively defined as follows:*

- $\epsilon \in San(n)$; and
- *if $w \in San(n), w' \in \Sigma^*, \hat{w}.w' \in n$, and for all $w'' \sqsubset w'$ we have $\hat{w}.w'' \notin n$, then $w.w'.s \in San(n)$.*

This definition ensures that a single sanction event is added after each violation. For example, if e_1, $e_1 e_2 \in n$, then $e_1 s$, $e_1 s e_2 s \in San(n)$. Note that $n = \{\hat{w} \mid w \in San(n) \setminus \{\epsilon\}\}$. Next, we define the concept of *sanctioned behavior* which extends words in the sanctioned norm with events that do not cause any further norm violations.

Definition 7. Sanctioned behavior. *Let $San(n)$ be a sanctioned norm. The set of sanctioned behavior, denoted as $San^+(n)$, is any non-violating extension of sanctioned norm. Formally $San^+(n) = \{w.w' \mid w \in San(n), w' \in \Sigma^*, \forall w'' \sqsubseteq w' : \hat{w}.w'' \notin n\}$.*

Given a norm specification, the set of sanctioned behaviors is included in the set of norm-compliant behaviors.

Definition 8. Norm Compliant Behaviors. *Let $n \subseteq \Sigma^*$ be a norm and s be a sanction event. The set of n-compliant behaviors in presence of s, denoted as $K_n^s = (\Sigma^* \setminus Viol_n) \cup San^+(n)$, contains all non-violating and sanctioned behaviors.*

Note that omitting s from strings in $San^+(n)$ results in the set of n-violating behaviors. Formally, $Viol_n = \{\hat{w} : w \in San^+(n)\}$. Observe that K_n^s consists of not only non-violating behaviors but also violating and sanctioned behaviors[1]. Moreover, as one can observe, K_n^s is defined *independently* of any specific plant.

In order to relate sanction-based compliant behaviors with a plant in which the sanction event does not occur, we first enrich the plant with the sanction event s and an auxiliary event $\dot{s}$, interpreted as no-sanction imposed. The introduction of

---

[1] We highlight that do not take sanctions to be permissible *events*, but consider an already sanctioned *behavior* as a norm-compliant one.

these two events enables us to prevent all violating behaviors (i.e., extensions of the norm without sanctions) while allowing norm compliant behaviors (including sanctioned behaviors). The natural question is how to enrich a plant with these two events. For this we, define the notion of sanction policy and virtual plant. A *sanction policy* determines when a sanction event may be added (i.e., after which sequences of events). A sanction policy F is therefore represented as a set of words, i.e., $F \subseteq (\Sigma \cup \{s, \dot{s}\})^*$. Note that the words in F may contain different occurrences of s and $\dot{s}$. Also, F is defined independent of any norm or plant. Let $\hat{w}$ be the same as w except that all occurrences of s and $\dot{s}$ are removed. Note that $\hat{w}$ is used before to remove all occurrences of s; we have to extend this operation here to remove $\dot{s}$ as well. We now define a virtual plant as a plant under specific sanction policy F by introducing states in the original plant where s and $\dot{s}$ are the only available events.

Definition 9. Virtual Plant. *A plant $\mathcal{G}$ under the sanctioning policy F, denoted by $F(\mathcal{G})$ and called virtual plant, generates the following behaviors:*

$$L(F(\mathcal{G})) = \{w \in L(\mathcal{G}) \mid \forall w' \sqsubseteq w \; : \; w' \notin F\} \cup$$
$$\{w.s.w', w.\dot{s}.w' \mid w, w' \in (\Sigma \cup \{s, \dot{s}\})^*, \hat{w}.w' \in L(\mathcal{G}), w \in F\}.$$

For our running example, one possible sanction policy is $F = \{I_u I_i W_m\}$. The following graph represents the virtual plant $F(\mathcal{G})$ that extends the original plant $\mathcal{G}$.

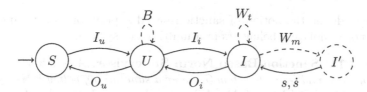

The introduction of virtual plant enables us to reduce the notion of *sanctioning* into *regimentation* by assuming s and $\dot{s}$ as the *only controllable events* in the plant under a given sanction policy. A supervisor can then control the plant under a given sanction policy by enabling either s or $\dot{s}$, but not both. As $\dot{s}$ is an auxiliary event (interpreted as no-sanction is imposed), we can ignore this event in the plant's behaviors. The set of behaviors of a virtual plant $F(\mathcal{G})$ from which all occurrences of the auxiliary event $\dot{s}$ are removed will be denoted as $L_s^F(\mathcal{G})$. It is crucial to note that this set includes all behaviors of the original plant as well as some new behaviors in which s occurs.

Given a plant $\mathcal{G}$ and a sanctioning policy F, not all norms are sanctionable. This is mainly due to presence of uncontrollable events and their potential to result in violating behaviors. The following definition circumscribes the class of sanctionable norms under a specific sanctioning policy.

Definition 10. Sanctionability. *A norm specified by n is sanctionable in $\mathcal{G}$ under sanctioning policy F, if $\overline{K_n^s}.\Sigma_u \cap L_s^F(\mathcal{G}) \subseteq \overline{K_n^s}$.*

Note that we are considering a norm to be sanctionable under a sanction policy. Hence, a norm may be sanctionable in a plant under a sanction policy F but not under $F' \neq F$. In other words, we dismiss the problem of finding/constructing an appropriate sanction policy that guarantees the sanctionability of a norm in a plant. The following proposition highlights that if the sanctioning policy F imposes s or $\dot{s}$ after any event, any norm will be sanctionable.

Proposition 3. Dictatorial Sanctioning Policy. *Any non-empty norm (specified by) n is sanctionable in plant $\mathcal{G}$ under sanctioning policy $F = \Sigma^*$.*

Proof. In this case, F includes all possible words $w \in \Sigma^*$. In other words, (under F) sanction operation s is imposed after any arbitrary event. Therefore, the sanctionability condition in Definition 10 always holds. Hence, for any nonempty $n \subseteq \Sigma^*$, we have that $\overline{K}_n^s . \Sigma_u \cap L_s^F(\mathcal{G}) \subseteq \overline{K}_n^s$.

The next proposition states that no non-empty norm will be sanctionable if the sanctioning policy never imposes the sanction event.

Proposition 4. Impotential Sanctioning Policy. *Any norm specified by a non-empty n is sanctionable in plant $\mathcal{G}$ under sanctioning policy $F = \emptyset$.*

Proof. In this case, F includes no word $w \in \Sigma^*$. In other words, sanction operation s can be imposed after no event. Therefore, the sanctionability condition in Definition 10 never holds. I.e. for no non-empty $n \subseteq \Sigma^*$, we have that $\overline{K}_n^s . \Sigma_u \cap L_s^F(\mathcal{G}) \subseteq \overline{K}_n^s$.

We now define the notion of sanction-based supervisor as a means of suppressing norm violating behaviors in a multi-agent system.

Definition 11. Sanction-Based Norm Supervisor. *A sanction-based norm supervisor for a multi-agent system $\mathcal{G}$ under a sanctioning policy F, is a function of the form $V_s : L(F(\mathcal{G})) \mapsto \{ \Sigma , \{s\} , \{\dot{s}\} \}$, where $V_s(w)$ denotes the set of events that are enabled next.*

Note that the set of events that a sanction-based norm supervisor enables includes all plant events (interpreted as non-controllable events) with either the controllable event s or the controllable event $\dot{s}$. This type of supervisor allows violating behaviors to take place but may impose the sanction event in order to punish violations.

Definition 12. Sanction-Based Supervisor. *Let $\mathcal{G}$ be a multi-agent system, F a sanctioning policy, and V_s a sanction-based norm supervisor for $\mathcal{G}$ under F. The sanctioned language of $\mathcal{G}$ under V_r is defined as $L(V_s/\mathcal{G}) = \{w.\sigma \mid w.\sigma \in L(F(\mathcal{G})), w \in L(V_s/\mathcal{G}), \sigma \in V_s(w)\} \cup \{\epsilon\}$.*

We emphasize that while our formerly introduced regiment-based norm supervisor uses the "real" behavior of the multi-agent system, the sanction-based norm supervisor considers a specific multi-agent behavior that is "virtually" extended under a given sanctioning policy. This is mainly because after (virtually) extending the multi-agent system under a policy, potential behaviors may include sanction events while they are not (really) events generated by the plant.

Theorem 2. *Let $\mathcal{G}$ be a multi-agent system, F a sanctioning policy, and $n \subseteq \Sigma^*$ be a norm such that $K_n^s \neq \emptyset$. Then, there exists a sanction-based norm supervisor V_s such that $L(V_s/\mathcal{G}) = \overline{K_n^s}$ iff norm n is sanctionable in $\mathcal{G}$ under F.*

Proof. The line of proof is analogous to the proof of Theorem 1 if we just replace $L(\mathcal{G})$ by the virtually extended behavior $L(F(\mathcal{G}))$ under sanctioning policy F.

In this sanction-based interpretation of supervision, n is enforceable when n-violating behavior can be sanctioned. Note that enforcing a norm via sanctions allows "bad" behaviors (of the multi-agent system) to take place after which sanction will incur. In our running example, any behavior that ends with W_m is a norm violating behavior. Using a sanctioning policy $F = \{\Sigma^*.W_m\}$, this theorem shows the existence of a sanction-based supervisor that imposes sanctions after any occurrence of W_m. It is observable that such a sanctioning mechanism does not prevent any norm-compliant behavior, e.g., watching a tutorial is now possible for the student (without paying any sanction). Given a plant, a norm may be not sanctionable under a specific sanction policy. Here, we define the concept of *supremal sanctionability* as the largest set of sanctionable behaviors (under a given sanction policy) in a plant.

Definition 13. Supremal Sanctionability. *Let $\mathcal{G}$ be a multi-agent system, $n \subseteq \Sigma^*$ a norm such that $K_n^s \neq \emptyset$, and F a sanctioning policy. The supremally sanctionable n-compliant behavior in $\mathcal{G}$ under F, denoted $K_n^{F,s\uparrow}$, is defined as $K_n^{F,s\uparrow} = \bigcup_{K \in R(K_n^s)} K$, where $R(K_n^s) = \{K \subseteq K_n^s : \overline{K}.\Sigma_u \cap L_s^F(\mathcal{G}) \subseteq \overline{K}\}$.*

That is, $K_n^{F,s\uparrow}$ represents the largest sublanguage of K_n^s that satisfies the sanctionability condition (Definition 10). Next, we point out that, at the technical level, we have basically transformed a norm enforcement via sanctions problem into a norm regimentation task, albeit in a modified multi-agent system plant. Doing so allows us to directly import Proposition 2 to the sanction-based framework.

Proposition 5. *Let $\mathcal{G}$ be a multi-agent system, F a sanction policy for which there exists a generator $\mathcal{G}_F$ such that $L(\mathcal{G}_F) = F$, and $n \subseteq \Sigma^*$ a norm for which there exists a generator $\mathcal{G}_n$ such that $L(\mathcal{G}_n) = n$. Suppose further that $K_n^s \neq \emptyset$. Then, a generator $\mathcal{R}$ such that $L(\mathcal{R}) = K_n^{F,s\uparrow}$ can be computed in polynomial time w.r.t. $\mathcal{G}$, $\mathcal{G}_F$ and $\mathcal{G}_n$.*

Proof. Because norm specification n is regular and implemented with $\mathcal{G}_n$, sets $Viol_n^s$ and K_n^s are regular as well. Since F is regular and generated by $\mathcal{G}_F$, we can once again directly apply the results in [26] and the thesis follows.

6   Reparation-Based Supervision

In this section, we consider some system events as "repairing" events, in the sense that any violating behavior followed by such events is considered as non-violating behavior. In our running example, one may consider watching a tutorial as repairing the violation of watching a movie. In addition to our assumption that the set of events consists of disjoint sets of controllable Σ_c and uncontrollable events Σ_u, we introduce an orthogonal partitioning over the set of events which makes distinction between reparation events Σ_p and non-reparation events Σ_{np}, i.e., $\Sigma = \Sigma_p \cup \Sigma_{np}$. For simplicity and without loss of generality, we assume $\Sigma_p = \{p\}$. Also, we only consider *immediate* reparation; we do not allow distant reparation. Allowing multiple (non-reparation) events between a violating behavior and its repair calls for a method that clarifies how to deal with multiple violations and their reparation priorities. Moreover, the specification of norms will be constrained to use only non-reparation events from Σ_{np}.

Definition 14. Norm Violating and Compliant behaviors. *Let $n \subseteq \Sigma_{np}^*$ be a norm and p be a repair event. The set of n-violating behaviors in presence of p is $Viol_n^p = n.\Sigma_{np}.\Sigma^*$, and the set of n-compliant behavior in presence of p is $K_n^p = \Sigma^* \setminus Viol_n^p$.*

Note that this view internalizes the reparation of norm violating behavior. Hence, we do not need any external set of sanction operations (as it was the case in Definition 8).

Definition 15. Repairability. *A norm specified by n is repairable in $\mathcal{G}$ with event p if $\overline{K_n^p}.\Sigma_u \cap L(\mathcal{G}) \subseteq \overline{K_n^p}$.*

In our running university example, norm $n = \Sigma^*.W_m$ is not repairable. This is because after some norm-compliant behaviors in $\overline{K_n^p}$, the occurrence of uncontrollable event W_m results in norm-violating behaviors (that are obviously not in $\overline{K_n^p}$). We later present a brief abstract example in which the norm is repairable.

We now define the notion of reparation-based supervisor as a mean of enabling the multi-agent system to repair possible violating behaviors.

Definition 16. Reparation-Based Norm Supervisor. *A reparation-based supervisor for a multi-agent system $\mathcal{G}$ is a function of the form $V_p : L(\mathcal{G}) \mapsto \{\Sigma_e \mid \Sigma_e \in 2^\Sigma, \Sigma_u \subseteq \Sigma_e\}$, where $V_p(w)$ denotes the set of events that are enabled (i.e., allowed) next.*

This type of supervisor can now allow violating behaviors that are immediately followed by a repair event, while regimenting all other violating behaviors.

Definition 17. Reparation-Based Supervision. *Let $\mathcal{G}$ be a multi-agent system, p be the repair event, and V_p a reparation-based norm supervisor for $\mathcal{G}$. The supervision of $\mathcal{G}$ by V_p obtains a multi-agent system, denoted as $V_p/\mathcal{G}$, that generates behaviors specified as $L(V_p/\mathcal{G}) = \{\epsilon\} \cup \{w.\sigma.p \in L(\mathcal{G}) \mid w \in L(V_p/\mathcal{G}), w.\sigma \in n\} \cup \{w.\sigma \in L(\mathcal{G}) \mid w \in L(V_p/\mathcal{G}), w.\sigma \notin n\}$.*

In reparation-based norm supervision, n is enforceable when violating behaviors that can not be immediately repaired are avoided. I.e., enforcing a norm via this approach only sees a behavior n-violating if after the occurrence of the norm, it is not immediately repaired. As shown in Sect. 4, in order to avoid violating behaviors, the regiment-based supervision of a plant may result in a subset of norm-compliant behavior by disallowing all the events that may result in violating behavior. In comparison, the reparation-based supervisor only disallows the events after which there is no reparation event in the plant. For instance, for $\Sigma = \{a, b, c, d, e, p\}$, $\Sigma_u = \{c\}$, $\Sigma_p = \{p\}$, and $n = \{abcd\}$, applying the regiment-based vision after a sequence of events $w = a$ results in loosing n-compliant behavior $abce$ in the following plant while the reparation-based approach allows it to take place. Although allowing b may result in n-violating behavior $abcd$, reparation is available afterwards.

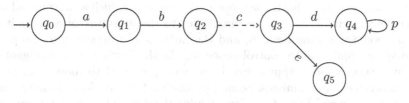

Theorem 3. *Let $\mathcal{G}$ be a multi-agent system, p be the repair event, and $n \subseteq \Sigma^*$ be a norm such that $K_n^p \neq \emptyset$. There exists a reparation-based norm supervisor V_p such that $L(V_p/\mathcal{G}) = \overline{K_n^p}$ iff norm n is repairable in $\mathcal{G}$.*

Proof. The line of proof is analogous to the proof of Theorem 1 if we just replace $L(\mathcal{G})$ by $L(V_p/\mathcal{G})$.

In our running example, any behavior that ends with W_m is a norm violating behavior. As the reparation-based supervisor is designed to allow norm-violating behaviors to take place, it does not prevent the event of watching a movie if this event is immediately followed by the repair event, which is in this case watching a tutorial W_t. The above theorem suggests the existence of a repair-based supervisor that ensures violations are either not take place or they are immediately followed by a repair event. It is observable that a repair-based supervisor is similar with a regimentation-based supervisor with a one-step look ahead function.

In a specific plant, a norm may be not repairable if it does not pass the repairability condition in Definition 15. Here, we define the concept of *supremal repairability* as the largest set of repairable behaviors in a plant.

Definition 18. Supremal Repairability. *Let $\mathcal{G}$ be a multi-agent system, $n \subseteq \Sigma^*$ a norm such that $K_n^p \neq \emptyset$, and p the repairing event. The supremally repairable n-compliant behavior in $\mathcal{G}$ with p, denoted $K_n^{p\uparrow}$, is defined as $K_n^{p\uparrow} = \bigcup_{K \in R(K_n^p)} K$ where $R(K_n^p) = \{K \subseteq K_n^p : \overline{K}.\Sigma_u \cap L(\mathcal{G}) \subseteq \overline{K}\}$.*

That is, $K_n^{p\uparrow}$ represents the largest sublanguage of K_n^p that satisfies the repairability condition (Definition 15). The following result mirrors that in Propositions 2 and 5 for the case of repairability.

Proposition 6. *Let $\mathcal{G}$ be a multi-agent system, p a repair event, and $n \subseteq \Sigma^*$ a norm for which there exists a generator $\mathcal{G}_n$ such that $L(\mathcal{G}_n) = n$. Suppose further that $K_n^p \neq \emptyset$. Then, a generator $\mathcal{R}$ such that $L(\mathcal{R}) = K_n^{p\uparrow}$ can be computed in polynomial time w.r.t. $\mathcal{G}$ and $\mathcal{G}_n$.*

7 Related Work

Our proposal contributes to the literature on normative multi-agent systems by re-purposing models and results from SCT to provide a formal, implementable and tractable semantics for the key normative concepts, such as norms and norm enforcement mechanisms. It also contributes to the literature of SCT as it provides a novel application domain, and the notions of sanctioning and repairing that may be applicable to control processes. In the normative multi-agent systems literature, various approaches have been proposed to model norms and norm enforcement mechanisms. Some approaches focus on logical characterization of normative multi-agents systems while others aim at designing frameworks to develop normative multi-agent systems. For example, [1] uses a linear-time temporal logic to represent norms and system behaviors. In such work, the idea of norm enforcement, which is enriched with lookahead possibilities, is characterized as decision problems with respect to specific classes of norms. Similar to our regiment-based supervisor function, [1] uses a guard function, that enables/disables options that (could) violate norms after a system history. However, the authors consider norm monitors to be imperfect while we assume that our supervisors have perfect observability over the behavior of the MAS. They also do not consider sanction- and repair-based norm enforcement mechanisms.

The idea of sanction-based enforcement mechanisms has been studied in several works, e.g., [3,12,14]. There, multi-agent systems are semantically modeled as transitions systems, where traces are interpretred as system behaviors. The enforcement of norms by means of sanctions is realized by identifying and sanctioning violating behaviors. This is done by modifying the valuation of states that occur in the violating behaviors. Our sanction-based approach is closely related except that in our approach sanctioning events are added to behaviors which are defined as event sequences.

Other approaches concern the development of normative multi-agent systems. For example, [16,18] takes into account the organizational structure of multi-agent systems in order to develop middle-wares for normative multi-agent organizations/institutions while we dismiss agent hierarchies and see a MAS as a plant that generates strings of discrete events. Moreover, [4] makes a distinction between regulative (deontic) and substantive (constitutive) norms while we define norms to be any arbitrary sub-language of event strings. Finally, [2] builds on the idea of norm enforcement and proposes a programming approach to develop norm-aware agents. These agents can deliberate on enforceable norms to decide whether they follow or violate the norms.

Our work clearly draws from (and hence is closely related to) some approaches in the DESs, e.g., [13], and SCT, e.g., [21,22]. We build on the *controllability condition* in [13] to introduce our three types of norm enforcement, namely, regimentation-, sanction-, and repair-based enforcement. However, we extend the classic concept of supervisor in DESs as a *violation precluding mechanism* by considering supervisors that allow violations to take place but are also able to impose sanction operations. This approach, i.e., allowing violations to occur, leads to a toolbox of norm enforcement mechanisms that are applicable in contexts that call for higher level of agent autonomy. Moreover, we introduce a normative dimension into reasoning about behavior of DESs. One noticeable contribution that considers decentralized control in multi-agent systems using SCT is [6] which mainly focuses on reformulating the results of SCT in terms of model checking problems in an epistemic temporal logic.

We would like to emphasize that our work differs from related but distinguishable approaches proposed in [7,28]. In our approach, we focus on coordination of a multi-agent systems, using the concept of norm-supervisors, in order to avoid/suppress some undesired but system-independent norm-violating behaviors. In contrast, [7,28] shows that some desired properties such as non-blocking (in a class of resource allocation systems) can be achieved using a supervisor that controls the plant's behavior. Although this approach might be similar to our regiment-based norm supervising mechanism, it should be emphasized that our norms are plant-independent. Hence, they do not necessarily reflect properties that are "good" in a plant, but represent "good" behaviors regardless of any plant.

8   Conclusion and Future Work

This paper presents a formal framework rooted in Supervisory Control Theory (SCT) *and* normative multi-agent systems. We show that three well-known types of norm enforcement mechanisms, namely, regimentation-, sanction-, and repair-based enforcement, can be modeled as special supervisor from SCT. Importing the controllability theorem from SCT, we prove the existence of supervisors that can either prevent, sanction or repair violating behaviors in a given multi-agent system. In addition to providing a semantics for norm and norm enforcement in formal languages, this work supports the direct use of available tools for SCT, such as TCT/STCT [27] or SUPREMICA [20] to synthesize supervisors. We intend to run experiments by developing norm-based supervisory systems using these tools. The fact is that by restricting to generator-based "regular" systems and properties, which are still fairly expressive, implementing SCT-based normative systems becomes amenable for computation (e.g., can be realized via the existing tools mentioned above) [9]. Hence, the possibility of automatically synthesizing SCT-based norm enforcement mechanisms that can be used for on-line norm monitoring/enforcement in multi-agent systems becomes a feasible.

Regarding the practicality of our approach we emphasize that, since we base our norm specification on given sequences of events, our presented norm enforcement mechanisms are applicable in domains where traces of violating behaviors are accessible (e.g., using data-oriented behavior models). We believe that such a set can be collected in big data projects, for example, by using data mining to extract and categorize instances of event sequences that are (un)desirable in a specific multi-agent system.

As future research, one can relax the full observability assumption and study the enforcement of norms under partial observability. In this line, dynamics of supervisor's belief-level can be incorporated by taking into account multiple belief worlds that are linked using *epistemic* event. An alternative approach would be to use a network of supervisors with local observability. Then having a class of communication events can enable them to collectively supervise the plant. Another possible extension is to relax the restriction on *immediate* reparations in reparation-based supervising mechanisms.

In this work, we merely focused on individual agents and reasoned about the normative behavior of a multi-agent plant in which supervisors can bring about desired behaviors by means of regimentation, sanctioning, or reparation mechanisms that controls individuals. The transition to collective actions, e.g. using concurrent structures, is left for future work. Such an extension may result in the introduction of mechanisms that take into account group potentials (e.g., for making collusion) and possible semantics of normative concepts in relation to collective actions.

Another possible extension would be to formalize "hybrid" supervisors. For instance, a supervisor that sanctions violating behaviors for a certain number of times, e.g., just once, and then starts preventing any further violations. In this case we are sensitive to sequence (and number) of imposed sanction operations. Roughly speaking, when the plant generates violating behaviors for which we already sanctioned it before, its behavior may trigger a meta-norm that allows the supervisor to use regiment-based supervision. Such a mixed supervisor may find application in some domains that can tolerate norm-violating behavior only to a given threshold, e.g., in safety-critical computer/industrial systems [11,25].

References

1. Alechina, N., Bulling, N., Dastani, M., Logan, B.: Practical run-time norm enforcement with bounded lookahead. In: Proceeding of the 2015 International Conference on Autonomous Agents and Multiagent Systems, pp. 443–451 (2015)
2. Alechina, N., Dastani, M., Logan, B.: Programming norm-aware agents. In: Proceeding of the 11th International Conference on Autonomous Agents and Multiagent Systems, vol. 2, pp. 1057–1064 (2012)
3. Alechina, N., Dastani, M., Logan, B.: Reasoning about normative update. In: Proceeding of the Twenty-Third International Joint Conference on Artificial Intelligence, pp. 20–26 (2013)

4. Alvarez-Napagao, S., Aldewereld, H., Vázquez-Salceda, J., Dignum, F.: Normative monitoring: semantics and implementation. In: De Vos, M., Fornara, N., Pitt, J.V., Vouros, G. (eds.) COIN -2010. LNCS, vol. 6541, pp. 321–336. Springer, Heidelberg (2011). doi:10.1007/978-3-642-21268-0_18
5. Andrighetto, G., Governatori, G., Noriega, P., van der Torre, L.W.: Normative Multi-Agent Systems, vol. 4. Schloss Dagstuhl-Leibniz-Zentrum fuer Informatik, Germany (2013)
6. Aucher, G.: Supervisory control theory in epistemic temporal logic. In: International conference on Autonomous Agents and Multi-Agent Systems, pp. 333–340 (2014)
7. Barkaoui, K., Chaoui, A., Zouari, B.: Supervisory control of discrete event systems based on structure theory of petri nets. In: 1997 IEEE International Conference on Systems, Man, and Cybernetics, 1997 Computational Cybernetics and Simulation, vol. 4, pp. 3750–3755. IEEE (1997)
8. Bicchieri, C.: The Grammar of Society: The Nature and Dynamics of Social Norms. Cambridge University Press, New York (2005)
9. Blondel, V.D., Tsitsiklis, J.N.: A survey of computational complexity results in systems and control. Automatica **36**(9), 1249–1274 (2000)
10. Boella, G., van der Torre, L.W.: Regulative and constitutive norms in normative multiagent systems. KR **4**, 255–265 (2004)
11. Bowen, J., Stavridou, V.: Safety-critical systems, formal methods and standards. Softw. Eng. J. **8**(4), 189–209 (1993)
12. Bulling, N., Dastani, M.: Norm-based mechanism design. Artif. Intell. **239**, 97–142 (2016)
13. Cassandras, C.G., Lafortune, S.: Introduction to Discrete Event Systems. Springer Science & Business Media, US (2009)
14. Dastani, M., Grossi, D., Meyer, J.C.: A logic for normative multi-agent programs. J. Log. Comput. **23**(2), 335–354 (2013)
15. Dastani, M., Grossi, D., Meyer, J.-J.C., Tinnemeier, N.: Normative multi-agent programs and their logics. In: Meyer, J.-J.C., Broersen, J. (eds.) KRAMAS 2008. LNCS, vol. 5605, pp. 16–31. Springer, Heidelberg (2009). doi:10.1007/978-3-642-05301-6_2
16. Esteva, M., Rosell, B., Rodríguez-Aguilar, J.A., Arcos, J.L.: AMELI: an agent-based middleware for electronic institutions. In: 3rd International Joint Conference on Autonomous Agents and Multiagent Systems, pp. 236–243 (2004)
17. Hopcroft, J.E., Ullman, J.D.: Introduction to Automata Theory Languages and Computation. Addison-Wesley, Reading (1979)
18. Hübner, J.F., Sichman, J.S., Boissier, O.: $S - \mathcal{M}oise^+$: A middleware for developing organised multi-agent systems. In: Boissier, O., Padget, J., Dignum, V., Lindemann, G., Matson, E., Ossowski, S., Sichman, J.S., Vázquez-Salceda, J. (eds.) AAMAS 2005. LNCS, vol. 3913, pp. 64–77. Springer, Heidelberg (2006). doi:10.1007/11775331_5
19. y López, F.L., Luck, M.: Modelling norms for autonomous agents. In: 4th Mexican International Conference on Computer Science (ENC 2003), 8–12 September 2003, Apizaco, Mexico, pp. 238–245 (2003)
20. Åkesson, K., Fabian, M., Flordal, H., Vahidi, A.: Supremica - a tool for verification and synthesis of discrete event supervisors. In: Proceeding of the 11th Mediterranean Conference on Control and Automation (2003)
21. Ramadge, P.J., Wonham, W.M.: Supervisory control of a class of discrete event processes. SIAM J. Control Optim. **25**(1), 206–230 (1987)

22. Ramadge, P.J., Wonham, W.M.: The control of discrete event systems. Proc. IEEE **77**(1), 81–98 (1989)
23. Reiser, C., da Cunha, A., Cury, J.: The environment GRAIL for supervisory control of discrete event systems. In: Proceeding of 8th International Workshop on Discrete Event Systems, pp. 390–391, July 2006
24. Ricker, L., Lafortune, S., Gene, S.: DESUMA: A tool integrating GIDDES and UMDES. In: Proceeding of 8th International Workshop on Discrete Event Systems, pp. 392–393 (2006)
25. Storey, N.R.: Safety Critical Computer Systems. Addison-Wesley Longman Publishing Co Inc., Reading (1996)
26. Wonham, W.M., Ramadge, P.J.: On the supremal controllable sublanguage of a given language. SIAM J. Control Optim. **25**(3), 637–659 (1987)
27. Zhang, Z., Wonham, W.M.: STCT: An efficient algorithm for supervisory control design. In: Symposium on Supervisory Control of Discrete Event Systems, pp. 249–6399 (2001)
28. Zouari, B., Barkaoui, K.: Parameterized supervisor synthesis for a modular class of discrete event systems. In: Proceeding of the IEEE International Conference on Systems, Man & Cybernetics, 5–8 October 2003, Washington, D.C, USA, pp. 1874–1879 (2003)

Formal Models of Conflicting Social Influence

Truls Pedersen and Marija Slavkovik[✉]

University of Bergen, Bergen, Norway
{Truls.Pedersen,Marija.Slavkovik}@uib.no

Abstract. Social influence is the process in which an agent is under pressure to form her opinion on an issue based on the opinions expresses by her peers. An obvious reaction to social influence is to change ones opinions to conform to the pressure. The study of formal models of social influence has been drawing attention in the literature. A comparatively under-explored aspect of social influence is its role as an instrument of social network change. Agents with an eclectic milieu of peers might find themselves under conflicting social pressures. In this case to conform to social influence by changing one's beliefs is no longer an option and the agent may seek to distance herself from some of her peers to relieve the pressure. We build a formal model of social influence that allows us to study social influence as a source of conflict and an instrument of network change. Within our framework different models of social influence can be defined but also compared to each other.

1 Introduction

Consider a society of individuals that perpetually expresses their opinions on various issues. Who "follows" whose expressed opinions in this society is described by a network and everyone in this society knows who "follows" who. To "follow" is taken as an indication of interest in the opinion being expressed. How do individuals in such a society influence each-other's opinions and behaviour is a question that has traditionally been studied by researchers in social science and humanities [2,7,8,11,17,23].

Recently the problem of social influence has also drawn the attention of researchers in artificial intelligence and multi-agent systems. The works [3,5,6,10,16], for example, are making important contributions towards advancing the state of the art in social influence research. The motivation for this development can easily be found in the increased distributivity of computation and the ubiquity of social network on-line services as a medium for commerce and broadcasting.

Social influence plays a substantial role in several phenomena that occur in social networks. In [5,6,16] it is studied how social influence is affecting the opinions and beliefs of the agents in the network. In [3] an epistemic dimension of influence is introduced to model the limitations of agents to have a complete knowledge of who "follows" whose opinions in a network. In [9] the focus is on models of strategic reasoning in situations of social influence.

© Springer International Publishing AG 2017
B. An et al. (Eds.): PRIMA 2017, LNAI 10621, pp. 349–365, 2017.
https://doi.org/10.1007/978-3-319-69131-2_21

Studies such as [3,5,6,9,16] use logic based models of social influence which allow for agent based reasoning to be analysed in a social network setting. In all of these works, social networks are static and it is the private and public opinions of the networked agents that change. It is also not considered that social influences can be conflicting.

Assume that you have a group of friends that are convinced that climate change is a hoax. You also have another equally dear to you group of friends that are climate change researchers devoted to slowing down climate change. It is quite clear that it would not be comfortable to invite both of these groups to the same dinner party. You would be under the pressure to choose an opinion to support and even if you resist to do so you have to be very careful never to post social media content that supports either of these climate positions in order not to offend some of your friends. Sooner or later you would however be pushed to make a choice. To avoid the conflict you would necessarily have to stop your relations with at least one of the groups. The social network can no longer be taken as static - opinions can change who "you are friends with".

There are three proposed logic-based models of social influence which can be encountered in the literature, two of which such that a conflicting social influence cannot be exerted on an agent. An agent can either be under social influenced to adopt an opinion about an issue or not. However, in these models it cannot happen that an agent is both influenced to adopt opinion φ and an opinion $\neg\varphi$ at the same time. Although the threshold model introduced in [3] does allow for a conflicting influence to occur, this is not explicitly considered as a situation of interest. We find that conflicting social influence can occur and it needs to be adequately modelled. Our first contribution is to propose social influence models that allow for conflicts to be represented.

In particular, we introduce a new model of influence based on a well known concept in social network analysis called "Simmelian tie", introduced by Krackhardt in [14]. While all existing logic-based social influence models look only to the adjacent agents to determine existence of social influence, our Simmelian model also takes into account relations among those adjacent agents. Our approach to model social influence allows for different models to be directly compared with each-other.

Schelling, in his seminal work [23], studied how individual members of two groups distribute themselves in neighbourhoods. Our agents resolve conflicts in influence by removing themselves from a neighbourhood. Similarly to Schelling's work, we are interested in studying what is the end effect of this removal of links in the social network. Ours is preliminary work in which we set the stage for a dynamic social network analysis of social influence. We are able to identify a property of social influence models that identifies whether conditions exist for agents to segregate themselves into like-minded neighbourhoods.

Our paper is structured as follows. In Sect. 2 we discuss related work. In Sect. 3 we give the basic definitions of concepts we use in Sect. 4 where we define different models of social influence and compare them. In Sect. 5 we consider the problem of conflicting social influence and detecting its existence. Section 6 is concerned with possible actions that resolve conflicts. Having observed that a conflict of social influence can be seen as a source of instability in a social network we build a temporal logic framework in which one can study the evolution of social network in reaction to conflict resolution in Sect. 7. Lastly, we outline our contributions, conclusions and directions for future work in Sect. 8.

2   Related Work

In mass-communication studies, it has been theorised that people care more about not being isolated by their peers than they care about being heard and being right. Thus it is a frequent occurrence that people progressively do not voice their opinion as to not appear in contradiction to what is public opinion, a phenomenon known as the *spiral of silence* [18]. A related phenomenon is the so called *pluralistic ignorance* [19], which refers to people having wrong beliefs about the beliefs of other people.

Recognising the relevance of understanding the information dynamics, logic-based models of social influence have been proposed in the literature. In [5, 6, 16] we find two types of influence, so called *strong influence* and *weak influence*. These strong and weak influence models are simplistic but they already capture the essence of social influence. We give their definitions.

An agent is *strongly influenced* to believe φ when that agent has at least one neighbour and all of her neighbours believe φ. An agent is *weakly influenced* to believe φ when some of her neighbours, and she has at least one, believe φ and none of her neighbours believe $\neg\varphi$. It can be observed that if an agent is strongly influenced to adopt φ, then she is also weakly influenced to adopt φ, but the implication in the other direction does not hold.

The definitions of strong influence and weak influence are such that a conflict of influence cannot occur. In [3], a third model of so called *threshold social influence* is considered. According to this model, an agent is influenced to adopt the opinion φ if a given proportion $\theta \in [0, 1]$ of his neighbours has stated that they support the opinion φ. In the threshold model, conflicting social influences can occur when $\theta < 0.5$. The strong social influence model is a threshold model for $\theta = 1$, assuming that the network is such that every agent has at least one neighbour.

We find a very interesting concept of Simmelian ties introduced by [14]. Krackhardt defines a *Simmelian tie* to be the relation between two agents that are both connected to at least one more agent, *i.e.*, a connection in a clique or more precisely, a *triad*. Krackardt argued that the formation of a clique funda-mentally restricts a member's options in terms of their public behaviour since once a triad is formed the group develops norms to which each member must conform to stay part of that group. Thus membership in certain cliques restricts how individuals can act in public. The more cliques an agent is part off, to more norms that agent would have to conform. Krackard writes about behaviour in general but his analysis applies also to expressed opinions. While the strong influence, weak influence, and threshold influence models "count" how many of the neighbours support an issue, Krackhard's Simmelian ties are more qualitative, in the sense that they take a bit broader view of a position an agent has within a social network.

Krackhardt [14] defines group norms as a set S_i of permissible behaviours in a group. An agent that is a member of n different cliques has at her disposal only as permissible behaviour the norms $\bigcap_i S_i$, of course to the extent that norm-bound behaviours are visible to members of all involved groups. Krackhardt, however does not identify the case when $\bigcap_i S_i = \emptyset$. The case of $\bigcap_i S_i = \emptyset$, namely when the agent is under equally strong but conflicting influences, we believe, is precisely the case when expressed influences shape the social network, which is opposite to what happens when social influence that occurs due to the social network structure shapes agent's beliefs.

3   Preliminaries

Our goal is to formalise and analyse the phenomenon of *conflicting social influence*. We intuitively understand social influence to be the pressure on an agent to not publicly express a truth judgement on an issue. We are here not concerned with the private beliefs of that agent, or any of the agents in the network.

We define N to be a finite, non-empty set of unique agent identifiers. Further we have a finite, non-empty set $\mathcal{I}$ of relevant issues represented as well formed propositional logic formulas. These are the issues for which agents my consider distancing themselves from their peers when a conflict of opinions occur. We use $\mathcal{I}^+$ to denote the set of non-negated formulas in $\mathcal{I}$, representing positive truth-value judgements to the issues. We require $\mathcal{I}^- = \{\neg\varphi | \varphi \in \mathcal{I}^+\}$, representing negative truth-value judgements to the issues, with $\mathcal{I}^+ \cap \mathcal{I}^- = \emptyset$ and $\mathcal{I}^+ \cup \mathcal{I}^- = \mathcal{I}$. We say the issues are binary, by which we mean that they come in pro/contra-pairs. We use $\sim\varphi$ to be $\neg\varphi$ if $\varphi \in \mathcal{I}^+$ and $\sim\varphi$ to be φ' when $\varphi = \neg\varphi'$ otherwise.

We model the publicly expressed judgements, or opinions, by a *support function*. The support function is a function that associates an opinion with the set of agents who have supported it. An agent cannot support two contradictory opinions simultaneously. We assume that the agents are always consistent in their statements, *i.e.*, the opinions they say they support are a consistent set of formulas.

Definition 1 (Support function). *Given a set of agents N and relevant issues $\mathcal{I}$, a support function* pro $: \mathcal{I} \to 2^N$ *maps every relevant issue to the set of agents which publicly support it. We require that* pro$(\varphi) \cap$ pro$(\sim \varphi) = \emptyset$. *For any $S \subset \mathcal{I}$, $\varphi \in \mathcal{I}$, if $S \models \varphi$, and $i \in$ pro(ψ) for all $\psi \in S$, then $i \in$ pro(φ).*

A social network is typically modelled as a graph in which the nodes are agents and there exists an edge between two agents if there is some form of social relationship between them. We also define a social network to be a graph in which the agents are represented with nodes. The information of two agents being aware of each-others publicly expressed opinion is represented as an edge e between those two nodes. The set E is a set of all the edges between agents

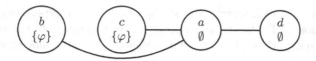

Fig. 1. An example of a social network

in the social network. We regard social networks to be symmetric, irreflexive relations over the agents, therefore an edge $e \in E$ is modelled as a set $e \subseteq N$ of size two ($|e| = 2$). A node in our social network graph is additionally labelled with the opinions from $\mathcal{I}$ which were publicly endorsed by that node's agent.

Definition 2 (Social network). *Given a set of agents N and a set of relevant issues $\mathcal{I}$, a social network is a tuple $G = (N, \mathcal{I}, \text{pro}, E)$ where pro is a support function and $E \subseteq \{\{i,j\} \mid i,j \in N, i \neq j\}$ is a set of edges. Given a social network $G = (N, \mathcal{I}, \text{pro}, E)$ we define the neighbours of agent $i \in N$ to be $n(i) = \{j \in N \mid \{i,j\} \in E\}$. The subset of i's neighbours which support (or "like") an opinion $\varphi \in \mathcal{I}$ is $l(i, \varphi) = n(i) \cap \text{pro}(\varphi)$.*

Example 1. Let G be a social network over four agents $N = \{a, b, c, d\}$ with $E = \{\{a,b\}, \{a,c\}, \{a,d\}\}$. The social network can be depicted as in Fig. 1. We see that the agents which support φ are $\text{pro}(\varphi) = \{b, c\}$. The neighbours of a are $n(a) = \{b, c, d\}$ and the neighbours of a which support φ are $l(a, \varphi) = \{b, c\}$.

4   Social Influence Models

Social influence exerted on an agent comes from her neighbours. The influence sources are those subsets of neighbours without which no social influence would exist. Given an agent $i \in N$ and $\varphi \in \mathcal{I}$ we define a "source of influence" as a pivotal set of neighbours. More than one set of neighbours can exert the same influence. That is why we consider a *set of pivotal sets* $\Omega(i, \varphi)$. We use pivotal sets as a proxy to model social influence. More precisely a pivotal set $A \in \Omega(i, \varphi)$ is a set of i's neighbours s.t., if all edges between i and the agents in A were removed, i would no longer experience social influence regarding φ.

Definition 3 (Social Influence Model). *A social influence model for a social network $G = (N, \mathcal{I}, \text{pro}, E)$ is an agent indexed family of functions: $\Omega^i : \mathcal{I} \to \mathcal{P}(\mathcal{P}(n(i)))$, where n is the function identifying the neighbours of agent i. We denote $\Omega^i(\varphi)$ as $\Omega(i, \varphi)$. The set $\Omega(i, \varphi)$ is called the set of pivotal sets for i regarding φ.*

The idea behind the social influence model is that it defines the presence of social influence by identifying exactly those groups of agents that are its sources. That is, when considering a social network G, we need to express the social influence exerted on an agent i by describing the sets of agents with which i needs to stop interacting if she wants to avoid experiencing influence to adopt opinion φ. By taking this approach, we can quantify the strength of a social influence experienced by an agent under different influence models and on different issues.

The *pivotal set* $A \in \Omega(i, \varphi)$ should reflect that *ceteris paribus*, after agent i has dropped all ties to the members of A, i is no longer under pressure to support φ. Further more, the set $\Omega(i, \varphi)$ should contain exactly and only these pivotal sets. Notice that if $\emptyset \in \Omega(i, \varphi)$, then the agent i is experiencing no influence regarding φ. This allows us to quickly verify whether an agent is under social influence for some opinion.

We can now define the existing social influence models as sets of pivotal sets and also introduce two new intuitive models of social influence. From now on, we shall use the terms social influence model and set of pivotal sets as synonyms. Since the strong influence is a special case of the threshold influence, we shall only give this latter's definition.

Definition 4 (Threshold social influence (TSI)). *Let G be a social network with agents N and issues $\mathcal{I}$. Let $i \in N$ be an agent and let $\varphi \in N$ be an issue. An influence threshold is a number $\theta \in [0, 1]$. The set of threshold pivotal sets Ω_t for i and φ is defined as*

$$\Omega_t(i, \varphi) = \left\{ A \subseteq n(i) \;\middle|\; \frac{|l(i, \varphi) \setminus A|}{|n(i) \setminus A|} \not\geq \theta \right\}.$$

Each set $A \in \Omega_t(i, \varphi)$ is such that after removing the connections between i and all the agents in A, the proportion of i's neighbours who support φ is below the influence threshold θ.

Example 2. Let G be the social network such that $\{a, b, c, d\} \in N$ as illustrated in Fig. 1. Let us take a quota of $q = 3/5$. We have that $\Omega_t(a, \varphi) = \{\{b\}, \{c\}, \{b, c\}, \{b, c, d\}\}$. Clearly, a is expected to support φ because $2/3 > 3/5$ of her neighbours support it. If the neighbourhood of a is changed to either $\{c, d\}$, $\{b, d\}$, $\{d\}$ or the empty set, the agent a would no longer be expected to support φ.

The strong, and threshold model in general, only take into account the neighbours with opinion φ to identify social influence regarding φ. Thus, when the quota is $\theta = 2/5$ an agent will experience conflicting influence when she has for example five neighbours out of which two support φ, one has no opinion on φ and two support $\neg\varphi$. In contrast, the weak influence model from [5, 6, 16] is different in the sense what the $\neg\varphi$ supporting neighbours also matter. In our little example, the agent a will no longer be under conflicting influence to support both φ and $\neg\varphi$, this agent will be under no social influence regarding any of these issues at all.

We generalise the weak influence into a new model which refines the threshold influence model, and we call it *opposition sensitive threshold social influence model* or OS-TSI. The OS-TSI intuitively says social influence exist to support

φ when the threshold social influence exists to support φ and none of the neighbours supports $\neg\varphi$. The weak social influence model is obtained as a special case of OS-TSI when $\theta > 0$.

Definition 5 (Opposition Sensitive TSI). *Let G be a social network with agents N and issues $\mathcal{I}$. Let $i \in N$ be an agent and let $\varphi \in N$ be an issue. A social influence threshold is a number $\theta \in [0,1]$. The set of threshold pivotal sets Ω_o for i and φ is defined as*

$$\Omega_o(i,\varphi) = \left\{ A \subseteq n(i) \;\middle|\; \frac{|l(i,\varphi) \setminus A|}{|n(i) \setminus A|} \not\geq \theta \text{ or } l(i,\neg\varphi) \setminus A \neq \emptyset \right\}.$$

Example 3. Consider again the social network G with $\{a,b,c,d\} \in N$ as illustrated in Fig. 1. Let $\theta = 2/5$. In this case $\Omega_o(a,\varphi) = \Omega_t(a,\varphi) = \{\{b\},\{c\},\{b,c\},$ $\{b,c,d\}\}$. Consider now the social network G' also with $\{a,b,c,d\} \in N$ and $\theta = 2/5$ as illustrated in Fig. 2. We now have that $\Omega_t(a,\varphi)$ is unchanged $\Omega_t(a,\varphi) = \{\{b\},\{c\},\{b,c\},\{b,c,d\}\}$, but $\Omega_o(a,\varphi) = \{\emptyset,\{b\},\{c\},\{b,c\},\{b,c,d\}\}$.

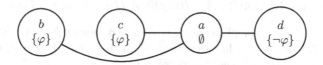

Fig. 2. Agent a is influenced under TIS, but not under OS-TIS

Unlike the TSI, the OS-TSI does not allow for a conflict of social influences to occur - if there is an opposing opinion among the neighbours there can be no social influence. It is also interesting to observe that, under the same threshold θ if the existence of OS-TSI for agent i on issue φ implies the existence of TSI on the same agent for the same issue, but the implication does not hold in the opposite direction.

An agent might not be influenced by proportions, but simply by the objective number of agents that expressed the same opinion. This number t may be seen as a personal tolerance of an agent. We assume always that the tolerance is at most the number of agents in the network. Thus if $|N| > t > n(i)$ we have a model of an agent who is never socially influenced.

Definition 6 (Accumulated Tolerance Social Influence (ATSI)). *Let G be a social network with agents N and issues $\mathcal{I}$. Consider an $i \in N$ and $\varphi \in \mathcal{I}$ and that i's tolerance is $0 < t < |N|$. We define the accumulated tolerance pivotal sets Ω_a for i and φ as $\Omega_a(i,\varphi) = \{A \subseteq n(i) \mid |l(i,\varphi) \setminus A| < t\}$.*

Example 4. Consider the same social network(s) as in the previous example given in Fig. 1 and let $t = 1$. This means that with only one friend supporting an issue, there is an active influence exerted upon the agent to support it. Now $\Omega_a(i,\varphi) = \{\{b\},\{c\},\{b,c\},\{b,d\},\{c,d\},\{b,c,d\}\}$. In fact, any set of neighbours containing at least b or c will suffice.

We lastly want to define the Simmelian social influence model that captures the idea of [14] about visible behaviour norms exerted by Simmelian ties.

An agent i has a Simmelian tie with an agent j when $\{i, j\} \in E$ and there exists an agent k such that both $\{i, k\} \in E$ and $\{j, k\} \in E$. A Simmelian influence to support φ is exerted on an agent i when that agent has a Simmelian tie with an agent j that supports φ and there exist an agent k that supports φ with whom both i and j are connected. To identify if there is Simmelian influence over i with respect to φ, we first identify all neighbours of i that support φ, $l(i, \varphi)$. Then we check if there is an edge between any two of the agent in $l(i, \varphi)$; these connected agents together with i form a clique and create the Simmelian influence over i. To remove the influence we need to remove edges so i is in no φ-supporting clique, or in other words, so that the remaining neighbours of i are no longer connected with each other.

Definition 7 (Simmelian Social Influence (SSI)). *Let* $G = (N, \mathcal{I}, \mathrm{pro}, E)$ *be a social network, with agents* N *and issues* $\mathcal{I}$. $\varphi \in \mathcal{I}$ *and agent* $i \in N$. *The Simmelian pivotal set of sets* $\Omega_s(i, \varphi)$ *is*

$$\Omega_s(i, \varphi) = \{A \subseteq n(i) \mid B = l(i, \varphi) \setminus A, G_B \subset G \text{ is s.t. } E_B \neq \emptyset\}$$

Example 5. Consider a social network with seven agents $N = \{a, b, c, d, e, f, g\}$ given on Fig. 3. The agent a has five Simmelian ties, given in green, with agents b, c, d, g and f. The set of neighbours for a is $n(a) = \{b, c, d, e, f, g\}$. The set of neighbours who support φ is $l(a, \varphi) = \{b, c, d, e\}$, given in red. The set of Simmelian pivotal sets for a and φ, $\Omega_s(s, \varphi)$, is the set containing $\{b, c\}, \{b, d\}, \{c, d\}$ and all supersets of these. Namely, if the agent a wishes to not be under Simmelian influence for φ, she then needs to remove at least two of her Simmelian ties with φ-supporting neighbours.

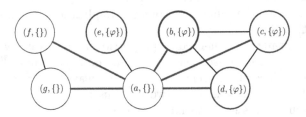

Fig. 3. An example of Simmelian ties and Simmelian influence. (Color figure online)

Let us define what it means for one social influence model to be weaker than another.

Definition 8. *Given two influence models represented with sets of pivotal sets* Ω_1 *and* Ω_2, *if for every network* $(N, \mathcal{I}, \mathrm{pro}, E)$, *every agent* $i \in N$, *and every issue* $\varphi \in \mathcal{I}$, *we have* $\Omega_1(i, \varphi) \subseteq \Omega_2(i, \varphi)$, *then we say that model 2 is weaker than model 1 and write* $\Omega_2 \preceq \Omega_1$.

It is obvious that for the same influence threshold θ it holds that $\Omega_t \leq \Omega_o$.

Lastly, we define the concept of purely social influence model. These are models under which the total hermit is not influenced to support any issue – no neighbours, no influence.

Definition 9 (Purely social influence models). *A set of pivotal sets Ω is purely social iff for every set of issues $\mathcal{I}$, and social network $(N, \mathcal{I}, \mathrm{pro}, E)$ over these issues, for every $i \in N$ and $\varphi \in \mathcal{I}$, $n(i) \in \Omega(i, \varphi)$.*

All social influence models we have introduced so far are purely social.

5   Conflicting Social Influences

Consider the social network on Fig. 3 and assume that agents f and g both support issue $\neg\varphi$. In this case, agent a would experience Simmelian influence to support φ from her Simmelian ties with b, c and d and another Simmelian influence to support $\neg\varphi$ from her Simmelian ties with f and g. We noted that under our social influence models, with the exception of OS-TSI, conflicting social influences to be experienced by the same agent. To be more specific, this is true in the case when the influence threshold is $\theta < 0.5$ and the tolerance is $t < n(i)/2$. To be even more specific, this is the case under the assumption that no two issues in $\mathcal{I}^+$ share variables, *i.e.*, the issues in $\mathcal{I}^+$ are logically independent.

Example 6. Consider a social network graph G of seven agents as given in Fig. 4. Under the TSI and OS-TSI models, for $\theta = 2/6$, the agent a is under the social influence to accept φ, $\neg\psi$, and $\varphi \rightarrow \psi$. This set of opinions is an inconsistent set of formulas.

Notice that if either of agents f and g also supported φ, there would have not been OS-TSI social conflict for a since there would have been no social influence to adopt $\neg\psi$.

From Example 6 we see that social conflict can occur in more complex forms than direct social influence to support two contradicting opinions. We therefore give a definition of *conflicting social influences*.

Definition 10 (Conflicting social influence). *Consider a consistent set of formulas $S \subset \mathcal{I}$. We define the closure of S, w.r.t. $\mathcal{I}$, as a set $S^{\mathcal{I}} = \{\varphi \in \mathcal{I} \mid S \models \varphi\}$. Let the set of all social influences experienced by $i \in N$ be $I_{\Omega}(i) = \{\varphi \in \mathcal{I} \mid \emptyset \notin \Omega(i, \varphi)\}$. We say that an agent $i \in N$ is under conflicting social influences when $(I_{\Omega}(i))^{\mathcal{I}}$ is an inconsistent set of formulas.*

It is clear that an agent that is experiencing conflicting social influences cannot resolve them by succumbing to the influence. Such an agent has to either persuade some of his influencers to change their statements or stop "following" their opinions. Of course an agent can exist under conflicting influence, but she has to be very careful that her expressed opinions do not involve the issue of

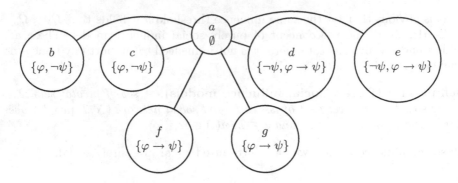

Fig. 4. Conflict of social influence under the OS-TSI model

conflict. We consider that this status quo in reality may be difficult to maintain. It may seem that severing ties is a drastic option, but it is a behaviour that we can witness in actual social networking services - one tends to "mute", "unfollow", "unfriend", etc. sources of opinions that one finds unreasonable or one does not identify with. While it takes at least two to make a relationship, one can single-sidedly end it. It is thus intuitive that conflicting social influences are a source of conflict in social networks.

Definition 11 (Unstable networks). *A social network G is called* unstable *if there exists an agent i in the network that is under a conflicting social influence on a relevant issue.*

An obvious question to ask at this point is: given a social network G and a social influence model Ω, how difficult is it to determine whether G is unstable? We can define the following decision problem.

Ω-Instability

Instance: Given is a social network $G = (N, \mathcal{I}, \mathrm{pro}, E)$ and a social influence model Ω.

Question: Is there an $a \in N$ such that $(I_\Omega(i))^{\mathcal{I}}$ is not consistent?

Note that the building of the set $(I_\Omega(i))^{\mathcal{I}}$ can be done in linear time with respect to the cardinality of the set of issues $|\mathcal{I}|$.

In the case of the TSI, OS-TSI, and ATSO models, checking for conflicts consists in visiting all of the nodes in G and checking the numbers $l(i, \varphi)$ and $l(i, \sim \varphi)$ for each non-negated $\varphi \in \mathcal{I}$. Thus for these models the instability problems are of linear time complexity with respect to $|N| \cdot |\mathcal{I}|$.

Interesting is the case of Ω_s-INSTABILITY problem, for the Simmelian social influence model, but this too is tractable.

It is simple to construct an algorithm that retrieves all agent-issue pairs where Simmelian social influence exists. The algorithm receives the social network $(N, \mathcal{I}, \mathrm{pro}, E)$ where we have given both sets of issues as input and returns a set $C \subseteq \{(i, \varphi) \mid i \in N, \varphi \in \mathcal{I}\}$ of all the agents that are under social influence for opinion φ. We then need to construct $C^{\mathcal{I}}$ and check whether it is a consistent set of formulas. The algorithm operates as follows. For each agent and for each node and each non-negated issue in $\mathcal{I}$ we find that node's neighbours who support φ. We then check if there are neighbours that are connected. The connected neighbours are potential sources of influence.

The following Proposition 1 is straightforward since the problem of finding all triangles in a graph is known to be solvable in quadratic time of the size of the graph [13].

Proposition 1. *The Ω-Instability problem is bounded by $O(|N| \cdot |\mathcal{I}| \cdot d^2)$, where d is the maximal degree of a node in G.*

6 Resolving Conflicts

It is reasonable to expect that a rational agent would try to resolve her conflicting social influences. Assuming autonomous agents, the agent may only change what she controls and not *e.g.,* other agents' support or beliefs. An agent i experiencing social conflict on φ has to remove ties to those neighbours that are the sources of the conflict. How to choose who to not "follow" any more?

An agent can avoid social influence by severing connections with the right neighbours. The main advantage of modelling social influence by means of pivotal sets is that they explicitly describe how to remove influence. A pivotal set $S \in \Omega(i, \varphi)$ can be seen as *influence avoiding action*, if we let the agent be able to remove edges she is involved in.

Definition 12 (Conflict avoiding actions). *Given is a social network $G = (N, \mathcal{I}, \mathrm{pro}, E)$, a social influence model defined via a set of pivotal sets Ω. Let $I_\Omega(i)$ be the set of all social influences experienced by $i \in N$, under the given social influence model. We define the minimal conflict set $MC(i)$ as*

$$MC(i) = \{C \subseteq I_\Omega(i) \mid C \models \bot \text{ and there is no } C' \subset C \text{ s.t. } C' \models \bot\}.$$

The set of influence avoiding actions can now be defined as

$$AC(i) := \{S \mid S \in \bigcup_{\varphi \in \bigcup MC(i)} \Omega(i, \varphi)\}.$$

Note that if $(I_\Omega(i))^{\mathcal{I}}$ is a consistent set of formulas, then $MC(i) = \emptyset$ and so $AC(i) = \emptyset$.

Recall that to restore consistency to a set it is sufficient to remove one element of its minimally inconsistent subset. This is how the set of avoiding actions is constructed. Each of the pivotal sets, that may be of varying size, are candidates of sets of agents to "unfriend". An agent that is convivial would like to remove a minimal set of its neighbours. To do so, such an agent would find (one of) the minimal set of agents $A \in AC(i)$ and remove edges precisely to those agents.

Example 7. Consider again the social network in Example 6 and that $\mathcal{I} = \{\varphi, \neg\varphi, \psi, \neg\psi, \varphi \to \psi, \neg(\varphi \to \psi)\}$. Under an influence threshold of $\theta = 2/6$ there is a TSI on a to adopt φ, $\varphi \to \psi$ and $\neg\psi$, namely $I_t(a) = \{\varphi, \neg\psi, \varphi \to \psi\}$. We have the following pivotal sets for a regarding each of these opinions:

$$\Omega_t(a, \varphi) = \quad \{\{b\}, \{c\}, \{b, d\}, \{b, e\}, \{b, f\}, \{b, g\}, \{c, d\}, \{c, e\}, \{c, f\}, \{c, g\}\}$$
$$\cup\{S \subset N \mid \{b, c, \} \subseteq S\}$$
$$\Omega_t(a, \neg\psi) = \quad \{\{d\}, \{e\}, \{d, b\}, \{d, c\}, \{d, f\}, \{d, g\}, \{e, b\}, \{e, c\}, \{e, f\}, \{e, g\}\}$$
$$\cup\{S \subset N \mid \{d, e, \} \subseteq S\}$$
$$\Omega_t(a, \varphi \to \psi) = \{\{d, e, f\}, \{d, e, g\}, \{d, f, g\}, \{e, f, g\}, \{b, d, e, f\}, \{b, d, e, g\},$$
$$\{b, d, f, g\}, \{b, e, f, g\}, \{c, e, f\}, \{c, e, g\}, \{c, f, g\}, \{c, e, f, g\},$$
$$\{b, c, d, e, f, g\}\}.$$

We have that $MC(a) = I_t(a)$. The set of actions is thus the union of $\Omega_t(a, \varphi)$, $\Omega_t(a, \neg\psi)$, and $\Omega_t(a, \varphi \to \psi)$. The smallest cardinality sets in this union are $\{b\}$, $\{c\}$, $\{d\}$, and $\{e\}$. A convivial agent a would thus remove her edge to one of these neighbours to resolve her conflict in social influences.

We can observe that since a conflict of social influences can never happen for an agent that has only one neighbour, an agent will never be put in a situation to isolate herself to avoid a conflict. However an agent might end up being isolated by the action of her neighbours. In Example 7, this can happen to any of the agents b, c, d and e.

Schelling observed that if an agent i moves to find a less diverse neighbourhood, since all agent move simultaneously, this agent i might end up in the same kind of neighbourhood that she tried to originally avoid [23]. We may ask a similar question here. If an agent removes edges to avoid a social influence, can she end up in a network in which the influence is still exerted on her as a result of the actions of her neighbours. To answer this question, we define a property of social influence models.

Definition 13 (Monotonic influence). *A social influence model represented with pivotal sets Ω is monotonic when for every $i \in N$ and $\varphi \in \mathcal{I}$, if $S \in \Omega(i, \varphi)$ then $S' \in \Omega(i, \varphi)$ for every $S \subseteq S' \subseteq n(i)$.*

It is easy to see that the TSI and OS-TSI models are non-monotonic. This is because these models take into account the proportion of neighbours. By removing connections to same "type" of neighbours, say those who support φ, we will never increase the proportion of neighbours that support φ. It is also immediate that the ATSI and SSI models are monotonic.

The agents resolve their influences individually, without coordination with other agents. To be able to study how the network changes over time with respect to conflict resolving actions, we propose a temporal logic framework, in the line with [9].

7   Temporal Model of Social Influence

Based on the notion of conflict avoiding actions, we give a simple version of linear-time temporal logic (LTL) [21] over our models. We have already defined what we will consider the possible actions, $AC(i)$, of a particular agent in the previous section.

Definition 14. *A* state *is a social network* $(N, \mathcal{I}, \text{pro}, E)$. *An* action profile *in a state, is an agent-indexed vector of sets of edges* $\alpha : N \rightarrow 2^N$ *such that for every agent* i, $\alpha(i) \in \{\{j, i\} | j \in A\} | A \in AC(i)\}$.

For every state, we have a set of actions which an agent can perform towards avoiding all conflicts she is experiencing. Every action profile gives rise to a next state in which exactly those edges have been removed. The definition of an action profile also needs to replace an agent's (i) targeted set of neighbours A with the corresponding edges $\{\{j, i\} | j \in A\}$.

Definition 15. *Given a state* $(N, \mathcal{I}, \text{pro}, E)$ *we define a* successor *to be a social network* $(N, \mathcal{I}, \text{pro}, E \setminus A)$ *such that for some action profile* α, $A \in \bigcup_{i \in N} \alpha(i)$. *A* history *is an infinite sequence of states* $H = H_0, H_1, H_2, \ldots$ *such that* H_{i+1} *is a successor of* H_i.

The successor is the union of some conflict avoiding action for each agent. We give a fragment of LTL in which we only provide the "next state" operator. Our atoms are of the form $\text{Infl}(i, \varphi)$ where $i \in N$ and $\varphi \in \mathcal{I}$.

$$\psi ::= \text{Infl}(i, \varphi) | \neg \psi | \psi \wedge \psi | \bigcirc \psi$$

We also define the abbreviation $\text{Conf}(i, \varphi)$ to denote that $\varphi \in MC(i)$. The satisfaction of these formulas is defined as usual for LTL, except that we fix a social influence model Ω and define $H, k \models \text{Infl}(i, \varphi)$ iff $\emptyset \notin \Omega(i, \varphi)$.

Proposition 2. *Given a history* H *over states with agents* N *and issues* $\mathcal{I}$ *under a social influence model* Ω, *if* Ω *is monotonic and purely social, then for any* $k \in \mathbb{N}$, $i \in N$, $\varphi \in \mathcal{I}$, $H, k \models \bigcirc \neg \text{Conf}(i, \varphi)$.

It suffices to give a sketch of the proof. Let $(N, \mathcal{I}, \text{pro}, E)$ be an arbitrary social network and Ω any purely social, monotonic influence model. Let $(N, \mathcal{I}, \text{pro}, E')$ be an arbitrary successor. Consider now whether there exists a conflict in this successor state. The set of edges E' was obtained by letting every agent delete edges so that to avoid conflicts for herself. No new conflicts could have been introduced, because if other edges were removed adjacent to that agent, these edges would be in some superset of the edges the agent herself chose to remove, hence no new conflict could have been introduced for her. To see that this is not always true when the influence model is not monotonic, consider the following example.

Example 8. Suppose we have the model shown in Fig. 5, with the influence threshold $\theta = 0.3$ and $N = \{a, a', b, b', b, c, c', d, d', e, e'\}$. Agent a is in conflict with respect to φ, and all of b, c, d and e are in conflict with respect to ψ. Every agent $i \in N$ has to select some action ($A \in AC(i)$) representing the edges to drop to avoid conflict. If Ω is not monotonic, then some other agent's choice may

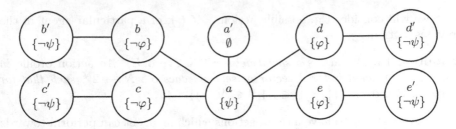

Fig. 5. a is in φ-conflict; b, c, d, e are in ψ-conflict.

introduce the action of deleting some edge which i depends on maintaining in order to avoid conflict. More concretely, assume a selects $\{b\} \in AC(a)$, b selects either $\{a\}$ or $\{b'\} \in AC(b)$, c selects $\{c'\} \in AC(c)$, d selects $\{a\} \in AC(d)$ and e selects $\{e'\} \in AC(e)$. Removing the edges $\{a, b\}$, $\{c, c'\}$, $\{a, d\}$, and $\{e, e'\}$ yields a new social network with a φ-conflict for a.

Social influence models which are not purely social, may give rise to states with no successor. If a model is not purely social, we may encounter situations which for some agent i, $AC(i) = \emptyset$. In this case, the agent has no way of performing a conflict avoiding action.

Proposition 3. *Given are issues $\mathcal{I}$, agents N and pivotal sets Ω. If Ω is not purely social, then there exists a state H, s.t. no history contains it.*

Consider the trivial influence model $\Omega_\emptyset$ which maps every agent and issue to the empty set. With only a single issue $\mathcal{I} = \{\varphi\}$ and a single agent $N = \{a\}$, we get $\emptyset \notin \Omega(a, \varphi) = \Omega(a, \neg\varphi) = \emptyset$, hence a has a conflict, but no friends and no available actions. A dire situation for a, and a dire situation for the prospect of analysing the evolution of the network.

Proposition 4. *Given a influence model Ω_1 and a history H under Ω_1, if Ω_2 is an influence model such that $\Omega_2 \leq \Omega_1$, then H is also a history for Ω_2.*

This final proposition states that a possible evolution under any social influence model Ω_1, is also a possible evolution under a weaker social influence model Ω_2.

8   Conclusions

Social influence over an agent to adopt one opinion is an interesting phenomena. We argue that the change of opinions is not the only way social influence can affect the agents in a social network. We argue that, particularly when social influences are a source of inconsistency, they can affect the edges in the social network.

In this work we primarily set the stage for the study of dynamic social networks, but we nonetheless make contributions to the field of formal social influence studies: we generalise the existing social influence models and introduce two new models of influence. While the ATSI models can be considered rather trivial, the Simmelian influence, has to the best of our knowledge not been considered before outside classic social network research. All the influence models we propose are purely social, but intuitively we are more likely to be influenced by our close friends than by acquaintances, although we might "follow" both. The Simmelian influence model, to a certain extent, helps us to identify closer friends through Simmelian ties. It is these new models, the Simmelian and the ATSI model, that help us identify the property of social influence models that instigates agent segregation, in the sense of [23], in a social network. We also give a temporal framework for further future investigations of social network dynamics social influence conflict resolution scenarios.

Our approach of modelling social influence via pivotal sets makes it easy for new models of social influence to be defined, particularly ones that are agent-subjective, issue-subjective, or both. An agent can discriminate between her neighbours and distinguish between neighbours she is curious about and those with whose opinions she generally agrees or whose opinions she holds in high regard. Then this agent can require much stricter conditions for becoming influenced by the first group than by the second. It is also easy to define a model discriminates between neighbours j of an agent i with respect to how similar the sets pro(i) and pro(j) are, again to model that we are more susceptible to be influenced by those with who we are alike.

We are ultimately interested in studying the dynamics of social networks, but so far we have only proposed a model of network change that just eliminates connections. It is also necessary to consider how new connections can be formed. An approach towards formation of connections is proposed by Smets and Velásquez-Quesada [25], who like us consider agents represented with a pro(i) support function. Smets and Velásquez-Quesada propose that similar agents become friends and go on to propose a similarity measure based on the support function.

In our model we do not account for the possibility of the agents changing their mind. Namely, once an agent expresses support for an issue, there is no mechanism by which they can change their mind and either become neutral on an issue of "flip sides" altogether. This is also an immediate direction in which we intend to extend our social influence models.

By having both the means for edge removal and adding, as well as opinion change, we can study network dynamics phenomena, such as for example group polarization. Group polarization occurs when like-minded individuals tend to segregate themselves and progressively get to support more radical opinions than the ones they initially supported. Group polarization is a topic that is also gaining interest. An interesting approach to this topic is [22], where argumentation frameworks are used to model how agents update their opinions.

Unlike other work on social influence models, *e.g.*, [3,5,6,10,16], we consider the case when the issues in $\mathcal{I}$ are logically related. Judgement aggregation [12] is concerned with methods for aggregating logically related issues and it is of interest in collective decision making problems in multi-agent systems [4], but has so far not studied socially related agents. The TSI model corresponds to a quota aggregator [9], but more methods are proposed in judgement aggregation [15] which could also be the basis of influence models. In particular we can observe that when an agent behaves in a convivial fashion and removes a minimal number of its neighbours, she gives preference to be influenced by those opinions that are more prevalent in the network. This is reminiscent of the aggregators based on the weighted majoritarian graph as studied in [15]. This relationship needs to be explored further.

We intend to investigate the behaviour of social networks over time with respect to influence conflicts. The work started by [9] points us to the interesting question of the cost of removing connections with respect to the strategic consequences of these actions. In the ATSI model, every agent had a contribution of 1 towards the agent's tolerance, but a more realistic model could replace this by a more reasoned value. This could be derived from network properties, such as an agent's centrality, or game theoretic notions such as the Shapley-Shubik value [24] of an agent. The action profiles defined in Definition 14 can readily be treated as the possible action profiles in an Coalition Logic [20] or Alternating Time Temporal Logic [1] model. Further, the framework can be extended to support predicates for more than one concurrent model of social influence to represent the option that different agents in the network can be differently influenced.

References

1. Alur, R., Henzinger, T.A., Kupferman, O.: Alternating-time temporal logic. J. ACM **49**(5), 672–713 (2002)
2. Asch, S.E.: Studies of independence and conformity: a minority of one against a unanimous majority. Psychol. Monogr. **70**(9), 1–70 (1956)
3. Baltag, A., Christoff, Z., Rendsvig, R.K., Smets, S.: Dynamic epistemic logic of diffusion and prediction in threshold models (2016)
4. Boella, G., Pigozzi, G., Slavkovik, M., Torre, L.: Group intention is social choice with commitment. In: Vos, M., Fornara, N., Pitt, J.V., Vouros, G. (eds.) COIN 2010. LNCS (LNAI), vol. 6541, pp. 152–171. Springer, Heidelberg (2011). doi:10. 1007/978-3-642-21268-0_9
5. Christoff, Z., Hansen, J.U.: A two-tiered formalization of social influence. In: Grossi, D., Roy, O., Huang, H. (eds.) LORI 2013. LNCS, vol. 8196, pp. 68–81. Springer, Heidelberg (2013). doi:10.1007/978-3-642-40948-6_6
6. Christoff, Z., Hansen, J.U., Proietti, C.: Reflecting on social influence in networks. J. Logic Lang. Inform. **25**(3), 299–333 (2016)
7. DeGroot, M.: Reaching a consensus. J. Am. Stat. Assoc. **69**(345), 118–121 (1974)
8. Festinger, L.: Informal social communication. Psychol. Rev. **57**(5), 271–282 (1950)
9. Grandi, U., Lorini, E., Novaro, A., Perrussel, L.: Strategic disclosure of opinions on a social network. In: Proceedings of the 16th International Joint Conference on Autonomous Agents and Multiagent Systems (AAMAS 2017) (2017)

10. Grandi, U., Lorini, E., Perrussel, L.: Strategic disclosure of opinions on a social network: (extended abstract). In: Proceedings of the 2016 International Conference on Autonomous Agents & #38; Multiagent Systems, AAMAS 2016, pp. 1391–1392. IFAAMAS (2016)

11. Granovetter, M.: Threshold models of collective behavior. Am. J. Sociol. **83**(6), 1420–1443 (1978)

12. Grossi, D., Pigozzi, G.: Judgment Aggregation: A Primer. Morgan and Claypool Publishers, San Rafael (2014)

13. Itai, A., Rodeh, M.: Finding a minimum circuit in a graph. SIAM J. Comput. **7**(4), 413–423 (1978)

14. Krackhardt, D.: The Ties that torture: Simmelian tie analysis in organizations. Res. Sociol. Organ. **16**, 183–210 (1999)

15. Lang, L., Pigozzi, P., Slavkovik, M., van der Torre, L., Vesic, S.: A partial taxonomy of judgment aggregation rules, and their properties. Soc. Choice Welfare **48**, 1–30 (2016)

16. Liu, F., Seligman, J., Girard, P.: Logical dynamics of belief change in the community. Synthese **191**(11), 2403–2431 (2014)

17. Moscovici, S., Personnaz, B.: Studies in social influence. J. Exp. Soc. Psychol. **16**, 270–282 (1980)

18. Noelle-Neumann, E.: The spiral of silence a theory of public opinion. J. Commun. **24**(2), 43–51 (1974)

19. O'Gorman, H.J.: The discovery of pluralistic ignorance: an ironic lesson. J. Hist. Behav. Sci. **22**(4), 333–347 (1986)

20. Pauly, M.: A modal logic for coalitional power in games. J. Log. Comput. **12**(1), 149–166 (2002)

21. Pnueli, A.: The temporal logic of programs. In: Proceedings of the 18th Annual Symposium on Foundations of Computer Science, SFCS 1977, pp. 46–57. IEEE Computer Society, Washington, DC (1977)

22. Proietti, C.: The dynamics of group polarization. In: Baltag, A., Seligman, J., Yamada, T. (eds.) Proceedings of the Logic, Rationality, and Interaction - 6th International Workshop, LORI 2017, Sapporo, Japan, 11–14 September 2015. (2017, Forthcoming)

23. Schelling, T.: Dynamic models of segregation. J. Math. Sociol. **1**, 143–186 (1971)

24. Shapley, L.S., Shubik, M.: A method for evaluating the distribution of power in a committee system. Am. Polit. Sci. Rev. **48**(3), 787–792 (1954)

25. Smets, S., Velázquez-Quesada, F.R.: How to make friends: a logical approach to social group creation. In: Baltag, A., Seligman, J., Yamada, T. (eds.) Proceedings of the Logic, Rationality, and Interaction - 6th International Workshop, LORI 2017, Sapporo, Japan, 11–14 September 2015. (2017, Forthcoming)

Argumentation in Multiagent Systems

Quantitative Argumentation Debates with Votes for Opinion Polling

Antonio Rago$^{(\boxtimes)}$ ⓘ and Francesca Toni ⓘ

Department of Computing, Imperial College London, London, UK
{a.rago15,ft}@imperial.ac.uk

Abstract. Opinion polls are used in a variety of settings to assess the opinions of a population, but they mostly conceal the reasoning behind these opinions. Argumentation, as understood in AI, can be used to evaluate opinions in dialectical exchanges, transparently articulating the reasoning behind the opinions. We give a method integrating argumentation within opinion polling to empower voters to add new statements that render their opinions in the polls *individually rational* while at the same time justifying them. We then show how these poll results can be amalgamated to give a *collectively rational* set of voters in an argumentation framework. Our method relies upon *Quantitative Argumentation Debate for Voting* (QuAD-V) frameworks, which extend QuAD frameworks (a form of bipolar argumentation frameworks in which arguments have an intrinsic strength) with votes expressing individuals' opinions on arguments.

1 Introduction

Two of the main aims of *e-Democracy* are to move from a *representative* to a *direct democracy*, shifting power to citizens, and to facilitate the necessary deliberations for direct democracy to function effectively [13]. These aims are shared by existing concepts of democracy, such as *Agonistic Pluralism* [19], which accepts and encourages conflicts on policy, and *Deliberative Democracy* [2], which allows the resolution of conflicts using *voting* if a rational consensus is not reached.

Voting is also core in *opinion polling*, a method for both obtaining information on people's sentiment and engaging them in the political process in a bottom up manner. In conventional opinion poll systems, a prominent example of which is *YouGov*[1], questions are put to users in a flat list format. More engaging user interfaces, as shown on the *WhichIt* platform[2], can be used, as well as the reverse wording of questions to ensure that responses are valid. Some systems, e.g. [18,23,24], integrate opinion polling with other techniques or systems, e.g. *Twitter* [23] or machine learning algorithms [18]. Moreover, *Deliberative Polling* [10] is a fully-fledged system for decision-making based on deliberation, incorporating aspects of deliberative democracy, e.g. samples of the users in the poll

---

[1] yougov.co.uk.
[2] www.getwhichit.com.

ⓒ Springer International Publishing AG 2017
B. An et al. (Eds.): PRIMA 2017, LNAI 10621, pp. 369–385, 2017.
https://doi.org/10.1007/978-3-319-69131-2_22

are given balanced information and are invited to deliberate with one another to improve the quality of the responses. To the best of our knowledge, no existing opinion polling system/method takes into account evaluation of the dialectical strength of the opinions based on voters' responses.

Argumentation, as understood in AI [22], can be used to evaluate the strength of opinions in dialectical exchanges, transparently articulating the reasoning behind them, when these exchanges are represented as *argumentation frameworks*. The simplest among such frameworks are *Abstract Argumentation* frameworks (AAFs), defined in terms of *arguments* and an *attack* relation between them [8], whereas *Bipolar Argumentation* frameworks (BAFs) [6] also include a *support* relation between arguments, and *Quantitative Argumentation Debate (QuAD)* frameworks [1], based on the IBIS methodology [15], distinguish answer, pro and con arguments and ascribe intrinsic strengths to arguments prior to debates. All frameworks are equipped with methods for evaluating the dialectical acceptability or strength of arguments.

Several argumentation frameworks have already been used to support collaborative debates and deliberation within e-Democracy or otherwise (e.g. see [3,5,7,12,14,16,17,20]). We propose *QuAD for Voting* (QuAD-V) frameworks and use them to support a novel, arguably more informative form of opinion polling in the spirit of deliberative democracy. Our *QuAD-V opinion polling* allows voters to provide information about the reasoning behind their opinions, while dynamically expanding the originally specified polls by eliciting information from users. The elicitation is driven by the semantic evaluation of voters' opinions, using a suitable notion of *strength* of arguments for QuAD-V frameworks that we define, instantiating the notion in [21]. The elicitation aims at rendering the opinions of the voters (i.e. their arguments and votes) *individually* and *collectively rational*.

This paper is organised as follows. In Sect. 2 we give a motivating example for our approach. In Sect. 3 we give necessary background on QuAD frameworks, the starting point for our approach. In Sect. 4 we define QuAD-V frameworks, and in Sect. 5 we study their properties. In Sect. 6 we discuss the convention we use to class voters as individually/collectively rational. In Sect. 7 we describe our opinion poll method, based on QuAD-V frameworks, and in Sect. 8 we conclude.

2   Motivation

To illustrate the motivation for this paper we look at two recent examples of political debate, "Brexit", the recent referendum on the UK exit from the European Union, and the US 2016 Presidential Election. In both examples, opinion polling failed to accurately predict the results of the voting[3,4] and the voters on the winning side felt that their voices were not being heard[5]. Many of the fundamental issues with the polling were related to statistical and sampling errors,

---

[3]   https://ig.ft.com/sites/brexit-polling/.

[4]   http://fivethirtyeight.com/features/the-polls-missed-trump-we-asked-pollsters-why/.

[5]   www.bbc.co.uk/news/election-us-2016-37943072.

but one of significance was voters being disingenuous or not fully expressing their opinions in the polls[6]. Improved sharing of this information could be achieved by more informed debates, rather than false promises, negative campaigning and scaremongering[7,8], which led to many voters expressing regret after voting under what they felt were false pretences[9]. We aim to address both disingenuous behaviour and disengagement of the public by developing a novel argumentation-based methodology supporting debating and voting in opinion polling to help ensure that information is shared and voters are more engaged.

In conventional opinion polls, users are asked to state (or grade) their agreement on statements by votes, e.g. users' votes may amount to *agree, neutral* or *disagree*. The aggregation of users' votes allows pollsters to obtain statistics on public agreement on issues the statements refer to. However, these methods ignore the relationships between statements and users' votes on statements have no bearing on their votes on related statements. Thus, the reasoning that may result from analysing users' votes given these relationships is neglected and opinion polls may disregard "irrationalities" in the voter's opinions.

For example, consider the following statements relating to the Brexit debate:

$S1$ - The UK should leave the EU.
$S2$ - The UK staying in the EU is good for its economy.
$S3$ - The EU's immigration policies are bad for the UK.
$S4$ - EU membership fees are too high.

Here, $S2$ may be deemed to *attack* $S1$, while $S3$ and $S4$ may be deemed to *support* it (where attack and support are *dialectical* relationships). So, if a user's votes indicate disagreement with $S1$, $S2$ and $S4$ but agreement with $S3$, the user may be disingenuous (hiding that she/he actually agrees with $S1$, but giving it away by agreeing with one of its supporters) or the poll may not provide sufficiently many statements to fully reflect the voter's opinions, e.g. the user may agree with some other argument (statement) attacking $S1$, such as:

$S5$ - The UK staying in the EU is good for world peace.

In both cases, we may deem the voter's opinions to be irrational.

Our opinion polling method interprets statements in opinion polls as arguments in a type of argumentation framework that we define. Moreover, it uses a measure of strength of arguments, based on both the *direct* votes on the statements/arguments and the *indirect* votes on their (dialectically) related statements/arguments. It then uses this measure to highlight voting that may be deemed as irrational and then gives voters the opportunity to become "rational"

---

[6] www.theguardian.com/commentisfree/2016/nov/09/polls-wrong-donald-trump-election.
[7] www.newyorker.com/news/john-cassidy/why-the-remain-campaign-lost-the-brexit-vote.
[8] www.theguardian.com/business/2016/sep/16/truth-lies-and-trust-in-the-age-of-brexit-and-trump.
[9] www.edition.cnn.com/2016/06/25/politics/uk-referendum-regrexit/index.html.

by dynamic transformations of the underlying argumentation framework. This information elicitation obtains additional data for the opinion poll while at the same time increasing engagement of its voters.

3   Background

As introduced in [1], a *Quantitative Argumentation Debate* (QuAD) framework is a 5-tuple $\langle \mathcal{A}, \mathcal{C}, \mathcal{P}, \mathcal{R}, \tau \rangle$ such that $\mathcal{A}$ is a finite set of *answer arguments*; $\mathcal{C}$ is a finite set of *con arguments*; $\mathcal{P}$ is a finite set of *pro arguments*; the sets $\mathcal{A}$, $\mathcal{C}$ and $\mathcal{P}$ are pairwise disjoint[10]; $\mathcal{R} \subseteq (\mathcal{C} \cup \mathcal{P}) \times (\mathcal{A} \cup \mathcal{C} \cup \mathcal{P})$ is an acyclic binary relation; for $\mathbb{I} = [0, 1]$, $\tau : (\mathcal{A} \cup \mathcal{C} \cup \mathcal{P}) \rightarrow \mathbb{I}$ is a total function: $\tau(a)$ is the *base score* of a, representing its intrinsic strength, prior to considering other arguments dialectically related to it. The Brexit debate from Sect. 2 can be represented as a QuAD framework $\langle \{S1\}, \{S2, S5\}, \{S3, S4\}, \{(S2, S1), (S3, S1), (S4, S1), (S5, S1)\}, \tau \rangle$, for any suitable τ. The relation component can be visualised as in Fig. 1.

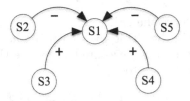

Fig. 1. Example QuAD framework

Pro and con arguments determine the attackers and supporters of arguments they are in relation with. Formally, for any argument $a \in \mathcal{A} \cup \mathcal{C} \cup \mathcal{P}$, the set of *attackers* of a is $\mathcal{R}^-(a) = \{b \in \mathcal{C} | (b, a) \in \mathcal{R}\}$ and the set of *supporters* of a is $\mathcal{R}^+(a) = \{b \in \mathcal{P} | (b, a) \in \mathcal{R}\}$.

Due to the acyclicity requirement, QuAD frameworks amount to sets of trees and each argument is the root of a (sub-)tree. For any argument $a \in \mathcal{A} \cup \mathcal{C} \cup \mathcal{P}$, we will use T_a to denote the tree with root a such that, for any node b in T_a, the children of b are the arguments in $\mathcal{R}^-(b) \cup \mathcal{R}^+(b)$.

The *Discontinuity-Free QuAD* (DF-QuAD) algorithm [21] aggregates the strengths of attackers and supporters of an argument in a QuAD framework using the *strength aggregation function*, which is defined as $\mathcal{F} : \mathbb{I}^* \rightarrow \mathbb{I}$, where for $S = (v_1, \ldots, v_n) \in \mathbb{I}^*$:

$$\text{if } n = 0 : \mathcal{F}(S) = 0$$
$$\text{if } n = 1 : \mathcal{F}(S) = v_1$$
$$\text{if } n = 2 : \mathcal{F}(S) = f(v_1, v_2)$$
$$\text{if } n > 2 : \mathcal{F}(S) = f(\mathcal{F}(v_1, \ldots, v_{n-1}), v_n)$$

---

[10] This requirement is imposed without loss of generality (see [1]).

with the *base function* $f : \mathbb{I} \times \mathbb{I} \to \mathbb{I}$ defined, for $v_1, v_2 \in \mathbb{I}$, as:

$$f(v_1, v_2) = v_1 + (1 - v_1) \cdot v_2 = v_1 + v_2 - v_1 \cdot v_2$$

Once the strengths of an argument's attackers and supporters have been aggregated separately using $\mathcal{F}$, the *combination function*, defined as $c : \mathbb{I} \times \mathbb{I} \times \mathbb{I} \to \mathbb{I}$, is used to combine the two (v^- and v^+) with the base score of the argument (v^0), in different ways depending on which of v^- and v^+ is larger, as follows:

$$c(v^0, v^-, v^+) = v^0 - v^0 \cdot |v^+ - v^-| \qquad \text{if } v^- \geq v^+$$
$$c(v^0, v^-, v^+) = v^0 + (1 - v^0) \cdot |v^+ - v^-| \qquad \text{if } v^- < v^+$$

The *score function*, $\sigma : \mathcal{A} \cup \mathcal{C} \cup \mathcal{P} \to \mathbb{I}$, determines the inputs for the combination function, giving the arguments' strength, as follows, for any $a \in \mathcal{A} \cup \mathcal{C} \cup \mathcal{P}$:

$$\sigma(a) = c(\tau(a), \mathcal{F}(\sigma(\mathcal{R}^-(a))), \mathcal{F}(\sigma(\mathcal{R}^+(a))))$$

where if $(a_1, \ldots, a_n)$ is an arbitrary permutation of the ($n \geq 0$) attackers in $\mathcal{R}^-(a)$, $\sigma(\mathcal{R}^-(a)) = (\sigma(a_1), \ldots, \sigma(a_n))$ (similarly for supporters).

For the framework in Fig. 1, if all arguments have a base score of 0.5, each of the arguments' resulting strength is 0.5, due to the framework's symmetry.

4   The QuAD-V Framework

We extend the QuAD framework defined in [1] to incorporate a set of *users* and their *votes* on arguments, while dropping the base score as given.

Definition 1. *A* QuAD *for Voting (QuAD-V) framework is a 6-tuple* $\langle \mathcal{A}, \mathcal{C}, \mathcal{P}, \mathcal{R}, \mathcal{U}, \mathcal{V} \rangle$ *such that:*

- *$\mathcal{A}$ is a finite set of* answer arguments;
- *$\mathcal{C}$ is a finite set of* con arguments;
- *$\mathcal{P}$ is a finite set of* pro arguments;
- *the sets $\mathcal{A}$, $\mathcal{C}$ and $\mathcal{P}$ are pairwise disjoint;*
- *$\mathcal{R} \subseteq (\mathcal{C} \cup \mathcal{P}) \times (\mathcal{A} \cup \mathcal{C} \cup \mathcal{P})$ is an acyclic binary relation;*
- *$\mathcal{U}$ is a finite set of* users;
- *$\mathcal{V} : \mathcal{U} \times (\mathcal{A} \cup \mathcal{C} \cup \mathcal{P}) \to \{-, ?, +\}$ is a total function; $\mathcal{V}(u, a)$ is the vote of user $u \in \mathcal{U}$ on argument $a \in \mathcal{A} \cup \mathcal{C} \cup \mathcal{P}$.*

Note that we impose that $\mathcal{V}$ is total and users explicitly specify ? as a vote. Alternatively, we could have allowed $\mathcal{V}$ to be partial, interpreting the absence of a vote by a user as ?.

In the remainder of the paper, unless otherwise indicated, we assume as given a QuAD-V framework $\mathcal{Q} = \langle \mathcal{A}, \mathcal{C}, \mathcal{P}, \mathcal{R}, \mathcal{U}, \mathcal{V} \rangle$.

Definition 2. *For any argument $a \in \mathcal{A} \cup \mathcal{C} \cup \mathcal{P}$, the set of users voting for a is $\mathcal{V}^+(a) = \{u \in \mathcal{U} : \mathcal{V}(u, a) = +\}$ and the set of users voting against a is $\mathcal{V}^-(a) = \{u \in \mathcal{U} : \mathcal{V}(u, a) = -\}$.*

The number of positive or negative votes on an argument are summated using the following functions:

Definition 3. *The* positive vote count *for an argument is* $\mathcal{N}^+ : (\mathcal{A} \cup \mathcal{C} \cup \mathcal{P}) \to \mathbb{N}$, *such that, for any argument* $a \in \mathcal{A} \cup \mathcal{C} \cup \mathcal{P}$, $\mathcal{N}^+(a) = |\mathcal{V}^+(a)|$. *The* negative vote count *for an argument is* $\mathcal{N}^- : (\mathcal{A} \cup \mathcal{C} \cup \mathcal{P}) \to \mathbb{N}$, *such that, for any argument* $a \in \mathcal{A} \cup \mathcal{C} \cup \mathcal{P}$, $\mathcal{N}^-(a) = |\mathcal{V}^-(a)|$.

We use both vote counts to calculate base scores of arguments, providing a measure of the *direct votes* on the arguments. It should be noted that this differs from the method of treating the positive counts as supporters and the negative count as attackers, as in [20].

Definition 4. *The* vote base score *(wrt $\mathcal{Q}$) is defined as* $\tau_v : \mathcal{A} \cup \mathcal{C} \cup \mathcal{P} \to \mathbb{I}$ *where, for any* $a \in \mathcal{A} \cup \mathcal{C} \cup \mathcal{P}$:

$$\tau_v(a) = \begin{cases} 0.5 & \text{if } |\mathcal{U}| = 0 \\ 0.5 + (0.5 \times \frac{\mathcal{N}^+(a) - \mathcal{N}^-(a)}{|\mathcal{U}|}) & \text{if } |\mathcal{U}| \neq 0 \end{cases}$$

This definition implies that the neutral or starting point for a vote base score is 0.5. A positive (negative, resp.) vote from a user will then add (subtract, resp.) 0.5 divided by the number of users in $\mathcal{U}$ to (from, resp.) this starting point of 0.5. A neutral vote will not have any effect on the vote base score. For example, for the framework in Fig. 1, if $\mathcal{N}^+(S1) = 3$ and $\mathcal{N}^-(S1) = 3$ and there are 10 users, then $\tau_v(S1) = 0.5$. For the same framework and number of users, if $\mathcal{N}^+(S2) = 8$ and $\mathcal{N}^-(S2) = 0$, then $\tau_v(S2) = 0.9$.

The score function from the DF-QuAD algorithm can then be used to calculate the strength of each argument using the vote base score as the base score. We refer to this instantiation of the DF-QuAD algorithm as the *QuAD-V Algorithm*. This strength provides a combined measure of the direct votes on the argument and its *indirect* votes. For an argument a, the indirect votes are those on any other argument in the tree T_a. These votes affect a through the attacking and supporting relations, with the underlying assumption that votes justified by "reasoning" (e.g. supporting arguments in the case of positive votes) are stronger than votes which are not. For example, for the framework in Fig. 1, the strength of argument $S1$ is increased if users agree with its supporter $S3$.

5   Properties of the QuAD-V Algorithm

Since the QuAD-V algorithm is an instantiation of the DF-QuAD algorithm, equivalent properties to those given in [21] for the latter hold for the former. We omit them here for lack of space to focus on new properties, specific to QuAD-V.

Firstly, in QuAD-V, an argument with more positive (negative, resp.) votes has a higher (lower, resp.) vote base score than an argument with fewer positive (negative, resp.) votes:

Property 1. For any $a, b \in \mathcal{A} \cup \mathcal{C} \cup \mathcal{P}$:

$$\tau_v(a) = \tau_v(b) \qquad \text{if } \mathcal{N}^+(a) = \mathcal{N}^+(b) \text{ and } \mathcal{N}^-(a) = \mathcal{N}^-(b)$$
$$\tau_v(a) > \tau_v(b) \qquad \text{if } \mathcal{N}^+(a) > \mathcal{N}^+(b) \text{ and } \mathcal{N}^-(a) = \mathcal{N}^-(b)$$
$$\tau_v(a) < \tau_v(b) \qquad \text{if } \mathcal{N}^+(a) = \mathcal{N}^+(b) \text{ and } \mathcal{N}^-(a) > \mathcal{N}^-(b)$$

Note that the "only-if" direction of the three statements in Property 1 does not hold in general. For example, if we have two arguments a and b such that $\mathcal{N}^+(a) = \mathcal{N}^-(a) = 2$ and $\mathcal{N}^+(b) = \mathcal{N}^-(b) = 3$, then $\tau_v(a) = \tau_v(b)$.

In the following properties, the attacking and supporting strengths of an argument $a \in \mathcal{A} \cup \mathcal{C} \cup \mathcal{P}$, i.e. $\mathcal{F}(\sigma(\mathcal{R}^-(a)))$ and $\mathcal{F}(\sigma(\mathcal{R}^+(a)))$, are represented, resp., as v_a^- and v_a^+.

An argument with more positive (negative, resp.) votes does not have a lower (higher, resp.) strength than an argument with fewer positive (negative, resp.) votes, equal negative (positive, resp.) votes, equal attacking strength and equal supporting strength:

Property 2. For any $a, b \in \mathcal{A} \cup \mathcal{C} \cup \mathcal{P}$, if $v_a^- = v_b^-$, $v_a^+ = v_b^+$, then:

$$\sigma(a) = \sigma(b) \qquad \text{if } \mathcal{N}^+(a) = \mathcal{N}^+(b) \text{ and } \mathcal{N}^-(a) = \mathcal{N}^-(b)$$
$$\sigma(a) \geq \sigma(b) \qquad \text{if } \mathcal{N}^+(a) > \mathcal{N}^+(b) \text{ and } \mathcal{N}^-(a) = \mathcal{N}^-(b)$$
$$\sigma(a) \leq \sigma(b) \qquad \text{if } \mathcal{N}^+(a) = \mathcal{N}^+(b) \text{ and } \mathcal{N}^-(a) > \mathcal{N}^-(b)$$

An argument with a higher attacking (supporting, resp.) strength does not have a higher (lower, resp.) strength than an argument with a lower attacking (supporting, resp.) strength, equal supporting (attacking, resp.) strength, equal positive votes and equal negative votes:

Property 3. For any $a, b \in \mathcal{A} \cup \mathcal{C} \cup \mathcal{P}$, if $\tau_v(a) = \tau_v(b)$, then:

$$\sigma(a) = \sigma(b) \qquad \text{if } v_a^- = v_b^- \text{ and } v_a^+ = v_b^+$$
$$\sigma(a) \leq \sigma(b) \qquad \text{if } v_a^- > v_b^- \text{ and } v_a^+ = v_b^+$$
$$\sigma(a) \geq \sigma(b) \qquad \text{if } v_a^- = v_b^- \text{ and } v_a^+ > v_b^+$$

An argument with stronger (weaker, resp.) attackers than supporters has a strength lower (higher, resp.) than the argument's vote base score, provided that this base score is not already minimal (maximal, resp.):

Property 4. For any $a \in \mathcal{A} \cup \mathcal{C} \cup \mathcal{P}$:

$$\sigma(a) < \tau_v(a) \qquad \text{iff } v_a^- > v_a^+ \text{ and } \tau_v(a) \neq 0$$
$$\sigma(a) = \tau_v(a) \qquad \text{if } v_a^- = v_a^+$$
$$\sigma(a) > \tau_v(a) \qquad \text{iff } v_a^- < v_a^+ \text{ and } \tau_v(a) \neq 1$$

If all users vote against (for, resp.) an argument, the vote base score is the minimum (maximum, resp.) value, while if equal numbers of users vote for and against an argument, the vote base score is the neutral value (0.5):

Property 5. For any $a \in \mathcal{A} \cup \mathcal{C} \cup \mathcal{P}$:

$$\tau_v(a) = 0 \qquad\qquad \text{iff } \mathcal{N}^-(a) = |\mathcal{U}| \qquad\qquad (1)$$
$$\tau_v(a) = 0.5 \qquad\qquad \text{iff } \mathcal{N}^+(a) = \mathcal{N}^-(a)$$
$$\tau_v(a) = 1 \qquad\qquad \text{iff } \mathcal{N}^+(a) = |\mathcal{U}| \qquad\qquad (2)$$

Our final property gives that for an argument to have the minimum (maximum, resp.) strength, either the supporters (attackers, resp.) have the minimum value and the attackers (supporters, resp.) the maximum or 100% of the users vote against (for, resp.) it with its attackers (supporters, resp.) at least as strong as its supporters (attackers, resp.).

Property 6. For any $a \in \mathcal{A} \cup \mathcal{C} \cup \mathcal{P}$:

$$\sigma(a) = 0 \quad \text{iff } [v_a^- = 1 \wedge v_a^+ = 0] \vee [\mathcal{N}^-(a) = |\mathcal{U}| \wedge v_a^- \geq v_a^+] \qquad (3)$$
$$\sigma(a) = 1 \quad \text{iff } [v_a^- = 0 \wedge v_a^+ = 1] \vee [\mathcal{N}^+(a) = |\mathcal{U}| \wedge v_a^- \leq v_a^+] \qquad (4)$$

We may deem an argument with a strength of 1 to be *accepted*, of 0.5 to be *neutral* and of 0 to be *rejected*. Then, directly from the properties above, an accepted argument either has universally positive votes from the users and supporters at least as strong as its attackers, or it has an accepted argument amongst its supporters and all of its attackers are rejected. Similarly, a rejected argument either has universally negative votes and attackers at least as strong as its supporters, or it has an accepted argument amongst its attackers and all of its supporters are rejected. This interpretation of arguments as accepted, neutral or rejected, depending on their strength, is a form of *bipolar labelling semantics*, in the spirit of the labelling semantics of [4] for abstract argumentation frameworks. There, arguments are labelled *in*, *undecided* or *out*, and, for a labelling to be *complete*, an argument is labelled *in* iff its attackers are all labelled *out* and an argument is labelled *out* iff at least one of its attackers is labelled *in*.

Overall, these properties show that the QuAD-V algorithm produces a notion of strength which is based on direct as well as indirect votes on arguments. Thus, if an argument has attackers and/or supporters then its strength is generally different from its base score, based exclusively on direct votes. This is only meaningful if the voters are voting rationally and the underlying argumentation frameworks are able to represent these opinions effectively, as discussed in the next section.

6   Rational Voters

QuAD-V frameworks offer the potential for characterising a user as rational. In this section we define rationality in a QuAD-V framework and some requirements which, if held, remove instances of irrationality.

In order to define rationality for individual voters we first reduce frameworks to *delegate frameworks* for each user, which are to QuAD-V frameworks with a single user.

Definition 5. *A* delegate framework *for a user u is* $Q^u = \langle \mathcal{A}^u, \mathcal{C}^u, \mathcal{P}^u, \mathcal{R}^u, \{u\}, \mathcal{V}^u \rangle$.

In the remainder of the paper, when given a delegate framework, we use $\tau_v(a)$, $\sigma(a)$, $\mathcal{R}^-(a)$, $\mathcal{R}^+(a)$, v_a^- and v_a^+ to indicate, resp., the vote base score, strength, attackers, supporters, attacking strength and supporting strength of an argument a wrt the delegate framework.

We posit that if a user votes for an argument, the supporters of that argument should be at least as strong as the attackers. This amounts to the user's reasoning for that argument being at least as strong as that against it, and therefore justifies the vote for the argument. Conversely, if a user votes against an argument, the attackers of that argument should be at least as strong as the supporters, amounting to the user's reasoning against that argument being at least as strong as that for it, therefore justifying the vote against the argument. If these conditions do not hold, we may therefore infer that either there is something missing from the framework or that the user is voting irrationally.

Definition 6. *Given a delegate framework* $Q^u = \langle \mathcal{A}^u, \mathcal{C}^u, \mathcal{P}^u, \mathcal{R}^u, \{u\}, \mathcal{V}^u \rangle$, *u is* strictly rational *(wrt Q^u) iff* $\forall a \in \mathcal{A}^u \cup \mathcal{C}^u \cup \mathcal{P}^u$:

$$if \ \tau_v(a) = 0 \ then \ v_a^- \geq v_a^+; \tag{5}$$

$$if \ \tau_v(a) = 1 \ then \ v_a^- \leq v_a^+. \tag{6}$$

There are a number of ways for a user in a QuAD-V framework to fail to satisfy strict rationality by this definition. Due to a lack of space, in this paper we chose one weaker definition of rationality and show how this instance (and, we predict, others) may be used to give more information about a voter's reasoning.

Definition 7. *Given a delegate framework* $Q^u = \langle \mathcal{A}^u, \mathcal{C}^u, \mathcal{P}^u, \mathcal{R}^u, \{u\}, \mathcal{V}^u \rangle$, *u is* individually rational *(wrt Q^u) iff*:

> **R1** : $\nexists a \in \mathcal{A}^u \cup \mathcal{C}^u \cup \mathcal{P}^u$ *such that:* $\mathcal{V}^u(u, a) = +,$
>
> $$\exists b \in \mathcal{R}^-(a) : \mathcal{V}^u(u, b) = +, and$$
>
> $$\forall c \in \mathcal{R}^+(a) : \mathcal{V}^u(u, c) = -$$

and:

> **R2** : $\nexists d \in \mathcal{A}^u \cup \mathcal{C}^u \cup \mathcal{P}^u$ *such that:* $\mathcal{V}^u(u, d) = -,$
>
> $$\exists e \in \mathcal{R}^+(d) : \mathcal{V}^u(u, e) = +, and$$
>
> $$\forall f \in \mathcal{R}^-(d) : \mathcal{V}^u(u, f) = -$$

If R1 is violated for some user u, then the user agrees with some argument a, agrees with one of its attackers b but disagrees with all of its supporters, which we see as being irrational. This violation can be avoided if the user also agrees with an argument (c) supporting a. Likewise, for requirement R2 to be violated, the user disagrees with the argument a, agrees with one of its supporters b but disagrees with all of its attackers, which we also see as being irrational. This violation can be avoided if the user also agrees with an argument (f) attacking d.

We can therefore characterise the situations where R1 and R2 are violated as those where either pro or con arguments are missing from the debate or the voter is voting irrationally. In the Brexit debate in Sect. 2, the addition of $S5$ is an example of enforcement of R2.

The following proposition shows that if a user in a QuAD-V framework fails to meet the requirements of being individually rational, then it also fails to meet those of being strictly rational.

Proposition 1. *Given a delegate framework* $Q^u = \langle \mathcal{A}^u, \mathcal{C}^u, \mathcal{P}^u, \mathcal{R}^u, \{u\}, \mathcal{V}^u \rangle$, *if* u *is not individually rational (wrt* Q^u*) then* u *is not strictly rational (wrt* Q^u*).*

Proof. For any user $u \in \mathcal{U}$, if u is not individually rational then one (or both) of R1 or R2 fail to hold.

If R1 does not hold then consequently $\exists a \in \mathcal{A}^u \cup \mathcal{C}^u \cup \mathcal{P}^u$ such that $\mathcal{V}^u(u,a) = +$, $\exists b \in \mathcal{R}^-(a) : \mathcal{V}^u(u,b) = +$ and $\forall c \in \mathcal{R}^+(a) : \mathcal{V}^u(u,c) = -$. By Property 5 (1) and (2), $\tau_v(a) = 1$, $\tau_v(b) = 1$ and $\tau_v(c) = 0$ (for any c). For u to be strictly rational, it must hold that $v_a^- \leq v_a^+$, by (6). By Property 4, $\sigma(b) = 1$ as if $\sigma(b) < \tau_v(b)$, then $v_b^- > v_b^+$, which itself causes u to fail to be strictly rational. Then, $\sigma(b) = 1$ implies, by the QuAD-V algorithm definition, that $v_a^- = 1$. Then, for u to be strictly rational, it must hold that $v_a^+ = 1$, which, by the QuAD-V algorithm definition, requires some $c \in \mathcal{R}^+(a) : \sigma(c) = 1$. Since $\tau_v(c) = 0$, by Property 4, this requires that $v_c^- < v_c^+$ but this itself causes u to fail to be strictly rational.

If R2 does not hold then consequently $\exists d \in \mathcal{A}^u \cup \mathcal{C}^u \cup \mathcal{P}^u$ such that $\mathcal{V}^u(u,d) = -$, $\exists e \in \mathcal{R}^+(d) : \mathcal{V}^u(u,e) = +$ and $\forall f \in \mathcal{R}^-(d) : \mathcal{V}^u(u,f) = -$. By Property 5 (1) and (2), $\tau_v(d) = 0$, $\tau_v(e) = 1$ and $\tau_v(f) = 0$ (for any f). For u to be strictly rational, it must hold that $v_d^- \geq v_d^+$, by (5). By Property 4, $\sigma(e) = 1$ as if $\sigma(e) < \tau_v(e)$, then $v_e^- > v_e^+$, which itself causes u to fail to be strictly rational. Then, $\sigma(b) = 1$ implies, by the QuAD-V algorithm definition, that $v_d^+ = 1$. Then, for u to be strictly rational, it must hold that $v_d^- = 1$, which, by the QuAD-V algorithm definition, requires some $f \in \mathcal{R}^-(d) : \sigma(f) = 1$. Since $\tau_v(f) = 0$, by Property 4, this requires that $v_f^- < v_f^+$ but this itself causes u to fail to be strictly rational.   □

Then, *collective rationality* amounts to individual rationality for all users.

Definition 8. *Given a QuAD-V framework* $Q = \langle \mathcal{A}, \mathcal{C}, \mathcal{P}, \mathcal{R}, \mathcal{U}, \mathcal{V} \rangle$, $\mathcal{U}$ *is collectively rational (wrt* Q*) iff* $\forall u \in \mathcal{U}$, u *is individually rational (wrt the delegate framework* $Q^u = \langle \mathcal{A}^u, \mathcal{C}^u, \mathcal{P}^u, \mathcal{R}^u, \{u\}, \mathcal{V}^u \rangle$*).*

Note that we assume that the given QuAD-V framework correctly represents dialectical relations between arguments and do not accommodate the possibility that a violation of the requirements may be due to a user actually disagreeing with the attack between two arguments it agrees with or the support between an argument it agrees with and one it disagrees with. We leave accommodating this possibility for future work.

Note also that other definitions of rationality, in addition to those shown here, may be possible but are left for future work.

In the next section we describe how QuAD-V frameworks can be used in opinion polls to highlight irrational voting and give the voters the opportunity to render their votes rational, if required.

7   QuAD-V Opinion Polls

QuAD-V opinion polls use an initial QuAD framework to specify (and relate) statements for users to vote on. The users may be asked to vote on the statements sequentially (and be unaware of the relations in the underlying QuAD framework) or may be presented with a graphical representation of the QuAD framework. Whichever the case, the result of the voting is a QuAD-V framework (referred to as *master framework* below). Users in this framework that are not individually rational are then asked *dynamic questions*. The users' responses to these dynamic questions transform their delegate frameworks iteratively until all of the individual irrationalities are removed and delegate frameworks become *stable*. A *revised master framework* is then created, which may be seen as the amalgamation of the stable delegate frameworks, and its set of users is guaranteed to be collectively rational. Multiple runs of this process may take place to allow voting on new arguments introduced on previous runs. Figure 2 summarises (a run of) this process, which is described in detail in this section.

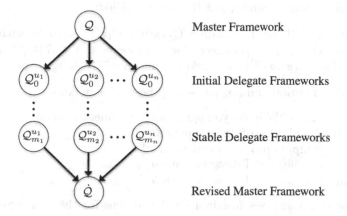

Fig. 2. QuAD-V opinion polling process for users u_1 to u_n

In the remainder of this section, $Q = \langle \mathcal{A}, \mathcal{C}, \mathcal{P}, \mathcal{R}, \mathcal{U}, \mathcal{V} \rangle$ is the master framework and $u_i \in \mathcal{U}$ is a generic user, where $1 \leq i \leq n$ and $n = |\mathcal{U}|$. Further, given any QuAD-V framework $Q^* = \langle \mathcal{A}^*, \mathcal{C}^*, \mathcal{P}^*, \mathcal{R}^*, \mathcal{U}^*, \mathcal{V}^* \rangle$, we denote $\mathcal{A}^* \cup \mathcal{C}^* \cup \mathcal{P}^*$ as $\mathcal{X}(Q^*)$.

7.1   Iteration and Initial Delegate Frameworks

Initial and iteration delegate frameworks are restrictions of the master framework and transformations thereof, resp.:

Definition 9. *For $j \geq 0$, $Q_j^{u_i} = \langle \mathcal{A}_j^{u_i}, \mathcal{C}_j^{u_i}, \mathcal{P}_j^{u_i}, \mathcal{R}_j^{u_i}, \{u_i\}, \mathcal{V}_j^{u_i} \rangle$ is the jth iteration delegate framework, defined as follows:*

- *If $j = 0$ then $\mathcal{A}_0^{u_i} = \mathcal{A}$, $\mathcal{C}_0^{u_i} = \mathcal{C}$, $\mathcal{P}_0^{u_i} = \mathcal{P}$, $\mathcal{R}_0^{u_i} = \mathcal{R}$ and, $\forall a \in \mathcal{X}(\mathcal{Q}_0^{u_i})$, $\mathcal{V}_0^{u_i}(u_i, a) = \mathcal{V}(u_i, a)$.*
- *If $j > 0$ then $\mathcal{A}_j^{u_i} = \mathcal{A}_{j-1}^{u_i}$, $\mathcal{C}_j^{u_i} \supseteq \mathcal{C}_{j-1}^{u_i}$, $\mathcal{P}_j^{u_i} \supseteq \mathcal{P}_{j-1}^{u_i}$, $\mathcal{R}_j^{u_i} \supseteq \mathcal{R}_{j-1}^{u_i}$, and there exists at most one argument $a \in \mathcal{X}(\mathcal{Q}_j^{u_i})$ such that if $\mathcal{V}_{j-1}^{u_i}(u_i, a) = +$ then $\mathcal{V}_j^{u_i}(u_i, a) = -$, if $\mathcal{V}_{j-1}^{u_i}(u_i, a) = -$ then $\mathcal{V}_j^{u_i}(u_i, a) = +$, and $\forall b \in \mathcal{X}(\mathcal{Q}_j^{u_i}) \setminus \{a\}$, $\mathcal{V}_j^{u_i}(u_i, b) = \mathcal{V}_{j-1}^{u_i}(u_i, b)$.*

We refer to $\mathcal{Q}_0^{u_i}$ as the initial delegate framework.

Note that at each iteration users may change their votes and/or add arguments and relations between arguments.

7.2   Dynamic Questions and Responses

In the remainder of this section, where there is no ambiguity, we will assume as given a jth iteration delegate framework $\mathcal{Q}_j^{u_i} = \langle \mathcal{A}_j, \mathcal{C}_j, \mathcal{P}_j, \mathcal{R}_j, \{u_i\}, \mathcal{V}_j \rangle$ for $j \geq 0$.

Dynamic questions are put to users that are found to be individually irrational. The allowed responses to these questions indicate how to remove the irrationalities from the delegate frameworks. We define two such questions. The first is produced when requirement R1 is not fulfilled:

Definition 10. A Type 1 Dynamic Question $\Omega_1(\mathcal{Q}_j^{u_i}, u_i, a, b)$ with possible responses $\rho_1(\alpha), \rho_2, \rho_3$ is produced for arguments $a, b \in \mathcal{X}(\mathcal{Q}_j^{u_i})$ such that $b \in \mathcal{R}_j^-(a)$ when $\mathcal{V}_j(u_i, a) = +$, $\mathcal{V}_j(u_i, b) = +$ and $\forall c \in \mathcal{R}_j^+(a)$, $\mathcal{V}_j(u_i, c) = -$.

Informally, question and responses may be read as follows:

- $\Omega_1(\mathcal{Q}_j^{u_i}, u_i, a, b)$ - "Why do you agree with argument a when you agree with its attacker b and none of its supporters?"
- $\rho_1(\alpha)$ - [User inputs pro argument α for a]
- ρ_2 - "I made a mistake, I disagree with a"
- ρ_3 - "I made a mistake, I disagree with b"

The first response gives insight into the reasons for the user agreeing with a by providing a supporting argument for a, which we envisage not to belong already to the (current) delegate framework. The second and third responses help to rectify mistakes or prevent users from voting randomly.

Responses are used to revise delegate frameworks:

Definition 11. Given a Type 1 Dynamic Question $\Omega_1(\mathcal{Q}_j^{u_i}, u_i, a, b)$, let ρ_* be its response. Then $\mathcal{Q}_{j+1}^{u_i}$ is the revision of $\mathcal{Q}_j^{u_i}$ by ρ_* to $\Omega_1(\mathcal{Q}_j^{u_i}, u_i, a, b)$ where[11]:

$$
\begin{aligned}
&\text{if } \rho_* = \rho_1(\alpha) &&\text{then } \mathcal{P}_{j+1} = \mathcal{P}_j \cup \{\alpha\}, \\
&&&\mathcal{R}_{j+1} = \mathcal{R}_j \cup \{(\alpha, a)\}, \\
&&&\mathcal{V}_{j+1}(u_i, \alpha) = +; \\
&\text{if } \rho_* = \rho_2 &&\text{then } \mathcal{V}_{j+1}(u_i, a) = -; \\
&\text{if } \rho_* = \rho_3 &&\text{then } \mathcal{V}_{j+1}(u_i, b) = -.
\end{aligned}
$$

---

[11] From here onwards, we give only the components of $\mathcal{Q}_{j+1}^{u_i}$ different to those in $\mathcal{Q}_j^{u_i}$.

The second question is produced when R2 is not fulfilled:

Definition 12. *A* Type 2 Dynamic Question $\Omega_2(\mathcal{Q}_j^{u_i}, u_i, a, b)$ *with possible responses* $\rho_1(\alpha), \rho_2, \rho_3$ *is produced for arguments* $a, b \in \mathcal{X}(\mathcal{Q}_j^{u_i})$ *such that* $b \in \mathcal{R}_j^+(a)$ *when* $\mathcal{V}_j(u_i, a) = -$, $\mathcal{V}_j(u_i, b) = +$ *and* $\forall c \in \mathcal{R}_j^-(a)$, $\mathcal{V}_j(u_i, c) = -$.

Informally, question and responses may be read as follows:

- $\Omega_2(\mathcal{Q}_j^{u_i}, u_i, a, b)$ - "Why do you disagree with argument a when you agree with its supporter b and none of its attackers?"
- $\rho_1(\alpha)$ - [User inputs con argument α against a]
- ρ_2 - "I made a mistake, I agree with a"
- ρ_3 - "I made a mistake, I disagree with b"

Definition 13. *Given a* Type 2 Dynamic Question $\Omega_2(\mathcal{Q}_j^{u_i}, u_i, a, b)$, *let* ρ_* *be its response. Then* $\mathcal{Q}_{j+1}^{u_i}$ *is the* revision *of* $\mathcal{Q}_j^{u_i}$ *by* ρ_* *to* $\Omega_2(\mathcal{Q}_j^{u_i}, u_i, a, b)$ *where:*

$$\text{if } \rho_* = \rho_1(\alpha) \qquad \text{then } \mathcal{C}_{j+1} = \mathcal{C}_j \cup \{\alpha\},$$
$$\mathcal{R}_{j+1} = \mathcal{R}_j \cup \{(\alpha, a)\},$$
$$\mathcal{V}_{j+1}(u_i, \alpha) = +;$$
$$\text{if } \rho_* = \rho_2 \qquad \text{then } \mathcal{V}_{j+1}(u_i, a) = +;$$
$$\text{if } \rho_* = \rho_3 \qquad \text{then } \mathcal{V}_{j+1}(u_i, b) = -.$$

Note that users are not allowed to give no response to either type of dynamic question, i.e. users are assumed to be cooperative.

When no more dynamic questions can be produced for arguments in a delegate framework then it is deemed stable:

Definition 14. $\mathcal{Q}_j^{u_i}$ *is* stable *iff no dynamic questions are produced for any arguments in* $\mathcal{X}(\mathcal{Q}_j^{u_i})$.

Stable delegate frameworks are guaranteed to exist and their users are guaranteed to be individually rational , provided that they change their vote on each argument at most once:

Proposition 2. *Let us assume that* u_i *is such that for every* $\mathcal{Q}_0^{u_i}, \ldots$, *for every* $a \in \mathcal{X}(\mathcal{Q}_0^{u_i})$, *there exists at most one* j, *for* $0 \leq j$, *such that* $\mathcal{V}_{j+1}(u_i, a) \neq \mathcal{V}_j(u_i, a)$. *Then* $\exists m_i \geq 0$ *and* $\mathcal{Q}_0^{u_i}, \ldots, \mathcal{Q}_{m_i}^{u_i}$ *such that* $\mathcal{Q}_0^{u_i}$ *is the initial delegate framework, each* $\mathcal{Q}_j^{u_i}$, *for* $0 < j \leq m_i$, *is the revision of* $\mathcal{Q}_{j-1}^{u_i}$ *(by some response to some dynamic question), and* $\mathcal{Q}_{m_i}^{u_i}$ *is stable. Further,* u_i *is individually rational (wrt* $\mathcal{Q}_{m_i}^{u_i}$*).*

Proof (Sketch). Each revision eliminates one violation of R1 or R2, and adds at most one argument (in the case of instances of ρ_1) which cannot introduce a violation. However, changing votes may do so. Each additional violation will give rise to an additional dynamic question and so votes on arguments would have to be changed back and forth for a delegate framework not to be reached. The order in which these questions and responses are produced is irrelevant, as the conditions for the dynamic questions are mutually exclusive. Thus convergence to $\mathcal{Q}_{m_i}^{u_i}$ is guaranteed, under the stated conditions. It is easy to see that users in stable frameworks are individually rational. □

7.3   Revised Master Framework

Once all delegate frameworks are stable, amalgamating the delegate frameworks gives the revised master frameworks.

Definition 15 *Let $\mathcal{Q}_{m_i}^{u_i}$ be the stable delegate frameworks for $u_i \in \mathcal{U}$, where $i \geq 1$. A revised master framework $\dot{\mathcal{Q}}$ is $\langle \mathcal{A}, \dot{\mathcal{C}}, \dot{\mathcal{P}}, \dot{\mathcal{R}}, \mathcal{U}, \dot{\mathcal{V}} \rangle$, where $\dot{\mathcal{C}} = \mathcal{C} \cup \mathcal{C}_+$ such that $\mathcal{C}_+ \subseteq \mathcal{C}_{m_1} \cup \ldots \cup \mathcal{C}_{m_n} \setminus \mathcal{C}$, $\dot{\mathcal{P}} = \mathcal{P} \cup \mathcal{P}_+$ such that $\mathcal{P}_+ \subseteq \mathcal{P}_{m_1} \cup \ldots \cup \mathcal{P}_{m_n} \setminus \mathcal{P}$, $\dot{\mathcal{R}} = \mathcal{R} \cup \mathcal{R}_+$ such that $\mathcal{R}_+ \subseteq \mathcal{R}_{m_1} \cup \ldots \cup \mathcal{R}_{m_n} \setminus \mathcal{R}$, and $\forall a \in \mathcal{X}(\dot{\mathcal{Q}})$ and $\forall u_i \in \mathcal{U}$, if $\exists a \in \mathcal{Q}_{m_i}^{u_i}$ then $\dot{\mathcal{V}}(u_i, a) = \mathcal{V}_{m_i}(u_i, a)$, otherwise $\dot{\mathcal{V}}(u_i, a) = ?$.*

Basically, each selection of "new" arguments, in the revised but not in the initial delegate frameworks, gives a revised master framework, with users' votes on "unseen" arguments (from other users' revised delegate frameworks) set to the neutral value.[12] The largest possible revised master framework includes all these arguments, whereas the smallest includes none. Our definition allows for human intervention to review the contents of the stable delegate frameworks and disregard, for example, "new" arguments that are not valid or relevant. We leave more sophisticated forms of amalgamation, e.g. taking into account duplications across users and natural language processing, for future work.

Irrespective of the choice of revised master framework, any given user is guaranteed to be at least as individually rational as they were in the master framework the process started with, as this process does not introduce any violations of requirements R1, R2.

Proposition 3 *Let $\dot{\mathcal{Q}}$ be a revised master framework. Let x be the number of violations of R1 and R2 in $\mathcal{Q}$ and y be the number of violations of R1 and R2 in $\dot{\mathcal{Q}}$. Then, $y \leq x$.*

If a user's new arguments have been integrated into the revised master framework then the user is guaranteed to be individually rational.

Proposition 4 *If $\mathcal{C}_{m_i} \subseteq \dot{\mathcal{C}}$ and $\mathcal{P}_{m_i} \subseteq \dot{\mathcal{P}}$ then u_i is individually rational (wrt $\dot{\mathcal{Q}}$).*

Finally, the largest possible revised master framework's set of users is collectively rational.

Proposition 5 *If $\dot{\mathcal{C}} = \mathcal{C} \cup \mathcal{C}_{m_1} \cup \ldots \cup \mathcal{C}_{m_n}$ and $\dot{\mathcal{P}} = \mathcal{P} \cup \mathcal{P}_{m_1} \cup \ldots \cup \mathcal{P}_{m_n}$ then $\dot{\mathcal{U}}$ is collectively rational (wrt $\dot{\mathcal{Q}}$).*

---

[12] Note that, as we state at the beginning of Sect. 7, users may change their votes on these "unseen" arguments if multiple runs of the process depicted in Fig. 2 occur. We leave the study of multiple runs to future work.

8   Conclusions

We have presented QuAD-V frameworks, extending QuAD frameworks [1] to incorporate voting, and applied them to support opinion polling.

QuAD-V frameworks can be also seen as extending the Social Argumentation Frameworks (SAFs) of [16] by also allowing support between arguments. Differently from QuAD-V frameworks, SAFs are not restricted to acyclic attack relations: we leave the relaxation of this restriction for QuAD-V frameworks as future work. Also, it would be interesting to study formal relationships between our vote aggregation mechanism and the one in [16] and our notion of strength and the evaluation of arguments in SAFs (determining, in particular, whether SAFs fulfil versions of the properties in Sect. 5). Like QuAD-V frameworks, mDICE frameworks [20] accommodate votes on arguments as well as attack and support relations, but keep votes and dialectical relations somewhat separate. Another approach for determining rationality in users' labellings of arguments is described in [11]. Differently from QuAD-V frameworks, the approach of [11] has not been applied to opinion polling (using dynamic questions and a revision process such as the one we have defined). Also, the aggregation function in [11] differs from, and exhibits different properties to, the QuAD-V algorithm. However, [11] also consider the relationship between direct and indirect opinions (votes, in our case) and their definition of "coherence" aligns with our definition of strict rationality (within the respective contexts). We plan to study relationships of QuAD-V frameworks with these approaches, along with their relative suitability to support opinion polling, in the future.

Our proposed QuAD-V opinion polling holds two main advantages over the flat, conventional approach which is almost universally adopted. Firstly, as we have shown, the use of an underlying QuAD-V framework to structure (semantically) statements in opinion polls paves the way to empower users to iteratively evolve polls so that they highlight, and potentially eradicate, irrationalities in users' opinions and, as a consequence, are more informative to the pollster. Secondly, the use of a method for determining the strength of opinions seen as arguments in QuAD-V frameworks can give useful additional measures of public sentiment on statements in a poll. We plan to develop the system further in future work, e.g. allowing users to respond to dynamic questions uncooperatively (e.g. "I don't know") or by disagreeing with the relation itself (e.g. "I don't agree that $S3$ supports $S1$", in the Brexit debate). The former may indicate irrational voting, while the latter would give an added dimension of dynamicity and self-correction to QuAD-V frameworks and could be implemented without losing the rationality properties by weighting relations (e.g. see [9]).

We have defined a basic notion of a user being strictly rational based on their voting and a weaker notion of a user being individually rational. We have shown how the latter may be beneficial for eliciting reasoning from users, highlighting "illogical" voting and filtering mistakes and random voting using our theoretical evaluation. It could be interesting to utilise strict rationality in this elicitation. An empirical evaluation of an implementation QuAD-V polling is also left as future work, along with comparisons with existing systems, e.g. [10], and verifying our assumption that users are cooperative.

Overall, we hope that our e-polling methodology will help to increase public engagement in a number of settings by letting users take an active part in debates that adapt to user opinions, rather than restricting these to predetermined opinions only.

References

1. Baroni, P., Romano, M., Toni, F., Aurisicchio, M., Bertanza, G.: Automatic evaluation of design alternatives with quantitative argumentation. Argum. Comput. 6(1), 24–49 (2015). http://dx.doi.org/10.1080/19462166.2014.1001791
2. Bessette, J.: Deliberative democracy: the majority principle in Republican government. How Democr. Const. 102, 109–111 (1980)
3. Buckingham-Shum, S.: Cohere: towards web 2.0 argumentation. In: Computational Models of Argument: Proceedings of COMMA 2008, Toulouse, France, 28–30 May 2008, pp. 97–108 (2008). http://www.booksonline.iospress.nl/Content/View.aspx?piid=9271
4. Caminada, M.W.A., Gabbay, D.M.: A logical account of formal argumentation. Studia Log. 93(2–3), 109–145 (2009). http://dx.doi.org/10.1007/s11225-009-9218-x
5. Cartwright, D., Atkinson, K.: Political engagement through tools for argumentation. In: Computational Models of Argument: Proceedings of COMMA 2008, Toulouse, France, 28–30 May 2008. pp. 116–127 (2008). http://www.booksonline.iospress.nl/Content/View.aspx?piid=9273
6. Cayrol, C., Lagasquie-Schiex, M.C.: On the acceptability of arguments in bipolar argumentation frameworks. In: Godo, L. (ed.) ECSQARU 2005. LNCS, vol. 3571, pp. 378–389. Springer, Heidelberg (2005). doi:10.1007/11518655_33
7. Conklin, J., Selvin, A.M., Shum, S.B., Sierhuis, M.: Facilitated hypertext for collective sensemaking: 15 years on from gIBIS. In: Proceedings of the 12th ACM Conference on Hypertext and Hypermedia, pp. 123–124 (2001). http://doi.acm.org/10.1145/504216.504246
8. Dung, P.M.: On the acceptability of arguments and its fundamental role in nonmonotonic reasoning, logic programming and n-person games. Artif. Intell. 77(2), 321–358 (1995). http://dx.doi.org/10.1016/0004-3702(94)00041-X
9. Dunne, P.E., Hunter, A., McBurney, P., Parsons, S., Wooldridge, M.: Weighted argument systems: basic definitions, algorithms, and complexity results. Artif. Intell. 175(2), 457–486 (2011). https://doi.org/10.1016/j.artint.2010.09.005
10. Fishkin, J.S., Luskin, R.C., Jowell, R.: Deliberative polling and public consultation. Parliam. Aff. 53(4), 657–666 (2000)
11. Ganzer-Ripoll, J., López-Sánchez, M., Rodriguez-Aguilar, J.A.: A multi-agent argumentation framework to support collective reasoning. In: Aydoğan, R., Baarslag, T., Gerding, E., Jonker, C.M., Julian, V., Sanchez-Anguix, V. (eds.) COREDEMA 2016. LNCS, vol. 10238, pp. 100–117. Springer, Cham (2017). doi:10.1007/978-3-319-57285-7_7
12. Gordon, T.F., Prakken, H., Walton, D.: The Carneades model of argument and burden of proof. Artif. Intell. 171(10–15), 875–896 (2007). http://dx.doi.org/10.1016/j.artint.2007.04.010

13. Gordon, T.F., Richter, G.: Discourse support systems for deliberative democracy. In: Traunmüller, R., Lenk, K. (eds.) EGOV 2002. LNCS, vol. 2456, pp. 248–255. Springer, Heidelberg (2002). doi:10.1007/978-3-540-46138-8_40
14. Krauthoff, T., Baurmann, M., Betz, G., Mauve, M.: Dialog-based online argumentation. In: Computational Models of Argument - Proceedings of COMMA 2016, Potsdam, Germany, 12–16 September 2016, pp. 33–40 (2016). http://dx.doi.org/10.3233/978-1-61499-686-6-33
15. Kunz, W., Rittel, H.W.: Issues as Elements of Information Systems, vol. 131. Institute of Urban and Regional Development, University of California Berkeley (1970)
16. Leite, J., Martins, J.: Social abstract argumentation. In: Proceedings of the 22nd International Joint Conference on Artificial Intelligence, IJCAI 2011, pp. 2287–2292 (2011). http://ijcai.org/papers11/Papers/IJCAI11-381.pdf
17. Loukis, E., Xenakis, A., Tseperli, N.: Using argument visualization to enhance e-participation in the legislation formation process. In: Macintosh, A., Tambouris, E. (eds.) ePart 2009. LNCS, vol. 5694, pp. 125–138. Springer, Heidelberg (2009). doi:10.1007/978-3-642-03781-8_12
18. Luna, G.D.I., López-López, A., Pérez, J.: Predicting preferences of voters from opinion polls by machine learning and game theory. Res. Comput. Sci. **77**, 121–131 (2014). http://rcs.cic.ipn.mx/2014_77/Predicting%20Preferences%20of%20Voters%20from%20Opinion%20Polls%20by%20Machine%20Learning%20and%20Game%20Theory.pdf
19. Mouffe, C.: Deliberative democracy or agonistic pluralism? Soc. Res. **3**, 745–758 (1999)
20. Patkos, T., Bikakis, A., Flouris, G.: A multi-aspect evaluation framework for comments on the social web. In: Principles of Knowledge Representation and Reasoning: Proceedings of the Fifteenth International Conference, KR 2016, Cape Town, South Africa, 25–29 April 2016, pp. 593–596 (2016). http://www.aaai.org/ocs/index.php/KR/KR16/paper/view/12885
21. Rago, A., Toni, F., Aurisicchio, M., Baroni, P.: Discontinuity-free decision support with quantitative argumentation debates. In: Principles of Knowledge Representation and Reasoning: Proceedings of the Fifteenth International Conference, KR 2016, Cape Town, South Africa, 25–29 April 2016, pp. 63–73 (2016). http://www.aaai.org/ocs/index.php/KR/KR16/paper/view/12874
22. Simari, G.R., Rahwan, I. (eds.): Argumentation in Artificial Intelligence. Springer, Heidelberg (2009)
23. Thapen, N.A., Ghanem, M.M.: Towards passive political opinion polling using Twitter. In: Proceedings of the BCS SGAI Workshop on Social Media Analysis 2013 Co-Located with 33rd Annual International Conference of the British Computer Society's Specialist Group on Artificial Intelligence (BCS SGAI 2013), Cambridge, UK, 10 December 2013, pp. 19–34 (2013). http://ceur-ws.org/Vol-1110/paper2.pdf
24. Zhu, J., Wang, H., Zhu, M., Tsou, B.K., Ma, M.Y.: Aspect-based opinion polling from customer reviews. IEEE Trans. Affect. Comput. **2**(1), 37–49 (2011). http://dx.doi.org/10.1109/T-AFFC.2011.2

Capturing Bipolar Argumentation in Non-flat Assumption-Based Argumentation

Kristijonas Čyras$^{(\boxtimes)}$ ⓘ, Claudia Schulz$^{(\boxtimes)}$ ⓘ, and Francesca Toni ⓘ

Department of Computing, Imperial College London, London, UK
{k.cyras,claudia.schulz,ft}@imperial.ac.uk

Abstract. Bipolar Argumentation Frameworks (BAFs) encompass both attacks and supports among arguments. We study different semantic interpretations of support in BAFs, particularly *necessary* and *deductive* support, as well as argument *coalitions* and a recent proposal by Gabbay. We analyse the relationship of these different notions of support in BAFs with the semantics of a well established structured argumentation formalism, Assumption-Based Argumentation (ABA), which predates BAFs. We propose natural mappings from BAFs into a restricted class of (non-flat) ABA frameworks, which we call *bipolar*, and prove that the admissible and preferred semantics of these ABA frameworks correspond to the admissible and preferred semantics of the various approaches to BAFs. Motivated by the definition of stable semantics for BAFs, we introduce a novel *set-stable* semantics for ABA frameworks, and prove that it corresponds to the stable semantics of the various approaches to BAFs. Finally, as a by-product of modelling various approaches to BAFs in bipolar ABA, we identify precise semantic relationships amongst all approaches we consider.

1 Introduction

Bipolar argumentation (as overviewed recently in [11,12]) extends Abstract Argumentation (AA) [15] by allowing a support relation between arguments, in addition to the standard attack relation. Bipolar argumentation is useful in a number of applications, for example to capture debates in social networks [7] and to support decision making [2]. Several alternative interpretations of support have been proposed in as many semantics for Bipolar Argumentation Frameworks (BAFs) in terms of "acceptable" extensions (i.e. sets of arguments) (e.g. see [4,6,11,16,19,20,26]) or in terms of numerical notions of strength (e.g. see [1,8,23]). These interpretations vary considerably. For example, for a and b arguments in a given BAF, if a supports b, denoted $a \Rightarrow b$, then:

- under the *deductive* interpretation of support [11], if a is accepted, then b must be accepted too;
- under the *necessary* interpretation of support [6,19,20], if b is accepted, then a must be accepted too.

© Springer International Publishing AG 2017
B. An et al. (Eds.): PRIMA 2017, LNAI 10621, pp. 386–402, 2017.
https://doi.org/10.1007/978-3-319-69131-2_23

These two interpretations give rise to different interplays between support and attack, and to different arguments being accepted in general. For example, if a supports b and a attacks itself, under the necessary interpretation of support neither a nor b can be accepted, no matter which semantics is adopted, whereas under the deductive interpretation b may be accepted (depending on the semantics). The following example illustrates the diverging intuitions behind these two interpretations.

Example 1. Consider a set of abstract arguments $\{a, b, c, d, e\}$ as well as the following attacks ($\rightsquigarrow$) and supports ($\Rightarrow$) among these arguments:

$$a \Rightarrow b \qquad a \Rightarrow c \qquad d \Rightarrow e \qquad e \rightsquigarrow b \qquad b \rightsquigarrow e \qquad e \rightsquigarrow c$$

The BAF consisting of these arguments, attacks and supports can be depicted as a graph below (here nodes are arguments, single-line arrows indicate attacks and double-line arrows indicate supports):

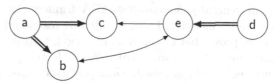

Under the deductive support interpretation, if we accept a, then we should accept *both* b *and* c. Instead, under the necessary support interpretation, accepting *either* b *or* c leads to accepting a. Also, under the first interpretation, if we accept d, then we are expected to accept e, while under the second interpretation, if we accept e, then we should accept d.

In addition to diverging intuitions and argument acceptance, different interpretations of support result in rather different semantic definitions for BAFs. This is mainly because support in BAFs is used alongside attacks to define new types of attacks, which differ across approaches due to their different interpretations of support. For example, the semantics for BAFs under the necessary interpretation of support [20] is defined in terms of a notion of *strong coherence* and an *extended* attack relation. Instead, the semantics for BAFs under the deductive interpretation of support [11] is defined in terms of relations of *supported* and *super-mediated* attack. Further, Gabbay's approach [16] uses the transitive and reflexive closure of the support relation to define yet another attack relation with respect to which argument acceptability is evaluated. As a final example, the support relation in BAFs is used, in [11], to provide a basis to form argument *coalitions*, where a coalition associated with an argument is simply the set of arguments supported by that argument. Such coalitions can then be seen as individual arguments in a 'meta' AA framework, where standard AA semantics defines the semantics of the original BAF. In the context of this multitude of concepts, the different semantics of BAFs have, so far, not been compared in detail (see [11] for some partial results, also discussed in Sect. 7).

In this paper we provide a cohesive view of this fragmented landscape by showing that the various aforementioned semantics of BAFs correspond to semantics of a well-known structured argumentation formalism predating BAFs, namely Assumption-Based Argumentation (ABA) [5,25]. As a by-product, we work out exactly how all aforementioned approaches relate. Several features of ABA make it a natural candidate for this correspondence: in ABA, as in other structured argumentation formalisms (see [3] for an overview), arguments are constructed from rules, which provide deductive support for the arguments' claims, rules can be chained to give transitive support, and acceptance of the consequent (or head) of a rule may require acceptance of the antecedent (or body); moreover, in ABA, arguments are also constructed from special premises, called *assumptions*, which can in turn be supported by other arguments.

It is known that AA frameworks can be mapped into ABA frameworks while preserving semantic correspondence [24,25]. In that case, the obtained ABA frameworks are guaranteed to be of a restricted type, namely *flat* [5]. Here, we generalise this mapping and define new mappings from BAFs into ABA frameworks, which in general yield *non-flat* ABA frameworks. However, these ABA frameworks are guaranteed to be of a different restricted kind, which we call *bipolar*. Indeed, we prove that the aforementioned interpretations of support in BAFs correspond, under the (respective) *admissible* and *preferred* extension semantics (where defined), to the admissible and preferred extension semantics of bipolar ABA frameworks. We also give a novel semantics of *set-stable* extensions for any (bipolar or non-bipolar) ABA frameworks. These set-stable extensions are equivalent to the standard stable extensions for flat ABA frameworks, and correspond to the stable extensions of BAFs under the interpretations of support for which the stable semantics has been defined.

The paper is organised as follows. In Sect. 2 we give basic background on ABA, AA and BAFs. In Sect. 3 we introduce bipolar ABA frameworks and prove some properties thereof. In Sects. 4 and 5 we map BAFs under the necessary and deductive interpretations, respectively, into bipolar ABA. Further, in Sect. 6, we map Gabbay's and the coalition approach into bipolar ABA. Then, in Sect. 7, we show formal relationships among the different approaches to BAFs we consider. We conclude in Sect. 8.

2   Background

Assumption-Based Argumentation (ABA) (see [5,14,25]). An *ABA framework* is a tuple $(\mathcal{L}, \mathcal{R}, \mathcal{A}, ^-)$, where:

- $(\mathcal{L}, \mathcal{R})$ is a deductive system with $\mathcal{L}$ a language (i.e. a set of sentences) and $\mathcal{R}$ a set of rules of the form $\varphi_0 \leftarrow \varphi_1, \ldots, \varphi_m$ with $m \geqslant 0$ and $\varphi_i \in \mathcal{L}$ for $i \in \{0, \ldots, m\}$; φ_0 is the *head* and $\varphi_1, \ldots, \varphi_m$ the *body*; if $m = 0$, then $\varphi_0 \leftarrow \varphi_1, \ldots, \varphi_m$ has an empty body, and is written as $\varphi_0 \leftarrow \top$, where $\top \notin \mathcal{L}$;
- $\mathcal{A} \subseteq \mathcal{L}$ is a non-empty set of *assumptions*;
- $^- : \mathcal{A} \rightarrow \mathcal{L}$ is a total map: for $\alpha \in \mathcal{A}$, the $\mathcal{L}$-sentence $\overline{\alpha}$ is referred to as the *contrary* of α.

For the remainder of this section, we assume as given a fixed but arbitrary ABA framework $\mathcal{F} = (\mathcal{L}, \mathcal{R}, \mathcal{A}, {}^{-})$.

- A *deduction for* $\varphi \in \mathcal{L}$ *supported by* $A \subseteq \mathcal{A}$ and $R \subseteq \mathcal{R}$, denoted $A \vdash^R \varphi$, is a finite tree with: the root labelled by φ; leaves labelled by $\top$ or assumptions, with A being the set of all such assumptions; the children of non-leaves ψ labelled by the elements of the body of some ψ-headed rule in $\mathcal{R}$, with R being the set of all such rules.
- $A \subseteq \mathcal{A}$ *attacks* $B \subseteq \mathcal{A}$, denoted $A \leadsto_{\text{ABA}} B$, iff there is a deduction $A' \vdash^R \overline{\beta}$, such that $\beta \in B$, $A' \subseteq A$.

If it is not the case that A attacks B, we may write $A \not\leadsto_{\text{ABA}} B$. (We will adopt an analogous convention for other attack relations throughout.) Let $A \subseteq \mathcal{A}$:

- The *closure* of A is $Cl(A) = \{\alpha \in \mathcal{A} \ : \ \exists A' \vdash^R \alpha, \ A' \subseteq A, \ R \subseteq \mathcal{R}\}$.
- A is *closed* iff $A = Cl(A)$.
- $\mathcal{F}$ is *flat* iff every $B \subseteq \mathcal{A}$ is closed.
- A is *conflict-free* iff $A \not\leadsto_{\text{ABA}} A$.
- A *defends* $\alpha \in \mathcal{A}$ iff for all closed $B \subseteq \mathcal{A}$ with $B \leadsto_{\text{ABA}} \{\alpha\}$ it holds that $A \leadsto_{\text{ABA}} B$. We also say A defends $B \subseteq \mathcal{A}$ iff A defends every $\beta \in B$.

We use ABA semantics as follows. A set $E \subseteq \mathcal{A}$, also called an *extension*, is:

- *admissible* iff it is closed, conflict-free and defends itself.
- *preferred* iff it is $\subseteq$-maximally admissible.
- *stable* iff it is closed, conflict-free and $E \leadsto_{\text{ABA}} \{\alpha\}$ for all $\alpha \in \mathcal{A} \setminus E$.

Abstract Argumentation (AA) (see [15]). An *AA framework* is a pair $(Args, \hookrightarrow)$ with a (finite) set $Args$ of arguments and a binary attack relation $\hookrightarrow$ on $Args$. Notions of conflict-freeness and defence, as well as semantics of admissible, preferred and stable extensions are defined verbatim as for ABA, but with (sets of) arguments replacing (sets of) assumptions and the closure condition dropped.

Bipolar Argumentation (see [9, 11, 12]). A *Bipolar Argumentation Framework* (BAF) is a tuple $(Args, \leadsto, \Rightarrow)$, where

- $Args$ is a (finite) set of *arguments*;
- $\leadsto$ is a binary *attack* relation on $Args$;
- $\Rightarrow$ is a binary *support* relation on $Args$.

The *inverse* $\Rightarrow^{-1}$ of $\Rightarrow$ is given by a $\Rightarrow^{-1}$ b iff b $\Rightarrow$ a, for a, b $\in Args$. Throughout, we assume the following conventions.

- For $S, T \subseteq Args$ and b $\in Args$: $S \leadsto$ b iff $\exists$a $\in S$ with a $\leadsto$ b; b $\leadsto S$ iff $\exists$a $\in S$ with b $\leadsto$ a; $S \leadsto T$ iff $S \leadsto$ c for some c $\in T$. (We adopt analogous conventions for other attack relations throughout the paper.)

- For $S \subseteq Args$ and b $\in Args$:
  - $S \Rightarrow$ b iff $\exists a_1 \Rightarrow \ldots \Rightarrow a_n \Rightarrow$ b with $n \geqslant 1$ and $a_1 \in S$;
  - S is *closed under* $\Rightarrow$ iff $S \Rightarrow$ b implies b $\in S$.

(We adopt analogous conventions for $\Rightarrow^{-1}$.)

3   Bipolar ABA

In this section, we define a class of restricted kind of (non-flat) ABA frameworks, called *bipolar ABA*. Later in the paper, we will relate BAFs and bipolar ABA frameworks.

Definition 1. *An ABA framework $(\mathcal{L}, \mathcal{R}, \mathcal{A}, ^{-})$ is bipolar iff every rule in $\mathcal{R}$ is of the form $\varphi \leftarrow \alpha$, where $\alpha \in \mathcal{A}$ and either $\varphi \in \mathcal{A}$ or $\varphi = \bar{\beta}$ for some $\beta \in \mathcal{A}$.*

Example 2. Consider $\mathcal{F} = (\mathcal{L}, \mathcal{R}, \mathcal{A}, ^{-})$ with

- $\mathcal{L} = \{\alpha, \beta, \gamma, \delta, \varphi, \psi, \chi\}$,
- $\mathcal{R} = \{\varphi \leftarrow \alpha, \quad \beta \leftarrow \gamma, \quad \chi \leftarrow \delta, \quad \chi \leftarrow \alpha\}$,
- $\mathcal{A} = \{\alpha, \beta, \gamma, \delta\}$,
- $\bar{\alpha} = \beta, \ \bar{\beta} = \varphi, \ \bar{\gamma} = \psi, \ \bar{\delta} = \chi$.

Clearly, $\mathcal{F}$ is bipolar. In $\mathcal{F}$, $\{\alpha\}$, $\{\beta\}$ and $\{\delta\}$ are closed, but $\{\gamma\}$ is not. Instead, $\{\beta, \gamma\}$ is closed. Among the attacks, we find $\{\alpha\} \rightsquigarrow_{\text{ABA}} \{\beta\}, \{\delta\}$; $\{\beta\} \rightsquigarrow_{\text{ABA}} \{\alpha\}$; $\{\gamma, \beta\} \rightsquigarrow_{\text{ABA}} \{\alpha\}$; $\{\delta\} \rightsquigarrow_{\text{ABA}} \{\delta\}$. It is thus easy to see that $\mathcal{F}$ has preferred extensions $\{\alpha\}$ and $\{\beta, \gamma\}$, but no stable extension.

In the remainder of this section, unless specified otherwise, we assume a fixed but arbitrary bipolar ABA framework $\mathcal{F} = (\mathcal{L}, \mathcal{R}, \mathcal{A}, ^{-})$. Note that bipolar ABA frameworks are in general non-flat, e.g., in Example 2, $\{\gamma\}$ is not closed.

It is immediate to see that attacks in bipolar ABA exhibit the following property, which will be of use later (for space reasons, we henceforth omit proofs of straightforward results):

Lemma 1. *For $\alpha, \beta \in \mathcal{A}$, $\{\alpha\} \rightsquigarrow_{\text{ABA}} Cl(\{\beta\})$ iff $Cl(\{\alpha\}) \rightsquigarrow_{\text{ABA}} Cl(\{\beta\})$.*

Differently from general, non-flat ABA frameworks [5,14], existence of admissible and preferred extensions is guaranteed for bipolar ABA frameworks:

Proposition 1. *$\mathcal{F}$ has admissible and preferred extensions.*

Proof. As no rule in $\mathcal{R}$ has an empty body, $\emptyset$ is closed, and hence admissible. Existence of a preferred extension then follows from [5, Theorem 4.9].

It is known that (the appropriately formulated version of) the Fundamental Lemma [15] holds for *flat* ABA frameworks, but not necessarily for non-flat ones [5]. We next show that (a version of) this lemma holds for bipolar ABA frameworks:

Proposition 2 (Bipolar Fundamental Lemma). *Let $E \subseteq \mathcal{A}$ be admissible and defend $Cl(\{\alpha\})$ and $Cl(\{\beta\})$, for $\alpha, \beta \in \mathcal{A}$. Then $E \cup Cl(\{\alpha\})$ is admissible and defends $Cl(\{\beta\})$.*

Proof. Due to the nature of $\mathcal{R}$, by Lemma 1, $E \cup Cl(\{\alpha\})$ is obviously closed, admissible and defends $Cl(\{\beta\})$.

We also introduce a new semantics for generic (possibly non-bipolar) ABA frameworks:

Definition 2. *Let $(\mathcal{L}, \mathcal{R}, \mathcal{A}, ^-)$ be an ABA framework. $E \subseteq \mathcal{A}$ is set-stable iff E is closed, conflict-free and $E \rightsquigarrow_{ABA} Cl(\{\alpha\})$ for every $\alpha \in \mathcal{A} \setminus E$.*

Differently from the standard stable extensions, set-stable extensions need not attack every (singleton set of) assumption, but only their closures. In Example 2, $\mathcal{F}$ has one set-stable extension, namely $\{\alpha\}$.

It is immediate to see from the definitions that set-stable extensions exhibit the following properties:

Proposition 3. *Let $(\mathcal{L}, \mathcal{R}, \mathcal{A}, ^-)$ be an ABA framework and let $E \subseteq \mathcal{A}$. (i) If E is stable, it is set-stable. (ii) If E is set-stable, it is preferred. (iii) If $\mathcal{F}$ is flat and E is set-stable, then E is stable.*

Note that, just like stable extensions in (bipolar) ABA, set-stable extensions are not guaranteed to exist in (bipolar) ABA. For instance, the bipolar ABA framework $(\mathcal{L}, \mathcal{R}, \mathcal{A}, ^-)$ with $\mathcal{L} = \{\alpha, \varphi\}$, $\mathcal{R} = \{\varphi \leftarrow \alpha\}$, $\mathcal{A} = \{\alpha\}$ and $\overline{\alpha} = \varphi$ has neither stable, nor set-stable extension: on the one hand, $\{\alpha\}$ is not conflict-free, so cannot be stable/set-stable; on the other hand, $\emptyset \not\rightsquigarrow_{ABA} \{\alpha\}$ and $Cl(\{\alpha\}) = \{\alpha\}$, so $\emptyset$ cannot be stable/set-stable either.

In the remainder of the paper, we show that the existing semantics for BAFs we consider (under the various interpretations of support in question) correspond, where applicable, to the semantics of admissible, preferred and set-stable extensions in bipolar ABA. By doing so, we also prove, as a corollary, that these existing semantics exhibit the properties we have identified in this section.

4 Necessary Support

In this section we investigate the correspondence between BAFs where support is interpreted as *necessary* [6,19,20] (referred to simply as *necessary support* from now on) and bipolar ABA. We give first (Sect. 4.1) background adapted from [6,19,20] and then (Sect. 4.2) our results.

4.1 Preliminaries

An *argumentation framework with necessities* (AFN) is a BAF $(Args, \rightsquigarrow, \Rightarrow)$ where $\Rightarrow$ is irreflexive and transitive. Throughout this section, unless stated otherwise, we assume as given a fixed but arbitrary AFN $\mathcal{N} = (Args, \rightsquigarrow, \Rightarrow)$.

The *extended attack* relation $\hookrightarrow$ is defined as follows: for $a, b \in Args$, $a \hookrightarrow b$ holds iff (i) either $a \rightsquigarrow b$, (ii) or $a \rightsquigarrow c$ and $c \Rightarrow b$, for $c \in Args$, (iii) or $c \rightsquigarrow b$ and $c \Rightarrow a$, for $c \in Args$.

A set $S \subseteq Args$ (also called an *extension*) is said to be:

- *coherent* iff S is closed under $\Rightarrow^{-1}$;
- *strongly coherent* iff S is coherent and $S \not\rightsquigarrow S$.

Given [20, Proposition 3], the semantics of $\mathcal{N}$ is as follows. $S \subseteq Args$ is:[1]

- *n-admissible* iff S is strongly coherent and for every $a \in Args \setminus S$ such that $a \rightsquigarrow S$ it holds that $S \hookrightarrow a$;
- *n-preferred* iff S is $\subseteq$-maximally n-admissible;
- *n-stable* iff S is strongly coherent and for every $a \in Args \setminus S$, either $S \rightsquigarrow a$, or $b \Rightarrow a$ for some $b \in Args \setminus S$.

Example 3. Consider the AFN $(Args, \rightsquigarrow, \Rightarrow)$ with $Args = \{a, b, c, d, e\}$, $e \rightsquigarrow c$, $b \rightsquigarrow e$, $e \rightsquigarrow b$, and $b \Rightarrow a$, $c \Rightarrow a$, $e \Rightarrow d$. (Note that this AFN has the arguments and attacks as in Example 1, but the support relation is inverted.) This AFN, together with its extended attack $\hookrightarrow$, can be graphically depicted as follows (where nodes hold arguments, single-lined solid arrows indicate $\rightsquigarrow$ attacks, double-lined arrows indicate support, and dotted arrows with the label *ext* indicate $\hookrightarrow$ attacks that are not $\rightsquigarrow$ attacks):

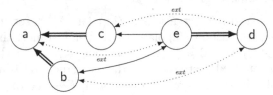

This AFN has n-preferred (and n-admissible) extensions $\{a, b, c\}$ and $\{d, e\}$, which are also n-stable. The other n-admissible extensions are $\emptyset$, $\{b\}$ and $\{e\}$.

4.2 Necessary Support in ABA

We map AFNs into ABA frameworks as follows.

Definition 3. *The* n-ABA framework corresponding to $\mathcal{N}$ *is* $(\mathcal{L}, \mathcal{R}, \mathcal{A}, ^{-})$ *with:*

- $\mathcal{L} = Args \cup \{a^c : a \in Args\}$,
- $\mathcal{R} = \{b^c \leftarrow a : a \rightsquigarrow b\} \cup \{a \leftarrow b : a \Rightarrow b\}$,
- $\mathcal{A} = Args$,
- $\bar{a} = a^c \; \forall a \in \mathcal{A}$.

Thus the support relation is "reversed" in the n-ABA framework, i.e. if $a \Rightarrow b$ is in $\mathcal{N}$, then $a \leftarrow b$ is a rule in the n-ABA framework corresponding to $\mathcal{N}$, and there is a deduction $\{b\} \vdash^{\{a \leftarrow b\}} a$. Clearly, any n-ABA framework corresponding to $\mathcal{N}$ is bipolar.

Example 4. The n-ABA framework corresponding to the AFN from Example 3 is $(\mathcal{L}, \mathcal{R}, \mathcal{A}, ^{-})$ as follows:

---

[1] We added the prefix n-, for 'necessary', for ease of reference.

- $\mathcal{L} = \{\mathsf{a}, \mathsf{b}, \mathsf{c}, \mathsf{d}, \mathsf{e}, \mathsf{a}^c, \mathsf{b}^c, \mathsf{c}^c, \mathsf{d}^c, \mathsf{e}^c\}$,
- $\mathcal{R} = \{\mathsf{c} \leftarrow \mathsf{a}, \quad \mathsf{b} \leftarrow \mathsf{a}, \mathsf{e} \leftarrow \mathsf{d}, \quad \mathsf{c}^c \leftarrow \mathsf{e}, \quad \mathsf{e}^c \leftarrow \mathsf{b}, \quad \mathsf{b}^c \leftarrow \mathsf{e}\}$,
- $\mathcal{A} = \{\mathsf{a}, \mathsf{b}, \mathsf{c}, \mathsf{d}, \mathsf{e}\}$,
- $\overline{\mathsf{a}} = \mathsf{a}^c, \ \overline{\mathsf{b}} = \mathsf{b}^c, \ \overline{\mathsf{c}} = \mathsf{c}^c, \ \overline{\mathsf{d}} = \mathsf{d}^c, \ \overline{\mathsf{e}} = \mathsf{e}^c$.

Note that the mapping from AFNs to n-ABA frameworks generalises the mapping from AA frameworks into ABA given in [24], in that we map the attacks in the same way and if the support relation is empty then the n-ABA framework is exactly as in [24].

In the remainder of this section, we assume $\mathcal{F}_n = (\mathcal{L}, \mathcal{R}, \mathcal{A}, ^-)$ to be the n-ABA framework corresponding to $\mathcal{N}$. Trivially:

Lemma 2. $S \subseteq Args$ is coherent (in $\mathcal{N}$) iff S is closed (in $\mathcal{F}_n$).

Extended attacks in AFNs and attacks in their corresponding n-ABA frameworks thus coincide, as follows:

Lemma 3. For coherent $S, T \subseteq Args$, $S \hookrightarrow T$ (in $\mathcal{N}$) iff $S \rightsquigarrow_{\mathrm{ABA}} T$ (in $\mathcal{F}_n$).

It then clearly follows that:

Lemma 4. $S \subseteq Args$ is strongly coherent (in $\mathcal{N}$) iff S is closed and conflict-free (in $\mathcal{F}_n$).

We can then prove semantic correspondences between AFNs and their corresponding n-ABA frameworks:

Proposition 4. $S \subseteq Args$ is an n-admissible extension of $\mathcal{N}$ iff S is an admissible extension of $\mathcal{F}_n$.

Proof. Let S be n-admissible. Then it is strongly coherent, and so, by Lemma 4, closed and conflict-free in $\mathcal{F}_n$. Let $T \subseteq \mathcal{A}$ be closed with $T \rightsquigarrow_{\mathrm{ABA}} S$. By Lemma 2, T is coherent. Thus, by Lemma 3, $T \hookrightarrow S$. As S is n-admissible, $S \hookrightarrow T$. Then, by Lemma 3, $S \rightsquigarrow_{\mathrm{ABA}} T$. So S is admissible in $\mathcal{F}_n$. Conversely, let S be admissible in $\mathcal{F}_n$. Then S is strongly coherent. Let $\mathsf{b} \in Args \setminus S$ be such that $\mathsf{b} \rightsquigarrow \mathsf{a}$ for some $\mathsf{a} \in S$. Let $T = Cl(\{\mathsf{b}\})$. Then $T \rightsquigarrow_{\mathrm{ABA}} S$, and, as S is admissible in $\mathcal{F}_n$, $S \rightsquigarrow_{\mathrm{ABA}} T$. By Lemma 3, $S \hookrightarrow T$. By definition of $\hookrightarrow$, $S \hookrightarrow \mathsf{b}$. So S is n-admissible.

From this it easily follows that:

Proposition 5. $S \subseteq Args$ is an n-preferred extension of $\mathcal{N}$ iff S is a preferred extension of $\mathcal{F}_n$.

The correspondence holds for n-/set- stable semantics too.

Proposition 6. $S \subseteq Args$ is an n-stable extension of $\mathcal{N}$ iff S is a set-stable extension of $\mathcal{F}_n$.

Proof. Let S be n-stable. By Lemma 4, S is closed and conflict-free in $\mathcal{F}_n$. Let $b \in A \setminus S$. Then $S \rightsquigarrow b'$ for some $b' \in Cl(\{b\})$, whence $S \hookrightarrow Cl(\{b\})$. By Lemma 3, $S \rightsquigarrow_{ABA} Cl(\{b\})$. Hence, S is set-stable. Conversely, let S be set-stable. By Lemma 4, S is strongly coherent. Let $b \in Args \setminus S$. Then $S \rightsquigarrow_{ABA} Cl(\{b\})$. By Lemma 3, $S \hookrightarrow Cl(\{b\})$. By definition of $\hookrightarrow$, $S \rightsquigarrow b'$ for some $b' \in Cl(\{b\})$. So either $b' = b$, or, by construction of $\mathcal{R}$ and transitivity of $\Rightarrow$, $b' \Rightarrow b$ (note $b' \notin S$ by strong coherence). Thus, S is n-stable.

As an illustration, the n-admissible, n-preferred and n-stable extensions of $(Args, \rightsquigarrow, \Rightarrow)$ from Example 3 are admissible, preferred and set-stable extensions, respectively, of the corresponding n-ABA framework from Example 4.

In this section we showed that BAFs under necessary support are instances of ABA. Particularly, we proved that AFNs with their *original semantics* can be easily captured in bipolar ABA. In the next section, we show that BAFs with support interpreted as deductive are similarly instances of ABA.

5   Deductive Support

In this section we investigate the correspondence between BAFs where support is interpreted as *deductive*, as in [11] (referred to simply as *deductive support* from now on) and bipolar ABA. We first give (Sect. 5.1) background adapted from [11] and then (Sect. 5.2) our results. Throughout this section, unless stated otherwise, we assume as given a fixed but arbitrary BAF $\mathcal{B} = (Args, \rightsquigarrow, \Rightarrow)$.

5.1   Preliminaries

Let $a, b \in Args$.

– The *supported attack* relation $\rightsquigarrow_{sup}$ is defined as: $a \rightsquigarrow_{sup} b$ iff $\{a\} \Rightarrow c$ and $c \rightsquigarrow b$, for $c \in Args$.
– The *super-mediated attack* relation $\rightsquigarrow_{s\text{-}med}$ is defined as: $a \rightsquigarrow_{s\text{-}med} b$ iff $\{b\} \Rightarrow c$, and either $a \rightsquigarrow c$ or $a \rightsquigarrow_{sup} c$.

Note that both notions are defined in terms of support from (singleton) sets ($\{x\} \Rightarrow c$) to take into account chains of supports (see Sect. 2). Given $\mathcal{B}$, the *complete associated AA framework for the deductive support* is the AA framework $\mathcal{D} = (Args, \hookrightarrow)$, where $\hookrightarrow = \rightsquigarrow \cup \rightsquigarrow_{sup} \cup \rightsquigarrow_{s\text{-}med}$. In what follows, unless stated otherwise, $\mathcal{D}$ is the complete associated AA framework for the deductive support, given $\mathcal{B}$. The semantics of $\mathcal{B}$ is then defined based on $\mathcal{D}$: $S \subseteq Args$ is a *d-admissible/d-preferred/d-stable extension* of $\mathcal{B}$ iff S is an admissible/preferred/stable extension of $\mathcal{D}$.[2]

---

[2] We added the prefix *d-*, for 'deductive', for ease of reference. These notions are not to be confused with the ones bearing the same names in [9].

Example 5. Consider the BAF from Example 1, that is, $(Args, \rightsquigarrow, \Rightarrow)$ with $Args = \{a, b, c, d, e\}$, $e \rightsquigarrow c$, $b \rightsquigarrow e$, $e \rightsquigarrow b$, and $a \Rightarrow b$, $a \Rightarrow c$, $d \Rightarrow e$. Given this BAF, the complete associated AA framework for the deductive support $(Args, \hookrightarrow)$ can be graphically depicted as follows (where nodes hold arguments and single-lined arrows denote $\hookrightarrow$ attacks):

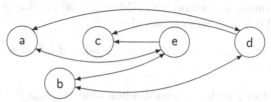

Then, $(Args, \rightsquigarrow, \Rightarrow)$ has d-preferred (and d-admissible) extensions $\{a, b, c\}$ and $\{d, e\}$, which are also d-stable. Additionally, $\emptyset$, $\{b\}$, $\{e\}$, $\{a\}$ and $\{d\}$ are also d-admissible. (Note that the d-preferred/d-stable extensions accord with the informal reading of deductive support in Example 1.)

5.2   Deductive Support in ABA

We map BAFs with deductive support into bipolar ABA as follows.

Definition 4. *The* d-ABA *framework corresponding to $\mathcal{B}$ is $(\mathcal{L}, \mathcal{R}, \mathcal{A}, ^-)$ with:*

- $\mathcal{L} = Args \cup \{a^c \; : \; a \in Args\}$,
- $\mathcal{R} = \{b^c \leftarrow a \; : \; a \rightsquigarrow b\} \cup \{b \leftarrow a \; : \; a \Rightarrow b\}$,
- $\mathcal{A} = Args$,
- $\overline{a} = a^c \; \forall a \in \mathcal{A}$.

Note that, differently from the mapping into n-ABA frameworks, this mapping preserves the direction of support. Still, as in the case of n-ABA frameworks, a d-ABA framework is clearly a bipolar ABA framework. Moreover, the mapping from BAFs to d-ABA frameworks also generalises the mapping from AA frameworks into ABA given in [24], in the same sense as in Sect. 4.2: if the support relation is empty then the d-ABA framework is exactly as in [24].

Example 6. The d-ABA framework corresponding to the BAF from Example 5 is the ABA framework $(\mathcal{L}, \mathcal{R}, \mathcal{A}, ^-)$ of Example 4.

In the remainder of this section, we assume $\mathcal{F}_d = (\mathcal{L}, \mathcal{R}, \mathcal{A}, ^-)$ to be the d-ABA framework corresponding to $\mathcal{B}$.

We first observe that standard and supported attacks in BAFs correspond to attacks in their corresponding d-ABA frameworks, as follows:

Lemma 5. *For $a, b \in Args$, $a \rightsquigarrow b$ or $a \rightsquigarrow_{sup} b$ (in $\mathcal{B}$) iff $\{a\} \rightsquigarrow_{ABA} \{b\}$ (in $\mathcal{F}_d$).*

Taking into account also super-mediated attacks, $\hookrightarrow$ corresponds to attacks in d-ABA frameworks, as follows:

Lemma 6. *For $a, b \in Args$, $a \hookrightarrow b$ (in $\mathcal{B}$) iff $\{a\} \rightsquigarrow_{ABA} Cl(\{b\})$ (in $\mathcal{F}_d$).*

Note that d-admissible extensions need not be closed under $\Rightarrow$ and thus they need not be admissible in the corresponding d-ABA framework: in Example 5, $\{a\}$ and $\{d\}$ are d-admissible, but not closed, and hence not admissible, in $(\mathcal{L}, \mathcal{R}, \mathcal{A}, ^-)$ from Example 6. Nevertheless, since trivially, by the definitions, $S \subseteq Args$ is closed under $\Rightarrow$ iff S is closed in $\mathcal{F}_d$, we have that if closure under $\Rightarrow$ is imposed, then d-admissible extensions of BAFs and admissible extensions of their corresponding d-ABA frameworks coincide:

Proposition 7. $S \subseteq Args$ *is closed under* $\Rightarrow$ *and a d-admissible extension of* $\mathcal{B}$ *iff* S *is admissible in* $\mathcal{F}_d$.

Proof. Let S be closed under $\Rightarrow$ and d-admissible. Then S is closed in $\mathcal{F}_d$ and, by Lemma 6, conflict-free in $\mathcal{F}_d$. Now let $T \subseteq \mathcal{A}$ be closed with $T \leadsto_{\text{ABA}} S$. That is, $\{b\} \leadsto_{\text{ABA}} \{a\}$ for some $b \in T$ and $a \in S$. As S is closed, $Cl(\{a\}) \subseteq S$, so, by Lemma 6, $b \hookrightarrow a$. As S is d-admissible, $S \hookrightarrow b$. That is, $\exists a' \in S$ with $a' \hookrightarrow b$. Then $\{a'\} \leadsto_{\text{ABA}} Cl(\{b\})$, by Lemma 6. As T is closed, $Cl(\{b\}) \subseteq T$, so that $S \leadsto_{\text{ABA}} T$. So, S is admissible in $\mathcal{F}_d$. The other direction is proven similarly.

Due to $\subseteq$-maximality, d-preferred extensions are always closed under $\Rightarrow$ and thus coincide with preferred extensions:

Proposition 8. $S \subseteq Args$ *is a d-preferred extension of* $\mathcal{B}$ *iff* S *is a preferred extension of* $\mathcal{F}_d$.

Proof. Let S be a d-preferred extension of $\mathcal{B}$. We first show that S is closed in $\mathcal{F}_d$. Suppose for a contradiction that it is not. So $S \vdash^R b'$ for some $b' \in \mathcal{A} \setminus S$. By construction of $\mathcal{F}_d$, $\{b\} \Rightarrow b'$ for some $b \in S$. As $b' \notin S$ and S is $\subseteq$-maximally d-admissible, it must be that $S \cup \{b'\}$ either (i) is not conflict-free in $\mathcal{D}$ or (ii) does not defend its elements in $\mathcal{D}$. In case (i), for some $a \in S$ either $a \hookrightarrow b'$ or $b' \hookrightarrow a$. Then either $a \hookrightarrow b$ or $b \hookrightarrow a$ follows from the definition of $\hookrightarrow$: contradiction. In case (ii), S does not defend b' in $\mathcal{D}$: $\exists a \in Args$ such that $a \hookrightarrow b'$ and $S \not\hookrightarrow a$. By definition of $\hookrightarrow$, $a \hookrightarrow b$, and, as S is admissible in $\mathcal{D}$, $S \hookrightarrow a$: contradiction. In both cases (i) and (ii), we get a contradiction, whence S is closed in $\mathcal{F}_d$. S is thus admissible in $\mathcal{F}_d$, by Proposition 7. So it suffices to show that S is $\subseteq$-maximally admissible. Suppose it is not and $S \cup T$ admissible in $\mathcal{F}_d$ for $T \subseteq \mathcal{A}$ with $T \setminus S \neq \emptyset$. Then, by Proposition 7, $S \cup T$ is d-admissible and $S \subsetneq S \cup T$ is not $\subseteq$-maximally d-admissible: contradiction.

Conversely, suppose S is a preferred extension of $\mathcal{F}_d$. By Proposition 7, S is closed under $\Rightarrow$ and d-admissible. Suppose that S is not $\subseteq$-maximal d-admissible, i.e. $\exists a \in Args \setminus S$ such that $S \cup \{a\}$ is d-admissible. Let $S' = Cl(S \cup \{a\}) = S \cup Cl(\{a\})$. S' is conflict-free in $\mathcal{D}$, as else $S \cup \{a\}$ would not be conflict-free in $\mathcal{D}$. Also, S' defends its elements in $\mathcal{D}$, for if $b \hookrightarrow Cl(\{a\})$ for some $b \in Args$, then $b \hookrightarrow a$, so $S' \hookrightarrow b$. Thus, S' is closed under $\Rightarrow$ and d-admissible, hence S' is admissible in $\mathcal{F}_d$, by Proposition 7. Thus, S is not $\subseteq$-maximally admissible in $\mathcal{F}_d$: contradiction.

Finally, d-stable and set-stable extensions coincide:

Proposition 9. $S \subseteq Args$ *is a d-stable extension of* $\mathcal{B}$ *iff* S *is a set-stable extension of* $\mathcal{F}_d$.

Proof. Let $S \in Args$ be a d-stable extension of $\mathcal{B}$. Then S is d-preferred (by the results in [15]), so by Proposition 7, S is admissible in $\mathcal{F}_d$. Let $b \in \mathcal{A} \setminus S$. Then $S \hookrightarrow b$, so $S \leadsto_{\text{ABA}} Cl(\{b\})$, by Lemma 6. Hence, S is set-stable. Conversely, if $S \subseteq \mathcal{A}$ is set-stable, then it is admissible, by Proposition 3, so closed under $\Rightarrow$ and d-admissible, by Proposition 7. Let $b \in Args \setminus S$. Then $S \leadsto_{\text{ABA}} Cl(\{b\})$. By Lemma 6, $S \hookrightarrow b$. So, S is d-stable.

As an illustration, the d-preferred and d-stable extensions of $(Args, \leadsto, \Rightarrow)$ from Example 5 are preferred and set-stable extensions, respectively, of the corresponding d-ABA framework from Example 6.

In this section we showed that BAFs under deductive support are instances of ABA. In the next section we show that two other notions of support can be captured in ABA, using the same mapping from BAFs to bipolar ABA as in this section.

6   Other Notions of Support

We next discuss two other notions of support: a recent proposal by Gabbay [16]; and (deductive) coalitions of Cayrol and Lagasquie-Schiex [11]. We show that these two approaches are immediately captured in bipolar ABA.

6.1   Preliminaries

We give preliminaries of both approaches. Let $\mathcal{B} = (Args, \leadsto, \Rightarrow)$ be given.

Gabbay's Approach. Let $\Rightarrow_*$ be the reflexive and transitive closure of $\Rightarrow$ and let $a, b \in Args$ and $S \subseteq Args$.

- *Gabbay's attack relation* $\leadsto_*$ is defined as: $a \leadsto_* b$ iff $a \Rightarrow_* a'$, $b \Rightarrow_* b'$ and $a' \leadsto b'$, for some $a', b' \in Args$.
- $S \subseteq Args$ is a *G-admissible extension* of $\mathcal{B}$ iff S is closed under $\Rightarrow_*$, conflict-free with respect to $\leadsto_*$, and defends its elements with respect to $\leadsto_*$.[3]

Coalitions. Let $a \in Args$. A *coalition associated with* a is the set $C(a) = \{a\} \cup \{b \in Args : \{a\} \Rightarrow b\}$; the *coalition framework*[4] corresponding to $\mathcal{B}$ is an AA framework $\mathcal{C} = (Coals, \leadsto_c)$, where:

- $Coals = \{C(a) : a \in Args\}$ is the set of all coalitions in $\mathcal{B}$;
- for $C(a), C(b) \in Coals$, it holds that $C(a) \leadsto_c C(b)$ if there are $a' \in C(a)$ and $b' \in C(b)$ such that $a' \leadsto b'$.

---

[3] Gabbay calls it simply an extension; we use G-admissible for ease of reference.
[4] The names 'd-coalition' and 'meta framework', respectively, are used in [11].

The semantics of coalition frameworks is defined via the semantics of AA frameworks. In addition, there is a one-to-one correspondence between the extensions of $\mathcal{C}$ and the extensions of $\mathcal{B}$ under the deductive interpretation of support, as shown in [11, Proposition 12]; using our terminology: $S = \{a_1, \ldots, a_n\} \subseteq Args$ is a d-admissible/d-preferred/d-stable extension of $\mathcal{B}$ iff $\{C(a_1), \ldots, C(a_n)\} \subseteq$ *Coals* is an admissible/preferred/stable extension of $\mathcal{C}$.

6.2   Other Notions of Support in ABA

We show that, (bipolar) d-ABA frameworks, as given in Sect. 5.2, correspond to both Gabbay's approach and coalitions. In this section, let $\mathcal{F}_d = (\mathcal{L}, \mathcal{R}, \mathcal{A}, ^-)$ be the d-ABA framework corresponding to $\mathcal{B}$ (see Definition 4), and let $\mathcal{C} = (Coals, \rightsquigarrow_c)$ be the coalition framework corresponding to $\mathcal{B}$.

Gabbay's Approach in ABA. It is plain that $\rightsquigarrow_*$ is simply $\hookrightarrow = \rightsquigarrow \cup \rightsquigarrow_{sup}$ $\cup \rightsquigarrow_{s\text{-}med}$, as in Sect. 5.1:

Lemma 7. *For* $a, b \in Args$, $a \rightsquigarrow_* b$ *iff either* $a \rightsquigarrow b$ *or* $a \rightsquigarrow_{sup} b$ *or* $a \rightsquigarrow_{s\text{-}med} b$.

Thus, Gabbay's semantics corresponds to the semantics of admissible extensions of d-ABA frameworks (by Lemmas 6 and 7 and Proposition 7):

Proposition 10. $S \subseteq Args$ *is a G-admissible extension of* $\mathcal{B}$ *iff* S *is an admissible extension of* $\mathcal{F}_d$.

In Example 5, the sets $\emptyset$, $\{b\}$, $\{e\}$, $\{a, b, c\}$ and $\{d, e\}$ are G-admissible extensions of $(Args, \rightsquigarrow, \Rightarrow)$, and they are exactly the admissible sets of the bipolar ABA framework $(\mathcal{L}, \mathcal{R}, \mathcal{A}, ^-)$ as in Example 6.

Coalitions in ABA. It is plain that for any $a \in Args$, the coalition $C(a)$ is the closure $Cl(\{a\})$ in $\mathcal{F}_d$, and that attacks in $\mathcal{C}$ and $\mathcal{F}_d$ coincide as follows:

Lemma 8. *For* $a, b \in Args$, $C(a) = Cl(\{a\})$. *Furthermore,* $C(a) \rightsquigarrow_c C(b)$ *iff* $Cl(\{a\}) \rightsquigarrow_{ABA} Cl(\{b\})$.

Hence, given that coalitions are closed under $\Rightarrow$, using Lemma 8 and Propositions 7, 8 and 9, as well as [11, Proposition 12], we have a one-to-one correspondence between extensions of the coalition framework and the d-ABA framework:

Proposition 11. $\{C(a_1), \ldots, C(a_n)\} \subseteq$ *Coals is an admissible/preferred/stable extension of* $\mathcal{C}$ *iff* $\bigcup\{C(a_1), \ldots, C(a_n)\} \subseteq \mathcal{A}$ *is an admissible/preferred/set-stable (respectively) extension of* $\mathcal{F}_d$.

In Example 1, the coalitions are $C(\{a\}) = \{a, b, c\}$, $C(\{b\}) = \{b\}$, $C(\{c\}) = \{c\}$, $C(\{d\}) = \{d, e\}$, and $C(\{e\}) = \{e\}$. The attacks among them in $(Coals, \rightsquigarrow_c)$ are $C(\{a\}) \rightsquigarrow_c C(\{e\}), C(\{d\})$; $C(\{b\}) \rightsquigarrow_c C(\{e\}), C(\{d\})$;

$C(\{e\}) \leadsto_c C(\{a\}), C(\{b\}), C(\{c\})$; $C(\{d\}) \leadsto_c C(\{a\}), C(\{b\}), C(\{c\})$. The preferred/stable extensions of $(Coals, \leadsto_c)$ are $\{C(\{a\}), C(\{b\}), C(\{c\})\}$ and $\{C(\{d\}), C(\{e\})\}$, corresponding to the preferred/set-stable extensions $\{a, b, c\}$ and $\{d, e\}$ of the bipolar d-ABA framework as in Example 6.

In this section we showed that Gabbay's [16] and coalition [11] approaches to BAFs are readily captured in ABA. In the next section, using all our results, we show how all the different approaches to BAFs that we considered relate.

7 Relationships

In this section we formally prove the relationships among different semantics of the various approaches to BAFs considered in this paper. The main result in this section says that the various approaches define respective semantics that yield essentially the same reasoning outcomes. The result follows from the results obtained in previous sections on mapping different approaches into bipolar ABA.

Theorem 1. *Let $\mathcal{B} = (Args, \leadsto, \Rightarrow)$ be such that $\Rightarrow$ is irreflexive and transitive. Let $\mathcal{N} = (Args, \leadsto, \Rightarrow^{-1})$ and let $\mathcal{C} = (Coals, \leadsto_c)$ be the coalition framework corresponding to $\mathcal{B}$.[5] For $S = \{a_1, \ldots, a_n\} \subseteq Args$:*

- *S is closed under $\Rightarrow$ and a d-admissible extension of $\mathcal{B}$ iff S is an n-admissible extension of $\mathcal{N}$ iff S is a G-admissible extension of $\mathcal{B}$ iff $\{C(a_1), \ldots, C(a_n)\}$ is an admissible extension of $\mathcal{C}$.*
- *S is a d-preferred extension of $\mathcal{B}$ iff S is an n-preferred extension of $\mathcal{N}$ iff $\{C(a_1), \ldots, C(a_n)\}$ is a preferred extension of $\mathcal{C}$.*
- *S is a d-stable extension of $\mathcal{B}$ iff S is an n-stable extension of $\mathcal{N}$ iff $\{C(a_1), \ldots, C(a_n)\}$ is a stable extension of $\mathcal{C}$.*

Proof. Let $\mathcal{F} = (\mathcal{L}, \mathcal{R}, \mathcal{A}, ^-)$ be the d-ABA framework corresponding to $\mathcal{B}$ (Definition 4), and observe that $\mathcal{F}$ is also the n-ABA framework corresponding to $\mathcal{N}$ (Definition 3). So, by Proposition 7, we have that S is closed under $\Rightarrow$ and a d-admissible extension of $\mathcal{B}$ iff S is an admissible extension of $\mathcal{F}$. Also, by Proposition 4, we have that S is an n-admissible extension of $\mathcal{N}$ iff S is an admissible extension of $\mathcal{F}$. In addition, by Proposition 10, S a G-admissible extension of $\mathcal{B}$ iff S is an admissible extension of $\mathcal{F}$. Further, by [11, Proposition 12], S is a d-admissible extension of $\mathcal{B}$ iff $\{C(a_1), \ldots, C(a_n)\}$ is an admissible extension of $\mathcal{C}$. Combining this last equivalence with Proposition 7, yields that $\{C(a_1), \ldots, C(a_n)\}$ is an admissible extension of $\mathcal{C}$ iff $S = \bigcup\{C(a_1), \ldots, C(a_n)\}$ is closed under $\Rightarrow$ and a d-admissible extension of $\mathcal{B}$. Lastly, by Proposition 11, $\{C(a_1), \ldots, C(a_n)\}$ is an admissible extension of $\mathcal{C}$ iff $\bigcup\{C(a_1), \ldots, C(a_n)\}$ is an admissible extension of $\mathcal{F}$. The first set of equivalences thus follows immediately.

The equivalences in the second item follow similarly by using Propositions 5, 8, 11 and [11, Proposition 12]. Likewise, the equivalences in the third item follow by using Propositions 6, 9, 11 and [11, Proposition 12]. □

---

[5] Note that $\Rightarrow^{-1}$ is irreflexive and transitive too; this condition is required to ensure that $\mathcal{N}$ is a well-defined AFN (see Sect. 4.1).

This result shows, first, that even though the semantics of BAFs under the deductive and necessary interpretation of support are defined in completely different ways, they lead to essentially the same results. The difference is how the "direction" of the support is used in the semantics. Second, it shows that Gabbay's approach to BAFs can be equivalently understood through admissible semantics of BAFs under either of the two interpretations of support. Finally, the result relates and shows correspondence of the semantics of coalition frameworks to the semantics of both BAFs under the deductive and the necessary interpretation of support, as well as to Gabbay's approach.

To exemplify, consider again $\mathcal{B} = (Args, \rightsquigarrow, \Rightarrow)$ from Example 1. Its d-preferred/d-stable extensions are $\{a, b, c\}$ and $\{d, e\}$ (see Example 5). These are precisely the n-preferred/n-stable extensions of $\mathcal{N} = (Args, \rightsquigarrow, \Rightarrow^{-1})$ from Example 3. They also correspond to the preferred/stable extensions of the coalition framework $\mathcal{C} = (Coals, \rightsquigarrow_c)$ corresponding to $\mathcal{B}$ from Example 1. In addition to these two extensions, $\emptyset$, $\{b\}$, $\{e\}$ are d-admissible and n-admissible in $\mathcal{B}$ and $\mathcal{N}$ respectively, G-admissible in $\mathcal{B}$ and correspond to the remaining three admissible sets in $\mathcal{C}$. Meanwhile, $\{a\}$ and $\{d\}$ are d-admissible in $\mathcal{B}$, but neither G-admissible, nor n-admissible in $\mathcal{N}$, nor correspond to admissible sets in $\mathcal{C}$, because they are not closed under either $\Rightarrow_*$, or $\Rightarrow^{-1}$, or $\Rightarrow$, respectively.

Note well that Cayrol and Lagasquie-Schiex [11] *do not* provide in full the semantic correspondence results exhibited in Theorem 1 (but provide the specific correspondence between the semantics of BAFs under deductive support and coalition frameworks, which is part of Theorem 1). Indeed, they do not consider the *original semantics* of AFNs at all. We, on the other hand, explicitly show how the original semantics of AFNs relates to the semantics of BAFs under deductive support. Thus, we also show how the original semantics of AFNs relates to the semantics of coalition frameworks. Still further, we show the correspondence of Gabbay's semantics with the other semantics.

8 Conclusions

We showed that four approaches to Bipolar Argumentation Frameworks (BAFs) can be naturally captured in Assumption-Based Argumentation (ABA). Particularly, we proved that the semantics of BAFs with (i) necessary [20], (ii) deductive [11], (iii) Gabbay's [16], (vi) and coalition [11] approaches to support are in one-to-one correspondence with the semantics of ABA. To this end, we identified a restricted type of ABA frameworks, called *bipolar*, as an exact fit for BAFs. We also identified a novel type of extensions for generic (possibly non-bipolar) ABA, called *set-stable*, to show correspondence with stable extensions of BAFs.

We showed that the concepts and semantics introduced for BAFs under various interpretations of support are already captured in the structured argumentation formalism ABA, predating BAFs. Further, as a by-product, we showed formally how the semantics of different approaches to BAFs relate, and provided means to establish properties (borrowed from (bipolar) ABA) of those semantics.

Our proposal is orthogonal to Prakken's [22], in that he shows how a well known structured argumentation formalism, ASPIC$^+$ [17], can be used to instantiate BAFs, whereas we show how ABA admits BAFs as instances. Note well that while *flat* ABA can be captured in ASPIC$^+$ [17], the same is *not* known for *non-flat* ABA, and hence BAFs are not automatically instances of ASPIC$^+$. It would be nonetheless interesting to study whether other structured argumentation formalisms (see [3]) could also admit BAFs as instances.

We leave the study of the relations between (possibly non-bipolar) ABA frameworks and BAFs under other interpretations of support as future work. In particular, we plan to study the *evidential argumentation frameworks* of [21], BAFs that employ attacks from sets of arguments, e.g. [18,26]), and works that aim to model defeasible and/or recursive support, e.g. [13,26]. Similarly, it would be interesting to analyse the relationship between bipolar ABA and the approaches that transform BAFs into abstract argumentation (AA) frameworks, such as [26]. For future work we also leave investigation of how other ABA semantics (such as grounded and ideal) relate to semantics of BAFs that we did not consider in this paper (e.g. grounded [10]). Still further, it would be interesting to study if research results pertaining to ABA computations, such as dispute derivations for flat ABA (see e.g. [25]), could be naturally extended to be applicable to bipolar ABA and thus to BAFs.

References

1. Amgoud, L., Ben-Naim, J.: Axiomatic foundations of acceptability semantics. In: Baral, C., Delgrande, J.P., Wolter, F. (eds.) 15th International Conference on Principles of Knowledge Representation and Reasoning, pp. 2–11. AAAI Press (2016)
2. Amgoud, L., Cayrol, C., Lagasquie-Schiex, M., Livet, P.: On bipolarity in argumentation frameworks. Int. J. Intell. Syst. **23**(10), 1062–1093 (2008)
3. Besnard, P., García, A.J., Hunter, A., Modgil, S., Prakken, H., Simari, G.R., Toni, F.: Introduction to structured argumentation. Argum. Comput. **5**(1), 1–4 (2014)
4. Boella, G., Gabbay, D.M., van der Torre, L., Villata, S.: Support in abstract argumentation. In: Baroni, P., Cerutti, F., Giacomin, M., Simari, G.R. (eds.) Computational Models of Argument. Frontiers in AI and Applications, vol. 216, pp. 111–122. IOS Press, Amsterdam (2010)
5. Bondarenko, A., Dung, P.M., Kowalski, R., Toni, F.: An abstract, argumentation-theoretic approach to default reasoning. Artif. Intell. **93**(97), 63–101 (1997)
6. Boudhar, I., Nouioua, F., Risch, V.: Handling preferences in argumentation frameworks with necessities. In: Filipe, J., Fred, A.L.N. (eds.) 4th International Conference on Agents and Artificial Intelligence, pp. 340–345. SciTePress (2012)
7. Cabrio, E., Villata, S.: A natural language bipolar argumentation approach to support users in online debate interactions. Argum. Comput. **4**(3), 209–230 (2013)
8. Cayrol, C., Lagasquie-Schiex, M.C.: Gradual valuation for bipolar argumentation frameworks. In: Godo, L. (ed.) ECSQARU 2005. LNCS (LNAI), vol. 3571, pp. 366–377. Springer, Heidelberg (2005). doi:10.1007/11518655_32
9. Cayrol, C., Lagasquie-Schiex, M.C.: On the acceptability of arguments in bipolar argumentation frameworks. In: Godo, L. (ed.) ECSQARU 2005. LNCS (LNAI), vol. 3571, pp. 378–389. Springer, Heidelberg (2005). doi:10.1007/11518655_33
10. Cayrol, C., Lagasquie-Schiex, M.C.: Coalitions of arguments: a tool for handling bipolar argumentation frameworks. Int. J. Intell. Syst. **25**(1), 83–109 (2010)

11. Cayrol, C., Lagasquie-Schiex, M.C.: Bipolarity in argumentation graphs: towards a better understanding. Int. J. Approx. Reason. **54**(7), 876–899 (2013)
12. Cohen, A., Gottifredi, S., García, A.J., Simari, G.R.: A survey of different approaches to support in argumentation systems. Knowl. Eng. Rev. **29**(5), 513–550 (2014)
13. Cohen, A., Gottifredi, S., García, A.J., Simari, G.R.: An approach to abstract argumentation with recursive attack and support. J. Appl. Logic **13**(4), 509–533 (2015)
14. Čyras, K., Fan, X., Schulz, C., Toni, F.: Assumption-based argumentation: disputes, explanations, preferences. In: Baroni, P., Gabbay, D.M., Giacomin, M., van der Torre, L. (eds.) Handbook of Formal Argumentation, vol. 1. College Publications (to appear)
15. Dung, P.M.: On the acceptability of arguments and its fundamental role in nonmonotonic reasoning, logic programming and n-person games. Artif. Intell. **77**, 321–357 (1995)
16. Gabbay, D.M.: Logical foundations for bipolar and tripolar argumentation networks: preliminary results. J. Logic Comput. **26**(1), 247–292 (2016)
17. Modgil, S., Prakken, H.: A general account of argumentation with preferences. Artif. Intell. **195**, 361–397 (2013)
18. Nouioua, F.: AFs with necessities: further semantics and labelling characterization. In: Liu, W., Subrahmanian, V.S., Wijsen, J. (eds.) SUM 2013. LNCS (LNAI), vol. 8078, pp. 120–133. Springer, Heidelberg (2013). doi:10.1007/978-3-642-40381-1_10
19. Nouioua, F., Risch, V.: Bipolar argumentation frameworks with specialized supports. In: 22nd IEEE International Conference on Tools with Artificial Intelligence, vol. 1, pp. 215–218. IEEE (2010)
20. Nouioua, F., Risch, V.: Argumentation frameworks with necessities. In: Benferhat, S., Grant, J. (eds.) SUM 2011. LNCS (LNAI), vol. 6929, pp. 163–176. Springer, Heidelberg (2011). doi:10.1007/978-3-642-23963-2_14
21. Polberg, S., Oren, N.: Revisiting support in abstract argumentation systems. In: Parsons, S., Oren, N., Reed, C., Cerutti, F. (eds.) Computational Models of Argument. Frontiers in AI and Applications, vol. 266, pp. 369–376. IOS Press, Amsterdam (2014)
22. Prakken, H.: On support relations in abstract argumentation as abstractions of inferential relations. In: Schaub, T., Friedrich, G., O'Sullivan, B. (eds.) 21st European Conference on Artificial Intelligence. Frontiers in AI and Applications, vol. 263, pp. 735–740. IOS Press (2014)
23. Rago, A., Toni, F., Aurisicchio, M., Baroni, P.: Discontinuity-free decision support with quantitative argumentation debates. In: Baral, C., Delgrande, J.P., Wolter, F. (eds.) 15h International Conference on Principles of Knowledge Representation and Reasoning, pp. 63–73. AAAI Press, Cape Town (2016)
24. Toni, F.: Reasoning on the web with assumption-based argumentation. In: Eiter, T., Krennwallner, T. (eds.) Reasoning Web 2012. LNCS, vol. 7487, pp. 370–386. Springer, Heidelberg (2012). doi:10.1007/978-3-642-33158-9_10
25. Toni, F.: A tutorial on assumption-based argumentation. Argum. Comput. **5**(1), 89–117 (2014)
26. Villata, S., Boella, G., Gabbay, D.M., van der Torre, L.: Modelling defeasible and prioritized support in bipolar argumentation. Ann. Math. Artif. Intell. **66**(1–4), 163–197 (2012)

Abstract Games of Argumentation Strategy and Game-Theoretical Argument Strength

Pietro Baroni[1] , Giulia Comini[1,2] , Antonio Rago[2(✉)] ,
and Francesca Toni[2]

[1] Università degli Studi di Brescia, Brescia, Italy
`pietro.baroni@unibs.it`
[2] Imperial College London, London, UK
{`giulia.comini16,a.rago15,ft`}`@imperial.ac.uk`

Abstract. We define a generic notion of *abstract games of argumentation strategy* for (attack-only and bipolar) argumentation frameworks, which are zero-sum games whereby two players put forward sets of arguments and get a reward for their combined choices. The value of these games, in the classical game-theoretic sense, can be used to define measures of (quantitative) *game-theoretic* strength of arguments, which are different depending on whether either or both players have an "agenda" (i.e. an argument they want to be accepted). We show that this general scheme captures as a special instance a previous proposal in the literature (single agenda, attack-only frameworks), and seamlessly supports the definition of a spectrum of novel measures of game-theoretic strength where both players have an agenda and/or bipolar frameworks are considered. We then discuss the applicability of these instances of game-theoretic strength in different contexts and analyse their basic properties.

1 Introduction

Argument strength can be conceived, at an intuitive level, as a measure of the capability of an argument to withstand challenges and to obtain support when other interacting arguments are produced. The assessment of argument strength evaluation can be regarded as a refinement of the traditional evaluation of arguments based on argumentation semantics [11] where, given a graph capturing the relationships among a set of arguments, a qualitative assessment of argument acceptability is produced, e.g. in terms of acceptance labels **IN**, **OUT**, and **UNDEC** [7]. Most existing approaches to the definition of argument strength, e.g. [4,9,13,15], adopt a sort of disinterested and non-dialogical view, in the sense that the evaluation of arguments is based on the underlying graph, without taking explicitly into account the possible existence of distinct self-interested agents supporting different arguments which may be part of the dialectical strategies of the agents themselves. Clearly this notion of strength is suitable for contexts where a neutral assessment of arguments is appropriate, e.g. when arguments are produced by some inference mechanism from a knowledge base, but does not

© Springer International Publishing AG 2017
B. An et al. (Eds.): PRIMA 2017, LNAI 10621, pp. 403–419, 2017.
https://doi.org/10.1007/978-3-319-69131-2_24

seem appropriate for the needs of self-interested evaluation of the strength of arguments when they are part of dialectical strategies in multi-agent contexts.

To address these needs Matt & Toni [14] pioneered the idea that argument strength can be formally expressed resorting to notions from *Game Theory* [17]. Briefly, the proposal in [14] considers dialectical contexts, where two agents (a proponent and an opponent) exchange sets of arguments, and formalises this exchange as a game. Each agent makes a *move* by putting forward a set of arguments, which represents one of its possible *strategies*. On the basis of its move and of the move of the other agent, each agent is *rewarded* with a *payoff*. The strength of an argument α can then be defined as the expected optimal payoff when an agent is committed to include α in its move.

While the proposal in [14] provides an original approach to argument strength evaluation, potentially suitable for multi-agent contexts, it also features two significant limitations. First, it focuses on Dung's *abstract argumentation frameworks* [11], encompassing only the relation of *attack* between arguments. However, other kinds of argument relations, in particular *support*, have been considered in the literature (e.g. in *bipolar argumentation frameworks* [3,8]) and can play a significant role for strength evaluation. Further, it adopts an asymmetrical perspective, with two distinct roles in the game, the proponent and the opponent, subject to different constraints and evaluation criteria. While this asymmetry reflects the nature of some kinds of debates, where one of the parties pursues an agenda related to a focal argument, and the other has a merely critical role, other symmetrical kinds of dialectical interactions can also be considered, where both parties competitively pursue different agendas.

To overcome these limitations and lay down the foundations of a general extensible approach to the definition of game theoretical argument strength measures for multi-agent contexts, in this paper we introduce the novel formal notion of *Abstract Games of Argumentation Strategy*, capturing the essentials notions underlying game theoretical measures of argument strength, while being parametric with respect to actual context-specific details, like the type of argumentation framework considered, the sets of strategies available to the two players and the actual form of the rewards. We also define symmetrical and asymmetrical notions of argument strength for abstract games of argumentation strategy and investigate a (non-exhaustive) spectrum of their possible instantiations. Besides encompassing the original proposal of [14] as a special case, this gives rise to three novel concrete games of argumentation strategy and strength measures, featuring different properties and fitting different application scenarios.

2   Motivations

Our approach belongs to the research trend concerning the quantitative evaluation of arguments based on their relations at an abstract level, the main ones considered in the literature being attack and support. In a nutshell, the starting point of the evaluation is a directed graph capturing these relations: Fig. 1a shows a simple example of such a graph, where the symbols + and − indicate support and attack relations respectively (e.g. γ supports α while δ attacks γ).

a.   **b.**

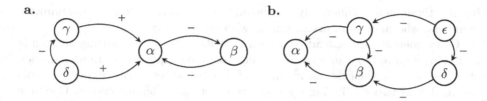

Fig. 1. Bipolar (**a**) and abstract (**b**) argumentation frameworks

Given such a graph, most approaches in the literature, e.g. [4,9,13,15], evaluate the strength of each argument *per se*, with respect to the other arguments, which serve as a sort of neutral background. In dialectical situations, however, arguments are put forward by different self-interested agents as parts of their positions and this difference may affect the evaluation criteria. Consider arguments α, γ, and δ in Fig. 1a: α is supported by both arguments γ and δ and benefits from both, for example using the method of [4,15], where each contributes to increasing the strength of α. However, in a debate an agent may not want to put forward both arguments γ and δ, since this could be viewed as an internally "inconsistent" position. Thus an agent with α in its agenda needs to decide whether to include γ or δ in its strategy: this calls for a different family of evaluation methods, where arguments are assessed as part of strategies including them, taking into account that adversarial strategies can be put forward by other agents, which may or may not have an agenda. To give an idea of the issues involved, if the agent decides to play δ in its strategy, it exploits the support of δ for α while discarding the support of γ. An adversary agent could then play β to attack α, but would refrain from playing γ since this would mean to support α, in the other agent's strategy, while being attacked by δ, also in the other agent's strategy. If instead the agent with α in its agenda decides to play γ, the adversary might choose to play δ in addition to β, but this is a bivalent move, given that it brings an attack against γ but also a support to α.

Assessing this kind of tradeoffs lies at the heart of the game-theoretical perspective we adopt, which generalizes the proposal of [14] in two main respects.

First, we aim at an abstract setting where argument strength is assessed in the context of a generic set of relations, thus being open to the consideration of any kind of argument interaction, in addition to or in replacement of those of attack and support.

Second, we aim at providing a general scheme encompassing different kinds of dialectical contexts where the involved agents play different roles.

To exemplify, some contexts are inherently "asymmetric", with an agent trying to defend its agenda against any possible criticism. To be credible, the agent is bound to be "consistent", while no constraint is posed on the arguments coming from the other agent(s). In human societies, this may be the case, for instance, in a *town hall*-style meeting, in which politicians try to defend their views with "coherent" arguments against a heterogeneous audience whose views may not be "coherent" with one another. Similarly, a Ph.D. candidate defending his/her thesis must "coherently" withstand any objections from the committee members, who may be in disagreement with one another.

Other contexts are instead "symmetric", with both sides featuring an agenda and being required to express a "coherent" position supporting it. In human societies, this may be the case, for instance, of debates between two parties attempting to defend two conflicting opinions, representing a binary choice. Concrete examples of these debates include a face-off between candidates for a presidential election, a political debate over implementing a policy, and a trial in a court of law where defence and prosecution argue over the innocence of a defendant. In these settings, the strength of an argument needs to be evaluated in relation to the other positions put forward rather than in absolute terms. For instance a presidential candidate will be elected if her/his position prevails over the positions of the other candidate(s), while s/he need not prevail over other possible positions which are irrelevant for electoral purposes.

To give a simple abstract example, consider the abstract argumentation framework in Fig. 1b where, in an "asymmetric" context, an agent playing α can be negatively affected by the fact that its adversary plays the arguments β, γ, both attacking α. Also, the agent cannot play the arguments α, δ, ϵ, which would counterattack both attackers β and γ, since δ and ϵ are in conflict. However, if also the adversary is required to be "consistent", then only β or γ individually can be played against α and for both cases there is a "consistent" defense strategy, namely $\{\alpha, \delta\}$ and $\{\alpha, \epsilon\}$ respectively.

Our motivation is thus the investigation of a general framework which can encompass the rich variety of dialectical contexts we have exemplified above in a systematic way, while at the same time providing guidelines for the exploration of further alternatives and supporting the analysis of general properties common to different instances, where possible. This framework and a set of instantiations will be illustrated in Sects. 4 and 5, respectively, building on the background notions presented next.

3 Background

3.1 Argumentation Frameworks

Following Dung [11], at a high level an argumentation framework captures some dialectical relations between arguments, while abstracting away from the arguments' structure and other aspects. In this paper we focus on *abstract* [11] and *bipolar* [3,8] argumentation frameworks, capturing, respectively, an *attack* relation alone and both *attack* and *support* relations, as follows:

Definition 1 (Argumentation Frameworks). *An Abstract Argumentation Framework (AF) is a pair $(\mathcal{A}, \mathcal{R}^-)$ where $\mathcal{A}$ is a set of arguments and $\mathcal{R}^- \subseteq \mathcal{A} \times \mathcal{A}$ is a binary attack relation on $\mathcal{A}$. A Bipolar Argumentation Framework (BF) is a triple $(\mathcal{A}, \mathcal{R}^-, \mathcal{R}^+)$ where $(\mathcal{A}, \mathcal{R}^-)$ is an AF and $\mathcal{R}^+ \subseteq \mathcal{A} \times \mathcal{A}$ is binary support relation on $\mathcal{A}$.*

It is clear that an AF $(\mathcal{A}, \mathcal{R}^-)$ can be seen as a BF $(\mathcal{A}, \mathcal{R}^-, \varnothing)$. Thus, in this section we will assume as given a BF $F = (\mathcal{A}, \mathcal{R}^-, \mathcal{R}^+)$, which may possibly be an AF.

AFs and BFs are equipped with semantics for accepting sets of arguments or for measuring the strength of arguments. In this paper we will make use of the weakest possible semantic notion, namely *conflict-freeness*, defined as follows:

Definition 2 *(Conflict-freeness)*. *A set of arguments $A \subseteq \mathcal{A}$ attacks a set of arguments $B \subseteq \mathcal{A}$ iff $\exists \alpha \in A, \beta \in B$ such that $(\alpha, \beta) \in \mathcal{R}^-$. A set of arguments $A \subseteq \mathcal{A}$ is conflict-free iff A does not attack itself.*

We will also use the following notions of *sets of attacks* or *supports* from sets of arguments against or towards (respectively) sets of arguments.

Definition 3 *(Set of attacks/supports)*. *Let $A, B \subseteq \mathcal{A}$. The set of attacks from A against B is defined as $B_F^{\leftarrow A} \triangleq (A \times B) \cap \mathcal{R}^-$. The set of supports from A towards B is defined as $B_F^{\leftarrow A} \triangleq (A \times B) \cap \mathcal{R}^+$.*

3.2   Two Player Zero-Sum Games of Imperfect Information

We will define various notions of strength for AFs and BFs in terms of the values of two player zero-sum games of imperfect information, in the spirit of and generalising the proposal of [14]. Here, we give essential game-theoretic background.

In the games we consider, *two players*, P and Q, are equipped with (finite and non-empty) sets of *(pure) strategies*, i.e. actions they can choose. The players have *imperfect information* as they choose their strategies without knowing in advance the choice of the other player. The players are also equipped with *reward functions*, assigning real numbers (utilities) to their combined choices. In this paper, reward functions always map pairs of strategies to a real number in the [0,1] interval. Moreover, our games of interest are *zero-sum*, namely such that each player's gain or loss of utility is balanced by the loss or gain of utility of the other. Formally, we consider the following games:

Definition 4 *(Two player zero-sum games of imperfect information)*. *A (two player zero-sum) game (of imperfect information) between players P and Q is a quadruple $(S_P, S_Q, \rho_P, \rho_Q)$ with S_P, S_Q the sets of (pure) strategies and ρ_P, ρ_Q the reward functions for P and Q, respectively, such that, for $*$ denoting either P or Q,*

- *S_* is non-empty and finite;*
- *$\rho_* : S_P \times S_Q \mapsto [0,1]$;*
- *for $X \in S_P$ and $Y \in S_Q$, $\rho_Q(X,Y) = 1 - \rho_P(X,Y)$.*

Players of these games need to choose their strategies so that they both maximise their minimum expected reward, given the strategy chosen by the other player. This reward is the *value* of the game. The *minimax theorem* [16] provides a characterisation of this value (for finite sets of strategies, as in our setting) in terms of *mixed strategies* for players, namely probability distributions over their (pure) strategies, as follows:

Definition 5 *(Value of a game).* *Given a game* $(S_P, S_Q, \rho_P, \rho_Q)$ *between* P *and* Q, *let*

- $S_P = \{P_1, \ldots, P_m\}$ *and* $S_Q = \{Q_1, \ldots, Q_n\}$;
- *for* $\mathcal{P}$ *and* $\mathcal{Q}$ *probability distributions over* S_P *and* S_Q, *respectively,* p_i *and* q_j *stand for* $\mathcal{P}(P_i)$ *and* $\mathcal{Q}(Q_j)$, *respectively, for* $i \in \{1, \ldots, m\}$ *and* $j \in \{1, \ldots, n\}$;
- $R = ((r_{i,j}))_{m \times n}$ *be the* reward matrix *for player* P, *where* $r_{i,j} = \rho_P(P_i, Q_j)$
- *player* P*'s* expected payoff *be defined as*[1]: $\mathcal{P}^T R \mathcal{Q} = \sum_{j=1}^{n} \sum_{i=1}^{m} r_{i,j} p_i q_j$.

Then the value *of the game is* v *such that*

$$v = max_{\mathcal{P}} min_{\mathcal{Q}} \mathcal{P}^T R \mathcal{Q} = min_{\mathcal{Q}} max_{\mathcal{P}} \mathcal{P}^T R \mathcal{Q}$$

Intuitively, P expects to obtain, as a result of playing the game, at least $min_{\mathcal{Q}} \mathcal{P}^T R \mathcal{Q}$ and will try to maximise this, and Q expects to obtain 1-$max_{\mathcal{P}} \mathcal{P}^T R \mathcal{Q}$ and will try to minimise $max_{\mathcal{P}} \mathcal{P}^T R \mathcal{Q}$. It is known that the value of a game is the solution of the linear programming problem of maximising variable p_{m+1}, subject to the $(n + m + 2)$ constraints: $\forall j \in \{1, \ldots, n\}$: $\sum_{i=1}^{m} r_{i,j} p_i - p_{m+1} \geq 0$; $\sum_{i=1}^{m} p_i = 1$; $p_1, \ldots, p_m, p_{m+1} \geq 0$.

4   Abstract Games of Argumentation Strategy

In this section we define a general form of games (that we call *abstract games of argumentation strategy*) for a generalised form of argumentation frameworks (that we call generalised argumentation frameworks (GAFs), defined below.

Definition 6 *(Generalised Argumentation Frameworks).* *A* Generalised Argumentation Framework *(GAF) is a tuple* $(\mathcal{A}, Rel_1, \ldots, Rel_l)$, *with* $l > 0$ *and* $Rel_i \subseteq \mathcal{A} \times \mathcal{A}$, *for* $i \in \{1, \ldots, l\}$.

Trivially, AFs are GAFs with $l = 1$ and Rel_1 an attack relation, and BFs are GAFs with $l = 2$, Rel_1 an attack relation and Rel_2 a support relation. *Support argumentation frameworks* [2] are also GAFs with $l = 1$ and Rel_1 a support relation. Other relations from the literature, e.g. defence or subargument, might be considered in future work.

Definition 7 *(Abstract games of argumentation strategy).* *Given a* *GAF* $(\mathcal{A}, Rel_1, \ldots, Rel_l)$, *an abstract game of argumentation strategy* between *players* P *and* Q *is a two player zero-sum game of imperfect information* $(S_P, S_Q, \rho_P, \rho_Q)$ *between* P *and* Q *such that* $S_P \subseteq 2^{\mathcal{A}}$ *and* $S_Q \subseteq 2^{\mathcal{A}}$.

Thus, in abstract games of argumentation strategy we only impose that players adopt sets of arguments as their strategies. The set of possible strategies of a player may be unconstrained and coincide with $2^{\mathcal{A}}$ (this is the case for the instances considered in this paper) but in general some sets of arguments can be excluded.

---

[1] Here $\mathcal{P}^T$ is the transpose of vector $\mathcal{P}$.

In this paper *concrete games of argumentation strategy* are obtained by instantiating the parameters of the abstract games, namely S_* and ρ_* for $*$ either P or Q, with the GAF either an AF or a BF. In all concrete games considered in this paper, for $X \in S_P$ and $Y \in S_Q$, $\rho_P(X, Y)$ is given along the following lines:

- if X, Y fulfil some specific *borderline conditions*, in terms of $Rel_1, \ldots, Rel_l$, then $\rho_P(X, Y)$ is some specific element of $[0,1]$;
- otherwise, $\rho_P(X, Y)$ is defined in terms of some *degree of acceptability* function $\phi : S_P \times S_Q \mapsto [0, 1]$, in turn defined in terms of $Rel_1, \ldots, Rel_l$.

Intuitively, $\rho_P(X, Y)$ measures the dialectical acceptability, in the GAF, of strategy X for player P given that Q plays Y. The borderline conditions capture special or possibly "pathological" situations where the outcome is fixed, while ϕ is in place to give a *gradual valuation* of the acceptability in "normal" conditions.

Games of argumentation strategies can be used to define notions of arguments' *strength* in terms of the value of the games. The idea is that the strength of each argument α can be assessed by considering a variant of the game where only the strategies including α are considered, i.e. the player has α as its agenda and hence commits to play α (possibly with other arguments). As discussed in Sect. 2, two scenarios can be considered depending on whether only one or both players have an agenda. The first case gives rise to an asymmetrical situation where one player (P) can be regarded as the *proponent* of some argument, say α, while the other, uncommitted, player (Q) plays just the role of *opponent*. The second case is symmetric, with both players being proponents of arguments, say α and β. Two different notions of strength are needed: in the asymmetrical case an absolute notion of strength is appropriate, assessing the ability of α to withstand a free-playing opponent, while in the symmetrical case a relative notion of strength is needed, since the adoption of α is assessed against the adoption of β (and vice versa). This gives rise to the following definition.

Definition 8 *(asymmetrical and symmetrical games and strength of arguments).* Given a GAF $(\mathcal{A}, Rel_1, \ldots, Rel_l)$ with $\mathcal{A}$ finite and a (concrete) game of argumentation strategy $G = (S_P, S_Q, \rho_P, \rho_Q)$ between players P and Q:

- *the (absolute) strength of $x \in \mathcal{A}$ with respect to G is the value of the asymmetrical game of argumentation strategy $G(x) = (\{X \in S_P | x \in X\}, S_Q, \rho_P, \rho_Q)$;*
- *the strength of $x \in \mathcal{A}$ relative to $y \in \mathcal{A}$ with respect to G is the value of the symmetrical game of argumentation strategy $G(x, y) = (\{X \in S_P | x \in X\}, \{Y \in S_Q | y \in Y\}, \rho_P, \rho_Q)$.*

Formally speaking, given a game of argumentation strategy G, Definition 8 involves two sets of derived games for strength assessment: the set $\{G(x) \mid x \in \mathcal{A}\}$ of asymmetrical games and the set $\{G(x, y) \mid x, y \in \mathcal{A}\}$ of symmetrical games. It must be noted, however, that although in principle for any G both derived games are automatically obtained, in concrete games the definition of the functions ρ_P and ρ_Q can be intrinsically oriented to the symmetrical or asymmetrical scenario, so that only one of the two kinds of strength assessment is appropriate, as we will exemplify in Sect. 5.

In the remainder, we will refer to the absolute and relative strength of arguments as *asymmetrical* and *symmetrical strength*, respectively. Moreover, we will assume that the set of arguments in all GAFs we will consider (i.e. AFs and BF) is finite.

5   Instantiating Abstract Games of Argumentation Strategy

Based on the general scheme defined in Sect. 4 we introduce four concrete games of argumentation strategy (two for AFs and two for BFs), by specifying the parameters of abstract games of argumentation strategy, namely the sets of strategies and the reward functions for the two players. As to the former, we adopt the simplest choice that in all games the set of strategies is exactly the powerset of the set of arguments in the given AF or BF. As to the latter, the four different reward functions are defined in terms of different borderline conditions and degree of acceptability functions, whose definitions arise from the combination of two dimensions: the type of formalism (AF or BF) and the asymmetrical or symmetrical (a or s) orientation of the game. Along the AF - BF dimension degree of acceptability functions ϕ^{AF}, ϕ^{BF} are used, while along the a-s dimension borderline conditions BC^a, BC^s are used. These alternatives are described in the following subsections.

5.1   Degree of Acceptability Functions

As to AFs, we define the degree of acceptability function (ϕ^{AF}) as in [14], taking into account "how much" each strategy attacks the other. Basically outgoing and incoming attacks make a positive and a negative contribution, respectively, as specified below:

$$\phi^{AF}(X,Y) = \frac{1}{2}[1 + f(|Y_{AF}^{\leftarrow X}|) - f(|X_{AF}^{\leftarrow Y}|)] \qquad (1)$$

where the function f is defined as

$$f(n) = 1 - \frac{1}{n+1} = \frac{n}{n+1}$$

and allows the scaling down of (arbitrarily large) cardinalities of sets to a normalized value between 0 and 1. In fact $f : \mathbb{N} \to [0,1]$ is such that $f(0) = 0$ and $lim_{n\to\infty} f(n) = 1$. Note that ϕ^{AF} returns 0.5 when outgoing and incoming attacks are balanced and a value closer to 0 (1) when incoming (outgoing, respectively) attacks prevail.

We extend the notion of degree of acceptability function to BFs by defining the novel ϕ^{BF} function as follows:

$$\phi^{BF}(X,Y) = \frac{1}{4}[2 + f(|Y_{AF}^{\leftarrow X}|) - f(|X_{AF}^{\leftarrow Y}|) + f(|X_{AF}^{\Leftarrow X\cup Y}|) - f(|Y_{AF}^{\Leftarrow X\cup Y}|)] \qquad (2)$$

where supports to X (either from X itself or from the other strategy Y) play a positive role, while supports to Y play a negative role. Note that other definitions of ϕ^{AF} and ϕ^{BF}, possibly using other definitions of f, may be possible: these are left for future work.

5.2 Borderline Conditions

For asymmetrical games, where P and Q can be seen as playing the distinct roles of proponent and opponent, respectively, we consider the setting proposed in [14], based on two main ideas: P's strategy is required to be conflict-free, but does not need to attack Q's strategy, while Q's strategy is not required to be conflict-free, but needs to attack P's strategy. This amounts to the borderline conditions expressed by the partially defined function $BC^{a} : 2^{\mathcal{A}} \times 2^{\mathcal{A}} \to [0,1]$ such that, for $X, Y \subseteq \mathcal{A}$:

1. if X is not conflict-free then $BC^{a}(X,Y) = 0$;
2. if X is conflict-free and Y does not attack X then $BC^{a}(X,Y) = 1$;
3. otherwise $BC^{a}(X,Y)$ is undefined.

For symmetrical games, conflict-freeness and attack requirements are applied equally to the two players, giving rise to the borderline conditions expressed by the partially defined function $BC^{s} : 2^{\mathcal{A}} \times 2^{\mathcal{A}} \to [0,1]$ such that, for $X, Y \subseteq \mathcal{A}$:

1. if X is not conflict-free and Y is conflict-free then $BC^{s}(X,Y) = 0$;
2. if X and Y are both not conflict-free then $BC^{s}(X,Y) = 0.5$;
3. if X is conflict-free and Y is not conflict-free then $BC^{s}(X,Y) = 1$;
4. if X and Y are both conflict-free and:
   (a) neither X nor Y attacks the other then $BC^{s}(X,Y) = 0.5$;
   (b) X attacks Y and not vice versa then $BC^{s}(X,Y) = 1$;
   (c) Y attacks X and not vice versa then $BC^{s}(X,Y) = 0$;
5. otherwise $BC^{s}(X,Y)$ is undefined.

5.3 A Spectrum of Strength Measures

The notions given in Sects. 5.1 and 5.2 provide the ingredients for defining four different game instances and strength measures, as detailed below. In all instances $S_P = S_Q = 2^{\mathcal{A}}$ and the reward function of player Q is the complement of that of player P (e.g. $\rho_Q^{AF,a}(X,Y) = 1 - \rho_P^{AF,a}(X,Y)$), so the latter is sufficient to characterize each instance.

Asymmetrical Strength for AFs. The first instantiation corresponds to the games of argumentation strategy of [14]: they are defined for AFs and distinguish the asymmetrical roles of proponent P and opponent Q with respect to the argument whose strength is assessed. This corresponds to the following definition.

Definition 9 (asymmetrical strength for AFs). *Let* $AF = (\mathcal{A}, \mathcal{R}^-)$ *be an AF and let* $G^{AF,a} = (S_P, S_Q, \rho_P^{AF,a}, \rho_Q^{AF,a})$ *be the concrete game of argumentation strategy where, for* $X, Y \subseteq \mathcal{A}$:

1. $\rho_P^{AF,a}(X,Y) = BC^a(X,Y)$ *if* $BC^a(X,Y)$ *is defined;*
2. $\rho_P^{AF,a}(X,Y) = \phi^{AF}(X,Y)$ *otherwise.*

Then the asymmetrical strength *of* $\alpha \in \mathcal{A}$ *(in* AF*), denoted* $\sigma^{AF,a}(\alpha)$*, is the value of the asymmetrical game of argumentation strategy* $G^{AF,a}(\alpha)$*.*

As an illustration, given the AF in Fig. 1b, $\sigma^{AF,a}(\alpha) = 0.333$. Thus, argument α has a fairly weak strength. This is due to P, the proponent of α, having no conflict-free strategy to fully counterattack its opponent's strategies. Table 1, a fragment of the full reward matrix for P in this example, shows P's rewards for its conflict-free strategies (the omitted non-conflict-free strategies give lower rewards), with respect to some of Q's strategies (we have omitted Q's strategies not playing a part in the problem of determining the value of the game in question, since they always give an equal or worse reward than those shown). The optimal strategy for P is to play $\{\alpha, \delta\}$ or $\{\alpha, \epsilon\}$ with equal probability. In the worst case situation (namely when the opponent plays $\{\beta, \epsilon\}$ or $\{\gamma, \epsilon\}$, respectively) this mixed strategy gives an average reward of 0.333, which is the value of the game in question and thus the asymmetrical strength of α.

Table 1. Fragment of the reward matrix for P in the asymmetrical game $G^{AF,a}(\alpha)$ for AF as given in Fig. 1b, with the proponent strategies (X) on the rows and opponent strategies (Y) on the columns. Cells give the relevant value of $\rho_P^{AF,a}(X,Y)$ (given by $\phi^{AF}(X,Y)$ in these cases).

Strategies	$\{\beta, \epsilon\}$	$\{\gamma, \epsilon\}$	$\{\beta, \gamma, \epsilon\}$
$\{\alpha\}$	0.25	0.25	0.167
$\{\alpha, \delta\}$	0.417	0.167	0.375
$\{\alpha, \epsilon\}$	0.25	0.5	0.417

Symmetrical Strength for AFs. As discussed in Sect. 2, symmetrical games are appropriate to assess argument strength in "one-against-all" contexts. Instead, in "head-to-head" contexts symmetrical games need to be considered. In the case of AFs, these games and the corresponding notion of strength are defined as follows.

Definition 10 (symmetrical strength for AFs). *Let* $AF = (\mathcal{A}, \mathcal{R}^-)$ *be an AF and let* $G^{AF,s} = (S_P, S_Q, \rho_P^{AF,s}, \rho_Q^{AF,s})$ *be the concrete game of argumentation strategy where, for* $X, Y \subseteq \mathcal{A}$:

1. $\rho_P^{AF,s}(X,Y) = BC^s(X,Y)$ *if* $BC^s(X,Y)$ *is defined;*
2. $\rho_P^{AF,s}(X,Y) = \phi^{AF}(X,Y)$ *otherwise.*

Then the symmetrical strength *of* $\alpha \in \mathcal{A}$ *(in AF) relative to* $\beta \in \mathcal{A}$, *denoted* $\sigma^{AF,s}(\alpha, \beta)$, *is the value of the symmetrical game of argumentation strategy* $G^{AF,s}(\alpha, \beta)$.

As an illustration, given the AF in Fig. 1b, $\sigma^{AF,s}(\alpha, \beta) = 0.417$ and $\sigma^{AF,s}(\alpha, \gamma) = 0.5$. Note that $\sigma^{AF,s}(\alpha, \beta) > \sigma^{AF,a}(\alpha)$ and $\sigma^{AF,s}(\alpha, \gamma) > \sigma^{AF,a}(\alpha)$, namely α has higher (relative) symmetrical strengths than its (absolute) asymmetrical strength, since Q is now penalised if it plays a non conflict-free strategy. Note also that $\sigma^{AF,s}(\alpha, \gamma) > \sigma^{AF,s}(\alpha, \beta)$, namely P fares worse when playing against β as opposed to γ, because it has no "good" strategy against $\{\beta, \epsilon\}$, while its strategy $\{\alpha, \epsilon\}$ fares well against the strategy $\{\gamma\}$ by Q, as shown in Table 2 (left) and (right), respectively (this table gives fragments of the corresponding reward matrices for P, after removing strategies for both P and Q, playing no role in the computation of strength, as done for Table 1).

Table 2. Fragments of the reward matrices for P in the symmetrical games $G^{AF,s}(\alpha, \beta)$ (left) and $G^{AF,s}(\alpha, \gamma)$ (right) for AF in Fig. 1b. Cells give the relevant value of $\rho_P^{AF,s}(X, Y)$ (given by $\phi^{AF}(X, Y)$ in these cases).

Strategies	$\{\beta\}$	$\{\beta, \epsilon\}$
$\{\alpha\}$	0	0
$\{\alpha, \delta\}$	0.5	0.4167
$\{\alpha, \epsilon\}$	0	0

Strategies	$\{\gamma\}$	$\{\gamma, \delta\}$
$\{\alpha\}$	0	0
$\{\alpha, \delta\}$	0	0
$\{\alpha, \epsilon\}$	0.5	0.5833

Asymmetrical Strength for BFs. We now move along the other design dimension in the definition of strength, considering also the support relation and hence focusing on BFs. The third concrete game of argumentation strategy corresponds to the adoption of the asymmetrical orientation in this context and gives rise to the following definition.

Definition 11 (asymmetrical strength for BFs). *Let* $BF = (\mathcal{A}, \mathcal{R}^-, \mathcal{R}^+)$ *be a BF and let* $G^{BF,a} = (S_P, S_Q, \rho_P^{BF,a}, \rho_Q^{BF,a})$ *be the concrete game of argumentation strategy where, for* $X, Y \subseteq \mathcal{A}$:

1. $\rho_P^{BF,a}(X, Y) = BC^a(X, Y)$ *if* $BC^a(X, Y)$ *is defined;*
2. $\rho_P^{BF,a}(X, Y) = \phi^{BF}(X, Y)$ *otherwise.*

Then the asymmetrical strength *of* $\alpha \in \mathcal{A}$ *(in BF), denoted* $\sigma^{BF,a}(\alpha)$, *is the value of the asymmetrical game of argumentation strategy* $G^{BF,a}(\alpha)$.

As an illustration, given the BF in Fig. 1a, $\sigma^{BF,a}(\beta) = 0.347$. Thus, β has a fairly weak strength. This is due to Q, the opponent, being able to play strategies $\{\alpha, \delta\}$ and $\{\alpha, \gamma, \delta\}$ despite the latter not being conflict-free. P then needs to resort to playing $\{\beta\}$ and, twice as often, $\{\beta, \delta\}$. This mixed strategy results in an average reward (and asymmetrical strength) of 0.347, as shown by Table 3 (a fragment of P's reward table, condensed in the same way as Table 1).

Table 3. Fragment of P's reward matrix in $G^{BF,a}(\beta)$ for BF in Fig. 1a.

Strategies	$\{\alpha,\delta\}$	$\{\alpha,\gamma,\delta\}$
$\{\beta\}$	0.375	0.333
$\{\beta,\gamma\}$	0.292	0.271
$\{\beta,\delta\}$	0.333	0.354

Symmetrical Strength for BFS. Finally, the fourth concrete game of argumentation strategy applies the symmetrical orientation to BFs, as follows.

Definition 12 (symmetrical strength for BFs). *Let* $BF = (\mathcal{A}, \mathcal{R}^-, \mathcal{R}^+)$ *be a BF and let* $G^{BF,s} = (S_P, S_Q, \rho_P^{BF,s}, \rho_Q^{BF,s})$ *be the concrete game of argumentation strategy where, for* $X, Y \subseteq \mathcal{A}$:

1. $\rho_P^{BF,s}(X,Y) = BC^s(X,Y)$ *if* $BC^s(X,Y)$ *is defined;*
2. $\rho_P^{BF,s}(X,Y) = \phi^{BF}(X,Y)$ *otherwise.*

Then the symmetrical strength of $\alpha \in \mathcal{A}$ *(in BF) relative to* $\beta \in \mathcal{A}$, *denoted* $\sigma^{BF,s}(\alpha,\beta)$, *is the value of the symmetrical game of argumentation strategy* $G^{BF,s}(\alpha,\beta)$.

As an illustration, given the BF in Fig. 1a, $\sigma^{BF,s}(\beta,\alpha) = 0.375$. Thus, β's (symmetrical) strength relative to α is higher than β's absolute (asymmetrical) strength (which is 0.347, as seen earlier). Indeed, Q, the player of α, now cannot play the strategy $\{\alpha,\gamma,\delta\}$, since it is not conflict-free, and so must choose between $\{\alpha,\gamma\}$ and $\{\alpha,\delta\}$, thereby weakening its attacks against β. This can be seen in Table 4 (condensing P's reward matrix as for earlier Tables).

Table 4. Fragment of P's reward matrix in $G^{BF,s}(\beta,\alpha)$ for BF in Fig. 1a.

Strategies	$\{\alpha,\gamma\}$	$\{\alpha,\delta\}$
$\{\beta\}$	0.375	0.375
$\{\beta,\gamma\}$	0.333	0.292
$\{\beta,\delta\}$	0.375	0.333

6 Properties of Game Theoretical Strength Measures

In this section we provide some properties[2] of the notions of strength introduced in Sect. 5, showing that they satisfy some basic desirable requirements. All of these properties hold independently of the type of framework (AF or BF), hence throughout this section, unless otherwise specified, we will assume as given a

---

[2] We omit proofs due to space limitations. Also, again for space limitations, we omit to consider other properties proposed in the extensive literature on properties of argumentation, e.g. [5,12]. The study of additional properties is left for future work.

generic $F = (\mathcal{A}, \mathcal{R}^-, \mathcal{R}^+)$, including the special case of AFs where $\mathcal{R}^+ = \varnothing$. For the sake of conciseness, $\sigma^{F,a}$ will stand for either $\sigma^{AF,a}$ or $\sigma^{BF,a}$ (similarly for $\sigma^{F,s}$) and, where appropriate, we will also use $*$ to stand either for a or s.

Some properties in this section refer to the *addition of an attack* to a framework: given $F=(\mathcal{A}, \mathcal{R}^-, \mathcal{R}^+)$ and $y \in \mathcal{A}$, the framework resulting from the addition of the attack (x, y) is defined as $F + (x, y)^- \triangleq F' = (\mathcal{A} \cup \{x\}, \mathcal{R}^- \cup \{(x, y)\}, \mathcal{R}^+)$. Similarly, the *addition of a support* (x, y), for $y \in \mathcal{A}$, is defined as $F + (x, y)^+ \triangleq (\mathcal{A} \cup \{x\}, \mathcal{R}^-, \mathcal{R}^+ \cup \{(x, y)\})$. Finally, some properties use the notion of *attackers of an argument*: for argument α, this is defined as $\alpha^- \triangleq \{\beta \in \mathcal{A} \mid (\beta, \alpha) \in \mathcal{R}^-\}$.

First, the strength of arguments is always guaranteed to be in $[0,1]$:

Proposition 1. *For every* $\alpha, \beta \in \mathcal{A}$, $0 \le \sigma^{F,a}(\alpha) \le 1$ *and* $0 \le \sigma^{F,s}(\alpha, \beta) \le 1$.

Also, only self-attacking arguments have absolute strength 0. Moreover, they have relative strength 0 with respect to non self-attacking arguments:

Proposition 2. *For any* $\alpha \in \mathcal{A}$, $\sigma^{F,a}(\alpha) = 0$ *if and only if* $(\alpha, \alpha) \in \mathcal{R}^-$. *Moreover, given any* $\beta \in \mathcal{A}$ *such that* $(\beta, \beta) \notin \mathcal{R}^-$, *if* $(\alpha, \alpha) \in \mathcal{R}^-$ *then* $\sigma^{F,s}(\alpha, \beta) = 0$.

Further, adding an attack cannot increase the (absolute or relative) strength of the attacked argument:

Proposition 3. *For any* $\alpha \in \mathcal{A}$, *let* $F' = F + (\beta, \alpha)^-$. *Then,* $\sigma^{F,a}(\alpha) \ge \sigma^{F',a}(\alpha)$ *and, for any* $\gamma \in \mathcal{A}$, $\sigma^{F,s}(\alpha, \gamma) \ge \sigma^{F',s}(\alpha, \gamma)$.

Still further, attacking an attacker of an argument cannot decrease its strength:

Proposition 4. *For any* $\alpha, \beta \in \mathcal{A}$ *with* $\beta \in \alpha^-$, *let* $F'=F+(\gamma, \beta)^-$. *Then,* $\sigma^{F,a}(\alpha) \le \sigma^{F',a}(\alpha)$ *and, for any* $\delta \in \mathcal{A}$, $\sigma^{F,s}(\alpha, \delta) \le \sigma^{F',s}(\alpha, \delta)$.

The next property is specific to the asymmetrical instantiations where unattacked arguments have strength 1 and are strictly stronger than attacked ones:

Proposition 5. *For every* $\alpha \in \mathcal{A}$ $\sigma^{F,a}(\alpha) = 1$ *if and only if* $\alpha^- = \varnothing$.

Proposition 5 shows an imbalance between attackers and supporters since, when an argument is unattacked, it already has the maximum strength value and adding supporter(s) does not change its score. The score of 1 is a direct consequence of the special conditions in the asymmetrical instantiations: given that the opponent role is purely critical in this case, if the proponent chooses an unattackable argument, there are no reasons for not awarding the top strength to it.

A corollary of Proposition 5 is that unattacked arguments are strictly stronger than attacked arguments:

Corollary 1. *For every* $\alpha, \beta \in \mathcal{A}$ *if* $\alpha^- = \varnothing$ *and* $\beta^- \ne \varnothing$ *then* $\sigma^{F,a}(\alpha) > \sigma^{F,a}(\beta)$.

The next properties are specific to the bipolar instantiations. First, adding a support will not decrease the strength of the supported argument:

Proposition 6. *For any $\alpha \in \mathcal{A}$, let $F' = F + (\beta, \alpha)^{+}$. Then, $\sigma^{F,a}(\alpha) \leq \sigma^{F',a}(\alpha)$ and, for any $\gamma \in \mathcal{A}$, $\sigma^{F,s}(\alpha, \gamma) \leq \sigma^{F',s}(\alpha, \gamma)$.*

Then, if one adds a supporter to an argument, the arguments it in turn attacks can only be weakened:

Proposition 7. *For any $\alpha, \beta \in \mathcal{A}$ with $\beta \in \alpha^{-}$, let $F' = F + (\gamma, \beta)^{+}$. Then, $\sigma^{F,a}(\alpha) \geq \sigma^{F',a}(\alpha)$ and, for any $\delta \in \mathcal{A}$, $\sigma^{F,s}(\alpha, \delta) \geq \sigma^{F',s}(\alpha, \delta)$.*

The next two properties are valid only for the symmetrical instantiation. Self-attacking arguments could be ignored for these instantiations:

Proposition 8. *If $(\alpha, \alpha) \in \mathcal{R}^{-}$, letting $\mathcal{A}' = \mathcal{A} \smallsetminus \{\alpha\}$ and $F' = (\mathcal{A}', \mathcal{R}^{-} \cap (\mathcal{A}' \times \mathcal{A}'), \mathcal{R}^{+} \cap (\mathcal{A}' \times \mathcal{A}'))$, then, for any $\beta, \gamma \neq \alpha$, it holds that $\sigma^{F,s}(\beta, \gamma) = \sigma^{F',s}(\beta, \gamma)$.*

The final property shows complementarity of the symmetrical instantiations:

Proposition 9. *Given $\alpha, \beta \in \mathcal{A}$, $\sigma^{F,s}(\alpha, \beta) + \sigma^{F,s}(\beta, \alpha) = 1$.*

7 An Application Example

We illustrate and discuss the use of alternative strength measures in an example about the Brexit referendum held in June 2016 in the UK, in which citizens voted on staying in or leaving the EU. Figure 2 shows a possible debate about the virtues of the two options, represented as a BF. This BF includes four economical reasons and implications concerning the UK currency in relation to Brexit. These are intricately linked by dialectical relations. The two main arguments x and y, representing the binary choice of the referendum (stay in the EU or leave it,

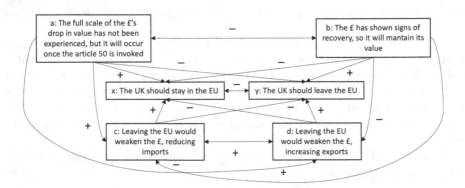

Fig. 2. Brexit debate BF example

respectively), are mutually exclusive. Moreover, two of the arguments, a and c, support x and attack y, while the converse holds for b and c. Further, a and b are in contrast with and attack one other, while c and d, despite supporting different theses, support each other. Then a supports both c and d, while b attacks them.[3]

We will now compare the behaviour of the (a)symmetrical strength measures, $\sigma^{BF,a}$ and $\sigma^{BF,s}$, in this example, with reference to the arguments x and y.

In the asymmetrical case, $\sigma^{BF,a}(x) = 0.361$ while $\sigma^{BF,a}(y) = 0.428$, thus the argument for leaving prevails. Indeed, it turns out from the reward matrix that the unique optimal strategy for x is $\{x, a, c\}$, which does not perform well against an opponent with a free choice of strategy; in particular the opponent may adopt a strategy where y is not included, such as $\{c, d\}$, which benefits from the mutual support between c and d and also from the support coming from a and attacks x through d. A proponent of y instead has a mixed strategy consisting of the sets $\{y, b\}$ (with probability 0.9091) and $\{y, d\}$ (with probability 0.0909), which gives rise to a higher strength value, since, on average, it performs fairly well against all other strategies, or, at least, better than $\{x, a, c\}$ does.

Turning to the symmetrical version, we obtain the opposite ranking, as x has a higher strength than y when they are compared "head-to-head": $\sigma^{BF,s}(x, y) = 0.533$ while $\sigma^{BF,s}(y, x) = 0.467$. This perhaps surprising result is due to the fact that in the symmetrical version the conflict-free strategies including x are faced only with the conflict-free strategies including y. As a result, $X = \{x, a, c\}$ is the optimal strategy for an agent putting forward x, which gives rise to a reward of 0.533 in the worst case (when $Y = \{y, d\}$). Conversely, the unique optimal strategy for an agent putting forward y turns is $Y = \{y, d\}$, with reward 0.467.

While this outcome has been obtained on a specific example with a specific instance of strength measure (both being debatable to some extent), some general considerations can be drawn. At a general level, this outcome strongly suggests that, at least in dialectical settings, there can be no such notion as the "right" strength assessment for arguments. In more detail, in the context of the game-theoretical approach, it shows that for a fixed framework and fixed degree of acceptability function (ϕ^{BF} in this case), the strength order of arguments may be different across the symmetrical and asymmetrical orientation. We suggest that, though at a preliminary level, this observation may be useful to explain (and provide a formal counterpart to) some phenomena occurring in actual dialectical contexts. For instance the fact that, in the political arena, some candidates prefer indirect to face-to-face TV debates (or vice versa) might be related to the context where they feel their arguments can be perceived as stronger. Also, the discrepancies between the preferences (and behavior) of the actual electoral body with respect to the previsions of "expert analysts" might be related to the fact that the latter may tend to adopt a more comprehensive

---

[3] Note that we resort here to an intuitive interpretation of the notions of attack and support, based on human understanding of the natural language description of the arguments. In other words, these relations are produced by manual annotation and we acknowledge that the relevant interpretation may not be univocal. Possible differences in this respect do not affect the main points of our discussion here anyway.

and symmetrical view, while a significant part of the electoral body may have a more limited analytic ability and tend to consider different aspects separately, in a sense mimicking the asymmetrical orientation. This might also explain the success of some electoral campaigning strategies in spite of the fact that they may look weak, if not absurd[4] from the perspective of some observers.

8   Conclusion

We have introduced a novel generic notion of game of argumentation strategy, extending the initial proposal of [14], and have shown how it supports the definition of a number of game-theoretical measures of argument strength, fitting different application scenarios. On the application side, we have discussed a simple real-world example suggesting how the consideration of alternative strength measures can be useful to provide a formal counterpart to the diversity of behaviours and (sometimes surprising) outcomes in actual dialectical scenarios like political debates. On the theoretical side, we have shown that the various measures satisfy a basic set of desirable properties, which are rooted in their common parametric definition. For future work we predict that there will be many potential directions for fruitful study. First, other reward functions can be investigated: we adopted the simple approach of considering conflict-freeness as a basic requirement and of counting attacks and supports, but more sophisticated reward functions, giving rise to different strength measures, can be considered. Second, the properties we have analysed here are by no means exhaustive and the definition of axiomatic requirements for game-theoretical strength measures is worth exploring, taking into account recent advancements concerning other families of argument strength measures (e.g. see [1,6]). Third, it could be interesting to study the relationships between our proposed semantics and other argumentation semantics in the literature, such as those of [11] for AFs or those overviewed in [10] for BFs. On the application side, it would be interesting to explore the problem of learning from past experiences (e.g. decisions made or election outcomes) the actual strength measure used in a given domain or by a given community. Finally, an analysis of the relationships between strength models and rhetorical strategies in the presentation of arguments would be extremely useful to further characterize the potential of our approach.

References

1. Amgoud, L., Ben-Naim, J.: Axiomatic foundations of acceptability semantics. In: Proceedings of the 15th International Conference on Principles of Knowledge Representation and Reasoning, KR 2016, pp. 2–11. AAAI Press (2016)
2. Amgoud, L., Ben-Naim, J.: Evaluation of arguments from support relations: Axioms and semantics. In: Proceedings of the 25th International Joint Conference on Artificial Intelligence, IJCAI 2016. AAAI Press (2016)

---

[4] Even the requirement of conflict-freeness seems to be overlooked in some cases.

3. Amgoud, L., Cayrol, C., Lagasquie-Schiex, M.-C., Livet, P.: On bipolarity in argumentation frameworks. Int. J. Intell. Syst. **23**(10), 1062–1093 (2008)
4. Baroni, P., Romano, M., Toni, F., Aurisicchio, M., Bertanza, G.: Automatic evaluation of design alternatives with quantitative argumentation. Argument Comput. **6**(1), 24–49 (2015)
5. Bonzon, E., Delobelle, J., Konieczny, S., Maudet, N.: Argumentation ranking semantics based on propagation. In: Computational Models of Argument - Proceedings of COMMA, 139–150 (2016)
6. Bonzon, E., Delobelle, J., Konieczny, S., Maudet, N.: A comparative study of ranking-based semantics for abstract argumentation. In: Proceedings of the 13th AAAI Conference on Artificial Intelligence, AAAI 2016, pp. 914–920 (2016)
7. Caminada, M.W.A., Gabbay, D.M.: A logical account of formal argumentation. Stud. Logica. **93**(2–3), 109–145 (2009)
8. Cayrol, C., Lagasquie-Schiex, M.C.: On the acceptability of arguments in bipolar argumentation frameworks. In: Godo, L. (ed.) ECSQARU 2005. LNCS (LNAI), vol. 3571, pp. 378–389. Springer, Heidelberg (2005). doi:10.1007/11518655_33
9. Cayrol, C., Lagasquie-Schiex, M.C.: Bipolar abstract argumentation systems. In: Simari, G., Rahwan, I. (eds.) Argumentation in Artificial Intelligence. Springer, Boston, MA (2009). doi:10.1007/978-0-387-98197-0_4
10. Cohen, A., Gottifredi, S., García, A.J., Simari, G.R.: A survey of different approaches to support in argumentation systems. Knowl. Eng. Rev. **29**(5), 513–550 (2014)
11. Dung, P.M.: On the acceptability of arguments and its fundamental role in nonmonotonic reasoning, logic programming and n-person games. Artif. Intell. **77**(2), 321–358 (1995)
12. Grossi, D., Modgil, S.: On the graded acceptability of arguments. In: Proceedings of the 24th International Joint Conference on Artificial Intelligence, IJCAI 2015, pp. 868–874. AAAI Press (2015)
13. Leite, J., Martins, J.: Social abstract argumentation. In: Proceedings of the 22nd International Joint Conference on Artificial Intelligence, IJCAI 2011, pp. 2287–2292. AAAI Press (2011)
14. Matt, P.-A., Toni, F.: A game-theoretic measure of argument strength for abstract argumentation. In: Hölldobler, S., Lutz, C., Wansing, H. (eds.) JELIA 2008. LNCS (LNAI), vol. 5293, pp. 285–297. Springer, Heidelberg (2008). doi:10.1007/978-3-540-87803-2_24
15. Rago, A., Toni, F., Aurisicchio, M., Baroni, P.: Discontinuity-free decision support with quantitative argumentation debates. In: Proceedings of the 25th International Joint Conference on Artificial Intelligence, IJCAI 2016, pp. 63–73. AAAI Press (2016)
16. von Neumann, J.: Zur Theorie der Gesellschaftsspiele. (German) (On the theory of games of strategy). Mathematische Annalen **100**, 295–320 (1928). (German)
17. von Neumann, J., Morgenstern, O.: Theory of Games and Economic Behavior. Princeton University Press, Princeton (1944)

ABAplus: Attack Reversal in Abstract and Structured Argumentation with Preferences

Ziyi Bao, Kristijonas Čyras$^{(\boxtimes)}$(iD), and Francesca Toni(iD)

Department of Computing, Imperial College London, London, UK
{ziyi.bao14,k.cyras,ft}@imperial.ac.uk

Abstract. We present ABAplus, a system that implements reasoning with the argumentation formalism ABA$^+$. ABA$^+$ is a structured argumentation formalism that extends Assumption-Based Argumentation (ABA) with preferences and accounts for preferences via attack reversal. ABA$^+$ also admits as instance Preference-based Argumentation which accounts for preferences by reversing attacks in abstract argumentation (AA). ABAplus readily implements attack reversal in both AA and ABA-style structured argumentation. ABAplus affords computation, visualisation and comparison of extensions under five argumentation semantics. It is available both as a stand-alone system and as a web application.

1 Introduction

Approaches to preferences in abstract argumentation (AA) [9] and structured argumentation [3] can be roughly classified as follows: 1. *discarding* attacks from attackers that are less preferred than attackees (see e.g. [1] for AA and ASPIC$^+$ [16,17] for structured argumentation); 2. *reversing* attacks from attackers that are less preferred than attackees (see Preference-based Argumentation Frameworks (PAFs) [2] for AA and Assumption-Based Argumentation with Preferences (ABA$^+$) [7] for structured argumentation); 3. comparing extensions by aggregating preferences over their elements (see e.g. [2] for AA and [21] for structured argumentation); 4. incorporating numerical weights of arguments or attacks into the definition of semantics (see e.g. [5] for AA and [12] for structured argumentation). Implementations of several approaches in classes 1. and 4. exist (see Sect. 6), but, to the best of our knowledge, implementations of approaches in classes 2. and 3. are lacking. In this paper, we present an implementation of approaches in class 2., i.e. implementation of *attack reversal* in both AA and structured argumentation with preferences.

Our system, *ABAplus*, implements reasoning with the recently proposed formalism ABA$^+$ [7]. ABA$^+$ extends Assumption-Based Argumentation (ABA) [6,20] with preferences and is the only structured argumentation formalism (to the best of our knowledge) to reverse attacks in structured argumentation due to preferences. To implement attack reversal in structured argumentation, ABAplus uses a semantics-preserving mapping from ABA$^+$ to AA and employs an off-the-shelf AA implementation, namely ASPARTIX [10], for determining extensions.

© Springer International Publishing AG 2017
B. An et al. (Eds.): PRIMA 2017, LNAI 10621, pp. 420–437, 2017.
https://doi.org/10.1007/978-3-319-69131-2_25

To this end, we advance a new mapping from ABA^+ frameworks to AA frameworks, which we call *assumption graphs*. In addition, we identify a novel property of ABA^+ frameworks, called *Weak Contraposition*, which distinguishes a class of ABA^+ frameworks in semantic correspondence with their assumption graphs. Subject to Weak Contraposition, assumption graphs guarantee a correct representation and implementation of ABA^+ (as well as ABA) under five semantics, and are used in ABAplus to provide concise graphical visualisation and comparison of ABA^+ (as well as ABA) frameworks.

To implement attack reversal in AA, ABAplus relies on a semantics-preserving mapping from PAFs into ABA^+. To this end, we consider a simple mapping from PAFs to ABA^+ frameworks, showing that ABA^+ admits PAFs as instances. Thus, ABAplus readily implements attack reversal in AA with preferences too.

ABAplus is freely available at https://github.com/kcyras/ABAplus as a stand-alone system, and at http://www-abaplus.doc.ic.ac.uk as a web application.

2 Background

ABA^+. We base the background on ABA^+ on [7].

An *ABA^+ framework* is a tuple $(\mathcal{L}, \mathcal{R}, \mathcal{A}, ^-, \leqslant)$, where:

- $(\mathcal{L}, \mathcal{R})$ is a deductive system with $\mathcal{L}$ a language and $\mathcal{R}$ a set of rules of the form $\varphi_0 \leftarrow \varphi_1, \ldots, \varphi_m$ with $m \geqslant 0$ and $\varphi_i \in \mathcal{L}$ for $i \in \{0, \ldots, m\}$; φ_0 is the *head* and $\varphi_1, \ldots, \varphi_m$ the *body* of the rule; if $m = 0$, then $\varphi_0 \leftarrow \varphi_1, \ldots, \varphi_m$ has an empty body, and is written as $\varphi_0 \leftarrow \top$, where $\top \notin \mathcal{L}$;
- $\mathcal{A} \subseteq \mathcal{L}$ is a non-empty set of *assumptions*;
- $^- : \mathcal{A} \to \mathcal{L}$ is a total map: for $a \in \mathcal{A}$, $\bar{a}$ is referred to as the *contrary* of a;
- $\leqslant$ is a preorder (i.e. reflexive and transitive) on $\mathcal{A}$, called a *preference relation*.

As usual, the strict (asymmetric) counterpart $<$ of $\leqslant$ is given by $\alpha < \beta$ iff $\alpha \leqslant \beta$ and $\beta \not\leqslant \alpha$, for any α and β. (We assume this for all preorders in this paper.) For assumptions $a, b \in \mathcal{A}$, $a \leqslant b$ means that b is at least as preferred as a, and $a < b$ means that a is strictly less preferred than b.

Assumptions in ABA^+ model defeasible information. For instance, assumptions can represent beliefs of an agent. In such a case, preferences in ABA^+ can be seen to represent the relative degrees of belief.

Example 1 (Preferences over beliefs). At a party, Zed is having a discussion about the outcome of a possible referendum in the Netherlands on whether to remain in the EU. Two of his interlocutors, Ann and Bob, have diverging views on the outcome of the referendum. Ann claims that the Dutch would vote to leave, whereas Bob maintains that they would vote to stay. Suppose Zed knows that Ann likes big claims based on dubious assumptions, so he trusts Bob more than Ann. This preference information should conceivably lead Zed to accepting Bob's argument, rather than Ann's.

We model Zed's knowledge as an ABA$^+$ framework $\mathcal{F} = (\mathcal{L}, \mathcal{R}, \mathcal{A}, ^-, \leqslant)$ with

- $\mathcal{L} = \{a, b, \textit{leave}, \textit{stay}\}$,
- $\mathcal{R} = \{\textit{leave} \leftarrow a, \quad \textit{stay} \leftarrow b\}$,
- $\mathcal{A} = \{a, b\}$,
- $\bar{a} = \textit{stay}, \quad \bar{b} = \textit{leave}$,
- $a \leqslant b, \quad b \nleqslant a$.[1]

Here, assumptions a and b stand for believing in Ann and Bob, respectively. Rules $\textit{leave} \leftarrow a$ and $\textit{stay} \leftarrow b$ represent the statements of Zed's interlocutors: for instance, $\textit{leave} \leftarrow a$ represents that if Zed were to believe in Ann, the outcome of the referendum would be the Dutch leaving the EU. The contraries indicate which information is conflicting: for instance, the contrary of b being $\textit{leave}$ models that the Dutch leaving the EU—$\textit{leave}$—conflicts with believing in Bob—b.[2] The degree of Zed's beliefs is represented through the preference $a < b$ (i.e. $a \leqslant b$, $b \nleqslant a$), which means that Zed trusts Ann strictly less than he trusts Zed.

Throughout the paper, we assume as given a fixed but otherwise arbitrary ABA$^+$ framework $\mathcal{F} = (\mathcal{L}, \mathcal{R}, \mathcal{A}, ^-, \leqslant)$, unless specified otherwise.

We next give notions of arguments (as deduction trees) and attacks in ABA$^+$.

An *argument for* $\varphi \in \mathcal{L}$ *supported by* $A \subseteq \mathcal{A}$ *and* $R \subseteq \mathcal{R}$, denoted $A \vdash^R \varphi$, is a finite tree with: the root labelled by φ; leaves labelled by $\top$ or assumptions, with A being the set of all such assumptions; the children of non-leaves ψ labelled by the elements of the body of some ψ-headed rule in $\mathcal{R}$, with R being the set of all such rules. $A \vdash \varphi$ is a shorthand for an argument $A \vdash^R \varphi$ with some $R \subseteq \mathcal{R}$.

Let $A, B \subseteq \mathcal{A}$. Then $A \subseteq \mathcal{A}$ *<-attacks* $B \subseteq \mathcal{A}$, denoted $A \rightsquigarrow_< B$, iff

- either there is an argument $A' \vdash \bar{b}$, for some $b \in B$, supported by $A' \subseteq A$, and $\nexists a' \in A'$ with $a' < b$;
- or there is an argument $B' \vdash \bar{a}$, for some $a \in A$, supported by $B' \subseteq B$, and $\exists b' \in B'$ with $b' < a$.

We call $<$-attack formed as in the first bullet point above a *normal attack*, and $<$-attack formed as in the second bullet point above a *reverse attack*. If it is not the case that A $<$-attacks B, we may write $A \not\rightsquigarrow_< B$. (We will adopt an analogous convention for other attack relations in this paper.)

To illustrate, in $\mathcal{F}$ from Example 1, $\{a\}$ 'tries' to attack $\{b\}$, but is prevented by the preference $a < b$. Instead, $\{b\}$ $<$-attacks $\{a\}$ (and also $\{a, b\}$) via reverse attack. Likewise, $\{a, b\}$ $<$-attacks both itself and $\{a\}$ via reverse attack.

---

[1] As a preorder, $\leqslant$ has to be reflexive, but for brevity purposes we often omit to specify the reflexive instances of any preorder.

[2] Other ways of formalising such examples in ABA are possible; we chose a natural and simple representation. Generally, knowledge representation in argumentation (and other formalisms) may be a complex problem, discussion of which is beyond the scope of this paper.

We next give auxiliary notions that will be used to define ABA$^+$ semantics.

Let $A \subseteq \mathcal{A}$. The *conclusions of* A is $Cn(A) = \{\varphi \in \mathcal{L} \; : \; \exists \, A' \vdash \varphi, \, A' \subseteq A\}$. We say that A is *closed* iff $A = Cn(A) \cap \mathcal{A}$. We say that $\mathcal{F}$ is *flat* iff every $A \subseteq \mathcal{A}$ is closed. We assume ABA$^+$ frameworks to be flat, unless specified otherwise.

Note that $\mathcal{F}$ from Example 1 is flat: no assumption can be deduced from the empty set of assumptions, so $Cn(\emptyset) = \emptyset$; the only assumptions deducible from $\{a\}$ and $\{b\}$ are a and b, respectively, so both $\{a\}$ and $\{b\}$ are closed; clearly, $\mathcal{A}$ is closed; hence, all sets of assumptions are closed.

Further, for $A \subseteq \mathcal{A}$, we say that: A is $<$-*conflict-free* iff $A \not\leadsto_< A$; also, A $<$-*defends* $A' \subseteq \mathcal{A}$ iff for all $B \subseteq \mathcal{A}$ with $B \leadsto_< A'$ it holds that $A \leadsto_< B$; and A is $<$-*admissible* iff it is $<$-conflict-free and $<$-defends itself.

We consider the following five ABA$^+$ semantics. A set $E \subseteq \mathcal{A}$, also called an *extension*, is:

- $<$-*complete* iff E is $<$-admissible and contains every set of assumptions it $<$-defends;
- $<$-*preferred* iff E is $\subseteq$-maximally $<$-admissible;
- $<$-*stable* iff E is $<$-conflict-free and for all b $\in \mathcal{A} \setminus E$ it holds that $E \leadsto_< \{b\}$;
- $<$-*ideal* iff E is $\subseteq$-maximal among sets of assumptions that are $<$-admissible and contained in all $<$-preferred sets of assumptions;
- $<$-*grounded* iff E is a $\subseteq$-minimal $<$-complete set of assumptions.

Throughout the paper, $\sigma \in \{\text{grounded, ideal, stable, preferred, complete}\}$, and we assume that $<$-σ denotes any of the above ABA$^+$ semantics.

To illustrate with Example 1, it is easy to see that $\{b\}$ is a unique $<$-σ extension of $\mathcal{F}$, leading Zed to accept Bob's argument, just as intended.

Note well that ABA$^+$ conservatively extends ABA in that, when preferences are absent, ABA$^+$ frameworks behave exactly like ABA frameworks [7]. Therefore, our implementation of ABA$^+$ will be an implementation of ABA too.

Abstract Argumentation (AA). We base the background on AA on [9].

An *AA framework* is a pair $(Args, \leadsto)$ with a set $Args$ of arguments and a binary attack relation $\leadsto$ on $Args$. Notions of conflict-freeness, defence and admissibility, as well as semantics of σ extensions, are defined verbatim as for ABA$^+$, but with sets of arguments replacing sets of assumptions and with $\leadsto$ replacing $\leadsto_<$.

Preference-Based Argumentation Frameworks (PAFs). We base the background on PAFs on [2].

A *Preference-based Argumentation Framework* (PAF) is a tuple $(Args, \leadsto, \preccurlyeq)$, where $(Args, \leadsto)$ is an AA framework and $\preccurlyeq$ is a preorder over $Args$. Given a PAF $(Args, \leadsto, \preccurlyeq)$, its *repaired framework* is an AA framework $(Args, \hookrightarrow)$ such that for a, b $\in Args$, a $\hookrightarrow$ b iff

- either a $\leadsto$ b and a $\not\prec$ b,
- or b $\leadsto$ a and b $\prec$ a.

The attack formed as in the second bullet pertains to attack reversal in AA.

From now on, unless specified otherwise, we assume a PAF $(Args, \leadsto, \preccurlyeq)$ as given, and denote its repaired framework by $(Args, \hookrightarrow)$.

Semantics of PAFs is defined via the semantics of their repaired frameworks: $E \subseteq Args$ is a σ *extension* of $(Args, \leadsto, \preccurlyeq)$ iff E is a σ extension of $(Args, \hookrightarrow)$.

Example 2. Zed's knowledge as in Example 1 can be modelled as a PAFs as follows. The arguments in $Args = \{a, b\}$ represent the statements of Zed's interlocutors, and the attacks $a \leadsto b$, $b \leadsto a$ represent the conflict between the two statements. The preference of Bob's argument over Ann's argument is expressed by $a \prec b$. For the resulting PAF $(Args, \leadsto, \preccurlyeq)$, the attack $a \leadsto b$ is reversed in $(Args, \hookrightarrow)$ to yield only $b \hookrightarrow a$. So $(Args, \leadsto, \preccurlyeq)$ has a unique σ extension $\{b\}$.

3 Implementing Attack Reversal in ABA⁺

The idea behind implementing attack reversal in ABA⁺ is to use a mapping from ABA⁺ to AA that preserves semantic correspondence, and then use an off-the-shelf AA solver, particularly ASPARTIX, to compute extensions of ABA⁺ frameworks by computing extensions of the corresponding AA frameworks. In this section, we provide one such mapping.

3.1 Assumption Graphs

Given an ABA⁺ framework, we construct its *assumption graph*—an AA framework with arguments being either singleton sets of assumptions, or sets of assumptions supporting (ABA⁺) arguments for contraries of assumptions, and with the attack relation being $\leadsto_<$ restricted to those arguments, as follows.

Definition 1. *Let $\mathcal{D}$ be the collection of sets of assumptions that support arguments for contraries of assumptions, i.e. $\mathcal{D} = \{S \subseteq \mathcal{A} : S \vdash \bar{a}, a \in \mathcal{A}\}$. The* **assumption graph** *of $\mathcal{F}$ is an AA framework $\mathcal{G} = (Args, \hookrightarrow)$ with*

- $Args = \mathcal{D} \cup \{\{a\} : a \in \mathcal{A}\}$,
- $\hookrightarrow = \leadsto_< \cap (Args \times Args)$,

where $\leadsto_<$ is the $<$-attack relation of $\mathcal{F}$.

Example 3. Consider the ABA⁺ framework $\mathcal{F} = (\mathcal{L}, \mathcal{R}, \mathcal{A}, ^-, \leqslant)$ with

- $\mathcal{L} = \{a, b, c, e, d, f\}$,
- $\mathcal{R} = \{d \leftarrow a, c, \quad e \leftarrow b, c\}$,
- $\mathcal{A} = \{a, b, c\}$,
- $\bar{a} = e, \ \bar{b} = d, \ \bar{c} = f$,
- $a < b$ (i.e. $\leqslant$ is a preorder with $a \leqslant b$, $b \not\leqslant a$).

In $\mathcal{F}$, $\{b,c\}$ supports an argument for the contrary e of a, and no assumption in $\{b,c\}$ is strictly less preferred than a. Thus, $\{b,c\}$ <-attacks $\{a\}$, as well as any set containing a, via normal attack. On the other hand, $\{a,c\}$ (supporting an argument for the contrary d of b) is prevented from <-attacking $\{b\}$, due to the preference a < b. Instead $\{b\}$, as well as any set containing b, <-attacks $\{a,c\}$ via reverse attack. Overall, $\mathcal{F}$ has a unique <-σ extension, namely $E = \{b,c\}$, with conclusions $Cn(E) = \{b,c,e\}$.

The assumption graph $\mathcal{G} = (Args, \hookrightarrow)$ of $\mathcal{F}$ has $Args = \{\{a\},\{b\},\{c\},\{b,c\},\{a,c\}\}$ and attacks $\{b,c\} \hookrightarrow \{a\}$, $\{b,c\} \hookrightarrow \{a,c\}$, $\{b\} \hookrightarrow \{a,c\}$, and is depicted below (here and henceforth, dashed arrows indicate normal attacks, dotted arrows indicate reverse attacks and solid arrows indicate <-attacks that are both normal and reverse).

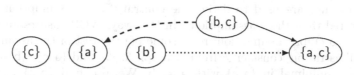

$(Args, \hookrightarrow)$ has a unique σ extension $\mathcal{E} = \{\{b\},\{c\},\{b,c\}\}$. Note that $\bigcup \mathcal{E} = E$.

In Example 3, the following semantic correspondence between ABA$^+$ frameworks and their assumptions graphs holds: $\mathcal{E} \subseteq Args$ is a σ extension of $(Args, \hookrightarrow)$ iff $E = \bigcup \mathcal{E}$ is a <-σ extension of $\mathcal{F}$. However, this correspondence does not hold in general, as the following example shows.

Example 4. Modify the ABA$^+$ framework $\mathcal{F}$ from Example 3 by removing the rule $e \leftarrow b,c$ from $\mathcal{R}$ to obtain the ABA$^+$ framework $\mathcal{F}' = (\mathcal{L}, \mathcal{R}', \mathcal{A}, \bar{}, \leqslant)$ with $\mathcal{R}' = \mathcal{R} \setminus \{e \leftarrow b,c\}$. Observe that, in $\mathcal{F}'$, all singleton sets of assumptions $\{a\}$, $\{b\}$ and $\{c\}$ are <-unattacked, and hence <-defended by any set. However, $\{a,b,c\}$ is not <-conflict-free, as $\{a,c\} \vdash \bar{b}$. Consequently, no set $A \subseteq \mathcal{A}$ can contain all sets of assumptions it <-defends and be <-conflict-free at the same time. Thus, $\mathcal{F}'$ has no <-complete extensions. Meanwhile, the assumption graph $\mathcal{G}'$ of $\mathcal{F}'$ (depicted below) has a unique complete extension $\{\{a\},\{b\},\{c\}\}$.

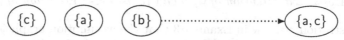

In the next section, we identify a property of ABA$^+$ frameworks, called the Axiom of Weak Contraposition,[3] satisfaction of which allows to preserve semantic correspondence between ABA$^+$ frameworks and their assumption graphs.

3.2 Weak Contraposition

The following axiom concerns contrapositive reasoning as understood in classical logic and is (strictly) weaker than *contraposition* as defined for ASPIC$^+$ in [17].

---

[3] Our notion of 'weak contraposition' bears no relationship with the notion by the same name used e.g. in [15], inspired by conditional entailment in Deontic Logic.

Axiom. $(\mathcal{L}, \mathcal{R}, \mathcal{A}, ^-, \leqslant)$ *satisfies* **the Axiom of Weak Contraposition** **(WCP** *for short) just in case for all* $A \subseteq \mathcal{A}$, $R \subseteq \mathcal{R}$ *and* $\mathsf{b} \in \mathcal{A}$ *it holds that*

> *if* $A \vdash \overline{\mathsf{b}}$ *and there exists* $\mathsf{a}' \in A$ *such that* $\mathsf{a}' < \mathsf{b}$,
> *then, for some* $\mathsf{a} \in A$ *which is* $\leqslant$*-minimal such that* $\mathsf{a} < \mathsf{b}$, *there is* $A_{\mathsf{a}} \vdash \overline{\mathsf{a}}$,
> *for some* $A_{\mathsf{a}} \subseteq (A \setminus \{\mathsf{a}\}) \cup \{\mathsf{b}\}$.

This axiom insists on contrapositive reasoning when an argument involves assumptions less preferred than the one whose contrary it supports. In essence, WCP plays the role of ensuring that, in a conflict arising from assumptions, contraries and rules, preferences help to pinpoint a culprit assumption that should be argued against. A culprit is identified as being least preferred among the assumptions that are used to derive the contrary of an assumption which is more preferred than those assumptions. In this way, WCP ensures an $<$-attack against such a culprit assumption from (some of) the rest of the assumptions.

As an illustration, consider $\mathcal{F}$ from Example 3. We find $\{\mathsf{a}, \mathsf{c}\} \vdash \overline{\mathsf{b}}$ and $\mathsf{a} < \mathsf{b}$, where a is $\leqslant$-minimal in $\{\mathsf{a}, \mathsf{c}\}$ with $\mathsf{a} < \mathsf{b}$. We also find $\{\mathsf{b}, \mathsf{c}\} \vdash \overline{\mathsf{a}}$, where $\{\mathsf{b}, \mathsf{c}\} = (\{\mathsf{a}, \mathsf{c}\} \setminus \{\mathsf{a}\}) \cup \{\mathsf{b}\}$. It is thus easy to see that $\mathcal{F}$ satisfies WCP. By contrast, in $\mathcal{F}'$ from Example 4, we find $\{\mathsf{a}, \mathsf{c}\} \vdash \overline{\mathsf{b}}$ and $\mathsf{a} < \mathsf{b}$, but there is no $A_{\mathsf{a}} \vdash \overline{\mathsf{a}}$ with $A_{\mathsf{a}} \subseteq (\{\mathsf{a}, \mathsf{c}\} \setminus \{\mathsf{a}\}) \cup \{\mathsf{b}\} = \{\mathsf{b}, \mathsf{c}\}$; hence, $\mathcal{F}'$ violates WCP.

Note well that ABA$^+$ frameworks with empty preferences (which can be seen as ABA frameworks) satisfy WCP trivially.

We next show that ABA$^+$ frameworks satisfying WCP are in semantic correspondence with their assumption graphs, in the following sense. (We omit lengthy proofs for space reasons.)

Theorem 1. *Suppose* $\mathcal{F} = (\mathcal{L}, \mathcal{R}, \mathcal{A}, ^-, \leqslant)$ *satisfies WCP and let* $\mathcal{G} = (\text{Args}, \hookrightarrow)$ *be the assumption graph of* $\mathcal{F}$ *with* $\text{Args} = \mathcal{D} \cup \{\{\mathsf{a}\} : \mathsf{a} \in \mathcal{A}\}$, *where* $\mathcal{D} = \{S \subseteq \mathcal{A} : S \vdash \overline{\mathsf{a}}, \mathsf{a} \in \mathcal{A}\}$, *as in Definition 1.*

- *If* $E \subseteq \mathcal{A}$ *is a* $<$-σ *extension of* $\mathcal{F}$, *then* $\{S \in \mathcal{D} : S \subseteq E\} \cup \{\{\mathsf{a}\} : \mathsf{a} \in E\}$ *is a* σ *extension of* $\mathcal{G}$;
- *If* $\mathcal{E} \subseteq \text{Args}$ *is a* σ *extension of* $\mathcal{G}$, *then* $\bigcup \mathcal{E}$ *is a* $<$-σ *extension of* $\mathcal{F}$.

For illustration, we saw in Example 3 that the assumption graph $\mathcal{G}$ of $\mathcal{F}$ has a unique σ extension $\mathcal{E} = \{\{\mathsf{b}\}, \{\mathsf{c}\}, \{\mathsf{b}, \mathsf{c}\}\}$, and $E = \bigcup \mathcal{E} = \{\mathsf{b}, \mathsf{c}\}$ is a unique $<$-sigma extension of $\mathcal{F}$. We also saw that WCP is necessary in Theorem 1: in Example 4, the assumption graph $\mathcal{G}'$ of $\mathcal{F}'$ has a unique complete extension $\{\{\mathsf{a}\}, \{\mathsf{b}\}, \{\mathsf{c}\}\}$, while $\mathcal{F}'$ has no $<$-complete extensions.

Theorem 1 provides a theoretical underpinning for the ABAplus system which we will describe in Sect. 5. Before that, we discuss how an ABA$^+$ framework that violates WCP to begin with, can be modified *by adding new rules* so as to satisfy WCP.

3.3   Enforcing WCP

Adding rules to an ABA^+ framework which violates WCP so that the framework with additional rules satisfies WCP is called *enforcing* WCP. In this section we detail how to enforce WCP on an ABA^+ framework.

A situation where an argument satisfies the antecedent of WCP while the consequent is false is called an *instance of WCP-violation* (*instance of WCP-v*, for short). More formally:

Definition 2. $A \vdash \overline{b}$ *is an **instance of WCP-v** just in case*

- $\exists a' \in A$ *such that* $a' < b$, *and*
- *for no* $a \in A$ *which is* $\leqslant$-*minimal such that* $a < b$ *there is* $A_a \vdash \overline{a}$, *for some* $A_a \subseteq (A \setminus \{a\}) \cup \{b\}$.

As an illustration, in $\mathcal{F}'$ from Example 4, $\{a, c\} \vdash d$ is an instance of WCP-v.

For WCP to be satisfied, it suffices, for every instance of WCP-v, to ensure *one* additional argument for the contrary of *some single* $\leqslant$-minimal assumption among those less preferred than the one whose contrary an instance of WCP-v is an argument for. We call any such $\leqslant$-minimal assumption a *witness*:

Definition 3. *Let* $A \vdash \overline{b}$ *be an instance of WCP-v and let* $a \in A$. *Then* a *is a **witness** to* $A \vdash \overline{b}$ *just in case* a *is* $\leqslant$-*minimal such that* $a < b$.

So, in $\mathcal{F}'$ from Example 4, a is a witness to the instance of WCP-v $\{a, c\} \vdash d$.

A witness to an instance of WCP-v can be seen as a candidate assumption with regards to which an additional argument is needed in order to satisfy WCP. This can be achieved by adding *enforcing rules*, defined as follows.

Definition 4. *Let* $A \vdash \overline{b}$ *be an instance of WCP-v and* $a \in A$ *a witness to* $A \vdash \overline{b}$. *Say* $A = \{a_1, \ldots, a_n\}$, *where* $a = a_i$ *for some* i. *The **enforcing rule**, denoted by* $\overline{a} \leftarrow A \setminus a, b$, *is the rule* $\overline{a} \leftarrow a_1, \ldots, a_{i-1}, a_{i+1}, \ldots, a_n, b$.

In Example 4, for the only instance of WCP-v $\{a, c\} \vdash d$ and its sole witness a, the enforcing rule is $e \leftarrow b, c$.

WCP can be enforced by adding an enforcing rule for every instance of WCP-v and its witness, as shown next.

Theorem 2. *Let* $(\mathcal{L}, \mathcal{R}, \mathcal{A}, ^-, \leqslant)$ *be an ABA^+ framework and let V be the set of instances of WCP-v (in $(\mathcal{L}, \mathcal{R}, \mathcal{A}, ^-, \leqslant)$). For any $A \vdash \overline{b} \in V$, let*

$$\mathcal{R}_{A \vdash \overline{b}} = \{\overline{a} \leftarrow A \setminus a, b \text{ is an enforcing rule } : \text{ } a \in A \text{ is a witness to } A \vdash \overline{b}\}$$

be the set of enforcing rules for $A \vdash \overline{b}$. *Let f be a function, defined for finite non-empty sets, that selects any one element from a given set. The ABA^+ framework* $(\mathcal{L}, \mathcal{R} \cup \mathcal{R}', \mathcal{A}, ^-, \leqslant)$, *where* $\mathcal{R}' = \{f(\mathcal{R}_{A \vdash \overline{b}}) \text{ } : \text{ } A \vdash \overline{b} \in V\}$, *satisfies WCP.*

Proof. Let $A \vdash \overline{b}$ be any instance of WCP-v (in $(\mathcal{L}, \mathcal{R}, \mathcal{A}, ^-, \leqslant)$) and let $\mathsf{a} \in A$ be a witness to $A \vdash \overline{b}$. The rule $\overline{\mathsf{a}} \leftarrow A \backslash \mathsf{a}, \mathsf{b}$ guarantees that in $(\mathcal{L}, \mathcal{R} \cup \mathcal{R}', \mathcal{A}, ^-, \leqslant)$ we can find the argument $(A \backslash \{\mathsf{a}\}) \cup \{\mathsf{b}\} \vdash^{\{\overline{\mathsf{a}} \leftarrow A \backslash \mathsf{a}, \mathsf{b}\}} \overline{\mathsf{a}}$. Note that no such argument can result in an instance of WCP-v (in $(\mathcal{L}, \mathcal{R} \cup \mathcal{R}', \mathcal{A}, ^-, \leqslant)$), precisely because the witness a is $\leqslant$-minimal. Therefore, $(\mathcal{L}, \mathcal{R} \cup \mathcal{R}', \mathcal{A}, ^-, \leqslant)$ satisfies WCP.

For illustration, to enforce WCP on $\mathcal{F}'$ from Example 4, add the enforcing rule $e \leftarrow \mathsf{b}, \mathsf{c}$ to $\mathcal{R}'$ to obtain $\mathcal{F}$ from Example 3, which satisfies WCP.

Several remarks regarding WCP are in place.

First, note well that enforcing WCP on an ABA$^+$ framework *does in general change* its semantics. For instance, $\mathcal{F}'$ from Example 4 has no $<$-complete extensions, whereas $\mathcal{F}$ from Example 3 obtained by enforcing WCP on $\mathcal{F}'$ has a unique $<$-complete extension. Using preferences to identify a culprit assumption to be argued against, and thus changing the semantics of an ABA$^+$ framework, is one of the objectives of enforcing WCP. Precisely this allows to obtain semantic correspondence between ABA$^+$ frameworks and their assumption graphs.

Second, observe that using WCP *does not* amount to 'making attacks symmetric'. Indeed, consider $A \rightsquigarrow \{\mathsf{b}\}$ and let $A \vdash \overline{b}$ be an instance of WCP-v with a witness $\mathsf{a}' \in A$ such that $\mathsf{a}' < \mathsf{b}$. Making this attack symmetric means imposing $\{\mathsf{b}\} \rightsquigarrow_< A$. However, WCP *does not* require $\{\mathsf{b}\} \rightsquigarrow_< A$. Instead, WCP requires that $(A \backslash \{\mathsf{a}'\}) \cup \{\mathsf{b}\} \vdash \overline{\mathsf{a}'}$, which in general amounts to $(A \backslash \{\mathsf{a}'\}) \cup \{\mathsf{b}\} \rightsquigarrow_< \{\mathsf{a}'\}$ (and hence $(A \backslash \{\mathsf{a}'\}) \cup \{\mathsf{b}\} \rightsquigarrow_< A$).

Third, the $\leqslant$-minimality of a witness assumption in enforcing WCP is crucial. In particular, it saves from generating redundant arguments when enforcing the axiom. For instance, consider $\mathcal{F} = (\mathcal{L}, \mathcal{R}, \mathcal{A}, ^-, \leqslant)$ with $\mathcal{R} = \{\overline{c} \leftarrow \mathsf{a}, \mathsf{b}\}$, $\mathcal{A} = \{\mathsf{a}, \mathsf{b}, \mathsf{c}\}$ and $\mathsf{a} < \mathsf{b} < \mathsf{c}$.[4] The argument $\{\mathsf{a}, \mathsf{b}\} \vdash \overline{c}$ is an instance of WCP-v. If $\leqslant$-minimality were not required in the conditions of the consequent of WCP, one could end up choosing b and adding the rule $\overline{b} \leftarrow \mathsf{a}, \mathsf{c}$ to $\mathcal{R}$ so as to generate the argument $\{\mathsf{a}, \mathsf{c}\} \vdash \overline{b}$ in $\mathcal{F}' = (\mathcal{L}, \mathcal{R} \cup \{\overline{b} \leftarrow \mathsf{a}, \mathsf{c}\}, \mathcal{A}, ^-, \leqslant)$. This would result in $\{\mathsf{a}, \mathsf{c}\} \vdash \overline{b}$ making the antecedent of the WCP true (because $\mathsf{a} < \mathsf{b}$) while keeping the consequent false, thus yielding an instance of WCP-v in $\mathcal{F}'$. Thus, to enforce WCP, one would need to ensure existence of yet another argument, for example, $\{\mathsf{b}, \mathsf{c}\} \vdash \overline{\mathsf{a}}$, by, for instance, adding the rule $\overline{\mathsf{a}} \leftarrow \mathsf{b}, \mathsf{c}$. By contrast, choosing a (necessarily $\leqslant$-minimal) witness to begin with, i.e. a, and adding a single rule, say the enforcing rule $\overline{\mathsf{a}} \leftarrow \mathsf{b}, \mathsf{c}$, generates the argument $\{\mathsf{b}, \mathsf{c}\} \vdash \overline{\mathsf{a}}$ in $\mathcal{F}'' = (\mathcal{L}, \mathcal{R} \cup \{\overline{\mathsf{a}} \leftarrow \mathsf{b}, \mathsf{c}\}, \mathcal{A}, ^-, \leqslant)$. Thus, the instance of WCP-v in question is eliminated in $\mathcal{F}''$ and no further instances of WCP-v are obtained in $\mathcal{F}''$.

The fourth remark concerns other ways to enforce WCP on a given ABA$^+$ framework. For example, given an instance of WCP-v $A \vdash \overline{b}$ with a witness $\mathsf{a} \in A$, one could add the rule $\overline{\mathsf{a}} \leftarrow \top$ to obtain the argument $\emptyset \vdash^{\{\overline{\mathsf{a}} \leftarrow \top\}} \overline{\mathsf{a}}$ as required to eliminate the instance of WCP-v in question, at the same time avoiding to create additional instances. This particular way seems rather ad hoc and also quite radical with respect to knowledge representation: it seems unintuitive to

---

[4] Unless specified otherwise, we omit $\mathcal{L}$ and $^-$, and adopt the following conventions: unless $\overline{\mathsf{x}}$ appears in either $\mathcal{A}$ or $\mathcal{R}$, it is different from the sentences appearing in $\mathcal{A}$ or $\mathcal{R}$; thus, $\mathcal{L}$ consists of all the sentences appearing in $\mathcal{R}$, $\mathcal{A}$ and $\{\overline{\mathsf{a}} : \mathsf{a} \in \mathcal{A}\}$.

have assumptions immediately 'rejected' (by arguing for their contraries from the empty set) just because they are involved in the argumentative process of arguing for contraries of more preferred assumptions. In contrast, enforcing WCP as in Theorem 2 is the least restrictive way that ensures satisfaction of WCP while leaving the user the option to restrict the knowledge further, if needed.

Finally, observe that, technically, imposing WCP on a flat ABA$^+$ framework may yield a non-flat ABA$^+$ framework. Indeed, consider $(\mathcal{L}, \mathcal{R}, \mathcal{A}, ^-, \leqslant)$ with $\mathcal{L} = \{a, b, c, x, y\}$, $\mathcal{R} = \{x \leftarrow a\}$, $\mathcal{A} = \{a, b, c\}$, $\overline{a} = c$, $\overline{b} = x$, $\overline{c} = y$, $a < b$. We find $\{a\} \vdash \overline{b}$ and $a < b$, so to enforce WCP, we need an argument $S \vdash \overline{a}$, for some $S \subseteq \{b\}$. Whatever the support S, we get an argument $S \vdash c$, whence S is not closed. Note, however, that this behaviour can be easily avoided and flatness guaranteed. Indeed, instead of defining the contrary mapping $^- : \mathcal{A} \to \mathcal{L}$ to map assumptions into elements of the language, we can assign new symbols for contraries of assumptions, while retaining the same behaviour (semantically) of ABA$^+$ frameworks: for each assumption a we take a new symbol a^c not in $\mathcal{L}$, and define the contrary mapping $\mathcal{C}$ so that $\mathcal{C}(a) = a^c$; then, for any intended contrary x of a in $\mathcal{L}$, we add a rule $a^c \leftarrow x$. We omit the details due to lack of space, and assume, without loss of generality, that enforcing WCP on an arbitrary flat ABA$^+$ framework always yields a flat ABA$^+$ framework that satisfies WCP.

4 Implementing Attack Reversal in PAFs

In this section, following the way ABA admits AA as an instance [19], we show how ABA$^+$ admits PAFs as instances. As a result, implementing attack reversal in ABA$^+$ will automatically give a way to implement attack reversal in PAFs.

To instantiate an ABA$^+$ framework with $(Args, \rightsquigarrow, \preccurlyeq)$, we map each argument $a \in Args$ into an assumption $a \in \mathcal{A}$, together with a new symbol $\overline{a}$ for the contrary, map each attack $a \rightsquigarrow b$ into a rule $\overline{b} \leftarrow a$, and transfer the preference ordering $\preccurlyeq$ to constitute $\leqslant$, as follows.

Definition 5. *Given a PAF $(Args, \rightsquigarrow, \preccurlyeq)$, an ABA$^+$ **framework corresponding to** $(Args, \rightsquigarrow, \preccurlyeq)$ is $\mathcal{F}_{\mathrm{PAF}} = (\mathcal{L}, \mathcal{R}, \mathcal{A}, ^-, \leqslant)$ with:*

- $\mathcal{L} = Args \cup \{\overline{a} \ : \ a \in Args, \ \overline{a} \notin Args\}$;
- $\mathcal{R} = \{\overline{b} \leftarrow a \ : \ a \rightsquigarrow b\}$;
- $\mathcal{A} = Args$;
- *for $a \in \mathcal{A}$, $\overline{a}$ is the contrary of a;*
- $\leqslant \ = \ \preccurlyeq$.

Note that $\mathcal{F}$ from Example 1 is an ABA$^+$ framework corresponding to the PAF $(Args, \rightsquigarrow, \preccurlyeq)$ from Example 2.

Henceforth, $\mathcal{F}_{\mathrm{PAF}}$ is an ABA$^+$ framework corresponding to $(Args, \rightsquigarrow, \preccurlyeq)$.

Note that $\mathcal{F}_{\mathrm{PAF}}$ is necessarily flat. However, $\mathcal{F}_{\mathrm{PAF}}$ need not in general satisfy WCP. Nonetheless, given that all (ABA$^+$) arguments for contraries in $\mathcal{F}_{\mathrm{PAF}}$ are supported by singleton sets, every instance of WCP-v $\{a\} \vdash \overline{b}$ (with $a < b$) has a unique witness a, so that enforcing WCP on $\mathcal{F}_{\mathrm{PAF}}$ as in Theorem 2 yields a unique ABA$^+$ framework $\mathcal{F}'_{\mathrm{PAF}}$ which has the same $<$-attack relation as $\mathcal{F}_{\mathrm{PAF}}$: for $A, B \subseteq \mathcal{A}$, $A \rightsquigarrow_< B$ iff $A \rightsquigarrow'_< B$, where $\rightsquigarrow_<$ and $\rightsquigarrow'_<$ are $<$-attack relations of $\mathcal{F}_{\mathrm{PAF}}$ and $\mathcal{F}'_{\mathrm{PAF}}$, respectively.

Observe further that since all (ABA$^+$) arguments for contraries in $\mathcal{F}_{\mathrm{PAF}}$ are supported by singleton sets, attacks in $(Args, \rightsquigarrow, \preccurlyeq)$ coincide with $<$-attacks in $\mathcal{F}_{\mathrm{PAF}}$ (in that for $\mathsf{a}, \mathsf{b} \in Args$, $\mathsf{a} \hookrightarrow \mathsf{b}$ iff $\{\mathsf{a}\} \rightsquigarrow_< \{\mathsf{b}\}$). We thus obtain the following correspondence result, which says that, under any semantics σ, every PAF is an instance of ABA$^+$, and that determining extensions of $(Args, \rightsquigarrow, \preccurlyeq)$ amounts to determining extensions of $\mathcal{F}_{\mathrm{PAF}}$, which amounts to determining extensions of $\mathcal{F}_{\mathrm{PAF}}$ with WCP enforced.

Theorem 3. *Let $(Args, \rightsquigarrow, \preccurlyeq)$ be a PAF, $\mathcal{F}_{\mathrm{PAF}}$ be an ABA$^+$ framework corresponding to $(Args, \rightsquigarrow, \preccurlyeq)$, and $E \subseteq Args$. E is a σ extension of $(Args, \rightsquigarrow, \preccurlyeq)$ iff E is a $<$-σ extension of $\mathcal{F}_{\mathrm{PAF}}$ iff E is a $<$-σ extension of $\mathcal{F}'_{\mathrm{PAF}}$, where $\mathcal{F}'_{\mathrm{PAF}}$ is obtained by enforcing WCP on $\mathcal{F}_{\mathrm{PAF}}$ as in Theorem 2.*

To illustrate Theorem 3, $(Args, \rightsquigarrow, \preccurlyeq)$ from Example 2 has a unique σ extension $\{\mathsf{b}\}$, and this is precisely the unique $<$-σ extension of the corresponding ABA$^+$ framework $\mathcal{F}$ from Example 1.

Theorem 3 implies that by implementing ABA$^+$, the ABAplus system described in the next section can readily compute σ extensions of PAFs.

5   ABAplus

ABAplus, both a stand-alone system an a web application, implements reasoning in (flat) ABA$^+$ (and its instances, including PAFs) subject to WCP. In this section, we describe and illustrate ABAplus. First, we describe the web application as well as the back-end of ABAplus. Then, we illustrate the use of ABAplus (as well as ABA$^+$) with a pair of examples that show how preferences over goals and rules can be accommodated in ABA$^+$ through preferences over assumptions.

5.1   System Description

To compute extensions of $\mathcal{F} = (\mathcal{L}, \mathcal{R}, \mathcal{A}, ^-, \leqslant)$, ABAplus feeds the assumption graph $\mathcal{G} = (Args, \hookrightarrow)$ (Definition 1) of $\mathcal{F}$ into ASPARTIX to compute extensions of $\mathcal{G}$ and maps the extensions obtained to extensions of $\mathcal{F}$. Such strategy is sound and complete, given that extensions of $\mathcal{F}$ and $\mathcal{G}$ are in one-to-one correspondence (Theorem 1), as long as ASPARTIX correctly computes the extensions of AA frameworks under any semantics σ. The following is a summary of how both the stand-alone system and the web application of ABAplus work.

Web Application. The web application http://www-abaplus.doc.ic.ac.uk takes a single ABA$^+$ framework $\mathcal{F}$ as input in the Prolog-like format:

- `myAsm(a).` specifies that a is an assumption from $\mathcal{A}$;

- `contrary(a, x)`. specifies that $x \in \mathcal{L}$ is the contrary $\bar{a}$ of assumption a;
- `myRule(h, [b₁,...,bₙ])`. specifies that $h \leftarrow b_1, \ldots, b_n$ is a rule from $\mathcal{R}$;
- `myPrefLE(b, a)`. specifies, for assumptions a, b, that $b \leqslant a$;
- `myPrefLT(b, a)`. specifies, for assumptions a, b, that $b < a$.

The input can either be entered in a textbox or uploaded as a file (.pl extension). Upon loading an ABA^{+} framework, its assumption graph is computed and visualised as follows. 1. Nodes hold sets of assumptions. 2. Arrows represent attacks: dashed arrows for normal attacks, dotted arrows for reverse attacks, solid arrows for <-attacks that are both normal and reverse. 3. An extension under any semantics can be selected to be highlighted. 4. A second graph can be displayed with any extension (under any semantics) highlighted for comparison.

Back-End. ABAplus back-end parses the Prolog-like representation of $\mathcal{F}$ into Python format. The next steps are as follows.

1. The input $\mathcal{F}$ is pre-processed: (a) checking if $\mathcal{F}$ is flat; (b) calculating and updating $\mathcal{F}$ with the transitive closure of $\leqslant$; (c) checking whether the strict counterpart $<$ of (the updated) $\leqslant$ is asymmetric; (d) computing (ABA^{+}) arguments for contraries of assumptions (bottom-up) to check whether $\mathcal{F}$ satisfies WCP, and if not, enforcing WCP as in Theorem 2.
2. Generation of $Args$ goes thus (a top-down recursive procedure is used to find the sentences that could label argument trees until assumptions are found):
   (a) For every assumption $a \in \mathcal{A}$, store $\{a\}$ in $Args$;
   (b) For every assumption $a \in \mathcal{A}$, generate all arguments for $\bar{a}$ and store the supports of those arguments in $Args$.
3. Generation of $\hookrightarrow$ goes thus:
   (a) For every $a \in \mathcal{A}$, for every $B \vdash \bar{a}$, check if $\exists b \in B$ such that $b < a$: (i) if no, store $B \hookrightarrow \{a\}$; (ii) else, store $\{a\} \hookrightarrow B$.
   (b) For any $A', B' \in Args$ such that $\{a\} \subseteq A'$ and $B \subseteq B'$, (i) if $B \hookrightarrow \{a\}$, store $B' \hookrightarrow A'$; (ii) if $\{a\} \hookrightarrow B$, store $A' \hookrightarrow B'$.
4. The assumption graph $\mathcal{G} = (Args, \hookrightarrow)$ thus constructed is fed to ASPARTIX (using clingo and DLV ASP solvers), represented via Prolog-like sentences:
   - `arg(A)`. represents an argument $A \in Args$;
   - `att(A, B)`. represents an attack $A \hookrightarrow B$.
5. For every semantics $\sigma \in \{$grounded, ideal, stable, preferred, complete$\}$, σ extensions of $\mathcal{G}$ are computed.
6. Each σ extension $\mathcal{E}$ of $\mathcal{G}$ is unpacked into a $<$-σ extension $E = \bigcup \mathcal{E}$ of $\mathcal{F}$.

Tools. ABAplus uses the following tools: Python 3.4.3; Gunicorn 19.6; Clingo 4.5.4; DLV ("deductive database system") version 17/12/2012; encodings of semantics (stable.dl, ideal.dl, comp.dl, prefex_gringo.lp, ground.dl) from ASPARTIX system page; D3 (graph visualisation) 3.5.17.

5.2 Examples

In this section, we exemplify the use of ABA$^+$ and ABAplus in two different scenarios. Specifically, in addition to having illustrated in Example 1 how preferences over beliefs are accommodated in ABA$^+$, we now consider how preferences over assumptions in ABA$^+$ can be used to model preferences over goals and rules. This illustrates how ABAplus supports computations pertaining to reasoning with preferences not only over beliefs and abstract arguments (by indirectly implementing PAFs), but also over goals and rules.

Preferences over goals express that certain goals are more desirable to be achieved in a particular situation. Goals in ABA$^+$ can be represented via assumptions, whence preferences over assumptions represent preferences over goals.

Example 5 (Preferences over goals). Consider ABAplus as a system to schedule meetings. Imagine a user who needs to schedule a meeting on one of two suggested time slots, t_1 and t_2. Suppose that t_1 is the time when the user usually has lunch, and that t_2 covers the user's standard coffee break. The user prefers to have lunch as usual over scheduling the meeting, but also deems the meeting to be more important than having coffee.

In ABA$^+$, we can represent the situation as follows. Let m, l and c be assumptions standing for having the meeting, lunch and coffee, respectively. Further, let t_1 and t_2 be assumptions standing for the two time slots in question. The rules $\overline{t_1} \leftarrow l$ and $\overline{t_2} \leftarrow c$ express that having lunch and coffee as usual make the two respective time slots unavailable. Additionally, the rule $\overline{m} \leftarrow \overline{t_1}, \overline{t_2}$ expresses that the meeting will not be scheduled if none of the time slots are available. Finally, user's preferences are expressed by letting $c < m < l$: having lunch as usual is (strictly) more important than scheduling the meeting, which is in turn (strictly) more important than taking a coffee break at a standard time.

The resulting ABA$^+$ framework, call it $\mathcal{F}$, can be input into ABAplus via the following specification:

```
myAsm(c).              contrary(c, c̄).          myRule(t̄₁, [l]).
myAsm(l).              contrary(l, l̄).          myRule(t̄₂, [c]).
myAsm(m).              contrary(m, m̄).          myRule(m̄, [t̄₁, t̄₂]).
myAsm(t₁).             contrary(t₁, t̄₁).        myPrefLT(c, m).
myAsm(t₂).             contrary(t₂, t̄₂).        myPrefLT(m, l).
```

Given this input, ABAplus recognizes that $\mathcal{F}$ does not satisfy WCP: there is $\{c, l\} \vdash \overline{m}$ with $c < m$, but there is no argument for $\overline{c}$ at all. Thus, ABAplus informs the user accordingly, and proposes to automatically enforce WCP on $\mathcal{F}$. ABAplus enforces WCP by adding the rule $\overline{c} \leftarrow m, l$, which expresses that having lunch and the meeting prevents having coffee. This results into a new framework, call it $\mathcal{F}'$. ABAplus then determines that $\mathcal{F}'$ has a unique σ extension $\{m, l, t_2\}$, with conclusions $\{m, l, t_2, \overline{t_1}, \overline{c}\}$, which indicate that the meeting should be scheduled at time t_2, at the expense of having coffee. The outcome of feeding $\mathcal{F}$ into ABAplus is depicted in the screenshot in Fig. 1 (cropped by cutting out the part with the editable window for the input).

Visualisation of the input ABA⁺ framework as an assumption graph

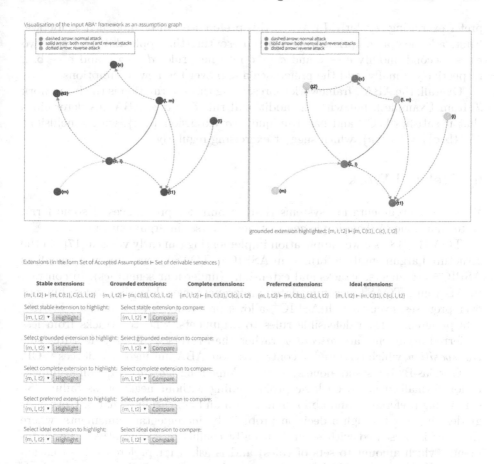

grounded extension highlighted: {m, l, t2} ⊢ {m, C(t1), C(c), l, t2}

Extensions (in the form Set of Accepted Assumptions ⊢ Set of derivable sentences)

Stable extensions:	Grounded extensions:	Complete extensions:	Preferred extensions:	Ideal extensions:
{m, l, t2} ⊢ {m, C(t1), C(c), l, t2}	{m, l, t2} ⊢ {m, C(t1), C(c), l, t2}	{m, l, t2} ⊢ {m, C(t1), C(c), l, t2}	{m, l, t2} ⊢ {m, C(t1), C(c), l, t2}	{m, l, t2} ⊢ {m, C(t1), C(c), l, t2}

Select stable extension to highlight: Select stable extension to compare:
[{m, l, t2} ▾] [Highlight]   [{m, l, t2} ▾] [Compare]

Select grounded extension to highlight: Select grounded extension to compare:
[{m, l, t2} ▾] [Highlight]   [{m, l, t2} ▾] [Compare]

Select complete extension to highlight: Select complete extension to compare:
[{m, l, t2} ▾] [Highlight]   [{m, l, t2} ▾] [Compare]

Select preferred extension to highlight: Select preferred extension to compare:
[{m, l, t2} ▾] [Highlight]   [{m, l, t2} ▾] [Compare]

Select ideal extension to highlight: Select ideal extension to compare:
[{m, l, t2} ▾] [Highlight]   [{m, l, t2} ▾] [Compare]

Fig. 1. Screenshot of ABAplus outcome for ABA⁺ framework $\mathcal{F}$ from Example 5

Preferences over rules indicate which rules should be followed in case application of multiple rules is impossible. In ABA⁺, preferences over rules can be expressed by adding new assumptions that stand for the applicability of the rules, and by imposing preferences over those assumptions.

Example 6 (Preferences over rules). Consider two general rules regarding healthy living: 'if you can afford it, you should follow a healthy diet' and 'if you can afford it, you should exercise regularly'. These two rules can be represented in ABA⁺ as $d \leftarrow c$ and $e \leftarrow c$, where e and d stand for exercising and diet, respectively, and the sentence c stands for affordability. Suppose that you are not able to both eat healthily and exercise regularly, as these habits require more time than you can afford. This can be considered as a constraint and modelled via the rule $\bar{c} \leftarrow d, e$.

Suppose that a certain authority declares that exercising regularly is more important than eating healthily. Thus, a preference of the second rule over the first rule can be formed, and given that you cannot follow both rules, you should prefer exercising regularly. In ABA$^+$ this preference can be modelled as follows. First, add new assumptions a and b representing the applicability of the two rules. Second, modify $e \leftarrow c$ and $d \leftarrow c$ into new rules $d \leftarrow a, c$ and $e \leftarrow b, c$, respectively. Finally, add the preference $a < b$ over the new assumptions.

Overall, the ABA$^+$ framework representing this information is the framework $\mathcal{F}$ from Example 3, but with the additional rule $\bar{c} \leftarrow d, e$. ABAplus determines that it satisfies WCP and has a unique $<$-σ extension $\{b, c\}$, with conclusions $Cn(\{b, c\}) = \{b, c, e\}$, which suggest exercising regularly.

6   Related Work

We discuss argumentation systems that account for preferences of some form. Note that none of them implements attack reversal in argumentation.

TOAST[5] [18] is a web application implementing (an early version [17] of) the structured argumentation formalism ASPIC$^+$. TOAST computes and visualises ASPIC$^+$ arguments, attacks and extensions (under four semantics). In contrast to ABAplus, TOAST accommodates preferences over defeasible rules, but not over premises, even though ASPIC$^+$ allows preferences over premises. TOAST lifts preferences from defeasible rules to arguments, whence attacks from less preferred arguments are *discarded*, rather than reversed. TOAST features rule *transposition*, which is related to contraposition. ABAplus instead enforces WCP.

Gorgias-B[6] is a stand-alone system implementing *Gorgias* [14]—an argumentation formalism based on logic programming without negation as failure [8], combining preferences and abduction. Given an application scenario, Gorgias-B guides the user through a decision problem by incremental refinements, where the user is presented with several (usually conflicting) alternatives (i.e. arguments, which amount to sets of rules) and is asked for preference information in order to determine which attacks succeed: a variant of *discarding* attacks is employed. Reasoning outcomes are evaluated essentially via preferred semantics, in contrast to multiple semantics available in ABAplus.

Gorgias-B asks the user to input preferences on the go whenever needed to solve conflicts, whereas ABAplus takes user information at once and provides reasoning outcomes, without the need for the user to specify any further information. Nonetheless, it may be a useful feature of ABAplus to be able to query the user for preferences. We leave this for future work.

DeLPclient[7] is a web application implementing reasoning in Defeasible Logic Programming (DeLP) [11]. It allows to specify logic programs with strict and defeasible rules, and preferences over the latter, which are accounted by *discarding* attacks. Given a program, DeLPclient answers queries and can also provide explanations of the answers in terms of arguments and counter-arguments for the warrant status of the query. We plan to explore in the future whether explanations could be implemented in ABAplus.

---

[5] http://toast.arg-tech.org.

[6] http://gorgiasb.tuc.gr/index.html.

[7] http://lidia.cs.uns.edu.ar/delp_client.

Carneades[8] [13] is a web application and a stand-alone system implementing the argumentation formalism of the same name [12]. Carneades supports weights on arguments (which are instantiations of argumentation schemes), and employs proofs standards and weighting functions to *balance* arguments and evaluate their acceptance via grounded semantics. Carneades also visualises argument graphs and indicates structural links within.

ConArg[9] [4] is a web application and a stand-alone system implementing *Weighted Argumentation Frameworks* (WAFs) [5]. ConArg allows for specifying (via graphical interface) WAFs—AA frameworks with weights on attacks—and computes their extensions under various semantics. Weights on attacks are accounted for by specifying *budgets* of how much conflict (within extensions) can be tolerated and defence can be relaxed.

7 Conclusions

We presented the system ABAplus that implements ABA^+ (and by extension, ABA), a formalism of structured argumentation with preferences. ABAplus implements attack reversal in ABA^+ as well as its instances, particularly Preference-based Argumentation Frameworks (PAFs). More specifically, ABAplus applies a new principle of Weak Contraposition (WCP) on flat ABA^+ frameworks, computes their extensions, visualises and allows for juxtaposing their assumption graphs. The theoretical backbone of the system is a semantics-preserving mapping from ABA^+ to abstract argumentation (AA), which allows to use off-the-shelf AA solvers (particularly, ASPARTIX) to determine extensions of ABA^+ (as well as ABA) frameworks. ABAplus is a freely available stand-alone system and a web application.

We aim to analyse the scalability and performance of ABAplus and to use it in applications of reasoning with preferences. It would also be interesting to find other classes of ABA^+ frameworks (possibly satisfying WCP) and/or mappings to e.g. AA that allow to determine ABA^+ extensions via AA or other formalisms (e.g. answer set programming). Implementing non-flat ABA^+ frameworks is a future research direction too. In addition to studying whether features of some other systems implementing argumentative reasoning with preferences can be of use in ABAplus (as discussed in Sect. 6), we plan to implement the following features: (a) relaxed syntactic requirements for input; (b) saving ABA^+ frameworks on the server; (c) query-based interface and computations; (d) interactive graphical representations; (e) improved session data handling. Finally, we have outlined possible uses of ABAplus in a number of settings. In the future we plan to investigate fully fledged applications of the system in general and in medical settings, e.g. to support reasoning with (possibly conflicting) guidelines and clinical pathways as well as preferences derived from resource constraints.

---

[8] http://carneades.fokus.fraunhofer.de/carneades.
[9] http://www.dmi.unipg.it/conarg.

Acknowledgements. This research was partially funded by the EPSRC project **EP/P029558/1** ROAD2H: Resource Optimisation, Argumentation, Decision Support and Knowledge Transfer to Create Value via Learning Health Systems. We also thank Jeff Thompson for helpful discussions on the use of ABAplus to schedule meetings (Example 5).

References

1. Amgoud, L., Cayrol, C.: A reasoning model based on the production of acceptable arguments. Ann. Math. Artif. Intell. **34**(1–3), 197–215 (2002)
2. Amgoud, L., Vesic, S.: Rich preference-based argumentation frameworks. Int. J. Approximate Reasoning **55**(2), 585–606 (2014)
3. Besnard, P., García, A.J., Hunter, A., Modgil, S., Prakken, H., Simari, G.R., Toni, F.: Introduction to structured argumentation. Argum. Comput. **5**(1), 1–4 (2014)
4. Bistarelli, S., Rossi, F., Santini, F.: ConArg: a tool for classical and weighted argumentation. In: Baroni, P., Gordon, T., Scheffler, T., Stede, M. (eds.) Computational Models of Argument. Frontiers in Artificial Intelligence and Applications, vol. 287, pp. 463–464. IOS Press, Potsdam (2016)
5. Bistarelli, S., Santini, F.: A Common computational framework for semiring-based argumentation system. In: Coelho, H., Studer, R., Wooldridge, M. (eds.) 19th European Conference on Artificial Intelligence. Frontiers in Artificial Intelligence and Applications, vol. 215, pp. 131–136. IOS Press, Lisbon (2010)
6. Bondarenko, A., Dung, P.M., Kowalski, R., Toni, F.: An abstract, argumentation-theoretic approach to default reasoning. Artif. Intell. **93**(97), 63–101 (1997)
7. Čyras, K., Toni, F.: ABA+: assumption-based argumentation with preferences. In: Baral, C., Delgrande, J.P., Wolter, F. (eds.) 15th International Conference on Principles of Knowledge Representation and Reasoning, pp. 553–556. AAAI Press, Cape Town (2016)
8. Dimopoulos, Y., Kakas, A.C.: Logic programming without negation as failure. In: Lloyd, J.W. (ed.) International Symposium on Logic Programming, pp. 369–383. MIT Press, Portland (1995)
9. Dung, P.M.: On the acceptability of arguments and its fundamental role in non-monotonic reasoning, logic programming and n-person games. Artif. Intell. **77**, 321–357 (1995)
10. Gaggl, S.A., Manthey, N., Ronca, A., Wallner, J.P., Woltran, S.: Improved answer-set programming encodings for abstract argumentation. Theory Pract. Log. Program. **15**(4–5), 434–448 (2015)
11. García, A.J., Simari, G.R.: Defeasible logic programming: DeLP-servers, contextual queries, and explanations for answers. Argum. Comput. **5**(1), 63–88 (2014)
12. Gordon, T.F., Prakken, H., Walton, D.: The carneades model of argument and burden of proof. Artif. Intell. **171**(10–15), 875–896 (2007)
13. Gordon, T.F., Walton, D.: Formalizing balancing arguments. In: Baroni, P., Gordon, T.F., Scheffler, T., Stede, M. (eds.) Computational Models of Argument. Frontiers in Artificial Intelligence and Applications, vol. 287, pp. 327–338. IOS Press, Potsdam (2016)
14. Kakas, A.C., Moraitis, P.: Argumentation based decision making for autonomous agents. In: 2nd International Joint Conference on Autonomous Agents & Multiagent Systems, pp. 883–890. ACM Press, Melbourne (2003)

15. Liao, B., Oren, N., van der Torre, L., Villata, S.: Prioritized norms and defaults in formal argumentation. In: Roy, O., Tamminga, A., Wille, M. (eds.) 13th International Conference on Deontic Logic and Normative Systems, pp. 139–154. College Publications, Bayreuth (2016)
16. Modgil, S., Prakken, H.: A general account of argumentation with preferences. Artif. Intell. **195**, 361–397 (2013)
17. Prakken, H.: An abstract framework for argumentation with structured arguments. Argum. Comput. **1**(2), 93–124 (2010)
18. Snaith, M., Reed, C.: TOAST: online ASPIC+ implementation. In: Verheij, B., Szeider, S., Woltran, S. (eds.) Computational Models of Argument. Frontiers in Artificial Intelligence and Applications, vol. 245, pp. 509–510. IOS Press, Vienna (2012)
19. Toni, F.: Reasoning on the web with assumption-based argumentation. In: Eiter, T., Krennwallner, T. (eds.) Reasoning Web 2012. LNCS, vol. 7487, pp. 370–386. Springer, Heidelberg (2012). doi:10.1007/978-3-642-33158-9_10
20. Toni, F.: A tutorial on assumption-based argumentation. Argum. Comput. **5**(1), 89–117 (2014)
21. Wakaki, T.: Assumption-based argumentation equipped with preferences. In: Dam, H.K., Pitt, J., Xu, Y., Governatori, G., Ito, T. (eds.) PRIMA 2014. LNCS (LNAI), vol. 8861, pp. 116–132. Springer, Cham (2014). doi:10.1007/978-3-319-13191-7_10

Early Innovation Short Papers

Repairing Socially Aggregated Ontologies Using Axiom Weakening

Daniele Porello[(✉)], Nicolas Troquard, Roberto Confalonieri, Pietro Galliani, Oliver Kutz, and Rafael Peñaloza

Free University of Bozen-Bolzano, Bolzano, Italy
{Daniele.Porello,Nicolas.Troquard,Roberto.Confalonieri,
Pietro.Galliani,Oliver.Kutz,Rafael.Penaloza}@unibz.it

Abstract. Ontologies represent principled, formalised descriptions of agents' conceptualisations of a domain. For a community of agents, these descriptions may significantly differ. We propose an aggregative view of the integration of ontologies based on Judgement Aggregation (JA). Agents may vote on statements of the ontologies, and we aim at constructing a collective, integrated ontology, that reflects the individual conceptualisations as much as possible. As several results in JA show, many attractive and widely used aggregation procedures are prone to return inconsistent collective ontologies. We propose to solve the possible inconsistencies in the collective ontology by applying suitable *weakenings* of axioms that cause inconsistencies.

1 Introduction

Social choice theory is a branch of economic theory that deals with the design and analysis of mechanisms for aggregating opinions of individual agents to arrive at a basis for a collective decision [6]. An ubiquitous example of such a mechanism is voting, usually intended as voting on preferences in standard social choice. Recently, the model of aggregation has been applied to judgements, or more generally to propositional attitudes, expressed in some logical setting, in an area termed Judgement Aggregation (JA) [11,13]. Ontologies are widely used in Knowledge Representation to provide principled descriptions of agents' knowledge, by presenting a clear formalisation of their conceptualisations. The meaning of the concepts is then represented by means of a number of axioms, which may be written in a variety of logical systems of varying expressivity [1,9]. With the exception of [15], the typical approaches to JA are usually applied to propositional logics, modal logics, or even more general logics, but they do not touch the problem of the possibly heterogeneous definitions of concepts used by the agents to formalise their individual conceptualisation. Understanding what is the meaning of a concept for a community of agents and deciding how to elect a common conceptualisation out of possibly conflicting ones is an interesting open problem that has several applications, for instance, in the context of political applications of JA. In this setting, understanding what is the meaning

B. An et al. (Eds.): PRIMA 2017, LNAI 10621, pp. 441–449, 2017.
https://doi.org/10.1007/978-3-319-69131-2_26

of a concept for a community of agents is crucial for modelling electoral campaigning, where parties try to maximise their electorate by appealing to widely shareable world views. In the context of ontology aggregation, we may think of each ontology as a vote submitted by a voter trying to 'elect' a collective ontology that adequately and fairly represents their conceptualisations. JA then provides the formal means to assess the suitable aggregation procedures for a given aggregation scenario, by defining a number of properties that aggregators may or may not satisfy. However, many results in JA show that a significant number of important aggregation procedures, e.g., the majority rule, fail to preserve the consistency of the individual inputs [13,15]. This means that, although we assume that all ontologies that agents submit for aggregation are consistent, the outcome of the aggregation may not be. A number of strategies to circumvent inconsistency have been pursued in JA, for instance, abandoning well-known aggregators in favour of aggregators that indeed preserve consistency, or restricting the set of propositions about which the agents cast their vote to those for which consistency can be ensured.

In this paper, we propose a novel approach. We present a well-known justified aggregation procedure that is actually used in real collective decision problems, viz. absolute majority rule, and we propose a computational viable methodology based on *axiom weakening* to repair its possibly inconsistent outcomes. The idea of axiom weakening is to generalise or specialise possibly conflicting concepts with concepts that are, in some sense, as close as possible to the original ones, but do not yield an inconsistency. Notice that, in order to generalise or specialise a concept in an informative manner, we need to rely on a certain amount of background information about the concepts, which shall be encoded in what we term in this paper the *reference* ontology. In case we have no information about the concepts at issue, the only way of weaken an axiom to a less constraining one is to replace it with a trivial (i.e. tautological) axiom, that in fact imposes no constraint at all on the agent's conceptualisation.

Preventing inconsistencies by appealing to 'general' concepts, which may then be prone to agreement although they have not been voted on by any individual, has been suggested and legitimated in the literature on social choice and deliberation [5,12,14]. This is an important issue, and it also relates to the distinction between fine vs. coarse integration of ontologies. In the case of a *coarse* integration, the ontology to be constructed will always contain some of the formulas included in the individual ontologies; in the *fine* integration, new formulas shall be constructed. The approach in [15] provides an example of coarse integration. In this paper, we are after a viable definition of fine integration.

To summarise, the contributions of this paper are as follows. We consider possible conceptualisations of agents' opinions represented by means of ontologies written in Description Logic (DL). In particular, we focus on the basic DL $\mathcal{ALC}$ [1], which is a popular language for ontology development. Secondly, we use the methodology of social choice theory and JA of [15] to define a framework for ontology aggregation. Thirdly, we use refinement operators for concept generalisations and specialisations [4], and we apply them to repair the collective ontology by selecting adequate refinements of the axioms that caused the inconsistency.

2   Ontologies and Description Logics

We take an ontology to be a set of formulas in an appropriate logical language, describing our domain of interest. A significant widely used basic description logic is $\mathcal{ALC}$, which is the logic we shall be working with here. For full details about this logic, we refer the interested reader to [1]. The language of $\mathcal{ALC}$ is based on an alphabet consisting of *atomic concepts names* N_C, and *role names* N_R. The set of *concept descriptions* is generated by the following grammar, where A represents atomic concepts and R role names:

$$C ::= A \mid \neg C \mid C \sqcap C \mid C \sqcup C \mid \forall R.C \mid \exists R.C$$

We collect all $\mathcal{ALC}$ concepts over N_C and N_R in $\mathcal{L}(\mathcal{ALC}, N_C, N_R)$. We assume a linear order $\prec_{\mathcal{ALC}}$ over $\mathcal{ALC}$ formulas. We do not need to attach any particular meaning to it, but it will be helpful for coping with non-determinism and for tie-breaking. A *TBox* is a finite set of concept inclusions of the form $C \sqsubseteq D$ (where C and D are concept descriptions). It is used to store terminological knowledge regarding the relationships between concepts. An *ABox* is a finite set of formulas of the form $A(a)$ ("object a is an instance of concept A") and $R(a, b)$ ("objects a and b stand to each other in the R-relation"). It is used to store assertional knowledge regarding specific objects. The semantics of $\mathcal{ALC}$ is defined in terms of *interpretations* $I = (\Delta^I, \cdot^I)$ that map each object name to an element of its domain Δ^I, each atomic concept to a subset of the domain, and each role name to a binary relation on the domain. The truth of a formula in such an interpretation is defined in the usual manner [1].

3   Aggregating Ontologies

Consider an arbitrary but fixed finite set Φ of $\mathcal{ALC}$ TBox statements over this alphabet.[1] We call Φ the *agenda* and any set $O \subseteq \Phi$ an *ontology*. We denote the set of all those ontologies that are *consistent* by $\mathrm{On}(\Phi)$. Let $\mathcal{N} = \{1, \ldots, n\}$ be a finite set of *agents*. Each agent $i \in \mathcal{N}$ provides a consistent ontology $O_i \in \mathrm{On}(\Phi)$. An *ontology profile* is a vector $\boldsymbol{O} = (O_1, \ldots, O_n) \in \mathrm{On}(\Phi)^{\mathcal{N}}$ of consistent ontologies, one for each agent. We write $N_\varphi^{\boldsymbol{O}} := \{i \in \mathcal{N} \mid \varphi \in O_i\}$ for the set of agents that include φ in their ontology under profile $\boldsymbol{O}$. Our object of study are *ontology aggregators*; that is, functions $F : \mathrm{On}(\Phi)^{\mathcal{N}} \to 2^{\Phi}$ mapping any profile of consistent ontologies to an ontology.

Observe that, according to this definition, the ontology we obtain as the outcome of an aggregation process might be inconsistent. Ontology aggregators

---

[1] The finite set of TBox formulas in Φ might be all TBox formulas of a certain maximum length or the union of all TBox formulas that a given population of agents choose to include in their TBoxes.

> LeftPolicy $\sqsubseteq$ RaiseWages
> LeftPolicy $\sqsubseteq$ RaiseWelfare
> RaiseWages $\sqcap$ RaiseWelfare $\sqsubseteq \bot$

Fig. 1. The TBox agenda of the agents

that are *consistent* would be very desirable in general. Unfortunately, they also suffer certain drawbacks. The *unanimous aggregator*, that accepts a formula if every individual does, is one of these. It indeed preserves consistency: if every ontology O_j is consistent, so is $F_{un}(O)$. However, if the individual ontologies are heterogeneous enough, the unanimous aggregator is likely to provide a very poor collective ontology. At the opposite side of the spectrum, we can define the *union* aggregator, that accepts any piece of information provided by at least one agent. In this case, the collective ontology is very likely to be inconsistent.

To balance the contributions of agents better than with the unanimous and the union aggregators, we can adopt the majority rule, which is widely applied in any political scenarios. In our setting, the majority rule is defined as follows: The absolute majority rule is the ontology aggregator F_m mapping any given profile $O \in \mathrm{On}(\Phi)^{\mathcal{N}}$ to the ontology

$$F_m(O) := \{\varphi \in \Phi \mid \#N_\varphi^O > \frac{n}{2}\}.$$

Under the absolute majority rule, a formula gets accepted if and only if more than half of the individual agents accept it. A simple generalisation of the majority rule provides the class of *quota* rules, where the threshold of $\frac{n}{2}$ is replaced by any threshold q. The majority rule, and more generally quota rules, return a consistent ontology only on very simple agendas [15].

4   Possibly Inconsistent Collective Ontologies

The following example shows that the absolute majority rule, which is widely used in practice, is not a consistent aggregator. Our example is a simple adaptation of the *doctrinal paradox* to the case of concept definitions [8,13].

Consider three left-wing political leaders, i.e., three agents 1, 2, and 3, who must agree on what is a left policy in order to coordinate their campaigns. They vote on possible definitions of left-wing policy by casting their votes on the TBox agenda shown in Fig. 1. Each individual ontology, in particular, formalises possible meanings that agents ascribe to what is a left-wing policy. Suppose that the agents vote as in Table 1.

Every individual set of axioms is consistent and the concept LeftPolicy is satisfiable in each of the individual ontologies. Agent 1, for instance, believes that a left policy must raise both the wages and the levels of welfare, accordingly this agent believes that it is possible to promote the levels of both. Agent 2 believes that a left policy only has to raise wages, not the level of

Table 1. A voting scenario

	LeftPolicy $\sqsubseteq$ RaiseWages	LeftPolicy $\sqsubseteq$ RaiseWelfare	RaiseWages $\sqcap$ RaiseWelfare $\sqsubseteq \bot$
1	Yes	Yes	No
2	Yes	No	Yes
3	No	Yes	Yes
Maj.	Yes	Yes	Yes

welfare, as they believe that it is not possible to do both. Agent 3 believes that what counts as a left policy is that it promotes the levels of welfare and that it is not possible to increase welfare and wages at the same time. Although all individual ontologies are consistent and the concept LeftPolicy is indeed satisfiable in each O_i, the ontology obtained by applying the absolute majority rule is not. The ontology $F_m(O_1, O_2, O_3)$ in this case coincides with the full agenda of Fig. 1. By accepting both LeftPolicy $\sqsubseteq$ RaiseWages and LeftPolicy $\sqsubseteq$ RaiseWelfare, we infer LeftPolicy $\sqsubseteq$ RaiseWages$\sqcap$RaiseWelfare, which together with RaiseWages $\sqcap$ RaiseWelfare $\sqsubseteq \bot$ makes the concept of LeftPolicy unsatisfiable. Moreover, as soon as we assume that there are indeed instances of left-wing policies, e.g., we add an ABox formula LeftPolicy(a), for some constant a, to the ontology $F_m(O_1, O_2, O_3)$, then the collective ontology becomes inconsistent.

To repair the outcome of the majority rule, we assume that the agents share a certain amount of background information about the concepts at issue, that is they appeal a *reference* ontology (Fig. 2). With respect to the reference ontology, there is more than one way of repairing the collective ontology. The concept ReduceInequality is a generalisation of RaiseWelfare, and of RaiseWages. So, one way of repairing is to weaken the axiom LeftPolicy $\sqsubseteq$ RaiseWages, by replacing the concept RaiseWages with ReduceInequality. Symmetrically, one can weaken LeftPolicy $\sqsubseteq$ RaiseWelfare, by generalising the concept RaiseWelfare also with ReduceInequality. In both cases, we obtain a consistent set of axioms. Another strategy is to weaken RaiseWages $\sqcap$ RaiseWelfare $\sqsubseteq \bot$, for instance by specialising the concept RaiseWages $\sqcap$ RaiseWelfare into $\bot$. However, the repaired ontology would contain the uninformative axiom $\bot \sqsubseteq \bot$. Although we effectively obtain a consistent ontology, a repair strategy would ideally avoid such an outcome when possible. Notice that if there is no viable reference ontology—that is, there is no information

LeftPolicy $\sqsubseteq$ RaiseWages	LeftPolicy $\sqsubseteq$ ReduceInequality
LeftPolicy $\sqsubseteq$ RaiseWelfare	ReduceInequality $\sqsubseteq$ Policy
RaiseWages $\sqsubseteq$ ReduceInequality	LeftPolicy $\sqsubseteq$ Policy
RaiseWelfare $\sqsubseteq$ ReduceInequality	

Fig. 2. A reference ontology

about the concepts that can be exploited for axiom weakening—replacing conflicting informative axioms with trivial or logical axioms is the only viable strategy.

5   Repairing Collective Ontologies

Our strategy for fixing the collective aggregated ontology relies on weakening the axioms present in a TBox w.r.t. an ontology. Weakening an axiom essentially amounts to refine its premise or its conclusion. In this setting, two types of refinement operators exist: specialisation refinement operators and generalisation refinement operators [3,10]. Given the quasi-ordered set $\langle \mathcal{L}(\mathcal{ALC}, N_c, N_R), \sqsubseteq \rangle$, a generalisation refinement operator is defined as follows:

$$\gamma_{\mathcal{T}}(C) \subseteq \{C' \in \mathcal{L}(\mathcal{ALC}, N_c, N_R) \mid C \sqsubseteq_{\mathcal{T}} C'\}.$$

Whereas a specialisation refinement operator is defined as follows:

$$\rho_{\mathcal{T}}(C) \subseteq \{C' \in \mathcal{L}(\mathcal{ALC}, N_c, N_R) \mid C' \sqsubseteq_{\mathcal{T}} C\}.$$

A generalisation refinement operator takes a concept C as input and returns a set of descriptions that are more general than C, according to $\mathcal{T}$. A specialisation operator, instead, returns a set of descriptions that are more specific.

We note $\gamma_{\mathcal{T}}^*(C)$ and $\rho_{\mathcal{T}}^*(C)$ the iterated generalisation and the iterated specialisation of the concept C, respectively. As a minimal requirement, we assume that for every concept C, we have $\top \in \gamma_{\mathcal{T}}^*(C)$ and $\bot \in \rho_{\mathcal{T}}^*(C)$.

The following strategy is designed to use the novel generalisation and specialisation refinement operators of [4].

5.1   Axiom Weakening

Weakening an axiom $C \sqsubseteq D$ amounts to *enlarging* the set of interpretations that satisfy the axiom. This could be done in different ways: Either by substituting $C \sqsubseteq D$ with $C \sqsubseteq D'$, where D' is a more general concept than D (i.e., its interpretation is larger); or, by modifying the axiom $C \sqsubseteq D$ to $C' \sqsubseteq D$, where C' is a more specific concept than C; or even by generalising and specialising simultaneously to obtain $C' \sqsubseteq D'$. Given an ontology O, we denote the set of concept names of O by N_C^O. We want to define a procedure to change axioms gradually by replacing them with less restrictive axioms. Recall that γ_O denotes the generalisation of a concept and ρ_O denotes its specialisation with respect to a given ontology O.

Definition 1 (Axiom weakening). *Given an axiom $C \sqsubseteq D$ of O, the set of weakenings of $C \sqsubseteq D$ in O, denoted by $g_O(C \sqsubseteq D)$ is the set of all axioms $C' \sqsubseteq D'$ such that*

$$C' \in \rho_O^*(C) \text{ and } D' \in \gamma_O^*(D).$$

Algorithm 1. Fixing ontologies through weakening.

Procedure FIX-ONTOLOGY(O,R)   ▷ O inconsistent ontology, R reference ontology
1: **while** O is inconsistent **do**
2:        $\mathcal{Y} \leftarrow$ MIS(O)   ▷ find all minimally inconsistent subsets of O
3:        **for** $Y \in \mathcal{Y}$ **do**
4:            **choose** $\psi \in Y, \psi' \in g_{\mathrm{R}}(\psi)$ with $Y \backslash \{\psi\} \cup \{\psi'\}$ consistent, $\lambda_O(\psi, \psi')$ minimal

5:            $O \leftarrow (O \backslash \{\psi\}) \cup \{\psi'\}$
6: **return** O

If the ontology O is consistent, the weakening of an axiom in O is always satisfied by a super set of the interpretations that satisfy the axiom. Let $I = (\Delta^I, \cdot^I)$ be an interpretation. By definition, the class of all entities that fulfill the axiom $C \sqsubseteq D$ is $(\Delta^I \backslash C^I) \cup D^I$. A weakening of $C \sqsubseteq D$ either specialises C, therefore restricting C^I, and accordingly extending $\Delta^I \backslash C^I$, or generalises D, therefore, extending D^I. Moreover, note that $\bot \sqsubseteq \top$ always belongs to $g_O(C \sqsubseteq D)$. We want to model how to repair any inconsistent set of axioms Y of $\mathcal{ALC}$, by appealing to a (consistent) reference ontology R. Notice that, even though it is not desirable, R can be dissociated from the axioms in the collective ontology.

Any inconsistent set of axioms Y can in principle be repaired by means of a sequence of weakenings of the axioms in Y with respect to R: in the worst case these axioms are weakened to become a tautology (e.g., $\bot \sqsubseteq \top$). However, we are interested in weakening axioms as little as possible to remain close to the original axioms. Since every axiom in $g_O(C \sqsubseteq D)$ is obtained by applying γ and ρ a finite number of times, we can define λ_O to be a *refinement distance* in an ontology O. Repair strategies can exploit this distance to guide the weakening of axioms that are the least stringent. Moreover, by trying to minimise the distance, we are trying to prevent non-informative (i.e., tautological) axioms to be selected as weakenings. In principle, we can also provide refined constraints on the generalisation and specialisation paths, e.g., by fixing an ordering of the concepts of the ontology O that determines which concepts are to be generalised or specialised first.

5.2   Fixing Collective Ontologies via Axiom Weakenings

When $F(O)$ is inconsistent, we can adopt the general strategy described in Algorithm 1 to repair it w.r.t. a given (fixed) reference ontology R.

The algorithm finds all the minimally inconsistent subsets $Y_1, \ldots, Y_n$ of $F(O)$ (e.g., using the methods from [2,16]) and repairs each of them by weakening one of its axioms to regain consistency. From all the possible choices made to achieve this goal, the algorithm selects one that minimizes the distance λ_O (line 4). This process corrects all original causes for inconsistency, but may still produce an inconsistent ontology [7]. Hence, the process is repeated until a consistent ontology is found. Notice that the algorithm is non-deterministic, since it depends on the choice of the axiom to weaken, and the weakening selected. As such, it can also be seen as a strategy returning a non-singleton *set* of ontologies (i.e. the procedure is termed non-resolute in social choice [15]). To make it resolute, two policies for breaking ties are required. For both, we can capitalize on the linear order over formulas $\prec_{\mathcal{ALC}}$ introduced earlier. We can define a linear order $\prec^x_{\mathcal{ALC}}$ over axioms as follows: $C \sqsubseteq D \prec^x_{\mathcal{ALC}} E \sqsubseteq F$ iff $C \prec_{\mathcal{ALC}} E$, or $C = D$ and $D \prec_{\mathcal{ALC}} F$.

Now, with a reference ontology R and the linear order $\prec_{\mathcal{ALC}}$ fixed, the strategy returns an aggregation procedure $g_{R,\prec_{\mathcal{ALC}}}(F(O))$: firstly, aggregate the individual ontologies in O, then generalise the axioms in any possible inconsistent set of $F(O)$ with respect to the reference ontology R, and obtain $g_{R,\prec_{\mathcal{ALC}}}(F(O))$. We leave a detailed presentation for future work.

5.3   An Application

We illustrate our strategy by discussing the example in Sect. 4. We have seen that the absolute majority rule returns an inconsistent collective ontologies. The inconsistent ontology $F_m(O)$ coincides, in this example, with the agenda of the agents (Fig. 1).

To apply our strategy, we have firstly to select a reference ontology R. Suppose we choose the ontology in Fig. 2. We exemplify how $g_R(F_m(O))$ works by assuming in this case that it is non-resolute. We start by choosing an axiom in a minimally inconsistent subset of $F_m(O)$ that needs to be weakened. The whole collective ontology $F_m(O)$ is a minimally inconsistent set. Assume we start by LeftPolicy $\sqsubseteq$ RaiseWages. Then, we have to select a concept to generalise or specialise. Suppose we select RaiseWages. Thus, to generalise the axiom LeftPolicy $\sqsubseteq$ RaiseWages we can replace it by LeftPolicy $\sqsubseteq$ ReduceInequality, since ReduceInequality is the closest generalisation to RaiseWages in the reference ontology R. We obtain the new ontology, where the axiom LeftPolicy $\sqsubseteq$ RaiseWages has been replaced by the weaker LeftPolicy $\sqsubseteq$ ReduceInequality.

Alternatively, we could have started by generalising RaiseWages $\sqcap$ RaiseWelfare $\sqsubseteq \bot$. In this case, we have two choices, either we generalise $\bot$, or we specialise RaiseWages $\sqcap$ RaiseWelfare. $\bot$ can be generalised by any concept in the reference ontology. RaiseWages $\sqcap$ RaiseWelfare can here be specialised only by replacing it with $\bot$, obtaining therefore $\bot \sqsubseteq \bot$, which is a (non-informative) logical axiom. By replacing an axiom with a logical one, the effect on the final ontology is the same as removing the original axiom (a logical axiom does not restrict the models of the ontology). Thus, in this case, the repaired ontology contains LeftPolicy $\sqsubseteq$ ReduceInequality and LeftPolicy $\sqsubseteq$ RaiseWelfare.

6   Conclusion and Future Work

We proposed a novel approach to repair an inconsistent ontology, obtained by aggregating the individual ontologies of a community of agents. Our approach is based on the notion of axiom weakening, which amounts to the generalisation or specialisation of concepts found in axioms that belong to minimally inconsistent subsets. Whilst we presented a viable solution, a more extensive evaluation is needed. Firstly, discussing good strategies for deciding a reference ontology is crucial for the present approach. Secondly, the study of the formal properties of the proposed algorithm and its computational complexity is required. Finally, it is important to extend the proposed approach to a large class of description logics and to a variety of important aggregation procedures. We leave these points for future work.

References

1. Baader, F., Calvanese, D., McGuinness, D.L., Nardi, D., Patel-Schneider, P.F. (eds.): The Description Logic Handbook: Theory, Implementation, and Applications. Cambridge University Press, New York (2003)
2. Baader, F., Peñaloza, R.: Axiom pinpointing in general tableaux. J. Logic Comput. **20**(1), 5–34 (2010). Special Issue: Tableaux and Analytic Proof Methods
3. Confalonieri, R., Eppe, M., Schorlemmer, M., Kutz, O., Peñaloza, R., Plaza, E.: Upward refinement operators for conceptual blending in $\mathcal{EL}^{++}$. Ann. Math. Artif. Intell. (2016). doi:10.1007/s10472-016-9524-8
4. Confalonieri, R., Kutz, O., Troquard, N., Galliani, P., Porello, D., Peñaloza, R., Schorlemmer, M.: Coherence, similarity, and concept generalisation. In: Proceedings of DL 2017. CEUR (2017)
5. Dietrich, F., List, C.: Judgment aggregation by quota rules: majority voting generalized. J. Theor. Polit. **19**(4), 391–424 (2007)
6. Gaertner, W.: A Primer in Social Choice Theory. Oxford University Press, Oxford (2006)
7. Horridge, M., Parsia, B., Sattler, U.: Justification masking in ontologies. In: KR 2012. AAAI Press (2012)
8. Kornhauser, L.A., Sager, L.G.: The one and the many: adjudication in collegial courts. Calif. Law Rev. **81**(1), 1–59 (1993)
9. Kutz, O., Mossakowski, T., Lücke, D.: Carnap, Goguen, and the Hyperontologies: Logical Pluralism and Heterogeneous Structuring in Ontology Design. Logica Universalis **4**(2), 255–333 (2010). Special Issue on Is Logic Universal?
10. van der Laag, P.R., Nienhuys-Cheng, S.H.: Completeness and properness of refinement operators in inductive logic programming. J. Logic Program. **34**(3), 201–225 (1998)
11. List, C., Pettit, P.: Aggregating sets of judgments: An impossibility result. Econ. Philos. **18**(1), 89–110 (2002)
12. List, C.: Deliberation and agreement. In: Rosenberg, S.W. (ed.) Deliberation, Participation and Democracy, pp. 64–81. Palgrave Macmillan UK, London (2007). doi:10.1057/9780230591080_4
13. List, C., Puppe, C.: Judgment aggregation: a survey. In: Handbook of Rational and Social Choice. Oxford University Press (2009)
14. Ottonelli, V., Porello, D.: On the elusive notion of meta-agreement. Politics Philos. Econ. **12**(1), 68–92 (2013)
15. Porello, D., Endriss, U.: Ontology merging as social choice: judgment aggregation under the open world assumption. J. Logic Comput. **24**(6), 1229–1249 (2014)
16. Schlobach, S., Cornet, R.: Non-standard reasoning services for the debugging of description logic terminologies. In: Proceedings of IJCAI 2003, pp. 355–362. Morgan Kaufmann (2003)

Collective Voice of Experts in Multilateral Negotiation

Taha D. Güneş[1,2](✉) [iD], Emir Arditi[2], and Reyhan Aydoğan[2,3,4]

[1] Agents, Interaction and Complexity Group,
University of Southampton, Southampton, UK
t.d.gunes@soton.ac.uk
[2] Department of Computer Science, Özyeğin University, Istanbul, Turkey
emir.arditi@ozu.edu.tr, reyhan.aydogan@ozyegin.edu.tr
[3] Interactive Intelligence Group, Delft University of Technology,
Delft, The Netherlands
[4] Frontier Research Institute for Information Science,
Nagoya Institute of Technology, Nagoya, Japan

Abstract. Inspired from the ideas such as *"algorithm portfolio"*, *"mixture of experts"*, and *"genetic algorithm"*, this paper presents two novel negotiation strategies, which combine multiple negotiation experts to decide what to bid and what to accept during the negotiation. In the first approach namely *incremental portfolio*, a bid is constructed by asking each negotiation agent's opinion in the portfolio and picking one of the suggestions stochastically considering the expertise levels of the agents. In the second approach namely *crossover strategy*, each expert agent makes a bid suggestion and a majority voting is used on each issue value to decide the bid content. The proposed approaches have been evaluated empirically and our experimental results showed that the crossover strategy outperformed the top five finalists of the ANAC 2016 Negotiation Competition in terms of the obtained average individual utility.

Keywords: Agreement technologies · Automated negotiation · Multilateral negotiation · Negotiation Competition · Multi-agent systems

Automated negotiation is a fundamental solution approach in multi-agent systems where there is a conflict of interest among parties [12]. It takes place to resolve the underlying conflicts for coming up with a joint agreement. Although there have been a number of negotiating agents designed in this area with varying strategies, heuristics and assumptions [4,5,7,8,20,21], the empirical evaluations in the negotiation literature have shown that each strategy performs significantly different in varying scenarios [6,10,17,22], due to their opponent's strategies and diverse characteristics of negotiation scenarios (e.g. size of outcome space, degree of conflicts). Some negotiation strategies may outperform other strategies in some negotiation scenarios while they may not perform well in other scenarios. Based on those observations, we investigate the question of how to devise an approach that combines the strengths of expert agents' strategies in order to achieve higher performance overall in a variety of negotiation scenarios.

© Springer International Publishing AG 2017
B. An et al. (Eds.): PRIMA 2017, LNAI 10621, pp. 450–458, 2017.
https://doi.org/10.1007/978-3-319-69131-2_27

The question of which strategy our agent should employ in the underlying negotiation is intriguing. Picking the best-performing strategy for a specific scenario resembles to the widely known "algorithm selection problem" [19], where an algorithm amongst a set of algorithms for a particular problem, which is expected to perform better than others, is selected. One common approach to this problem known as "winner-take-all" [14], is to select the algorithm whose overall performance is the best on a given problem distribution. Following this approach in the context of negotiation might not be appropriate since the performance of the negotiation strategies may significantly vary regarding to their opponents as well as the negotiation scenarios.

Inspired from "*algorithm portfolio*" approach [15], Ilany and Gal [11] develop a meta-agent, which aims to guess the performance of a set of bilateral negotiation strategies based on distinctive features of domains such as the size of the outcome space, the competitiveness of the given scenario, and degree of conflicts among preferences and so on, and accordingly adopt the strategy expected to perform best for the given scenario. However, more complex automated negotiations such as multilateral negotiations are not covered by this work.

Instead of following a one-shot strategy determination, an agent may combine multiple strategies of expert agents on-the-fly to achieve higher performance similarly to "*mixture of experts*", combining multiple learners approach in machine learning [1]. Accordingly, this paper studies how to combine multiple experts in multilateral negotiation settings in which more than two agents aim to reach a joint consensus by following Stacked Alternating Offer Protocol (SAOP) [2]. In the light of aforementioned motivations, this paper introduces two techniques to merge the strength of the experts: *incremental portfolio strategy* and *crossover voting strategy*. In the former approach (incremental portfolio), our strategy assigns a weight to each expert denoting how reliable they are, and choose one of the experts to ask what action to take at each negotiation round by taking their associated weights into account. Inspired from genetic algorithm and mixture of expert, the latter strategy, namely crossover voting strategy, asks each expert's opinion on what to bid and merges the given bids by voting the values per each issue. That is, a bid is constructed from other bids like generating a genome by using genetic algorithm except there is no mutation operation in our case and crossing over is done by means of voting. It is worth noting that our agent employing incremental portfolio strategy, *Caduceus* participated in ANAC 2016 competition[1], and got the first place amongst ten finalist agents.

We evaluate the performance of our strategies against a variety of negotiation scenarios (i.e., different domains, different opponents) in General Environment for Negotiation with Intelligent multi-purpose Usage, [16] GENIUS[2], a testbed also used in International Competition Automated Negotiating Agents Competition (ANAC) [9,13]. The benchmark provided by the competition has been used in our tests. The conducted results show that our agent employing *crossover*

---

[1] http://web.tuat.ac.jp/%7Ekatfuji/ANAC2016/.
[2] http://ii.tudelft.nl/genius/.

voting strategy yields higher performance overall in a variety of different negotiation settings regarding the gained average individual utility.

The rest of the paper is organized as: First, we elaborate on related work in Sect. 1 and our problem setting in Sect. 2. Our negotiation strategies for multilateral negotiation setting are explained in Sect. 3. Section 4 provides empirical evaluation of our findings. Lastly, we conclude our work with future work directions in Sect. 5.

1   Related Work

Alpaydin proposes to combine multiple machine learning algorithms in order to increase the performance of the overall learning process [1]. One of the techniques mentioned in this paper is voting where each learner has a weight and their votes have an impact on the overall decision accordingly. In our work, we adopt a similar approach. In our incremental portfolio approach, each negotiation strategy has a weight denoting their expertise level and the bid is made stochastically by asking each strategy in our portfolio by taking their weights into account. In crossover approach, we again use voting but slightly different way. Each agent suggests a bid and we use the majority voting on each issue to decide their values in the final bid to be made.

Another study [11] also discusses the positive effects of using different algorithms in different domains in order to achieve better outcomes in the context of automated negotiation. The study mainly focuses on selecting a negotiation strategy based on the characteristics of the negotiation strategy. They apply machine learning algorithms to predict which strategy would work better in the given negotiation scenario. The main difference between that study and our work is that they pick the best negotiation strategy guessed by a machine learning algorithm, and employ this study in the entire negotiation whereas our approach is using multiple strategies and these strategies collectively determine what to bid and what to accept during the negotiation.

Furthermore, Aydoğan *et al.* pursue the problem of selecting the most effective negotiation mechanism for a given negotiation scenario [3]. While Ilany and Gal address the problem of selecting the best negotiation strategy, Aydoğan *et al.* studies which negotiation mechanism (i.e., negotiation protocol and compatible strategies) should be adopted under the given negotiation problem. They define a set of scenario metrics to capture the characteristics of the negotiation problems and apply machine learning techniques to guess which mechanisms work better with which scenarios. That work also focuses on bilateral negotiations while our approach is for multilateral negotiations.

Faratin *et al.* propose a number of negotiation tactics such as time-based concession tactics and behavior-based tactics, which mimics opponent's behavior [21]. They also provide a meta-strategy, which makes a counter proposal by linear combination of tactics. This approach is similar to our approach since both approaches take more than one tactics/strategies into account to make a counter offer during the negotiation. However, our approach also asks each expert's opinion in the decision of acceptance of a given bid. Another difference is that they consider only numeric issues in a specific range [min, max] so that they can construct a counter offer by taking the linear combination of the bid values suggested by each tactic. On the other hand, our approach works well with the discrete issues as well as the integer issues.

Matsune and Fujita combines multiple existing opponent modeling algorithms by using boosting based on the least square method and nonlinear programming in multilateral negotiation settings [9]. In that sense, our work is complementary. While we are combining bidding and acceptance strategies of multiple negotiation strategies, they are combining existing opponent models.

2   Problem Setting

In this work, we focus on non-mediated multilateral negotiations in which more than two negotiating agents, Agents=$\{1, 2, ..., n\}$, aim to reach a joint agreement on a set of issues denoted by L. Each issue $j \in L$ can take a value v_j from a predefined set of valid values for that issue denoted by D_j; that is $v_j \in D_j$. This domain information is shared between each negotiating party. However, preferences of a negotiating party is private; that is, none of the agents does not know their opponents' preferences. Particularly, the utility function of an opponent is unknown to the negotiating agent. A bid $b = (b_1, ..., b_{|L|})$ is an assignment of values to all issues where $b_1 \in D_1$.

In our setting, the utility of a given bid is modelled in terms of additive utility function as shown in Eq. 1 where $o_i(v_j)$ denotes agent i's valuation of the value of issue j in the given bid and the weights of that issue is represented by $w_{i,j}$. In other words, agents sum up their weighted valuation of each issue value to calculate the overall utility.

$$u_i(b^t) = \sum_{j \in L} o_i(b_j^t) \cdot w_{i,j} \tag{1}$$

Each party complies to *Stacked Alternating Offers Protocol* (SAOP) [2], which is a turn-taking fashion protocol where each agent i is expected to provide an action a_i in its turn during a negotiation session. Type of an action is denoted as $type(a)$ which can take $type(a) = \{I^{bid}, I^{accept}, I^{end}\}$; that is, the agent can make a counter offer, accept the offer in the negotiation table or walk away from the negotiation respectively. The session ends whenever the offer on the table is accepted by all parties, the deadline is reached or a party walks away. If an agreement on the bid b is reached, the utility of the agent i at the time t is estimated as formulated in Eq. 2. As seen obviously, the utility of a given bid goes down over time.

$$u_i(b^t) = [\sum_{j \in L} o_i(b_j^t) \cdot w_{i,j}] \cdot \delta_i^t \tag{2}$$

In the case of not reaching a consensus, the utility that every agent is simply equal to $r_i \cdot \delta_i^t$ where r_i is the reservation value and δ_i^t is the discount factor of at time t. The reservation value and the discount factor information is provided within the preference profile. Each agent is self-interested: the agent wants to maximize its individual utility $u_i(b^t)$ at the end of a negotiation session.

We follow the negotiation settings of ANAC 2016 competition for our empirical evaluations. The winner agent is picked after a *tournament* where the participants enter a series of negotiation sessions with all possible settings (e.g. a variety of negotiation domains with varying preference profiles, different combination of agents, etc.). It is important to note that the agents are not allowed to save any domain information throughout the tournament and identities of the participants are not shared. According to the competition, the best agent is the one that achieves the highest total utility after all negotiation rounds.

3   Proposed Negotiation Strategies

Here, we describe our meta strategies based on the opinions of multiple negotiation experts. *Incremental portfolio* strategy in which actions of experts agents are gathered and only a single action from all collected actions is picked stochastically by taking the expertise level of the experts into account while *crossover* strategy combines the suggested actions by using majority voting.

3.1   *Incremental Portfolio* Strategy

As shown in Algorithm 1.1, *Incremental Portfolio* strategy separates negotiation process into two major phases. In the first phase, our agent chooses the best possible offer for itself (i.e., the offer with the highest utility) and sends this bid to its opponents up to $T \cdot \beta$, where T is the maximum negotiation duration (deadline) and β is the parameter controlling how long the first phase will endure (Lines 6–9). To decide the best value for β, we did some experiments and chose the value giving the highest utility. Note that we observed that involving such an eager phase enables our agent to yield higher utilities in practice.

In the second phase, each expert agent is informed by the received action a, which is one of our opponents' most recent action, and asked to make a decision on which action to be taken: *accept* or *make a counter bid* (Line 12). The response of each agent a'_i can be either a counter-offer I^{bid} or an accept action I^{accept}. In the case of I^{bid}, action is added into candidate bid set, B. Votes of expert agents for actions ℓ_{bid} and ℓ_{accept} are counted (Lines 13–15). Finally, the output action is decided based on those votes. If majority of the votes are in favor of accept action, the agent accepts the opponent's offer a (Line 16); otherwise, a bid is chosen from the set B by Monte Carlo sampling where the weights of each expert agent are taken in account (Line 18).

3.2   *Crossover* Strategy

Similar to *Incremental Portfolio* Strategy, *Crossover* strategy also consists of two phases. Since the first phase is identical in both strategies, we will focus on how agent will act in the second phase. The valuable information during the

---

Algorithm 1.1. *Incremental Portfolio Strategy*

1: **Input:** Action a {one of an opponent action}
2: **Output:** Action b' {for the negotiation table}
3: **Initialization:** $A \leftarrow \{set\ of\ expert\ agents\}$;
4: $\Omega \leftarrow (\omega_i, ..., \omega_{|A|})$; {impact weights of each expert agent}
5: $B \leftarrow \{\}$; {set of bids suggested by the expert agents}
6: **Waiting phase:**
7: **if** $t < T \cdot \beta$ **then**
8:     return B^{max}; {return best bid for agent itself}
9: **Voting phase:**
10: **for each** $i \in A$ **do**
11:     $a'_i \leftarrow$ query agent i with action a in time t;
12:     **if** $type(a'_i) = I^{bid}$ **then**
13:         $B \leftarrow B \cup \{a'_i\}$ $\ell_{bid} \leftarrow \ell_{bid} + 1$;
14:     **else**
15:         $\ell_{accept} \leftarrow \ell_{accept} + 1$;
16: **if** $\ell_{accept} > \ell_{bid}$ **then return** I^{accept};
17: **else**
18:     **return** a bid b' from weighted random sample set B by Ω;

---

generation of a counter-offer action is not preserved and utilised well enough in our *incremental portfolio* strategy since only a single bid is chosen from a set of expert agents' bids. To address this, we extended our strategy by combining offers from the expert agents. We call this new approach, *crossover* strategy by being inspired by *"genetic algorithms"* [18]. The *crossover* strategy, as shown in Algorithm 1.2, combines bids from expert agents by picking the most favourable values of an issue by applying majority voting on each issue value.

As previously described, all expert agents have a weight value to impact the final bid action. The value of an each issue is voted (Lines 19–22) and the value that gets the majority of the votes is then picked in this strategy (Lines 23–24). Therefore not only which action to take is decided collectively by expert agents, but also what to offer is collectively made with this strategy.

4   Performance Evaluation

To evaluate our strategies empirically, we conducted a number of experiments in GENIUS negotiation testbed environment. We compare the performance of the proposed negotiation strategies against the best five agents from ANAC 2016 Negotiation Competition[3] namely: ParsCat, YXAgent, Farma, MyAgent and Atlas3. We ran 14400 different negotiation sessions (6 agents, 3 participants per sessions, 5 repetitions per session, 6 domains, 3 preference profiles per domain and four differently configured *Caduceus*.) in GENIUS platform with version 7.1.2. Each run per domain took around 24 h, and conducted within similar machine configurations.

---
[3] http://web.tuat.ac.jp/~katfuji/ANAC2016/.

Algorithm 1.2. *Crossover Strategy*

1: **Input:** Action a {one of an opponent action}
2: **Output:** Action b' {for the negotiation table}
3: **Initialization:** $A \leftarrow \{set\ of\ expert\ agents\}$;
4: $\Omega \leftarrow (\omega_i, ..., \omega_{|A|})$; {impact weights of each expert agent}
5: $B \leftarrow \{\}$; {set of bids suggested by the expert agents}
6: Same as Algorithm 1.1;
7: **if** $\ell_{accept} > \ell_{bid}$ **then return** I^{accept};
8: **else** $b' \leftarrow (\emptyset, ..., \emptyset)$ {create an empty bid}.
9:     **for each** $j \in L$ **do**   {each issue in negotiation scenario}
10:         **for each** $v_j \in D_j$ **do**   {each valid value for issue j}
11:             **for each** $i \in A$ **do**   {each expert agent}
12:                 $\ell_{v_j} = \ell_{v_j} + \mathbb{1}_{b_i}(v_j) \cdot \omega_i$;
13:         **for each** $j \in L$ **do** {each issue in the domain}
14:             $b'_j = \arg \max_{v_j} \ell_{v_j}$; {pick the value that got the highest vote}
15:     **return** b';

Figure 1 shows the average individual utilities gained by each agent over 14400 different negotiations. We created two versions of each negotiation strategy. First, we use equal weights for each agent in our portfolio while in the second version we set different weights for each agent regarding to their past performance. It is obviously seen that Caduceus agent with *crossover* strategy with equal weights (CE) and with ordered weights (CO) outperforms all of the agents in overall. The performance of our *incremental portfolio* strategy suffered slightly with the given equal weights, which were giving more chance to all consisting expert agents (0.727 versus 0.721).

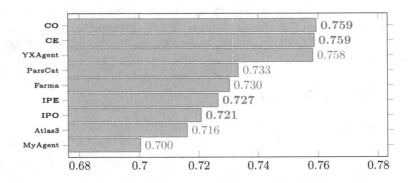

Fig. 1. The performance of the agents

It is worth noting that the ranking order of the other top five agents from the competition in our experiments changed, but the utility range was similar and stayed above 0.7 as in competition. This is because the performance of the negotiating agents highly depend on their opponent sets. In the competition, there were 10 finalist agents. However, we have 5 top agents and the variants of Caduceus. Since this competition is harder than ANAC 2016, some of the agents' rank may be different from their rank in the competition.

5   Conclusion and Discussion

In this paper, we have introduced two novel negotiation strategies, which ask negotiation expert's opinion to collectively decide which action to be taken. To our knowledge, this is the first work that uses existing expert agents progressively in multilateral negotiations. Our results have shown that the *crossover* strategy that employs previous years top five agents from ANAC 2015 with varying impact weights outperformed top five agents (excluding *Caduceus* from ANAC 2016. Thus, we have shown the feasibility of utilising pre-existing expert agents to devise better negotiation behaviors to achieve higher utilities, even by using dated expert agents. When calculating the votes for the acceptance, the weights were not taken into account. We can try to consider weights in this process too. Furthermore, the same weights of experts are used for the entire negotiation. As a future work, the agent may aim to observe its opponent's behavior and adapt these weights accordingly during the negotiation.

Acknowledgments. We thank Burak Atalay and Bahadır Kırdan for their help in implementation of the initial agent. This work was supported by the ITEA M2MGrids Project, grant number ITEA141011.

References

1. Alpaydin, E.: Techniques for combining multiple learners. In: Proceedings of Engineering of Intelligent Systems, pp. 6–12 (1998)
2. Aydoğan, R., Festen, D., Hindriks, K.V., Jonker, C.M.: Alternating offers protocols for multilateral negotiation. In: Fujita, K., Bai, Q., Ito, T., Zhang, M., Ren, F., Aydoğan, R., Hadfi, R. (eds.) Modern Approaches to Agent-based Complex Automated Negotiation. SCI, vol. 674, pp. 153–167. Springer, Cham (2017). doi:10.1007/978-3-319-51563-2_10
3. Aydogan, R., Marsa-Maestre, I., Klein, M., Jonker, C.M.: A machine learning approach for mechanism selection in complex negotiations. In: Proceedings of The 8th International Workshop on Agent-based Complex Automated Negotiations (2015)
4. Aydoğan, R., Yolum, P.: Effective negotiation with partial preference information. In: Proceedings of the 9th International Conference on Autonomous Agents and Multiagent Systems (AAMAS 2010), Toronto, Canada, May 10–14, 2010, vol. 1–3. pp. 1605–1606 (2010)
5. Baarslag, T., Gerding, E.H., Aydoğan, R., Schraefel, M.: Optimal negotiation decision functions in time-sensitive domains. In: 2015 IEEE/WIC/ACM International Conference on Web Intelligence and Intelligent Agent Technology (WI-IAT), vol. 2, pp. 190–197. IEEE (2015)
6. Baarslag, T., Hindriks, K., Jonker, C., Kraus, S., Lin, R.: The first automated negotiating agents competition (ANAC 2010). In: Ito, T., Zhang, M., Robu, V., Fatima, S., Matsuo, T. (eds.) New Trends in Agent-Based Complex Automated Negotiations. SCI, vol. 383, pp. 113–135. Springer, Heidelberg (2012). doi:10.1007/978-3-642-24696-8_7

7. Beam, C., Segev, A.: Automated negotiations: a survey of the state of the art. Wirtschaftsinformatik **39**(3), 263–268 (1997)

8. Fatima, S., Kraus, S., Wooldridge, M.: Principles of Automated Negotiation. Cambridge University Press, Cambridge (2014)

9. Fujita, K., Aydoğan, R., Baarslag, T., Hindriks, K., Ito, T., Jonker, C.: The sixth automated negotiating agents competition (ANAC 2015). In: Fujita, K., Bai, Q., Ito, T., Zhang, M., Ren, F., Aydoğan, R., Hadfi, R. (eds.) Modern Approaches to Agent-based Complex Automated Negotiation. SCI, vol. 674, pp. 139–151. Springer, Cham (2017). doi:10.1007/978-3-319-51563-2_9

10. Fujita, K., et al.: The second automated negotiating agents competition (ANAC2011). In: Ito, T., Zhang, M., Robu, V., Matsuo, T. (eds.) Complex Automated Negotiations: Theories, Models, and Software Competitions. SCI, vol. 435, pp. 183–197. Springer, Heidelberg (2013). doi:10.1007/978-3-642-30737-9_11

11. Ilany, L., Gal, Y.: Algorithm selection in bilateral negotiation. Auton. Agent. Multi-Agent Syst. **30**(4), 697–723 (2016)

12. Jennings, N., Faratin, P., Lomuscio, A., Parsons, S., Wooldridge, M., Sierra, C.: Automated negotiation: prospects, methods and challenges. Group Decis. Negot. **10**(2), 199–215 (2001)

13. Jonker, C.M., Aydoğan, R., Baarslag, T., Fujita, K., Ito, T., Hindriks, K.: Automated negotiating agents competition. In: Proceedings of the Thirty-First AAAI Conference on Artificial Intelligence (AAAI-17), pp. 5070–5072. AAAI Press (2017)

14. Lazzaro, J., Ryckebusch, S., Mahowald, M.A., Mead, C.A.: Winner-take-all networks of O (n) complexity. In: Advances in neural information processing systems, pp. 703–711 (1989)

15. Leyton-Brown, K., Nudelman, E., Andrew, G., McFadden, J., Shoham, Y.: A portfolio approach to algorithm selection. In: IJCAI, pp. 1542–1543 (2003)

16. Lin, R., Kraus, S., Baarslag, T., Tykhonov, D., Hindriks, K., Jonker, C.M.: Genius: an integrated environment for supporting the design of generic automated negotiators. Comput. Intell. **30**(1), 48–70 (2014)

17. Marsa-Maestre, I., Klein, M., Jonker, C.M., Aydoğan, R.: From problems to protocols: towards a negotiation handbook. Decis. Support Syst. **60**, 39–54 (2014)

18. Melanie, M.: An Introduction to Genetic Algorithms, vol. 5, pp. 62–75. MIT Press, Cambridge, London (1999)

19. Rice, J.R.: The algorithm selection problem. Adv. Comput. **15**, 65–118 (1976). Elsevier

20. Sanchez-Anguix, V., Aydogan, R., Julian, V., Jonker, C.: Unanimously acceptable agreements for negotiation teams in unpredictable domains. Electron. Commer. Res. Appl. **13**(4), 243–265 (2014)

21. Sierra, C., Faratin, P., Jennings, N.R.: A service-oriented negotiation model between autonomous agents. In: Padget, J.A. (ed.) Collaboration between Human and Artificial Societies 1997. LNCS, vol. 1624, pp. 201–219. Springer, Heidelberg (1999). doi:10.1007/10703260_12

22. Williams, C.R., Robu, V., Gerding, E.H., Jennings, N.R.: An overview of the results and insights from the third automated negotiating agents competition (ANAC2012). In: Marsa-Maestre, I., Lopez-Carmona, M.A., Ito, T., Zhang, M., Bai, Q., Fujita, K. (eds.) Novel Insights in Agent-based Complex Automated Negotiation. SCI, vol. 535, pp. 151–162. Springer, Tokyo (2014). doi:10.1007/978-4-431-54758-7_9

An Approach to Characterize Topic-Centered Argumentation

Maximiliano C.D. Budán[1,2]([⊠]), Maria Laura Cobo[3], Diego C. Martinez[1], and Guillermo R. Simari[1]

[1] Department of Computer Science and Engineering,
Institute for Computer Science and Engineering (UNS - CONICET),
Universidad Nacional del Sur, Bahía Blanca, Argentina
{mcdb,dcm,grs}@cs.uns.edu.ar
[2] Department of Mathematics, Universidad Nacional de Santiago del Estero,
Santiago del Estero, Argentina
[3] Department of Computer Science and Engineering,
Universidad Nacional del Sur, Bahía Blanca, Argentina
mlc@cs.uns.edu.ar

Abstract. As we engage in a debate with other parties, it is usual that several subjects might come under discussion. In this work, we propose an extension of classic abstract argumentation frameworks which includes a set of interrelated topics decorating arguments. These topics represent what the arguments are addressing and provide a supporting structure for the analysis of multi-topic argumentation. A notion of "proximity" of an argument to the focus of the debate is introduced, leading to a notion of *distance* between the topics of the arguments, which is used for proximity-based semantic elaborations.

Keywords: Argumentation · Topics related · Proximity semantics

1 Introduction

The relevance of argumentation in the area of Knowledge Representation and Reasoning has grown steadily for the past three decades, providing a computationally amenable method to model human decision making. In particular, *abstract argumentation systems* are formalisms for defeasible reasoning where some components remain unspecified, being the structure of arguments the central abstraction. In these systems, the semantic notion of finding the set of acceptable arguments becomes the primary issue. In this direction, Dung in [4], presented the notion of *Abstract Argumentation Frameworks (AFs)* that only considers abstract arguments and an attack relation defined between them; in this seminal work, semantic consequences of the interaction among arguments through the defeat relation were considered characterizing several ways of obtaining the set of *acceptable arguments*. Later on, this formal framework was expanded by considering the inclusion of several elements such as preferences

© Springer International Publishing AG 2017
B. An et al. (Eds.): PRIMA 2017, LNAI 10621, pp. 459–467, 2017.
https://doi.org/10.1007/978-3-319-69131-2_28

between arguments [8], new argument relations [7], temporal dimensions [6], or different notions of weight for its components [3], to mention just a few of the possible extensions.

However, in the scenario just described, several representational aspects of the argumentation process still require further attention. Here, we are interested in introducing the notion of the *topics* associating these with an argument and acknowledge the fact that arguments could be linked with different topics, which in turn might not be closely related to each other affecting the pertinence of introducing them, or their relevance to the discussion. For example, suppose four persons, say P_1, P_2, P_3 and P_4 are debating global warming:

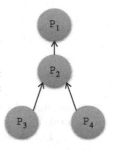

- P_1 *says that no control on pollution is needed, since global warming is a hoax.*
- P_2 *says that global warming is real, there is an unquestionable rise in the atmosphere and sea temperatures, plus the recent demonstration of ocean acidification.*
- P_3 *says that global warming is not real since there is not enough historical data on atmospheric temperature and what is observed in the ocean since the 90's does not suggest significant temperature changes.*
- P_4 *says that global warming is an invention of foreign countries to reduce the American industrial activity.*

The argument of P_2 is contradicting what P_1 holds, by referring to actual data on global warming evidence. Arguments P_3 and P_4 defend the initial proposition of P_1 by attacking P_2, but both with different reasons. The argument of P_2 and its attacker P_3 refer to topics that are *closed*: environmental temperature, oceanic water, historical records. The fourth person, however, to dispute P_2, proposes an argument that is about the competition among nations. Whether this last argument makes sense or not, clearly it is referring to topics that are not considering the environment and its variables. Should this last argument be considered in a debate? This is unclear since its reasons are not related to the central topics discussed by P_2 and P_3. In most debates, it is important to stay "focused" when providing the arguments in order to avoid distraction from important issues. In this example, P_3 proposes a defense argument for P_1 that is closer to its original topics, while P_4 does not. What are the semantic consequences of considering only closely-related argument defense?

To address these issues, we propose an extension of the abstract argumentation frameworks that includes a set of interrelated topics which decorate the arguments in the framework, reflecting what they are addressing while providing a supporting structure for the analysis of multi-topic argumentation. The pertinence of arguments to the debate leads to the evaluation of "proximity" of the topic of an argument to the focus of the debate. This can be modeled by a notion of *distance* between the topics of the arguments, wich is the basic element for proximity-based semantics.

2   Hashtagged Argumentation

In an organized dialogue or debate, the most relevant unit of expression is the *argument*, which is a single, tentative piece of reasoning that introduces new (defeasible) information in the argumentation process. Here, we will add to the abstract framework a formalization of the notion of *topics* which are addressed (or referred to) by an argument. As it is usual in abstract frameworks, arguments are considered as tentative pieces of reasoning with no reference to the underlying logic; however, we are interested in giving relevance to *what* an argument refers, not as a set of literal constructions but as a whole. We define a *topic tag*, or simply *hashtag*, as a single label denoted with the prefix #.

Definition 1. *Let Ht be a finite non-empty set of hashtags. A hashtagged argument structure is a pair* $\langle A, H_A \rangle$, *where* A *is an argument and* $H_A \subseteq Ht$. *We will say that* $\langle A, H_A \rangle$ *is tagged* on Ht.

A hashtag is as general as it is in social networks, and when inside an argument structure they define concepts (implicitly or explicitly) referred in the argument. They may be objects in the real world, agency entities (such as goals and desires), bibliographical references or even articles in civil law.

Example 1. *Consider a scenario where the set of hashtags is* $Ht = \{\#world\ cup, \#soccer, \#aliens, \#scandal, \#bermudaTriangle, \#pyramids, \#believe, \#bribe, \#island, \#moneyLaundering, \#offshoreCompany, \}$. *The following are three abstract arguments hashtagged in Ht:*

$\mathbb{A} = \langle A, \{\#worldcup, \#soccer, \#scandal, \#bribe, \#moneyLaundering\}\rangle$
$\mathbb{B} = \langle B, \{\#offshoreCompany, \#bermudaTriangle, \#island\}\rangle$
$\mathbb{C} = \langle C, \{\#aliens, \#pyramids, \#believe\}\rangle$

Here, argument $\mathbb{A}$ *refers to an alleged corruption case related to the World Cup Organization, while argument* $\mathbb{B}$ *is focused on Bermuda as an offshore jurisdiction which simply does not impose any form of taxation on companies. Finally, the argument* $\mathbb{C}$ *refers to some particular theories about aliens building great pyramids a long time ago.*

Hashtags are not isolated entities, and they could be related to each other in several ways. A possible conceptual relation of the hashtags associated to the Example 1 is shown as a graph in Fig. 1. Since hashtags are involved in a *semantic* network, also the arguments of this example are somehow related according to the intended meaning of the hashtags. For instance, the argument structure $\mathbb{C}$ refers to extraterrestrial life, which sometimes is used as an alternative theory for the mysterious disappearances in the Bermuda Triangle, referred in argument structure $\mathbb{B}$. This relation between $\mathbb{B}$ and $\mathbb{C}$ seems to be weak, since both arguments are supposedly referring to different topics, but there is a conceptual connection which should be somehow captured. Nevertheless, there is an apparently stronger connection between $\mathbb{A}$ and $\mathbb{B}$, since political corruption is

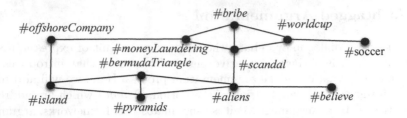

Fig. 1. Connections between hashtags

sometimes related to offshore financial activities, and both arguments seem to be talking about money and illicit issues.

Thus, a notion of proximity between arguments can be considered which is inherited by the distance that exists between the referred topics and the set of hashtags of each argument. It is important to note that an argument may refer to distant, not directly-connected hashtags; for example, an argument $\mathbb{D} = \langle D, \{\#island, \#soccer\} \rangle$ refers to hashtags with no direct link between them, moreover, hashtags in an argument may be not connected at all.

With hashtags as an abstract formalization of argument topics, we are interested in exploring the semantic issues which emerge from probing the abstract notion of *closeness* between arguments. The following definition provides the formal framework for hashtagged argumentation.

Definition 2. *A hashtagged argumentation framework Ω is a tuple $\langle Ht, \mathbb{A}rgs, \mathbb{A}ttacks, Hr \rangle$, where Ht is a finite non-empty set of hashtags, $\mathbb{A}rgs$ is a set of hashtagged arguments on Ht, $\mathbb{A}ttacks \subseteq \mathbb{A}rgs \times \mathbb{A}rgs$, and $Hr \subseteq Ht \times Ht$. We will call* hashcloud *of Ω to the pair $\langle Ht, Hr \rangle$, and will be denoted $\#_\Omega$.*

As stated before, the hashtags in the framework may be connected according to $\#_\Omega$. An edge $(\#\alpha_1, \#\alpha_2) \in Hr$ is an abstract semantic connection between $\#\alpha_1$ and $\#\alpha_2$, representing the "closeness" between the concepts symbolized by $\#\alpha_1$ and $\#\alpha_2$. Other hashtags may not be connected at all, since the hashcloud is not necessarily a connected graph. For example, if hashtags represent words, the relation can be as in a thesauri, an interesting source for building a semantic network. However, hashtags can represent more complex notions than words, such as web pages or bibliographical references and the specific meaning of this link should be stated then.

The set of hashtags $H_\mathbb{A}$ for an argument $\mathbb{A}$ also provides semantic information about the underlying structure of the argument, specially regarding the dispersion of interrelated topics. The definition below borrows three relevant concepts from Graph Theory (see for instance [1,2,5] for the notion of distance in graphs).

Definition 3. *Let Ω be a hashtagged framework, and a set $H \subseteq Ht$ be a finite non-empty set of hashtags. Then: the* eccentricity *of a hashtag in H is the maximum of the distances to all other hashtags in H, according to $\#_\Omega$. If a hashtag is not connected its eccentricity is infinite; the* radius *of H is the minimum eccen-*

tricity of the hashtags in H; and the diameter *of H is the maximum eccentricity of the hashtags in H.*

Note that, if H has a single element then the eccentricity, the radius, and the diameter is zero. In this work, the distance between two hashtags is the number of edges in a shortest path (also called a graph geodesic) connecting them. However, a different interpretation of distance can be used; for example, the cost associated to a shortest path if weighted links are used.

Definition 4. *Let Ω be a hashtagged framework, $\mathbb{A} = \langle A, H_{\mathbb{A}} \rangle$ be a tagged argument structure of Ω. The* radius *and* diameter *of $\mathbb{A}$ is the radius and diameter of $H_{\mathbb{A}}$ respectively.*

The definition above provides an approximation to a certain sense of the *size of an argument*. This is according to the referred topics, and not to the underlying linguistic structure, which is not relevant here given our abstract approach. For instance, a relatively small diameter could indicate that the argument is more *focused*, since it refers to hashtags not very distant to each other. Thus, since different arguments are attached to sets of possible diverse hashtags, a notion of distance *between arguments* emerges. We use the classical definition of metric space in graphs applied to tagged frameworks.

Definition 5. *A* metric *or* distance *function on a set $\mathbb{A}rgs$ is defined as $D_\Omega : \mathbb{A}rgs \times \mathbb{A}rgs \to \Re_0^+$, where for all $\mathbb{A}, \mathbb{B}, \mathbb{C} \in \mathbb{A}rgs$, the following conditions are satisfied: (1) $D_\Omega(\mathbb{A}, \mathbb{B}) \geq 0$ (non-negativity); (2) $D_\Omega(\mathbb{A}, \mathbb{B}) = 0$ iff $\mathbb{A} = \mathbb{B}$ (identity of indiscernibles); (3) $D_\Omega(\mathbb{A}, \mathbb{B}) = D_\Omega(\mathbb{B}, \mathbb{A})$ (symmetry); (4) $D_\Omega(\mathbb{A}, \mathbb{C}) \leq D_\Omega(\mathbb{A}, \mathbb{B}) + D_\Omega(\mathbb{B}, \mathbb{C})$ (triangle inequality); and (5) $0 \leq D_\Omega(\mathbb{A}, \mathbb{B}) \leq diameter(H_{\mathcal{A}} \cup H_{\mathcal{B}})$ (arguments boundaries).*

The metric function is based on the topology of the hashcloud considering only hashtags of the involved arguments. The conditions presented in Definition 5 are denoting intuitive notions about the concept of distance. On one hand, the distance between different hashtags is positive, and the distance from α to β is the same as the distance from β to α. On another hand, the triangle inequality means that the distance from α to δ via β is at least as great as from α to δ directly. Furthermore, any notion of hashtagged distance between arguments is bounded by the minimal distance possible between two hashtags and the diameter of the set of hashtags of both arguments. Then, two arguments cannot be closer than the minimal distance between their hashtags, nor could be farther than their maximally distant hashtags. Several notions of distance may be obtained; for example, two possible definitions of $D_\Omega(\mathbb{A}, \mathbb{B})$ where $\mathbb{A} = \langle A, H_{\mathbb{A}} \rangle$ and $\mathbb{B} = \langle B, H_{\mathbb{B}} \rangle$ are:

- $D_\Omega(\mathbb{A}, \mathbb{B}) = min(dist(\#a, \#b))$ where $\#a$ and $\#b$ are hashtags of $\mathbb{A}$ and $\mathbb{B}$ respectively. Here, the distance is zero if both arguments share at least one hashtag.

- $D_\Omega(\mathbb{A}, \mathbb{B}) = average(dist(cent(\mathbb{A}), cent(\mathbb{B})))$, where $cent(\mathbb{X})$ is the set of central hashtags in $\mathbb{X}$. A hashtag α is a *central* hashtag in $\mathbb{X}$ if eccentricity(α) = radius($\mathbb{X}$). The average distance between central hashtags is used.

In the last case, common hashtags are ignored and the distance between the rest is taken into account. Note that the pair $(\mathbb{A}rgs, D_\Omega)$ associated to the tagged framework Ω denotes a metric space. This is sound since we are defining a notion of distance between arguments.

The notion of proximity can be applied to the basic element of admissibility semantics: the attack and defense of arguments. On one hand, an attack produced by an argument $\mathbb{A}$ will be considered in a dialogue or debate if their topics are close to those referred by the attacked arguments, since closer attackers are relevant in sensitive context semantics. On another hand, a defender $\mathbb{C}$ of an argument $\mathbb{A}$ closer to $\mathbb{A}$ is desirable, since what is stated in $\mathbb{A}$ can be defended by using knowledge *around* the same topics presented by $\mathbb{A}$. Argument $\mathbb{C}$ may not be using *exactly* the same topics but, according to the hashtags involved, the knowledge used to construct this supporter argument is not distant to the knowledge used to construct $\mathbb{A}$.

In summary, the hashcloud corresponding to a tagged argumentation framework is the semantic map of topics addressed by any argument in the framework. In the example of Sect. 1, the arguments of P_2 and P_3 are intuitively closer to each other than the argument of P_4. In a dialogue or debate it is very important to stay focused around a set of topics, avoiding the introduction of a lateral issue or *red herring*; in such a case, arguments like the one exposed by P_4 may not be taken into account. This is because the potential counterarguments must attack the reasons or conclusions exposed by P_4, opening a new discussion that will be branching out. In this case, the interest of foreign nations, which is not closely related to the discussion on scientific evidence concerning global warming. If this is admitted, the dialectical analysis starts to diverge. In these type of *focused* dialogues, an off-topic argument introduces "noise" in the dialectical process and could be discarded. Hence, proximity is an important feature in defining rational positions of argument acceptance.

3   Proximity-Based Semantics

The semantic notions developed for abstract argumentation frameworks AF (see for more detail [4]), can be applied to hashtagged argumentation because arguments in a Dung's framework can be thought as black-boxed tagged arguments structures. However, the presence of hashtags leads to proximity-based evaluations of argument extensions. First, we need to introduce a few definitions.

Definition 6. *Let* S *be a set of hastagged arguments. The set of all hashtag used in* S *is defined as* $ht(S) = \{\#\alpha \mid \#\alpha \in H_\mathcal{A}, \langle \mathbb{A}, H_\mathcal{A} \rangle \in S\}$.

The set $ht(S)$ simply captures all the topics addressed in a particular set of arguments. Thus, this set inherits distance metrics regarding the corresponding hashcloud. The diameter of an extension is an indication of how widespread is the set regarding the topics involved in the discussion; in this sense, it is interesting to characterize sets of arguments devoid of unrelated or distant topics. Here, we are focused in the reinterpretation of Dung's semantic formalisms by introducing the consideration of the "proximity" between arguments. By starting with the basic semantic concept of admissibility semantics, the notion of argument acceptability can be refined to capture the idea that, for any argument, a *closer attacker* is more relevant or offensive over a more distant one, and a *closer defender* is more preferable or strong over a more distant one. Naturally, this represents a more restricted notion of attack and defense since some genuine attackers or defenders could be disregarded due to their distance to the focus. Consequently, an admissible set which contains arguments and their closer defenders will be more focused on certain topics.

Definition 7. *Let $\Omega = \langle Ht, \mathbb{A}rgs, \mathbb{A}ttacks, Hr \rangle$ be a hashtagged framework, D_Ω be a metric function, and $\epsilon \in \Re_0^+$ be a threshold. Then:*

- *A set $S \subseteq \mathbb{A}rgs$ is said to be ϵ-conflict free if there are no hashtagged arguments $\mathbb{A}, \mathbb{B} \in S$ such that $\mathbb{B}$ attacks $\mathbb{A}$ and $D_\Omega(\mathbb{A}, \mathbb{B}) \leq \epsilon$.*
- *A hashtagged argument $\mathbb{A} \in \mathbb{A}rgs$ is ϵ-acceptable with respect to S if for every argument $\mathbb{B} \in \mathbb{A}rgs$, if $\mathbb{B}$ attacks $\mathbb{A}$ then there is a hashtagged argument $\mathbb{C} \in S$ such that $D_\Omega(\mathbb{A}, \mathbb{C}) \leq \epsilon$, $D_\Omega(\mathbb{C}, \mathbb{B}) \leq \epsilon$ and $\mathbb{C}$ attacks $\mathbb{B}$.*
- *S is said to be ϵ-admissible if every hashtagged argument in S is ϵ-acceptable with respect to S.*

Note that under this interpretation of "defense and attack by proximity", a potential defender or attacker argument that is beyond that threshold will not be considered as such.

As usual in abstract argumentation, Definition 7 leads to different notions providing proximity-based interpretations of classical admissibility.

Definition 8. *Let $\Omega = \langle Ht, \mathbb{A}rgs, \mathbb{A}ttacks, Hr \rangle$, be a hashtagged framework, with a metric function D_Ω, and threshold $\epsilon \in \Re_0$. Then:*

- *An ϵ-admissible set S is a ϵ-complete extension iff S contains each argument that is ϵ-acceptable with respect to S.*
- *A set $S \subseteq \mathbb{A}rgs$ is the ϵ-grounded extension of Ω iff S is a $\subseteq$-minimal ϵ-complete extension.*
- *A set $S \subseteq \mathbb{A}rgs$ is an ϵ-preferred extension of Ω iff S is a $\subseteq$-maximal ϵ-complete extension.*
- *A set $S \subseteq \mathbb{A}rgs$ is an ϵ-stable extension of Ω iff S is an ϵ-conflict free set and S attacks every argument in $\mathbb{A}rgs \setminus S$ such that $D_\Omega(\mathbb{A}, \mathbb{B}) \leq \epsilon$ where $\mathbb{A} \in S$ and $\mathbb{B} \in \mathbb{A}rgs \setminus S$.*

Note that the proximity approach to admissibility discards argument defenders and attackers which are not close enough to the attacked argument; however, as expected, if the proximity threshold is big enough, Dung's admissibility and *ϵ-admissibility* coincide.

Proposition 1. *Let $\Omega = \langle Ht, \mathbb{A}rgs, \mathbb{A}ttacks, Hr \rangle$ be a hashtagged framework, and $\epsilon \in \Re$ be a proximity threshold. If the threshold $\epsilon \geq diameter(Ht)$ then it holds that every ϵ-{admissible, complete, grounded, preferred, stable} extension is an {admissible, complete, grounded, preferred, stable} extension respectively.*

In classical argumentation, the grounded extension is the skeptical position of acceptance. It is unique for the entire framework. In our proposal, since the notion of defense is bounded to a threshold ϵ, the skeptical position is attached to ϵ. Different thresholds lead to different ϵ-grounded extensions. However, as in classical frameworks the extension always exists.

Proposition 2. *Let $\Omega = \langle Ht, \mathbb{A}rgs, \mathbb{A}ttacks, Hr \rangle$ be a hashtagged framework, D_Ω be a proximity function, and $\epsilon \in \Re$ be a threshold. Then, considering a fixed threshold ϵ, there always exists a unique ϵ-grounded extension.*

Since hashtagged argumentation frameworks are an extension of Dung's frameworks, if hashtags information is discarded, a classical Dung's framework emerges. Topologically, classical and proximity semantics should be related, i.e., there exists a link between proximity-based semantics and its corresponding abstract framework counterpart, remarking that the former is a refinement of the latter. This connection will be explored in future works.

4   Conclusions and Future Works

We have presented an extension of Dung's abstract argumentation frameworks that adds a set of interrelated topics that will be used to decorate arguments. These topics reflect what the arguments are addressing and provide a supporting structure for the analysis of multi-topic argumentation; using this novel framework, new argumentation semantics are formalized. A notion of distance between arguments which is derived from the attached topics is introduced and this distance is used for new, proximity-based semantic elaborations. The central aspects in these semantics is the initial idea that an argument should be defended by arguments closely related to the same addressed topics. The relation between these new semantic formalizations and the classical admissibility semantics was analyzed. Several directions for future work are open; new semantics can be defined taking the *dispersion* of arguments into account, an aspect that was not fully considered in the proposals contained in this work but it is interesting since it affects the diameter of the extensions. Hence, although a particular semantic may introduce several extension sets (such as preferred semantics), a quality among them may be distinguished according to centrality of debate. It is our intuition that these notions may rise a new family of proximity-based semantics. We are also interested in applying information retrieval concepts in order to establish the importance of arguments according to its own set of hashtags in a given hashcloud. This will help to answer some interesting semantic questions such as whether some topics in a given set S are more *important* than others. If this is the case, does it makes sense to defeat an important argument by using an almost non-relevant argument? Finally, as usual when introducing new argumentation semantics, we are interested in the computational complexity behind these novel extensions. For instance, the focused extension presented here is a formalism intended to achieve completeness while considering proximity between arguments, which requires an evaluation of distances within the set.

Acknowledgments. This work has been partially supported by EU H2020 research and innovation programme under the Marie Sklodowska-Curie grant agreement No. 690974 for the project MIREL: MIning and REasoning with Legal texts, and by funds provided by CONICET, Universidad Nacional del Sur and Universidad Nacional de Santiago del Estero, Argentina.

References

1. Bondy, A., Murty, U.S.R.: Graph Theory. Graduate Texts in Mathematics, 3rd edn. Springer-Verlag, New York (2008)
2. Buckley, F., Harary, F.: Distance in Graphs. Addison-Wesley Publishing Company Advanced Book Program, Redwood (1990)
3. Budán, M.C.D., Simari, G.I., Viglizzo, I., Simari, G.R.: An approach to characterize graded entailment of arguments through a label-based framework. Int. J. Approximate Reasoning **82**, 242–269 (2016)
4. Dung, P.M.: On the acceptability of arguments and its fundamental role in non-monotonic reasoning and logic programming and n-person games. Artif. Intell. **77**, 321–357 (1995)
5. Goddard, W., Oellermann, O.R.: Distance in graphs. In: Dehmer, M. (ed.) Structural Analysis of Complex Networks, Chapter 3, pp. 49–72. Birkhäuser Basel, Boston (2011)
6. Pardo, P., Godo, L.: t-DeLP: an argumentation-based temporal defeasible logic programming framework. Ann. Math. Artif. Intell. **69**(1), 3–35 (2013)
7. Prakken,H.: A study of accrual of arguments, with applications to evidential reasoning. In: International conference on Artificial intelligence and law, pp. 85–94. ACM, 2005
8. Visser, W., Hindriks, K.V., Jonker, C.M.: An argumentation framework for qualitative multi-criteria preferences. In: Modgil, S., Oren, N., Toni, F. (eds.) TAFA 2011. LNCS, vol. 7132, pp. 85–98. Springer, Heidelberg (2012). doi:10.1007/978-3-642-29184-5_6

A Multi-agent Proposal for Efficient Bike-Sharing Usage

C. Diez[1(✉)], V. Sanchez-Anguix[2], J. Palanca[1], V. Julian[1], and A. Giret[1]

[1] Dpto. Sistemas Informáticos y Computación,
Universitat Politécnica de Valencia, Valencia, Spain
{cardieal,jpalanca,vinglada,agiret}@dsic.upv.es
[2] School of Computing, Electronics, and Maths, Coventry University, Coventry, UK
ac0872@coventry.ac.uk
http://www.gti-ia.upv.es

Abstract. Urban transportation systems have received a special interest in the last few years due to the necessity to reduce congestion, air pollution and acoustic contamination in today's cities. Bike sharing systems have been proposed as an interesting solution to deal with these problems. Nevertheless, shared vehicle schemes also arise problems that must be addressed such as the vehicle distribution along time and across space in the city. Differently to classic approaches, we propose the architecture for a muti-agent system that tries to improve the efficiency of bike sharing systems by introducing user-driven balancing in the loop. The rationale is that of persuading users to slightly deviate from their origins/destinations by providing appropriate arguments and incentives, while optimizing the overall balance of the system. In this paper we present two of the proposed system's modules. The first will allow us to predict bike demand in different stations. The second will score stations and alternative routes. This modules will be used to predict the most appropriate offers for users and try to persuade them.

Keywords: Multi-agent systems · Vehicle sharing systems

1 Introduction

Transportation systems have become one of the most important areas of application for artificial intelligence paradigms [3,4,11,13]. There are several reasons behind this trend such as the scale of the problem, the need to optimize a pool of limited resources, or the necessity to include models of human behavior in the loop. Among all the available transportation systems, urban transportation systems have received a special interest, boosted by public and government initiatives. With an increasing population in urban areas comes a rise for the need of urban transportation [7]. This rise is problematic as it may lead to problems such as congestion, air pollution, investment into expensive infrastructures, and so forth [7]. In many cases, the investment is two-sided as it also potentially involves citizens acquiring new transportation vehicles for individual use. Hence,

© Springer International Publishing AG 2017
B. An et al. (Eds.): PRIMA 2017, LNAI 10621, pp. 468–476, 2017.
https://doi.org/10.1007/978-3-319-69131-2_29

optimizing current resources has become an area of great interest for both the public and the private transportation sector.

Shared vehicle schemes, such as bike or car sharing systems, have been proposed as a solution to both optimize the number of existing vehicles, traffic, and as a mean of contributing to a cleaner environment. Despite its advantages, shared vehicle schemes also arise other problems that must be addressed. For instance, one of the problems with bike sharing systems is the bike distribution along time, creating some areas that agglutinate most of the bikes, thus making parking very difficult, and some areas lacking bikes, thus making it very difficult to borrow a bike from that location. In the specific case of bike sharing systems, this can lead to potential dissatisfaction of users, which in the end may result in loss of service subscribers, and an increase in the use of non-shared vehicles like personal cars. Of course, that is usually translated into several problems including traffic jams, rise in pollution problems, or even less healthy citizens due to a more sedentary form of transportation. Moreover, bike sharing providers often need to balance bikes across stations by using trucks or other types of motorized transportation. This incurs in an additional cost for the service provider, as well as more traffic if balance is not done properly.

The problem of optimizing bike sharing systems' resources (i.e., bikes, stations, transportation trucks) has caught the attention of researchers [9,10,14,15], who have proposed many architectures and algorithms that allow service providers to both predict the incoming/outgoing demand from bike sharing stations, as well as educated balancing strategies that optimize the service provider's resources. All of these proposals are pieces of a global strategy that aims to smartly balance bikes according to future demand. All of the actions and strategies are applied from a service provider perspective, while taking the user behavior as granted. This means that resources are optimized by modeling the user behavior, and accepting that behavior as an external effect that will change the system. As a result, actions aiming at balancing the state of the system are solely carried out by the service provider. This paper takes a slightly different point of view to this problem. What if, instead of taking the user behavior for granted, we attempt to slightly modify the user's planned trip for optimizing the overall bike sharing system?

The paper defines the architecture of a multi-agent system aimed at improving the efficiency of bike sharing system by introducing user-driven balancing in the loop. While predicting the future demand and smartly balancing bikes across stations are seen as important components of the system, we also envision the inclusion of a negotiation and argumentation [6,12] module that aims to slightly modify the behavior of users.

2   A General MAS Proposal for Bike Sharing

As mentioned in Sect. 1, our aim is that of providing a MAS system for efficiently managing resources (i.e., bikes, stations, transportation trucks, etc.) in bike-sharing systems. The problem of optimizing bike-sharing systems is that of making sure that bikes are available in stations when users decide to start their trips, and parking positions are available when users reach their destinations. Due to the nature of cities and their lifestyle, bikes and parking positions become unequally distributed across stations. In order to cope with that situation, the service provider needs to redistribute bikes making use of transportation trucks. However, late distribution of bikes may end up in user dissatisfaction. Therefore, the real challenge for service providers is predicting future demand to redistribute bikes accordingly.

Balance operations carried out by the service provider will always be an integral part of bike sharing system, specially for preparing for rush hour. However, in some scenarios we may be able to employ users as balancing agents if individuals are persuaded to slightly deviate[1] from their planned destination/origin. The reasons by which these users may be persuaded vary and include reasons such as the fact that their destination station may be full at arrival, the adoption of healthier habits, or the inclusion of small rewards (e.g., extra rental minutes, badges, lotteries, etc.). Small deviations can act in benefit of the system by carrying out pre/after rush hour balancing, and acting as real time balance for unplanned demands.

In order to tackle this scenario, we propose a multi-agent based architecture. The proposed system will run on top of *SURF* [5], an agent support framework for open fleet management. The work we are presenting in this paper is part of a broader research project, in which the main goal is to provide a set of tools and applications that foster the efficient and sustainable management of urban

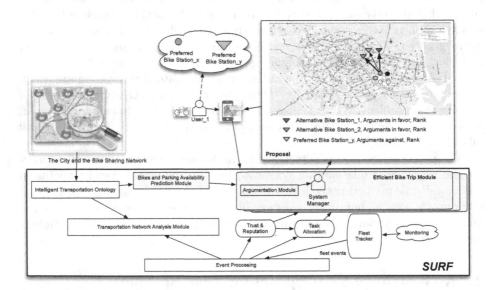

Fig. 1. General view of the proposed MAS architecture

---

[1] We would never expect drastic deviations.

fleets. One of such applications is the one presented in [8] for last mile delivery in urban areas.

SURF was designed to support general urban transportation fleets, and it provides modules for most general and shared functionalities. As a result, part of the proposed architecture is supported by these general modules. However, we need to include some extra modules to support some of the particular functionalities of this bike sharing system. Figure 1 shows the general view of the proposed architecture, the gray components being the modules specially designed for the application of bike sharing, and the other modules being part of the services and utilities provided by *SURF* for open fleet management. The two main components that distinguish our approach to bike sharing are: **The Efficient Bike Trip Module** and the **Bikes and Parking Availability Prediction Module**.

Both the **Bikes and Parking Availability Prediction Module** and the **Efficient Bike Trip Module** will support how users' trips are managed. In order to understand the logic behind the module, let us focus on an example:

1. $User_1$ agent wants to ride from $PreferredBikeStation_x$ to $Preferred$ $BikeStation_y$. The user employs a mobile app to query the availability of bikes at the origin station, and the availability of slots in the destination station.
2. The request is received by the System Manager agent, and then it is analyzed to find out the availability by the time $User_1$ agent may arrive to both preferred origin and destination stations. The expected times are calculated taking into consideration the current GPS location of $User_1$ agent, the possible route that leads to the origin station, the possible route that leads to the destination station, and all the information from the Intelligent Transportation Ontology from SURF concerning traffic, traffic lights, weather, and so forth.
3. With this time frame the System Manager agent requests to the **Bikes and Parking Availability Prediction Module** an estimation for the number of free bikes at $PreferredBikeStation_x$ by the expected departure time. At the same time, the System Manager agent also requests an estimation for the number of free parking slots at $PreferredBikeStation_y$ by the expected arrival time.
4. The prediction module also computes whether or not $PreferredBike$ $Station_x$ or $PreferredBikeStation_y$ are likely to suffer from bikes/slots shortage in the short/medium term. In that case, the prediction module retrieves a set of available nearby stations to $PreferredBikeStation_x$ and a set of available nearby stations to $PreferredBikeStation_y$. If they are not likely to suffer from bikes/slots shortage in the short term, then they are also suggested to the System Manager agent.
5. The System Manager agent collects the suggestions from the **Bikes and Parking Availability Prediction Module** and sends those suggestions to the **Efficient Bike Trip Module**. Within this module, the alternatives for both origin and destination are analyzed. The module will select pairs of origin and destination stations, along with arguments or incentives in favor of the slight trip change.

6. The System Manager agent receives the offers from the **Efficient Bike Trip Module** and presents them to the user, who finally selects the one that he/she considers more appealing.

In this paper, we introduce the **Bikes and Parking Availability Prediction Module** and on the **Efficient Bike Trip Module**. The **Bikes and Parking Availability Prediction Module** will predict the occupation of the stations using a machine learning model that will be trained to solved the regression problem. The features that will be used in order to achieve that in our case study are discussed on Sect. 3. The predictions for the user preferred stations, and the predictions for alternative routes if needed, will be passed to the **Efficient Bike Trip Module**. This module, using the mentioned predictions will score the stations and the alternative routes taking into account the objective of balancing the stations. This scores, and the user's behavior model provided by the trust and reputation module, will be used to generate the arguments or incentives for the user.

3   Case Study: Valencia's Bike Sharing System

The aforementioned architecture is abstract and general, making it applicable to a wide range of urban systems and cities. Nevertheless, as part of the verification of the architecture, our intention is to test the proposed architecture in some realistic scenarios. As an on-going work we focus on the future application of the architecture to Valencia's bike sharing system. The reasons to focus on this domain are varied: access to domain expertise, possibility of linking the bike sharing system with other urban transportation methods, access to data, and the scale of the proposed system.

Valencia's population is close to 800,000 inhabitants, and it exceeds the 1.5 million inhabitants when considering its metropolitan area [1]. This makes Valencia a large/medium-sized city, which makes it appropriate for the verification of our architecture. On top of that, its flat landscape and availability of dedicated bike lanes foster the use of bikes as an urban transportation method. Valencia's bike sharing system consists of 276 bike stations whose capacity varies between 14 and 50 slots, with an average of 20 slots per station. Therefore, there are 5,500 parking slots for a total of 2,750 bikes available to users. The operations of the bike sharing system started in 2011, rapidly gaining around 100.000 subscribers in it's first two years. In the next two years, as seen in most of these bike sharing systems, the number of user subscriptions dropped and stabilized around 45,000 users [2].

We have collected open access data from all the stations in Valencia[2], containing information about the number of slots and bikes available at each station. This information is collected periodically with a frequency ranging from one to ten minutes[3]. In total, we have collected 617 days of activity starting from 26th

---

[2] http://gobiernoabierto.valencia.es/en/.

[3] Sometimes technical issues and systems overload preclude from sampling at the same frequency.

September 2014 to 15th February 2017. This results in a total of 62,130,711 records containing information about the occupation of a station in a particular point in time.

As suggested by [9], weather conditions may influence the demand for bike sharing systems. As a consequence, we collected information about the weather conditions[4] in Valencia, including attributes such as temperature, rainfall and wind speed. The information is collected with a granularity of 30 min and then merged with the station data. In total, we have collected 1141 days of weather data starting from 1st January 2014 to 15th February 2017.

We merged together both data sources, resulting in a single dataset whose samples contained information about the status of the station and weather conditions at a certain timestamp. With this dataset, we endeavored to analyze what variables could help us with the task of predicting bike usage in our case study.

Firstly, we attempted to analyze whether or not the day of the week could influence bike demand. Our initial hypothesis was that the day of the week would influence how people move around the city. During the week, stations in popular work areas are most likely to receive incoming and outgoing traffic than during the weekend. Similarly, leisure areas are more likely to receive traffic during the weekend. With that goal in mind, we plotted the average number of available bikes for each day of the week. In Fig. 2 (a), it can be appreciated that our reasoning was correct. The figure shows the average number of available bikes for *UPV Informática*, one of the most transited bike stations due to its proximity to one of the largest universities in the city. It is shown that, during the weekend, barely no bikes are available at the station, while the rest of the week the station acts like a sink. This behavior was aligned with common sense, as universities tend to be more active on the weekdays. Although not shown in the graph, we could observe this and similar patterns in other stations throughout the city.

Then we proceeded to analyze the influence of temperature on bike demand. Our initial hypothesis was that colder and extremely warm days are less propitious for riding bikes, specially in days when environmental conditions are harsher. Those days, individuals are most likely to refrain from using the bike sharing system and use other transportation methods that are more sheltered from the outside conditions. With that idea in mind, we plotted the average number of available bikes at *UPV Informática* during the daytime. Figure 2 (b) shows our initial hypothesis. Before analyzing the graph, one must consider that this station usually acts as a sink during the daytime. Therefore, reduced demand is translated into less bikes arriving to the station. This is exactly what is shown in the figure. In colder days, demand tends to be minimum, and it gradually increases as temperature becomes more comfortable. There is again another drop in the demand when days become hotter. Despite not being shown in the graph, we could observe this behavior in other stations throughout the city.

---

[4] https://www.wunderground.com/.

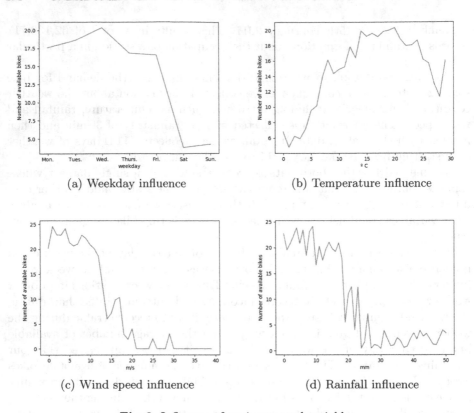

(a) Weekday influence

(b) Temperature influence

(c) Wind speed influence

(d) Rainfall influence

Fig. 2. Influence of environmental variables

Our rationale for the wind speed was similar. Stronger winds make it difficult to handle bikes, with even the risk of falling off in case of a very strong gust of wind. Hence, users may be more hesitant to use the bike sharing system in those particular days. We plotted a similar graphic to describe the relation between the bike demand and the wind speed. Figure 2 (c) shows the relationship between the average number of bikes at *UPV Informática* during the daytime for different ranges of wind speed. As we expected, bike demand in the station is reduced as the wind speed increases, supporting our initial guess. Again, we found a similar pattern in other stations.

Following our thoughts regarding the effect of wind speed on bike demand, we made a similar conjecture with regards to rainfall precipitation. When rain is absent, users should employ the system as usual. However, as rain becomes more prominent, demand should decrease since users will feel less comfortable riding a bike. In extreme conditions, rain may make the ground slippery, thus making bike riding a dangerous activity. In Fig. 2 (d) the average number of available bikes at *UPV Informática* during daytime is shown for different levels of precipitation. Our rationale was again supported by data. For no or light rain the station's demand is unaffected, but less bikes tend to arrive (thus, reducing demand) when the rain becomes heavier.

All of these insights were taken into consideration when deciding what variables should be part of the final dataset that will be used for training our proposed prediction module. More specifically, the records in the resulting dataset consisted of a station id, a timestamp decomposed into year, month, day, hour, minute, second, and weekday of the measurement, temperature, rainfall precipitation, wind speed, and the number of free parking slots and bikes available in the station.

4   Conclusions

This paper has presented a multi-agent system architecture to improve the efficiency of bike sharing systems. The main novelty of the approach comes from the introduction of user-driven balancing in the loop: attempting to persuade users to slightly deviate from their origin/destination stations, and balancing the system in the process. We expect that this architecture will help to provide a better service, increase user satisfaction, and optimize the management of the bike network by reducing the number of balancing operations carried out by the service providers' trucks.

The proposed architecture has two main components: an *efficient bike trip module* and a *bikes and parking availability prediction module*. The prediction module will use a machine learning approach to estimate the foreseen bike station status based on real historic data of a given bike sharing service. The output of this module will be used by the *efficient bike trip module* to score the stations and the alternative routes. The module final function is to persuade the user to use the most appropriate stations according to the user preferences and the system balancing.

As ongoing work, the *bikes and parking availability prediction module* and the *efficient bike trip module* are being built to be included in the bike sharing system of the city of Valencia (Spain). Moreover, the proposed approach will be integrated with other applications running on top of the *SURF* framework, such as [8].

References

1. Ayuntamiento de valencia: Estadisticas del area metropolitana. https://www.valencia.es. Accessed 6 Dec 2017
2. Valenbisi gana usuarios. http://www.levante-emv.com/valencia/2017/04/29/valenbisi-gana-usuarios-primera-vez/1560137.html. Accessed 6 Dec 2017
3. Bast, H., Delling, D., Goldberg, A., Müller-Hannemann, M., Pajor, T., Sanders, P., Wagner, D., Werneck, R.F.: Route planning in transportation networks. In: Kliemann, L., Sanders, P. (eds.) Algorithm Engineering. LNCS, vol. 9220, pp. 19–80. Springer, Cham (2016). doi:10.1007/978-3-319-49487-6_2
4. Bazzan, A.L., Klügl, F.: A review on agent-based technology for traffic and transportation. Knowl. Eng. Rev. **29**(03), 375–403 (2014)

5. Billhardt, H., Fernández, A., Lujak, M., Ossowski, S., Julián, V., De Paz, J.F., Hernández, J.Z.: Towards smart open dynamic fleets. In: Rovatsos, M., Vouros, G., Julian, V. (eds.) EUMAS/AT -2015. LNCS, vol. 9571, pp. 410–424. Springer, Cham (2016). doi:10.1007/978-3-319-33509-4_32

6. Costa, A., Heras, S., Palanca, J., Jordán, J., Novais, P., Julián, V.: Argumentation schemes for events suggestion in an e-Health platform. In: de Vries, P.W., Oinas-Kukkonen, H., Siemons, L., Beerlage-de Jong, N., van Gemert-Pijnen, L. (eds.) PERSUASIVE 2017. LNCS, vol. 10171, pp. 17–30. Springer, Cham (2017). doi:10.1007/978-3-319-55134-0_2

7. Farahani, R.Z., Miandoabchi, E., Szeto, W., Rashidi, H.: A review of urban transportation network design problems. Eur. J. Oper. Re. **229**(2), 281–302 (2013). http://www.sciencedirect.com/science/article/pii/S0377221713000106

8. Giret, A., Carrascosa, C., Julian, V., Rebollo, M.: A crowdsourcing approach for last mile delivery. Transp. Res. Part C Emerg. Technol. (2017). in press

9. Kull, M., Ferri, C., Martínez-Usó, A.: Bike rental and weather data across dozens of cities. In: ICML 2015 Workshop on Demand Forecasting (2015)

10. O'Mahony, E., Shmoys, D.B.: Data analysis and optimization for (citi)bike sharing. In: Proceedings of the Twenty-Ninth AAAI Conference on Artificial Intelligence, AAAI 2015, pp. 687–694. AAAI Press (2015). http://dl.acm.org/citation.cfm?id=2887007.2887103

11. Rigas, E.S., Ramchurn, S.D., Bassiliades, N.: Managing electric vehicles in the smart grid using artificial intelligence: a survey. IEEE Trans. Intell. Transp. Syst. **16**(4), 1619–1635 (2015)

12. Sanchez-Anguix, V., Aydogan, R., Julian, V., Jonker, C.: Unanimously acceptable agreements for negotiation teams in unpredictable domains. Electron. Commer. Res. Appl. **13**(4), 243–265 (2014). http://www.sciencedirect.com/science/article/pii/S1567422314000283

13. Satunin, S., Babkin, E.: A multi-agent approach to intelligent transportation systems modeling with combinatorial auctions. Expert Syst. Appl. **41**(15), 6622–6633 (2014)

14. Schuijbroek, J., Hampshire, R., van Hoeve, W.J.: Inventory rebalancing and vehicle routing in bike sharing systems. Eur. J. Oper. Res. **257**(3), 992–1004 (2017)

15. Yoon, J.W., Pinelli, F., Calabrese, F.: Cityride: a predictive bike sharing journey advisor. In: 2012 IEEE 13th International Conference on Mobile Data Management (MDM), pp. 306–311. IEEE (2012)

A Distributed Algorithm for Dynamic Break Scheduling in Emergency Service Fleets

Marin Lujak[1]([⊠]) and Holger Billhardt[2]

[1] IMT Lille Douai, Douai, France
marin.lujak@imt-lille-douai.fr
[2] University Rey Juan Carlos, Madrid, Spain
holger.billhardt@urjc.es

Abstract. The quality of service and efficiency of labour utilization in emergency service fleets, such as police, fire departments, and emergency medical services (EMS), depends, among other things, on the efficiency of work break scheduling. The workload of such fleets usually cannot be forecasted with certainty and its urgency requires an immediate response. However, prolonged focused work periods decrease efficiency with related decline of attention and performance. Therefore, break schedule should be regularly updated as the work shift progresses to allow frequent and sufficiently long time for rest. In this paper, we propose a distributed and dynamic work break scheduling algorithm for crews in emergency service vehicle fleets. Based on the historical intervention data, the algorithm rearranges vehicles' crews' work breaks in a manner considering individual crews' preferences. Moreover, it dynamically reallocates stand-by vehicles for best coverage of a region of interest. We analyze the proposed algorithm and show its performance and efficiency on the EMS use-case.

Keywords: Emergency service · Dynamic break scheduling · Dynamic shift scheduling · Vehicle crew assignment · Service operations scheduling

1 Introduction

Fatigue causes decreased levels of alertness and performance deficits that can have hazardous results on the activities that require high concentration and attention. Its control is especially relevant in the case of emergency vehicle crews (e.g., fire brigades, police, and ambulances) that spend most of their workday in a vehicle addressing critical and constantly changing situations.

Usually, the number of breaks, their start times, and duration are regulated by labor rules. Traditionally, break scheduling is performed off-line, before a work shift begins. However, in the emergency fleet context, the workload of vehicle crews is unknown in advance, i.e., both the arrival rate and the geographical location of emergency events needing assistance is stochastic while the urgency of assistance requires an immediate response. As a result, a predefined break schedule often cannot be accomplished since the attendance of emergency events prevails. It might happen that certain crews may not have taken their assigned

© Springer International Publishing AG 2017
B. An et al. (Eds.): PRIMA 2017, LNAI 10621, pp. 477–485, 2017.
https://doi.org/10.1007/978-3-319-69131-2_30

breaks, which leads to deterioration of attention and performance, or that certain areas are "uncovered" in a certain moment because too many vehicle crews in that area are taking a break.

This is why the breaks of emergency vehicle crews should be dynamically scheduled as the day unrolls and should guarantee frequent and sufficiently long time for rest. This is especially the case in 24-hour emergency shifts where eating and sleeping patterns are altered. Consequently, such emergency systems require efficient decision support for dynamic "on-the-fly" break scheduling.

In this paper, we study the problem of dynamically scheduling breaks for emergency fleet's vehicles such that they do not deteriorate the response time of emergency activity and yet increase the rest time for the fleet's vehicle crews. The considered dynamic break scheduling problem consists of determining which vehicle crews should be scheduled a break for the remaining time periods of the shift based on the workload dynamics and taking into account the coverage of an area of interest by available vehicles and the constraints on the work hours and the number of work breaks for each individual vehicle crew.

For this problem, we propose a distributed dynamic break scheduling algorithm that balances the crews' workload and break-related satisfaction based on the geographical vicinity in a Voronoi diagram. Since vehicles respond to emergency events based on their geographical closeness, we model the interrelations among vehicles in break scheduling and their geographical distribution based on Delanauy triangulation. The motivation for this approach is the requirement on the minimization of arrival time of an emergency vehicle and the intrinsic area of responsability of each of the vehicles based on the closeness to an emergency event in Voronoi diagrams. The objectives are increasing the well-being of the crew members while reducing absenteeism and related costs.

This paper is organized as follows. In Sect. 2, we describe State-of-the-Art practice in break scheduling. In Sect. 3 we formulate the break scheduling problem for dynamically changing work environments. Section 4 presents the proposed dynamic break scheduling algorithm. Section 5 contains a use case example in emergency medical assistance. We draw conclusions in Sect. 6.

2   Preliminaries and Related Work

In practice, work break times are usually fixed around breakfast, lunch, and dinner time. In the case of an incident, the emergency management system applies a First-Come-First-Served (FCFS) strategy and locates the nearest available vehicle of necessary characteristics and dispatches it to assist the incident independently of the past crew's break and workload dynamics and if it is momentarily in a break or not. This approach may induce a delay of up to several minutes in the arrival to incidents, which in critical cases can be hazardous.

As an example, target arrival time of ambulances to out-of-hospital patients in the European Union is set to 15 min. An additional delay, even if counted in minutes can significantly worsen the patients chances for survival. In the simultaneous presence of multiple urgent patients, support for optimized EMS coordination based on real-time information is necessary for efficient patient assistance. In this context, we tackled various issues in our previous work, like dynamic patient assignment and dynamic reallocation of stand-by ambulances [5,6,14], and coordination between ambulances, hospitals and out-of-hospital surgery teams for the assistance of urgent surgery patients [15,16]. However, due to human fatigue, the scheduling of breaks is another crucial element to guarantee efficiency of patient assistance.

A review of the literature on personnel scheduling problems can be found in [3], while the review of rostering problems in specific application areas and the models and algorithms that have been reported in the literature for their solution is presented in [10].

Many works are based on optimizing break schedules in advance. Beer et al. [2] address complex real-world break-scheduling problem for supervisory personnel and present a scheduling system that can help professional planners create high-quality shift plans. The objective is to assign breaks to employees such that various constraints reflecting legal demands or ergonomic criteria are satisfied and staffing requirement violations are minimised. Similarly, Di Gaspero et al. [9] also consider the problem of scheduling breaks that fulfill different constraints about their location and lengths, and Musliu et al. in [21] propose a memetic algorithm for the assignment of breaks. Rekik et al. in [19] consider a break scheduling problem that includes different forms of flexibility in terms of shift starting times, break lengths and break placement. Huisman et al. in [11] and Mesquita et al. in [18] present different models and algorithms for the integrated vehicle and crew scheduling problem, where crews can be assigned to different vehicles. In their algorithms, they take into account several complicating constraints corresponding to workload regulations for crews.

Many service systems display non-stationary demand: the number of customers fluctuates over time according to a stochastic though to some extent predictable pattern. Crew work schedules are typically created several days or weeks in advance. However, after schedules are created, staffing managers receive additional information that can affect forecasted workload and resource availability. In [8], Defraeye and Van Nieuwenhuyse provide state-of-the-art overview of research in the period 1991–2013 on personnel staffing and scheduling approaches for systems with a stochastic demand with a time-varying rate.

In [17], Mehrotra et al. develop a flexible heuristic framework for call center managers to make intra-day resource adjustment decisions that take into account updated call forecasts, updated agent requirements, existing agent schedules, agents' schedule flexibility, and associated incremental labor costs. In [12], Hur et al. define the modification between available worker capacity and the actual demand in a certain period as the real-time work schedule adjustment decision. They propose mathematical formulations and develop efficient heuristic approaches for this decision. Moreover, they evaluate the effectiveness of these heuristics in terms of profit. Regarding the call center scenario that concerns only uncertain time-varying customer demand, Bhandari et al. in [4] and Robbins and Harrison in [20] deal with the problem of reducing staff costs while maintaining an acceptable level of customer service. In order to cost-effectively satisfy their service level goals in the face of this uncertainty, call centers may employ a certain number of permanent operators, and a number of temporary operators who provide service only when the call center is busy. This gives the call center manager the flexibility of dynamically adjusting the number of operators providing service in response to the time-varying demand.

As presented, break scheduling is a very researched area with off-line mathematical models using efficient optimal or heuristic algorithmic approaches that compute the schedules in advance before an actual shift begins. However, to the best of our knowledge, none of the related works tackles the issue of equity among vehicles in "on-the-fly" break scheduling in emergency service fleets with unpredictable workload dynamics. As a result, following the State-of-the-Art approaches, it can happen that emergency vehicles positioned close to incidents do not take a break while the vehicles away from the incidents have extended break periods each work day.

3   Dynamic Break Scheduling Problem

We study the problem of break scheduling in a dynamic emergency service fleet context with a time- and location-varying (stochastic) incidence demand that has to be assisted within a given maximum allowed arrival time τ_{max}.

Considering a time horizon made of T break periods $1, \ldots, T$, given is a set of n collaborative agents $A = \{a_1, \ldots, a_n\}$ representing a fleet of capacitated identical vehicles with assigned in-vehicle crews. By a break period, we consider a minimum time period in which each break can be assigned and performed without interruption. For example, if a break period is 30 min, then a break of 1 hour could be assigned as 2 consecutive break periods of 30 min.

The vehicle-crew agents can refer to, e.g., ambulances, police cars, and fire trucks that mutually coordinate to assist events appearing in the region (incidents). Moreover, they are positioned, w.l.o.g., in a 2D square environment $Env = [0, l]^2 \subset \mathbf{R}^2$ of side length $l > 0$.

We assume that each agent $a \in A$ knows the position $p_a(t)$ (through GPS) and state $s_a(t)$ of itself and of all the fleet at every time $t \in T$. Possible states are: *idle* - a vehicle is waiting for new incidents; *unassigned idle* - an idle vehicle that has requested a break for the present period but has not yet been assigned one; *on break* - presently on a break; and *occupied* vehicles that are currently attending an incident. Furthermore, we assume that each agent has an ordered break preference set $R_a(t)$ for remaining work break periods $t \in T$ of the shift.

At every time period $t \in T$, *idle* vehicles are considered for assistance of pending incidents. From the fleet's perspective, the objective is to schedule breaks such that there are always enough idle vehicles in each area to assure the coverage of upcoming incidents and to reduce possible break interruptions. However, if the emergency situation requires it, a vehicle currently *on break* may also be called to assist an incident. Then, its break period is interrupted and, after attending an incident, its state changes to *unassigned idle* - waiting for a new break assignment. Moreover, a crew is assumed to be working at any time when not *on break*. From the individual vehicle's crew point of view, the breaks should be scheduled considering both its personal balance between its workload and breaks, and the global balance among all the fleet's vehicle-crew agents $a \in A$. Additionally, the break scheduling approach should update the break schedule rapidly and regularly in real-time considering equity regarding the workload of vehicles' crews and the satisfaction with the dynamics of the work breaks so far.

4   Dynamic Break Scheduling Approach

Since we search for an equitable approach to balance the workload and breaks individually and among the emergency fleet's crews and to keep track of their performance, we base our approach on the concept of satisfaction with past and present break dynamics. Satisfaction of an agent $a \in A$ at a given time $t \in T$ is made of three components:

$S_a^p(t)$: **satisfaction with meeting agent's break preferences** if it has been assigned a break at time t:

$$S_a^p(t) = 1 - \frac{N_{ord}(t) - 1}{T}, \tag{1}$$

where $N_{ord}(t)$ is the rank of the assigned break period t in ordered break preference set $R_a(t)$. If no break assignment at time t, $S_a^p(t) = 1$.

$S_a^w(t)$: **satisfaction with agent a's workload** in relation to the average workload of the rest of the fleet:

$$S_a^w(t) = \frac{\Delta\tau_{fl}^{wl}(t)}{\Delta\tau_a^{wl}(t)}, \tag{2}$$

where $\Delta\tau_a^{wl}(t) > 0$ is the duration agent a has worked so far (in the periods 1 to t, both inclusive) and $\Delta\tau_{fl}^{wl}(t) = \left(\sum_{a_i \in A \setminus \{a\}} \Delta\tau_{a_i}^{wl}(t)\right)/(|A| - 1)$.

$S_a^i(t)$: **satisfaction with break interruptions**:

$$S_a^i(t) = \frac{\Delta\tau_a^{wb}(t)}{\Delta\tau_{fl}^{wb}}, \tag{3}$$

where $\Delta\tau_a^{wb}(t)$ is the actual duration of agent a's breaks taken up to time t and $\Delta\tau_{fl}^{wb}$ is the given predefined total duration of the brakes.

All three satisfaction components $S_a^x(t)$, with $x \in \{p, w, i\}$ are accumulated over time with $S_a^x := w_x \cdot S_a^x(t) + (1 - w_x) \cdot S_a^x(t - 1)$, where $w_x \in [0, 1]$ are weights given to the present values with regard to the previous values.

Finally, the overall satisfaction S_a of each agent $a \in A$ is then calculated by $S_a = \sqrt[3]{S_a^p \cdot S_a^w \cdot S_a^i}$. We choose geometric mean for calculating S_a, since it balances the values among the three presented break satisfactions in a more strict way than the arithmetic mean value. Specifically, it is sufficient that at least one value is zero, for the whole term to have a zero value.

4.1   Break Scheduling Using Delaunay Triangulation

We use Delaunay Triangulation (DT) to constrain a break schedule of each vehicle crew in respect to the rest of the fleet. DT can be presented by a connected graph $G = (A, E)$ made of a set A of nodes representing vehicle crew agents and a set E of DT edges connecting minimum distance adjacent nodes. Neighbors of each agent $a \in A$ are considered to be its adjacent agents on its incident DT edges. The DT of a node set A corresponds to the dual graph of the Voronoi diagram for A, where each node is surrounded by its Voronoi cell. Note that for any point within the edges of a Voronoi cell, the belonging (vehicle agent) node is the closest to that point in respect to all the neighboring nodes in terms of a given distance function. If the point represents an incident appearing within the cell, the vehicle node is the closest and responsible for attending the incident. In real-world road networks, travel time depends on multiple factors as, e.g., congestion, vehicle flow, road distance, etc. These factors influence the travel time function and the weights in the weighted Voronoi diagram. Hence, the choice of the travel time function should consider these factors and the DT structure.

4.2   Proposed Distributed Break Scheduling Algorithm

At the beginning of each break period $t \in T$, each *unassigned idle* agent uses the following algorithm for break scheduling. For the initiation purposes, all the initial satisfaction values are assumed 1 so that the initial break assignment process (at time $t = 0$) is lexicographic.

Step 1. Each *unassigned idle* agent finds the edges of its Voronoi cell [1] considering its and the momentary positions of its idle neighbors. Then, it computes its arrival time to the most distant point on each edge. If all the arrival times are within the maximum allowed arrival time τ_{max}, the agent's Voronoi cell is assumed to have sufficient coverage.

Step 2. Each agent with sufficient coverage finds a new Voronoi diagram with only the positions of its idle neighbors and without considering its position. Then, it checks the coverage of its neighbors' Voronoi cells, and if they are all covered by its neighbors without its presence, the agent is considered eligible for break assignment.

Step 3. Each eligible agent is ranked for priority in break assignment in a non-decreasing ordered set O based on the value of its satisfaction S_a through a distributed randomized gossip ranking algorithm [7].

Step 4. Each ranked agent $a \in O$ is considered for the assignment to the present break period starting from the agent with the lowest satisfaction. Once an agent is assigned a break, it takes it while its neighbors recompute Voronoi diagram without it and update their eligibility for break assignment (Step 3). Step 5 is repeated until all eligible agents are assigned a break.

Step 5. Each agent $a \in A$ updates its satisfaction S_a at the end of period t.

In the first step, each *unassigned idle* agent essentially checks the coverage of its local area in collaboration with its neighbors. Then, in Step 2, it checks its eligibility for break assignment based on the coverage of its area by its neighbors.

Steps 3 and 4 keep track of the coverage and assure a distributed assignment of breaks. Besides the specification in the algorithm, each idle agent continuously moves towards the centroid of its Voronoi cell by Lloyd's algorithm [13], thus covering possibly uncovered areas. This causes the whole fleet to move towards their optimal positions in the weighted centroidal Voronoi diagram.

5   Functioning Example

We show the functioning of the proposed break scheduling algorithm on a simple use-case example. Let us assume that there are 3 time periods for break assignment and the duration of each break is 1 time period. Moreover, there are 4 vehicle agents randomly positioned in a 2D environment, Fig. 1. Their ordered break preference sets are $R_1(1) = \{2,1,3\}$, $R_2(1) = \{2,3,1\}$, $R_3(1) = \{3,2,1\}$, and $R_4(1) = \{2,1,3\}$.

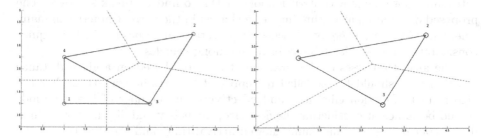

Fig. 1. Left: Four agents in a Voronoi diagram with cells in full blue line and DT triangulation in red dash-dot line. Right: The control of coverage of the neighbors of agent 4 for its break assignment eligibility (Color figure online)

Each agent that requests a break for the present period, changes its status from *idle* to *unassigned idle*. Let us assume that all 4 agents do so and follow the steps of the algorithm in Sect. 4.2. In Step 1, they mutually find the edges of their Voronoi cells by using algorithm in [1] and compute the arrival times to the most distant point on their every edge. Let us assume that all the arrival times of all agents are within τ_{max} such that all the agents have sufficient coverage.

Then, in Step 2, each agent computes a new Voronoi diagram without considering its presence in it. In Fig. 1, it is shown how the Voronoi diagram looks with and without agent 1. Let us assume that it is eligible (its neighbors cover completely its Voronoi cell) and that all its neighbors are also eligible for break assignment.

For the ranking of priority in break assignment in ordered set O, initially, since all agents have the same satisfaction value $S_A(0) = 1$, the break assignment at time $t = 1$ is lexicographic, so agent 1 starts the assignment and is assigned a break at break period $t = 1$. Then, agents 2, 3, and 4 mutually recompute Voronoi diagram without it and each one updates its eligibility for break assignment considering the coverage of their new Voronoi cell without their presence in it. Since now there are too few idle agents, none of them is eligible for a break. Therefore, they move towards the centroids of their Voronoi cells and wait for the end of the period to update their satisfaction (Step 5). The remaining idle unassigned agents restart the break algorithm again in each remaining time period until all agents have taken a break or the shift is over.

6 Conclusions

In this paper, we proposed a dynamic and distributed break-scheduling algorithm for emergency service fleets that is based on Delaunay triangulation (DT) and that considers the area coverage for efficient incident assistance and equity among vehicle crews in the break assignment. The objective was to assure that the arrival times to upcoming incidents are within some maximum allowed arrival time in any part of the region of interest by stand-by vehicles while optimizing the number and duration of breaks based on the requirements for fatigue minimization.

In our model, each vehicle crew is represented by an agent that communicates and coordinates with its neighbors in DT to find its break schedule. The proposed distributed algorithm implies a change in the current practice in many emergency services, where break-scheduling is static and does not include equity consideration for workload/break balance among vehicles.

The algorithm assesses the coverage of the area based on a given distance function that should be modelled to represent real traffic conditions. For the algorithm to function efficiently and effectively, the number of break periods should be sufficient considering the fleet size, frequency and distribution of incidence appearance, the maximum allowed arrival time, and the structure of the road network. The performance of the proposed algorithm also depends on the flexibility of vehicles for break assignment. The higher the number of idle vehicle crews that request a break at every break period, the more efficient is the break algorithm and the lower is the number of unsatisfied crews.

Additionally, based on the modelling of the proposed three satisfaction functions (for break preference, workload, and break interruptions), the preference ordering of agents in the break assignment, and therefore, the performance of algorithm may change significantly.

In future work, we plan to further analyze the algorithm's sensitivity to performance variation based on different function types. We also plan to evaluate the algorithm through simulations of sufficiently complex emergency fleet scenarios on road networks with congestion.

References

1. Bash, B.A., Desnoyers, P.J.: Exact distributed Voronoi cell computation in sensor networks. In: Proceedings of the 6th International Conference on Information Processing in Sensor Networks, pp. 236–243. ACM (2007)
2. Beer, A., Gartner, J., Musliu, N., Schafhauser, W., Slany, W.: An AI-based break-scheduling system for supervisory personnel. IEEE Intell. Syst. 25(2), 60–73 (2010)
3. Van den Bergh, J., Beliën, J., De Bruecker, P., Demeulemeester, E., De Boeck, L.: Personnel scheduling: a literature review. Eur. J. Oper. Res. (EJOR) 226(3), 367–385 (2013)

4. Bhandari, A., Scheller-Wolf, A., Harchol-Balter, M.: An exact and efficient algorithm for the constrained dynamic operator staffing problem for call centers. Manage. Sci. **54**(2), 339–353 (2008)

5. Billhardt, H., Fernández, A., Lemus, L., Lujak, M., Osman, N., Ossowski, S., Sierra, C.: Dynamic coordination in fleet management systems: toward smart cyber fleets. IEEE Intell. Syst. **29**(3), 70–76 (2014)

6. Billhardt, H., Lujak, M., Sánchez-Brunete, V., Fernández, A., Ossowski, S.: Dynamic coordination of ambulances for emergency medical assistance services. Knowl.-Based Syst. **70**, 268–280 (2014)

7. Chiuso, A., Fagnani, F., Schenato, L., Zampieri, S.: Gossip algorithms for distributed ranking. In: American Control Conference (ACC), 2011, pp. 5468–5473. IEEE (2011)

8. Defraeye, M., Van Nieuwenhuyse, I.: Staffing and scheduling under nonstationary demand for service: a literature review. Omega **58**, 4–25 (2016)

9. Di Gaspero, L., Gärtner, J., Musliu, N., Schaerf, A., Schafhauser, W., Slany, W.: Automated shift design and break scheduling. In: Uyar, A., Ozcan, E., Urquhart, N. (eds.) Automated Scheduling and Planning. SCI, vol. 505, pp. 109–127. Springer, Heidelberg (2013). doi:10.1007/978-3-642-39304-4_5

10. Ernst, A.T., Jiang, H., Krishnamoorthy, M., Sier, D.: Staff scheduling and rostering: a review of applications, methods and models. Eur. J. Oper. Res. **153**(1), 3–27 (2004)

11. Huisman, D., Freling, R., Wagelmans, A.P.: Multiple-depot integrated vehicle and crew scheduling. Transp. Sci. **39**(4), 491–502 (2005)

12. Hur, D., Mabert, V.A., Bretthauer, K.M.: Real-time work schedule adjustment decisions: an investigation and evaluation. Prod. Oper. Manage. **13**(4), 322–339 (2004)

13. Lloyd, S.: Least squares quantization in PCM. IEEE Trans. Inf. Theory **28**(2), 129–137 (1982)

14. Lujak, M., Billhardt, H.: Coordinating emergency medical assistance. In: Ossowski, S. (ed.) Agreement Technologies. LGTS, vol. 8, pp. 597–609. Springer, Dordrecht (2013). doi:10.1007/978-94-007-5583-3_35

15. Lujak, M., Billhardt, H., Ossowski, S.: Optimizing emergency medical assistance coordination in after-hours urgent surgery patients. In: Bulling, N. (ed.) EUMAS 2014. LNCS, vol. 8953, pp. 316–331. Springer, Cham (2015). doi:10.1007/978-3-319-17130-2_21

16. Lujak, M., Billhardt, H., Ossowski, S.: Distributed coordination of emergency medical service for angioplasty patients. Ann. Math. Artif. Intell. **78**(1), 73–100 (2016)

17. Mehrotra, V., Ozlük, O., Saltzman, R.: Intelligent procedures for intra-day updating of call center agent schedules. Prod. Oper. Manage. **19**(3), 353–367 (2010)

18. Mesquita, M., Moz, M., Paias, A., Paixão, J., Pato, M., Respício, A.: A new model for the integrated vehicle-crew-rostering problem and a computational study on rosters. J. Sched. **14**(4), 319–334 (2011)

19. Rekik, M., Cordeau, J.F., Soumis, F.: Implicit shift scheduling with multiple breaks and work stretch duration restrictions. J. Sched. **13**(1), 49–75 (2010)

20. Robbins, T.R., Harrison, T.P.: A stochastic programming model for scheduling call centers with global service level agreements. EJOR **207**(3), 1608–1619 (2010)

21. Widl, M., Musliu, N.: An improved memetic algorithm for break scheduling. In: Blesa, M.J., Blum, C., Raidl, G., Roli, A., Sampels, M. (eds.) HM 2010. LNCS, vol. 6373, pp. 133–147. Springer, Heidelberg (2010). doi:10.1007/978-3-642-16054-7_10

Negotiation for Incentive Driven Privacy-Preserving Information Sharing

Reyhan Aydoğan[1,2,3](✉), Pinar Øzturk[4], and Yousef Razeghi[1]

[1] Department of Computer Science, Özyeğin University, Istanbul, Turkey
reyhan.aydogan@ozyegin.edu.tr
[2] Interactive Intelligence Group, Delft University of Technology,
Delft, The Netherlands
[3] Frontier Research Institute for Information Science,
Nagoya Institute of Technology, Nagoya, Japan
[4] Norwegian University of Science and Technology, Trondheim, Norway
pinar@ntnu.no

Abstract. This paper describes an agent-based, incentive-driven, and privacy-preserving information sharing framework. Main contribution of the paper is to give the data provider agent an active role in the information sharing process and to change the currently asymmetric position between the provider and the requester of data and information (DI) to the favor of the DI provider. Instead of a binary yes/no answer to the requester's data request and the incentive offer, the provider may negotiate about excluding from the requested DI bundle certain pieces of DI with high privacy value, and/or ask for a different type of incentive. We show the presented approach on a use case. However, the proposed architecture is domain independent.

Keywords: Data and information sharing · Incentive-driven · Secrecy and privacy risk · Negotiation · Privacy-preserving agent systems

1 Introduction

E-commerce and ubiquitous-application companies aim to increase their revenues through providing tailored services to their customers. In order to achieve this goal, companies need to know about customers' needs, habits, interests, and their pattern of behavior toward the services provided by these companies. Despite the fact that the users could benefit from this kind of personalization, consumer behaviour research reports that people are reluctant to share their personal DI[1] due to fear for possible illegal and unethical usage of their DI [6,7]. Sometimes people can anticipate what the possible uses and harms may be while other times they don't even know for what *purposes* their DI may be used.

---

[1] From now on we use DI to refer to "data and information" but also interchangeably use only "data" or only "information" as well.

© Springer International Publishing AG 2017
B. An et al. (Eds.): PRIMA 2017, LNAI 10621, pp. 486–494, 2017.
https://doi.org/10.1007/978-3-319-69131-2_31

It has been contended that privacy risk beliefs on one side and the entice-ment beliefs and utility perceptions on the opposite side jointly determine a per-son's decision to provide private DI [8]. The well established theory of "privacy calculus" studies the factors that influence individuals' risk-benefit analysis and how these factors interact with each other [18,20]. Most privacy calculus mod-els agree that privacy concerns have an inhibitory influence on DI disclosure decisions [8,20,23]. These studies typically rely on users' answers to prepared questionnaires which are then aggregated. However, it has been observed that the behaviour of users in actual information disclosure situations deviates from these aggregated responses, a fact called as "privacy paradox" [1,4,5]. This may partially been explained by the differences across individuals. Some individuals may be more risk aversive or more preoccupied with uncertainty [17] than others do. Existing information sharing practices and tools deployed by the companies do not involve the specific constructs and the process necessary for dealing with differences between individuals. For example, a data requester company pro-poses the same incentives to everybody regardless of individuals' preferences and beliefs.

Another main downside of the information acquisition practice employed by the companies (i.e., data consumer/requester) is that the data provider can only accept or reject the possible incentive offered by the data requester. To have to give an accept/reject (i.e., only a binary option) type of answer for giving to data requesters access right to their data may create uncertainty and hence reluctance on data provider's side. Being in a passive situation where the data provider is involved neither in the selection of the data pieces to disclose nor the amount of the incentive blocks the information disclosure.

The main contribution of the paper is to give the DI provider an active role in the information sharing process and to change the currently asymmet-ric position between the DI provider and the requester to the favor of the data provider. Instead of a binary yes/no answer to the requester's data request and incentive offer, the provider may negotiate about excluding from the to-be dis-closed DI bundle certain pieces of DI with high privacy value, and/or ask for a different type of incentive. The proposed approach inherently takes into con-sideration that people vary in what they consider as secret and risky data and how they value it. Furthermore, we develop a preference elicitation tool for the data provider and consumer and illustrate the proposed idea on an example from Telecommunication domain.

The rest of this paper is structured as follows: Sect. 2 provides an overview of related work and Sect. 3 explains the proposed information sharing scheme. A case study in telecommunication domain is illustrated in Sect. 4. Finally, we conclude the paper with a direction to future work in Sect. 5.

2   Related Work

There have been a number of works focusing on service consumer's privacy con-cern about their personal data, which they need to provide in order to get some services from service providers for invoicing, shipment, etc. [9,21]. Those works point out that service provider's traditional "take it or leave it" approach (i.e., service consumer needs to provide this information to get the underlying service) or "one-size-fits-all" approach (i.e., acting each service consumer in the same way without considering their sensitivity about their personal information may vary) would have a negative impact on user satisfaction. Therefore, they focus on more flexible approaches based on privacy negotiation.

El-Khatib presents a privacy negotiation protocol where the service provider and consumer negotiates on privacy policy. According to that negotiation protocol, the service provider (i.e., data consumer in our case) initiates the negotiation with an offer and the service consumer (i.e., data provider in our case) could accept this offer or reject this offer with an explanation why the given bid is rejected. In this set-up, an offer contains how the consumer's information will be used (e.g. shared with other department or only shared with the billing office etc.) and a discount rate as an incentive. Furthermore, Preibusch models this interaction like a dynamic game [21]. In that study, four types of users have been defined according to their characteristics. Although both studies present more flexible way of building privacy policy than the traditional approach, service consumer still cannot negotiate actively as service provider does. Service consumer can only accept or reject an offer whereas s/he can make offers in our framework.

A more recent study also proposes a negotiation scheme for permission management [2]. Baarslag *et al.* suggest a negotiation in which the service consumer (i.e., data provider) makes a partial offer and asks the service provider to complete this partial offer with the remaining issues such as price discount. The service consumer then may accept the given complete offer or make another partial offer. In the proposed framework, asking for completing the partial offer has a penalty (cost) for service consumer; in this way, the service provider avoids to reveal its entire cost structure. In that study, an agent's preferences are represented by means of additive utility functions and the given cost is subtracted from this utility. Implicitly it is assumed that there exist no preferential interdependencies between issues. However, we believe that there might be such interdependencies. For example, the evaluation of how the data can/will be used may depend on the type of data. Therefore, in our work we consider a number of factors to evaluate a bid such as the secrecy level of the given information, the risk of sharing it as well as the gained profit from the received incentives. On the other hand, our focus is only on the information type and the given incentives whereas [2] also consider other issues such as how the data will be used etc. It can be interesting to extend our work in that direction.

There are also other work focusing on detection of the privacy violation rather than preserving such as PRIGUARD [16] and PROTOSS [14]. Those works are complementary to our work. After negotiation, our information sharing framework may check whether both parties act in line with their agreements. In case of violation of the agreement, the agent violating the agreement may get penalized (e.g. a low reputation is assigned to that agent and so on).

3   Negotiation Based Information Sharing Approach

We define the notion of privacy in terms of two components. The first is **desire for secrecy** and captures that the DI owner may be reluctant to share a certain pieces of DI content just because she likes to keep it for herself. An example is that a person may not want others to see her falling down from a horse. Sharing a video record of this event would not lead to any harm but would make her uncomfortable. The second component relates to the **risk/fear of harm** and uncertainty about possible unethical and improper usage of DI by others without her consent. These together determine the **privacy value** attained by the data provider/owner to a certain DI content.

The proposed information sharing approach is founded on the following two constructs. First, a data consumer (e.g. a company) must have specific *goals* and a purpose for wanting to access/use the concerned DI. **Utility of information** for the data consumer depends on how much this DI is needed to achieve their goals, e.g., a company's business goal(s). Second, a data provider (e.g. customer) must have a **motivation** for sharing her personal/private DI despite privacy concern. **Incentives** offered to data owners/providers play a motivating role for DI sharing.

People show significant differences regarding which type of DI[2] has high secrecy level, perception of the risk of sharing certain DI, as well as how they value their private DI. Certain types of DI are considered secret by everybody, such as personal id numbers while there are many differences across individuals (or individual companies) regarding secrecy of other types of DI. Similarly, certain DI may be perceived as bearing high threat for privacy breaches by some people while others may feel quite relaxed about the same DI. Hence, people value their DI differently. To sum up, an effective information sharing approach should be sensitive to individuals' peculiarities.

The following requirements guide us towards the design of an architectural model: (1) The data provider should be able to behave in coherence with their *level of secrecy* and *risk value* which reflects the individual's *risk averseness* and *uncertainty avoidance inclination*, etc. (2) The data provider should be given an **active** role in the information sharing processes. More specifically, the provider agent can take initiative for bargaining *(i)* to exclude the pieces of DI with high privacy value for herself from the shared bundle of DI, and *(ii)* to ask for more incentive to disclose the requested DI. (3) The data consumers should model the *goals* of their owner and map each goal with a set of *DI types* required to achieve that goal. The agents should also attach a utility to each type of DI,i.e. how important a specific DI is for the goal and the maximum incentives the consumer can use to persuade the data provider to disclose that DI.

Putting together these requirements, the information-sharing framework should allow individual reasoning about privacy. A decentralized, agent-based

---

[2] Note the distinction between DI and DI types where the former refers to the data itself while the latter is about the type of data, where 'age' is a DI type and '68' is a corresponding piece of DI.

solution is needed where the DI requester and provider can interact through a standardized protocol to communicate their preferences and to bargain for an optimal solution for both parties. We propose a negotiation-based DI sharing where DI requester and provider agents model their owners' preferences and needs and involve in a bargaining process in accordance with these models.

In the proposed framework, both agents have a knowledge base and a data base. The knowledge base of the provider agent has its preferences and beliefs about the secrecy and risk value of the knowledge in its knowledge base while the knowledge base of the consumer agent contains its goals (e.g., business goals if a company) and the mapping between these goals with the type of DI necessary to achieve these goals. On the other side, the data base of the provider agent has its personal/private DI, while consumer agent's data base comprise the DI it gathered from various providers. This database is often used for data analytics to infer knowledge for revising their business models or to create new models.

The main function of the negotiation in information sharing is to facilitate the trade-off between a data consumer and a provider agent. Negotiation goal of the consumer is to obtain all data it needs at a minimum cost whereas the provider aims to preserve its privacy as much as possible while maximizing the gained incentives, which can be a promotion (e.g. free service) or a monetary benefit (e.g. a certain amount of money to be received).

The data consumer and the provider negotiate on sharing some private/personal information in exchange for an incentive in a bilateral fashion. Both agents have an access to a shared ontology which provides the common vocabulary for their communication. Briefly, the shared ontology defines the type of information such as age, birth date as well as the types of potential incentives in the given domain such as promotion types (e.g. free one hour phone call). The negotiation between the data consumer and the provider is governed by the Alternating Offer Protocol [22]. The data consumer initiates the negotiation with a request and the data producer agent may accept this offer or make a counter offer. This process continues in a turn-taking fashion till the termination condition is met such as reaching a joint agreement or deadline.

In this negotiation, a bid structure can be formalized as follows: $o :< IB, Incentive >$ where IB denotes a set of information types under trade-off and an $Incentive$ denotes the incentives to be given for the considered information. In the shared ontology, the set of all possible information types, I is defined formally and $IB \subseteq I$. $Agent_C$, the data consumer initiates the negotiation with an offer such as $o_1 =< \{Age, Birth date\}, \text{"3-month free phone call"} >$. $Agent_P$ needs to evaluate this offer to decide either to accept or to make a counter offer.

For the data consumer agent, the utility of an offer depends on two values: *the value of the bundle of information types* and *the value of the cost of the incentives*. Therefore, the expected utility of an offer for the data consumer can be estimated as follows:

$$\mathcal{EU}(o < IB, Incentive >) = Value_{info}(IB) - Value_{cost}(Incentive) \quad (1)$$

When the data consumer agent ($Agent_C$) generates its offer or evaluates the data provider's counter offer, it ensures that the content of the information bundle,

IB, is sufficient for achieving its targeted goals. The set of $Agent_C$'s goals are represented as $G = \{g_1, g_2, \ldots g_k\}$ where k denotes the total number of goals. A goal $g \in G$ relies on some information to be achieved. For instance, $i_1, i_2, i_3 \in I$ are necessary for achieving g_1 while achieving g_2 may require only i_3. $Agent_C$ aims to obtain this information from $Agent_P$ through the negotiation. On the opposite side, if the parts of the information has a high privacy value for $Agent_P$, then, $Agent_P$ may either try to avoid sharing this data or ask for more incentives.

Usually, each goal may have different importance level for $Agent_C$. Therefore, a weight value, w_i is associated to each goal $g_i \in G$, denoting the importance of g_i for $Agent_C$. The sum of the goal weights is equal to one; $\sum_i^k w_i = 1$. In this context, a goal is considered as *satisfiable* if $Agent_C$ has access to the information required for satisfying that goal. Accordingly, Eq. 2 defines the value of information bundle $Value_{info}(IB)$ as the weighted sum of the satisfiable goals with IB where $Satisfiable(g_i, IB)=1$ if IB comprises all data that g_i requires; otherwise, $Satisfiable(g_i, IB)=0$.

$$Value_{info}(IB) = \sum_i^k w_i \times Satisfiable(g_i, IB) \qquad (2)$$

Note that this formulation assigns a value to the entire bundle and does not consider each data item constituting the bundle separately. The rationale behind this is that a specific data item may be worthless without having other one(s). For example, consider that $Agent_C$ needs both i_1 and i_2 for achieving g_1 meaning that the lack of either i_1 or i_2 jeopardizes g_1. However, we conceive that more refined methods are needed to handle the data interdependency.

Recall that an offer consists of two components: information bundle and incentives offered to the data provider agent. The incentive incurs a cost. Without doubt, $Agent_C$ aims to minimize this cost. The value of the cost of the incentives for $Agent_C$ is a function, which maps the cost of the incentives for the obtained information types IB to a real value between zero and one $[0, 1]$. A high value mean it incurs a high cost to provide the chosen incentive in exchange for the information bundle. Note that the value of cost would be less than one if the cost of the incentive to be provided by $Agent_C$ is less important for the $Agent_C$ than the value of information to be provided by $Agent_P$.

During the negotiation, the data provider agent takes into consideration both the utility of the incentive provided by $Agent_C$ and the level of privacy violation incurred while sharing its personal/private information requested by $Agent_C$. Accordingly, Eq. 3 shows how $Agent_P$ estimates the expected utility of a given bid. We consider that $Agent_P$ has a utility function, $Value(Incentive)$, which maps each potential incentive to a real value $[0, 1]$ according to its user's needs or interests.

$$\mathcal{EU}(o < IB, Incentive >) = Value(Incentive) - Value_{privacy}(IB) \qquad (3)$$

While estimating $Value_{privacy}$, the value of privacy violation, $Agent_P$ considers level of secrecy of the information and how risky (i.e., harmful consequences) is to share the requested information. Secrecy has a psychological aspect and has to do with a person's preference to keep a certain personal information for herself, independently from whether it may be used against herself. In our framework, the level of secrecy for each information type will be elicited from the data provider. Accordingly, Eq. 4 shows how the value of privacy is estimated in our framework where $Risk(x)$ denotes how risky is to share the requested item x and SL represents the normalized secrecy level of the given information type.

$$Value_{privacy}(IB) = \max_{x \in IB}(SL(x) * Risk(x)) \qquad (4)$$

In our formulation, we chose to take the value of maximum privacy violation instead of taking the average privacy violation of each information in the given bundle. This is because the bundle may consist of information types whose privacy violation might be very high and very low, then the average may not accurately capture how significant the violation actually is.

Once the agents are able to evaluate expected utility of each bid, then they can employ any state of art negotiation strategy proposed for bilateral negotiations – particularly compatible with the alternating offers protocol [3,10–12,15]. There may either be a data consumer agent (i.e., bot) negotiating with a human counterpart directly, or alternatively, the information sharing system can be built in a fully automated manner.

4   Case Study

As a use case, we consider a telecommunication company, which aims to do some data analytics on their customer's data in order to gauge customer needs and satisfaction better, and accordingly to provide more targeted services/products for their customers. According to the laws, they need to ask for their customers' permission to store and use their personal/sensitive data. In order to get their customers' permission, they may offer some incentives such as "1GB Fee Internet", "100 SMS for one month", and so on. A customer may accept this offer or reject it. When the customer rejects to give permission to the company regarding his/her personal data, the conversation ends in most of the cases.

However, we suggest a more interactive way of information sharing for such kind of scenarios. That is, the company (i.e., data consumer) may initiate a negotiation process with their customers (i.e. data providers) in a bilateral fashion and they together decide what to share and the incentive to drive sharing. In order to develop such a mechanism, we first need to define the types of information of interest, and the kind of incentives the company may provide in exchange for the requested information types. Afterwards, the company and their customers should be able to express their preferences as explained in previous section.

Similar to other negotiation frameworks such as *Genius* [19] and *Pocket Negotiator* [13], this framework provides stakeholders an interface to describe the underlying negotiation domain (i,e., negotiation issues and outcome space) and to express their preferences. In Genius, the stakeholders represent their preferences by means of additive utility functions, which are compact models but cannot capture interdependencies among negotiation issues. However, in our case, the company agent needs to evaluate some negotiation issues such as DI types in groups where the intersection of these groups is not mandatory to be an empty set. That is, the agent should be able to say that a subset of information types may contribute to achieving a particular goal while other subset might contribute another goal. Therefore, it would not be appropriate to adopt additive utility functions for representing such kind of preferences in our framework.

Similar to the approach followed by Pocket negotiator (e.g. expressing users' interests and associating negotiation issues with the specified interests), we define goals of the DI consumer with varying weights, and associate the necessity of the information types with the specified goals. In addition to goal specification, a company agent also needs to indicate the cost of incentives. After preference elicitation, both party can negotiate by following the alternative offer protocol.

5 Conclusion

In this work, we have introduced a negotiation-based privacy preserving information sharing framework, in which data consumers offer some incentives in exchange for being authorized to store and use data provider's personal data. Different from other existing framework, the data provider (i.e., service consumer in e-commerce) plays an active role in the negotiation. We consider Internet of Things as an attractive application area for the presented framework. In this scenario, IoT entities in various levels, sensor-owners, business entities (retailers, manufacture companies), governmental organizations (road and traffic management), non-profit institutions, research units all can come together around a data market place where data and information can be sold according to the conceptual model and principles introduced in this paper. As a future work, it would be interesting to add more elements such as duration of permission, limitation on the scope of the usage, and so on. In addition, the data requester agents may provide their use-intention and some arguments to convince the data provider.

Acknowledgement. We would like to thank Murat Sensoy and Pinar Yolum for our fruitful discussions. This work was supported by the ITEA M2MGrids Project, ITEA141011.

References

1. Acquisti, A., Grossklags, J.: Privacy and rationality in individual decision making. IEEE Secur. Priv. **3**(1), 26–33 (2005)
2. Baarslag, T., Alan, A.T., Gomer, R., Alam, M., Perera, C., Gerding, E.H., et al.: An automated negotiation agent for permission management. In: Proceedings of the 16th Conference on AAMAS, pp. 380–390 (2017)
3. Baarslag, T., Gerding, E.H., Aydoğan, R., Schraefel, M.: Optimal negotiation decision functions in time-sensitive domains. In: Web Intelligence and Intelligent Agent Technology (WI-IAT), vol. 2, pp. 190–197. IEEE (2015)
4. Barnes, S.: A privacy paradox: social networking in the united states. First Monday **11**(1) (2006)

5. Barth, S., de Jong, M.D.: The privacy paradox investigating discrepancies between expressed privacy concerns and actual online behavior a systematic literature review. Telematics and Informatics (2017, in press)
6. Becker, M.C., Knudsen, T.: The role of routines in reducing pervasive uncertainty. J. Bus. Res. **58**(6), 746–757 (2005)
7. Culnan, M.J., Armstrong, P.K.: Information privacy concerns, procedural fairness, and impersonal trust: an empirical investigation. Organ. Sci. **10**(1), 104–115 (1999)
8. Dinev, T., Hart, P.: An extended privacy calculus model for e-commerce transactions. Inf. Syst. Res. **17**(1), 61–80 (2006)
9. El-Khatib, K.: A privacy negotiation protocol for web services. In: Workshop on Collaboration Agents: Autonomous Agents for Collaborative Environments, pp. 85–92. Halifax (2003)
10. Faratin, P., Sierra, C., Jennings, N.R.: Using similarity criteria to make issue trade-offs in automated negotiations. Artif. Intell. **142**(2), 205–237 (2002)
11. Fatima, S., Kraus, S., Wooldridge, M.: Principles of Automated Negotiation. Cambridge University Press, Cambridge (2014)
12. Jonker, C.M., Aydoğan, R., Baarslag, T., Fujita, K., Ito, T., Hindriks, K.: Automated negotiating agents competition. In: Proceedings of the Thirty-First AAAI Conference on Artificial Intelligence (AAAI-17), pp. 5070–5072. AAAI Press (2017)
13. Jonker, C.M., Robu, V., Treur, J.: An agent architecture for multi-attribute negotiation using incomplete preference information. Auton. Agent. Multi-Agent Syst. **15**(2), 221–252 (2007)
14. Kafalı, Ö., Günay, A., Yolum, P.: Protoss: A run time tool for detecting privacy violations in online social networks. In: ASONAM, pp. 429–433 (2012)
15. Kawaguchi, S., Fujita, K., Ito, T.: AgentK: compromising strategy based on estimated maximum utility for automated negotiating agents. In: Ito, T., Zhang, M., Robu, V., Fatima, S., Matsuo, T. (eds.) New Trends in Agent-Based Complex Automated Negotiations. SCI, vol. 383, pp. 137–144. Springer, Heidelberg (2012). doi:10.1007/978-3-642-24696-8_8
16. Kokciyan, N., Yolum, P.: PRIGUARD : a semantic approach to detect privacy violations in online social networks. IEEE Trans. Knowl. Data Eng. **28**(10), 2724–2737 (2016)
17. Krasnova, H., Veltri, N.F., Günther, O.: Self-disclosure and privacy calculus on social networking sites: the role of culture. Bus. Inf. Syst. Eng. **4**(3), 127–135 (2012)
18. Li, H., Sarathy, R., Xu, H.: The role of affect and cognition on online consumers' decision to disclose personal information to unfamiliar online vendors. Decis. Support Syst. **51**(3), 434–445 (2011)
19. Lin, R., Kraus, S., Baarslag, T., Tykhonov, D., Hindriks, K., Jonker, C.M.: Genius: an integrated environment for supporting the design of generic automated negotiators. Comput. Intell. **30**(1), 48–70 (2014)
20. Culnan, M.J., Bies, R.J.: Consumer privacy: balancing economic and justice considerations. J. Soc. Issues **59**(2), 323–342 (2003)
21. Preibusch, S.: Implementing privacy negotiation techniques in e-commerce. In: Seventh IEEE International Conference on E-Commerce Technology, CEC 2005, pp. 387–390. IEEE (2005)
22. Rubinstein, A.: Perfect equilibrium in a bargaining model. Econometrica **50**(1), 97–109 (1982)
23. Taddei, S., Contena, B.: Privacy, trust and control: which relationships with online self-disclosure? Comput. Hum. Behav. **29**(3), 821–826 (2012)

Crowdsourcing Mechanism Design

Yuko Sakurai[1]($\boxtimes$), Masafumi Matsuda[2], Masato Shinoda[3], and Satoshi Oyama[4]

[1] National Institute of Advanced Industrial Science and Technology, Tsukuba, Japan
yuko.sakurai@aist.go.jp
[2] NTT Communication Science Laboratories, Kyoto, Japan
matsuda.masafumi@lab.ntt.co.jp
[3] Nara Women's University, Nara, Japan
shinoda@cc.nara-wu.ac.jp
[4] RIKEN Center for Advanced Intelligence Project, Hokkaido University,
Sapporo, Japan
oyama@ist.hokudai.ac.jp

Abstract. Crowdsourcing is becoming increasingly popular in various tasks. Although the cost incurred by workers in crowdsourcing is lower than that by experts, the possibility of errors in the former generally exceeds that of the latter. One of the important approaches to quality control of crowdsourcing is based on mechanism design, which has been used to design a game's rules/protocols so that agents have incentives to truthfully declare their preferences, and designers can select socially advantageous outcomes. Thus far, mechanism design has been conducted by professional economists or computer scientists. However, it is difficult to recruit professional mechanism designers, and developed mechanisms tend to be difficult for people to understand. Crowdsourcing requesters have to determine how to assign tasks to workers and how to reward them. Therefore, a requester can be considered to be an "amateur mechanism designer". This paper introduces the "wisdom of the crowd" approach to mechanism design, i.e., using crowdsourcing to explore the large design space of incentive mechanisms. We conducted experiments to show that crowd mechanism designers can develop sufficiently diverse candidates for incentive mechanisms and they can choose appropriate mechanisms given a set of candidate mechanisms. We also studied how the designers' theoretical, economic, and social tendencies, as well as their views on the world, justifiably affect the mechanisms they propose.

1 Introduction

Crowdsourcing is becoming increasingly popular in various tasks, such as classifying data, gathering opinions, and reviewing products. A requester can ask many workers around the world to do his/her tasks at relatively low cost by using crowdsourcing services, such as Amazon Mechanical Turk (AMT). Crowdsourcing has also been attracting attention from artificial intelligence (AI) and multi-agent systems (MAS) researchers as a platform for *human computation*, which tackles problems that can only be solved by computers. Human computation is based on the idea of the wisdom of crowds and solves problems by

© Springer International Publishing AG 2017
B. An et al. (Eds.): PRIMA 2017, LNAI 10621, pp. 495–503, 2017.
https://doi.org/10.1007/978-3-319-69131-2_32

combining the forces of many people. It utilizes human intelligence as functions in computer programs [6,12,13]. Although an advantage of crowdsourcing is that a large workforce is available at relatively low cost, the quality of the results is occasionally problematic. For example, workers in image classification label sample images that are used as training data in machine learning. Although the cost of the labels incurred by workers in crowdsourcing is lower than that by experts, the possibility of errors in the former generally exceeds that of the latter.

There have been many methods proposed to overcome the issue of quality control. Most studies on quality control have been based on machine learning and statistics. They have treated workers as "noisy information sources" and have tried to obtain high quality results from error prone results produced by workers. However, regarding workers as static information sources has been rather simplistic and has sometimes failed to capture important properties of crowdsourcing, such as motivation and incentives by workers, and their strategic behaviors.

There are various ways of incentivizing workers in crowdsourcing services, e.g., monetary incentives and improving rank. A requester in typical commercial crowdsourcing services provides a monetary incentive to workers. These commercial crowdsourcing services apply two basic rewarding options: fixed and performance-based rewards. Incentives can be given to workers in several different ways, such as punishing low quality work by disapproving of it, or encouraging high quality work by giving bonuses. In practice, a requester has to choose from vast design options and combine them in a coherent way.

There has been a large volume of studies in the areas of microeconomics and game theory called mechanism design that has pursued principled ways of designing such systems by considering people's incentives. Mechanism design has been used to study the design of a game's rules/protocols so that agents have incentives to truthfully declare their preferences, and designers can select socially advantageous outcomes. Such studies have recently been attracting a great deal of attention from computer scientists along with the popularization of network environments. Studies related to mechanism design for crowdsourced workers have particularly been advanced by AI and MAS researchers [1,2,8].

Thus far, mechanism design has been conducted by professional economists or computer scientists, who have been able to design high quality mechanisms with theoretical guarantees. However, it is difficult to recruit professional mechanism designers for each task, considering the great variety and volume of crowdsourcing tasks. In other words, the number of such experts is limited and not sufficient for exploring numerous design choices.

Another weakness of the mechanism design approach thus far is that developed mechanisms tend to be difficult for people to understand. For example, the Vickrey-Clarke-Groves (VCG) mechanism [3,4,15] is well-known as the king of mechanisms since it satisfies theoretically advantageous properties such as strategy-proofness, individual rationality, and Pareto optimality. However, the VCG mechanism has unfortunately not yet widely been applied to real-world applications. The two main reasons for this is that it has been difficult to calculate the winner's payments and it has been very far from being intuitive. No participants can immediately understand the calculations. Recently, Lee and Baykal reported that the results of mathematically-proved fair mechanisms do not always perceived fair by the participants [7]. Similarly, although computer scientists have already developed many mechanisms to attain quality control in crowdsourcing, they are rarely used in practice.

Crowdsourcing requesters have to determine how to assign tasks to workers and how to reward them. Therefore, a requester can be considered to be an *amateur mechanism designer*. A mechanism designer designs a mechanism so that it will satisfy some advantageous properties such as strategy-proofness, but he/she also has to consider several preconditions that are not only determined by economic rationality, but also by the sense of value of the requester and workers, or social and economic practice in society.

This paper introduces the "wisdom of the crowd" approach to mechanism design, i.e., using crowdsourcing to explore the large design space of incentive mechanisms. Our four research questions are:

- Can crowd mechanism designers develop sufficiently diverse candidates for incentive mechanisms?
- Can crowd mechanism designers choose appropriate mechanisms given a set of candidate mechanisms?
- How do the designers' theoretical, economic, and social tendencies, as well as their views on the world, justifiably affect the mechanisms they come up with?

While there exists a study in which crowdworkers tried to create personality questionnaire items, which are normally written by experts in personality theory or psychometrics [9], this is the first study to analyze the mechanisms proposed by amateur designer by using his/her personal tendency, as far as the authors know. We specifically performed crowdsourcing tasks that asked workers to propose a quality-control mechanism for a task to count the number of points which is traditionally well-executed micro-tasks. We also asked them questions framed by a psychologist about their personal tendencies. We then used crowdsourcing to evaluate the proposed mechanisms. The workers who developed the highly-ranked mechanisms were best characterized by the economic scale, among the four psychological scales used in the experiments.

2 Experimental Setting to Collect the Mechanisms Proposed by the Crowdworkers

Here, we introduce our experimental problem setting in which we asked workers to propose a mechanism for a task related to image analysis. We posted the task on Lancers (http://www.lancers.jp/), which is a crowdsourcing platform in Japan. We collected answers from 30 workers and each of them was paid 300 Japanese yen (2.7 US dollars). We asked each worker in our task to describe the

Fig. 1. Counting number of points

mechanism for a task to count the number of points and then asked him/her to answer questionnaires about his/her age, academic background, and personal value scales.

We asked the workers to propose a mechanism to count the number of points Fig. 1. This task was relatively easy and the solution to it was unique. We gave workers the following instructions to design a mechanism for counting.

Instructions to Design Mechanism for Task of Counting: You need to know the numbers of black, red, and blue points in Fig. 1. You have a 1,000 Japanese yen (9.1US dollars) budget for each worker and have to try to accurately estimate the numbers from those counted by crowdsourcing workers. Even if you do not pay them all the 1,000 Japanese yen, the remaining money cannot go to you. Please respond to:
- How many workers will you hire,
- How will you distribute the budget among workers as rewards, and
- How will you estimate the answers?

We applied theoretical, economic, and social scales from the six dimensions of values (theoretical, economic, aesthetic, religious, social, and political) proposed by Spranger [14]. We used the questions developed by Sakai et al. [11] to measure these three questions. We asked participants twelve questions on each of the theoretical, economic, and social value scales. Furthermore, we measured a worker's just world scale proposed by Rubin and Peplau [10]. We used the questions developed by Konnno and Hori [5]. We asked four questions for measuring a just world scale. We applied a five-level Likert scale to all the questions.

3   Mechanisms Proposed by Crowdworkers

In this section, we present the results by analyzing the mechanisms proposed by crowdworkers.

3.1   Analyses of Personal Value Scales

We will first present the statistical results of workers' backgrounds listed in Table 1. While we expected that many twenty-something workers would execute this task, there were only four workers. Typical workers were middle age and highly educated.

Table 1. Personal background

	Age						Education			
Category	10's	20's	30's	40's	50's	$\geq$60's	Junior	High	Bachelor	Master
Num. of workers	1	4	10	11	3	1	1	7	18	4

Next, we present four histograms in Fig. 2 to indicate the distribution of workers' average scales for four scales. The average scale for the just world was lower than that for the other scales. We also calculated correlations between scales and found that economic and the just world were almost independent of each other, since it was -0.0057. The economic scale was used to measure a person's consciousness to save time and effort while the just world scale was used to measure a person's tendency to believe in a just world in which people get what they deserve and deserve what they get. Thus, we used the mechanisms

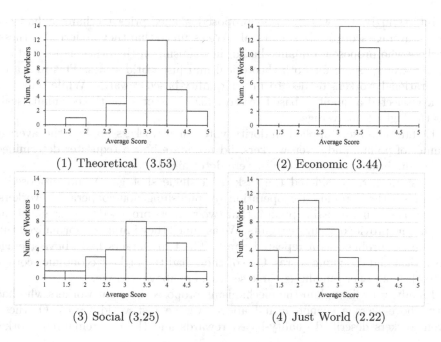

(1) Theoretical (3.53)   (2) Economic (3.44)

(3) Social (3.25)   (4) Just World (2.22)

Fig. 2. Histogram for each value scale

proposed by eight workers who had both an above-average economic score and an above-average just world score in the analyses that follow.

3.2   Proposed Mechanisms

We categorized reward plans proposed by the workers into the three categories listed in Table 2. Eleven workers adopted fixed rewards and 18 workers adopted quality-based rewards. The remaining worker planned to use quantity-based rewards. Of the 18 workers who adopted quality-based rewards, 14 planned to reject low-quality results, one worker planned to be awarded an additional bonus in achieving high-quality results, two workers offered to continue hiring people who attained accurate results, and the one remaining worker did not mention how a requester rewarded/punished workers according to their quality of tasks.

Table 2. Relationships between proposed mechanism and average value score in a task of counting number of points

	Num. of workers	Theory	Economics	Society	Just world
Fixed reward	11	3.40	3.33	3.28	2.08
Quality-based reward	18	3.61	3.50	3.22	2.31
Quantity-based reward	1	3.58	3.83	3.17	1.25

Interestingly, the workers who proposed a fixed-price mechanism had the highest average score on the social scale. We assumed that they preferred fairness. Workers who proposed a quality-based mechanism, on the other hand, had the highest average score for both theoretical and just-world scales. This indicated that rational workers tended to prefer quality-based rewards. While only one worker selected a quantity-based reward, his/her scores for the economic scale was the highest on average.

Eighteen workers applied majority votes, five workers applied the average number of points, and seven workers did not state how a requester determined the results in how the final results were determined.

Most workers considered the task as a single shot game and proposed a mechanism that promoted cooperation by punishing non-cooperative workers. Furthermore, an interesting point is that two workers proposed to continue hiring people who provided accurate results. We assumed they implicitly formalized this task design problem as a repeated game. The two workers had above-average theoretical and economic scores. One of them had the highest economic score of all workers and her remaining three scales were above average.

Finally, we will explain the mechanisms proposed by eight workers who had both above-average economic and above-average just-world scores. Of these, seven workers described quality-based rewards and the one remaining worker described quantity-based rewards. Furthermore, four workers described a majority vote, two workers described the average number of points, and two workers did not describe anything to determine the final results. We found that they preferred quality-based rewards to fixed prices from statistical analysis. We considered that these results met worker tendencies.

4   Evaluations of Proposed Mechanisms by Using Crowdworkers

We asked crowd workers to evaluate the proposed mechanisms to confirm their appropriateness. We asked 30 workers to evaluate the proposed mechanisms and each worker was paid 200 Japanese yen (1.8US dollars). Each task was evaluated on a five-point Likert scale. The final score for each mechanism was calculated by averaging all the scores provided by workers in evaluating the mechanisms.

We also administered workers with the same questionnaire as we had given to workers who designed the mechanisms. We used different sets of workers for each kind of task because we had to evaluate 30 mechanisms for each task.

Here, we present the results on how workers evaluated the proposed mechanisms for the task of counting the number of points. First, we found that each of the average scores of personal value scales for these workers was 3.70 for theory, 3.73 for economics, 3.27 for society, and 2.23 for the just world. Compared with the workers' described mechanisms, each score was higher, but the difference for each score was small.

We found the highest-ranked and lowest-ranked mechanisms had been proposed by workers who had both above-average economic and above-average just world scores.

Highest-ranked mechanism for counting number of the points: We ask 30 workers to count the number of points. The final answers are determined by taking the majority votes for each color. We also give instructions to workers that if the numbers of points are not accurately counted or irresponsibly answered, no awards will be paid. Each worker is paid 50 Japanese yen if their answers are considered to be unproblematic.

Lowest-ranked mechanism for counting number of points: We ask three workers to count the numbers of points. If two or more workers agree on the numbers of all three colors, the numbers are regarded as being correct and we pay 333 Japanese yen to each worker who respond with the correct numbers of points.

Furthermore, of the four lowest ranked mechanisms, one used fixed rewards, two used achievement-based rewards, and one used quantity-based rewards. This indicated that amateur mechanism designers do not favor high-risk high-return mechanisms.

5 Conclusion

This paper introduces the "wisdom of the crowd" approach to mechanism design, i.e., using crowdsourcing to explore the large design space of incentive mechanisms. We performed crowdsourcing tasks that asked workers to propose a quality-control mechanism for a task to count the number of points. We also asked them questions framed by a psychologist about their personal tendencies. We then used crowdsourcing to evaluate the proposed mechanisms. The workers who developed the highly-ranked mechanisms were best characterized by the economic scale, among the four psychological scales used in the experiments. Our future work includes larger scale experiments with more crowd workers as well as studies using more complex tasks such as text summarization and translation.

Acknowledgment. This work was partially supported by JSPS KAKENHI Grant Numbers JP15H02751, JP15H02782.

References

1. Bacon, D.F., Chen, Y., Kash, I., Parkes, D.C., Rao, M., Sridharan, M.: Predicting your own effort. In: Proceedings of the 11th International Conference on Autonomous Agents and Multiagent Systems (AAMAS 2012), pp. 695–702 (2012)
2. Chandra, P., Narahari, Y., Mandal, D., De, P.: Novel mechanisms for online crowdsourcing with unreliable. In: Proceedings of 29th AAAI Conference on Artificial Intelligence (AAAI 2015), pp. 1256–1262 (2015)
3. Clarke, E.H.: Multipart pricing of public goods. Public Choice (1971)
4. Groves, T.: Incentives in teams. Econometrica **41**, 617–631 (1973)
5. Konno, H., Hori, H.: Effects of justice beliefs on injustice judgement. Institute of Psychology, University of Tsukuba, Departmental Bulletin Paper, vol. 20, pp. 157–162 (1998). (in Japanese)
6. Law, E., Ahn, L.V.: Human Computation. Morgan & Claypool Publishers, San Rafael (2011)
7. Lee, M.K., Baykal, S.: Algorithmic mediation in group decisions: fairness perceptions of algorithmically mediated vs. discussion-based social division. In: Proceedings of the 2017 ACM Conference on Computer Supported Cooperative Work and Social Computing (CSCW 2017), pp. 1035–1048 (2017)
8. Liu, Y., Chen, Y.: Sequential peer prediction: learning to elicit effort using posted prices. In: Proceedings of 31st AAAI Conference on Artificial Intelligence (AAAI 2017) (2017, to appear)
9. Loe, B.S., Smart, F., Firtova, L., Brauner, C., Lueneborg, L., Stillwell, D.: Validating the quality of crowdsourced psychometric personality test items. In: Proceedings of the 4th AAAI Conference on Human Computation and Crowdsourcing (HCOMP 2016), pp. 119–128 (2016)
10. Rubin, Z., Peplau, L.A.: Who believes in a just world? J. Soc. Issues **31**(3), 65–89 (1975)
11. Sakai, K., Hisano, M.: Construction of value-intending mental act scale. Educ. Psychol. Res. **45**(4), 388–395 (1997). (in Japanese)
12. Shaw, A.D., Horton, J.J., Chen, D.L.: Designing incentives for inexpert human raters. In: Proceedings of the ACM 2011 Conference on Computer Supported Cooperative Work (CSCW 2011), pp. 275–284 (2011)

13. Snow, R., O'Connor, B., Jurafsky, D., Ng, A.Y.: Cheap and fast - but is it good? Evaluating non-expert annotations for natural language tasks. In: Proceedings of the Conference on Empirical Methods in Natural Language Processing (EMNLP 2008), pp. 254–263 (2008)
14. Spranger, E., Pigors, P.J.W.: Types of Men: The Psychology and Ethics of Personality (1928)
15. Vickrey, W.: Counter speculation, auctions, and competitive sealed tenders. J. Fin. **16**, 8–37 (1961)

A Theory to Devise Dependable Cooperative Encounters

Humbert Fiorino$^{(\boxtimes)}$ and Damien Pellier

Univ. Grenoble Alpes, LIG, 38000 Grenoble, France
{humbert.fiorino,damien.pellier}@imag.fr

Abstract. In this paper, we investigate the question of how to characterize "fault tolerance" in cooperative agents. It is generally admitted that cooperating agents can achieve tasks that they could not achieve without cooperation. Nevertheless, cooperating agents can have "Achilles' heels", a *cooperative encounter* can eventually fail to achieve its tasks because of the collapse of a single agent. The contribution of this paper is the study of how cooperating agents are affected by *dependability* issues. Specifically, our objectives are twofold: to formally define the concepts of dependability in cooperative encounters, and to analyze the computational complexity of devising dependable cooperative encounters.

Keywords: Collaboration & coordination · Teamwork · Cooperation theory

1 Introduction

In this paper, we investigate the question of how to characterize "fault tolerance" in cooperative agents. It is generally admitted that cooperating agents can achieve tasks that they could not achieve without cooperation. For instance, a group of agents is committed in achieving a common task that none of them is able to fulfill. As a consequence, they decompose the initial common task into subtasks which are easier to handle separately. With this divide-and-conquer strategy, they can examine different alternatives, that is, redundant ways of achieving their subtasks [7,10,11,17]. In this framework, the risk of failures is disseminated over the multiagent system because agents commit to tasks corresponding to their skills.

Nevertheless, cooperative encounters have "Achilles' heels". Some agents are much more involved in the encounter's outcome than others, and thus, deserve a closer consideration. A whole group can eventually breakdown because of the collapse of a single agent. Much work has been done in investigating cooperation representations, dependency relations between agents' activities [7,10,11,17], conflict resolution [4] and task allocation [15]. Acting coherently despite partial or erroneous knowledge, partner failures and unpredictable events is central to multi-agent research works. But, they provide few arguments to identify and

© Springer International Publishing AG 2017
B. An et al. (Eds.): PRIMA 2017, LNAI 10621, pp. 504–513, 2017.
https://doi.org/10.1007/978-3-319-69131-2_33

anticipate strengths and weaknesses in a group of cooperating agents. The main contribution of this paper is the study of how cooperating agents are affected by dependability issues. Specifically, our objectives are twofold:

- to formally define the concept of *dependability in cooperative encounters*,
- to characterize the computational complexity of achieving dependable encounters.

We introduce the fundamental concepts for our framework and define the *Cooperative Encounter Problem* as a decision problem combining task decomposition and allocation (Sect. 2). Then, we prove that this problem is intractable in principle (Sect. 3). Section 4 presents the related works, and some conclusions and future works are proposed in Sect. 5.

2   Cooperative Encounter Formalization

In this section, we define the fundamental concepts on which our search procedures are based.

2.1   Definitions

Cooperative encounters involve a set of agents, $\mathcal{A} = \{A_0, \ldots, A_n\}$ and a set of tasks, $\mathcal{T} = \{T_0, \ldots, T_m\}$. A task is either *primitive* or *composite*. This is represented as a set of *decomposition rules* $\mathcal{R}$ such that $(op, T_i, \rho) \in \mathcal{R}$: $\rho = [\tau_1, \ldots, \tau_k]$ is the decomposition of the composite task T_i into a list of k subtasks $\tau_i \in \mathcal{T}$, and $op \in \{AND, OR\}$: the AND operator means that a task is achieved if and only if all its subtasks are achieved; the OR operator signifies that at least one subtask has to be achieved in order to realize the composite task. We require that composite tasks appear only once in decomposition rules and we strictly forbid recursion. The primitive tasks do not have decomposition rules.

Each agent A_i has a set of $S_i \subseteq \mathcal{T}$ of **primitive** tasks that it can achieve, i.e. its *skills*: $\mathcal{S} = \{S_1, \ldots, S_n\}$ represents what each agent can do. Furthermore, we consider that agents can be *mutually exclusive* (mutex) in order to take into account conflicts, incompatible interests or unwillingness to work together, etc. $\nabla_i \subseteq \mathcal{A} - \{A_i\}$ denotes the set of A_i's mutually exclusive agents: $A_j \in \nabla_i$ if and only if $A_i \in \nabla_j$. Let $\mathcal{O} = \{\nabla_1, \ldots, \nabla_n\}$ be the set of mutually exclusive agents. (Ω_i, T_i) is the *assignment* of a set of agents $\Omega_i \subseteq \mathcal{A}$ to a task T_i. A task T_i is *achievable* if and only if there is no mutually exclusive agent in Ω_i and T_i is a skill of all the agents of Ω_i (otherwise it is *unachievable*). We use the term "achievable" rather than "achieved" on purpose: it means that T_i can be achieved if, at least, one of the agents of Ω_i does not collapse. Or, equivalently, T_i is not achieved if all the agents collapse. Our formalization does not constrain the meaning of the agent's collapse in any sense: it can be a rational decision to abandon, a failure, a malicious attack etc.

Now, we give a formal definition of the problem we want to address:

Definition 1. *A Cooperative Encounter Framework is a tuple $CEF = (\mathcal{A}, \mathcal{T}, \mathcal{S}, \mathcal{R}, \mathcal{O})$. A Cooperative Encounter Problem is a tuple $\wp = (CEF, \lambda)$ with $\lambda = [T_0]$. T_0 is the initial task. A cooperative encounter $\Delta = [(\Omega_0, T_0), \ldots, (\Omega_k, T_k)]$ is a list of assignments.*

In the following defintions, $e \cdot S$ stands for "in the list $e \cdot S$, e is the head and S is the tail", $R + S$ is the concatenation of R and S lists, $|A|$ is the cardinality of the set A and $A \bigotimes B = \{a \cup b \mid a \in A, b \in B\}$ is the cartesian product: $\{\{x\}, \{x'\}\} \bigotimes \{\{x''\}\} = \{\{x, x''\}, \{x', x''\}\}$. Then, we define how cooperative encounters are solution for Cooperative Encounter Problems as follows:

Definition 2. *A cooperative encounter Δ is a solution for a Cooperative Encounter Problem $\wp = (CEF, \lambda)$ if and only if either:*

1. *$\Delta = []$ and $\lambda = []$, or*
2. *Given $\Delta = (\Omega, T).\Delta'$ and $\lambda = T.\lambda'$, at least one of the following conditions is satisfied:*
   (a) T is primitive:
      T is achievable by Ω and Δ' is a solution of (CEF, λ');
   (b) $\exists (AND, T, \rho) \in \mathcal{R}$:
      Δ' is a solution of $(CEF, \rho + \lambda')$. That is, T is a composite task and all its subtasks have solutions;
   (c) $\exists (OR, T, \rho) \in \mathcal{R}$:
      $\exists t \in \rho$ such that Δ' is a solution of $(CEF, t.\lambda')$. That is, T is a composite task and at least one of its subtasks has a solution.

Definition 2 is recursive: it defines the achievement of the initial task T_0 as a decomposition process of T_0 into achievable primitive tasks. From here, the expression "cooperative encounter" will stand for "a cooperative encounter that is solution of a Cooperative Encounter Problem".

Figure 1 represents a cooperative encounter for the preparation of a meal consisting of an appetizer and an entree [10]. In this specification, cooking chicken means cooking a sauce and grilling the chicken. There are two alternatives for the sauce: either a tomato sauce or a pesto sauce. The tomato and pesto sauces are respectively performed by Kate and Mary; Joe is in charge of grilling the beef or the chicken. With respect to the *dependability* of their encounter, this role distribution is not the most appropriate because if Joe eventually does not attend the dinner (whatever the reason), the entree will not be done and the meal preparation will fail. A more adequate role distribution regarding the encounter's dependability, assuming that Joe and Kate have equivalent skills, is to assign the beef grilling task to Kate. As a consequence, whatever the failure of one of the invitees, the meal will be done. In this new role distribution, at least two agents (Joe and Kate) must fail to cause the meal to collapse. Hence, the resulting encounter is more dependable because the simultaneous failure of two agents is more improbable than one isolated failure (assuming that the probabilities of failure are independent).

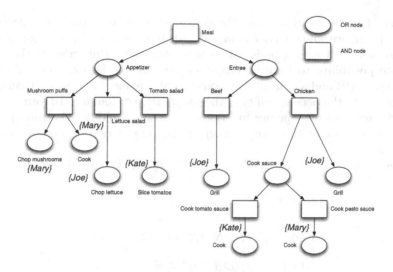

Fig. 1. A Cooperative Encounter Tree for the meal preparation.

The key idea of this paper is that role distributions define critical set of agents that are responsible for the vulnerability of cooperative encounters to failures. We name *conspiracy* the set of agents that must *simultaneously* fail to prevent the encounter's success. Thus, *the bigger the conspiracy, the more dependable the cooperative encounter.* Therefore, we define a dependable cooperative encounter is an optimization problem consisting in calculating a role distribution maximizing the conspiracy's size. In the meal scenario, the participating agents are Kate, Mary and Joe. However, the largest possible conspiracy is composed of Joe and Kate (Fig. 2).

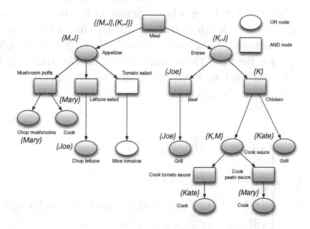

Fig. 2. Maximizing the conspiracy. The explored nodes appear in grey. {...} represents the conspiracies.

Then, how do we determine the conspiracies in a cooperative encounter? At this point, we know that the initial task is achievable by a decomposition into subtasks and agents assigned to these subtasks. But, not all the agents have the possibility to form a conspiracy because of the existence of various alternatives (OR nodes). Intuitively, some agents are more important than others with respect to the dependability of the cooperative encounter. To formalize this intuition, we need two "helper functions", $\top$ ("top") and $\bot$ ("bottom"), which will be used later in the computation of the cooperative encounters and the conspiracies.

Given $CEF = (\mathcal{A}, \mathcal{T}, \mathcal{S}, \mathcal{R}, \mathcal{O})$, $\wp = (CEF, [T_0])$ and Δ, we define $\bot$ and $\top$ as follows:

Definition 3

$$
\top(T) = \begin{cases}
\bigotimes_{t \in \rho} \top(t) & if\,(AND, T, \rho) \in \mathcal{R}, \\
\bigcup_{t \in \rho} \top(t) & if\,(OR, T, \rho) \in \mathcal{R}, \\
\{\emptyset\} & if\,T\,is\,primitive\,and\,achievable\,by\,\Omega, \\
\{T\} & if\,T\,is\,primitive\,and\,unachievable.
\end{cases}
$$

In Definition 3, $\top(T)$ represents the set of tasks that have to be achieved in order to achieve T, and $\emptyset$ means that there is nothing to do to achieve T as shown by the following theorem:

Theorem 1. *Let* $\wp = (CEF, [T_0])$ *be a Cooperative Encounter Problem.* $\Delta = [(\Omega_0, T_0), \ldots, (\Omega_k, T_k)]$ *is a solution of* $\wp$ *if and only if* $\emptyset \in \top(T_0)$.

Proof idea: the proof is by induction on the task decomposition depth k. For a single node tree ($k = 0$), it is easy to see from the Definition 3 that the theorem is true: proof sets of achievable leaf nodes contain the empty set element. Hence, the theorem is admitted for trees whose depth is inferior or equal to k. The theorem is proved for $k + 1$ depth trees by showing that achievable roots have k depth subtrees – all subtrees being achievable if that root is an AND node and at least one otherwise. Because these subtrees verify the theorem by induction hypothesis, it is not difficult to conclude from the Definition 3 that the proof sets of achievable $k + 1$ depth trees also contain $\emptyset$.

Definition 4

$$
\bot(T) = \begin{cases}
\bigcup_{t \in \rho} \bot(t) & if\,(AND, T, \rho) \in \mathcal{R}, \\
\bigotimes_{t \in \rho} \bot(t) & if\,(OR, T, \rho) \in \mathcal{R}, \\
\{\Omega\} & if\,T\,is\,primitive\,and\,achievable\,by\,\Omega, \\
\{\emptyset\} & if\,T\,is\,primitive\,and\,unachievable.
\end{cases}
$$

Definition 4 recursively computes the set of agents committed to the achievement of T. The smallest elements of $\bot(T)$ are "the most critical sets of agents", i.e. the agents that have the possibility to form conspiracies and collapse T (if $\emptyset \in \bot(T)$ then there is no set of agents able to achieve T). Then we define the **conspiracy set** $\chi(t)$ as follows:

Definition 5. $\chi(T) = \{x \in \bot(T) | \forall x' \in \bot(T), |x| < |x'|\}$

In Fig. 1, the meal is achievable because all its subtasks ("Appetizer" and "Entree") are achievable. Consider for instance the appetizer preparation: this is a composite taks, which is achievable unless {Mary, Joe, Kate} (the only conspiracy in the conspiracy set of the task "Appetizer") do not realize their tasks.

3   The Cooperative Encounter Problem Complexity

Now, consider the question of the Cooperative Encounter Problem satisfiability: given a CEP, does it admit a cooperative encounter Δ?

Let CE-SAT $= \{(CEF, [T_0]) | T_0$ is achievable$\}$. Not surprisingly,

Theorem 2. CE-SAT *is NP-complete.*

Proof: To show that CE-SAT is NP-complete, we must show that it is in NP and that all NP-problems are polynomial time reductible to it [16]. The first part consists in showing that, given a cooperative encounter Δ, there is a polynomial time algorithm that verifies that it is a solution of $(CEF, [T_0])$. The last part of the proof is based on a polynomial time reduction from 3SAT to CE-SAT.

CE-SAT is in NP. The proof by induction is based on the length k of the cooperative encounter Δ: $|\Delta| = k$.

- Basis: Proving that Δ is a solution for $k = 0$ is immediate. Here is a procedure that runs in polynomial time:
  1. If $k = 0$, test whether $\lambda = []$.
  2. If the test passes, *accept*; otherwise, *reject*.
- Induction step: For each $k \geq 0$, assume that CE-SAT satisfaction is in P for k (induction hypothesis) and show that it is also true for $k+1$. If $|\Delta| = k+1$, Δ is a solution iff case (2) in Definition 2 is true. We specifically analyze condition (2–a), the other conditions are similar. We give the following procedure:
  1. Test whether $(\Omega, T) = head(\Delta)$ and $T = head(\lambda)$.
  2. Test whether $tail(\Delta)$ is a solution of $(CEF, tail(\lambda))$.
  3. If both pass, *accept*; otherwise, *reject*.

The first test is decidable in polynomial time, so is the second because $|tail(\Delta)| = k$.

Here are the details of the reduction from 3SAT to CE-SAT that operates in polynomial time. Let $\phi = C_1 \wedge C_2 \wedge \cdots \wedge C_n$ where C_1 is a clause of formal parameters (for instance $a_1 \vee b_1 \vee c_1$) and each parameter corresponds to a propositional variable $a_1 = a$, $b_1 = \neg b$ etc. The reduction maps a Boolean formula ϕ to a CEP $\wp = (CEF, [\phi])$. The set of agents $\mathcal{A}$ in the

$CEF = (\mathcal{A}, \mathcal{T}, \mathcal{S}, \mathcal{R}, \mathcal{O})$ contains all the propositional variables. The set of tasks $\mathcal{T}$ is $\{a_1, b_1, c_1, \ldots, a_n, b_n, c_n\}$. Each agent's skill in $\mathcal{S}$ is defined by the mapping between the formal parameters and the propositional variables. The decomposition rules $\mathcal{R}$ are as follows: $(AND, \phi, [C_1, \ldots, C_n])$, $(OR, C_1, [a_1, b_1, c_1])$, $\ldots$, $(OR, C_n, [a_n, b_n, c_n])$. The mutex of an agent a in $\mathcal{O}$ is the negation of the corresponding propositional variable. For instance, $\nabla_a = \{\neg a\}$ etc.

We show that ϕ is satisfiable iff $\wp$ has a solution. If ϕ is satisfiable, there exists at least a true variable in each clause and an assignment of non contradictory variables. As a consequence, the corresponding agents are not mutexes. Let each of these agents commit to the leaves of the OR nodes and $\Delta = [(\Omega_0, \phi), (\Omega_1, C_1), \ldots, (\Omega_n, C_n), (\{a\}, a_1), (\{\neg b\}, b_1), \ldots]$. This is a solution of $\wp = (CEF, [\phi])$ because at least one agent commits to one of the leaves of all OR-type rules. Conversely, if $\wp = (CEF, [\phi])$ admits a solution Δ, by construction, at least one agent commits to a leaf in each OR node. We then assign *true* to each corresponding propositional variable. This assignment is consistant because agents are not mutexes in cooperative encounters (the corresponding variables are not contradictory) and at least one literal is true in each clause. Hence, ϕ is satisfiable.

4   Related Work

The Cooperative Encounter Tree is a cooperative structure very similar to those used elsewhere. The main difference is that CET are the result of a decision process when pre-defined cooperative structures are used in the literature as support for group activity. In their work on collaborative plans for complex group action [7], B. J. Grosz and S. Kraus rely on *recipes* to represent actions at different levels of abstraction, agents commit to them etc. In this framework, agents must decide what recipes to use and, if an agent is unable to perform an assigned action then the group revises its recipe. Recipes have been then extended to *Probabilistic Recipe Trees* [10] where each branch of an OR node to one of its children has an associated probability representing the likelihood of being selected. As a consequence, the agents implement decision-making strategies about the relevance of communicating information and perform actions helpful to their partners.

STEAM framework [17] focus is on devising general models of *teamwork* for the agents. Such models give them the ability to have appropriate behaviors whenever they discover unexpected opportunities or unexpectedly fail in fulfilling responsabilities. Group activity is represented by a hierarchy of team or individual *operators* that have rules of application and terminaison. Quite similarily to our approach, a *role* is an abstract specification of the set of activities an individual or a subteam undertakes in service of the team's overall activity; operators are connected to their sub-operators by AND-combination, OR-combination and role dependency relations.

Generalized Partial Global Planning (GPGP) [11] is also associated with a Hierarchical Task Network representation. This representation called TÆMS is an AND/OR goal tree with relations to data and resources that are needed to solve specific subgoals. Furthermore, interpendencies relations among goals are allowed in order to indicate that one goal may facilitate the achievement of another goal or may hinder it. TÆMS representation allows the agents to reason on how their local decisions influence other agents' activites and help them to schedule tasks in the most appropriate way.

More generally, mathematical treatment of cooperation are based on either game-theoric or modal logic formulations. d'Inverno et al. [6] have defined a graph structure of goals and discussed its properties for representing cooperation. Then, they have shown that the problem of determining whether cooperation structures are avalaible to achieve an agent's goal is NP-complete.

Contingent planning is the task of generating a conditional plan given uncertainty about the initial state and action effects, but with the ability to observe some aspects of the current world state. Contingent planning can be transformed into an And-Or search problem in belief space, the space whose elements are sets of possible worlds [1, 8, 13]. In online contingent planning under partial observability, an agent decides at each time step on the next action to execute, given its initial knowledge of the world, the actions executed so far, and the observation made. Such agents require some representation of their belief state to determine which actions are valid, or whether the goal has been achieved. Efficient maintenance of a belief state is, given its potential exponential size, a key research challenge [2]. In [5], the authors consider a general concept of undoability, asking whether a given action can always be undone, no matter which state it is applied to. This generalizes previous concepts of invertibility, and is relevant for search as well as applications.

Another related research area is multi-agent planning [3, 12]. Multi-agent planning deals with the problem of classical planning for multiple cooperative agents who have private information about their local state and capabilities they do not want to reveal [14]. Two main approaches have recently been proposed to solve this type of problem: one is based on reduction to distributed constraint satisfaction, and the other on partial-order planning techniques. In classical single-agent planning, constraint-based and partial-order planning techniques are currently dominated by heuristic forward search. The question arises whether it is possible to formulate a distributed heuristic forward search algorithm for privacy-preserving classical multi-agent planning. In [9], multiagent planning for cooperative agents in deterministic environments intertwines synthesis and coordination of the local plans of involved agents. Both of these processes require an underlying structure to describe synchronization of the plans. A distributed planning graph can act as such a structure, and the authors propose a general negotiation scheme for multiagent planning based on planning graphs.

5 Conclusion and Perspectives

Cooperation is a central issue in multi-agent systems and the research effort has focused mainly on trying to understand with models and experiments which are their desirable features. In this paper, we have emphasized some possible short-comings of cooperation. We have formally introduced the concepts of dependability and conspiracy in cooperative encounters. We have shown that achieving dependable encounters is a hard problem.

We are investigating the search algorithms and the heuristics to find and maximize dependable encounters. The idea is to build solutions with the highest vulnerability at first and then to reduce it by making conspiracies as large as possible (anytime approach).

References

1. Botea, A., Braghin, S.: Contingent versus deterministic plans in multi-modal journey planning. In: Proceedings of the Twenty-Fifth International Conference on Automated Planning and Scheduling, ICAPS 2015, Jerusalem, Israel, 7–11 June 2015, pp. 268–272 (2015)
2. Brafman, R.I., Shani, G.: Online belief tracking using regression for contingent planning. Artif. Intell. **241**, 131–152 (2016)
3. Cardoso, R.C., Bordini, R.H.: A distributed online multi-agent planning system. In: Proceedings of the Workshop on Distributed and Mutiltiagent Planning (ICAPS), pp. 15–23 (2016)
4. Cox, J.S., Durfee, E.H.: An efficient algorithm for multiagent plan coordination. In: AAMAS 2005: Proceedings of the Fourth International Joint Conference on Autonomous Agents and Multiagent Systems, pp. 828–835. ACM, New York, NY, USA (2005)
5. Daum, J., Torralba, Á., Hoffmann, J., Haslum, P., Weber, I.: Practical undoability checking via contingent planning. In: Proceedings of the Twenty-Sixth International Conference on Automated Planning and Scheduling, ICAPS 2016, London, UK, 12–17 June 2016, pp. 106–114 (2016)
6. d'Inverno, M., Luck, M., Wooldridge, M.: Cooperation structure. In: Proceedings of the Fifteenth Intenational Joint Conference on Artificial Intelligence, Nagoya, Japan, pp. 600–605 (1997)
7. Grosz, B., Grosz, B.J., Kraus, S.: Collaborative plans for complex group action. Artif. Intell. **86**, 269–357 (1996)
8. Hoffmann, J., Brafman, R.I.: Contingent planning via heuristic forward search with implicit belief states. In: Proceedings of the Fifteenth International Conference on Automated Planning and Scheduling (ICAPS 2005), 5–10 June 2005, Monterey, California, USA, pp. 71–80 (2005)
9. Tozicka, J., Jakubuv, J., Durkota, K., Komenda, A.: Multiagent planning by iterative negotiation over distributed planning graphs. In: Proceedings of the Workshop on Distributed and Mutiltiagent Planning (ICAPS), pp. 7–15 (2014)
10. Kamar, E., Gal, Y., Grosz, B.J.: Incorporating helpful behavior into collaborative planning. In: AAMAS 2009: Proceedings of The 8th International Conference on Autonomous Agents and Multiagent Systems, pp. 875–882. International Foundation for Autonomous Agents and Multiagent Systems, Richland, SC (2009)
11. Lesser, V., Decker, K., Wagner, T., Carver, N., Garvey, A., Horling, B., Neiman, D., Podorozhny, R., Prasad, M.N., Raja, A., Vincent, R., Xuan, P., Zhang, X.Q.: Evolution of the GPGP/TÆMS domain-independent coordination framework. Auton. Agents Multi-Agent Syst. **9**(1–2), 87–143 (2004)

12. Luis, N., Borrajo, D.: Plan merging by reuse for multi-agent planning. In: Proceedings of the Workshop on Distributed and Mutiltiagent Planning (ICAPS), pp. 38–46 (2014)
13. Maliah, S., Brafman, R.I., Karpas, E., Shani, G.: Partially observable online contingent planning using landmark heuristics. In: Proceedings of the Twenty-Fourth International Conference on Automated Planning and Scheduling, ICAPS 2014, Portsmouth, New Hampshire, USA, 21–26 June (2014)
14. Nissim, R., Brafman, R.I.: Distributed heuristic forward search for multi-agent planning. J. Artif. Intell. Res. **51**, 293–332 (2014)
15. Shehory, O., Kraus, S.: Methods for task allocation via agent coalition formation. Artif. Intell. **101**(1–2), 165–200 (1998)
16. Sipser, M.: Introduction to the Theory of Computation. Thomson Course Technology, Boston (2006)
17. Tambe, M.: Towards flexible teamwork. J. Artif. Intell. Res. **7**, 83–124 (1997)

An Algorithm for Simultaneous Coalition Structure Generation and Task Assignment

Fredrik Präntare$^{(\boxtimes)}$, Ingemar Ragnemalm, and Fredrik Heintz

Linköping University, 581 83 Linköping, Sweden
fredrik.prantare@liu.se

Abstract. Groups of agents in multi-agent systems may have to cooperate to solve tasks efficiently, and coordinating such groups is an important problem in the field of artificial intelligence. In this paper, we consider the problem of forming disjoint coalitions and assigning them to independent tasks simultaneously, and present an anytime algorithm that efficiently solves the *simultaneous coalition structure generation and task assignment* problem. This NP-complete combinatorial optimization problem has many real-world applications, including forming cross-functional teams aimed at solving tasks. To evaluate the algorithm's performance, we extend established methods for synthetic problem set generation, and benchmark the algorithm using randomized data sets of varying distribution and complexity. Our results show that the presented algorithm efficiently finds optimal solutions, and generates high quality solutions when interrupted prior to finishing an exhaustive search. Additionally, we apply the algorithm to solve the problem of assigning agents to regions in a commercial computer-based strategy game, and empirically show that our algorithm can significantly improve the coordination and computational efficiency of agents in a real-time multi-agent system.

Keywords: Coalition formation · Task allocation · Multi-agent system · Artificial intelligence · Optimal assignment

1 Introduction

An important research challenge in the domain of artificial intelligence and multi-agent systems is to solve the problem of how to organize and coordinate agents to improve their efficiency and capabilities when solving problems. Many partial solutions to this problem have already been suggested, including methods for *task allocation*, and algorithms based on the formation of organizations (e.g. coalitions, teams, hierarchies) [1,8,11]. For example, *coalition formation* is a technique that has been used to enable cooperation among agents in multi-agent environments by forming coalitions of agents. This technique involves evaluating different coalition structures, and forming the coalitions in the coalition structure that has the highest performance measure (utility value). The formed coalitions may then be used to perform tasks that require several agents to be accomplished efficiently. Optimal *coalition structure generation* is NP-complete, and

© Springer International Publishing AG 2017
B. An et al. (Eds.): PRIMA 2017, LNAI 10621, pp. 514–522, 2017.
https://doi.org/10.1007/978-3-319-69131-2_34

many algorithms have been presented that solves this problem, including algorithms based on dynamic programming, evolutionary approaches, and branch-and-bound [5–7,12].

The *optimal assignment* problem is an important optimization problem in which the goal is to assign workers to tasks to maximize the overall performance measure [2]. In certain settings this problem can be solved in polynomial time (e.g. using the Hungarian algorithm) [3].

In this paper, we consider the simultaneous (or combined) coalition structure generation and task assignment problem. This problem can be solved by first forming coalitions, and then assigning them to tasks. However, this approach may generate suboptimal solutions—even if the coalition structure generation and task allocation algorithms in themselves are optimal, since the generated coalitions may not be the best coalitions for the tasks at hand. The reason for this is that, during the generation of coalition structures, the performance measure of a coalition is given by its members, and not by the task that the coalition is potentially assigned to. Perhaps even worse is the consequence that any generated solution could potentially be arbitrarily worse than the optimal solutions. Additionally, this approach would generally require two different utility functions: one for each of the two subsequent steps, since coalition structure generation algorithms do not consider the tasks that each coalition is to be assigned to. This is disadvantageous, since it may not be a simple task to create good utility functions (or to generate realistic performance measures), and it could potentially be hard to predict how the two utility functions affect the quality of the generated solutions.

To address these issues, we present an efficient anytime algorithm that integrates task assignment into the formation of coalitions. We accomplish this by generating coalition structures where each coalition is assigned to exactly one task. Our algorithm can thus be used to create structured collaboration in multi-agent systems by utilizing task allocation. Furthermore, our algorithm only requires one utility function, has the ability to prune large subspaces of the search space, can give worst-case guarantees on generated solutions, and always generates optimal solutions when run to exhaustion.

To evaluate the algorithm's performance, we extend established methods for synthetic problem set generation provided by Sandholm and Larson [4], and benchmark our algorithm against simple brute-force and branch-and-bound implementations, since there are no algorithms that solves the problem under our assumptions that we can compare to. Such experiments can be replicated by anyone, and are conducted to deduce whether the presented algorithm can handle difficult data sets efficiently. Additionally, we apply our algorithm to solve the problem of assigning groups of agents to regions in the commercial strategy game *Europa Universalis 4*, and empirically show that our algorithm can be used to optimally solve real-world simultaneous coalition structure generation and task assignment problems efficiently. Apart from solving problems that exist in strategy games, our algorithm can potentially be used to solve many important real-world problems. It could, for example, be used to form optimal cross-functional teams aimed at solving a set of problems, to assist in the organization and coordination of subsystems in an artificial entity, or to allocate tasks in multi-robot systems.

We begin by formalizing the simultaneous coalition structure generation and task assignment problem in Sect. 2. Then, in Sect. 3, we give a presentation of our algorithm. In Sect. 4, we evaluate our algorithm, and present results from our experiments. In Sect. 5, we conclude with a summary of our results.

2 Problem Formalization

The simultaneous coalition structure generation and task assignment problem is formalized as:

Input: A set of agents $A = \{a_1, ..., a_n\}$, a set of tasks $T = \{t_1, ..., t_m\}$, and the performance measure $v(C, t)$ for assigning a coalition $C \subseteq A$ to a task $t \in T$.

Output: A set of coalitions $\{C_1, ..., C_m\}$ that maximizes the sum $\sum_{i=1}^{m} v(C_i, t_i)$, such that $C_i \subseteq A$, $C_i \cap C_j = \emptyset$ for all $i \neq j$, and $\bigcup_{i=1}^{m} C_i = A$.

3 Algorithm Description

To solve this problem, we propose an anytime algorithm based on branch-and-bound, a novel representation of the search space, and a guided sequential search for solutions. By using branch-and-bound, our algorithm can generate both optimal solutions, and high-quality anytime solutions with worst-case guarantees. The algorithm consists of the following three steps:

 I. **Partitioning of the search space.**
    To discard unnecessary parts of the search space that only contain suboptimal solutions, we first partition the search space into disjoint subspaces.
 II. **Calculation of the upper and lower bounds for the partitions.**
    We cannot know whether a subspace can be discarded if we don't have a way to deduce whether the best possible solution in that subspace can be discarded (if we want to be able to guarantee the optimality of our solutions).
III. **Searching for the optimal solution.**
    We search for the best solution by sequentially searching the partitions, and discarding unnecessary suboptimal subspaces using branch-and-bound.

3.1 Partitioning of the Search Space

Before we describe how our partitioning scheme works, note that an integer partition of an integer $k \in \mathbb{N}$ is a way of writing k as a sum of positive integers. Now, given a set of agents $A = \{a_1, ..., a_n\}$, and a set of tasks $T = \{t_1, ..., t_m\}$, we use the following three steps to partition the search space:

1. First, generate sets from all of the possible distinct integer partitions of the number $|A| = n$ that has $|T| = m$ or fewer addends. For example, if we have that $|A| = 4$ and $|T| = 3$, we generate $\{4\}, \{3, 1\}, \{2, 2\}$ and $\{2, 1, 1\}$.

2. Insert zeros to the sets that we generated during *step 1* until they have as many members as there are tasks. For example, given the sets from the example in *step 1*, we generate $\{4, 0, 0\}, \{3, 1, 0\}, \{2, 2, 0\}$, and $\{2, 1, 1\}$.

3. Now, let each possible multiset permutation of each of the sets generated during *step 2* represent partitions of the search space by letting each number represent a task. For example, the multiset permutation $\langle 4, 0, 0 \rangle$ corresponds to assigning 4 agents to t_1, 0 agents to t_2, and 0 agents to t_3, while $\langle 0, 4, 0 \rangle$ corresponds to assigning 0 agents to t_1, 4 agents to t_2, and 0 agents to t_3.

The multiset permutations in *step 3* can efficiently be generated using the algorithm based on tree-traversal proposed by Takaoka [9], or the algorithm based on loopless generation proposed by Williams [10].

The reason to why the generated partitions cover the whole search space is the fact that any coalition structure with n agents can be directly mapped to one of the possible distinct integer partitions of the integer n (for proof, see [7]). For instance, $\{\{a_i, a_j\}, \{a_k\}\}$ can be mapped to $\{2, 1\}$, and $\{\{a_i, a_j, a_k\}\}$ to $\{3\}$. In *step 1*, we generate the partitions that correspond to these mappings. We then remove unnecessary coalition structures in *step 2*, so that we only look at coalition structures that can represent valid solutions. Finally, in *step 3*, we refine the representation of the search space generated by *step 2*, by taking advantage of the fact that we are only interested in bijections of coalitions to tasks.

3.2 Calculation of the Upper and Lower Bounds for Partitions

To calculate the bounds for partitions, let $\mathbb{A}_p = (X \subseteq A : |X| = p)$, and define:

- $M(p, t) = \max \{v(C, t) : C \in \mathbb{A}_p\}$
- $Avg(p, t) = \frac{1}{|\mathbb{A}_p|} \sum \{v(C, t) : C \in \mathbb{A}_p\}$

Now, given a multiset permutation $P = \langle p_1, ..., p_m \rangle$ that represents a partition (subspace) of the search space, we can calculate an upper bound U_P for the partition that corresponds to P as the sum $U_P = \sum_{i=1}^{m} M(p_i, t_i)$. This is a valid upper bound for the partition that corresponds to P, since given a set of tasks $T = \{t_1, ..., t_m\}$, and any possible solution $S_P = \{C_1, ..., C_m\}$ induced by P with the performance measure $V(S_P) = \sum_{i=1}^{m} v(C_i, t_i)$, then $v(C_i, t_i) \leq M(|C_i|, t_i)$, of which $V(S_P) \leq U_P$ follows.

Similarly, we can calculate a lower bound L_P for the partition that corresponds to P as the sum $L_P = \sum_{i=1}^{n} Avg(p_i, t_i)$, with the intuition that a solution that has a value that is as good as the arithmetic mean of the solutions induced by P is always worse than or equal to the optimal solution induced by P.

3.3 Searching for the Optimal Solution

To search for the optimal solution, we expand one partition at a time, and base the precedence order for expanding partitions on the upper bound of the partitions: $U_{P_i} > U_{P_j} \implies P_i \prec P_j$, where $P_i \prec P_j$ denotes that partition P_i should be expanded before partition P_j. If two partitions have the same upper bound, we use a second ordering criterion based on the lower bound of the partitions: $U_{P_i} = U_{P_j}$ and $L_{P_i} > L_{P_j} \implies P_i \prec P_j$.

Now, given this order of precedence for the expansion of partitions, we sequentially search through each expanded partition using branch-and-bound. When a partition has an upper bound that is lower than or equal to the value of the best solution that we have found so far, simply discard the entire partition and terminate the search. Since the partitions are "sorted" on their upper bound, it is possible to terminate the search and still guarantee optimality.

To address the high memory requirements for generating and storing many multiset permutations (required for generating the precedence order), we can generate and store multiset permutations into blocks. These blocks can sequentially be generated and searched during partitioning. The more blocks we use, the less memory is required. In our case, we use each set generated in *step 2* during the partitioning phase to represent a block. In other words, each possible group of multiset permutations that has the same members is searched in sequence according to the aforementioned order of precedence.

4   Evaluation

A common approach to evaluating the performance of search algorithms is to use standardized problem instances for benchmarking. In the case of simultaneous coalition structure generation and task assignment, no such standardized problem instances exist. Therefore, we look at standardized problem instances from a similar domain. More specifically, we translate standardized problem instances used for benchmarking coalition structure generation algorithms to the domain of simultaneous coalition structure generation and task assignment.

Larson and Sandholm [4] provided standardized synthetic problem sets for the optimal coalition structure generation problem by using normal and uniform probability distributions to provide randomized coalition (utility) values. Following Rahwan et al. [7], we denote these NPD and UPD, respectively. Since our algorithm's performance depends on its ability to discard suboptimal subspaces of the search space, it is important that we benchmark it using problem sets with different characteristics. As such, we suggest using NPD and UPD for benchmarking our algorithm. In addition to NPD and UPD, we also use NDCS, a probability distribution that was proposed by Rahwan et al. [7] for benchmarking coalition structure generation algorithms, since both NPD and UPD generate biased results. Translating these probability distributions to our domain is simple, and the translations are presented below, where $v(C, t)$ denotes the performance measure of assigning a coalition C to a task t:

- **NPD:** $v(C, t) \sim |C| \times \mathcal{N}(\mu, \sigma^2)$, where $\sigma = 0.1$ and $\mu = 1$.
- **NDCS:** $v(C, t) \sim \mathcal{N}(\mu, \sigma^2)$, where $\sigma = \sqrt{|C|}$ and $\mu = |C|$.
- **UPD:** $v(C, t) \sim |C| \times \mathcal{U}(a, b)$, where $a = 0$ and $b = 1$.

Furthermore, the result of each experiment is produced by calculating the average of the resulting values (e.g. time measures or utility values) from 100 generated problem sets per probability distribution and experiment. We deem this to be sufficient to give a clear indication of the behavior of the algorithm. Finally, we compare our algorithm to simple brute-force and branch-and-bound implementations, since there are no existing algorithms that solves the problem under our assumptions that we can compare to. However, this is not possible when there are many agents and tasks, since simple algorithms based on brute-force and branch-and-bound are too slow.

4.1 Implementation and Equipment

The algorithms were implemented in C++11 using the C++ standard library. All probability distributions were generated using the random number distribution generator `std::random::normal_distribution<double>` for NDCS and NPD, and `std::random::uniform_real_distribution<double>` for UPD. The tests were conducted using a computer with Windows 10 (x64), an Intel 7700 K 4200 MHz CPU, and 16 GB of DDR4 memory (3000 MHz CL15).

4.2 Results

The execution time to find an optimal solution for the fixed number of 8 tasks is plotted using a logarithmic scale in Fig. 1. Plots of the search times for the plain branch-and-bound (denoted **pBNB**) and brute-force algorithms are used as a comparison to the presented algorithm (denoted **iBNB**). In Fig. 2, we fix the number of agents to 10, and look at how the number of tasks affect performance. Finally, in Fig. 3, we look at the quality of the anytime solutions generated by our algorithm. We used 12 agents and 8 tasks for this purpose, and interrupted the

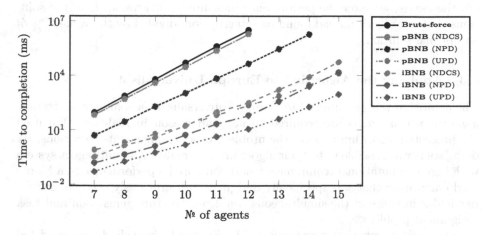

Fig. 1. The execution time to find an optimal solution in problems with 8 tasks.

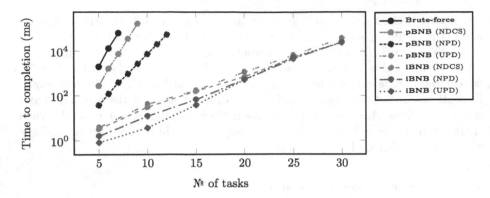

Fig. 2. The execution time to find an optimal solution in problems with 10 agents.

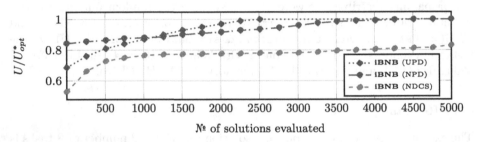

Fig. 3. The quality of anytime solutions when the algorithm is interrupted prior to finishing an exhaustive search when solving synthetic problem sets with $8^{12} \approx 7 \times 10^{10}$ possible solutions.

algorithm during search by only allowing it to evaluate a fixed number of solutions. The total number of solutions for 12 agents and 8 tasks is $8^{12} \approx 7 \times 10^{10}$. On the y-axis, we show the performance measure (utility value) U of the solutions that our algorithm had found on interruption, divided by the value U^*_{opt} of an optimal solution.

4.3   Applying the Algorithm to Europa Universalis 4

The algorithm was also applied to Europa Universalis 4—a commercial strategy game in which agents are required to act and reason in real-time. We used the presented algorithm to solve the problem of assigning agents to regions. By doing so, it was possible to test our algorithm in a real-world multi-agent system with high computational requirements, and compare its performance to a Monte Carlo algorithm that was specifically designed (and previously used) to solve a particular instance of the simultaneous coalition structure generation and task assignment problem.

The problem sets that were generated by Europa Universalis 4 each consisted of up to 8 agents and 35 regions (tasks). As such, the problem sets were rather small, with $|A| \in [2,8]$ and $|T| \in [2,35]$. In total, 13922 problem sets were generated, each reflecting a problem instance from the game. With this in mind, our algorithm managed to increase both the quality of the solutions, and the performance of the computer-based players, compared to using the specialized Monte Carlo algorithm that was developed and designed by the developers of the game. The quality of the solutions was increased by, on average, 565%, and the search time for the best possible solution was improved by, on average, 422%.

4.4 Discussion

As empirically shown, our algorithm is considerably faster (by many orders of magnitude) than both brute-force and plain branch-and-bound—for all problem sets and distributions. The reason is that our algorithm discards huge portions of the search space, and almost always terminates searches before it generates unnecessary solutions, even when solving extremely difficult problem sets (NDCS). For the same reasons, and due to our order of precedence for expanding partitions, it doesn't take our algorithm many evaluations before it finds close-to-optimal solutions for any of the three probability distributions.

The presented algorithm solves problem sets generated by UPD the fastest, followed by the sets generated by NPD, and then NDCS. This is not surprising, since it is reasonable to expect that our algorithm exhibits performance characteristics that are similar to those exhibited by similar algorithms used for coalition structure generation. In the case of 8 tasks, 8 agents, and problem sets generated by UPD, our algorithm is, on average, roughly 2416 times better than brute-force (i.e. it takes approximately 0.041% of the time to find the optimal solution). As the number of agents increases, this factor also increases. For example, in the case of 8 tasks and 12 agents and UPD, our algorithm is, on average, 280882 times better than brute-force (i.e. it finds optimal solutions in approximately 0.00035% of the time it takes for the brute-force algorithm). As such, if we increase the number of tasks or agents, the relative gains in performance increases considerably, which is also true in comparison to plain branch-and-bound.

5 Conclusions

In this paper, we presented an anytime algorithm that efficiently solves the simultaneous coalition structure generation and task assignment problem by integrating task assignment into the formation of coalitions. To benchmark our algorithm, we extended established methods for benchmarking coalition structure generation algorithms to our domain, and then used synthetic problem sets to empirically evaluate its performance. We used brute-force and plain branch-and-bound algorithms for comparison, since we didn't find any specialized algorithms that solves the problem under the same assumptions as we do.

Our results clearly demonstrate that our algorithm is far superior to brute-force and plain branch-and-bound, and that our algorithm doesn't have to search for very long before it can find good solutions. This is beneficial in many real-time systems (e.g. real-world multi-agent systems), in which optimal solutions are not always required. Apart from these properties, our algorithm is also able to give worst-case guarantees on anytime solutions due to taking advantage of branch-and-bound. Finally, by using our algorithm to improve agent-to-region assignment in Europa Universalis 4, we demonstrated that our algorithm can be used to efficiently solve a common real-world simultaneous coalition structure generation and task assignment problem.

References

1. Bryan, H., Lesser, V.: A survey of multi-agent organizational paradigms. Knowl. Eng. Rev. (2004)
2. Gerkey, B.P., Matar, M.J.: A formal analysis and taxonomy of task allocation in multi-robot systems. Int. J. Robot. Res. **23**(9), 943 (2004)
3. Kuhn, H.W.: The Hungarian method for the assignment problem. Naval Res. Logist. Q. **2**(1–2), 83–97 (1955)
4. Larson, K.S., Sandholm, T.W.: Anytime coalition structure generation: an average case study. J. Exp. Theoret. Artif. Intell. **12**(1), 23–42 (2000)
5. Rahwan, T., Jennings, N.R.: An improved dynamic programming algorithm for coalition structure generation. In: Proceedings of the 7th International Joint Conference on Autonomous Agents and Multiagent Systems, vol. 3. International Foundation for Autonomous Agents and Multiagent Systems (2008)
6. Rahwan, T., Michalak, T.P., Wooldridge, M., Jennings, N.R.: Coalition structure generation: a survey. Artif. Intell. **229**, 139–174 (2015)
7. Rahwan, T., Ramchurn, S.D., Jennings, N.R., Giovannucci, A.: An anytime algorithm for optimal coalition structure generation. J. Artif. Intell. Res. **34**, 521–567 (2009)
8. Shehory, O., Kraus, S.: Methods for task allocation via agent coalition formation. Artif. Intell. **101**(1–2), 165–200 (1998)
9. Takaoka, T.: An O(1) time algorithm for generating multiset permutations. In: International Symposium on Algorithms and Computation. Springer (1999)
10. Williams, A.: Loopless generation of multiset permutations using a constant number of variables by prefix shifts. In: Proceedings of the Twentieth Annual ACM-SIAM Symposium on Discrete Algorithms. Society for Industrial and Applied Mathematics (2009)
11. Yamada, T., Nasu, Y.: Heuristic and exact algorithms for the simultaneous assignment problem. Eur. J. Oper. Res. **123**(3), 531–542 (2000)
12. Yang, J., Luo, Z.: Coalition formation mechanism in multi-agent systems based on genetic algorithms. Appl. Soft Comput. **7**(2), 561–568 (2007)

Argument-Based Bayesian Estimation of Attack Graphs: A Preliminary Empirical Analysis

Hiroyuki Kido[1](✉) and Frank Zenker[2]

[1] Institute of Logic and Cognition, Sun Yat-sen University, Guangzhou, China
kido@mail.sysu.edu.cn
[2] Department of Philosophy, Lund University, Lund, Sweden

Abstract. This paper addresses how to identify attack relations on the basis of lay arguers' acceptability-judgments for natural language arguments. We characterize argument-based reasoning by three Bayesian network models (coherent, decisive, and positional). Each model yields a different attack relation-estimate. Subsequently, we analyze to which extent estimates are consistent with, and so could potentially predict, lay arguers' acceptability-judgments. Evaluation of a model's predictive ability relies on anonymous data collected online ($N = 73$). After applying leave-one-out cross-validation, in the best case models achieve an average area under the receiver operating curve (AUC) of .879 and an accuracy of .786. Though the number of arguments is small ($N = 5$), this shows that argument-based Bayesian inference can in principle estimate attack relations.

1 Introduction

According to Moens [5], "argumentation mining can be defined as the detection of the argumentative discourse structure in text or speech and the recognition or functional classification of the components of the argumentation." Detection of attack relations between arguments is important insofar as it potentially impacts sentiment analysis (or opinion mining) and persuasive technology in general. While sentiment analysis extracts information about lay arguers' opinions from discourse, detecting attack relations further enables extracting information why opinions are held, and thus how they might be changed.

As two major approaches to argumentation mining, computational linguistics (aka natural language processing) starts from textual discourse in order to identify individual arguments, their internal structure, and how they interact (see, e.g., [4,7]), while computational argumentation starts from the acceptability status of arguments in order to identify abstract attack relations between arguments (see, e.g., [3,6,8]). Riveret and Governatori [8], for instance, formalize the learning of such abstract structures via probability theory, thus aiming at a synthesis of structural and probabilistic approaches. Solutions to such learning-problems are qualified by their expected explanatory utility towards maximizing the similarity between an argumentation graph and its observed labeling. Moreover, Niskanen et al. [6] address the argument framework (AF) synthesis-problem for

© Springer International Publishing AG 2017
B. An et al. (Eds.): PRIMA 2017, LNAI 10621, pp. 523–532, 2017.
https://doi.org/10.1007/978-3-319-69131-2_35

constructing an AF from partial knowledge of argument statuses. Their problem-solutions are based on realizability (Dunne [2]) and become a function of the cost of minimizing the semantic distance between partial knowledge and a synthesized AF. Finally, Kido and Okamoto [3] have provided a Bayesian network that characterizes abstract argument-based reasoning. Here, attack relations are estimated by their posterior probability given the acceptability status of arguments. In addition to inferential (causal) relations, this network also handles inferences to the best explanation.

This paper focuses on the approach presented in [3] as a well-founded instance of Bayesian statistical inference. A critical weakness of this work, however, is that it lacks empirical justification. So it remains unclear whether lay arguers find compelling how the network estimates the attack relations between arguments. (The term 'argument' here refers the combination of a claim and reasons.) Addressing this lacuna, our study therefore asks to which extent lay arguers' revealed acceptability-judgments of arguments are consistent with how the Bayesian network estimates the attack relations.

To answer this question, we instantiate the general Bayesian network of [3] with three specific models, called coherent, decisive and positional models. Models differ in the number of their extensions, which intuitively correspond to self-consistent standpoints that explain the acceptability status of arguments. We represent an extension by a random variable situated between a model's parent variable (representing an attack relation between arguments) and its child variables (representing an argument's acceptability status). We evaluate the models' predictive ability on two criteria, namely the area under the receiver operating curve (AUC) and accuracy, after applying a method called leave-one-out cross-validation (LOOCV) .

To anticipate the main result: given 5 arguments pro or con government-control of a casino, we estimated attack relations between pairs of arguments (using the three models) on the basis of 73 data-sets obtained online from anonymous lay arguers. Results show a maximum AUC of .879 and maximum accuracy of .786. The scale of the study is admittedly small. Results nevertheless suggest that Bayesian models are useful towards identifying attack relations, although the semantic content of an argument is not analyzed. To our knowledge, this is the first study in argument-based Bayesian inference [3] that distinguishes coherent, decisive and positional models to represent different standpoints that explain the acceptability status of an argument. Moreover, this also demonstrates for the first time the use-value of Dung's abstract argumentation framework for purposes of statistically estimating attack relations.

2 Preliminaries

2.1 Abstract Argumentation

An abstract argumentation framework (AF) [1] is defined as a pair $\langle Arg, Att \rangle$, where Arg denotes a set of arguments and Att denotes a binary relation on Arg. Att represents an attack relation between arguments, i.e., $(a, b) \in Att$ means

"a attacks b." Suppose $a \in Arg$ and $S \subseteq Arg$. S attacks a if, and only if (iff), some member of S attacks a. By contrast, S is conflict-free iff S attacks none of its members. Further, S defends a iff S is conflict-free and S attacks all arguments that attack a. A characteristic function $F : Pow(Arg) \rightarrow Pow(Arg)$ is defined by $F(S) = \{a|S \text{ defends } a\}$. Given an AF, acceptability semantics [1] thus defines four types of extensions that correspond to intuitively rational sets of arguments. Here, S is a complete extension (abbreviated CE) iff S is a fixed point of F. S is a grounded extension (GE) iff it is a minimum complete extension with respect to set inclusion. S is a preferred extension (PE) iff it is a maximum complete extension with respect to set inclusion. S is a stable extension (SE) iff it is a complete extension that attacks all members in $Arg \setminus S$.

Example 1. We assume an abstract argumentation framework $AF = \langle Arg, Att \rangle$, where $Arg = \{a, b, c, d\}$, and $Att = \{(b, c), (c, b), (c, d), (d, d)\}$. The acceptability semantics defines the four types of extensions: preferred extensions $\{a, b\}$ and $\{a, c\}$, stable extension $\{a, c\}$, grounded extension $\{a\}$, and complete extensions $\{a\}$, $\{a, b\}$ and $\{a, c\}$.

To define logical expressions for the possible acceptability statuses of arguments in Arg, we introduce the propositional language L_{Arg}.

Definition 1 (Language). *For all arguments $x \in Arg$, x is a formula of L_{Arg}. If x and y are formulas of L_{Arg}, then $(x \wedge y)$, $(x \vee y)$, $(x \rightarrow y)$, and $\neg x$ are formulas of L_{Arg}.*

In this study, $s(AF), p(AF), g(AF)$, and $c(AF)$ respectively denote the sets of all stable, preferred, grounded, and complete extensions of AF.

2.2 Bayesian Network for Argument-Based Reasoning

We assume that four types of random variables Att, Sem, Ext, and Acc respectively represent attack relations, acceptability semantics, extensions, and acceptability statuses. We moreover assume that Arg represents a set of arguments. The domain of Att is defined as a set of binary relations on Arg, i.e., $dom(Att) \subseteq Pow(Arg \times Arg)$, and the domain of Sem is defined as a set of the acceptability semantics, i.e., $Sem \subseteq \{s, p, g, c\}$. Here, s, p, g, and c respectively represent stable, preferred, grounded, and complete semantics. The domain of Ext is defined as a subset of the power set of arguments, i.e., $dom(Ext) \subseteq Pow(Arg)$, and the domain of Acc is defined as a set comprising a formula and its negation, i.e., $dom(Acc) = \{x, \neg x\}$ where $x \in L_{Arg}$.

A Bayesian network is a directed acyclic graph. Each node represents a random variable and each edge represents an independence relation between the former. The Bayesian network structure of [3] is defined as follows:

Definition 2 (Bayesian network structure). *[3] Let Att, Sem, Ext_i, and Acc_{ij} be random variables of, respectively, attack relations, semantics, extensions, and acceptability statuses, for all $i(1 \leq i \leq m)$ and $j(1 \leq j \leq n)$. A Bayesian network structure for argument-based reasoning is defined as shown in Fig. 1.*

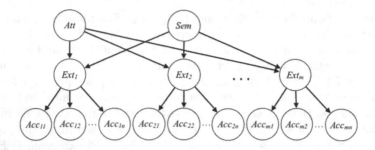

Fig. 1. The Bayesian network structure for argument-based reasoning [3].

To estimate an attack relation, Bayes' theorem computes the posterior probabilities of all hypothetical attack relations given observed acceptability statuses. If α denotes a normalization constant for $dom(Att)$, then the posterior probability of the attack relation att given the observed acceptability statuses $acc_{11}, acc_{12}, ..., acc_{mn}$, itself denoted $\boldsymbol{acc}$, is calculated as follows:

$$P(att|\boldsymbol{acc}) = \frac{P(\boldsymbol{acc}|att)P(att)}{P(\boldsymbol{acc})} = \alpha \sum_{\boldsymbol{ext}} \sum_{sem} P(\boldsymbol{acc}, \boldsymbol{ext}, sem, att)$$

$$= \alpha P(att) \sum_{sem} P(sem) \prod_{i=1}^{m} \sum_{ext_i} P(ext_i|att, sem) \prod_{j=1}^{n} P(acc_{ij}|ext_i).$$

3   Coherent, Decisive and Positional Models

This section introduces three specific models instantiating the Bayesian network introduced in the previous section.

Definition 3 (Coherent model). *Let Arg be a set of arguments and L a possible number of observations. A coherent model is a Bayesian network with the structure shown in Fig. 2 where n is the cardinality of Arg and, for any argument $x \in Arg$, there are two random variables Acc_i and Acc_j such that their domain is $\{x, \neg x\}$.*

A plate notation is used to represent Bayesian network structures. The random variable in each box exists as often as the number in the bottom right corner specifies. Variables have the same parent and the same conditional probability table (defined below). In contrast to other models (also defined below), the coherent model has a single extension. We call the model coherent because any acceptability status of *all arguments* is defined by an extension. So a single rational belief, as it were, provides an interpretation of all arguments.

Definition 4 (Decisive model). *Let Arg be a set of arguments and L be a possible number of observations. A decisive model is a Bayesian network with the structure shown in Fig. 3, where m is the cardinality of Arg and, for any argument $x \in Arg$, there is a random variable Ext_i such that the domain of the random variables Acc_{i1} and Acc_{i2} is $\{x, \neg x\}$.*

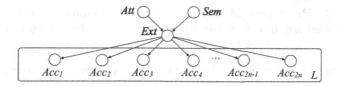

Fig. 2. The coherent model having a single extension.

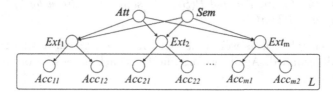

Fig. 3. The decisive model having as many extensions as the number of arguments.

In contrast to the other two models, the decisive model has as many extensions as the number of arguments. We call the model decisive because, for any acceptability status of *each argument*, there is an extension defining the status. Thus, for any argument, a rational belief provides an interpretation of the argument.

Definition 5 (Positional model). *Let Arg be a set of arguments and L be a possible number of observations. A positional model is a Bayesian network with the structure shown in Fig. 4 where m is the cardinality of Arg and, for any argument $x \in Arg$, there are two random variables Ext_i and Ext_j such that the domain of the random variables Acc_i and Acc_j is $\{x, \neg x\}$.*

In contrast to the other two models, the positional model has as many extensions as the number of possible positions, depending on whether a given formula takes the values True or False with respect to every argument. We call the model positional because, for any acceptability status of *each position* on a given argument, an extension defines the status. Thus, for any position, a rational belief provides an interpretation of the position.

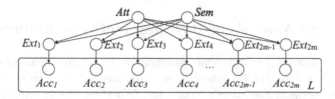

Fig. 4. The positional model having as many extensions as the number of positions.

We now define conditional probability tables for the three models, assuming that every attack relation occurs with the same probability, respectively.

Definition 6 (Prior probability of attack relations). *Let att* ∈ *dom(Att).* *The prior probability of att, denoted P(Att = att), is defined by 1/N, where N is the cardinality of dom(Att).*

Similarly, we assume that acceptability semantics occur with the same probability.

Definition 7 (Prior probability of semantics). *Let sem* ∈ *dom(Sem). The prior probability of sem, denoted P(Sem = sem), is defined by 1/N, where N is the cardinality of dom(Sem).*

Once an attack relation as well as its semantics are given, a set of extensions is uniquely determined. Again, we assume that each extension occurs with the same probability.

Definition 8 (Conditional probability of extensions). *Let sem* ∈ *dom(Sem), att* ∈ *dom(Att) and ext* ∈ *dm(Ext). The posterior probability of ext, given att and sem, denoted P(Ext = ext|Att = att, Sem = sem), is defined as 1/N if ext* ∈ *sem(⟨Arg, att⟩), and as 0 otherwise, where N is the cardinality of sem(⟨Arg, att⟩).*

Given an extension, the acceptability status of each argument is thus uniquely determined. Intuitively, we must define the posterior probability of an argument's logical expression as 1 iff the extension satisfies the formula in terms of the entailment relation ⊨. This may lead to a zero-frequency problem, however, if the posterior probability of a dependent variable is 0, and provided we observe merely one formula that is not satisfied by the extension. We therefore use an m-estimator, here assuming m samples some of which are satisfied by the extension, while others are not. The proportion p of each of these m samples occurring, finally, is assumed to be the same.

Definition 9 (Conditional probability of acceptability statuses). *Let ext be an extension and acc be an acceptability status. The posterior probability of acc given ext, denoted P(Acc = acc|Ext = ext), is defined as (1+mp)/(1+m) if ext ⊨ acc, and as mp/(1 + m) otherwise.*

Hereafter, we use a Laplacian estimator assuming $m = 2$ and $p = .5$.

4   Empirical Analysis of Bayesian Network Models

We used the following five arguments pro/contra public-management of casinos: (a) "A casino should not be owned by a state because it becomes a hotbed of crime and causes pathological gambling;" (b) "No state should enter a commercial business because efficient and effective management cannot not be expected without competition by private companies;" (c) "A casino has no global demand because the number of people who enjoy gambling is limited and there are many people, especially young adults, who do not like gambling;" (d) "A casino has global demand because some countries own publicly-managed gambling sports, *e.g., horse racing, making a stable profit;"* (e) *"A casino should be owned by a state because it is an effective strategy to earn foreign exchange and create new jobs."*

We collected lay arguers' data online, using a (Google forms) questionnaire consisting of two parts. In Part 1, respondents answered a variant of the following questions, in this order, for every possible pair of arguments $x, y \in \{a, b, c, d, e\}$, and in Part 2 for every individual argument $x \in \{a, b, c, d, e\}$.

Part 1 *Do you think arguments x and y conflict? Please choose either "Yes" or "No."*

Part 2.1 *How much do you agree with argument x? Please choose an approximate value from 0 (meaning no agreement) to 5 (meaning complete agreement).*

Part 2.2 *How much do you disagree with argument x? Please choose an approximate value from 0 to 5.*

	a	b	c	d	e
a	0 (0%)	24 (32.9%)	22 (30.1%)	41 (56.2%)	59 (80.8%)
b	24 (32.9%)	0 (0%)	19 (26.0%)	50 (68.5%)	58 (79.5%)
c	22 (30.1%)	19 (26.0%)	0 (0%)	52 (71.2%)	46 (63.0%)
d	41 (56.2%)	50 (68.5%)	52 (71.2%)	0 (0%)	13 (18.8%)
e	59 (80.8%)	58 (79.5%)	46 (63.0%)	13 (18.8%)	0 (0%)

degree	votes to a for	against	votes to b for	against	votes to c for	against	votes to d for	against	votes to e for	against
0	6 (8.2%)	22 (30.1%)	5 (6.8%)	18 (24.7%)	5 (6.8%)	16 (21.9%)	9 (12.3%)	11 (15.1%)	19 (26%)	7 (9.6%)
1	9 (12.3%)	15 (20.5%)	13 (17.8%)	10 (13.7%)	8 (11%)	14 (19.2%)	8 (11%)	12 (16.4%)	6 (8.2%)	8 (11%)
2	9 (12.3%)	10 (13.7%)	13 (17.8%)	8 (11%)	12 (16.4%)	19 (26%)	10 (13.7%)	13 (17.8%)	11 (15.1%)	18 (24.7%)
3	11 (15.1%)	10 (13.7%)	8 (11%)	21 (28.8%)	14 (19.2%)	14 (19.2%)	26 (35.6%)	17 (23.3%)	22 (30.1%)	14 (19.2%)
4	16 (21.9%)	11 (15.1%)	16 (21.9%)	10 (13.7%)	19 (26%)	6 (8.2%)	10 (13.7%)	10 (13.7%)	10 (13.7%)	9 (12.3%)
5	22 (30.1%)	5 (6.8%)	18 (24.7%)	6 (8.2%)	15 (20.5%)	4 (5.5%)	10 (13.7%)	10 (13.7%)	5 (6.8%)	17 (23.3%)

Fig. 5. Participants' revealed attack relations (top) and acceptability-judgments (bottom)

Data from 94 anonymous participants (obtained via a recruiting agency) were recorded, placing no restriction on attributes such as age and gender. For practical and computational reasons, we limited the number of arguments to five, thus generating 15 questions and answers (10 in Part 1; 5 in Part 2). We treated data-sets as implausible only if the same answer was supplied to all questions in Part 1, or if answers to questions 2.1 and 2.2 were the same for all arguments. We thus retained 73 valid data-sets.

Data obtained in Part 1 are presented in the adjacency matrix at the top of Fig. 5. Each cell states the number of total acceptability-judgments, or votes, along with each vote's probability. Similarly, data from Part 2 are presented at the bottom of Fig. 5. Answers to questions 2.1 and 2.2 correspond to votes for or against an argument. We thus obtained various conflict relations as defined by different thresholds of argument-acceptability. Obviously, the number of conflicts increases if the conflict threshold is lowered, and vice versa. In discussing the stability of these models, we therefore consider a *dynamic* conflict threshold.

Our analysis relied on the leave-one-out cross validation-method (LOOCV) along with the two criteria AUC (the area under the receiver operating characteristic curve) and accuracy. LOOCV treats the presence of conflicts among a given pair of arguments as "hidden" information, and estimates this from the presence of conflicts among all remaining pairs of arguments. Figure 6 shows an average receiver operating characteristic curve (ROC) of the 73 data-sets. In all models, except GE (grounded extension), the use of SE (stable extensions), PE (preferred extensions) and CE (complete extensions), does on average exceed AUC = .8. This means these models are stable with respect to changing the conflict threshold. Notice that GE performs badly because, due to its uniqueness, random variables for GE can only take one value.

With respect to accuracy, it is equally obvious that the number of estimated conflicts increases as the accuracy threshold is lowered, and vice versa. We there-

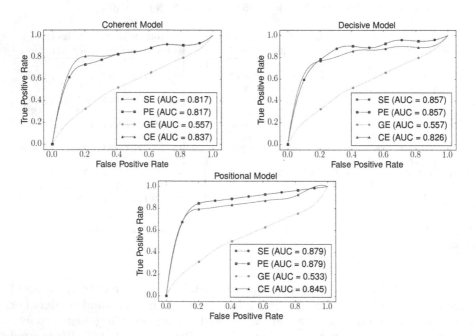

Fig. 6. Average ROC curves of 73 data-sets. Each of the 73 data-sets is averaged on conflict-thresholds ranging from .2 to .8, in steps of .1, and interpolated to smooth out the curves.

fore proceed to analyze the models' accuracy with respect to changing both the conflict and accuracy thresholds. Given the use of SE, PE and CE in any model, if the conflict-threshold is .5, then the accuracy value is 1. in an accuracy threshold. Averaging accuracy on each conflict threshold, the best use is CE in the positional model where the best accuracy value is .786 in an accuracy threshold. Except for GE, the worst use is SE and PE in the decisive model where the best accuracy value is .686 in an accuracy threshold.

These results imply that we can in the best case identify an attack relation between arguments with an accuracy of nearly 80%. In terms of accuracy, moreover, the coherent model turns out to be inferior to both the decisive and the positional model. In terms of the stability of accurately estimating attack relations when changing the threshold, finally, the decisive model proves to be inferior to the positional one.

5   Conclusion

This paper has formalized coherent, decisive and positional models as instances of the Bayesian network described in [3], which characterizes argument-based reasoning. Applying LOOCV and using the criteria AUC and accuracy on 73 data-sets recording lay arguers' acceptability judgments for five pro/con arguments, the models' best predictive ability was estimated as AUC = .879 and accuracy = .786. Results show that, despite not semantically analyzing an argument, the use of argumentation in Bayesian inference in principle succeeds at estimating attack relations. In our view, this sufficiently motivates further broadening the study of argument-based Bayesian inference. Future work should increase the number of arguments and data-sets, may apply various approximate inference algorithms (e.g., Gibbs sampler) to advanced Bayesian network models.

Acknowledgements. This study was supported by JSPS KAKENHI Grant Number 15KT0041, awarded to H.K. F.Z. acknowledges funding from HANBAN, the Volkswagen Foundation (90 531), and the European Union (1225/02/03).

References

1. Dung, P.M.: On the acceptability of arguments and its fundamental role in non-monotonic reasoning, logic programming, and n-person games. Artif. Intell. **77**, 321–357 (1995)
2. Dunne, P.E.: Computational properties of argument systems satisfying graph-theoretic constraints. Artif. Intell. **171**(10–15), 701–729 (2007)
3. Kido, H., Okamoto, K.: A Bayesian approach to argument-based reasoning for attack estimation. In: Proceedings of the 26th International Joint Conference on Artificial Intelligence, pp. 249–255 (2017)
4. Lawrence, J., Reed, C.: Argument mining using argumentation scheme structures. In: Proceedings of the 6th International Conference on Computational Models of Argument, pp. 379–390 (2016)

5. Moens, M.F.: Argumentation mining: Where are we now, where do we want to be and how do we get there? In: Proceedings of the 5th Forum on Information Retrieval Evaluation (2013)
6. Niskanen, A., Wallner, J.P., Järvisalo, M.: Synthesizing argumentation frameworks from examples. In: Proceesings of the 22nd European Conference on Artificial Intelligence, pp. 551–559 (2016)
7. Palau, R.M., Moens, M.F.: Argumentation mining: the detection, classification and structure of arguments in text. In: Proceedings of the 12th International Conference on Artificial Intelligence and Law, pp. 98–107 (2009)
8. Riveret, R., Governatori, G.: On learning attacks in probabilistic abstract argumentation. In: Proceedings of the 15th International Conference on Autonomous Agents and Multiagent Systems, pp. 653–661 (2016)

Alternating Offers Protocol Considering Fair Privacy for Multilateral Closed Negotiation

Hiroyuki Shinohara(✉) and Katsuhide Fujita

Department of Computer and Information Sciences, Faculty of Engineering,
Tokyo University of Agriculture and Technology, Tokyo, Japan
shinohara@katfuji.lab.tuat.ac.jp

Abstract. In multi-agent systems, a multilateral closed negotiation, where the opponent's strategy and utility are closed, is an important class of automated negotiations. However, most existing negotiation protocols haven't addressed the private information revealed by agents. During negotiations, such private information as agents preferences must be revealed fairly because each agent loses utility in them. In this paper, we propose a negotiation protocol that addresses the fairness of revealing each agent's private information. First, we propose a new measure of revealing each agent's private information, which is based on the accuracy of estimating opponents' utility functions. Next, the negotiation protocol adjusts the number of offers by each agent based on a new measure. This adjustment encourages agents who reveal less private information than other agents to reveal more offers. In the experiments, we compared and investigated the fairness of revealing private information by tournaments among state-of-the-art agents in ANAC2016 using our proposed negotiation protocol. The experimental results demonstrate that our proposed negotiation protocol with the adjustment improves the fairness of the revealed private information and a trade-off between the revealed private information and individual utility exists.

1 Introduction

Automated negotiation, which originates from various disciplines including economics, social science, and game theory, has played an important role in artificial intelligence ([8, 12–14]). Automated negotiating agents will enable automatic negotiations and act cooperatively against conflicts. The developments of automated negotiating agents for realistic situations are also expected to support negotiations among people and achieve decision support systems.

Motivated by the challenges of bilateral negotiations among agents, the automated negotiating agents competition (ANAC) was first organized in 2010 to facilitate research in automated multi-issue closed negotiation [1]. The ANAC setup is based on realistic models that include time discounting, closed negotiation, and alternative offering protocols. By analyzing the ANAC results, the trends of the automated negotiating agents' strategies and critical factors for developing competition have been shown [4]. Many effective automated negotiating agents have also been proposed through competitions [5,6].

© Springer International Publishing AG 2017
B. An et al. (Eds.): PRIMA 2017, LNAI 10621, pp. 533–541, 2017.
https://doi.org/10.1007/978-3-319-69131-2_36

Multi-issue closed negotiation, including multiple parties, is crucial for achieving automated negotiations because their settings closely resemble negotiations in real life. Many real-world negotiation problems assume multiparty situations because web negotiations are becoming more common. Although an automated negotiation strategy can be effective for bilateral negotiations, it is not always possible or desirable to apply it to multiparty negotiations [7]. In other words, designing more efficient automated negotiation strategies against various negotiating opponents in multiparty situations remains an open and interesting question. Therefore, several negotiation protocols are proposed including multilateral situation [2,3,10,15,16]. However, most existing negotiation protocols haven't considered the private information revealed by agents. In negotiations, revealing such private information as agent offers should be kept fair because each agent loses utility in negotiations. In addition, the existing measure of revealed agents' private information failed to consider the effectiveness of private information for negotiations [9].

In this paper, we propose a negotiation protocol that addresses the fairness of revealing the private information of agents. First, we propose a new measure of revealed private information of each agent, which is based on the accuracy of estimating opponents' utility functions. In this, the estimation is done by a simple estimation method that counts opponent's offers. A simple estimation method that counts opponent's offers is one common estimation method in multi-issue closed negotiations [11]. In this method, the utility function is predicted by counting and normalizing the occurrences of each element in proposed bids. An example of counting the elements of 500 proposals is shown in Table 1 for the utility function given in Table 2. After that, the negotiation protocol adjusts the number of offers by each agent based on a measure that revealed private information. This adjustment encourages agents who reveal less private information than other agents to reveal more offers.

Table 1. Example of predictions based on counting values of each issue

Issue	Value	Occurrence	Normalized value
Issue 1	Value (1,1)	230	1.00
	Value (1,2)	130	0.57
	Value (1,3)	140	0.61
Issue 2	Value (2,1)	30	0.09
	Value (2,2)	80	0.24
	Value (2,3)	60	0.18
	Value (2,4)	330	1.00

We experimentally compared and investigated the fairness of the revealed private information by tournaments among state-of-the-art agents at ANAC2016 using our proposed negotiation protocol. Our results demonstrate that our

Table 2. Example of utility space

Issue	Issue weight	Value	Value evaluation
Issue 1	0.4	Value (1,1)	1.00
		Value (1,2)	0.35
		Value (1,3)	0.55
Issue 2	0.6	Value (2,1)	0.80
		Value (2,2)	0.10
		Value (2,3)	0.40
		Value (2,4)	1.00

proposed negotiation protocol improves the fairness of the revealed private information and a trade-off between the revealed private information and individual utility exists.

This paper makes the following two contributions:

1. We proposed a novel measure of revealed private information considering the importance in negotiation;
2. We proposed a new negotiation protocol that considers fair privacy.

The remainder of this paper is organized as follows. First, we describe describe the negotiation environments. Next, we propose a new measure of revealing private information as well as an adjustment method of the number of offers based on this measure. Finally, we demonstrate our experimental results and provide a conclusion.

2   Negotiation Environments

We assume that more than three agents (A_1, A_2, A_3) are involved in a negotiation. The parties negotiate about *issues*, each of which has an associated range of alternatives or *values*. A negotiation outcome consists of a mapping of every issue to a value, and set Ω of all possible outcomes is called the negotiation *domain*, which is the common knowledge shared by the negotiating parties and remains fixed during a single negotiation session. All parties have certain preferences, prescribed by a *preference profile* over Ω, which can be modeled by utility function U that maps possible outcome $\omega \in \Omega$ to a real number in range $[0, 1]$. In contrast to the domain, a preference profile is private information.

A negotiation lasts a predefined time in seconds (*deadline*). The timeline is normalized, i.e., time $t \in [0, 1]$, where $t = 0$ represents the negotiation's start and $t = 1$ represents its deadline. Except for a deadline, a scenario may feature discount factors that decrease the utility of the bids under negotiation as time passes. Let δ in $[0, 1]$ be the discount factor, and let t in $[0, 1]$ be the current normalized time, as defined by the timeline. We compute discounted utility U_D^t of outcome ω from undiscounted utility function U as follows:

$$U_D^t(\omega) = U(\omega) \cdot \delta^t.$$

At $t = 1$, the original utility is multiplied by the discount factor. If $\delta = 1$, the utility is not affected by time, and such a scenario is undiscounted.

A bid is a set of chosen values $s_1 \ldots s_{|||}$ for each issue. Each value is assigned evaluation value $eval(s_i)$ in the utility function, and each issue is assigned normalized weight (w_i, $\sum_{i \in I} w_i = 1$) in the utility function. The utility is the weighted sum of the normalized evaluation values. When three agents negotiate, each agent has its own utility function.

According to issue's element s_i and s_i's evaluation $eval(s_i)$, the utility function is expressed as

$$U(\vec{s}) = \sum_{i \in I}(w_i \times eval(s_i)). \tag{1}$$

The utility function refers to each agent's preference, which is calculated by the weights of the issues and the evaluation value of the elements for each issue.

Table 2 shows an example of the weighted-summing utility function. Bid $\vec{s} = (Value(1,1), and\ Value(2,2))$'s utility is $U(\vec{s}) = 0.4 \times 1.0 + 0.6 \times 0.1 = 0.46$. When the discount factor is considered, the actual utility values are reduced as time passes.

3   Alternating Offers Protocol Considering Fair Privacy

3.1   Measure of Agent's Revealed Private Information

We proposed a new measure of revealed agent's revealed private information in negotiations based on the following two concepts:

1. The critical private information in negotiations is defined as that information that reveals the agent's utility of each offer.
2. The information predicted by a common estimated method is almost the same as the revealed information.

In our new revealing measure, we consider the importance of each agent's private information for the negotiation. The utility space means an agent's preference information and should remain concealed because the opponents can advantageously conduct their negotiation. In addition, the situations, where the private utility function is predicted by opponents with the common method, are already the same as revealing their private information. Therefore, the accuracy of estimating an opponent's utility function is a critical measure of the revealed private information.

Based on the above, the measure of the revealed private information for each agent is defined by the accuracy of estimated utility function for all of the agents. In our new measure, we assume that the estimated method, which counts the opponent's offers, is a common estimation method of the opponent's utility function.

When I means the set of issues, $Value(i)$ means the set of values for issue i, $Value(i, j)$ means value j for issue i, $eval(Value(i, j))$ means the evaluation function of $Value(i, j)$, and $Estimated(Value(i, j))$ means the estimated evaluation function of $Value(i, j)$, N means the total count of the values in each issue, i.e., $N = \sum_{i \in I} |Value(i)|$, and the accuracy rate of estimating the opponent's utility function is calculated as follows:

$$(Privacy\ Score) = \sum_{i \in I} \sum_{j \in Value(i)} \frac{|eval(Value(i, j)) - Estimated(Value(i, j))|}{N \times |eval(Value(i, j))|}.$$

(2)

For example, the privacy score of Tables 1 and 2 is $(Privacy\ Score) = \{|1.00 - 1.00|/1.00 + |0.35 - 0.57|/0.35 + ... + |1.00 - 1.00|/1.00\}/7.0 = 0.511$. When the privacy score is high, the agent doesn't reveal much private information. When the privacy score is low, the agent reveals more private information.

3.2 Adjustment of Order of Proposals Based on Privacy Scores

In our proposed method, the number of offers by each agent is adjusted by the new privacy measure. This adjustment encourages agents who haven't revealed much private information to reveal more of it. This adjustment protocol is performed as follows:

1. Calculate the current privacy measures of each agent.
2. Normalize the privacy measures of all agents.
3. Determine the probability that each agent will make new bids using the normalized privacy measure.

First, the current privacy measure of each agent is calculated as a fair privacy score based on the measure of the revealed private information. As described in Sect. 3.1, when the privacy measure is high, the agent doesn't reveal much private information. Second, the calculated privacy measure is normalized as 1.0 to be the total of each agent's privacy measure. After that, the agent who proposed the next offer is decided based on the probability of offering new bids by each agent using the normalized privacy measure.

4   Experimental Results

4.1   Settings

In experiments, about our proposed negotiation protocol, we compared differences in the fairness of the revealed private information depending on the presence or absence of the adjustment of the number of offers using a tournament among the state-of-the-art agents. The following are the detail settings of the experiments:

- Tournament setting: round-robin competitions;
- Number of agents in negotiations: 3;
- Opponents: top six state-of-the-art agents in the individual utility categories in ANAC 2016: *Caduceus, YXAgent, ParsCat, Farma, MyAgent, and Atlas3*;
- Negotiation scenarios: party_domain (profiles 1~6) scenario, which includes six issues with three to six elements in each issue;
- Discount factor: 1.0;
- Deadline: 180 sec;
- Reservation value: 0;
- Number of negotiations per tournament: 2400;
- Tournament repetitions: 20.

4.2   Experimental Results

Figure 1 shows the average and standard deviations of our proposed privacy measure. In addition, Fig. 2 shows the differences between the maximum and minimum privacy measures in the negotiation. In Fig. 1, each agent's revealed private information fluctuates due to the adjustment of the number of offers. Even though *YXAgent* revealed less information than the other agents, it revealed more private information after the number of offers was adjusted. At the same time, the amount of information revealed by *ParsCat* decreased more than the method without any adjustment. In Fig. 2, the difference between the maximum and minimum revealed information decreased more than the method without adjusting. Therefore, our Alternating Offers Protocol considering Fair Privacy

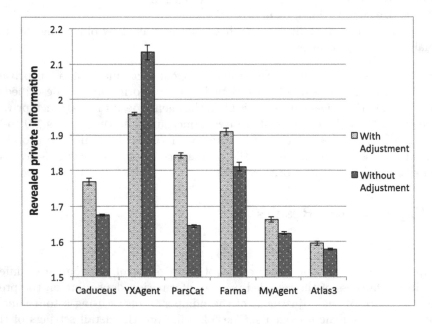

Fig. 1. Revealed private information of each agent

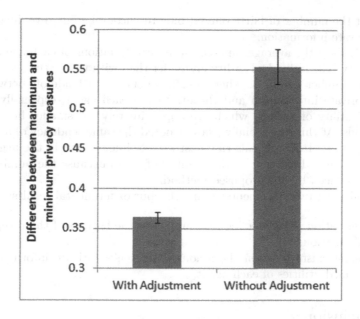

Fig. 2. Difference between maximum and minimum privacy measures in negotiation

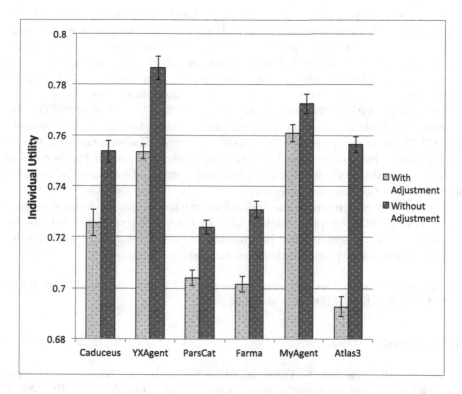

Fig. 3. Individual utility when agreements are made

can adjust the number of fairly offered bids to encourage fair revealing of each agent's private information.

Figure 3 show the averages and the standard deviations of each agent's individual utility. The individual utility is smaller than with the method that didn't adjust the number of offers. Therefore, we identified a trade-off between the revealed private information and the utilities of each agent, especially for the individual utility of *Atlas*3, which are approximately 5% smaller between the two methods. At this, the social welfare denoted the same tendency of individual utility. In Fig. 1, *Atlas*3 reveals the most private information in the negotiation regardless of the adjustment of the number of offers because the number of its offers was reduced by our proposed method.

The following two statements summarize our experimental results:

1. Our negotiation protocol effectively improves the fairness of the revealed private information.
2. A trade-off exists between the amount of revealed private information and the obtained utilities of each agent.

5   Conclusion

In this paper, we proposed a negotiation protocol that considers the fairness of revealing each agent's private information. First, we proposed a new measure of each agent's revealed private information that is based on the accuracy estimating opponents' utility functions. Next, our negotiation protocol adjusted the number of offers by each agent based on our new measure. This adjustment encourages agents who reveal less private information than other agents to reveal more of it. In experiments, we compared and investigated the fairness of revealing private information in tournaments among state-of-the-art agents in ANAC2016 using our proposed negotiation protocol. The experimental results demonstrated that our proposed negotiation protocol improved the fairness of the revealed private information and identified a trade-off between the revealed private information and social welfare.

Future work will improve the individual utility and social welfare of each agent. Our negotiation protocol will also include preferential treatments for agents that reveal more private information. Another important task is comparisons between our proposed measure and existing measures.

Acknowledgements. This work was supported by CREST, JST, and JSPS KAKENHI Grant Numbers 15H01703 and 26730116.

References

1. Aydoğan, R., Baarslag, T., Fujita, K., Hindriks, K., Ito, T., Jonker, C.: The seventh international automated negotiating agents competition (ANAC 2016) (2016). http://www.tuat.ac.jp/~katfuji/ANAC2016/

2. Aydoğan, R., Festen, D., Hindriks, K.V., Jonker, C.M.: Alternating offers protocols for multilateral negotiation. In: Fujita, K., Bai, Q., Ito, T., Zhang, M., Ren, F., Aydoğan, R., Hadfi, R. (eds.) Modern Approaches to Agent-based Complex Automated Negotiation. SCI, vol. 674, pp. 153–167. Springer, Cham (2017). doi:10.1007/978-3-319-51563-2_10

3. Aydoğan, R., Hindriks, K.V., Jonker, C.M.: Multilateral mediated negotiation protocols with feedback. In: Marsa-Maestre, I., Lopez-Carmona, M.A., Ito, T., Zhang, M., Bai, Q., Fujita, K. (eds.) Novel Insights in Agent-based Complex Automated Negotiation. SCI, vol. 535, pp. 43–59. Springer, Tokyo (2014). doi:10.1007/978-4-431-54758-7_3

4. Baarslag, T., Fujita, K., Gerding, E., Hindriks, K., Ito, T., Jennings, N.R., Jonker, C., Kraus, S., Lin, R., Robu, V., Williams, C.: Evaluating practical negotiating agents: Results and analysis of the 2011 international competition. Artif. Intell. J. **198**, 73–103 (2013)

5. Baarslag, T., Hindriks, K.V.: Accepting optimally in automated negotiation with incomplete information. In: Proceedings of the 12th International Conference on Autonomous Agents and Multi-Agent Systems (AAMAS 2013), pp. 715–722 (2013)

6. Chen, S., Ammar, H.B., Tuyls, K., Weiss, G.: Conditional restricted boltzmann machines for negotiations in highly competitive and complex domains. In: Proceedings of the 23th International Joint Conference on Artificial Intelligence (IJCAI 2013), pp. 69–75 (2013)

7. Fatima, S., Kraus, S., Wooldridge, M.: Principles of Automated Negotiation. Cambridge University Press, New York (2014)

8. Fatima, S.S., Wooldridge, M., Jennings, N.R.: Multi-issue negotiation under time constraints. In: Proceedings of the First International Joint Conference on Autonomous Agents and Multiagent Systems (AAMAS 2002), New York, NY, USA, pp. 143–150 (2002)

9. Fujita, K., Ito, T.: An analysis of computational complexity of the threshold adjusting mechanism in multi-issue negotiations. Int. Trans. Syst. Sci. Appl. **4**(4), 305–311 (2008)

10. Hemaissia, M., El Fallah Seghrouchni, A., Labreuche, C., Mattioli, J.: A multilateral multi-issue negotiation protocol. In: Proceedings of the 6th International Joint Conference on Autonomous Agents and Multiagent Systems, AAMAS 2007, pp. 155:1–155:8. ACM, New York (2007). doi:10.1145/1329125.1329314

11. Kakimoto, S., Fujita, K.: Preliminary estimating method of opponent's preferences using simple weighted functions for multi-lateral closed multi-issue negotiations. In: Bai, Q., Ren, F., Fujita, K., Zhang, M., Ito, T. (eds.) Multi-agent and Complex Systems. SCI, vol. 670, pp. 181–192. Springer, Singapore (2017). doi:10.1007/978-981-10-2564-8_13

12. Kraus, S.: Strategic Negotiation in Multiagent Environments. MIT Press, Cambridge (2001)

13. Kraus, S., Wilkenfeld, J., Zlotkin, G.: Multiagent negotiation under time constraints. Artif. Intell. **75**(2), 297–345 (1995)

14. Osborne, M.J., Rubinstein, A.: Bargaining and Markets (Economic Theory, Econometrics, and Mathematical Economics). Academic Press, London (1990)

15. Rubinstein, A.: Perfect equilibrium in a bargaining model. Econometrica **50**(1), 97–109 (1982)

16. Rubinstein, A.: A bargaining model with incomplete information about time preferences. Econometrica **53**(5), 1151–1172 (1985)

Author Index

Printed in the United States
By Bookmasters